Onondaga River

Oneida Lake

Ft. Stanwix

Onondaga•

Mohawk River

Ft. Schuyler

S. A.

Canajoharie•

Springfield

Cherry Valley

Schenectady

Albany

•Schoharie

Otsego Lake

•Cherry Valley

NEW YORK

Catherines Town

Susquehanna River

Delaware R. (Mohawk Br.)

Hudson (North) River

Kingston•

hemung

Owego

a

PENNSYLVANIA

NEW YORK

Wyalusing

Lackawanna River

Susquehanna R

Great
Swamp

Newburgh• •Fishkill

West Point•

Wyoming
Valley

Minisink•

NEW YORK

NEW JERSEY

Susquehanna R

PENNSYLVANIA

NEW JERSEY

SUSSEX
COUNTY

NORTHAMPTON
COUNTY

•Morristown

New York City

ry/Ft. Augusta

Nazareth•

Easton•

Camp

Long Island

BERKS
COUNTY

Northampton•

Middlebrook

Perth Amboy

TER
TY

•Lebanon

•Reading

Delaware River

NEW
JERSEY

Sandy Hook

dleton

Coryells Ferry

Trenton

Schuylkill R.

•Lancaster

•Burlington

k

Philadelphia•

ATLANTIC OCEAN

SYLVANIA

YLAND

Wilmington

Christiana •

New Castle

DEL.

Mullica River

•Batsto Furnace

Little Egg Harbor

THE PAPERS OF
General Nathanael Greene

Nathanael Greene by Charles Willson Peale; from this original most of the portraits of Greene were copied or derived
(Courtesy of Independence National Historical Park)

THE PAPERS OF
General Nathanael Greene

VOLUME III
18 October 1778–10 May 1779

Richard K. Showman
EDITOR

Robert E. McCarthy
ASSOCIATE EDITOR

Elizabeth C. Stevens
ASSISTANT EDITOR

*Assisted by Margaret Cobb, Nathaniel N. Shipton,
and Mary MacKechnie Showman*

THE UNIVERSITY OF NORTH CAROLINA PRESS
Chapel Hill

Published for the
RHODE ISLAND HISTORICAL SOCIETY

Library of Congress Cataloging in Publication Data
(Revised for volume 3)

Greene, Nathanael, 1742–1786.
   The papers of General Nathanael Greene.

   Includes bibliographical references and indexes.
   CONTENTS: v. 1. December 1766–December 1776.—
v. 2. 1 January 1777–16 October 1778.—v. 3. 18 October
1778–10 May 1779.
   1. Greene, Nathanael, 1742–1786.   2. United States—
History—Revolution, 1775–1783—Sources.   I. Showman,
Richard K.   II. Rhode Island Historical Society.
E302.G73   1976   973.3'3'0924   76-20441
ISBN 0-8078-1285-4 (v. 1)
ISBN 0-8078-1384-2 (v. 2)
ISBN 0-8078-1557-8 (v. 3)

TABLE OF CONTENTS

ILLUSTRATIONS

MAPS

INTRODUCTION

Volume II of the Nathanael Greene Papers carried him to mid-October 1778, when he had just rejoined Washington's army at Fredericksburg, N.Y., after an absence of two and a half months in Rhode Island, the highlight of which had been his participation in the battle of Rhode Island. This volume starts at 18 October, as he resumed his quartermaster duties, and ends at 10 May 1779. For the seven-month period, 583 documents have been located—as many as have been found for the two previous war years. Approximately 40 percent are letters *from* Greene, the great majority in his hand. There are no formal orders, but a dozen documents, signed by aides, conveyed his informal orders.

Not surprisingly, the greatest number of documents are concerned with quartermaster matters, including a few items that are neither to nor from Greene. How many letters he actually wrote or received during the period cannot be estimated with any accuracy; as is evident from the number of references in this volume to letters "not found," the number of missing ones is substantial—possibly a third as many as have been found. Many of the missing ones have been destroyed, but some few are still hidden in public repositories, and many more are in private hands. (For the history of Greene's papers, see the first volume, pages xxvii–xxxiii.)

Of the 583 documents in this volume, space limitations have made it necessary to calendar 274, many of them of a routine nature and most written *to* Greene. The rest, except for a few duplicates, have been printed in full. Since the complete text of the calendared documents would be useful to some scholars—especially to the social or economic historian—the Rhode Island Historical Society plans eventually to make typescripts of all manuscripts available in microform, noting the locations of the originals for those who might want to consult them.

During the seven months covered by this volume, Nathanael Greene was absorbed by the problems of the quartermaster department, which he administered from Washington's headquarters. Despite his preoccupation with his quartermaster duties, however, few days went by on which Washington did not confer with him on other matters, including strategic problems. This is not to say that in the absence of Councils of War, which Washington had given up, he did not confer with other general officers, but he seems to have drawn somewhat closer to Nathanael Greene. On one occasion Greene was the only general officer from whom Washington requested a written opinion on the campaign of 1779.

The seven-month period was a quiet one for Washington's army of twenty thousand men, although for some weeks in the autumn of 1778, Sir Henry Clinton, commander of the British army, kept Washington and his staff on tenterhooks trying to fathom Clinton's next move. First, there were fears of an attack on Boston, which led Washington to dispatch part of the army toward that city before he learned that the British fleet had sailed for the West Indies in pursuit of the French fleet. Then followed a month of puzzling activity among British troops in New York City, leading some of Washington's general officers—though Nathanael Greene was not among them—to believe the enemy was preparing to evacuate the city and even to withdraw from America. When a large contingent of British troops sailed from New York, however, their destination proved to be Georgia, not England. In late December 1778 they captured Savannah, and soon thereafter they took the adjoining coast and the Savannah River as far as Augusta. They were unable to take Charleston, but Georgia was to remain in British hands until the end of the war.

Clinton remained in New York City with sufficient troops to secure the city against an American attack and to serve as a threat to any nearby American unit caught off guard. It was apparent, however, that he was not about to give up the amenities of the city for the rigors of a winter campaign in the North. With the British firmly entrenched in New York and Newport, R.I., Washington could do little more than keep his army in the field and prepare for any British sorties.

An army of twenty thousand was not needed for such strictly defensive purposes, but Washington was reluctant to release any troops lest they fail to reenlist in the spring. Moreover, with an army of that size, he could still contemplate some kind of offensive move. At one point he even indulged in the somewhat fanciful dream of attacking New York City, although how seriously is not known. Throughout the autumn he did seriously consider a winter invasion of Canada over the frozen waters of the Connecticut River or Lake Champlain—a pet project of a group of New York and New England delegates to Congress, encouraged by General Schuyler and some New Hampshire militiamen, all of whom believed that once the British army was out of the war, French Quebec would rush to join the union.

Washington had many doubts about the success of such an

expedition, but he was slow to abandon the project. From the first, many of his general officers thought it a foolhardy venture. Nathanael Greene went further. After thoroughly studying the distances involved and taking shortages into account, he informed Washington that it would be virtually impossible to supply such an expedition. Jeremiah Wadsworth, the commissary general, agreed. In the end, they persuaded Washington that such an attack was out of the question.

Despite the disappointment of the pro-Canada faction in Congress, Washington kept their support by converting plans for a Canadian invasion into a proposed 1779 expedition against the Iroquois Indians and Tories in upstate New York, an expedition that New York and Pennsylvania delegates had first suggested after the July 1778 massacre at Wyoming Valley, Pa., and had strongly urged after the November 1778 massacre at Cherry Valley, N.Y. In January 1779, Congress gave its blessing to the expedition as the only practicable offensive the army could consider for the coming campaign. In March, after Gates refused the command, Washington appointed John Sullivan to lead the expedition. The magnitude of the planned expedition would put a crushing demand on the quartermaster department.

In the meantime, there was an army of twenty thousand men to be fed and supplied. One division was in Rhode Island, one in southwestern Connecticut, and one in the New York Highlands. This left some eight thousand men in and around Camp Fredericksburg, N.Y., who were not needed to protect the area. Because of shortages of food for men and forage for beasts in New England and the Hudson Valley, Greene made a convincing case for moving the eight thousand men to New Jersey, where they would be closer to the sources of supply to the south.

On 25 November the first contingent set off on the one-hundred-mile march to Camp Middlebrook, N.J., a good defensive position north of the Raritan River at the base of the Watchung Mountains, where the army had encamped in 1777. Greene not only had to oversee their march, but during the early days of December, he spent long hours in laying out the camp and getting construction started on huts and roads. Washington made his headquarters at the Wallace house, while Greene settled in nearby at the Van Veghten house, where he was soon joined by his wife Catharine. Other wives, including Martha Washington, joined their husbands and there ensued considerable socializing—teas, dinners, dances, "frolics," commemorative events. Although there were no such social occasions for the troops, the men were far more comfortable and well fed than during the same months at Valley Forge, thanks primarily to improvements in the quartermaster and commissary departments. The army remained at Middlebrook until June.

Although the period from October to May was a quiet one for the army, with time for conviviality among the officers, it was far from an easy period for Nathanael Greene. It is true that he had not previously enjoyed such a high income, sharing as he did with his two assistants, Charles Pettit and John Cox, a 1 percent commission on all quartermaster purchases. But he had to pay dearly for his improved financial condition.

In the first place, he was reluctant to accept the post of quartermaster general in March 1778 because, in becoming, as he said, a staff officer, he was "taken out of the line of splendor." And it was the vision of battlefield laurels that had motivated him, as it had many officers, to join the army in the first place and to continue to endure the hardships and dangers of war. Moreover, as quartermaster his days were long, laborious, and frustrating. Not only was he responsible for supplying the army with an enormous variety of items, but even more burdensome was the task of transporting all of those supplies as well as the food, clothing, and ordnance purchased by other departments. In a period of severe shortages that also saw the Continental dollar continue its fall from twenty-five cents in October 1778 to less than six cents in May 1779, it is a miracle that Greene and his deputies were able to assemble the necessary components to transport supplies—men, wagons, carts, sleighs, horses, oxen, boats, ships, etc. Although the department was chiefly occupied with land transport (including building roads), there was one notable exception in 1779. As the correspondence reveals, Nathanael Greene and Charles Pettit spent innumerable hours between January and May arranging for ships to bring rice from Charleston, S.C., to New England, where crop failures had brought great hardship. Although fewer than half the vessels got through the British blockade, an enormous amount of rice did reach New England.

The most difficult task in land transport was to provide forage, the grain and hay that constituted the power for horse-drawn vehicles—the eighteenth-century equivalent of a modern army's oil. Aside from war-time demands, crop failures in 1778 made forage even scarcer. The correspondence is filled with the desperate search for sources of forage and, when a supply was located, the efforts to persuade state and county officials to use their powers to pry it from reluctant sellers, many of whom preferred British specie to Continental dollars or promissory notes. Some army horses died from starvation, and many that survived were too weak to pull a load. Nevertheless, somehow, enough forage was scrounged to keep the army supplied.

Ironically, few people credited the quartermaster department with success, much less miracles. Indeed the majority had nothing but unkind words for the deputies and their assistants. Those citizens with something to sell blamed the deputies for not paying enough; the remaining critics accused them of paying too much in order to increase their commissions. And everyone envied them their income even when honestly gained. There were some assistant deputies and agents who did pay higher prices than necessary to increase their commissions, but they were in the minority, and there is no evidence that those directly under Greene were guilty of the same thing, although some of them were lax with subordinates. The fact is that during this period, the cost of supporting a soldier in the field as measured in specie (rather than in Continental dollars) actually decreased. Only a few knowledgeable people, however, recognized this.

Criticism of the department became more widespread during the winter and spring of 1779, some of it directed at Nathanael Greene personally—especially for the large commissions he was collecting (albeit in paper money). Whether directed at him or the department, it was this growing criticism, some of which reached the newspapers, that made his post most onerous. He had not developed a thick skin in the face of criticism. In November 1778, to meet the general criticism, Congress had appointed a committee to oversee the quartermaster and commissary departments. The committee was not unfriendly to Greene, but faced by the continued need to finance the war with paper money, the committee had no suggestions for improving conditions. Greene spent six weeks in mid-winter in Philadelphia pleading with Congress for help in coping with rising prices, especially in meeting the needs of the underpaid wagoners, artificers, and hundreds of others in his department. Congress made helpful gestures, but it was as powerless as its committee in solving Greene's supply problems. It did give him a full vote of confidence, which it later repeated, but at the same time it continued to criticize the deputies and agents in his department for whom he was responsible. There were even a few delegates who ludicrously blamed the rise in prices on the high prices the quartermasters paid instead of on the paper money they had voted for.

Toward late spring more and more of Greene's and his deputies' time was spent on the Indian expedition. An army of several thousand men under the command of Gen. John Sullivan was to approach the Iroquois by way of Pennsylvania and the Susquehanna River; it was to join an army half its size under Gen. James Clinton, approaching from the Mohawk Valley in New York. Such a cumbersome force would require dozens and dozens of boats and hundreds of pack horses to carry the supplies it would have to haul through the trackless wilderness. When this volume closes on 10 May, not even half of the supplies had been assembled, and it would be another three months before the so-called Sullivan-Clinton expedition actually got under way.

Providence, R.I.   RICHARD K. SHOWMAN
January 1983   *Editor*

ACKNOWLEDGMENTS

As the editors have pointed out in previous volumes, a title page contains but a fraction of the names of persons who make such documentary editions possible. Our indebtedness to those who contributed previously has been acknowledged in Volumes I and II; here, we take the opportunity of thanking those who have contributed for the first time or who have continued to assist us.

We are obligated to our own Rhode Island Historical Society staff in countless ways. Only a few can be mentioned by name: Director Albert Klyberg, who has continued to assume responsibility for financing and housing the Greene Papers and to lend his sound judgment and encouragement; Helen Hodde, who has good-naturedly kept tabs on our income and expenditures; Kate Waterman, Carolyn Brown, and Linda Levin, who have kept the world informed of our needs as well as our achievements; Glenn W. LaFantasie, who has shared his expertise and advice; Deborah Doolittle, who has come to our rescue when extra typing was to be done; Paul Campbell, who has kept his bookman's eye open for pertinent items, and his library staff, who have aided us on many occasions; David Shields, who, when a student at Brown University, helped part-time with editorial chores; and finally Clifford Cone and his maintenance staff of John Rymill and Al Papino, who collectively have made our quarters in the Aldrich House the most pleasant imaginable. One staff member whose name appears on the title page should also be mentioned here; this is Margaret Cobb, who retired in June after having been with the project since its inception. We were saddened to learn in January 1983 of her death in Santa Clara, California. Her leaving was an immense loss to the Greene Papers, although the work she has done in accessioning and transcribing documents will be evident through the final volume in the series.

Staff members of a number of libraries and archives have also aided the Greene Papers in various ways. We are especially indebted to Madeline F. Gross, John D. Rockefeller, Jr., Library, Brown University. We have continued to receive help from the staff of the Providence Public Library; the staff of the John Carter Brown Library; Phyllis Silva, Rhode Island State Archives; the librarians at the University of Rhode Island Extension Library, Providence; Roland M. Baumann, Pennsylvania Division of Archives and Manuscripts; and Don Skemer of the New Jersey Historical Society.

To the many institutions and to their staffs, whom we have previously thanked for providing us with copies of documents, we should like to add Joseph R. Chrostowski, Archives of the City of Providence, and E. Jane Townsend, Washington's Headquarters, Newburgh, N.Y. We should also like to thank the following private collectors who have made copies of documents available: for this volume, David H. Coblentz, Chase City, Va., and Mary Lynn McCree, Chicago, Ill.; for future volumes, Dr. Thomas N. Cross, Ann Arbor, Mich., Horace G. Stepp, High Point, N.C., and Cary Whitfield, Tallahassee, Fla. We are grateful to two autograph dealers who have recently permitted us to print documents in their possession: Bruce Gimelson, Chalfont, Pa., and Doris Harris, Los Angeles, Calif. And finally in the acquisition of additional Greene documents we are favored by several persons who have steered us to obscure documents or have served as intermediaries between a collector and the Greene Papers: Peter Agnew, Port Washington, N.Y.; Professor Lawrence E. Babits, Armstrong College, Savannah, Ga.; Professor Bruce Daniels, University of Winnipeg; Charles H. Lesser, South Carolina Department of Archives and History; Jerry Patterson, executive vice president, Sotheby Parke Bernet; and Robert Schnare, librarian of the U.S. Military Academy at West Point.

We are obliged to Director Frank Burke of the National Historical Publications and Records Commission and to the members of his staff, who have never failed to respond to calls for assistance: Roger Bruns, George L. Vogt, Richard N. Sheldon, Mary Giunta, Sara Dunlap Jackson, and Joyce E. Eberly.

In addition to the groups of persons named above we should like to express our appreciation to a number of individuals: John Dann, director of the William L. Clements Library, who has shared with us copies of recent additions to the library's superb collection, as well as having aided in fund-raising efforts; Charles M. Destler of West Hartford, Conn., for permitting us to quote from the manuscript of his biography of Jeremiah Wadsworth; Dennis P. Ryan, co-editor of the William Livingston Papers, who has aided us in locating Greene documents in New Jersey; Mrs. Elizabeth H. Drew, Dr. Howard Brown, and Col. Robert Allen Greene for their fund-raising efforts; Sandy Strand for her maps; and the Rhode Island Chapter of the Sons of the American Revolution for their gift of the five-volume Index to the Papers of the Continental Congress.

And finally we give our heartfelt thanks to those who have contributed financially to the project as "Benefactors of the Papers of General Nathanael Greene":

BENEFACTORS OF
The Papers of General Nathanael Greene

Norris G. Abbott, Jr.
John and Margaret Adams
Mrs. Samuel Adams (in memory
of Col. Samuel Adams)
Peter R. Agnew
John Alden
Anonymous
Mr. and Mrs. Lawrence E. Babits
John D. Bacon
Mrs. J. C. Baxter
Dorothy Blankenburg
Frederick W. Bogert
Col. Robert Graham Bosworth
O. G. Boynton
William G. Bradshaw
Francis J. Buckley, III
John P. Cady
Shirley E. Calkins
A. Watson Cocroft
Robert S. Cocroft
Mrs. Mary Costantino
Elizabeth H. Drew
Mrs. Philip Drinker
Robert F. Eddy
Mr. and Mrs. Louis A. Fazzano
Carolyn A. Fitzgerald
Mr. and Mrs. Dixwell Goff
Mrs. Charles F. Gormly
Ruth H. Green
Miss Margaret Greene
Richard A. Greene
Col. Robert Allen Greene
Thomas Casey Greene, Jr.
Robert A. Greene II
Todd A. Greene
Mr. and Mrs. L. James
Halberstadt
Clarence DeW. Herreshoff
Eric Hertfelder
Doris Greene Holmes
David Ingram

Karl P. Jones
Ralph H. Keeney
Kentish Guards, R.I. Militia
Mrs. Albert A. Klyberg
Mrs. B. Leonard Krause
Mrs. Marguerite N. Lambert
Mrs. Royal D. Leith
Charles King Lennig, Jr.
John S. Lopes
James H. McFarland, Jr.
Capt. F. McMaster, USN, Ret.
Cathay Greene MacRae
Mr. and Mrs. Donald Greene
McRae
Dr. Alden C. Manchester
Cameron G. Marshall
Massachusetts and Rhode Island
Booksellers Association
Frank Mauran III
Mr. and Mrs. Wilbur N. Melin
William D. Metz
Charles T. Miller
Patricia and Thomas Murdoch
Mr. and Mrs. W. A. Newcomb
Mrs. A. Dean Perry
Mr. and Mrs. Edward C. Prest
Rhode Island State Chapter
Daughters of the American
Revolution
Mr. and Mrs. H. Roland Rich
Marion W. Ricketson
Mr. and Mrs. Ezra Schneider
Mrs. William A. Sherman
Nathaniel Shipton
Miss Sarah Greene Smith
Sons of the Revolution
in the State of Rhode Island
Sons of the American Revolution
Standard Oil of Ohio
Lucy Rawlings Tootell
John Tottenham

Ronald G. Tracey

Mrs. W. F. Twaddell

Dr. and Mrs. Lee D. Van Antwerp

David Whieldon

Dorothy Whitaker

David R. Whitesell

Jeremiah Wadsworth Whitney

Charlotte Wolfe

EDITORIAL METHOD

Arrangement of Material

Letters and documents are arranged chronologically. If two or more related items are dated the same day they are arranged in sequence; if unrelated to each other, they are arranged as follows:

1. Military orders and documents (as opposed to letters)
2. Letters from NG, alphabetically by recipient
3. Letters to NG, alphabetically by sender

Undated Items

If a date omitted by the writer can be determined, it is printed in brackets, and the item takes its place chronologically. A doubtful conjecture is followed by a question mark.

If a precise day cannot be established, the shortest conjecturable time span is placed in brackets and the item arranged as follows:

Conjectured Time Span	Chronological Arrangement
[10–18] September 1776	Placed at 10 September 1776
[April] 1776	Placed at end of April 1776
[November 1775–February 1776]	Placed at end of November 1775
[1775]	Placed at end of 1775
[1776–78]	Placed at end of 1776
[before 12 December 1776]	Placed at end of 11 December documents

All such conjectures are explained in footnotes. If no time period can be conjectured, the item will be placed at the end of the last volume of the series.

Misdated Items

If a correct date can be determined for a misdated item, it follows the incorrect date in brackets; if a date is suspected of being incorrect, a question mark in brackets follows.

Form of a Letter

The form of a letter is rendered as follows, regardless of the original:

1. Place and date is at top right.

2. Complimentary close is set continuously with the body.

3. Paragraphs are indented, and paragraphing is sometimes introduced to relieve long, unbroken segments.

4. Author's interlineations or brief additions in the margin are incorporated into the text silently unless of unusual significance, when they are explained in a footnote.

5. Scored-out or erased passages are ignored unless mentioned in a footnote.

6. Address sheet and docketing are normally omitted.

Calendared Items

Many less important items are calendared, with an abstract of the contents set within brackets. The item is arranged according to date. If the writer's original wording is included, it is set off by quote marks, or if in a lengthy passage, by indentation.

MANUSCRIPT TEXTUAL POLICY

Following the practice established by Julian Boyd, Leonard Labaree, and other modern editors, manuscripts are rendered in such a way as to be intelligible to the present-day reader while retaining as much as possible the essential form and spirit of the writer. The following guidelines reflect this compromise.

Spelling

Spelling is retained as written. If a misspelled word or name is not readily recognizable, the correct spelling follows in brackets. Names are correctly spelled in notes and index.

Obvious slips of the pen and inadvertent repetition of words are corrected silently.

Capitalization

The only instance in which an author's capitalization is always followed is the eighteenth-century practice of capitalizing words within sentences—usually, but not confined to, nouns. In other cases an author's capitalization is changed where necessary to conform to the following rules:

1. All sentences begin with initial capitals.

2. Personal names and titles used with them, honorifics (such as

"His Excellency"), geographical names, and days of the week and months are capitalized.

Abbreviations and Contractions

1. Shortened word forms still in use or those that can easily be understood (as "t'was" or "twixt") are rendered as written.

2. Those no longer readily understood are treated thus: "cmsy [commissary]" or "warr[an]t."

3. Abbreviations of names or places—forms known only to the correspondents or their contemporaries—are also expanded in brackets, as in S[amuel] A[dams] or Chsn [Charleston].

Symbols Representing Letters and Words

When any of the following symbols are expanded they are done so silently:

1. The ampersand is expanded to "and" except in "&c," "&ca.," and "& Co." in business firms.

2. The thorn, which by 1750 had been debased to "y" as in "ye," is expanded to "th." Such abbreviations as "ye" "yᵗ" or "yᵐ" are rendered as "the," "that" or "them."

3. The tilde is replaced by the letter(s) it represents—as in com̄ission.

4. The ℬ sign is expanded to the appropriate letters it represents (e.g., per, pre, or pro).

5. Superscript letters are brought down to the line as in 9ᵗʰ to 9th or Regᵗ to Regt.

Punctuation

Where necessary, punctuation is changed to conform to the following rules:

1. A period or question mark is placed at the end of every sentence.

2. Within a sentence, punctuation is sparingly added or deleted in order to clarify a confusing or misleading passage.

3. Dashes used in place of commas, semicolons, periods, or question marks are replaced with appropriate punctuation; dashes are retained when used to mark a suspension of the sense or to set off a change of thought.

4. No punctuation is used after a salutation.

Missing or Indecipherable Passages

If such passages cannot be conjectured, they are indicated by italicized editorial comments in brackets, such as [*mutilated*], [*indecipherable*], [*remainder of paragraph (or letter) missing*], [*several words missing*].

If missing or indecipherable portions can be conjectured they are treated in one of the following ways:

1. If no more than four letters are missing they are supplied silently.
2. If more than four letters are conjectured they are inserted in brackets. If there is some doubt about the conjecture, it is followed by a question mark: Ch[arleston?].
3. If such portions can be supplied from a variant version of the manuscript they are set in angle brackets: ⟨Washington⟩.
4. A blank left by the author is so depicted.

PRINTED MATERIAL

In reprinting documents from printed sources the capitalization, spelling, punctuation, and paragraphing have been faithfully followed—except for obvious printer's errors.

The earlier practice of italicizing names, however, is dropped, as are the italicization of passages by the former editor.

SOURCE NOTE

An unnumbered source note directly follows each document. For manuscript material it consists of a symbol describing the type of manuscript, followed by the symbol or name of the repository that owns the document, or the name of an individual owner. Pertinent facts or conjectures concerning the manuscript are added when required. A list of manuscript symbols and a list of the Library of Congress repository symbols follow the section on annotation below.

ANNOTATION

The editors have set several goals for themselves in annotating the documents. The most important of these is to explain a document sufficiently to make it intelligible to the modern reader who may be unfamiliar with the subject. In a sense, the editor puts the reader in the place of the eighteenth-century recipient. He may, at times, give the reader an advantage over both author and recipient of a document by alluding to facts that were unknown or unknowable to them. Another goal is the correction of errors in a document, since many a myth has found its source in "documentary evidence" that was false or inaccurate. Then, too, for the reader's convenience, the editor should relate the document at hand with other documents or notes in the series by the use of cross-references. And there is a final goal: to provide continuity and understanding to the reader by filling significant gaps in the documents before him.

A few procedural points need emphasis:

1. Identification of persons is usually made at the first appearance of their names and is not repeated. References to these biographical notes are found in the index. Identifications are omitted for such leading figures as Washington or Franklin, as well as for obscure persons who played an insignificant role in NG's career.

2. Cross-references to an earlier volume are designated by volume and page number, as in "See above, vol. 2: 418n." Otherwise, cross-references are to documents, as in "See above, NG to Washington, 30 November 1778." If the reference is to a document within the same year, the year is often omitted, as in "See above, NG to Washington, 5 January." If the reference is to future volumes, the year is always given, as in "See below, NG to Washington, 25 January 1782."

3. When a page number does not appear in a citation, the reader can assume the work is in dictionary form.

DESCRIPTIVE SYMBOLS FOR MANUSCRIPTS

Following are the symbols employed in source notes to describe the kinds of manuscripts used in the texts.

AD	Autograph document
ADS	Autograph document signed
ADf	Autograph draft
ADfS	Autograph draft signed
AL	Autograph letter
ALS	Autograph letter signed
D	Document
DDf	Document draft

DS   Document signed
Df   Draft
DfS   Draft signed
LS   Letter signed
LB   Letter book copy
FC   File copy
Cy   Copy (made contemporaneously with original)
ACy   Autograph copy
ACyS   Autograph copy signed
Tr   Transcript (later copy made for historical record)
[A]   Indicates some uncertainty about the autograph
[S]   Indicates signature has been cropped or obliterated
(No symbol is given to printed letters or documents)

LIBRARY OF CONGRESS SYMBOLS OF REPOSITORIES

The following institutions have provided copies of manuscripts that are printed or calendared in volume three:

CSmH Henry E. Huntington Library, San Marino, Calif.
CtHi   Connecticut Historical Society, Hartford, Conn.
CtHWa at CtHi Wadsworth Atheneum Collection at Connecticut Historical Society, Hartford, Conn.
CtNIC Connecticut College, New London, Conn.
CtY   Yale University, New Haven, Conn.
DLC   U.S. Library of Congress, Washington, D.C.
DNA   U.S. National Archives, Washington, D.C.
MH   Harvard College Library, Cambridge, Mass.
MHi   Massachusetts Historical Society, Boston, Mass.
MWA American Antiquarian Society, Worcester, Mass.
MiU-C William L. Clements Library, University of Michigan, Ann Arbor, Mich.
N   New York State Library, Albany, N.Y.
NBLiHi Long Island Historical Society, Brooklyn, N.Y.
NHi   New-York Historical Society, New York, N.Y.
NNC   Columbia University, New York, N.Y.
NNPM Pierpont Morgan Library, New York, N.Y.
NcD   Duke University, Durham, N.C.
NhHi New Hampshire Historical Society, Concord, N.H.
Nj   New Jersey State Library, Trenton, N.J.
NjHi   New Jersey Historical Society, Newark, N.J.
NjMoW Morristown National Historical Park, Morristown, N.J.

NjP   Princeton University, Princeton, N.J.
NjR   Rutgers—The State University, New Brunswick, N.J.
OClWHi   Western Reserve Historical Society, Cleveland, Ohio
OMC   Marietta College, Marietta, Ohio
PHC   Haverford College, Haverford, Pa.
PHi   Historical Society of Pennsylvania, Philadelphia, Pa.
PPAmP   American Philosophical Society, Philadelphia, Pa.
PPIn   Independence Hall National Park, Philadelphia, Pa.
RHi   Rhode Island Historical Society, Providence, R.I.
RPB   Brown University, Providence, R.I.
WaU   University of Washington, Seattle, Wash.

SHORT TITLES FOR WORKS FREQUENTLY CITED

Alden, *Lee* — Alden, John Richard. *General Charles Lee: Traitor or Patriot?* Baton Rouge: Louisiana State University Press, 1951.

Bartlett, *Records* — Bartlett, John Russell, ed. *Records of the State of Rhode Island and Providence Plantations in New England.* 10 vols. Providence, 1856–65.

BDAC — *Biographical Directory of the American Congress, 1774–1961.* Rev. ed. Washington: United States Government Printing Office, 1961.

Bemis, *Diplomacy* — Bemis, Samuel Flagg. *The Diplomacy of the American Revolution.* New York: D. Appleton-Century Co., 1935.

Bezanson, *Prices* — Bezanson, Anne. *Prices and Inflation during the American Revolution: Philadelphia, 1770–1790.* Philadelphia: University of Pennsylvania Press, 1951.

Boatner, *Encyc.* — Boatner, Mark Mayo, III. *Encyclopedia of the American Revolution.* New York: David McKay Co., 1974.

Bowman, *Captive Americans* — Bowman, Larry G. *Captive Americans: Prisoners during the American Revolution.* Athens, Ohio: Ohio University Press, 1976.

Boyer, *Early Forges* — Boyer, Charles S. *Early Forges & Furnaces in New Jersey.* Philadelphia: University of Pennsylvania Press, 1931.

Brunhouse, *Pennsylvania* — Brunhouse, Robert Levere. *The Counter-Revolution in Pennsylvania, 1776–90*. Philadelphia: University of Pennsylvania Press, 1942.

Buel, *Dear Liberty* — Buel, Richard, Jr. *Dear Liberty: Connecticut's Mobilization for the Revolutionary War*. Middletown, Conn.: Wesleyan University Press, 1980.

Burnett, *Congress* — Burnett, Edmund Cody. *The Continental Congress*. New York: The Macmillan Co., 1941.

Burnett, *Letters* — Burnett, Edmund C., ed. *Letters of Members of the Continental Congress*. 8 vols. Washington: Carnegie Institution of Washington, 1921–36.

Butterfield, *Adams Family* — Butterfield, L. H., et al., eds. *Adams Family Correspondence*. Cambridge, Mass.: Belknap Press of Harvard University Press, 1963–.

Clarke, *Greenes* — Clarke, Louise Brownell. *The Greenes of Rhode Island, with Historical Records of English Ancestry, 1534–1902*. New York: Knickerbocker Press, 1903.

Clinton, *Papers* — Clinton, George. *Public Papers of George Clinton, First Governor of New York*. Edited by Hugh Hastings. 10 vols. Albany, 1899–1914.

Clinton, *American Rebellion* — Clinton, Henry. *The American Rebellion: Sir Henry Clinton's Narrative of His Campaigns, 1775–82*. Edited by William B. Willcox with an appendix of original documents. New Haven, Conn.: Yale University Press, 1954.

Coleman, *Georgia* — Coleman, Kenneth. *The American Revolution in Georgia, 1763–89*. Athens, Georgia: The University of Georgia Press, 1958.

Columbia Encyclopedia — *The Columbia Encyclopedia*. Edited by William Bridgewater and Seymour Kurtz. 3d ed. New York: Columbia University Press, 1967.

Conn. Men in Rev. — *Record of Service of Connecticut Men in the War of the Revolution*. Hartford, 1889.

DAB | Johnson, Allen, and Malone, Dumas, eds. *Dictionary of American Biography.* 21 vols. New York: Charles Scribner's Sons, 1928–36. 5 supplements, 1944, 1958, 1973, 1974, and 1977.

Deane Papers | Deane, Silas. *The Deane Papers.* New-York Historical Society, *Collections.* 5 vols. New York, 1886–91.

Destler, "Wadsworth" | Destler, Chester McArthur. "Jeremiah Wadsworth." An unpublished biography.

Dupuy and Hammerman, *People* | Dupuy, Trevor N., and Hammerman, Gay M., eds. *People and Events of the American Revolution.* New York and London: R. R. Bowker Co., 1974; Dunn Loring, Va.: T. N. Dupuy Associates, 1974.

Ferguson, *Power of Purse* | Ferguson, E. James. *The Power of the Purse: A History of American Public Finance, 1776–90.* Chapel Hill: University of North Carolina Press, 1961.

Fitzpatrick, *GW* | Washington, George. *The Writings of George Washington, from the Original Manuscript Sources, 1745–1799.* Edited by John C. Fitzpatrick. 39 vols. Washington: United States Government Printing Office, 1931–44.

Flexner, *GW* | Flexner, James Thomas. *George Washington in the American Revolution (1775–1783).* Boston and Toronto: Little, Brown and Co., 1967.

Freeman, *GW* | Freeman, Douglas Southall. *George Washington.* 7 vols. The last volume by John C. Alexander and Mary W. Ashworth. New York: Charles Scribner's Sons, 1948–57.

Furman, *Letters* | Furman, Moore. *The Letters of Moore Furman.* Compiled and edited with genealogical notes by the New Jersey Society of the Colonial Dames of America. New York: Frederick H. Hitchcock, 1912.

Gérard, *Dispatches* | Gérard, Conrad Alexandre. *Dispatches and Instructions of Conrad Alexander Gerard, 1778–1780.* With historical introduc-

Gottschalk, *Lafayette*

Greene, *Greene*

Gruber, *Howe Brothers*

GWG Transcript
Hammond, *Sullivan*

Heitman, *Register*

Higginbotham, *War*

Hoadly, *Records*

Hoffman, *New Jersey*

Idzerda, *Lafayette Papers*

Ives, *Headquarters*

tion and notes by John J. Meng. Baltimore: The Johns Hopkins Press, 1939.
Gottschalk, Louis. *Lafayette Joins the American Army*. Chicago: University of Chicago Press, 1937.
Greene, George Washington. *The Life of Nathanael Greene, Major-General in the Army of the Revolution*. 3 vols. 1871. Reprint. Boston and New York: Houghton, Mifflin and Co., 1897–1900.
Gruber, Ira D. *The Howe Brothers and the American Revolution*. New York: Atheneum, 1972.
Greene, George Washington.
Sullivan, John. *Letters and Papers of Major-General Sullivan, Continental Army*. Edited by Otis G. Hammond. 3 vols. Concord: New Hampshire Historical Society, 1930–39.
Heitman, Francis B., comp. *Historical Register of Officers of the Continental Army during the War of the Revolution*. 1914. Reprint. With addenda by Robert H. Kelby. Baltimore: Genealogical Publishing Co., 1967.
Higginbotham, Don. *The War of American Independence: Military Attitudes, Policies, and Practice, 1763–1789*. New York: The Macmillan Co., 1971.
Hoadly, C. J., and others, eds. *Public Records of the Colony of Connecticut, 1636–1776*. 15 vols. Hartford, 1850–90. *Public Records of the State of Connecticut, 1776–1803*. 11 vols. Hartford, 1894–1922.
Hoffman, Robert V. *The Revolutionary Scene in New Jersey*. New York: The American Historical Co., 1942.
Lafayette, Marquis de. *Lafayette in the Age of the American Revolution: Selected Letters and Papers, 1776–90*. Edited by Stanley J. Idzerda et al. Ithaca, N.Y.: Cornell University Press, 1977–.
Ives, Mabel Lorenz. *Washington's Head-*

quarters. Upper Montclair, N.J.: Lucy Fortune, 1932.

JCC — Ford, Worthington C., et al., eds. *Journals of the Continental Congress, 1774–1789.* 34 vols. Washington: Government Printing Office, 1904–37.

Johnson, *Dictionary* — Johnson, Samuel. *A Dictionary of the English Language.* 2 vols. 1755. Reprint. New York: AMS Press, 1967.

Johnson, *Greene* — Johnson, William. *Life and Correspondence of Nathanael Greene, Major General of the Armies of the United States.* 2 vols. Charleston, S.C., 1822.

Kemble, *Journal* — Kemble, Stephen. "Journal." In *Kemble Papers,* New-York Historical Society, *Collections.* 2 vols. New York, 1884.

Lee Papers — Lee, Charles. *The Lee Papers.* New-York Historical Society, *Collections.* 4 vols. New York, 1872–75.

Leiby, *Hackensack* — Leiby, Adrian C. *The Revolutionary War in the Hackensack Valley: The Jersey Dutch and the Neutral Ground, 1775–1783.* New Brunswick, N.J.: Rutgers University Press, 1962.

Lesser, *Sinews* — Lesser, Charles H., ed. *The Sinews of Independence: Monthly Strength Reports of the Continental Army.* Chicago: University of Chicago Press, 1976.

Lundin, *Cockpit* — Lundin, Leonard. *Cockpit of the Revolution: The War for Independence in New Jersey.* 1941. Reprint. New York: Octagon Books, 1972.

MacKenzie, *Diary* — MacKenzie, Frederick. *The Diary of Frederick MacKenzie.* 2 vols. Cambridge, Mass.: Harvard University Press, 1930.

Mackesy, *War* — Mackesy, Piers. *The War for America, 1775–1783.* Cambridge, Mass.: Harvard University Press, 1964.

Md. Archives — *Archives of Maryland.* Documents published by the authority of the state. Baltimore: Maryland Historical Society, 1883–.

Murdoch, *Annual Register* — Murdoch, David H., ed. *Rebellion in*

	America: A Contemporary British Viewpoint, 1765–83. Selections from the *Annual Register.* Santa Barbara, Calif.: American Bibliographical Center-Clio Press, 1979.
Nelson, *Gates*	Nelson, Paul David. *General Horatio Gates: A Biography.* Baton Rouge: Louisiana State University Press, 1966.
N.J. Archives	*New Jersey Archives. Documents Relating to the Revolutionary History of the State of New Jersey.* 2nd series. 5 vols. Trenton, N.J.: State of New Jersey, 1901–17.
N.J. Rev. Correspondence	*Selections from the Correspondence of the Executive of New Jersey from 1776 to 1786.* Newark, N.J., 1848.
OED	*Oxford English Dictionary.*
Pa. Archives	*Pennsylvania Archives. Selected and Arranged from Original Documents in the Office of the Secretary of the Commonwealth.* 119 vols. Philadelphia and Harrisburg, 1852–1935.
Pa. Col. Records	The *Pennsylvania Colonial Records* constitute the first sixteen volumes of the *Pennsylvania Archives.* See above, *Pa. Archives.*
PCC	Papers of the Continental Congress. Unless otherwise noted, all citations are from Record Group 360, M247.
Peckham, *Toll*	Peckham, Howard H. *The Toll of Independence: Engagements & Battle Casualties of the American Revolution.* Chicago and London: University of Chicago Press, 1974.
Pierce, *Iron in the Pines*	Pierce, Arthur D. *Iron in the Pines: The Story of New Jersey's Ghost Towns and Bog Iron.* New Brunswick, N.J.: Rutgers University Press, 1957.
PMHB	*Pennsylvania Magazine of History and Biography.*
Proceedings of Arnold's Court Martial	*Proceedings of a General Court Martial for the Trial of Major General Arnold.* Edited with an introduction, notes, and index by Francis Suydam Hoffman. New York, 1865.

Reed, *Reed* — Reed, William B. *Life and Correspondence of Joseph Reed.* 2 vols. Philadelphia, 1847.

R.I. Acts — *Rhode Island Acts and Resolves, 1747–1800.* 31 vols. Providence: State of Rhode Island, 1908–25.

R.I. Biog. Cycl. — *Biographical Cyclopedia of Representative Men of Rhode Island.* Providence, 1881.

RIHS, *Coll.* — *Collections* of the Rhode Island Historical Society (1827–1902). Rhode Island Historical Society, *Collections* (quarterly 1918–41).

Roche, *Reed* — Roche, John F. *Joseph Reed: A Moderate in the American Revolution.* New York: Columbia University Press, 1957.

Rossman, *Mifflin* — Rossman, Kenneth R. *Thomas Mifflin and the Politics of the American Revolution.* Chapel Hill: University of North Carolina Press, 1952.

Thacher, *Journal* — Thacher, James. *Military Journal of the American Revolution.* Hartford, Conn., 1862.

Wallace, *Traitorous Hero* — Wallace, Willard M. *Traitorous Hero: The Life and Fortunes of Benedict Arnold.* New York: Harper and Row, 1954.

Ward, *Weedon* — Ward, Harry M. *Duty, Honor or Country: General George Weedon and the American Revolution.* Philadelphia: The American Philosophical Society, 1979.

Wharton, *Correspondence* — Wharton, Francis, ed. *The Revolutionary Diplomatic Correspondence of the United States.* 6 vols. Washington, 1889.

Whittemore, *Sullivan* — Whittemore, Charles P. *A General of the Revolution: John Sullivan of New Hampshire.* New York and London: Columbia University Press, 1961.

WMQ — *William and Mary Quarterly.*

WRMS — War Department Collection of Revolutionary War Records, Record Group 93.

A GLOSSARY OF MILITARY TERMS

ABATIS
: A barrier of felled trees, with limbs pointing toward the enemy; usually temporary.

ARTILLERY PARK
: An encampment for artillery.

ARTILLERY TRAIN
: An army's collection of cannon and the material for firing them.

BARBETTE
: A platform or mound of earth for artillery, usually separated from a main fortification.

BASTION
: An outward projection of a fort enabling gunners to fire along the wall of the fort at an enemy.

BATEAU
: A light, flat-bottomed river craft with raked bow and stern.

BATTALION
: See Regiment.

BOMB, BOOMBE
: A powder-filled iron sphere that is fired from a mortar and fused to explode after falling.

BREASTWORK
: An improvised fortification, usually consisting of a trench and earthen barrier.

BRIGADE
: A formation of two or more regiments.

BROADSIDE
: The firing of all artillery on one side of a warship.

CANISTER
: A tin cylinder containing metal balls that scattered when fired from a cannon.

CARCASS
: An incendiary device fired from a cannon at wooden structures or ships.

CARTOUCHE
: Cartridge made of a paper cylinder, containing powder and lead ball.

CHANDELIER
: Wooden frame filled with fascines, for protection where earth could not be dug.

CHEVAL-DE-FRISE
: Used usually in the plural; a portable defense barrier bristling with long, iron-tipped wooden spikes. An underwater version consisted of a rock-filled wooden frame, on which sharpened timbers were set at an angle to rip the hull of a vessel.

COLOURMAN
: Traditionally, a soldier who assisted in preparing a new camp site; also often used for one who was responsible for disagreeable cleaning and sanitation tasks.

DIVISION
: A unit of two or more brigades.

DRAGOON
: Once a mounted infantryman, by 1775 term was used interchangeably with cavalryman.

DURHAM BOAT	A shallow-drafted boat developed to transport iron ore. Varying in length from forty to sixty feet and around eight feet in width, it could carry a company of troops and was usually poled.
EMBRASURE	An opening through which cannon were fired.
ENFILADE	To sweep with gunfire along a line of works or troops from end to end.
FASCINE	A firmly tied bundle of wooden sticks or small limbs.
FATIGUE	Manual and menial duty performed by troops.
FIREBOAT	A vessel filled with a variety of combustibles for burning enemy vessels.
FLECHE	An outwork of a fort, shaped like an arrow, the point toward the enemy.
FRIGATE	A two-decked warship built for swift sailing, mounting twenty to thirty-eight guns on the upper deck.
GLACIS	A bank sloping away from a fortification.
GRENADE	A hand-thrown metal device that exploded when the lighted fuse reached the powder inside.
GRENADIERS	Once hurlers of grenades, by 1775 an elite corps.
GUN	Although technically used to describe a cannon, the term was also regularly used in the colonies for a musket or rifle.
INVALIDS	Disabled soldiers who were assigned to limited duties.
JÄGER	German light infantry chosen for their marksmanship with the German rifle (not the German-American long-barreled rifle).
LIGHT INFANTRY	Lightly equipped, highly mobile troops.
MARÉCHAUSÉE	Mounted provosts, responsible for policing a camp.
MARQUEE	A canvas tent designed especially for officers; also, a cover for another tent.
MATROSS	Assistant to an artillery gunner.
MORTAR	A short-barreled cannon used for lobbing shells, bombs, etc., over an obstacle.
MUSQUETEER	Soldier armed with a musket.
ORDNANCE	Military equipment and supplies.
OUTWORK	A defensive work outside a fort.
PALISADE	Timbers set in the ground, close together and sharpened at the top.
PAROLE	A prisoner's oath on being freed that he will not bear arms until exchanged.

PETTY AUGER	An open, flat-bottomed boat, generally two-masted, carrying some thirty tons.
PICKET, PICQUET	An outguard to warn of an enemy approach.
PIKE	Wooden spear of varying length, with a steel point.
PIONEERS	Men responsible for digging trenches, repairing roads, preparing fortifications, etc.
PLATFORM	A wooden bed upon which a cannon was placed.
PRIVATEER	A privately owned armed vessel commissioned to take enemy merchantmen as prizes.
REGIMENT	During this period, regiment and battalion were used interchangeably. Usually composed of eight companies and at full strength numbering from 520 to 780.
REVETMENT	A wall to retain an earthen rampart or side of a ditch.
ROW GALLEY	A low, flat vessel with one deck, varying in length up to 130 feet; manned by oarsmen and carrying several small cannon.
SCHOONER	A small fore-and-aft-rigged vessel with two masts.
SCOW	A flat-bottomed boat with square ends.
SHIP	A large vessel with three masts, each composed of a lower mast, top mast, and top gallant mast.
SLOOP	Small, one-masted vessel.
SNOW	Generally a two-masted vessel with small mast behind the main mast.
SUBALTERN	Commissioned officer below the rank of lieutenant.
SUTLER	A provisioner for an army camp who operates for profit.
TRANSPORT	A vessel for carrying troops.
XEBEQUE	A three-masted ship with long overhanging bow and stern which originated in the Mediterranean.

1778	13 October	NG rejoins Washington's army at Fredericksburg, N.Y.
	Late October	Washington assigns NG responsibility for supplying Convention army en route to Virginia.
	10 November	Congress appoints committee to oversee quartermaster and commissary departments.
	27–30 November	NG oversees removal of main army to Middlebrook, N.J.
	1–6 December	NG establishes headquarters at Van Veghten house and lays out Camp Middlebrook.
	Mid-December	Catharine Greene and son George arrive at the Abraham Lotts at Beverwyck, N.J.
	Late December	The Greenes stay with the John Coxes in Trenton en route to Philadelphia.
1779	1 January	NG arrives in Philadelphia to consult with Congress during a six-week period.
	Mid-January	Catharine and son George join NG in Philadelphia.
	9 February	The Greenes return to Camp Middlebrook.
	4 April	Partnership established with Jeremiah Wadsworth and Barnabas Deane.
	21–27 April	NG in Philadelphia to consult with Congress.
	10 May	Decides to share in purchase of Batsto furnace.

THE PAPERS OF
General Nathanael Greene

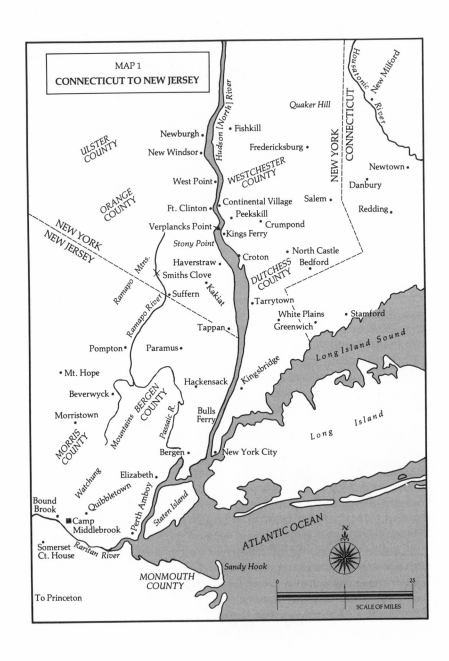

MAP 1
CONNECTICUT TO NEW JERSEY

Hudson [North] River

Quaker Hill

ULSTER
COUNTY

Newburgh •   • Fishkill

New Windsor •   Fredericksburg •

ORANGE
COUNTY

West Point •   WESTCHESTER
                 COUNTY

Ft. Clinton •   • Continental Village   Salem •

                 • Peekskill

Verplancks Point   • Crumpond

                 • Kings Ferry

NEW YORK
NEW JERSEY

Stony Point

Haverstraw •   • Croton   • North Castle
                             Bedford

Ramapo Mtns.

Smiths Clove   DUTCHESS
                             COUNTY

• Suffern   Kakiat

Ramapo River   • Tarrytown

                 • White Plains   • Stamford
                 Greenwich •

Tappan •

Pompton •   Paramus •

Long Island Sound

• Mt. Hope

Hackensack •   Kingsbridge

Beverwyck •

BERGEN
COUNTY

Morristown

Mountains

Passaic R.

Bulls
Ferry

Long   Island

MORRIS
COUNTY

Bergen •   • New York City

Watchung

Elizabeth •

Quibbletown •

Perth Amboy

Staten Island

Bound
Brook
■ Camp
Middlebrook

ATLANTIC OCEAN

Somerset
Ct. House   Raritan River

MONMOUTH
COUNTY   Sandy Hook

To Princeton

NEW YORK

CONNECTICUT

Housatonic River

New Milford •

Newtown •

Danbury •

Redding •

0   25

SCALE OF MILES

To George Washington

Sir   Camp at Fredricksburg [N.Y.] Octo 18th 1778

Your Excellencys queries laid before the Council held the 16th of this instant Has been duly considerd and I shall endeavor to give them an answer as far as I am able to comprehend the subject.[1]

The first query is whether it will be prudent and adviseable to make a detachment from this Army for Boston and of what force? A detachment to move towards Boston can only be necessary upon the supposition that the Enemies preparations now makeing in the City of New York for a movement somewhere is designd against that place and the French Fleet in the Harbour. The ballance of Evidence is greatly against the probabillity of such an intention being in contemplation with the Enemy. The Town of Boston is very difficult of access and strongly fortified within and well securd without upon all the approaches. The French Fleet is securely posted at the entrance of the Harbour, Formidable in itself and greatly strengthened by Land Fortifications. There is a numerous and spirited Militia in the Neighbourhood of Boston that can be hastily drawn together to secure it against any sudden dessent of the Enemy. General Sullivan also lies within two Days march and can give them early support with a part of his Troops if it should be found necessary.[2] The Town thus guarded and the Fleet thus securd, there is not a bare probabil[i]ty of the Enemys attempting anything against either the Town or the Fleet with any detachments they are able to make and hold the Posts of New York and Rhode Island. Besides these reasons it is now late in the season and the navigation in Boston Bay difficult and Hazzardous.

From the state of the British West India Islands and from the late accounts from thence, it is almost reducd to a certainty that the Troops geting in readiness for embarcation are bound there. Therefore I dont think it advisable to make any more detachments to the Eastward than Poors brigade, and for them to proceed no farther than Conecticut River unless we get some further evidence of the Enemies preparations being designd against Boston.[3]

The second query is whether the Army shall be held in a collected state and where? This query involves in it so many consequences. The reasons are so numerous for it, and the objections so strong against it, and these so complicated and difficult to decide upon that I find a great difficulty in forming an Opinion.

To have the Army in a collected state would render it secure against any attempts of the Enemy; and at the same time it would be in readiness to take such advantages of them as the season and the condition they may be in may offer. The dicipline of the Troops will also be preservd and improvd. The Cattle of the Army may be all

[3]

sent out into the Country to recruit which will save the Forage in the neighbourhood of the Camp.[4] These Reasons offer themselves strongly in favor of the plan for holding the Army in a collected state and on this side of the North River, too. But when I consider the state of our Magazines; the difficulty with which we now feed the Army; The late season of the year; The scarcity of Flour from the Eastward; The long transportation to bring a supply from the Westward;[5] The scarcity of Forage in New Jersey; The barrenness of the Country from Morris Town to Kings Ferry; The difficulty of crossing the North [Hudson] River at certain seasons; and the great quantity of Flour that will be wanted Eastward for the Troops at Rhode Island and Boston, I am afraid to recommend the Armies takeing a position on this side the North River, Notwithstanding the reasons that operate in favor of it.

But if it should be thought most advisable to take a position on this side and risque the consequences of failing in geting a supply of Flour and Forage, I recommend a position not far distant from the White Plains. Such a situation will be more favorable for drawing in supplies than any one I can conceive off. Our communication with the Western States can be kept open longer at Kings Ferry than any other place. The communication with Tarry Town can be kept up by Water and if a covering party could be kept about Hakensack we might receive stores by the way of Tappan which would save near or quite 20 Miles Land carriage. A position at or near the White Plains is well situated to cover Conecticut and Newyork State and keep the Enemy within their Lines.

Let us take what Position we may, the Horse must go into the State[s] of Conecticut and Pensylvania. I would send Sheldons[6] into the former and all the rest into the latter except such a party as will be necessary to accompany our advance Parties.

If it should be found that the Army cannot be subsisted on this side the North River I would propose leaveing a good Garrison at West Point for the security of that important pass. Two or three Brigades should take post at Danbury, there Hut and fortify themselves immediately. The rest of the Army should cross the North River and take post in Bergen County or at our old Middle Brook Camp.[7] In either place to Hut and fortify themselves as soon as possible. Should the Troops take a position in Bergen County they will be at hand to support the Garrison at West Point and well situated to keep up the communication from Kings Ferry to Morristown. But as all the Forage upon the upper and lower communication will be wanted for the Cattle employed in transporting stores Eastward, and as the position in Bergen County will be forty miles farther from the source of our supplies than that at Middle Brook I would prefer the later position to the former. Middle Brook is situated in a plentyful

Country, naturally strong and difficult of access and surrounded with a great plenty of Wood. Great security will also be given to this Camp by the militia of the Country. The Post at West Point will also be greatly strengthened by the Militia of Ulster and Orange Counties, and Danbury has a formidable militia in its Neighbourhood.

I think there will be very little or no danger of the Enemies makeing an attack upon either of those Posts, more specially if they make a detachment from N York. However if they should, they will in all probabillity fail in the attempt. But if we should take a position all on this side the North River, and the Enemy should march out and intercept our Line of communication and cut of [off] our supplies it would go near to starve the Army as all our Bread must come from the Westward.

There can be but two modes of covering the Troops; one is, to quarter them in small Towns and the neighbouring Houses to those Villages. The other is, to erect such Huts as they did the last Winter. The season is so far spent, Boards so difficult to be got, That it will be utterly impossible to procure materials for Barracking the whole Army. Besides which if it was practicable it would be attended with a most enormous expence. If the Troops take the foregoing position recommended, Forage may be had from the respective States for the support of the Cattle belonging to each Post.

It will be found absolutely necessary to strip the Army of all superfluous and unnecessary Horses which must be sent to the Interior Country where they will be supported at a much less expence and get in good order for the opening Campaign.

The influence of Money has become so feeble, People so reluctantly part with their property and are so indifferent about engageing in the service that I am really afraid without force or the aid of the Civil Magistrate[s] we shall hardly be able to support the Army.

As I have to consider the subject before me in a double capacity, I have made a calculation to accompany this that your Excellency may at one view see the difficulties of subsisting the Army all on this side of the North River. This calculation is made only for the Articles of Flour and Forage.[8] When that of Salted Provisions, Spirits, Stores of all kinds and Clothing comes to be added to the account It will greatly augment the number of Teams. I am with great respect Your Excellencys most obedient humble Servt

NATH GREENE

ALS (Washington Papers: DLC).
    1. The council minutes are printed above, vol. 2: 548–49.
    2. Sullivan was in command at Providence.
    3. As seen in the note on British strategy above, vol. 2: 549–50n, NG was remarkably prophetic. Washington, however, received faulty intelligence on 19 October which

led him to order Gates to march with the rest of his division toward Boston, Gen. Enoch Poor's brigade having already started for Hartford on the recommendation of the council. (Fitzpatrick, *GW*, 13: 100–101, 112–13)

4. As used here, "cattle" was synonymous with "livestock;" to "recruit" was to "restore the health of."

5. See cross reference in note 8, below.

6. Col. Elisha Sheldon of the Connecticut Light Horse.

7. Middlebrook, N.J., on the Raritan River, had been the site of the American camp in the early summer of 1777. As seen in Washington's letter of 29 October, below, he followed NG's advice on quartering the army.

8. NG refers to Pettit's estimate, a final draft of which was not delivered to Washington for several days and which is printed below, "Before 27 October."

See Maps 1 and 2 for geographic references above.

From Colonel Robert H. Harrison

[Fredericksburg, N.Y., 19 October 1778. Washington asks that expresses to Boston be ready to "start at a moments warning." Intelligence suggests British evacuation of New York City.[1] Washington also requests establishment of expresses to Elizabethtown, N.J.[2] ALS (PHi) 1 p.]

1. See above, vol. 2: 549–50n.

2. On the route of the expresses see note at NG to Washington, 30 November, below.

From Colonel Robert H. Harrison

[Fredericksburg, N.Y., 19 October 1778. Washington has letter for Lord Stirling when expresses are established to Elizabethtown. ALS (MH) 1 p.]

From Colonel Ephraim Bowen

[Providence, R.I., 20 October 1778. Has borrowed $140,000 from General Sullivan; a large number of tents sent to Nehemiah Hubbard; Sullivan refuses to pay damages to Rhode Island inhabitants. "Your further Directions in this matter will be agreeable as it seems hard that individuals should Suffer in such Cases."[1] ALS (RHi) 1 p.]

1. NG answered 27 October, below.

To Colonel James Abeel

[Fredericksburg, N.Y., 21 October 1778. Of watch that Abeel took for repair in May he says, "I am much in want of her." Cautions that

returns be accurate "for they will all be laid before Congress." ALS
(RHi) 1 p.]

To Governor George Clinton of New York

Sir,   Fish Kills [N.Y.] Oct. 21 1778.

Your Excellency is sensible how necessary it is for a General to
know the resources of a Country in which he means to canton his
Troops. I was mentioning to His Excellency General Washington the
necessity of haveing an account of all the Grain taken in this State
and that the best mode to effect it would be to get your Excellency to
appoint proper Persons for the purpose in every Town. The General
promised me he would write your Excellency upon the subject; and
that he would engage the expences to be defrayed by the Public. If it
meets with your Excellency's approbation I wish it may be executed
as soon as possible. It is a very interesting question to the quarter
master's department. In takeing the account there must be no dependance upon the information of the Proprietors; but the Persons must
see and examin for themselves. All kinds of Grain should be taken
into the account that will answer either for bread or Forage.[1]

I am well perswaded from the feeble influence of money that
both the Commisaries and quarter masters department will stand in
need of the aid of Civil Government to procure sufficient supplies for
the Army.

However, this is a question that will come upon the carpet
hereafter.

The Enemy appear to be preparing for a general evacuation of
New York; and most people think they are all going off, but I cannot
help thinking they will leave a Garrison. However if they should
we must endeavor to serve them as they did us, drive them out by
Force.[2]

I beg your Excellency to make my most respectful compliments
to Mrs. Clinton. I am with great respect Your Excellency's Most
Obedient humble Serv't

NATH GREENE

Reprinted from Clinton, *Papers*, 4: 179–81.

1. Washington wrote a detailed letter to Clinton the same day, amplifying NG's
request and asking if the legislature might approve taking such an inventory. (Fitzpatrick, *GW*, 13: 121–22)

No answer to NG's letter has been found, but the New York Senate rejected his
request indirectly on 30 October by approving a committee report made in response to
Washington's letter and to an earlier one from Udny Hay, NG's deputy, who had
undoubtedly suggested that NG also write. The report declared that "to take an
Estimate of all grain and Forage in this State would be a Task of great Labor and

consequently take Much time." Clinton sent the resolution to Washington without commenting on NG's request. His letter instead concerned an Act of 31 October that authorized the commissary to seize wheat and flour under certain conditions. He also asked Washington, on behalf of the Senate, to inquire into wrongdoing in the commissary department. A copy of the Senate resolution of 30 October is in the Washington Papers, DLC, as is the Act of 31 October and Clinton's letter to Washington of 1 November.

2. See above, vol. 2: 549–50n.

To George Washington

Sir   Fish Kill [N.Y.] Octo 21, 1778

Upon examination into the state of the Forage department I find there is wanted 200 men to mann a number of Battaues [Bateaux] which are to go up the [Hudson] River single and then be lashed together and come down double. Six tuns of Hay may be brought upon two Battaues in this way. The weather is now good for the business and the greater exertions are necessary as the Time will be short. There is Fifty Fatigue men wanted also to assist in screwing the Hay. The whole of these will be wanted for some time, and as it will be constant duty, the men must have some extraordinary allowance. Besides the foregoing there is 20 Carpenters and 20 masons wanted to forward the Barracks now on hand. If there is a regular draft made from each Brigade, that is an equal number, according to their Strength, it will be very trifleing.

Your Excellency is sensible how much business an Army creates, and how necessary it is to have that business done rapidly to keep pace with the Seasons. You are also sensible how difficult it is to get men, and what feeble influence Money has to effect it. It would be my wish if it was practicable to transact all the business of my department Independant of the Army. But I believe it is the Universal custom of all Armies to give temporary aid to the great departments of Provision and Forage. If it was possible (which it is not) to procure men, it must be at an expence that would soon be too burthensome for the Continent to support. To keep a great number of men always in Pay to be equal to all the Emergencies of business would often leave a considerable number Idle upon our hands.

There is a great number of Vessels employed in transporting Flour, Forage, Wood &c &c. And the Garrison at West Point [MAP 1] takes up a great number of our Artificers upon the Works which leaves us weaker than we shall be by and by. There is also a considerable number of Battaue men employed in furnishing the Garrison with Materials for the Works and provisions for the Troops. Upon the whole our People are all employed, and all we can get we have engagd without giving some very extraordinary pay. Therefore Necessity obliges me to solicit your Excellency for a farther Aid from the

Line of the Army, That everything may be done, that can be done, to draw together a sufficiency of Forage to supply the demands of the Army.

If your Excellency thinks proper to detach the men, let them be orderd to Col Hay who will give them the proper instructions and put them in the different branches of business. Both men and officers that are detached for the Battaues should be acquainted with that service or with sea service if such can be had; but if they cannot, we must take raw hands and learn them. This will render it necessary to have no shift of men until the season of business is over.[1] I am with great respect Your Excellencys Most Obedient humble Servant

NATH GREENE

ALS (Washington Papers: DLC).
1. On 23 October, Washington ordered Baron de Kalb at Fishkill (Map 1) to furnish Colonel Hay with 250 men from the Maryland division to "assist in getting forage" down the river and to send Hay 20 carpenters and 20 masons if available. (Fitzpatrick, GW, 13: 140)

From Oliver Wendell

[Boston, 21 October 1778. Concerns an account owed by the quarter-master department. ALS (PPAmP) 1 p.]

From Colonel James Abeel

Sir   Morris Town [N.J.] Oct 22d 1778
This Morning recd your favour of the 19th Instant and find that there was Several Mistakes in the last Invoice of Goods sent to Camp.[1] The Horse Shoes all Except five Boxes came from Colo [Jacob] Morgan and were never Unloaded or Examined. Likewise the Harness, as Mr Weiss ordered me to Send all the Harness, Horse Shoes &c I did not think it Right to have them Unpacked as It would Detain the Waggons.[2] Any Articles that are put [up] here I can Swear to the Contents of the Packages as the[y were] Put up by myself principally. It is very Certain the Waggoners plunder when ever they have an Opportunity. For the future no Stores shall go through my hands without first Examining them. Those that Come from Morgan shou'd have been Examined, but it was in the hight of the Trouble of Moving the Stores from hence they were sent off. Every Article I put in from this place were packed by myself and the Invoices Principally made out by me likewise. I am convinced no man pays more Attention to his Duty and the Interest of the Publick than I do. My Acco'ts shall be Regular and Clear and hope I shall put it out of the Power of any Man to Complain. The Express is waiting. I shall wrote more fully by next

Opportunity. The Articles Mr Pettit orders shall be sent on soon as Waggons can be procured which are Difficult getting at Present. I have Apply'd to Mr Burnsides for them.[3] I am in Haste yr most Hble Servt

LB (NjHi).
1. Letter not found.
2. Jacob Weiss served as a deputy quartermaster in various locations during NG's tenure. In September 1780, NG selected him to assist Pettit in the preparation of an audit of the department. (See below, NG to Weiss, 8 September 1780.) Weiss's letterbook covering the period is in the Lehigh County Historical Society, Allentown, Pennsylvania.
3. John Burnside was an assistant quartermaster for the artillery brigade. He resigned his post in early 1780. (See below, Burnside to NG, 18 January 1780.)

From Colonel William Smith Livingston[1]

[Beverwyck, N.J., 23 October 1778. Regrets he must retire from the army, but since his regiment is to be consolidated with another in the new arrangement, he would be subject to a senior colonel. "I confess I part with those Military Honors conferred upon me by our worthy General [Washington] with great regret." ALS (N) 2 pp.]

1. In the identification of William Smith Livingston in volumes 1 and 2 of the *Papers of General Nathanael Greene*, he was confused with William Livingston, Jr., the son of Governor William Livingston of New Jersey. He was, rather, the son of Robert James Livingston and Susan Smith Livingston. His mother was the daughter of the eminent New York jurist, William Smith (1697–1769) and the sister of the even more famous William Smith (1728–1793), jurist, loyalist historian of New York, and, after the war, chief justice of Canada. William Smith Livingston was born in 1755, was graduated from Princeton in 1772 at age seventeen, and four years later was a major in Lasher's New York militia. At age twenty-two he became an aide to NG.
   In January 1777 he joined Samuel B. Webb's "additional" regiment as lieutenant-colonel and fought with him in the battle of Rhode Island, where he was wounded. In 1777 he married Catherine Lott, daughter of the Greenes' friends, the Abraham Lotts; at the time he wrote this letter he was staying at Beverwyck, the Lotts' home, where Catharine Greene had been a frequent guest. Until 1780, when his correspondence with NG stopped, he seems to have been in business with his father-in-law. He later practiced law in New York. He died in 1794. (Ruth Lawrence, ed., *Colonial Families of America*, 27 vols. (New York: National Americana Society, 1928–48), 11: 113.)

To Colonel Ephraim Bowen

[Fredericksburg, N.Y., 24 October 1778. Not his intention that "Mr. Mitchel" be kept on as brigade quartermaster contrary to a resolve of Congress.[1] Hopes another place in the department can be found for Mitchel "because of his lameness" and "because I think him an honest, faithful officer." From Greene, *Greene*, 2: 399]

1. See below, NG to Varnum, 24 October. A resolve of 27 May 1778 stated that a brigade quartermaster was to be appointed by the quartermaster general from the captains and subalterns in the brigade to which he was to be appointed. (*JCC*, 11: 542)

To William Smith

[Fredericksburg, N.Y., 24 October 1778. Has sent him all available money. Washington has put six brigades "in motion towards" Boston.[1] Smith to give all necessary aid if they go beyond Connecticut River. ALS (RHi) 2 pp.]

1. See below, NG to Varnum, 24 October. Smith was deputy quartermaster at Springfield, Mass.

To General John Sullivan

Sir   Camp at Fredricksburg [N.Y.] Octo 24th 1778

It gives me great pleasure to hear the Rhode Island expedition spoke on with so much respect as I find it is. I thought it was honorable but I find it meets with applause. Give me leave to assure you that your Name stands high very high upon the list of Fame. I had a Letter from a member of Congress a few days since in which he speaks of your conduct in the highest terms of approbation.[1]

I remember Cardinal de Retz advice was, that upon any turn of good fortune to prepare for bad.[2] I wish you may never meet with a reverse. But Fortune is a fickle Jade and often gives us a tumble when we least expect it.

The Enemy have embarked a large part of their Army at N York. Their destination is unknown. Many think they are bound to Boston, but I am not of that number. Preparations are makeing for a second embarkation. Most people think there will be a total evacuation of Newyork; I am of a contrary opinion.

General Gates and General McDougall are on their march with Six Brigades for Boston, and we are holding ourselves in readiness to follow if ocassion requires it.[3]

Make my compliments agreeable to the Gentl of the Army and to those of your Family in particular. I am with great respect Your most Obedient humble Servt

NATH GREENE

ALS (NhHi).

1. Letter not found. In a resolution of 9 September, Congress had thanked Sullivan, his officers, and his men "for their fortitude and bravery, displayed in the action of 29th August, in which they repulsed the British forces and maintained the field" in Rhode Island. Congress also praised Sullivan's retreat as "prudent, timely, and well conducted." (JCC, 12: 894) The battle is described above, vol. 2: 499–503n.

2. Jean François de Retz (1613–79), the French prelate, whose Memoirs, published in 1717, are considered a classic description of politics in France during the time of Mazarin. (Columbia Encyclopedia)

3. As noted above, vol. 2: 549–50n, Sir Henry Clinton's plans for the British navy continued to baffle the Americans. On receiving reports that 150 ships had sailed from New York on 19 and 20 October, Washington ordered McDougall with three brigades to join Gates at Hartford, where they would be prepared to march to Boston if necessary.

(Fitzpatrick, *GW*, 13: 126n, 133–34) The division had marched only ten miles from Fredericksburg to New Milford, Conn., when Washington, learning that his intelligence was faulty, ordered it to halt. (Washington to McDougall, 25 October; McDougall to Washington, 28 October and 3 November, Washington Papers, DLC) There, the division stayed for a month until threats to Boston were past. On 24 November, McDougall was ordered back with his division to the Highlands while Gates went on to take command in Boston. (Fitzpatrick, *GW*, 13: 320–22)

See Maps 1 and 2 for geographic references above.

To General James M. Varnum

Dear Sir   Camp at Fredricksburg [N.Y.] Octo 24, 1778
When I left Rhode Island I directed Mr Bowen to apply to you and General Glover to nominate some Persons in your brigade to act as brigade quarter masters. I receivd a letter from him this day in which he says that Mr Mitchel claims a promise to be continued and that you confirmd it.[1] I am fully perswaded both you and he are entirely mistaken in the matter. I remember a promise for a temporary continuance, and the grounds upon which it was made. The Resolve of Congress was then in its infancy and it was uncertain whether the establishment of the Army would be gone into or not. While things remain in that situation I was willing Mr Mitchel should continue because there was no other person that I should have wished to have taken his place, but to comply with the Order of Congress. But the establishment is now gone into in all its forms and necessity obliges me to a conformity in my department. Or else I shall lay myself liable for all the extra pay and perhaps be impeached for contempt of Authority. Mr Mitchels circumstances and fidelity would make me wish to continue him if I could consistently. But I cannot and therefore must beg you to nominate some Person belonging to the Line to supply his place. I have wrote to Mr Bowen that if there is any department that he can be usefully employed in, to continue him in the Publick service.

A large part of the Enemy at N York have embarked, their destination is unknown. Many conjecture they are bound to Boston. I am rather of an opinion they are going to the West Indies. Another embarkation is said to be geting in readiness. Most People are of an opinion there will be a total evacuation of N York; but I am not of the number; I think they will have a Garrison if it is but a small one.[2]

General Gates and General McDougal have marched with Six brigades towards Boston.[3]

Make my compliments agreeable to Mrs Varnum and to the Officers of your brigade. I am Sir your humble Sert

NATH GREENE

NB I was at Capt Drakes a few Days since.[4] Patty says you must come and fetch your Slippers.

ALS (MiU-C).
1. See above, NG to Bowen, 24 October.
2. See note at NG to Washington, 18 October, above.
3. On Gates and McDougall, see above, note at NG to Sullivan, 24 October.
4. Greene and Varnum had spent time at Drake's home. See above, vol. 2: 458.

To George Washington

Sir   Camp Fredericksburg [N.Y.] October 24th 1778
    Agreeable to your Excellencys commands I have been in company with Colo Putnam and examined all the Country from this place to Fish Kill from FishKill to Peeks Kill and from Peeks Kill to Crumpond, Croten and Bedford and from thence up through Salem to this Place and can find but one Tract of Woodland of sufficient extent to Hut the Army collectively.[1] That is called the Furnace Lot and lies a little below Kings Ferry upon the Post Road from Peeks Kill to New York. This Tract contains near 1500 Acres and is well Wooded and Watered and is advantageously situated to receive supplies from the Western States. The Ground is broken and intersected with a great number of Sloughs.
    There is besides the Furnace Lot several other Pieces of Woodland adjoining of much the same make.
    An Army might be Huted by Brigades in the Highlands from Peeks Kill to Fishkill but there is no Ground where the Army can be Huted collectively, besides which it will be a difficult Position to supply the Troops with Provisions and Forage in the Winter; I think also the situation would be rather unhealthy and there is no ground to exercise and Manouvre the Troops upon. Their Situation in the High Lands will be little better than in a Goal.
    The Troops may also be Huted by Brigades in the Neighbourhood of Crumpond or Croten perhaps in a circle of Six or Eight Miles. The Country appears to be all divide[d] into small Farms of about 200 Acres principally cleared up, with only a sufficiency of Wood reserved for the use of the Farms.
    I had a full View of all the Country as low down as North Castle. Lower than which I have not examined; But Major Lee of the Light Dragoons promises to examine the lower Country down as low as the White Plains, being instructed what observations to make. He is to report the beginning of the Week.
    Here I think proper to observe that almost all the Forage that can possibly be spared by the Farmers from Kings Ferry to the White Plains and from Peeks Kill to Danbury has been already consumed.

Indeed all the Forage below the Danbury route is nearly spent clear down to the Sound. I am with due respect Your Excellencys Most Obedient humble Servant

NATH GREENE

LS (RG 93, WRMS: DNA). An ADfS is at PHi.
1. Washington had probably given his orders in person. NG and Col. Rufus Putnam of the engineers had traveled almost a hundred miles within a twenty-mile radius south and west of Fredericksburg. NG did not favor hutting the army collectively in the area, nor, in the end, did Washington. See NG to Washington, 18 October, above.

See Map 1 for geographic references above.

From Captain John Gooch

[Boston, 24 October 1778. Gooch complains that Thomas Chase, deputy quartermaster in Boston, has consistently refused to reimburse him for money that was advanced to engage teamsters in 1777. Accounts are still in arrears to the teamsters and to himself.[1] "People are loath to work for nothing." Needs money. ALS (PPAmP) 2 pp.]

1. See below, Gooch to NG, 25 October.

From George Lux

Dear General   Baltimore [Md.] 24 October 1778 (Saturday)
I was told last night by Mr Custis that you had joined the Army under his Exc'y Genl Washington before he left it; this induces me to drop you a line to congratulate you upon your safe and honourable retreat from Rhode Island, where Death or Captivity stared you full in the face, but you were preserved by valour and good Conduct. I am pleased that you and Genl Sullivan have so well acquitted yourselves of the duty you owed to your Country: now the tongues of malice and defamation will be stopt, and His Exc'y and You will no more be caballed against. I am lately returned from Reading, whither I went to see my Dulcinea, who has agreed in due time to take me for better and for worse.[1]
Genl M lives within 2 miles of it, and I often happened in Company with him—once when he was pretty merry in consequence of a plentiful infusion of the juice of Grape.[2] He began to talk about (what he called) the injustice done him by Congress: he asked me, what was generally thought of it in Maryland, and I candidly answered his Conduct was very generally censured. He then said, he could easily prove that imbezzelment of Public Money could not be

laid to his charge, and I told him, Report did not alledge it against him, but it did, that he caballed against our illustrious Genl; he then declared solemnly, he never did, but acknowledged he was *sometimes* displeased at the General's not following his own opinion, rather than that of others; yet he thought him the properest Person on the Continent for his important Station, and that he dearly loved and greatly esteemed him. I asked him, if he had said, *you* were the Favourite that ruled at Head Quarters and he answered, in *some capital cases* you had. He said, that after his Trial was over, he should bring to light those, who had injured the Public and him, but descended not to particulars: I saw, tho tipsy as he was, he was evasive. I am told by some of his Friends that he talks of challenging some Persons *in due time* and suspect, you are included in his *black list*, but dont think he means seriously to do it, as he puts it off so long. This I can assure you, that he is now disliked by most of the leading Gentlemen in Pens'a on acc't of his Cabals, although they make much of him at present in order to make an advantage of his influence among the populace, that they may amend their present absurd, ridiculous and tyrannical system of Government.

I must beg of you, my Dear Sir, not to mention my Author of the report of his saying you were not fond of Bullets, because it will probably prevent my getting the Girl of my Heart—as you mentioned it to him as a *mere Report,* let it rest as such—if it is necessary, I should acknowledge having wrote it to you as a *mere Report,* you may do it, but I promised Major S. not to mention *him.* My only reason for telling you was, to evince my Confidence in you and to put you on your guard. As the matter stands, *he,* is now generally censured and *you* applauded, so *you* need not be uneasy. He took uncommon pains to ingratiate himself with me, and I *seemed* captivated with it, in order that he might talk freely to me, but he would not do it; had he, I would have boldly stood forth and told You of it, for I should not mind having his ill will, though could not bear drawing my Dearest Friend on earth into a scrape. I should be glad of an answer to the above as soon as possible. Write by Post, that it may not miscarry, unless you know a *safe* opportunity directly to this place.

I refer you to my Letter to Dr McHenry[3] for news from this quarter and am Dr Sir Yr oblig'd Friend and Servt

G L

ALS (NNC).
1. His fiancée, Catharine Biddle.
2. Gen. Thomas Mifflin was one of Lux's favorite subjects of gossip. Mifflin, cleared by Congress of any wrongdoing as NG's predecessor, proved again to be a very popular person in Pennsylvania, and he was later elected to various offices—including

three terms as governor. Rossman's *Mifflin* treats the subject with objectivity. On Mifflin's differences with Joseph Reed and the Pennsylvania Council, see below, note at Reed to NG, 5 November.

3. See biographical note, McHenry to NG, 8 November, below.

From Colonel James Abeel

[Morristown, N.J., 25 October 1778. Will try to find NG's watch.[1] Returns are done "in as correct a manner as possible." Needs invoices so he can tell what is missing from Sussex County; some stores intended for him were sent by Colonel Hooper to John Mitchell in Philadelphia; will send someone through Sussex to see if any can be found, but fears "foul play somewhere."[2] LB (NjHi) 2 pp.]

1. See above, NG to Abeel, 21 October.
2. See follow-up, 31 October, below.

From Captain John Gooch

Dear General   Boston Octr 25, 1778

I'm almost afraid to trouble you with another Letter, but will engage not to write one in a long time again by way of attonement for thus often intruding on your Patience. I'm now going to do what some may censure me for as not belonging to my Department, but as I presume not to do it Officially but mearly as a Member of the Community, I think it a Duty as incumbent on me as any Individual to represent everything that may serve the Publick.

I mean to informe you of the situation of the Quarter Masters Department in this Post. I was appointed in July 1777 an A[sst. Deputy] QMGl and stationd at Springfield. At that time the Department was greatly in Debt, and ever since the Debt has been increasing even in the Department at Springfield. When I left it, which was in the Novr. following my Appointment, the Debt that was there contracted amounted to more than ten thousand Dollars, above half which remains unpaid at this Day, and all the other Posts have increased their Debts in full Proportion. This keeps a continual murmuring amongst those that have money due. They tell it [to] their Neighbours, insinuate the Publick, or their Officers keep them out of their Money with some sinister Views. This brings a discredit on the Publick, and the Officer is at once stigmatized as unfaithfull. This makes People cautious of trusting either the Officer or the Publick, being suspicious of both, by which means Publick Stores are often unavoidably delay'd, it not being Possible to procure Teams, knowing they will not recive their pay on their return. While at the same time they are interceding and sometimes even under biding each other to transport private Property, that on any extraordinary demand [for] Teams, Application must be made to Councill for Warrants to impress, which does not inspire a more favorable Idea of the Publick. Whereas had it been Duly paid, Press Warrants would have been useless [i.e., unnecessary], for the Teamsters would have been fond of the Publick's imploy, and Teams never wanted for transporting Stores.

Duns for Debts due from the Publick continually [arrive] at the Office Door, cursing all publick Business, damning themselves if ever they cart for the Continent again; this is humilliating to the Officers and degrading to the Publick. I have even known an Instance where a Number [who] had agreed to take publick Stores, on heareing these Dunns making their complaints, refused to take the Stores and Loaded with Private Property and I'm well inf[ormed] divers Instances of Like nature have happend from Sim[ilar] causes. These are Grievances that greatly injure the Publick by retarding every kind of Business, creates a General discontent and reduces the Officers to the Most ridiculous Situation. All these Evills arrise in consequence of moneys not being duly remitted to the Officers of this Department. It has ever been kept short above one half what the Dissbursements have amounted to.[1]

I observe Congress have granted Genl Mifflin tw[o] Million Dollars to discharge his Publick Debts.[2] This Department will require not less than half a Million, and should the other Departments be as much in Debt as this, it will go but [a] small way towards liquidateing his accounts. But I hope tha[t is] not the case, as I'm inform'd the other Departments have [been] much better supplied with Cash. This post only seems to have been forgotten. I have known the DQMr here to be destitute [of] money for above six weeks together, and at this time is not in a much better situation. For my Part I have not Received one hundred[th] part sufficient to supply this Post, and have not at this time one farthing, and inform'd to Day Hay is sold for thirty pounds Pr Ton which will require Just double the sum to supply this post it would when I came into Office. I could then have Purchased ten thousand pounds what will now require twenty thousand [had?] I been properly furnished with money. I'm now lossing the chance for Purchasing Oates. Their is in this Harbour twenty thousand Bushls that came round from Salem in the Prizes I mention'd in my former Letter. I could now purchase for a whole twelvemonth at a tolerable Rate had I money.[3] Twenty four thousand Dollars would purchase what Oates would be necessary here.

For want of money to purchase in proper time, the Publick Debt is vastly increased. Of consequence the large sums taken to discharge them, by making a great Plenty of money daily, Depreciates it's value, that what it will finally come to I fear, but fear even to

Prophecy; confident I am this Department could never have been sufferd to remain in such a situation, had it ever been properly Represented. From a certainty of that I have undertaken the Task, and have
thus far proceeded and I hope no person can take Offence, as I mean
to give none. Thus much further I can say that the People at large
stick not to say that the money is Depreciated as much by the Publick
[ie., government], as by the Averice of Individualls.

I would beg to be informd wether the Officers on the Staff are
intituled to draw Clothing from the Continental Store. General Heath
being uncertain declines granting any Orders for that purpose. The
Staff in the other Departments have that indulgence. If we are obliged
to Purchase at the present exorbitant price our pay will not be sufficient to furnish us with Clothing and I can see no Reason why we
must be excluded.[4] I am Dr Genl with the greatest Respect Your much
obliged and most obedt Servant

JOHN GOOCH

ALS (PPAmP). Since original is deteriorated at edges, many words with
missing final letters have been restored—usually silently.

1. In his letter to NG of 24 October, above, Gooch had blamed Thomas Chase,
under whom he had served at Springfield, for the lack of payment. On 25 December
1778 the executive council of Massachusetts ordered Chase to pay the past accounts
due to teamsters and drivers to insure "that in future emergencies people may be
induced to turn out to serve the public." This letter is in PPAmP.

2. Congress on 17 September granted Mifflin one million dollars to settle his
accounts. (JCC, 12: 921)

3. Gooch's letter of 24 October, above, does not mention prizes. His reference
could be to those taken by the French fleet.

4. If NG wrote to Heath about this, the letter has not been found.

To Joseph Reed

Dear Sir   Camp at Fredricksburg [N.Y] Octo 26th 1778

Inclosd is the arrangement of Col [Christopher] Greens battallion
which he desird me to forward to you for the approbation of Congress.[1]

I have seen several paragraphs of Letters from you to Mr Pettit. I
thank you kindly for the hints you give. What you recommend will
take place.[2] The change would have been long before this, had I not
been detaind to the Eastward longer than I expected. Mr Pettits
prudence, knowledge of business and constant attention I hope will
go a great way to silence all complaints. I never was more happy in
my life at any circumstance than that Mr Pettit belongs to the department. His knowledge, his manners and attention to business, are all
so well adapted to the duties of the office that he is of the highest
importance to me. I shall be always happy to receive your advice and
information at all Times as well upon the business of my department
as other matters that may effect my interest or reputation.

I am told General Mifflin is striveing to get into the *President's Chair*. Every body wishes you to accept it; and no one more than myself providing it was consistent with your views and interest.[3] I am happy to hear the Rhode Island expedition is spoke on with some degree of approbation. General Sullivan is the most unlucky man in the World. I thought it almost impossible for him to fail in the object of the expedition.[4] Indeed I was dreaming of whole Hosts of men and Cargoes of Generals to grace our triumph. But all at once the prospect fled like a shadow. I was very happy that the General and I had a good agreement during the siege. At my leaving Rhode Island he wrote me one of the highest Letters of thanks you ever saw pennd.[5] I have not time to add more at present. I will send you a Journal kept by Major Gibbs who was one of my family during the expedition.[6] I am dear Sir your most obedient humble Servt

NATH GREENE

ALS (NHi).
    1. The arrangement of Col. Christopher Greene's Black Regiment has been lost. NG must have known that Reed had resigned his seat in Congress on 12 October to run for the Pennsylvania executive council, but apparently felt that Reed still had influence to get Colonel Greene's arrangement approved.
    2. Reed's letter to his brother-in-law, Charles Pettit (NG's assistant), undoubtedly relayed criticism of the quartermaster department agents. On abuses in the department, see note at Marchant to NG, 5 November, below.
    3. Reed had been elected to the executive council in October, had taken his seat on 24 November, and on 1 December was selected by that group to become its president—the equivalent of being the governor of Pennsylvania. (See note at Reed to NG, 5 November, below.)
    4. The campaign in Rhode Island.
    5. See above, vol. 2: 541–42.
    6. Caleb Gibbs had been a member of Washington's Guards. (Fitzpatrick, *GW*, 12: 82n) Part of his journal is reprinted in *Pa. Archives*, 6: 734–36.

To Colonel Charles Stewart[1]

[Fredericksburg, N.Y., 26 October 1778. Lists amounts of rations to be allowed artificers. Excerpted from Greene, *Greene*, 2:400.]

    1. Stewart was commissary general of issues 1777–81.

Estimate of Teams Required to Transport Provisions and Forage from Trenton to Kings Ferry[1]

[Camp near Fredericksburg, N.Y., before 27 October 1778]
    It is supposed that about 50,000 Rations per Day are required for the Supply of the Army and its Appendages on the East Side of Hudson's River, including the Troops at Boston and other Places in New England, and the Convention Troops.[2] These, computing six Barrels to one thousand Rations, will call for a daily Delivery of 300

Barrels of Flour. The New England States can furnish no part of this Supply, not having enough within themselves for the Consumption of the Inhabitants. New-Jersey, from the Failure of the late Crop, can scarcely be relied on for any considerable Quantity. The Produce of New York may be thought to be not more than a sufficient Reserve for contingent Demands which may arise from calling out the Militia or other emergenc[i]es, especially while the French Fleet remains at Boston. The daily Supply for the Army must therefore come from the West Side of [the] Delaware; and from Trenton to Hudson's River must be transported by Land.

Allowing the Waggons to carry on an Average 7 1/2 Barrels each; to transport 300 Barrels will require 40 Waggons.

The Distance from Trenton to King's Ferry is about 105 Miles; supposing the Teams to travel ten Miles per Day, it will take 21 Days to perform the Trip: therefore to deliver 300 Barrels each Day will require the constant Employment of 840 Waggons.

These will require at 4 to a Team . . . 3360 Horses
One Riding Horse to every 10 Teams . . 84
Forage Teams, as Forage must also be
    brought from Trenton, say . . . . . <u>2056</u>
                    5500 Horses

Allowing these Horses Forage equal to one Peck and a half of Grain per Day, the daily Consumption will be upwards of 2000 Bushels. This, on a medium, must be transported half the Distance from Trenton to Hudson's River, say 50 Miles; and, allowing the Teams to carry about 40 Bushels each, and ten Days to perform the Trip, will require the constant Employment of 500 Teams.

Suppose the Army to take such a Position as that all the Team-Horses may be sent away except such as may be necessary for the mere Camp Duty, there will remain, together with those for the Saddle, at least 1000 Horses. Allowing these each one Peck per Day, will require a daily issue of

                          250 Bus [Bushels] of Grain

Suppose 18,000 Bushels can be
procured on the East Side of
Hudson's River, this on an
Average of 180 Days or Six
Months, will allow a Deduction of . . . . . <u>100</u> [Bushels]
          The remaining . . . . .150 Bushels per Day must come from Trenton; to transport which will require at
4 Loads per Day . . . . 84 Teams
Additional Forage Teams in Proportion . . . . <u>50</u>
                       134 Teams

The number of Teams necessary to be employed between Trenton and King's Ferry, will therefore be

To deliver 300 Barrels of Flour per Day 840
To Forage these and the Forage Teams 500
To deliver 150 Bushels of Grain per day . . . 84
To Forage these and the Forage Teams 50   134
                                                  ————
                                         1474 Teams
                                         [5896 Horses][3]

Estimate of Horses to be detained with the Army

The Commander in Chief and his Family 30
6 Major Generals . . . . each 6 36
12 Brigadiers . . . . each 4 48
48 Regiments . . . . each 3 144   258 [Horses]
                                                  ————
Paymaster Genl and Assistants , , , , , , , , , , 5
Quarter Master Genl and Family, and Spare
   Horses for occasional Service 20
Brigade Quarter Masters 12
Commissary's Line 12
Muster Master and Assistants 6
Auditors . , ... 4
Forage Department 20
Hospital 10
Expresses 20
Judge Advocate, Chaplains, Engineers
   and others not mentioned, say 20
Occasional Visitors on Business &c 100
                                                  ————
               Riding Horses   [229]   229
          [Total Riding Horses]   ————
                                             487
          Teams
For His Excellency's Family 2
6 M. Generals 6
12 Brigadiers 12
12 Brigades each 4 48
Q'ur Mr Genl and Assistants 2
Com'y Genl of Forage 1
2 Comm'y Generals 2
Reserve Teams 10
Teams daily arriving 40
Detention by accidents equal to 10   50
                                                  ————
                                         133 at 4
                                  Horses each 532
                                         1019 Horses
                     [Total number of horses 6915][4]

D (Washington Papers: DLC).

1. This undated document is in the hand of Charles Pettit, NG's assistant. NG mentioned in his letter to Washington of 18 October, above, that he had made such a "calculation" to accompany that letter, but he did not enclose it. It is likely that Pettit had prepared the calculation since he had had to cope with transportation and forage problems during the two and a half months that he headed the department in NG's absence. NG, moreover, would hardly have had time to make a detailed study before writing to Washington on the eighteenth, having arrived from Rhode Island only two days earlier. He may, however, have contributed to it, and in any case before delivering this final draft to Washington, he obviously approved it. Washington docketed it under "Maj. Gen. Greene," while Varick's transcript, copied later, headed it "M. General Greene's Estimate." Washington dated his copy (probably later) as between 19 and 27 October, although NG spoke in his letter of the twenty-seventh of its having been delivered to Washington "a few Days since."

Few documents reveal so forcefully the army's dependence on horses and forage. It is the basis for NG's 27 October letter to Washington below, also written by Pettit.

2. The figure of 50,000 rations is extremely conservative, considering the number of men to be fed. In October, Washington listed 22,291 troops fit for duty east of the Hudson—in New York, Rhode Island, and Connecticut. (Lesser, *Sinews*, pp. 88–90) With 5,000 British prisoners (the Convention troops) in Massachusetts, the total would have been approximately 28,000. NG had estimated in a letter to John Brown, 6 September 1778 that "a well appointed" army would draw three times as many rations as it had men, an "irregular" army even more. See above, vol. 2: 510.

3. In the first figures listed above, Pettit had allowed one riding horse for every ten wagons. For 1,474 teams, therefore, an additional 147 riding horses should have been listed.

4. Pettit did not carry out this total, which, with the 147 riding horses mentioned in note 3 above, would have brought the number to 7,062.

See Map 1 for geographic references above.

To Colonel Ephraim Bowen[1]

Dear Sir   Camp at Fredricksburg [N.Y.] 27th Octo 1778

Your favor of the 23d this moment came to hand.[2] I am sorry it is not in my power to enable you to repay the Money borrowed from the Military Chest. The first supply of money that comes to hand shall be appropriated to that purpose. General Sullivan was very obligeing in lending the Money and I wish to repay it in a way agreeable to his wishes.

With respect to damage done by the Troops. The common mode has been to get some good substantial free holders to view the damages, make an account thereof, and certify it before some Civil Magistrate; and these accounts are transmited to the *Board of War*: who will direct payment hereafter, so as to do equal justice to all Inhabitants of the United States that have been injurd by Military operations.[3]

With regard to the Carts, Cattle, Yokes, Chains &ca. that were lost upon the Rhode Island expedition. I am sensible it is a great hardship upon the People to lose their property and get no satisfaction. I think General Sullivan should give orders for payment after being acquainted fully with the circumstances. However if he will not, such Teams as were impressed into the service and sustaind real losses properly provd, you may make them satisfaction.[4] You must be very careful in the payment of these accounts as there will be a critical examination. The Reasons must appear clear and the facts fully ascertaind That no doubts may remain of the losses sustaind or of the Justice of payment.

I intended to have orderd you a party of Artificers; but at my return, I found it impossible to spare them from this Army, without doing more injury to us, than they could be of service to you. You must therefore endeavor to do without them.

You will forward us a copy of your accounts as soon as you possibly can with conveniency. We are anxious to lay a state of our expenditure before the Congress, Least they should think from the very great sums that have been granted us there is some misapplication. I have forgot whether I told you that I was to pay for the Horse Col [John] Laurens had, he haveing given me an order on his Father for the Money at Philadelphia. I am Sir your humble Sert

NATH GREENE

ALS (RHi).
1. Ephraim Bowen, Jr. (1753–1842), NG's deputy quartermaster for Rhode Island, had won local fame before the war as one of the youngest participants in the destruction of the *Gaspee*. (On that incident, see above, vol. 1: 29n.) He lived on for seventy years to become the sole survivor of the episode. A lieutenant in NG's brigade from its inception in May 1775, he was promoted to captain in January 1776. On NG's recommendation he was given leave in September 1776 in New York to become an assistant deputy quartermaster under Hugh Hughes for the area east of the Hudson River. In 1777 he resigned from his regiment when General Mifflin appointed him deputy quartermaster for Rhode Island, a post he continued to hold throughout NG's tenure as quartermaster general. He was NG's friend as well as his deputy. (Biographical information taken from depositions of Charles F. Tillinghast, Stephen Olney, and John Dexter before clerk of the Court of Common Pleas, Providence, 1832. RAr)
2. Since this letter appears to be an answer to Bowen's of 20 October, above, there may have been no letter of the twenty-third.
3. On this mode of settlement, see above, vol. 2: 419–20n.
4. Sullivan was not persuaded to give such orders and the matter dragged on until February 1779. (See Bowen to NG, 6 January, below.) In the meantime, NG changed his mind about Bowen's making "satisfaction" for such losses, as seen below, Burnet to Bowen and NG to Sullivan, 9 February 1779.

To Colonel Thomas Chase

[Fredericksburg, N.Y., 27 October 1778. In response to Chase's letter of 21 October,[1] NG is too far removed to judge whether valuable wharf space should be used as barracks. Chase must take directions from General Heath in this, as well as in the matter of paying rent for its use. ADfS (NHi) 2 pp.]

1. Letter not found.

To George Washington

Sir   Camp near Fredricksburg [N.Y.] 27th October 1778

The Campaign being near a Close, the Cantoning of the Troops for the Winter is probably under Your Excellency's Consideration. In the Choice of a Position I doubt not due Regard will be paid to the Practicability of obtaining Supplies of Provisions and Forage; But as the Means of furnishing these Capital Articles fall much within my Department, and I am apprehensive of some Difficulties which may not have occurred to Your Excellency, I think it incumbent on me to lay before you the present state of our Resourses, and to suggest a Plan which appears to me to afford a better Prospect of ensuring a Supply of Provisions for the Army and the Eastern Posts than that now in use.

The Seat of War having continued for nearly three Years in the States of New York, New Jersey and Pennsylvania, the Husbandmen of these States have been so much engaged in the Publick Service as Militiamen, Teamsters, Artificers &c, and the Country has been so much exposed to the Depredations of the Enemy, and no inconsiderable Part of it at Times in their actual Possession, that a very large Proportion of Land has remained unimproved, and the Residue has not been cultivated with the accustomed Vigor. Hence the Resourses of these States, for Provisions and Forage, are greatly reduced, more especially in New-York and New-Jersey where the Ravages as well as the Burden of the War have been peculiarly great and distressing. In Proportion as the Resourses have become scanty, the Demand for Land Carriage has increased, the Supplies for the Army being necessarily drawn from greater Distances. This in Turn, has increased the Consumption of Forage to so great a Degree that the Country on every Side of the Army within a convenient Distance of the Lines of Communication is almost entirely exhausted.[1]

The Quantity of Flour necessary to supply the Grand Army and the Troops and Prisoners in Massachusets[2] Bay and Rhode Island, is estimated at 300 Barrels per Day. Of this perhaps no Part can with Propriety be drawn from the Country eastward of [the] Delaware, the quantity which can be procured in that Region being not more than may be absolutely necessary for other Purposes; the whole must therefore come from the west Side of [the] Delaware. I have already shewn to Your Excellency by a Calculation delivered in a few Days since, that to convey this Daily Supply from Trenton to Kings Ferry only, would require the constant Employment of 1340 Waggons with about 5500 Horses, including the Forage Teams necessary to support those immediatly transporting the Flour.[3]

The Deputy Quarter Master General for the State of New-Jersey is a Gentleman of great Industry, well acquainted with Business and stands fair with the People;[4] he has been engaged for several Months past in forming Magazines at different Posts on the Roads through his District; but the constant Consumption has been so great that, with the Aid of the Grain he has received from the Westward, he has not been able to retain a single Bushel in Store, nor will the Country he is in afford him any farther Supply worth mentioning. As to Hay, he has some collected at different Magazines, but the whole he can procure will scarcely be sufficient to supply the estimated Number of Horses for two Months.[5] Instances have already been not unfrequent of Teams being delayed several Days merely through Want of Forage to enable them to proceed, and in some Cases the Loads have been discharged by the Way and the Teams returned, from the same Cause. The Forage to support the Teams in New-Jersey must therefore come chiefly from the West Side of [the] Delaware also, and the greater Part of it from Chesapeak Bay. The Distance it must travel is so great that, even while the Rivers continue open, it is with Difficulty a Quantity equal to the current Demand can be got forward, and the Magazines are yet empty; so that on the least Obstruction of the Navigation, Disappointment must ensue, and the Land Carriage through New-Jersey in a great Measure Cease.

This, however, is not the only Way in which we may meet Disappointment. Land Carriage through so great an Extent of Country abounding with Rivers, Mountains and difficult Passes, is liable to numerous Accidents, Delays and Obstructions of various Kinds which the utmost Precaution cannot altogether avoid. If, under the favourable Circumstances of mild Weather and good Roads, we find it difficult to bring forward a bare Sufficiency for a current Supply, but cannot accumulate a Stock to guard against any accidental Delay, what must be our Condition when the Winter Season arrives in which the Roads are commonly so bad as to render the Passage of Waggons very precarious, and the Rivers impassable perhaps for Weeks together?

But supposing a sufficient Quantity of Forage to be attainable and that no other Obstacle should remain but the Expence; this alone would be worthy of Consideration. The Hire of a Team and Driver, fed by the Publick, is now established at 55s Pennsylvania Currency per Day;[6] the Drivers Ration with little Allowances which must be made to such People, will not cost less than 5s; the Forage for each Team will cost the Publick about 6 Dollars per Day. The daily Expences for each Team will therefore be fourteen Dollars: which for 1340 Teams estimated for the Transportation from the Delaware to Hudson's River will amount to 18,760 Dollars per Day, equal to more than half a Million per Month for that Distance only.[7] The Expence of

Transportation farther Eastward may be inferred. According to this Estimate the Land Carriage of a Barrel of Flour will cost but little less than six Dollars for every ten miles, which, extravagant as it may appear, and though more than it may have heretofore cost, will not be found far from the Truth in Future if so great a Quantity must be urged on in Teams hired by the Day, and the Forage to support them imported from other States.

The Difficulty of transporting so great a Distance by Land the Quantity of Flour necessary for the current Demand, would, in common Times and in the Summer Season, render such a supply too precarious to be relied on without the previous Establishment of Magazines to guard against accidental Delays. I therefore take it for granted that under the present Circumstances the Necessity of establishing such Magazines, as well in the Neighbourhood of Hudson's River as within a convenient Distance from Boston, must be too apparent to admit of Doubt. To form such Magazines by Land Carriage only, appears to me utterly impossible, and no Expedient seems to be left but at all Hazards to attempt it by Water.[8] A sufficient Quantity of Flour I am told may readily be collected on Chesapeake or the Delaware. I would therefore beg Leave to suggest the Propriety of purchasing or hiring of a Number of small Vessels carrying from 200 to 500 Barrels each and loading them with Flour and other Necessaries for Boston or such other Port as may be proper; they may sail separately which will make the Risk the smaller, and they may occasionally run into Harbours to avoid Cruisers. If only one out of four of these Vessels should arrive safely it would be a Saving in Point of Expence; but with proper Management I cannot but imagine the Arrival of at least two, if not three out of four may be fairly counted upon. With the greatest Respect I have the Honor to be Your Excellency's most Obedient and most humble Servant

NATHANAEL GREENE

LS (Washington Papers: DLC). This letter, like the estimate above of "Before 27 October," is in Pettit's hand. From the style, it would appear that Pettit had also composed most of it. If so, he certainly conferred with NG, as he did in preparing the estimate above.

1. In his letter to Washington of 18 October, above, NG had pointed out the scarcity of provisions north and east of the Delaware and the difficulties in crossing the Hudson.

2. Although NG was not aware of it, Congress had already ordered the five thousand British prisoners of the Convention army to move from Massachusetts to Virginia. See below, NG to Davenport, 9 November.

3. See "Estimate" cited in source note above.

4. Moore Furman.

5. Udny Hay, deputy quartermaster general at Fishkill, N.Y.

6. Nominally, about $7.50.

7. NG's figures are in Continental dollars, which had sunk to about one fourth of their value.

8. The advocacy of water transport was more typical of NG's thinking than

Pettit's. (See vol. 2: 319–20n. See also his letter to Lord Stirling, 31 December, below.) Since July, Jeremiah Wadsworth, a former sea captain, had also been advocating the use of ships to transport flour to New England, which was suffering from a greater than usual shortage of flour. Congress had authorized Wadsworth in August to purchase twenty thousand barrels of flour in the South, to acquire vessels, and to confer with the Marine Committee for a protective convoy. (*JCC*, 11: 831–32). Nothing, however, seems to have come of plans for acquiring vessels or arranging for a convoy. (For a thorough discussion of New England's food shortages during 1778–79, see section on "The Grain Crisis" in Buel, *Dear Liberty*, pp. 159–65.) NG was probably correct in his estimates of the percentage of vessels—especially small vessels—that could get through the British blockade. Britain had far too few naval vessels to guard a thousand miles of coastline, especially with the additional responsibility of supporting the army. Thus the American war effort had been largely sustained by military supplies that slipped through the blockade. It has been estimated that between 80 and 90 percent of the gunpowder used before 1777 was obtained from abroad. (Mackesy, *War*, pp. 98–102; Gruber, *Howe Brothers*, pp. 103–4)

By the late winter of 1778–79, however, the blockade was greatly strengthened by British privateers, which in NG's words had become "as thick upon the coast as grass hoppers." (NG to Wadsworth, #1, 19 March, below) British privateers also entered Chesapeake Bay and hindered the shipment of flour from Virginia. (Finnie to NG, 11 February 1779, below)

See Maps 1 and 4 for geographic references above.

From Joseph Webb

[Wethersfield, Connecticut, 27 October 1778. Has arranged to finish stores, which he will deliver to Nehemiah Hubbard as ordered. Sorry he missed NG's visit. ALS (PPAmP) 1 p.]

To George Washington

Sir   Camp Fredricksburg [N.Y.] 28th Octo 1778
    Inclosd is General Schuylers Letter, which I have read.[1]
    The utillity of the plan which he recommends being altogether dependant upon the Canada expedition, and that being rather in contemplation than agreed upon, I think it will be necessary before I give any orders upon the matter to receive your Excellencys instructions upon that head.
    Your Excellency expressed a desire to have all the Battaues [Bateaux] collected and repaird that were not in actual service that are now upon the North River. I could wish to know where you would have them collected, and how soon to have the repairs compleated.
    As soon as your Excellency has determind in your own mind, the line of cantonment I could wish to receive a private intimation of it because it would enable me to make many previous and necessary preparations, not explanatory of your Excellencys intentions.[2] I have the honor to be with great respect Your Excellencys most Obedient humble Sert

NATH GREENE

ALS (Washington Papers: DLC).

1. The subject of General Schuyler's letter of 9 October, a possible invasion of Canada, was not a new one. Pressure for such a venture had been steadily mounting in recent weeks. Advocates in and out of Congress, in fact, had kept the pot simmering since Lafayette's abortive "irruption" into Canada the previous winter. (See above, vol. 2: 276n) Washington's correspondence on the subject between August 1778 and January 1779 (especially with Congress) reveals a great ambivalence on his part about such an expedition. This uncertainty was partly the result of changing circumstances as well as conflicting advice from military advisers. It also grew out of Washington's attempt to please certain members of Congress and his young friend, the Marquis de Lafayette, even while going against his own judgment at times.

Both Washington and NG, who had disapproved of Lafayette's ill-prepared expedition of January 1778 (Washington had called it a "child of folly"), agreed that the "emancipation" of Canada was a highly desirable objective—as long as it did not weaken the army or bring about a permanent return of the French to Quebec. Not only did the specter of another British offensive from the north loom as a possibility while Canada remained in British hands, but Canada was the base for Indian and Tory raids along the frontiers of New York and Pennsylvania. Finally, of course, the "emancipation" of Canada would add a fourteenth state that was rich in resources and strategically located. (Justin H. Smith's classic two-volume work, *Our Struggle for the Fourteenth Colony* [1907] is still the best general study of the subject.)

Not surprisingly, interest in Canada was strongest among upstate New Yorkers and New Englanders—and among the latter, especially those from New Hampshire and Massachusetts whose territory bordered Canada. To the Canada watchers, the summer of 1778 had seemed a propitious time for reviving the project, because of the arrival of d'Estaing's fleet with its contingent of French marines (although the French fleet was to prove a disappointment), and because of the resignation of Sir Guy Carleton, the able governor and commander in chief of Canada, whose fairness in the treatment of French dissenters had kept Quebec from falling like a ripe plum into America's lap. In July he was replaced by the Swiss-born Gen. Frederick Haldimand, whose ignorance of English civil government and his harshness as an official was apparently alienating many of the French Canadians.

Although Canada had never been at the center of Washington's concerns, there was no dearth of military men to encourage the "Canada faction" in Congress. Chief among these were three major generals, all of whom hoped to lead an invasion force—Schuyler, Gates, and Lafayette. They were abetted by even more ardent military men, who were familiar with the Canadian border country, Col. Moses Hazen of the Continental army's volunteer "Canadian Regiment" (also known as "Congress's Own") and two New Hampshire militiamen, Gen. Jacob Bayley and Col. Timothy Bedel, both of whom had extensive land holdings on either side of the upper Connecticut River in an area called Co'os. (Map 2) All three had patriotic as well as personal reasons for wanting a union with Canada.

Of the three major generals, Schuyler of New York was the most knowledgeable about Canada. He was frank to suggest to Washington the desirability of an invasion over the frozen waters of Lake Champlain in the winter of 1778–79. Gates and Lafayette, who were antagonistic contenders for Congress's favor, were more secretive than Schuyler. They favored the approach by Co'os. With the arrival of d'Estaing, it had been Lafayette's hope to lead American and French soldiers into Canada in the summer or fall of 1778 in collaboration with d'Estaing's fleet. After d'Estaing's failure in the attack on Newport in August 1778 forced a postponement of such a venture, Lafayette was still effective with many members of Congress in pushing for a joint venture in 1779, with himself at the head of the invasion force when he returned from a temporary visit to France in the spring.

Also during the summer of 1778, General Gates had been working through Colonel Bedel to gain intelligence of the border area on the upper Connecticut River and to advance his own plans for a September invasion. In mid-summer he sent Bedel to Philadelphia to inform interested members of Congress of the timeliness and practicality of his plans. Bedel was an effective promoter. (Nelson, *Gates*, pp. 200–201) When it seemed that French help for the time being was out, a majority in Congress expressed interest in Gates's plan, while keeping possible French participation in mind for the following spring.

In early September, Congress asked Washington for his opinion of such an invasion in the autumn or the winter. On 10 September, Washington, who was aware of Gates's interest but not of his secret plans, called a meeting with Gates, Hazen, and Bayley to ask for their written opinions. After reiterating the advantages of such an invasion, they proposed three invasion routes, all based from Co'os and to begin in January. As Washington learned later, Bayley (and his informant Bedel) greatly exaggerated local supplies that would be made available at Co'os. Washington dispatched Hazen to Congress in Philadelphia with the report so that he would be available to answer delegates' questions. (Allan S. Everest, *Moses Hazen and the Canadian Refugees in the American Revolution* [Syracuse, N.Y., Syracuse University Press, 1976], pp. 62–63) Hazen also carried Washington's letter of 12 September to Congress with his comments on the report. Washington judged that their plan, though "attended with many difficulties, affords a reasonable prospect of success." He qualified his support by saying the undertaking would depend on "the enemy's evacuating these states [New York and New England]" and added, "While they keep their present footing, we shall find employment enough in defending ourselves, without meditating conquests." (Fitzpatrick, *GW*, 12: 434–35) He went on somewhat ambiguously, however, to declare, without again mentioning the necessity of British withdrawal from New York as a condition, that preparations should begin at once if a winter invasion were planned: magazines of stores should be established, warm clothing and snow shoes obtained, etc.

Washington's 12 September letter was the beginning of a series of exchanges with Congress on the invasion of Canada that must have consumed most of his free time for the following three months. Some delegates from New England, paying slight heed to Washington's conditions, were ready to urge an immediate invasion, but Congress as a whole was more cautious. President Laurens wrote Washington on 16 September that he was "directed to intimate that Congress highly approve laying up Magazines of forage and Provisions . . . if the Motions of the Enemy shall render the measure expedient." Washington was to make every preparation he should "deem necessary." (Fitzpatrick, *GW*, 12: 436n)

NG was still in Boston when this letter reached camp, but Washington undoubtedly discussed the project with Charles Pettit, NG's assistant. On 26 September, Washington authorized General Bayley in Co'os to obtain fifteen hundred snow shoes and skins for "at least four thousand mocosons." (Ibid, 12: 507) On 3 October he reiterated his requests, warning Bayley to keep his moves secret. (Ibid, 13: 19) Schuyler's 9 October letter to Washington argued against an expedition from Co'os and the upper Connecticut River and pushed for the Lake Champlain route. When NG returned to camp in mid-October, he probably heard about the project for the first time, although there is no record of his reaction.

Schuyler's arguments against the Co'os approach undoubtedly caused Washington to have some second thoughts about proceeding by that route. Moreover, he had begun to have reasons to suspect the accuracy of the intelligence he was receiving from General Bayley and Colonel Bedel, especially on the amount of local supplies available, as he noted in his letter to NG on 29 October, below. In a letter to Washington on 5 November, Bayley admitted that flour was not as plentiful as he had earlier thought. (Washington Papers, DLC) If most supplies were to be hauled from southern New England to the upper Connecticut River region, NG was convinced that the means of transportation were far from adequate. Moreover, Commissary Wadsworth could not promise sufficient food.

On 11 November, Washington informed Congress that "zeal for the expedition" had made Bayley and the others at Co'os "much too sanguine in the matter" of local supplies. (Fitzpatrick, *GW*, 13: 241) Without local supplies, he wrote, "The difficulties of transportation, as represented by the Quarter Masters and Commissaries, supported by facts that speak for themselves, are so great and complicated, that I should have no hope of our being able from remote parts of the Continent, to throw in the quantity requisite for subsisting these troops during the Winter." (Ibid.) At the same time, he discouraged Schuyler from counting on his support for the Champlain route. NG and Wadsworth had convinced Washington that a winter invasion by any route was impractical.

On 24 November, Washington wrote Gates that "Several circumstances conspire to render an expedition into Canada this Winter impracticable." Even if the enemy had withdrawn men from New York and Newport, he said, "want of provisions only, in proper time, would have been an insuperable bar." (Fitzpatrick, *GW*, 13: 319) The following day he wrote General Bayley that the condition of supplies "with some other weighty considerations, make it necessary to suspend the expedition to Canada for this winter." (Ibid, pp. 326–27)

Congress was apparently satisfied that a winter invasion was out of the question, but by no means had it abandoned plans for collaborating with the French in such a venture during the spring or summer of 1779 as Lafayette had been urging. On 27 October, the Foreign Affairs Committee wrote Washington that they were enclosing a plan for such a joint effort on which they wished his opinion. (The letter is in the Washington Papers, DLC; the plan, in the form of a letter of instruction to Benjamin Franklin in Paris, was printed on 22 October 1778, *JCC*, 12: 1039–48.) The plan was a long, unbelievably complicated one, which, among other things, boldly called for a joint invasion of Quebec and Halifax, with side expeditions to Niagara and Detroit.

The Foreign Affairs Committee could hardly have been unaware of the imposition they had placed on Washington. To respond knowledgeably on the many points raised in the letter to Franklin would have required an expertise possessed by no single person, not to mention months of Washington's time to search out basic facts. Washington, nevertheless, set about nobly to respond the best he could. His thoughtful response, which he discussed with NG and other general officers at Fredericksburg, was contained in a twenty-six page letter, dated 11 November. (Fitzpatrick, *GW*, 13: 223–44) Although he pointed out the multiplicity of difficulties involved in such a broad offensive, he did not absolutely rule it out, and, in fact, perhaps to soften his criticisms, he agreed to do his utmost to have supplies sent northward during the winter in preparation for a possible joint spring offensive.

He set about on the task at once, although the burden fell largely upon the quartermaster and commissary departments. A winter invasion was a thing of the past, but the task of getting supplies to the frozen northland remained to plague NG, as the correspondence below during December testified. (See NG to Morgan Lewis, 6 December; Washington to NG, 15 and 17 December; NG to and from Jeremiah Wadsworth, 17 December; NG to Pettit, 17 December; and Abeel to NG, 21, 24, 27 and 30 December.)

In the meantime, plans for a spring or summer invasion had hit some snags in Congress. Immediately after writing Congress on 11 November, Washington had written privately to President Laurens, whom he knew he could trust, saying he had one reservation he did not include (because he did not want Lafayette to see it) in his long letter to Congress. This was his fear of having a large number of French soldiers in Canada, which might lead to the French recovery of Quebec. To put them in that province, he said, "attached to them by all the ties of blood, habits, manners, religion and former connexion of government," he feared, "would be too great a temptation, to be resisted by any power actuated by the common maxims of national policy." (Fitzpatrick, *GW*, 13: 254) Laurens agreed, saying he believed that the scheme "originated in the breast of the Marquis de lafayette, encouraged probably by conferences with Count d'Estaing." Since Laurens, like Washington, had the greatest respect and affection for Lafayette, he believed the young Frenchman had the "purest motives." Lafayette never knew of their reservations about a collaborative invasion, and despite Washington's and Laurens's fears, there is no evidence that France had any ambitions to reclaim Quebec. (Laurens's letter is quoted in Fitzpatrick, *GW*, 13: 257–58n.)

Washington's twenty-six page letter of 11 November must have caused many delegates to reconsider the Franco-American expedition; Laurens undoubtedly influenced a few delegates close to him. At any rate, on 1 January, Laurens wrote a diplomatically phrased letter to Lafayette, stating that Congress had directed him to inform the Marquis that a number of reasons—including the conditions of American finances, "the nature of the country, the defect of supplies, and the impossibility of transporting them thither; to say nothing of the obstacles which a prudent enemy might throw in the way"—make it "not only imprudent but unjust" to enter into such a joint venture with their ally. (*JCC*, 13: 14)

A contemplated invasion of Canada was not completely dead, but thenceforth as noted below at NG to Washington, 5 January 1779, preparations for a spring invasion were being turned into a plan for an expedition against the Iroquois Indians in upstate New York.

2. For Washington's response, see below, 29 October.

See Map 2 for geographic references above.

To Colonel Ephraim Bowen

[Fredericksburg, N.Y., 29 October 1778. Money sent to repay General Sullivan. Is having portmanteaus and valises sent for officers in Glover's and Varnum's brigades, who are to pay for them if Congress refuses.[1] Excerpt from Greene, *Greene*, 2: 406–7.]

1. As noted below at NG to Board of War, 27 February 1779, Congress finally agreed to pay for them.

To Colonel Thomas Chase

[Fredericksburg, N.Y., 29 October 1778. Has sent money. General Gates is to command the Eastern district.[1] Chase should be on "good footing with the Commanding Officer under whom you serve for your own ease and for the reputation of your department." ALS (MiU-C) 1 p.]

1. At Boston; see Congress's resolution of 22 October in *JCC*, 12: 1038.

From George Washington

Dear Sir   Head Quarters [Fredericksburg, N.Y.] 29th October 1778

I have your favr of last evening. From present appearances and a variety of circumstances, I think we may conclude that nothing can be done towards the Canada expedition this Winter. It appears now, notwithstanding Genl Baileys assurances, that the Country, upon the head of Connecticut River, will afford but a scanty if any supply of provision. Genl Bailey has lately, upon a supposition that the expedition would be carried on at all events, called upon the Commissary at Albany to send up supplies of flour from thence. This I shall forbid.[1]

I rather meant that the Batteaus should be collected than repaired, as I understand that they are much scattered. The place is not material, so it be above the Highlands. When they are collected, if the persons who have the care of them, know anything of the business, they may repair them.[2]

Upon a full consideration of the subject, and a comparison of the opinions of the General Officers upon cantoning the Army for the Winter, I am led to fix upon three places—Danbury, West Point and its vicinities upon both sides the River, and Middle Brook in Jersey.[3] At the first I think we may determine upon two or three Brigades or thereabouts. At the others, the numbers will depend upon the Strength of the Enemy in New York this Winter. Should they, contrary to appearances and our expectations, remain there with *their* whole force, *ours* must be in proportion upon the North River; but should they send off the detachment which is now embarked, we may safely remove a greater number to Middle Brook than we would otherwise have done. There probably may be a Regiment or two thrown directly into the Clove near Sufferan [Suffern] where there are Barracks already built; and, if circumstances will admit, a Brigade at Albany &c. But there being very good Barracks there also and that Country ordered not to be drained but in case of necessity you will have no preparations to make in that quarter.

I think we may venture to assert the following position: That if the enemy do keep a Garrison at New York it will be of sufficient Strength to repel any attack that we can make with prudence during the Winter. I would therefore lay aside all thought of collecting our force suddenly for such a purpose and extend my views to more remote Cantonments than the above, should our necessities require it and circumstances justify it.

There are good Barracks at Trenton and Burlington, and the adjacent Country abounding in Wheat and Mills to manufacture it. Also, the troops stationed there being fed upon the spot, would consequently ease us in the article of carriage—our greatest difficulty.

I hope I have said sufficient to explain my meaning and intentions generally. You may therefor be making the necessary previous preparations at the three capital Points. Mr Caldwell some little time ago mentioned that there were very considerable quantities of salt and fresh Forage upon the Sound which Colo Biddle should immediately give orders to have removed to the foot of the Mountain, or at least so far from the Water, that it may be easily brought during the Winter to Camp. The necessity of reconnoitering proper positions for hutting will naturally strike you, and of collecting Tools, Boards, Stone and such materials as are requisite to make Barracks comfortable. I am Dear Sir Sincerely Yours

GO: WASHINGTON

LS (PPAmP).

1. On Bayley and the Canadian expedition, see above, NG to Washington, 28 October.

2. For more on the collection and repair of bateaux, see below, NG to Morgan Lewis, 30 October, as well as their correspondence in November and December 1778.

3. NG had suggested these areas for the army's winter quarters in his letter to Washington of 18 October, above.

See Maps 1 and 2 for geographic references above.

To Colonel Morgan Lewis

[Fredericksburg, N.Y., 30 October 1778. Washington requests that all bateaux on the North River be collected and repaired, if possible, although NG is unclear as to his reason.[1] A brigade may be quartered for the winter in Albany. Compliments to General Schuyler. ALS (NHi) 1 p.]

1. See above, NG to Washington, 28 October, and Washington to NG, 29 October. NG wrote this letter before receiving Washington's of 29 October, which answers the questions concerning repair of bateaux and reasons for collecting.

From Otis & Andrews

[Boston, 30 October 1778. Will send "quarter Cask of Red port" and dishes; also their corrected accounts. LS (PPAmP) 1 p.]

From Colonel William Shepard[1]

[Providence, R.I., 30 October 1778. Complains of "Mr Charles Whittelsey," formerly his regimental quartermaster and now quartermaster of Glover's brigade.[2] When some officers in the brigade "took a miff" at General Sullivan's orders, Whittelsey, "in Sted of trying to apease the officers and Settel the matter Tryed all in his Power to make the Breach greatier." Seventy six officers submitted resignations. Sullivan refused to accept them and "in Some measure Convinced them of there error and mistake." With difficulty "wee Stopt the matter from going any further." Whittelsey and others, who are left out of the new arrangement, are "trying to make all the mischief in there Power." He deserves to be "turned out of the Service."[3] ALS (PPAmP) 2 pp.]

1. William Shepard (1737–1817), colonel of the Fourth Massachusetts Regiment in Glover's brigade, had distinguished himself in the battle of Rhode Island in August. He later served three terms in the U.S. House of Representatives. (*DAB*)

2. Charles Whittlesey (so spelled in Heitman, *Register*) had the rare distinction of having been advanced from noncommissioned officer to ensign.

3. He was subsequently dismissed. (See NG to Bowen, 14 November, below.) The "new arrangement," which so displeased some officers, was not approved until 24 November. By it, Congress finally hammered out "rules" that it fondly hoped would stop squabbles over rank. (*JCC*, 12: 1154–60)

From Colonel James Abeel

[Morristown, N.J., 31 October 1778. Cannot get returns from Sussex County (Map 3); since he is sure valuable stores are there, he will have to "scour that Country" himself.[1] Tent cloth sent on to Philadelphia. Three thousand sets of horseshoes, twelve to fifteen hundred axes, many shoes, and some wedges and frows[2] are now being loaded. LB (NjHi) 2 pp.]

1. See above, Abeel to NG, 25 October.
2. A cleaving tool for splitting cask staves and shingles from a block of wood.

From Colonel James Abeel

[Morristown, N.J., 2 November 1778. Will send bed and table linens when finished, along with NG's watch, which he located.[1] LB (NjHi) 1 p.]

1. See above, NG to Abeel, 21 October and Abeel to NG, 25 October.

To Royal Flint[1]

Sir   Camp at Fredricksburg [N.Y.] November 3d 1778

In a Letter just receivd from Mr Nehemiah Hubbart [Hubbard] DQMG at Hartford, is the following paragraph.[2]

NB. "General Gates desires me to inform you that we have no Flour at this Post but what is taken from private people."

Hubbart then goes on and says I can furnish any Number of Teams to transport it to this place if I was directed where to send them.

I wish to know whether you have any particular orders you would wish to be given in consequence of the above information. I shall wait your answer before I write to Mr Hubbart.[3] I am Sir your humble Sert

NATH GREENE

ALS (CtHi).
1. Royal Flint, a former merchant, was assistant commissary for Connecticut troops until May 1778 when Jeremiah Wadsworth, commissary general, appointed Flint as his assistant. He resigned in early 1780 when Wadsworth resigned. In the meantime, NG and Flint had become close friends.
2. Hubbard's letter not found.

3. This letter illustrates the difficulties encountered by the supply services in a period when contradictory intelligence kept troops marching and countermarching. At the time Hubbard wrote, Gates was encamped near Hartford with six brigades of over ten thousand men awaiting developments to the East. Before Flint could respond to NG, however, provisions were no longer needed at Hartford because the six brigades were on their way back to Danbury (Map 1)—Gates then being en route alone to take command in Boston. (Troop movements from 20 October to 15 November are detailed in the Washington Papers, DLC, especially in Washington's correspondence with Generals Gates, Putnam, Parsons, and McDougall.)

To Colonel Ephraim Bowen

[Fredericksburg, N.Y., 4 November 1778. Requests a bill for cloth and hat and Bowen's accounts. Anxious that his New England deputies "may appear faithful stewards." Many feel British will leave New York; NG doubtful. From Greene, *Greene*, 2: 408.]

To Colonel James Abeel

[Fredericksburg, N.Y., 5 November 1778. Abeel's favor of the second received; NG is glad sheets are being made and his watch found. Abeel should stop buying horseshoes since Colonel Cox has contracted for enough. Frows, crosscut saws, and grindstones needed. ALS (RHi) 2 pp.]

From Colonel William S. Livingston

[Philadelphia, 5 November 1778. Congratulates NG on birth of daughter. Sorry Boston "is hurrying into the same Extravagence" as Philadelphia. Enemy's hopes rest on depreciation of dollar. Believes they will not evacuate U.S., but if they do, New York will be last. Disaffected members of New Jersey Assembly hope to displace the governor.[1] Has NG seen "Address" of New York Assembly to governor?[2] States must confederate before enemy leaves. Some members of Congress have said others who appear to favor confederation are keeping up feuds and dissensions "underhandedly." Criticizes Massachusetts for not changing representatives oftener. [Charles] Lee trying to "make a Party" against Washington; he and his "Family say [Washington] is an old Woman," without stability, judgment, etc.[3] "Give my Love to him." ALS (PPAmP) 3 pp.]

1. Governor Livingston had drawn the enmity of a small group by writing a series of articles for the *New Jersey Gazette* under the signature of "Hortentius," attacking loyalists and others hopeful of eventual British victory. (Lundlin, *Cockpit*, chapter 8, details the web of jealousies and intrigues in New Jersey.)
2. The address refers to the dissident residents of northeastern New York who styled themselves citizens of Vermont. (Clinton, *Papers*, 4: 176–78)
3. On Lee's court-martial, see below, NG to McDougall, 8 November.

From General Alexander McDougall

[Near Fredericksburg, N.Y.,[1] 5 November 1778. Needs grain for horses and tools for "blowing up rocks." Believes it is "morally certain" the enemy will not attempt a campaign east of New York before severe weather sets in. Fragment of an ALS (MiU-C) 1 p.]

1. He was encamped at this time at Second Hill, New Milford, Conn.

From Henry Marchant

Dear Sir   Philadelphia Nov 5th 1778

Yours of the 15th of October by Dr Hutchinson I rec'd. In my last I mentioned to you that I could have wished to have [damaged] the Business of your Department [had?] allowed you to have visited this City. I think the Heads of Departments should now and then put themselves near Congress. Much advantage might result thereby. The Members might be better informed of the Situation and wants of the Departments, and you would more clearly see the Views and Wishes of Congress, and be perhaps usefully informed of many Matters, and abuses which reach Our Ears; if not as a Body [then as?] Individuals.[1] That there are some [damaged] business in all the Departments I am sure of, and L. Chesterfields Observation can hardly be admitted.[2] For I believe the Fraud and Abuses are infinitely beyond what they are known to be. We are in the pursuit of some few, tho' of a deep die.

The Complaints in Maryland and Delaware are of the most grevious abuses of Swarms of Deputy Quarter masters, or such as pretend to be so—Assistants, Deputy assistants &c &c.[3] Their Insolence and [damaged] upon the Peoples one Letter for [damaged] Congress immediately to take into Consideration the Greviances they labour under that the great Disproportion of Disaffected in that State, are increased by these People and even good Whigs staggered. That the publick Monies are in private use may not be doubted of and either will [do] well to consider how they will support a Character with the Publick who, while they hold important offices under Congress with great Perquisites and entirely in the money way, They are launching out in Trade foreign and domestick, and of the most [damaged]. In vain may they say they trade [damaged] private Fortune. For if true, their Characters will not be screened from great Suspicion, and with Truth it will be said their Commissions and perquisites are sufficient to demand all their Time and attention, which cannot be, if privately imbarked in extensive business. You will inquire if Things are so round you. Let me beg that your Eyes and Ears may be fully open, retaining (as I know you will) an unbiased Mind [damaged] determination. I have a Regard [*damaged*] Publick, and I have, I do assure you, a Regard for your Honor and Character, and am very desirous it should continue not only to deserve, which I am sure it will, the Applause of your Country, but that it should not suffer Reflections from any, for the misconduct of others.[4] Tis from these Principles I write so freely. I mean it for your private use not to promote unnecessary Jealousies, but to promote a Scrutiny and proper Examination, and If I in some good Measure serve the Honor of your Department, and the Publick I shall be [amply rewarded?] for these few Moments [spent in doing it?][5]

I expect to return in about a fortnight, I shall be happy to meet you on my way, but fear you'l be rather [?] too far Northward.[6] I am Dear Sir Yr Friend and Servt

H'Y MARCHANT

ALS (MiU-C). Letter damaged.

1. He followed Marchant's advice in late December, when he went to Philadelphia for six weeks.

2. NG had likened the agents in his department to the state ministers about whom Lord Chesterfield was reported as saying that they were "not so good as they should be, and by no means as bad as they are thought to be." (See above, vol. 2: 546.)

3. Much of the criticism of the quartermaster department in 1778–79 concerned agents in Delaware and Maryland. See below, Hollingsworth to NG, 10 February 1779.

4. There is evidence that Marchant, although a fellow Rhode Islander, was critical of NG behind his back. For example, see below, Bowen to NG, 13 June 1779.

5. As a delegate to Congress, Marchant was candid in relaying criticism of the quartermaster department. He was one of the first to do so—in a letter of 16 September that has not been found. He undoubtedly wrote of the same "Fraud and Abuses," for NG had responded in a letter of 15 October by defending the agents and deputies in his department as "men of principle, honor, and honesty." He was especially confident of those in New England. He did promise, however, to keep a "watchful eye" over all branches, pointing out at the same time that he was "at so great a distance from many parts of the business, abuses may prevail for some time, unless my friends will be kind enough to give me seasonable information." (vol. 2: 547)

NG, in truth, had been out of touch with his deputies and agents for most of the four months that had elapsed since the British evacuated Philadelphia in mid-June. Except for the last two weeks in July, when the army was settling in at White Plains, Charles Pettit and John Cox, NG's assistants, administered the department. It was a period during which the quartermaster and commissary departments came under increasing fire, mainly as a result of the depreciation of the continental currency. Depreciation put a constant pressure on the most honest agent to keep his expenditures within reasonable limits; it could also cover the misdeeds of the fraudulent agent. As acting quartermaster general, Pettit was in no position in the camp in New York to check on the honesty of agents and deputies—especially further south. He was not, however, out of touch with the gossip that was circulating in Philadelphia. He even informed Cox of the criticisms. On 6 October he wrote Cox of "some Blows" aimed at Cox. "It has been said," he wrote, "or broadly insinuated, in Philadelphia that when the Expenditures in the Qu'r Master General's Department are so great as to afford monstrous Commissions, the Person at the Head of the Business there is spending his Time in pursuit of private Concerns, leaving those of the Publick to be conducted by a Person not chosen by them, nor equal to the Business." When he first heard such things, Pettit added, "I treated the information with some Degree of Neglect, but being lately told they have crept into Congress, and that they are not uncherished by some Persons there, I must confess I felt a serious Alarm. When the Tongue of Malevolence

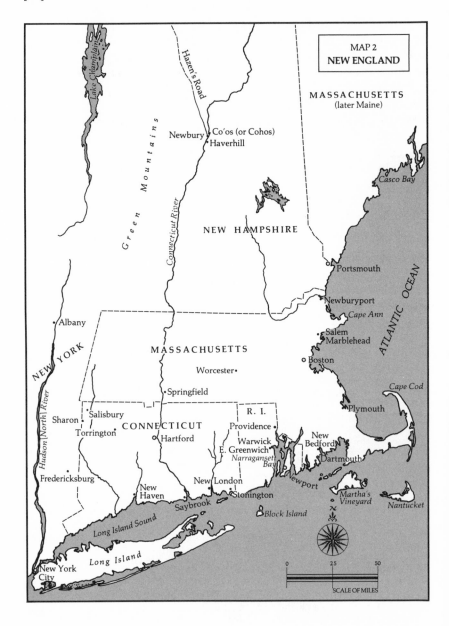

Henry Marchant, 1741–1796, artist unknown
(Courtesy of Newport Historical Society, photograph by Betsy Ray)

has proceeded thus far, you may be assured it's Influence has extended farther." (Pettit to Cox, PHi)

On 31 October, Congress formed a committee to investigate charges of fraud in the quartermaster department and named Samuel Adams, Nathaniel Scudder, and Roger Sherman as members. (JCC, 12: 1083) There is no evidence that the committee functioned, and on 10 November, Congress named another committee to superintend both the commissary and quartermaster departments. See below, NG to Bowen, 12 November.

6. He thought NG would be participating in the invasion of Canada. See note at NG to Washington, 28 October, above.

From Joseph Reed

⟨My dear General,   Philad. Nov. 5. 1778.

It is with very great satisfaction I set down to answer your Favor of the 26th October, exclusive of all concerns of business, or Politicks. I am happy to find you safely return'd from an expedition, from which I confess I expected nothing and am therefore not one of the disappointed.[1] I have no idea that Gen. Sullivan ever will shine as a military officer, and I have learn'd so much of military matters that the thanks of Congress or the puffs of the Camp (which in this case we have not had) have little influence on my Mind. Untill I heard you was gone, I had not the most distant hope of any advantage, and I cou'd not help believing that his ill luck, and other circumstances wou'd be an over Match for every thing you cou'd do. However I am told (indeed that we know here) that he has beprais'd *you all* in such a manner, that like the Continental Money it takes a great Deal to purchase any Respect or Value. I believe I may venture to say this much, that Congress will be more sparing of their Thanks upon another occasion. One thing I imagine will not be so easily pass'd over, I mean disgusting our Allies: there are certain occasions when we ought neither to see nor hear; much less to express what we see or feel, and tho' it might and I suppose did wound certain Feelings very much which our Hero elect may have—I think he would have done well to have suppress'd them. He should have considered, that God almighty may have made some other Creatures in the same mould with himself. I do not mean by this to condemn the Count d'Estaing, from all the Evidence, I should *now* say that he did right, but whether I should have thought so *then* is not so clear.[2]

As to your Department, perhaps the part I had in framing it, the Hopes I had form'd and express'd, the support I had given it in and out of Congress may have occasion'd an overweening and undue anxiety that you shou'd discharge it with Honour to yourselves and advantage to your Country.[3] Perhaps this anxiety may have induced me to lay greater stress upon Incidents than they really deserved. If it shou'd be so, and I have been too tremblingly alive to every Circumstance that tended to) impede or disparage it, I can only say it was an Emanation of Friendship and Affection the Effects of which could not injure tho it might serve the Department. You must be sensible that my delicate Situation will forbid me to say much in a Letter, but yet I will trust a few Sentiments upon Paper and shall rejoice to find that Events prove me totally mistaken.

I think there has been a constant subsisting Opposition between the old Department and yours from the Beginning, and in Congress the Marks appeared very evident. Mr. [William] Duer and the Party adhering to the Old Qr Mr [Mifflin] set out with predicting that you would never be able to move the Army, being disappointed in this, and the Accounts from Camp not answ[er]ing their Wishes they have been since predicting a Distress this Winter equal to the last, and that for a very plain Reason that the Distress of the Army last winter will then be ascribed to unavoidable Misfortune and not to any Delinquency ever accompanying their Argum[en]ts with irritating Remarks upon the Amount of the Expenditure and running a Parallel in this Respect with the last Year. The Absurdity, Injustice and even Wickedness of this Sentiment does not prevent their repeating it over and over again upon every Application for Money. Under this View therefore I confess I never was able to discern the Policy or Wisdom of continuing under you Men devoted at all Points to those who were the fixed and inveterate Enemies of the Department, who were quite in another Interest and who I firmly believe only remained in Office to cover more effectually their own Conduct and embarrass and betray you.[4] That there are some of these I suppose you cannot be ignorant, but the Person whom I principally refer to is Col. Hooper and who I verily believe was brought in for the above Purposes.[5]

You must be sensible also that one of the great Complaints against Genl Mifflin was employing Persons under him of known Disaffection to the Interests of America and openly hostile to the Authority of the State in which they were to act. This is now brought against your Department and verified in a very remarkable and recent Instance. The Brother of the infamous Doctr Smith and equally infamous with him for the Part he has acted in the publick Cause, has, since Danger of Disobliging the British Interest is removed, been appointed Qr Master of a County: under the Influence and Credit which this gave him, he is now returned (with several to whose Election he greatly contributed) in the Assembly to destroy and counteract that Interest upon which your Honour and even Safety as a publick Officer depends, for Integrity itself is not allways a Match for the malevolent Views of a Party.[6] Col. Ross at Lancaster used also every Influence his Office gave him to effect a Return of Members under the same Influence, but finding it impracticable, a Mob was raised which threw the whole into Confusion.[7] Col. Hooper not only harangued and exerted every Power but the Clerks of Office were employed in writing Tickets and then march'd off with all their Dependants for the like Purpose. In short in this City, and every Part of this State the whole Weight of the Department was given and ever exerted against your Friends with what real Effect Time only can determine. One Effect is obvious, to wit, throwing every Thing into Confusion, a Circumstance I imagine which will not contribute much to your Ease and Honour.

You say in your Letter before me "that you understand Genl Mifflin wants the Presidents Chair [of Pa. Executive Council], that every Body wishes me to accept it, and none more than yourself." That the Chair would be very convenient to a publick Delinquent there can be no Doubt, and it is really diverting to observe the Windings and Turnings he takes to recover lost Popularity. That he would sacrifice every Thing for his own Safety and gratify his inordinate Ambition at any Rate is very obvious. But all his Artifices would fail, and he would have sunk into utter Contempt if he had not been bolster'd up by many who derive their Importance from their Connection with you.

The Chair was in my offer all last Summer. Neither Ambition or Interest inclined me to accept it, but I now plainly see that there is a settled fixed System to subvert the Whig Interest and that in a little Time the very Name will be reproachful, if there are not very spirited Exertions.[8] You have undoubtedly heard into what Line Gen. Arnold has thrown himself. If Things proceed in the same Train a few Months longer I would advise every continental Officer to leave his Uniform at the last Stage, and procure a Scarlet Coat as the only Mode of insuring Respect and Notice.[9]

The Whigs are not depress'd, tho' the Tories are unhumbled and I still hope and believe if our own Friends will not take Part against us we shall rise superior to all their Efforts.

I do not pretend to say from what Cause it has proceeded or how it has happened, but I am inclined to think our Friends have been overreached. Little Attentions, great seeming Respect, and treacherous Professions, have led them into the Snare, and there is often so much Pride in the human Heart, that it will persist in the Error rather than acknowledge the Imposition. I am inclined to think Congress will soon suspend Hooper for some Practices not very honourable to himself or the Department, but as they are mingled with the Transactions of the former Department we could not disclose them to you.[10] Indeed from their Nature, yourself and the Department generally must appear exempt from Suspicion. After having suggested upon two Occasions to Mr Cox my Apprehensions that the Depart-

ment might suffer from certain Measures, and meeting with a different Reception than I expected, I could not trouble him any farther,
with any similar Remarks, but resolving to preserve private Friendship have constantly avoided the Subject. For the same Reason I must
request you to use this Letter consistently with my Views. The Honesty of his Heart has made him very averse to doubt that of others,
and he seems to think it disrespectful to himself that the Probity of
any one appointed by him should be doubted. For these Reasons and
others which are obvious you will see that what I say is to *you*.

As I have not been in Congress for 3 or 4 Weeks I did not know
till since I had wrote the above that a Complaint of some kind has
been formally made against the Department, and a Committee actually appointed thereupon.[11] But hearing that the Committee on the
former Departm[en]t (of which I am one) had Evidences of some Mal-
Practices of Hooper this Summer they sent to me for them but I
evaded it; I shall make further Inquiry and let you know whether it is
of any Consequence. Had I thought of it in Time I would have wrote
you to caution your People against meddling too much in the Election
either Way, as it has a manifest Tendency to raise Enemies to the
Department unnecessarily. Indeed I thought you had express'd yourself so clearly to them on your Intention not to embroil yourself with
any State Disputes that they would have avoided every Thing of the
kind. However they have done it, and most evidently against the
Interest you favour. They already talk of a Sett of Delegates from this
State, which if I thought there was any Probability of their carrying, I
should advise Mr Pettit immediately to prepare himself to leave the
Department, as I am sure his Connection with me [i.e., brother-in-
law] and their unprovoked Enmity would induce them to give you
every Opposition in their Power. What would you think of Mr Chew
the late Kings Chief Justice, whom we kept Prisoner as an Enemy till
within these 3 months upon full Evidence of his Enmity to us, and
that so great that he could not be trusted on Parole?[12] But if Pettit was
out of the Way, you would not be much better off as they are in the
same Interest and I believe with not very different Views than the
Reading Junto last Winter.

Gen. Lee is making his Court and I believe successfully to the
same Interests, at least if we may judge from personal Civilities and
Attention. We are totally out. After laboring to convince me that he
had great Merit at Monmouth, and I to convince him that he had
behaved very ill, which I knew from his own Mouth and my own
observation, we have parted mutually unconvinced.[13] I only added
one Piece of Advice to him to forbear any Reflections upon the
Commander in Chief of whom for the first Time I have heard Slander
on his private Character, viz, great Cruelty to his Slaves in Virginia

and Immorality of Life tho they acknowledge so very secret that it is difficult to detect. To me who have had so good Opportunities to know the Purity of the latter and equally believing the Falsehood of the former from the known Excellence of his Disposition, it appears so nearly bordering upon Frenzy that I can pity the wretches rather than despise them. However they help to make up the Party. New Characters are emerging from Obscurity like Insects after a Storm. Treason, Disaffection to the Interests of America and even Assistance to the British Interest is called openly only Error of Judgment, which Candour and Liberality of Sentiment will overlook, these are Gen. Cadwallader's Sentiments and that all Distinction should be laid aside under a perfect oblivion for past Offences, if such Practices deserve the name of Offences.[14]

Out of the great Number of Pilots, Guides, Kidnappers, and other Assistants of the British Army two of the most notorious were convicted, but it would astonish you to observe the Weight of Interest exerted to pardon them, and virtually every other, for none could be more guilty, but these being rich and powerful (both Quakers) we could not for shame have made an Example of a poor Rogue after forgiving the rich. The same Gentlemen publickly pronounced their Execution a horrid Barbarity infamous Carnage &c.[15] So much and so soon do Party Views change the Minds of Men, and of so little Consequence do they estimate the Lives and Safety of Officers and Soldiers who are so often destroyed by these treacherous Practices, when the Considerations of Power and Ambition intervene.

There is a considerable Majority of real Whigs in the [Pa.] House, a Number of *new* Converts to the Independence of America and a few real inveterate but concealed Tories. The Council who are also the Representatives of the People are Whigs to a Man. The only Disadvantage the Whigs have is the Want of Speakers.

From some Inquiries I have made since I began this Letter I imagine Smith got into Office last spring under the Influence of the Junto then form'd against the General and has been continued by [John] Davis who is appointed by you.

It is reported here that Mr Cox has proposed to Congress an Alteration of the Commissions as making the office too lucrative even beyond his Desire. I suggested an Idea of his [this] Nature to Mr Pettit when I was at Camp as a thing worthy your Consideration when you were all together. If Mr Cox has conveyed any Sentiments of this kind to Congress I am sure they must have proceeded from a Belief that they would promote the common Interest and might be necessary to obviate any Prejudices against the Department. I said in Congress and say now that unless any Man will declare that he believes the Commissaries and Qr Masters enhance the Prices in order to increase the Commissions I think the latter should not be diminished on Acct of the Expenditure because it was Value not Quantity that was to be the Reward of publick Duty. The Measure would certainly be disinterested and generous on the Part of the Staff, but I am clear the States cannot in Justice demand it, and I am sorry to add farther that the Prejudices which prevail with Respect to the Advantages Mr Cox has had in Bargains, Privateering &c, would in the Eyes of some lessen the Value of the offer because it would be suspected to proceed from a less honourable Motive than it really did. I need not say more.[16]

Col. Cox sometimes throwing out Ideas of Resignation leads me to say a few words upon that point. He cannot resign. I mean he cannot resign with Honour, and therefore I hope he will dismiss every Idea of that Kind. I will not say that such an Event would break up the Department tho' it would injure it, but if Mr Pettit was to consult me upon such a Point I should be against it as to him, and no Prejudices have gone forth against him or you. Much more should I dislike such a step if there had.

I am very glad you have found in Mr Pettit those Qualities which I think will cement your Friendship and Interests; tho' he is my Brother [in-law] I believe I may say without Partiality that he will wear well and that you will find him not only a Man of Business and Temper but unquestionable Honour and Patriotism. I look back with some Surprize at the Quantity I have wrote, but there is one material Fact respecting yourself which I ought to add tho' it will swell my Letter, already beyond all reasonable Size. In Mifflins Attempts to reestablish himself he found his Enmity to the General was a fatal Objection; he has therefore been obliged to recur to his old Ground that he did not oppose the Commander in Chief, but his Favourites (yourself and Knox) who had ⟨an undue⟩ Influence over him. This is the Language he is obliged to talk or he would have been utterly rejected, and this is the Language which some of your People have talked for him.

I am yet at a loss to say what will be the Result of our present Measures. I am in the Council and shall now accept the Chair if offered to me with a tolerable Salary because I see plainly that unless I make this Sacrifice of my Interest and Ease, the Whig Interest must be materially injured. Will you not think it extraordinary that Gen. Arnold made a publick Entertainment the Night before last of which not only ⟨numerous⟩ Tory Ladies but the Wives and Daughters of Persons proscribed by the State and now with the Enemy at New York, formed a very considerable number? The fact is literally true.

Adieu. I hope our Friendship founded ⟨on our mutual attachment⟩ to our Country and cemented by mutual Dangers and kind offices will not easily be shaken. My Love to Mr Pettit. I will write him very soon and am Dr Sir Your Affect. Friend and Hbble Servt

JOS. REED

ALS (MiU-C). Portions in angle brackets taken from *Lee Papers*, 3: 245–53.
1. The expedition to Rhode Island.
2. For Sullivan's relations with the French in Rhode Island, see above, vol. 2: 526–27.
3. The "yourselves" to which Reed refers are NG, Charles Pettit, and John Cox. Reed's advice and counsel had been essential in persuading NG to accept the quartermaster post. See above, vol. 2: 307–310n.
4. Reed was correct in his observation that NG retained most of Mifflin's appointees; and this despite the mutual distrust and dislike that he and Mifflin had for one another, which grew out of the "Conway Cabal." (See above, vol. 2: 277–79n.) As noted earlier, NG's reluctance to rid the department of "Mifflin men" may have been in part because he found it difficult to discharge anyone. But it was also not his nature to hold a grudge or to condemn someone through guilt by association. He not only relied heavily upon deputies that had served under Mifflin, but since most were effective in getting supplies, he seems to have developed respect and even an affection for them. He refused, moreover, to become involved in Pennsylvania politics and later warned his deputies to refrain. (See Circular, 26 March 1779, below.)
    Joseph Reed, on the other hand, who was caught up in the maze of Pennsylvania politics, was far from objective about Mifflin appointees. He too had opposed Mifflin for his criticism of Washington, but he now had more at stake than the memory of the "Cabal." Ambitious to become president of the executive council—Pennsylvania's equivalent of the chief executive—he had laid the groundwork to switch his alignment from the Conservative Republicans to the Radicals then in power. In the October elections he had run for both the Assembly and the executive council. That he waited six weeks to resign the assembly post was imputed, Robert Brunhouse has written, "to his desire to see which house offered the best chance for advancement." (Brunhouse, *Pennsylvania*, p. 56) In any case, he accepted a post in the council, and a month after he wrote the above letter, he was inaugurated as its president. In taking an oath to uphold the Radical constitution, he thus "formally deserted the Republicans and became a bulwark of the Radical party." (ibid., p. 57)
    As a Radical, or a Whig as he called himself, Reed had nothing good to say about anticonstitutionalists, or Republicans, as they styled themselves. In the Radical lexicon they were always Tories—said with a strong implication that they were neutralists at best and traitors at worst. Quakers were especially apt to be so classified. The tone of this letter reflects Reed's new affiliation, as does his position on the John Mitchell–Benedict Arnold affair, described in note at NG to Reed, 31 January #1, below. As seen there, Reed did not succeed in winning over NG or his assistant, Charles Pettit (Reed's brother-in-law) to his point of view. By 1780, Reed and the Radicals had begun to lose ground to the Republicans, and by the end of 1781 Reed found himself out of favor politically. Despite his apparent opportunism and his differences with NG, they remained good friends.
5. Robert Lettis Hooper was deputy quartermaster at Easton, Pa. (Map 3). On his background and his quarrels with the Radicals, see above, vol. 2: 331n, 425n, and 430n. For later charges against him, see note at NG to Hooper, 29 April 1779, below.
6. He has not been identified, but he was probably the brother of William Smith, an Anglican minister and loyalist sympathizer who headed the Old College, later the University of Pennsylvania. (*DAB*) On William Smith's relations with his father-in-law, whose loyalty had also been questioned, see below, William Moore to NG, 10 November.
7. George Ross was deputy quartermaster at Lancaster.
8. On Reed's efforts to obtain the presidency, see note 4, above.
9. As Reed later wrote, Arnold had been accused by the Whigs of entertaining known loyalists and their families. Arnold responded to the accusations in his letter to NG of 10 November, below. Many of Arnold's later critics pointed out, with perfect

hindsight, that such activities were but a portent of his eventual treason. On Reed's continuing animosity toward Arnold, see below, note at NG to Reed, #1, 31 January 1779.

10. Hooper disproved Reed's suspicions by remaining.

11. See above, note at Marchant to NG, 5 November.

12. Benjamin Chew (1722–1810) had been chief justice of the Pennsylvania Supreme Court until the Revolution. Due to his less than wholehearted support of the Declaration of Independence, he was first held prisoner in his own house and then moved out of Pennsylvania with John Penn. While away, his house became a landmark as a British stronghold at the battle of Germantown. (See vol. 2: 174–75n, above.) Chew later resumed his judicial career. (*DAB*)

13. For details of Lee's court-martial, see below, NG to McDougall, 8 November.

14. John Cadwalader (1742–86), a brigadier general in the militia, twice refused a similar commission in the Continental army. As a supporter of Washington, he had wounded Conway in a duel over the "Conway Cabal." (*DAB*) Political differences and misunderstandings had by this time split the once close friendship of Reed and Cadwalader. Mutual enmity culminated in the threat of a duel near the end of the war. (Roche, *Reed*, pp. 204–8)

15. He refers to the trials of Abraham Carlisle and John Roberts, whom Reed as prosecutor had helped to convict of treason. Presiding Justice Thomas McKean ordered them to be hanged—the only two hanged of forty-five tried for the same offense that year. The executive council was deluged with memorials by leading Pennsylvanians asking for leniency, but the council, believing the evidence of guilt to be overwhelming, ordered the sentences carried out to deter similar acts. The men were hanged on 4 November. (Reed, *Reed*, 2: 33–37; Roche, *Reed*, pp. 146–47)

16. As noted at Marchant to NG, 5 November, above, the three principal officials of the quartermaster department were well aware of the widespread criticism of the commissions paid on items purchased. On NG's efforts to allay congressional criticisms, see his letters to Pettit of 23 and 29 November, below; on the offer he and his assistants later made to work for a salary, see below, NG to Jay, 15 February 1779.

To Nehemiah Hubbard

[Fredericksburg, N.Y., 6 November 1778. Convention troops are on the march. Need a person immediately to accompany them to the North [Hudson] River[1] who is "acquainted with accounts, polite in his manners, and of a firm and resolute disposition, to be able to do justice to the department and honor to himself." If no one has all these requisites Hubbard may need to lower the requirements. Pass on the enclosed letter to William Joyce.[2] ALS (PHi) 2 pp.]

1. See below, Hubbard to NG, 9 November, and NG to Davenport, 9 November.
2. See below, William Joyce to NG, 9 November.

From Nehemiah Hubbard

[Hartford, Conn., 7 November 1778. Six-month teamsters will engage again but must have $4 per day to support their families.[1] They are ones he and Wadsworth hired and are much better than new ones; "generally honest," with good conductors and good teams. Sorry to have to raise wages so much. Excerpt (RG 93, WRMS: DNA) 1 p.]

1. In a letter of 14 November, below, NG approved the sum.

To General Alexander McDougall

Dear Sir   Camp at Fredricksburg [N.Y.] November 8th 1778
Your favor of the 5th of this instant was handed me yesterday.[1]

I have given orders to Col Baldwin to get the Tools made, and to have them forwarded as soon as possible.[2] I shall also make an immediate enquiry into the Forage allowed the Horses sent out to recruit [i.e., to be refreshed].

What you observe respecting the Enemies operateing East of N York I believe to be founded in truth and reason. It has been my opinion all along that Boston was not his object. What confirms me in this opinion is part of the Fleet has already Saild about 108 Sail. They put to Sea some days since. The force that is on board this Fleet must be too small for the attempt.

If he had any designs upon Boston he never would embark only such a part of his Fleet as would only serve to explain his intentions, and then have to wait for the remainder of his Force. You and I have been and still are of the same Sentiments with respect to this expedition being intended against Boston.[3]

Our intelligence from N York is altogether equivocal and uncertain. There are appearances of a second embarcation; but it remains very uncertain whether a total evacuation is intended. I have been of a contrary opinion hitherto and have no very substantial reason for changeing my sentiments yet. Lord Sterling and General [Charles] Scott from whom we receive all our intelligence are clearly of opinion N York will be evacuated; but when I examin the intelligence upon which the opinion is form'd I cannot jump in judgment with them. However this notion is very prevalent at Headquarters and among all the officers.

I have read your plan for cantoning the Troops for the Winter and like it much; but I am for Cantoning more Troops in the Jerseys than even you propose. An active vigilant General can guard against every kind of evil but that of the want of Provision and Forage. In takeing a position therefore regard must be had to the resources of the Country and the means of drawing them to his Camp. Under this consideration I recommended to the General the following line of Cantonment.[4] Three Brigades at Danbury, a good Garrison at West Point and all the rest of the Troops at Middle Brook New Jersey. Your reasons are so conclusive upon the improbabillity of the Enemys moveing out of his quarters in the Winter to make an attack upon any of our Forts or fortifications or even upon any of our Posts that I think it unnecessary to shew upon what principles I gave my opinion and advice to the General. Perhaps I have a little exceeded you in presumption; but our opinions are founded upon the same principles and reasons. I think the plan I have recommended will be adopted. But this is *under the rose*.[5]

I had heard of the famous Connecticut bill before the receipt of your Letter. It is founded in ignorance and Wickedness. Was this measure to take place it would soon disband the Army, ruin our cause and leave the marks of everlasting disgrace upon the contriveers.[6]

The Jamaca expedition is not yet confirmd.[7] Genl Lees sentence is not yet confirmd or rejected; he is forming a strong party at Congress. General Schuylers and St. Clairs cause is obligd to wait the issue of General Lees.[8] I believe you have guessed the true cause of General Gates going to Boston. Hitherto he has found himself surrounded with flatterers until the junction of the two Armies. Since which he has been like Samson after his Head was shaveed. His strength has been no more than another mans. This is a situation his pride and ambition cannot brook.

General Schuyler is not in Camp. Our good General [Washington] is in health, but not happy; things dont go to his mind. Some where I can plainly see the marks of distress. He intends to have his Lady at Camp this Winter.

I wish it was in my power to feast you with news, but this is a barren Time. I love the Army and could wish to gratify them but for want of matter, must leave them starveing.

My compliments to the officers under your command. I am with great respect and regard Your most obedient humble Sert

N GREENE

ALS (NHi).
1. Letter not found.
2. Jeduthan Baldwin of Massachusetts (1732–88) was a practical man of great competence who held a dual commission as colonel of engineers and colonel of the quartermaster artificers. As head of the latter he was successful in recruiting many skilled craftsmen, chiefly from Connecticut and Massachusetts. Later, he assisted Kosciuszko in constructing the defenses at West Point. (Boatner, *Encyc.*, under BALDWIN and ARTIFICERS. His *Revolutionary Journal*, edited by Thomas W. Baldwin in 1906, has been reprinted by Arno Press [1971].)
3. NG and McDougall had expressed the same opinion in their answers to Washington's queries at the 16 October Council of War. (See NG to Washington, 18 October, above, and McDougall to Washington, 21 October, Washington Papers, DLC). For a summary of British strategy in the autumn of 1778, see above, vol. 2: 549–50n. McDougall responded to NG's comments on 12 November, below.
4. See above, NG to Washington, 18 October.
5. It was adopted. See note, Washington to NG, 29 October, above.
6. The reference is to an unfounded rumor that Connecticut was not accepting Continental currency as legal tender.
7. A report of the French capture of Jamaica was unfounded.
8. Lee's fate had been in the hands of Congress since he had been convicted by court-martial in August 1778 and sentenced to be suspended from any command in the armies of the United States for twelve months. The sentence was debated in Congress between 23 October and 5 December, with Congress finally approving the findings of

the court-martial. (*JCC*, 12: 1195. On Lee's actions at Monmouth, see above, vol. 2: 452–56n.)

Congress took up the case of Schuyler on 3 December and that of St. Clair on 16 December, again approving the findings of the courts-martial by which both men were cleared of any culpability in the loss of Ft. Ticonderoga in 1777. (*JCC*, 12: 1186, 1225–26)

See Map 1 for geographic references above.

From Colonel James Abeel

[Morristown, N.J., 8 November 1778. Has taken a good horse for an express rider and one needed for a wagon. If NG does not approve it "shall be immediately sent down." ALS (PPAmP) 1 p.]

From Colonel Alexander Hamilton

[Fredericksburg, N.Y., 8 November 1778. Washington requests tools for General McDougall to enable him to "blow up rocks which greatly impede his carting &c." ALS (PPAmP) 1 p.]

From Colonel Morgan Lewis

[Albany, N.Y., 8 November 1778. Unable to procure lumber at agreed-upon price. Lewis had asked Governor Clinton for his aid, but by Clinton's attached reply, NG can see "the Ill success" of his "Expedient."[1] Since it will soon be impossible to communicate with Fishkill by water,[2] Lewis asks if he should meet price being asked or be content with what he has bought. Relates a long tale of a farmer who had his home first occupied by troops and then used as a fort. What compensation should he be given for lost income?[3] Sending returns. ALS (PPAmP) 4 pp.]

1. Lewis's letter to Clinton of 28 October is printed in Clinton, *Papers*, 4: 218–19. In his reply, Clinton agreed the practice was "certainly unjust and injurious to the Public," but he knew no way to stop it, since they were "Merchants and as the Demand for their Commodities increases so will their Price." (ibid., 4: 219)
2. The Hudson normally froze in this area in December.
3. NG's reply to Lewis's questions has not been found.

From Doctor James McHenry[1]

[Fredericksburg, N.Y., 8 November 1778. Colonel [Theodorick] Bland has been appointed to superintend the movement of the Convention army. Washington wishes NG to appoint a quartermaster to accompany the group to Virginia.[2] ALS (PPAmP) 1 p.]

1. James McHenry (1753–1816) emigrated from Ireland in 1771. He studied medicine under Benjamin Rush and in 1775–76 was surgeon in the Fifth Pennsylvania

Regiment. Captured at Ft. Washington in November 1776, he was not exchanged until March 1778. In May 1778 he became a secretary to Washington, serving without pay. During the next two years he and NG became fast friends, and had NG been able to obtain a colonelcy for him in the fall of 1780, McHenry would have accompanied him to the South. (See below, McHenry to NG, 21 October 1780) He was, in fact, associated with NG's southern campaign as Lafayette's aide, in which post he was finally commissioned a major. McHenry became secretary of war under President John Adams. (*DAB*)
2. See below, NG to James Davenport, 9 November.

To James Davenport[1]

Sir,   Camp, near Fredericksburg, [N.Y.] 9th November, 1778.

With this you will receive an appointment as deputy quartermaster-general, for the special purpose of providing for, and conducting the British prisoners, lately commanded by General Burgoyne, and the guards attending them from New England to Virginia.[2] If you find it necessary to have an assistant, or assistants, in this business, you will appoint some suitable person, or persons, for the purpose, being careful to appoint no more than are really necessary; nor to keep any one longer in pay than the public service absolutely requires it.

You will take your instructions as to the route, orders of march, and halting places, from Col. Bland, or the officer commanding the troops of the United States, on the march; you will also take his instructions from time to time, for such articles as he shall think proper to order the troops to be furnished with. The deputy quartermasters-general, of the several districts, through which you will march, will have orders to give you any assistance in their power. You will apply to them for such articles as you may have occasion for, in their respective districts. A list of their names, and the respective districts assigned them, will be hereto subjoined.

You will be careful to keep an exact account of all your expenditures, taking receipts, or other vouchers, for all payments. I am, sir, your most humble servant,

N. G., Q.M.G.

List of the Deputy Quarter-masters general, and the districts assigned them, through which it is probable the within-mentioned may pass.

Nehemiah Hubbard, Esq., State of Connecticut.

Col. Udney Hay, Fish Kill, State of New York.

Col. R.L. Hooper, Easton, Sussex county, in New Jersey, and Northampton, in Pennsylvania.

Col. Jacob Morgan, Reading, Berks county, Pennsylvania.

Col. Geo. Ross, Junr., Lancaster, Lancaster and its neighborhood.

Robert Patton, Esq., Lebanon, upper part of Lancaster county.

Col. John Davis, Carlisle, all the western side of the Susquehanna, in Pennsylvania. His assistant at York Town is Mr. George Echleberger.

Charles Beatty, Frederick Town, Frederick county, Maryland.
William Finnie, Williamsburg, State of Virginia.

Reprinted from Theodorick Bland, *The Bland Papers*, ed. Charles Campbell,
2 vols. (1840–43), 1:107.

1. James Davenport (1758–97), a Yale graduate, at this time was serving in the
commissary department. He entered the legal profession after the war and became a
justice of the Connecticut Court of Common Pleas. (*Conn. Men in Rev.*, p. 376)

2. The British prisoners captured at Saratoga in 1777, known as the Convention
army, had been in Massachusetts for a year, most of them by this time having been
moved inland from the Boston area. On 16 October, Congress ordered them to Charlottesville, Va., because of the scarcity of provisions in Massachusetts. It had warned
Sir Henry Clinton in September it would do so if he refused either to give passports to
American supply vessels from the South or to provision the men directly. It was an
arduous march of some seven hundred miles, taking almost three months in mid-
winter. It was also a challenge to the commissary and quartermaster departments,
especially at a time when a large part of Washington's army was moving to a new camp
and provisions were increasingly scarce.

Of the 5,863 men captured in October 1777, some 800 had deserted before the
march began. By August 1779 another 1,200 had deserted, and by the end of the war
half were gone. Desertion was especially heavy among the German troops, who were
able to settle unobtrusively into German communities in Pennsylvania and Maryland
as new Americans. See Alexander J. Wall, "The Story of the Convention Army,
1777–83," *New-York Historical Society Quarterly Bulletin* 11 (1927): 67–99 and William
Dabney, *After Saratoga: The Story of the Convention Army* (Albuquerque: University of
New Mexico Press, 1954).

See Maps 1, 3, and 4 for geographic references above.

From Colonel James Abeel

[Morristown, N.J., 9 November 1778. NG's of the fifth received;
sheets and NG's watch to be sent; has contracted for twenty to thirty
thousand sets of horseshoes; has axes, wedges, frows, and crosscut
saws; hopes to get grindstones nearby; requests tents be dried before
sending for repairs to prevent rotting. LS (PPAmP) 2 pp.]

From Nehemiah Hubbard

[Hartford, Conn., 9 November 1778. Has appointed James Bull to
accompany the Convention army troops through Connecticut.[1] "Was
oblig'd to make some abatement in the Accomplishments of this
Gentleman, from the discription in your letter, not so much however,
as to disgrace the Department."[2] The head of the guards will no
doubt be able to instruct Bull as to what is needed. Asks what Bull is
to be allowed for his services and for those of his assistants. Sends
response of William Joyce to NG.[3] ALS (PPAmP) 3 pp.]

1. James Bull of Hartford had been appointed by the Connecticut Council of Safety
to assist the militia in the Northern Army in August 1777. That October he was made
quartermaster of the First Connecticut Brigade. (Hoadly, *Records*, 1: 387, 426)

2. See above, NG to Hubbard, 6 November.
3. See below, William Joyce to NG, 9 November.

From William Joyce

Sir   Middletown [Conn.] Novemr 9th 1778
    Yours of the 6th Inst't is now before me, forwarded by QM
Hubbard.[1] I have been, as it were Idle for some [time], but have
within ten days past given Encouragement for a Cruise in the Privateer Brig'n *Middletown* now fitting with all Possable Dispatch, and will
be Ready to Sail the latter end of this Month. My offers [officers?] on
board are three shears [sharers] w'ch I look upon to be very great. I
wou'd [have] waited on you myself agreeable to your desire, but the
time Rideing to Camp and back again if we did not agree on Terms
wou'd be a great detriment to my getting myself in readiness for
the Cruise.
    I am much Oblig'd to Mr Flint for Recommending me to you, and
am Sensiable he is a Gentleman much Acquainted with my Abillities.
Truly Sir I have in times past spared no pains to make myself well
Acquainted in every branch of Book Keeping in the Merchantile way,
and that Attended with great Cost and dint of Study. My Ussuall
price per day was One Silver dollar w'ch at that time wou'd Purchase
me one and an half bushells Wheat. Now sir, if you will make me
whole agreeable to a bushell and an half Wheat per day and my
Keeping and Insure me your Business untill May next, I will leave the
Privateer and undertake with you. My Reasons for not waiting on
you myself I have above mentioned and my Terms you have as fully
as if present and Your Answer to this very soon will be greatly
Regarded by Sir Your Most Obt Servt[2]

WILLIAM JOYCE

ALS (PPAmP).
    1. Letter not found.
    2. Joyce remained under consideration for the post of clerk until NG decided that
his qualifications were not adequate and that his terms for acceptance were excessive.
See below, NG's letters to Nehemiah Hubbard, 14 November and 4 December, and to
Charles Pettit, 23 November.

From Colonel Morgan Lewis

Dr General   Albany [N.Y.] 9th November 1778
    Since closing my Letter of yesterday Date, yours of the 30th Ulto
was handed me. Your Express deserve a severe Reprimand for being
so excessively dilatory. Ten Days from Fredericksburgh to Albany is
unpardonable.[1]
    There are no Batteaux in this District which fall under the Gen-

erals Discription, excepting Two or three, which are too Old to be repaired. The small number We have here, not exceeding Thirty, are almost always in Constant employ. The few that are not, are so well secured with Chains that there is no Possibility of their receiving Injury.

In the fall of the year 'tis a Constant practice with us, to have them taken Out of the River and removed a sufficient distance from the Banks to protect them from the Ice. It may not Perhaps be amiss to make Enquiry into the state of the Batteaux; for Should a greater number than we at Present have, be wanted for the Ensuing Campaign, the Winter is the Proper Season for having the Timber &c prepared. I shall want to employ at least one Company of Batteaumen or Laborours at this Post the Ensuing Winter. Their Times of Enlistment are Out on the last of December. I find there is no possibility of engaging them for another year unless they can be provided with a Suit of Cloaths at a Certain fixed Price, as they are now literally naked and incapable of remedying the Evil. I should be glad to know if Cloathing could not be drawn for Thirty Men at the Clothier Genls store at Camp or if an Order could not be Obtained for that Purpose on the agents in Boston, the Men Paying Prime Cost and Charges therefor.

My Money is nearly expended. Should be glad you would Transmit me about Thirty Thousand Dollars, which I imagine will be Sufficient to last me till my former Accounts are settled, when there will be a very Considerable Ballance coming to me. In Case any Troops should be sent this way, tis necessary to Inform you that we have Barracks in this Town for four Hundred and forty Men, and at Schenectady and Saratoga for as many more at each Place.[2] I am Most Respectfully Sir your Most Obt Servt

MOR'N LEWIS

PS. I have only Eleven Sheets of money left and expect in a few Days to have none.

ALS (PPAmP).
1. The distance was about one hundred miles, normally a two-day trip for an express.
2. NG's answer has not been found, although he did respond in his letter of 6 December, below, to questions about bateaux, which Lewis had repeated in a lost letter of 27 November.

From General George Weedon

My Dear Genl   Fredericksburg [Va.] Nov 9th 1778
    I am this day Honored with your fav. 14th Ulto by Mr Custis,[1] and snatch a moment before the post leaves Town, to thank you for it,

and also to congratulate you on the growing prospect of your Family and your lady's being well after her Delivery of a Daughter.[2] This, if I count right, is the Effect of her Vissit to Valley Forge. I would have given my Hatt, and I have but one, it had been a boy, he no doubt would have cut a figure in the profession of Arms as he might with propriety have said he was on Picket before he was born.

I wrote you a long letter since my geting home, for which you are indebted an Answer,[3] but as I have your promise to communicate everything worthy Notice, shall not be over particular in my Account against you, but reserve the Ball[ance] (if any there be) till you come to Virginia and as you have given me hopes towards the close of your letter, that I shall see that happy day, shall keep the credit open. I have leased a farm a very small Distance from Town, and in full view, where I shall retire to in a few months, and where I shall always keep as good Cheer as the Circumstances of a disbanded Officer will afford, and tho' the [indecipherable] are not the most Ellegent, you shall find a clean bed, good Beef and Mutton, and a hearty welcome under their roof, and I'll promise Mrs Green a Ball every Week while she honors us with her Company.

No doubt your expectations were great, from every Circumstance that presented itself at the opening of the Rhode Island Expedition. Nor did I think any thing short of a finnishing Stroke to the War, could have happened, but who is there amongst us that can avert the designs of Providence who often disappoints in order to awake us to a knowledge of a Ruling power to whose pleasure we must Submit.

The State of the Army, with the New Arrangement in the Virginia,[4] The results of the Court Martial,[5] The Eastern pole Tax with your private Sentiments on each will be very Acceptable; tell me also what your oppinion is respecting the future operations of the British. Where do they mean to expose themselves Next, or are they leaving us to go to the Devil our own way (as they once said). I fancy they are pritty Sick of us, and would gladly quit scores if they knew how to bring it about. Our Assembly has been long Siting, and shall in my next Communicate the heads of these deliberations. I have only time to make a tender of Mine and Kitty Compliments to you and when you write Mrs Green, I beg you'll present our loves and warmest Congratulations to her also. Believe me Very Affectionatly yr Sincere friend and Hb st

G WEEDON

ALS (PPAmP).
1. Letter not found.
2. Cornelia was born on 23 September.
3. See above, 5 October, vol. 2: 543–45.
4. For details on the arrangement of the Virginia Line—the cause of Weedon's leaving active service until June 1780—see above, vol. 2: 362–64.

5. The outcome of General Lee's court-martial is recounted above, NG to Mc-
Dougall, 8 November.

To General John Cadwalader

Dear Sir   Camp Fredricksbg [N.Y.] November 10, 1778

Since the battle of Monmouth I have never had the pleasure to
see you, or even to hear of you only by accident. I mean such as
shooting People through the Head. Your duel made a great noise in
the American World. Most People rejoiced at Mr Conways fate. The
only pain that I ever felt upon the ocasion was on account of your
delicate situation if the wound had happend to prove mortal. I wish
every such restless discontented spirit may meet with such a seasonable check.[1]

General Lees tryal seems to be suspended. It is as the Lawyers
sais in a state of abeyance. We are told here parties run high in
Congress upon the subject. I have ever thought myself happy in not
being connected with that tryal. There would have been many ungenerous insinuations, besides being subject to the fire of all General
Lees Artillery of satire.[2]

It has been lately hinted to me that the Congress are growing
more jealous of the Army than ever. Some of our officers are not
altogether as prudent and respectful towards Congress as they ought
to be. But their observations are generally unmeaning and their
remarks rather flow from the luxuriance of fancy than from serious
intention. I cannot help feeling mortifyed that the indiscretion of a
few should bring under imputation the Whole. It is not good policy
for a Master to suspect the fidelity of a servant without good cause. It
hurts his pride and destroys a necessary confidence. The Officers
sufferings are great. Their merit conspicuous. But it is not improbable
but that they may over rate their own consequence. Men are easily
perswaded to think favorably of their services and sometimes perhaps may claim a consideration for them that is incompatible with the
good of society to grant. However it is a pity that the merit of many
should be sullied by the folly of a few. Factions I dread, the secret
fomentors often lies conceald, and makes tools of those, to effect their
designs, who in principle would abhor their measures if they could
but see their views.

The fate of a British Parliament and the conduct of a Cromwell is
a good lesson of caution to a Legislature. But I am perswaded a generous confidence and a just conduct towards the American Army will
forever keep it from swerveing from the Laws of honor or honesty.

General Gates is gone to Boston. He had rather be the first in a
Village than the second man in Rome. "Ye gods what havock does
Ambition make among your creatures."

I am told General Arnold is become very unpopular among you oweing to his associateing too much with the Tories. Pray how is the fact? At this distance it is difficult to get at the truth. I should be sorry to hear that he had done any thing to forfeit the good opinion of the truly deserving. But all men have their Friends and Enemies.[3]

General Mifflin because he could not get at the Head of the Army has turnd Legislator again. I suppose he is aiming after the chief seat in Government. He is a restless spirit and like Belzebub would rather be chief in H— than a servant in Heaven.

How is the French Ambasador approvd on at Court? Our first operations in conjunction with the French were rather unfortunate.[4] The Rhode Island expedition once promised a rich harvest of honor and laurels. But the Winds and the Weather blasted the crop. General Sullivan has a strange mixture of good and ill fortune. He is ever unsuccessful as to the principal object and yet comes off free from disgrace. Pray what is the general opinion of people of understanding with respect to the conducting that expedition?

Every body seems to be in high expectations of the Enemies leaveing N York. The ballance of evidence at this time greatly favor this opinion and yet I cannot bring myself to believe it. Nothing could be more agreeable than such an event and from its being so I am afraid we put too favorable construction upon the intelligence we receive. It would be very happy for America to have the Enemy go off at this time. Public virtue is upon the decline. Our money dayly depreciateing, a growing discontent prevailing in the Army. Provisions and forage growing scarce, Factions and jealousies in our Councils, all conspire to make me wish most heartily for a little breathing spell.

I am well informd the Governor and Council of Conecticut sent down a bill to the lower House for passing a Law that the Continental bills should not be a tender in Law. This would put a finishing stroke to all further opposition. What think you of this policy?[5]

I shall be happy to hear from you. Please to make my compliments agreeable to General Dickason [Dickinson] and Col Lambert.[6] I am sincerely yours

N GREENE

ALS (PHi).
1. In a duel with Thomas Conway on 4 July 1778, Cadwalader wounded Conway in the mouth. The incident is related in Freeman, *GW*, 5: 39. Conway's role in the "Cabal" is discussed above, vol. 2: 277–79n.
2. See above, NG to McDougall, 8 November.
3. For accusations against Arnold, see above, Joseph Reed to NG, 5 November. Arnold responded to the charges in his letter to NG on 10 November. See also note on the Mitchell-Arnold affair, NG to Reed, #1, 31 January 1779.
4. On Ambassador Gérard and his arrival in America, see above, vol. 2: 470, 472n. For the French role in the Rhode Island expedition, see ibid., 477–513 passim and 526–27.

5. See above, note at NG to McDougall, 8 November.

6. Lambert Cadwalader (1743–1823) was, like his brother John, an early patriot who had been a member of the Provincial Convention of Pennsylvania in 1775. As colonel of the Third Pennsylvania Regiment in 1776, Cadwalader was taken prisoner in the capture of Ft. Washington but was soon released. He resigned from the service in 1779. (*DAB*) His bitter criticism over the loss of Ft. Washington can be found above, vol. 1: 354n.

To Colonel John Davis

[Fredericksburg, N.Y., 10 November 1778. The Convention army will be passing through his district on its way to Virginia.[1] Asks that he assist it. LS (Davis Papers: DLC) 1 p.]

1. His district included Cumberland and York Counties, which were west of the Susquehanna River (Map 3).

To Colonel Walter Stewart

[Fredericksburg, N.Y., 10 November 1778. Concerns lottery tickets they had purchased. ALS (NjMoW) 1 p.]

From General Benedict Arnold

Dear General   Philadelphia Novr 10 1778

    A few days since I was favoured with your's of the 16th Ulto and was happy to hear you were well.[1] The history you alude to is short; some Gentlemen, or rather Officers of the Army, and Members of Congress, were offend'd with my paying a polite attention to the Ladies of this City, without first discovering if they were whigs at *Bottom*. Those Gentlemen who avow such Illiberal sentiments, I shall treat with the Contempt which I think they deserve by takeing no Notice of them.[2] I have no News to Communicate, except Political, and Our affairs both at home and abroad are in so deplorable a situation as forms a Picture too horrid to dwell upon, and must give Pain to every Man who is interested in the safety of his Country; which in my Opinion was never in a more Critical Situation than at present. The great Council of the Nation Distracted and torn with Party and faction, the Publick Credit lost and Debt accumulated to an Amaseing and Incredible Sum, the Currency daily Depreciateing, and Congress if Possible depreciateing still faster, haveing lost the Confidence of the Army, and Publick in General, and abused or neglected their most faithful Servants, these are the outlines of the Picture. For the rest your knowledge of Matters will Supply, from impending Ruin may God defend us.

My best wishes attend you. Adieu my Dear General and believe me with great Sincerity Your Friend and Obedt Servt

B ARNOLD

ALS (MH).
1. Letter not found.
2. In the missing letter, NG apparently repeated some of Joseph Reed's comments on Arnold's activities in Philadelphia. See above, Reed to NG, 5 November.

From Colonel Ephraim Bowen

[Providence, R.I., 10 November 1778. Mr. Mitchel has refused other employment in the department.[1] "Have got a pr of Breeches and Wiscoat making for you." ALS (PPAmP) 2 pp.]

1. See above, NG to Bowen and NG to Varnum, 24 October.

From Colonel William Grayson

[West Point, N.Y., 10 November 1778. Believes General Knox took a book that NG is looking for. ALS (MH) 1 p.]

From William Moore[1]

Sir   Moore hall [Pa.] the 10 November 1778
   This is intended to meet you in Winter Quarters. It's then and I suppose not untill then you'l be at leasure to read what may be offerd you that does not Imediatly concern you in the military department. I must informe you I have been most shamefully treated by Mr Clem Biddle, the forage Master Genl, in a grate many Instances too Numerous to mention in a letter. I shall therefore only mention three or four out of near one hundred Articles and then when well considered, I think will appear to you in the blackest dye.
   On the 21st day of Septr 1777 my Team, Equal to any taken into the Servis of the State was press'd, so that on the 21st of this Instant w'ch I suppose will be before this reaches your hands, it will have been in the Servis of the State 426 days as by the receipt Biddle has or Ought to have in his hands will fully appear (how he came by the rec'ts I at present forbare to mention) said Biddle also in a base [manner?] detains from me severall other Valuable rec'ts pretending he has either lost or mislayed them whereby I am deprived of the hire of my *Valuable* Team, my Horses or pay for my Blanketts &c none of which have ever yet been return'd me nor do I believe ever will. I make no doubt but a handsome allowance has been made for the use of my

mill for the 7 mo Biddle and his deputy had it, and a very grate part of my House in their possession. They have totaly [destroyed?] my Mill and every article in it to a very large amount, and for which he had the assurence (an expression very aplicable to him) to offer me by Colo Sheriff[2] one hundred dollars Only. To do Colo Sheriff justice I believe he was ashamed to make the offer, indeed he was advised not to make it, but as he acted under Biddle thought himself oblig'd to do it, and when he did do it recd. such an answer as it well deserved. Colo Sheriff has on every Occasion behaved civily towards me and I hope I have not been wanting in my behavior towards him; we have lived friendly.

No consideration being made me by Biddle gives me just cause to say I have been cruelly used and I must think it's alltogether owing to Clem Biddle and his conections ill will towards me and my distressed Family. My behavior towards him was becoming a Gentleman in his own House and not like that of a man of Biddle's own Rank or perhaps I had been better treated. I verily believe Biddle has recd not only the pay for the hire of my Team but the full price of it, but that he has likewise rec'd the Cash for my other rects. &c. I hope you'l excuse the liberty I have taken with you; I have no one else to apply to that has weight or Influence in the military department. On your friendship and the Friendship of the two worthy Gentlemen your assistants in the QMG department I fully rely.[3] My case Sir has been particularly hard, falln on me in extreem old age and under grate infirmity of body, therefore deserves particular attention. I have not a blade of Hay or Sheaff of Straw, a Horse Collar or geer of any kind, my fields and valuable meadows lay dust and when you left them, I am told every person has been allowed Rent for their Houses, Barnes, stables and out Houses &ca. I have not been considered in that way, nor the least allowance made me for [the] distruction of my Hous hold furniture which is very grate.

You know I with held not from the officers of the Army a single Article that my House, Farme or Garden afforded; during the time the Committee of Congress occupied my House (upwards of three months) many, very many Articles were furnished them by me. The beds they lay on were mine, grate part of their dyet was mine, no part of the linnen they used (one pair of Sheets only excepted that Genl Read had) but were mine, they had not a Towell to wipe their hands on but what was mine. Much more I have to offer, but that can only be done when we meet togeather. God grant it may soon be in peace and good will.[4] I am Sr your most humble Servt

WM

P S I had one very valuable Horse Taken from me for which I had no rec't, but was much abused by the Horseman that took it. He broke open my mill to get at it. He said it was for Gen. Greens division. The Horse was Equal in Value to any Coach Horse in the Governmt: 6 yrs old. Mine and Mrs Moores Compliments to Mrs Green. We congratulate you on the birth of your little Daughter w'ch Doctr Hutchison tells us is very Butifull.[5]

ADfS (PHi).

1. William Moore (1699–1783) was the owner of Moore Hall (near Valley Forge), which the Committee of Congress at camp used in the late winter of 1778 and where NG and Catharine stayed later that spring. See above, vol. 2: 282n.

The harsh treatment received by the seventy-nine-year-old Moore had undoubtedly sprung from strong suspicions of his loyalty, which, in turn, had grown out of partisan rivalries of the French and Indian War. As a county judge, Moore had led in criticizing the Assembly for failing to provide protection against the Indians. This led to a three-months imprisonment in 1757, along with the Reverend William Smith, first provost of the College of Philadelphia, who defended Moore. (Smith later married Moore's daughter, Rebecca.) Moore continued as a judge but spent most of his time thenceforth overseeing his farm at Moore Hall. (*DAB*) His loyalist sympathies did not prevent him or his family from demonstrating deep affection for NG and Catharine. (See above, vol. 2: 425.)

2. Cornelius Sheriff was a deputy quartermaster.

3. Charles Pettit and John Cox.

4. While encamping the army, NG lost track of Moore's letter, and during his stay in Philadelphia in January, he asked Moore's grandson to refresh his memory by restating Moore's claims. (William Smith to NG, 28 January 1779, below) Although sympathetic, NG apparently recommended that Smith petition Congress, since the damages occurred during Thomas Mifflin's tenure. This, Smith did. On 6 August 1779 Congress directed Mifflin to pay Moore for all the items "taken for the army and committee of Congress." (*JCC*, 14: 927)

5. James Hutchinson. See below, NG to Biddle, 26 February.

To George Washington

[Fredericksburg, N.Y., 11 November 1778. "Exceedingly distressed for want of Waggoners." NG hopes that soldiers in the hospitals who are "incapable of doing Soldiers duty" will be assigned to this task when they are finished with treatment.[1] ALS (Washington Papers: DLC) 1 p.]

1. See below, Meade to NG, 11 November.

From James Abeel

Sir   Morris Town [N.J.] 11th Novr 1778

I wrote you 9th Inst in Answer to your Letter of 5th Inst but for fear it shou'd not come to hand in Time I now inclose you a Copy to which I refer.

I have had a Second Person sent into Sussex County in search of Stores, he can find no other than some belonging to the Clothiers Dept. which have laid there a long time, and will still remain there as the Clothier Genl knows nothing of their being there.[1] I shall inform him soon as possible. Stephens, Col. Hoopers Asst, says that all the Stores that came from the Eastward were forwarded to Colo Hooper, a part of which were sent to Philada and the rest came to this Place.

I am extremely sorry to tell you that we are suffering much at this Post for Forrage. The Waggons are often detained three days for want of it and I am convinced Mr Furman does his utmost, but there is a Law in this State prohibiting the Forrage Master from seizing it from the Farmers and they ask such an enormous price that it exceeds the Limits of the Forrage Masters as they are restricted.[2] You cannot concieve how much the Service suffers for want of Forrage and unless some other Method is divised to procure forrage, the Supplys of the Army must of course Stop. It is impossible to get the private Teames to Stir untill they are supplyed. There is a very great abuse in the Waggon Department. Waggons are loitering four or five days longer on [the] Road than is necessary. Some go only 8 and 10 miles a day to my Certain knowledge, and no one takes notice of it. The Waggon Masters are afraid of their Waggoners and are hale fellow well met with them. It is a pitty there was not proper Persons appointed at different Places to take notice of them and make them perform a days Journey and if they did not, deduct it from their pay Roles, or if a Certain Number of Miles was alloted them it would save that expence. I am well assured that I can provide 100 Grin[d] Stones. A Person is now gone to purchase them. I am Sr your most hble Sert

JAS ABEEL

ALS (PPAmP).
1. The clothing had probably "laid there" since winter—a time when men were going naked at Valley Forge. See above, vol. 2: 246n.
2. On the problems that one forage master had with a New Jersey justice of the peace over the impressment of forage, see below, NG to Governor Livingston, 14 February 1779.

From Colonel Richard Kidder Meade

[Fredericksburg, N.Y., 11 November 1778. Washington approves using invalid soldiers as wagoners.[1] Will notify director of hospitals. ALS (Washington Papers: DLC) 1 p.]

1. See above, NG to Washington, 11 November. Washington covered this in his general orders the next day. (Fitzpatrick, GW, 13: 248)

To Colonel Ephraim Bowen[1]

Sir   Camp Fredricksburg [N.Y.] Nov 12th 1778

On the receipt of this you will forward me your accounts up to the first of this month; also, a return of all the stores in your district, specifying where deposited, in whose care, and in what condition. These returns are wanted as soon as possible to lay before a committee of Congress.[2]

From this time forward you will make monthly returns of all your disbursements, (to the last of each month), of the stores in your district, and of the number and occupation of people employed in the Quarter-Master General's Department. I am, Sir, Your humble servant,

NATHANAEL GREENE

Reprinted from RIHS, *Coll.* 6 (1867): 220. This circular letter was enclosed with NG's letter to Bowen of 12 December, below, written from Middlebrook, N.J.

1. NG sent similar letters to deputies east of the Hudson River and asked Pettit to circularize the rest of the deputies. See NG to Pettit, 23 November, below.

2. Only two days before NG wrote to his deputies, Congress had authorized a new committee to superintend the quartermaster and commissary departments. The committee was a response to reported abuses and frauds such as Marchant had relayed to NG on 5 November, above, but congressional action appears to have been immediately triggered by a letter from NG to Congress on 6 November, which was read to Congress on the tenth. (*JCC*, 12: 1114–15)

NG's letter, unfortunately, has not been found. He undoubtedly echoed the hopes he had expressed to Henry Marchant on 15 October that there were few, if any, of his agents or deputies who were not "men of principle, honor, and honesty." (See above, vol. 2: 547) He must also have pointed out that inflation was the principal culprit, although he may have been convinced by this time that something had to be done to monitor the conduct of agents. It is doubtful, however, if he went so far as recommending a committee to oversee his department. In any case, Congress based its decision not only on the conviction that "speedy and vigorous measures should be taken to regulate the commissary's and quarter master's departments, but also that a constant attention should be paid to those departments."

On the same day, it appointed Nathaniel Scudder of New Jersey, Gouverneur Morris of New York, and William Whipple of New Hampshire to the committee, any two members being empowered to "take such steps . . . as they shall think most [advantageous] for the public service." (*JCC*, 12: 1114–15) They wasted no time in getting down to work. The following day, 11 November, they sent a series of letters to the executives of each state concerning inventories of scarce items, the waste of distilling grain, and the prosecution of engrossers and public officials (in the supply departments) who used the monies entrusted to them in speculation. "This seething of the Kid in its Mothers milk," they declared, "calls for the most exemplary punishment," which, they hoped, would be instituted by the legislatures. In the meantime, they requested that each executive secure such guilty persons "in safe and close Custody" for trial. (Burnett, *Letters*, 3: 492–93; the letters start on 489.)

None of the committee appeared to bear any animus toward NG or Wadsworth; and all were fully aware of the effects of depreciation on purchases. At the same time, they were agreed on the need to oversee the departments. Gouverneur Morris was an especially warm friend, yet in his letter of 16 November, below, he did not underestimate the criticisms directed at NG. During the following year, the committee underwent a number of changes in personnel, but newer members also tended to be understanding of the problems faced by the two departments during a period that saw the continental dollar drop to one fortieth of its face value. The committee was active until its duties were turned over to the Board of War on 25 November 1779. (*JCC*, 15: 1312) As seen below in NG's correspondence during the year, it was rarely effective in achieving its objectives. Since Congress did not give a formal name to the committee, the editors have designated it henceforth as the Supply Departments Committee.

To Nehemiah Hubbard

[Raritan, N.J.,[1] 12 November 1778. Circular letter virtually identical to above letter to Bowen. (MiU–C) 1 p.]

1. On 12 November, NG was still at Fredericksburg, N.Y. He probably failed to send Hubbard his circular at this time and back-dated it when he arrived at Raritan. It was signed for NG by Ichabod Burnet and enclosed in NG to Hubbard, 12 December, below.

From Henry Laurens,
President of the Continental Congress

[Philadelphia, 12 November 1778. Encloses two congressional resolutions: one directs the quartermaster department to pay for horses purchased for a recent expedition; the other directs the department to ship ten tons of bar iron to Charleston, S.C.[1] Cy (PCC, item 13, vol. 2: 160, DNA) 1 p.]

1. JCC, 12: 1109, 1119–21. The iron was to be sent aboard one of Capt. John Barry's armed galleys, which were to accompany General Lincoln in a proposed expedition against East Florida.

From General Alexander McDougall

Camp Second Hill [Near New Milford, Conn.][1]

My dear Sir   12th Novr 1778

I have been favored with yours of the 8th Current. I am not so Sanguine as to expect the Enemy will totally evacuate the United States, till the Ministry have time to form and transmit a new System of National conduct on the loss of Dominica.[2] And not even then. Its a question with me whether they will evacuate. If they do on such an Event, it will be the Latter end of December before it will take effect in America. General Scotts character for combining particulars and ballancing evidence I am a stranger to. But I have my doubts about my Lords capacity at this day, for those purposes; and therefore I am an Infidel as to some articles of his present creed. I think him very hasty to make a calm comparison of Facts, and draw the best conclusion. I belive it certain, Large detachments are making and no more.[3] The Fears of the Tories, and the Hopes of the whigs in N York both conspire to consider those appearances as Evidence of a totall evacuation being near.

But if he leaves a respectable Garrison there, I dont altogether like your proposed Cantonments. There should be as many Troops at Fish Kill as the Barracks will quarter; and at Peeks Kill and Crompond to Kings Ferry, as many as the Houses will comfortably contain, otherwise the repose of your Three Brigades at Danbury may be disturbed by Alarms for the safety of the stores at Fish Kill. For you are to remember the Garrison at West Point at Certain seasons may not be able to cross the river to protect them. But by Troops being disposed as above, the Tories will Estimate them at triple their number, which will prevent any insult on either side of the river, and promote the repose of the whole. If the Enemy should presume to move out, by those Troops falling back into the Gorge of the Mountains time will be given for the March of those from Danbury. From my recollection of the Houses from Kings Ferry to Crompond and Peeks Kill and near those places in a circle of eight miles, three regiments of 300 Each may be quartered, and two in the Lower Barracks [at] Fish Kill upon your plan, as the Majority of the Army go to Jersey. His Excellency goes there of course.

In that Case General Putnam will play the Devil on the East side if his command is not circumscribed within very narrow Limits. Flags [of truce] in abundance will be continually passing from him and New York and every kind of disorder and Folley. Every traytor and whore in that city will be permited to come out, and to return, and as many of the like cast will obtain the Same permission to go in. In short my dear Sir, no man's reputation who has the immediate Command on the River will be safe; nor the Corps under his command if the Enemy can disturb them, if that Gentleman is not tightly and closely bound with orders, and these he will hardly obey. For my part I hope the Lott will not fall on me to be the man. If it should I shall follow the Army, be the Consequence what it may, unless he is confined in his Command within such Limits as will not endanger my reputation or whatever Troops I may command.

I intend to-morrow morning if its fair to Sett out for Hartford, to Visit Mrs Macdougal for a few days and shall return soon [in] time [?] enough to be at your Heels going into Newyork, or to Follow the Division to Winter Quarters. I mentioned to you some time ago, my desire to have a pair of Good Bay trotting Horses, well matched for the Tongue of my Wagon and that I could replace them with two very good public Horses, altho not well matched as to Colour. If those can be picked I wish you will be so kind as to direct the Wagon Master to do it; and if he accomplishes it, let one of your Family advise Major Platt of it.[4] I am my dear Sir with Esteem and regard, Your affectionate Humble Servant

ALEX M'DOUGALL

P S What has removed General Putnam from the right wing to Hartford?[5] Are the Virginians tired of him? Or is it too hot for him among them?

ALS (MiU-C).
    1. On McDougall's being stationed at New Milford, see note at NG to Sullivan, 24 October, above.
    2. The British garrison of five hundred men on the West Indian island of Dominica was captured during 7–8 September 1778 by the Marquis de Bouille with a force of two thousand troops from Martinique.
    3. The reference is to NG's observations concerning Scott's and Lord Stirling's intelligence of British activities in New York.
    4. Richard Platt, McDougall's aide.
    5. Putnam was then in command of three brigades at Hartford, but the following week he was ordered to winter with them at Danbury. (Fitzpatrick, *GW*, 13: 195–290 passim)

See Map 1 for geographic references above.

Major Ichabod Burnet to Colonel James Abeel

[Camp Fredericksburg, N.Y., 13 November 1778. If bed sheets not sent, Abeel should keep them, since Burnet will be in New Jersey in ten days. NG wishes twenty pounds of "Coffee and *refined Sugar*" and "firkin of good Butter." He depends on Abeel for such articles [for his official family]. No news from New York. Relates news and speculations on Admiral Byron and d'Estaing. Reports sinking of British ship *Somerset* of sixty-four guns with loss of sixty of her crew and capture of four hundred men by militia.[1] NG is satisfied that error in Abeel's invoice to Colonel Hay "did not arise from inattention in you." ALS (NjMoW) 4 pp.]

    1. The British officer, Frederick MacKenzie, in Newport agreed with Burnet's figure of 60 men lost. He reported ten days later that 180 of the *Somerset's* crew were being exchanged for a like number of captive Americans, who were "suffering greatly from Sickness, & want of cloathing." (MacKenzie, *Diary*, 18 and 28 November, vol. 2: 421, 426.)

Major Ichabod Burnet to Colonel Ephraim Bowen

[Fredericksburg, N.Y., 13 November 1778. Apologizes for requesting aid in obtaining clothing. Sends money owed by NG, including a sum for John Laurens's horse.[1] Pleased that Bowen has obtained some cashmere; would appreciate some swanskin,[2] stockings, and linen. Asks for accounts for items shipped. ALS (RHi) 3 pp.]

    1. Laurens had participated in the battle of Rhode Island.
    2. A fabric resembling flannel and having a soft nap.

To Catharine Greene

My dear Angel   Camp at Fredricksburg [N.Y.] November 13, 1778
    The Eastern jaunt I am afraid will prove very unfriendly to my wishes, as I am all impatient to see you.[1] Never did I experience more anxious moments. Col Cox and Mr Pettit are gone to Philadelphia. They both desire their most respectful compliments and insist upon the pleasure of seeing you at Trenton this Winter. You know how polite and cleaver these Gentlemen are and they affirm they are the worst part of the family. What a happy set. Great deductions is to be made from peoples professions in polite life, but I veryly believe these Gentlemen have a great respect and regard for you. The Col says Mrs Cox is very desireous of being one of your acquaintances. I din'd yesterday with His Excellency who enquird very particularly after you and renewed his charge to have you at Camp very soon. Your last Letter containd expressions of doubt and fears about the matter.[2] To be candid with you I dont believe half a Kingdom would hire you to stay away; but at the same Time I as candidly confess I most earnestly wish it, as it will greatly contribute to my happiness to have you with me. However this pleasure I would willing[ly] forgo rather than expose you too much in coming to Camp.[3] Should you think upon the whole of seting forward come on by the way of Kings Ferry that will be the safest and best route. In the Clove there has been several Roberies commited lately by *Tories and other Vilians*. Apply to General Putnam who will command at Kings Ferry for a small escort of Light Horse to guard you on to Paramus or Pompton.[4] I have spoke to him upon the subject. Bring Washington[5] with you if the Weather is not too cold.
    I have many matters to write you but my Time is so taken up upon matters of business that I can hardly spare a moment to write a friend.
    You will make my compliments agreeable to all friends. Yours affectionately

                                                        NG

ALS (NjP).
    1. The "Eastern jaunt" was a trip proposed by Catharine to Boston and Newburyport on 15 November. NG had asked his aide, William Blodget, to accompany her. In an amusing letter to a friend, Blodget expressed the hope that the phaeton would not break down nor the "Horses founder." (Blodget to John Cushing, 10 November 1778, MB) On Catharine's journey to camp in New Jersey, see below, NG to Griffin Greene, 21 November and NG to Pettit, 4 December.
    2. Letter not found.
    3. He planned to leave soon to establish the camp at Middlebrook, N.J.
    4. As noted above, NG to Sullivan, 24 October, Putnam was ordered the following week to winter with his division at Danbury, Conn.
    5. Their son, George, who would be three in January, did accompany Catharine.

In a letter to NG of 10 November (too mutilated to transcribe in its entirety) NG's brother Jacob had written that George "Says he Wants to See his dada." (This letter is at MiU-C.)

See Maps 1 and 2 for geographic references above.

From Colonel Clement Biddle

Sir   Quaker Hill [N.Y.] Nov: 13, 1778
Since the arrival of the Troops at Fredericksburg I have used my utmost Endeavours to provide Forage for the horses from the vicinity of Camp, that I might collect some stock beforehand for our winter magazines at other places. I have hitherto in a great measure succeeded, but am now under the necessity of drawing supplies of Grain from whence it will be much wanted, unless some method can be fallen on to oblige the Farmers to part with a reasonable share of their Forage.

The Resolve of Congress prohibiting the use of Wheat for Forage, even in the neighbourhood of the army, will make it extremely difficult to provide a sufficiency of Forage, and we should have every aid that the Country can give, of Grain of other kinds and of Hay.[1] But my purchasers complain that the people in general keep back their Grain and hay in hopes of higher prices, tho' they now receive very exorbitant rates, and when I have directed them to apply to the magistrates throughout this state, to impress Forage agreable to Law, it has not answered our purpose, as we get but a small part of what we want and it is attended with much Delay. The person who purchases in this district round here assures me there are considerable quantities of Hay and Grain yet to spare, but the Neighbours judging for each other, do not direct a sufficient share to be spared for the army and they will not part with more.

Unless some remedy is found immediately I must draw Forage from a distance to this place if we remain here and it is equaly necessary to fall on some for the supply of Fish Kill, where we can not get any Quantity of Grain beyond the present Consumption there.

As I am of Opinion the Country round us may yet subsist us for some time I request you will obtain such warrant or Orders from his Excellency Genl Washington as may answer the purpose or favour me with your Orders herein.[2] I am with great respect Yr: mo: ob: hum serv

                                                    CLEMENT BIDDLE

ALS (Washington Papers: DLC).
1. The resolution of 26 October was intended to reserve wheat for human consumption. (JCC, 12: 1064)

2. Biddle asked for impressment powers with reluctance. He had discovered what NG pointed out to Washington in his letter of 14 November, below, that New York's forage law had not worked well, partly because of local magistrates' "tenderness to their Neighbours." Some farmers, however, were also unwilling to part with hay and grain because of their disaffection. Quaker Hill (Map 1), where Biddle was stationed, was considered by some to be a virtual hotbed of neutralism or even disloyalty. Dr. James Fallon, who could not obtain transportation for sick soldiers in his hospital, believed the Quaker inhabitants were especially guilty. "Quaker-hill," he wrote Governor Clinton, "has been the Rendevouz of . . . tory vagrants." He quoted a local magistrate as saying he could not enforce his own warrant without a military guard because of "the disaffection of the generality of the Inhabitants on Quaker-hill" (Fallon to Clinton, 3 January 1779, Clinton, *Papers*, 4: 465, 467)

Washington was even more reluctant than Biddle in resorting to impressment. Only after a second and more urgent request from Biddle did he comply. See below, Biddle to NG and NG to Washington, 20 November.

Major Ichabod Burnet to Colonel James Abeel

[Camp Fredericksburg, N.Y., after 13 November 1778.[1] Has received sheets. Laments loss of Abeel's valuable plate. Hopes Abeel will see NG when he is on his way to Middlebrook to reconnoiter a camp. ALS (NjMoW) 2 pp.]

1. Burnet did not date his letter. The arrival of sheets to which Burnet referred in his letter of 13 November above establishes the date.

To Colonel Ephraim Bowen

[Fredericksburg, N.Y., 14 November 1778. Due to a lack of forage, all horses, wagons, and carriages that are unfit for service should be sold. He should obtain accounts from brigade quartermasters. Mr. Whittlesea [Whittlesey] to be dismissed from the service. "He has been dabbling in politics and creating mischief."[1] From Greene, *Greene*, 2: 410–11.]

1. See above, William Shepard to NG, 30 October.

To Nehemiah Hubbard

[Fredericksburg, N.Y., 14 November 1778. Has Hubbard's of 7 November. Tents to be made immediately. Instructions on paying for carting flour ordered by General Gates. All expenses of moving Convention army through Connecticut must be paid.[1] Reengage teamsters at $4 per day, if they cannot be hired for less.[2] Express riders "are a set of troublesome fellows"; their wages must not be raised. Asks for reference on William Joyce as clerk.[3] From Greene, *Greene*, 2: 410.]

1. See above, NG to James Davenport, 9 November.
2. See Hubbard to NG, 7 November, above.
3. See above, Joyce to NG, 9 November.

To George Washington

Sir　　　　　　　　Camp Fredericksburg [N.Y.] 14 Novemb [17]78

Inclosed is Colo Biddles Letter to me upon the distressed state of the Forage Department.[1] Our Cattle [i.e., livestock] for this ten days past have not had one half the necessary allowance of Forage. The Resolution of Congress prohibiting the use of Wheat and the Restrictive Laws in the several States, in the neighbourhood of Camp, renders it impossible to subsist the Cattle, unless some further aid can be given to the Forage Master General and his Deputies.

The Law of this State, appointing certain Persons in every Town to collect Forage and to say how much every Farmer shall spare, is not attended with that advantage that the Legislature designed in passing the Law. Men judge so differently from one another, and many from motives of tenderness to their Neighbours take so sparing from the People, that our supplies are very deficient notwithstanding we see the Country full of Forage. I am therefore under the necessity to call upon your Excellency for a Warrant to impress such Quantities of Forage from Time to Time as we find ourselves deficient in obtaining in the regular modes pointed out by Law.[2] I have the Honor to be Your Excellencys respectful Humble Servt

NATH GREENE

LS (Washington Papers: DLC).
1. See above, 13 November.
2. See note at Biddle's letter above.

From Colonel James Abeel

[Morristown, N.J., 14 November 1778. Has enough tools and other articles needed by the army. To prevent neglect of last year, asks if tents should not be sent to him for washing and repair when men are hutted. Expects to buy grindstones. LB (NjHi) 1 p.]

From Colonel Ephraim Bowen

[Providence, R.I., 14 November 1778. Forwarding his accounts. Has been careful to get vouchers for funds spent. Paid General Sullivan $65,000 of the $160,000 he owed. ADfS (RHi) 2 pp.]

From Henry Laurens,
President of the Continental Congress

[Philadelphia, 14 November 1778. Presented NG's letter of 6 November to Congress, which turned it over to a committee.[1] LB (PCC, item 13, vol. 2: 164, DNA) 1 p.]

1. On NG's letter and the new committee see above, note at NG to Ephraim Bowen, 12 November.

To Colonel Jeremiah Wadsworth

[Fredericksburg, N.Y. [?] 15 November 1778. NG had misplaced Wadsworth's letter of 5 November and has just read it. Wadsworth can tell him what has been done about getting bread to Sharon [Map 2] when NG returns to camp "to Night."[1] ALS (CtHi) 1 p.]

1. The bread was intended for the Convention army, which had been slated to march through Sharon, Conn. Wadsworth's letter not found.

Major Robert Forsyth to Moore Furman

[Fredericksburg, N.Y., 16 November 1778. Directed by NG to inform him that the army will soon be in motion by "Lower Route."[1] (Map 1) ALS (Nj) 1 p.]

1. It was 25 November before the army left. The lower route was via Fishkill and Kings Ferry, thence through Paramus and Elizabethtown, N.J. (Fitzpatrick, *GW*, 13: 323, 347)

To Colonel Charles Pettit

Dear Sir   Camp Fredricksburg [N.Y.] November 16th 1778
We are preparing with all immaginable diligence to move the Army into Winter quarter, Our Stores are on their way for Middle Brook.

I have seen Col Wadsworth and had a long conversation with him upon the subject of forage and the late Resolution of Congress prohibiting the use of Wheet.[1] The Col says he is perfectly disposd to concur with every measure that shall appear to be calculateed to promote the joint interest of the Commisary and Forage department. He has no wish to engross Grain or Flour to form Magizines that cannot be removed to the Army for want of Forage. But he thinks such is the scarcity of Wheet that every measure should be taken to forage the Army without the use of it. I enquird after the subject of dispute between him and Mr Wade.[2] He says Mr Wade wrote something to some person in Philadelphia reflecting upon the conduct of the Commisarys department that was not true.[3] He also says there is one Ohara an assistant to Mr Wade either in the quarter Matters [Masters] or Forage department who there has been a complaint entered against for selling Flour that should have been deliverd over to the Commisary. Doctor Scudder is possessd of the Papers.[4] The charge has been mentioned to some Members of Congress. I wish the matter to be diligently enquird into, This will be necessary to secure Mr Wade from any unjust imputations. Other wise as it happened in his district the charge will naturally [be] leveled at the Head.

Col Wadsworth says Mr Colhoun [Calhoun] is one of the best deputies he ever saw. He does his business very silently and expeditiously. I wish the affair of Mr Baty may not take place without first consulting him upon the subject.[5]

I am out of Money and obligd to stop payment. You know I cannot bear duning and therefore must beg you to forward me a supply.

From several circumstances I foresee it will be necessary for us to see each other very soon. When I arrive at Middle Brook I will advertize you to meet me at Trenton (Map 1). Col Cox has already agreed to be there. I shall have a double motive for coming both business and pleasure.

My best respects to Col Cox and his family to your family Mr Mitchel and his family. I am with sinsire regard Your most Obedient humble Servant

N GREENE

ALS (Original in possession of Doris Harris, Los Angeles, 1981).
1. See note at Clement Biddle to NG, 13 November, above.
2. Nothing more is known about the dispute between Wadsworth and Francis Wade, NG's Delaware deputy, than is revealed here. For biographical information on Wade, see above, vol. 2: 418n.
3. In the original, which NG wrote in a hurry, the phrase "that was not true" appears to be a separate sentence. Since, however, he was a friend of Wadsworth and had no way of knowing what Wade might or might not have written to someone in Philadelphia, it is most unlikely that he would have written anything that was such a flat contradiction.
4. Scudder was a member of the Supply Departments Committee.
5. Charles Beatty was a deputy quartermaster in Maryland. For more on this issue, see below, Beatty to NG, 27 November and NG to Pettit, 12 December.

To George Washington

Sir   Camp at Fredricksburg [N.Y.] November 16, 1778

The repeated instances of violence commited by Officers of inferior rank in the line, upon Waggon Masters, In direct violation of your Excellency orders, render it necessary that some check should be given to this unwarrantable practice. The warrant officers begin to think their situation so very disagreeable that they are determined one and all to quit the service unless they can find some freedom from such acts of oppression and injustice. Waggon Masters have been repeatedly put under guard for the most trifleing offences. Notwithstanding your Excellency hath again and again directed that they should only be subject to the same modes of tryal and arrest for misconduct which officers in the line were.

There is now a regular complaint made to me by Mr Byers, Waggon Master for the 2d Pennsylvania brigade against Mr Knox, quarter master of the 9th Pennsylvania Regiment. The Waggon Master was in the line of his duty agreeable to the orders he had received from the commanding officer of the brigade, when the quarter master interferd and prevented him from pursueing his orders. This the Waggon Master took as an injury and wrote him a note, not the most polite, nor yet very insolent. The quarter master no sooner receivd the note than he sent a file of men, took the Waggon Master prisoner and confind him in the quarter guard all night.

I wish not to urge this complaint. I am sensible of the danger of opening disputes between the commision[ed] and Warrant Officers, but the lat[t]er declarye they will leave the service, unless they can find some protection from the violence of the former.

What I have to request of your Excellency upon this occasion is that you would be pleas'd to repeat your former orders upon this subject, for the protection of Warrant Officers, Forbidding the Officers of the Line in the most pointed Terms and under the severest penalties from presuming to confine them otherwise than by arrest for any offence what ever.

I hope such a declaration will check the evil and satisfy the party who bring forward the complaint. If your Excellency approve of the proposition, please to found the order upon a representation made by the quarter master General of the great injury done the public service by the violence offer'd by some indiscreet commisioned Officers to Warrant Officers in the Waggon department.[1] I have the honor to be with great respect Your Excellencys Most humble Servt.

NATH GREENE

ALS (Washington Papers: DLC).
1. There is no evidence that Washington complied with NG's request.

To George Washington

Sir   Camp Fredricksburg [N.Y.] November 16, 1778

I wish when your Excellency gives your orders for the Troops to march from Fishkills that those employed in transporting forage may continue in that service until the Troops that are to Winter there, arrive and furnish a party to releive them.

There are also a few Masons now employed in building Chimneys to the Barracks. These I wish may be left for about a fortnight.

There will be wanted for a few days about 40 men to facilitate the Armies crossing the River. They should be good oresmen if to be got. Great part of our Waterman are employed in the forage business and cannot be called off with out great injury to that service. We have only about thirty men at Kings Ferry [Map 1] to man the Boats. These will be found insufficient to cross with as much expedition as I could wish.

Will your Excellency be so kind as to furnish me with a clue to find out the person in the forage department who you hinted to me the other day had betrayed his trust. No Person in any branch of my department shall escape with impunity if it is possible to detect him, who either neglects his duty or missapplies the public money.[1] I have the honor to be with great respect Your Excellencys Most Obedient humble Sert

NATH GREENE

ALS (Washington Papers: DLC).
1. Washington answered on 17 November, below.

From Royal Flint

[Fredericksburg, N.Y., 16 November 1778. Colonel Wadsworth requests NG to direct his deputy in New Jersey to consult with commissaries as to where to deposit provisions for troops on march to winter quarters. FC (CtHi) 1 p.]

From Gouverneur Morris

Dr Sir   Phila 16th Novr 1778

I have written a long Letter to the Genl. The Burthen of the Song is divide your Army and come hither.[1] I am more and more convinced that unless something of the former Kind be done we shall find the Distresses in your and Wadsworth's Departments insurmountable. I wish much that He and you should be here not meerly for the sake of the Public but that in addition to that which is indeed also for the public advantage. Prejudices may be removed, Suspicions quietd,

Jealousies stifled, Calumny destroyed, and Friendship and Harmony and Confidence awakened and kept alive.[2] The General hath Enemies as who is it that hath not. You have Enemies. The Army I am told hath Jealousies and Suspicions about it detrimental to Congress and to the Public Welfare. I hope not. But at any Rate let those who know best what they suffer and how they feel be on the spot to say in the Language of a Soldier: do this Act of Justice and that of Generosity; I have served you faithfully, reward therefore these Men for they have also most faithfully served. Besides all this perhaps it might be full as proper for him to meet Mrs Washington here as in any Camp under Heaven.[3] Adieu. I am your Friend

GOUV MORRIS

ALS (NjP).
1. Morris had written Washington on 11 November with suggestions of possible locations for quartering the army during the winter. (Washington Papers, DLC)
2. NG had received similar advice from William S. Livingston, Henry Marchant, and Joseph Reed, 5 November, above. He went to Philadelphia at the end of December.
3. Martha Washington went to Philadelphia in mid-December and was joined by her husband in January 1779.

From Colonel James Abeel

[Morristown, N.J., 17 November 1778. Wagons are dispatched to bring grindstones to this place. LB (NjHi) 1 p.]

From George Washington

Sir   Headquarters [Fredericksburg, N.Y.] Novr. 17th. 1778
    The information I gave you respecting the Forage department, was only meant to excite a close attention to the conduct of those who are employed in the execution of this branch of business; suspicion of unfair dealing in some of them, having been imbibed.
    No direct charges, or regular information, was lodged against the forage Master in this department; for if there had, I should have proceeded in a different manner, than barely suggesting suspicion. Genl. Scott of this state,[1] to the best of my recollection, was the Gentn. who intimated that there was reason to apprehend, that from the Wheat which was run through the Mills for forage, a small quantity of the finest Flour was taken from every Bushel, without crediting the public for it. It is possible, upon application to him, a clue may be had to the discovery, if the suspicions are well founded.
    One thing I can relate to you with certainty, and that is, that it is a matter of suprize to every body, that a Mr. Bostick[2] (I think he is called) who never could take such care of his own affairs as to escape a Goal, should be entrusted with the management of public business.

Such a choice, independant of every other consideration, is sufficient to create suspicions of Public injury from neglect or inability, if no other cause. I am Sir Yr Most Obedt Hbl Servt

GO: WASHINGTON

ALS (Mr. Edward W. Smith, Darien, Conn., 1981).
    1. For Gen. Charles Scott's criticism of the quartermaster department in Delaware, see below, Scott to NG, 8 December 1778.
    2. If the reference was to Andrew Bostwick, deputy forage master at Fishkill, it was apparently false; Bostwick had been appointed on the recommendation of General McDougall, and he remained in the post throughout NG's tenure.

To Colonel Clement Biddle

Sir   Camp at Fredricksburg [N.Y.] Novem 19, 1778
    Supposing His Excellency should have it in contemplation to carry on an expedition against Newyork. Is the Forage department in such a situation as to be capable of aiding the operations?[1]
    The Army may possibly consist of 12000 men besides the Artillery.[2] These will be [have] to be fed with Provisions transported at a great distance. The Teams requisite for this purpose will consume a great quantity of forage.
    There will be besides the Teams employed upon the communications upwards of 5000 Horses to be fed that are necessary to move the Army. You will add to these the Forage Teams employed in and out of Camp in drawing Forage to the communications and to the Army.
    If you think it is practicable to aid such an expedition with a sufficient supply of Forage, Please to point out the place where it is to be drawn from and the ways and means by which you propose to draw it together.
    As very important consequences may depend upon your Answer I would wish you to be very particular in your account. On the one hand I want to know what the resources of the Country can afford but on the other great care should [be] taken not to promise more than you can perform.
    It may be attended with destructive consequences to deceive the General into an attempt upon N York and have his operation fail for want of a sufficient supply of Forage.[3] I am Sir your humble Servt

NATH GREENE

ALS (RG 93, WRMS, MS. 25484: DNA).
    1. Although most of the general officers, including NG, considered the mere contemplation of attacking New York City at this time as unrealistic, the possibility of retaking New York was never completely absent from Washington's thinking, even at a time when he was still toying with a plan to invade Canada. (See note at NG to Washington, 28 October, above.)
    2. NG inadvertently reversed the first two numerals. In Washington's report of

Continental troop strength in November, with which NG was familiar, 21,476 men were listed as "PRESENT FIT FOR DUTY & ON DUTY," including 933 in the artillery. (Lesser, *Sinews*, pp. 92–94, quoting Washington's reports in Record Group 93, DNA, and elephant folios, MiU-C)

3. See Biddle's reply, same date, below.

From Colonel Clement Biddle

Sir   Camp Fredericksburg [N.Y.] Nov. 19, 1778

I have considered your Letter respecting the Resources for supplying Forage in Case an Expedition should take place against New York.

By my late Letters from Jersey that State could with difficulty furnish Forage for the Teams then passing with Provisions, and great part of the Grain which was consumed by the Teams in that State was brought from Pennsylvania and the southern States to Trenton.

A Quantity of Grain will arrive at Trenton before the River closes [i.e., freezes] but by my last Accounts from thence there was no quantity on hand and I could not depend on such Supplies at that post in time as would be sufficient to keep the Provision and Forage Teams in motion.

From this State I cannot draw a sufficiency to subsist the number of horses that would be Requisite for our Army if collected together for any length of time. The Roads are now becoming so bad that Forage cannot be speedily brought from any distance.

As there would be near 5000 horses with the Army if collected together and at least Eight hundred Teams employd in furnishing supplies of Provisions and Forage, I am of Opinion that with every supply of Forage that the Country could yield it would be impossible to subsist the horses if the Army should be collected together and remain for any length of Time.

I found my Opinion on the Letters I have Received from my different purchasers in this State, Jersey and Connecticut; And if all that could be got was Collected, it would leave us under great difficulties for our supplies for Winter.

If a sudden movement of the Army towards New York should be thought necessary, the Country might furnish a supply for a short Time by impressing Forage of every kind, but this would only answer for a very few Days.[1] I am with great Respect Your most Obedt Servt

CLEMENT BIDDLE

ALS (RG 93, WRMS, MS 25485: DNA).

1. For more on Biddle's plight see below, Biddle to NG, 20 November and NG to Washington, 20 November.

From Colonel Clement Biddle

Sir   Quaker Hill [N.Y.] Novr 20, 1778

It will be impossible to subsist the horses at this Post if we remain here longer than tomorrow unless I have a warrant to impress Forage. I beg you to represent this to his Excellency the General and request his warrant to impress what Forage may be necessary in the Vicinity of Camp both in this state and the borders of Connecticut. I am with respect Yr Mo Ob Serv

CLEMENT BIDDLE

It will be necessary to extend the warrant so as to serve on our march to Jersey.[1]

ALS (Washington Papers: DLC).
1. See below, NG to Washington, 20 November, in which this letter was enclosed.

To George Washington

Sir   Camp Fredricksburg [N.Y.] Nov. 20, 1778

Inclosd is Col Biddles Letter to me upon the subject of Forage.[1] I shall only add that a great number of our Horses for Ten days past have been falling away to such a degree for want of a sufficient supply that those which were in good order then are now almost unfit for duty.

I am perswaded it will be impossible to subsist the Cattle [i.e., livestock] belonging to the Army here unless there is a Press Warrant granted to aid the Forage Master. I shall take great care that no improper use is made of the Warrant.[2] I have the honor to be with great respect your Excellency obedient humble Sert

NATH GREENE

ALS (Washington Papers: DLC).
1. See above, Biddle to NG, 20 November.
2. Washington had failed to issue a press warrant as Biddle had requested on 13 November (above); and he was apparently still reluctant to do so. Nevertheless, he did comply the same day out of "absolute necessity." It could be used in the areas through which the army would march, but he limited it to one month and warned the agents to have regard "to the real wants of the inhabitants." (Fitzpatrick, *GW*, 13: 296–97) Biddle was no less considerate. Even when armed with the warrant, he asked his deputy, Thomas Mitchell, to try persuasion with the people in order to avoid using force among them, which, he stressed, "I am very anxious to prevent." (Biddle to Mitchell, 20 November 1778, PHi.) It was only the beginning of a difficult winter for the foragemaster and the quartermaster.

From General Henry Knox

[Fredericksburg, N.Y., 20 November 1778. Requests that NG give directions to his deputy at Springfield [Mass.] to pay for such lumber and coal as will be needed for the ordnance works[1] there. ALS (PPAmP) 1 p.]

1. The so-called Elaboratory.

To Colonel Ephraim Bowen

[Fredericksburg, N.Y., before 21 November 1778.[1] Still in need of a person "in the stile of an Auditor" to direct clerks on how "to Methodese Accounts." Asks if Bowen can persuade George Olney to take the post.[2] ALS (MiU-C) 1 p.]

1. Date is determined by NG's letter to Bowen of 12 December, below, in which he refers to two lost letters of Bowen's of "21st and 28th ultimo." Bowen, it is implied, responded in both of them to NG's request concerning Olney.
2. Olney, a member of a prominent Providence family, did accept the post. (See below, NG to Bowen, 12 December, and Olney to NG, 2 January 1779.) An able auditor as well as a sometime assistant, Olney remained until NG resigned as quartermaster. In 1780 they held joint shares in the privateer *Tartar*. (See below, Olney to NG, 30 August 1780.) Although their wives quarreled openly in March 1781, the men seem to have remained on friendly terms. Olney was later made receiver of continental taxes in Rhode Island and in October 1789 became "sole commissioner" to receive claims of Rhode Islanders against the United States. (Bartlett, *Records*, 9: 661, 10: 364)

To Griffin Greene

Dear Sir   Camp at Fredricksburg [N.Y.] November 21, 1778
    I am anxious to hear how your son is. Jacob wrote me he was very ill and that he thought he could not recover.[1] However as Jacob is one of Doctor Youngs diciples I am in great hopes he has overrateed the danger. I hope Sally is in a better state of health than when I left Coventry. She must not confine herself at Home. Traveling and freedom from care can alone restore her to perfect health.
    Jacob proposd to purchase Daniel Gardner's place. I think it will answer a good purpose. It is a very good pi[e]ce of Meadow ground. But Mr Gard'r proposd one condition in the purchase that Jacob did not care to comply with, which was for him to hold the farm until next Spring come twelve months and allow the interest of the Money for the rent. I would try to get possession next Spring if possible, but if I could not I think it will be for your interest to take it providing you [*several words missing*] considerable stroke of business at Coventry with the Iron Works.
    However I am clear in my opinion that you two ought not both to live at that place. The business done there is too triffling an object for

such a sacrifice of Time and attention as you are both obligd to pay to it.

Was you in Boston or in any great Tradeing Town the advantages you might have there more than you can have in your present situation would more than four-fold pay the difference in the expence of living. Coventry from the Nature of the Country, from its Inhabitants and produce dont admit nor never can any great stroke of business being drove on there. The Inhabitants are poor and thin, Labour is high and difficult to be got that there must in the nature of things be always a ballance of Trade against whatever business is done there. But as you own the interest and it cannot be sold for its Value, necessity will oblige one of you to stay there. Indeed it will support one family very genteelly with proper industry and good oeconomy. I should recommend therefore that one of you thought of Some other plan of business.[2] You are now in the prime of life and have got good Talents for business and are tolerably well acquainted with the World. I think it will fall to your lot to turn out [i.e., leave], especially as you have got over local prejudices and enjoy a much better state of health than Jacob does.

However if I was you I would make myself Master of the English grammar. A few months application will give you an amazing advantage in writing correctly and spelling properly.

My love to your Wife and all friends. Pray advise Mrs Greene what to do whether to come to camp or not. You know the state of things at Home and know the distance and ground she will have to travel over.[3] Yours Aff

N GREENE

ALS (OMC).
    1. In Jacob's letter, almost all of which is too mutilated to transcribe, he had said that Griffin's little son "lies At the Point of death" and that it was "next to Impossible he Can Recover." (Jacob Greene to NG, 10 November 1778, MiU-C) The boy did recover, however, as seen below, NG to Griffin, 25 January 1779. Griffin and Sarah Greene lost a child in April 1782, but its name was not recorded. (Clarke, *Greenes*, p. 197)
    2. NG had presented similar arguments to Griffin and Jacob in May 1778. See above, vol. 2: 380, 406.
    3. Catharine left for camp on 26 November. See below, NG to Pettit, 4 December.

From Nehemiah Hubbard

[Hartford, Conn. (?), 22 November 1778. Wishes NG's directions on wages for James Bull and assistants.[1] Asks if wagon conductors should be paid subsistence. LB (RG 93, WRMS: DNA) 1 p. extract.]

    1. See above, Hubbard to NG, 9 November.

To Colonel Charles Pettit

Dear Sir   Camp Fredricksburg [N.Y.] November 23d 1778

I waited upon his Excellency immediately on the receipt of yours of the 15th at Elizabeth.[1] He consented that Col White should go to Baltimore, but not without some difficulty, for he is apprehensive they will run mad with pleasure as the situation will be favorable for diversions of all kinds.[2]

I expected to have left this ground some days since, but the General thinks it prudent to remain in our present situation until the Convention Troops have passed the North River. The first division I expect will cross next day after to morrow.[3]

We are more and more distressed for want of forage every day. The General has given us a press Warrant to enable us to procure a present supply.[4] Great exertions must be made to the Westward or ruin awaits us. The restrictive Laws in the several States, the prohibition of Congress, The depreciation of money, and the Avarice of the People all seem to conspire to distress us. I am well convinced without the helping hand of Government our utmost exertions will be ineffectual, unless we agree to give the most extravagant price for things.

If the Congress has in contemplation any plan for restoreing the credit of their currency, the sooner they give a check to the evil the better. The People must agree to submit to some seeming arbitary Edicts or else diminish their Army.

The President of Congress writes me the subject of my Letter to them is referd to a Committee with full powers to act upon it as they shall think proper. Go[u]verneuer Morris, Doctor Skudder [Scudder] and General Whipple compose the Committee. You will please to wait upon them, and give them a full History of the Forage department.[5]

Col Bowen and Col [Morgan] Lewises Accounts will accompany this. Inclosd you have a Copy of a Letter from the Secretary of the board of *War* with sundry Resolutions of Congress by which you'l see the demand.[6] You will therefore give the necessary directions to all the Deputies West of the North River for obtaining the proper returns agreeably to the Resolution of Congress. Our Deputies for the future must make their Assistants send in their Accounts at the close of every month. This will enable them to send us Monthly returns, Which by the by I believe would be a very pleasing circumstance to the Congress and go a great way towards reconcileing them to the expence. The prejudices of a certain order of people are so deeply rooting respecting the misapplication of Public Money that nothing short of occular demonstration can convince them to the contrary. I shall demand the returns to the Eastward.

There has been more applications for money since you left me than there was all Summer before. I hope there is some on the way or the Lord knows how I shall reconcile the people to the disappointment. It is surprising to me that the people has such an avidity for what they seem to set so little store by.

Upon Weighing the matter more fully I am of opinion it will not be for the interest of the Department to put the management of it under Col Finney to the Westward.[7] The People to the Southward have high notions and it is not improbable but that the same men who would willingly hold the Office under the principal would refuse it from a Deputy. I wish that appointment not to take place until you hear further from me upon the subject.

I think it will be necessary for you to consult freely with Mr Biddle and if there has been any misconduct of the deputies or agents employed under him, let them be treated as their conduct deserves. I am inform'd from pretty good authority there has been some regular complaints laid before Congress respecting our department.

The person I wrote to in Connecticut dont appear upon farther enquiry to be altogether quallified for the office of Auditor. He has a perfect knowledge of Book keeping but dont seem to be acquainted with business. Besides which his Terms are such as cannot be complied with.[8]

I must request you therefore ⟨to endeavor to engage one⟩ in Philadelphia. You know the necessity and ⟨therefore⟩ I need not urge it.

The complaints are so loud and so numerous from New Jersey that I am almost afraid to go there. Trenton must save us, as it has done once before,[9] or else there will be an end of the poor quarter Master.

Remember I have a draft upon you for one hours writing every day. I dont intend to lose the pleasure of your conversation and not have some compensation for it. My best respects to Col Cox. I am Sir your Most Obedient humble Sert

NATH GREENE

ALS (NHi). Enclosure missing. Portion in angle brackets taken from *Greene*, Greene, 2: 416.

1. Letter not found.

2. Pettit had stopped in Elizabeth Town (Map 1) with Lord Stirling, who had been there since late September to guard against British incursions. (Fitzpatrick, *GW*, 12: 513–14) In early October, Moylan's Fourth Continental Dragoons joined Stirling, with Lt. Col. Anthony Walton White in command in place of the ill Moylan. Forage from the lower Chesapeake was presumably available in Baltimore. Washington's apprehension that the men would "run mad with pleasure" in Baltimore was apparently based on cavalrymen's reputation for rowdyism.

Lord Stirling objected to the regiment's going to Baltimore, but only because he insisted they were needed in Elizabeth Town. On NG's advice, however, Washington decided to send the regiment to Lancaster, Pa., as originally recommended by Colonel

Biddle. (See below, NG to Washington, 30 November, and Washington's response, 4 December. Washington's orders of 7 December to White are in the Washington Papers, DLC.) Forage, however, was not as plentiful in Lancaster as Biddle thought. (See NG to Pettit, 17 December, below.)

3. On the Convention army see above, NG to Davenport, 9 November. The Pennsylvania Line and Artillery left Fredericksburg on 25 November. (Fitzpatrick, *GW*, 13: 323) NG left the next day.

4. See above, NG to Washington, 20 November.

5. On the formation of the committee, see above, NG to Bowen, 12 November.

6. Letter not found.

7. William Finnie served as deputy quartermaster for Virginia until the end of the war, although he was sometimes the target of sharp criticism. Washington's stepson, John Parke Custis, for example, accused him of paying excessive prices in order to increase his commissions. (Washington to Custis, 2 January 1779, Fitzpatrick, *GW*, 13: 478) He was also criticized for his handling of the Convention army in Virginia; see Finnie to NG, 11 February 1779, below.

8. See above, William Joyce to NG, 9 November.

9. As the battle of Trenton had saved Washington's army in December 1776.

From Samuel Hodgdon[1]

[Danbury, Conn., 23 November 1778. Defends himself against criticism of Wagonmaster Thompson on taking horses and harness from old wagons to use with new ammunition wagons. Cy (RG 93, WRMS: DNA) 1 p.]

1. Hodgdon was a deputy commissary of military stores. (Heitman, *Register*)

To George Washington

Sir   Headquarters [Fredericksburg, N.Y.] Novem 24, 1778

There is great complaints from Fish Kill and other Posts among the Waggoners and Artificers on account of the Commisarys being directed to issue a Gill of Rice in lieu of half a pound of flour and being cut off of their usual allowance of Rum. Col Hay writes me the Waggoners are actually leaveing the service on account of the Rice and the Country People refuse to work without the allowance of a gill of Rum. There must be some alteration in these matters or it will work a great injury to the public service.[1]

If your Excellency will give me authority, I will put the matter upon as oeconomical a plan as the nature of the service can admit. I am your Excellencys very hum'e Sert

N GREENE

ALS (Washington Papers: DLC).

1. It was not the amount of rice about which the men complained (a gill being half a cup), but simply that they did not like rice. The shortage of flour during the winter would force many to eat rice, but in the meantime NG got Washington's approval to furnish them with flour and to restore their rum ration. (See NG's letter to Samuel Gray, 5 December, below.)

To General Anthony Wayne

[Fredericksburg, N.Y., 24 November 1778. Has ordered a hundred axes for Wayne. NG is "astonnished" that Wayne had been unable to get any. "Sure I am there must have been a great neglect either in the Brigade quarter Masters or the Store keepers" for there has been "a great plenty." Warns against men losing or selling axes. He hopes to have "friendly hints" if Wayne sees other deficiencies. ALS (PHi) 2 pp.]

To Colonel John Cox[1]

Dear Sir   Camp Fredricksburg [N.Y.] Nov 25th 1778

By yours of the 19th[2] I see the burden of the song is change the System of the department or the expence will become intollerable. Observe the policy: they began upon the Deputies, but if the principals could be brought to manage the business upon Sallary it would greatly facilitate bringing the Deputies onto the measure. Great pains will be taken to find out which of us favors the new System most, to encourage it will be popular for a Time, but mark the end.[3]

As soon as ever I can get the Army to their several Posts, I intend to Visit Philadelphia, and if it appears to me that the conditions proposd to us are unequal to the trouble and fatigue, or if the Terms we shall have to offer to the Deputies will not engage good men, I shall leave the department for I will not continue in it unless it is upon such conditions as will enable me to employ such.

Col Mitchel sent us 200,000 dollars; it arrivd very seasonally, for the Deputies began to paint their distress from every quarter. Indeed the Teamsters began to refuse to work any longer unless they were paid. I mean those which were impressed by the Law of this State. We shall want large Sums more to the Eastward and very shortly too. Bowen, Chace and Smith has had none of this and Hubbart but a very small pittance and yet I have not 5000 dollars left of the whole 200,000 dollars sent me.[4]

I had a Letter from the Committee of Congress appointed upon the quarter masters and Commisary's departments. They mention nothing respecting the new arrangement but wish to see me as soon as possible.[5]

I had one also from Go[u]verneuer Morris, but he carefully avoids touching upon that string also.[6]

I thank you kindly for your polite invitation to Bloomsbury.[7] It is yet very uncertain whether Mrs Greene will come to Camp. If she does, doubtless it will be agreeable for her to spend a few Days there while I am in Philadelphia.

I shall be glad to hear from you by every opportunity. We are this moment going to set out for the Jerseys. We are packing up bag and baggage and all in confusion. You will therefore excuse my not writing you more largely. I am with sincere regard Your Most Obedient humble Sert

NATH GREENE

ALS (NHi).
1. Little has been published about John Cox (1731–93). One of NG's two assistants, he was a successful merchant in Philadelphia and iron manufacturer in New Jersey before the war. In 1760 he had married Esther Bowes, whose older sister, Theodosia, was the mother of Joseph Reed—a connection that first brought him to NG's attention. (See above, vol. 2: 310n.) Through his wife's father, Francis Bowes, who was part owner of the Black Creek Forge at Bordentown, Cox first became involved in iron making. In 1770 he and a partner bought the Batsto furnace, Cox becoming sole owner in 1773. (For a description of Batsto and the shares that NG, Cox, and Pettit later owned, see below, NG to Jacob Greene, 20 March 1779.)
Cox's businesses did not prevent his taking an active part in patriot affairs, first as a member of Pennsylvania's General Committee of Correspondence and of the Council of Safety, then as a major in the Second Battalion of the Philadelphia Associators. When his nephew, Joseph Reed, resigned from the battalion, Cox succeeded him as lieutenant colonel. During the early war years his iron business thrived, although a second furnace—at Mt. Holly—was demolished by the British in June 1778. He also did a brisk business in salt, a business that he continued to run while serving as NG's assistant. (See invoices for salt from June 1778 to March 1779 in the Jonathan Potts Papers, vol. 4, PHi.) On accepting the post as NG's assistant in March 1778, it was Cox who insisted on being paid a commission as recompense for his giving up various enterprises, including the Batsto furnace.
After selling Batsto, he purchased "Bloomsbury Court," a mansion south of Trenton that had been built by William Trent in 1721. Here, Esther Cox, a renowned hostess, brought up their six daughters and saw them married to a variety of prominent young men. Ill health plagued Cox during the winter of 1778–79, but he continued as AQMG throughout NG's tenure. From 1781 to 1783 he served in the New Jersey Legislative Council, part of the time as vice president. He kept a hand in business until his death. (Biographical information on Cox, his wife, and daughters is found in Boyer, *Early Forges*, pp. 134, 177–80. Additional facts are in Pierce, *Iron in the Pines*, pp. 121–26, 128–31; Reed, *Reed*, 1: 26, 364n; and in his correspondence with NG.)
2. Letter not found.
3. On 20 October, Congress had ordered that the "Commissary and Quarter Master General be directed forthwith to contract with their Deputies and Assistants respectively, and allow them fixed salaries." NG and Wadsworth were to be exempt, but nothing was said about Pettit and Cox. (*JCC*, 12: 1030–31) It is clear in the second paragraph of NG's letter that he had not yet put the directive into effect and that, in fact, he was virtually threatening to resign rather than to do so.
In the same resolution, Congress had suggested that, as an inducement to deputies and assistants to save money, they be given a percentage of their savings. One could sympathize with Congress for seeking incentives to save money, but since there were no standard prices by which to measure savings, their suggestion bordered on the ludicrous—especially in a period of a rapidly depreciating dollar.
In a letter to President Jay, 15 February 1779, below, NG did present a proposal for compensating the principals in his department by salary.
4. The men were NG's New England deputies.
5. Letter not found.
6. See above, 16 November.
7. As seen in note 1 above, Bloomsbury was the Cox's home near Trenton, N.J.

John Cox, 1731–1793, engraving of a miniature by unknown artist, reproduced from Anne Hollingsworth Wharton, Salons Colonial and Republican, *Philadelphia, 1900*

The William Trent House; John Cox named it "Bloomsbury" when he moved there
(Courtesy of the Trent House Association)

The Van Veghten House, Greene's Headquarters at Camp Middlebrook
(Courtesy of the Somerset Historical Society)

From Colonel Jeremiah Wadsworth

Dear Sir   [   ] Nov 25, 1778
My House being founded on a Rock I fear neither Storms of detraction or Hurricanes of Calumny. If my [military] Family are Wicked let them Answer for their Sins. I am not anxious about being classed with your very Wicked Department. The "feelings of my Heart" decide in Your and my own favour. My opinion of other People you know already.[1] I dine at Hd Quarters today and will take Yours in my way. With sincerity I remain. Your very H St

JERE WADSWORTH

ALS (PPAmP).
1. The commissary department had received even more criticism than the quarter-master department.

To General Anthony Wayne

[Kings Ferry, N.Y., 27 November 1778. Since the Convention troops require many regular ferrymen, NG requests forty men of Wayne's brigade to assist [the American army] in "crossing the Troops and Waggons at this Ferry."[1] He will allow each a "Dollar per Day and half pint of Spirits." LS (PHi) 2 pp.]

1. The army was en route to Middlebrook, N.J. On the Convention army, which was crossing at Fishkill, some twenty miles upstream, see above, NG to Davenport, 9 November.

See Map 1 for geographic references above.

From Charles Beatty

[Frederick Town, Md., 27 November 1778. As NG requests, he will assist the Convention army to get through his district.[1] Asks that NG or Cox answer his letters as to whether his district will be enlarged to include Frederick County as it "formerly Stood." If not, he does not "chose to Act any longer."[2] ALS (PPAmP) 1 p.]

1. On the Convention army, see above, NG to Davenport, 9 November.
2. Beatty's earlier letters to Cox and NG have not been found. On 30 March 1778, ten days before John Cox had appointed Beatty as DQM for Frederick County, NG had appointed James Calhoun as DQM of an area defined only as the "Western shore of Maryland" (i.e., of Chesapeake Bay), without any delimitations to the west. Beatty's district of Frederick County extended from the unsettled area of western Maryland eastward to within ten miles (in some places) of the "Western shore." In the interim, Frederick County had been divided into Washington, Montgomery, and Frederick counties—all bordering the Potomac. A jurisdictional conflict was inevitable.
Although neither NG nor Cox resolved the matter, Beatty did not resign as

threatened. In September 1779 the Maryland Council found that the territories of the two men still overlapped, which the council quite properly saw as an "Inconsistency in different People acting in the same Place, in the same Business, with equal Powers." (*Md. Archives*, 21: 530. Excerpts from the commissions of Calhoun and Beatty are printed on pages 513 and 524.)

See Map 4 for geographic references above.

From Colonel Stephen Moylan

[Elizabeth Town, N.J., 27 November 1778. Thanks NG for his letter.[1] Is recovering and hopes to see NG again soon. ALS (NNPM) 1 p.]

1. Letter not found. During Moylan's illness, Lt. Col. Anthony Walton White was commanding Moylan's Dragoons. See NG to Pettit, 23 November, above.

To Colonel Charles Pettit

Dear Sir   Elizabeth Town [N.J.] Nov 29, 1778
The Army are on their march for Middle Brook Camp. I came to this place last night and am just going to set out for the place where we design to Hutt.

Not a line have I receivd from you since you left this place. I should be glad to hear from you by every opportunity. The Committee of Congress have requested my attendance in Philadelphia as soon as possible.[1] I shall attend them immediately after geting the Troops fixt in their Winter quarters, but that will take a fortnight at least. You will please to hasten in the returns and the accounts of all the Western deputies. I am perswaded the Committee of Congress intend to change the System of the quarter masters department and the Commisarys too from paying a commision to allowing a Sallary.

I think we shall be very delicately situated. To refuse a reasonable sallary will expose us to the cry of the People; but there is no sallary that the Congress dare give that will bear any propotion to the fatigue and difficulties incident to the Office.[2]

I have found the Memorandum which I mentiond to you.

My respects to Col Cox and all others of my acquaintance. I am sincerely yours

NATH GREENE

ALS (NHi).
1. NG did not go to Philadelphia until the end of December.
2. In a letter to John Jay, 15 February 1779, below, NG agreed that he, Pettit, and Cox would accept salaries.

To George Washington

Sir   Bound Brook [N.J.] Novr 30, 1778
I got to this place last night but too late to take a survey of any
part of the Country. I waited upon Lord Sterling as I came through
Elizabeth Town and to my great surprise found Col Moylans Light
Dragoons had not been sent off.[1] I spoke to his Lordship upon the
necessity of sending them away immediately. He refusd to let them
go, and said he would not remain at the Post if they were order'd
away. He also informd me that he had wrote your Excellency upon
the subject which he did not doubt would be very satisfactory to you.
Every consideration must yield to necessity. If the Horse are continued there, the Post must be abandoned by and by for want of
Forage. There is less danger of a surprise there than ever there was.
The Enemy upon Statten Island are all collected at the North end and
their numbers greatly diminished. The Garrison at N York much
weakened and not the least appearance of any offensive operations in
view. Under these circumstances I cannot see the propriety of continueing the Horse where it is attended with such destructive circumstances to guard against so remote an event.
      If there must be that number of Horse or any think [thing] like it
kept there during the Winter, The Post had much better be abandoned. The expence in the single article of Wood is upwards of 300
dollars a day.
      I consulted the Field officers upon the necessity of haveing the
Horse kept there. They all agree to whom I mentioned the matter that
there is not the least necessity for their being continued. There are not
wanting insinuations that they are kept for Parade and that only; but
as this is an ungenerous insinuation and as it comes from those who
feel themselves injurd by the Horse being kept at the Post I would not
lay any stress upon it.[2]
      Bad as I had conceivd of the Forage department in this quarter I
find it much worse than I expected. There is none at all collected here
and I am afraid not a great deal too collect. Col Berry who is a man
well acquainted with the resources of this County gives but poor
encouragement of geting a supply of forage.[3] I only mention this to
shew the necessity of dismissing every useless mouth that destroys
forage. Mr [Moore] Furman has already been obligd to dismiss near
300 teams that have been employed in transporting Provisions Eastward for want of provender.
      It now rains very fast. As soon as ever it slakens a little I shall
immediately go out to take a view of the ground towards Steels
Tavern to fix upon a place for Huting. We have a considerable quantity of Boards collected here and a great many more coming in. I am in

hopes nothing will be wanting but the Article of Forage; and as to that I cannot promise any great things. However there shall be no want of industry to get every thing the Country can furnish or the people are willing to part with.

Col [Robert L.] Hooper and Col [Jacob] Morgan in the State of Pennsylvania whose districts are both Forage Counties complain of a great scarcity of it. Col Hooper says we must not depend much upon him; he is already so much drain'd that little more will be to be got in his district.

I suppose your Excellency has heard of the Tories takeing off Col Ward from Mr Hardens.[4] I lodg'd that night at Mr Hoppers at Paramus. An Express came to me at Three oClock in the morning and acquainted me of the accident. I immediately sent all the Light Horse I had with me in persuit of the Vilians. I also directed Col Febiger at Hakensack to send out parties on Horseback and to guard all the passes leading into N York. Whether any of the parties came across the thieves I have not heard as I came off early the next morning.

The impudence of these rascals is without example. It appears to me that it will be necessary to have a small guard at Paramus and Coes Tavern to secure the communication with the Eastern States. Our Expresses and all dispaches will otherwise be greatly exposd. I was told as I came through that part of the Country that the Commanding Officer in N York had offerd a considerable sum to any person that would intercept the dispaches from Congress to your Excellency or from you to them.[5] There must also be a guard at Kings Ferry otherwise the Stores there on this side the River will be greatly exposd. Had not one of Col Clarkes Regiments better take post there at once and prepar themselves for wintering there? I find from every late piece of intelligence out of N York there is less hope of the Enemys going off than ever and by my Lords [Stirling's] account of their numbers still remaining in the City and the other out Posts their strength is very considerable.

Col Febiger makes them much less. Major Burnet thinks his account is better than my Lords but as my Lord has got the particular Corps his account must be better than the Colonels. However, the Major founds his opinion upon the Bergen intelligence which he thinks is and ever has been the most to be depended upon of any that has ever been opened. I have the honor to be with great respect your Excellencys most obedient humble Sert

NATHL GREENE

ALS (Washington Papers: DLC).
1. Because of Moylan's illness (Moylan to NG, 27 November, above) his dragoons were under Lt. Col. Anthony Walton White.

2. For disposition of the regiment, see note at NG to Pettit, 23 November, above and postscript to Washington's letter of 4 December, below.

3. Sidney Berry was an assistant deputy quartermaster and foragemaster in New Jersey.

4. On their capture, see note 5, below.

5. As supervisor of express riders, NG was especially concerned about the security of the communication route west of the Hudson, which ran southwest through the Highlands and Bergen County, N.J. Not only was it vulnerable to British raids and foraging parties, but sections of it teemed with disaffected Tories and outlaw gangs. The group of Tories who captured Col. Joseph Ward, in fact, had been sent from New York City a week earlier to waylay an express rider. They waited near the village of Kakiat, where express riders frequently stayed; when none appeared, they raided the Harding house, capturing Ward and his deputy, Capt. William Bradford, Jr. The two prisoners were put on their own horses and the party set off for Bull's Ferry on the Hudson—twenty some miles to the south.

Col. Christian Febiger received NG's orders at 4:00 A.M. He immediately dispatched a party of horsemen, but the Tories eluded them and narrowly escaped in a boat to New York City. There they received a hundred guineas from the British command for their exploit. Leiby, *Hackensack*, pp. 188–91 covers the episode thoroughly; NG's orders to Febiger, who had fought under him at Brandywine and Germantown, are cited in Febiger to Washington and Taliafero to Febiger, 29 November 1778, Washington Papers, DLC. Ward remained a prisoner on Long Island until exchanged late in 1779. (*JCC*, 13: 195, 425; 15: 1368)

See Map 1 for geographic references above.

From General George Weedon

Dear General   Fredericksburg [Va.] Novr 30th 1778.

I am to thank [you for] your favr 25th ulto which was handed me th[is morning?] by Major Monroe.[1] I observe the disappointment [that you] met with at Rhode Island still hangs heavy o[n your mind?].[2] For shame. You shd learn to brook such [disappointments?] with Christian patience, and Adhere to the Old proverb, ["Worse] luck now, The better another time." I know you'll laugh to hear me Philosophize, but can assure you am much altered; in so much that I have become a Socratas, and I find, for the real ease, and peace of mind (without which life is a burthen) It is absolutely Necessary to imbibe more, or less, of that Sage Old fellows principles.

The Actions of Brandy Wine, and Germantown, I have frequently considered, and have fully Anticipated your feelings. My Ideas coincide exactly with yours respecting the Genl Orders, which however did not so forcable strike me, till you Delineated their meaning, and tho' you are the only man I ever complained to—Or ever will—I do say boath you, and myself ware differently treated to what Military Characters in Similar Cases have experienced, whose Services ware not more important, or displayed more prudence or firmness.[3] [Your?] not getting even a *Glove* wounded in this Service [has been a?] misfortune. I had the top of my Shoe cut of [*several words missing*] Shoes ware scarce, and hard to be got [*three lines damaged*].

The measure I adopted with Congress, was streniously recommended to me by my friends or I should not have consented.[4] I do not see it can be drawn into a precedent that will be attended with any future bad consequences, and should the Enemy ever [Operate] in this State, there may be Occation for every [able man?] turning out. And my present Situation leaves me [able to?] Accept, or not Accept of Service abroad, and the [changing?] circumstances and situations may here after make [affairs now?] displeasing quite plesent.

I wish you [could be more?] Sanguine in your conjectures respecting a general [withdrawal?] of the Enemy. Should it take place depend upon [it they'll?] leave the Continant. But I must confess to you, I do not think they will totally evacuate N.Y. Many Cogent reasons leads me to this Opinion. There Tory Connections has now become formidable, and will not be given up, Or should they have in Contemplation concilitary Measures, New York will be held as a place of Negociation, or at least a reserve post till things are finally Settled. I do with you, most Sincearly wish them away for the sake of a little respite, for it is realy Alarming to see the distress of the Country. I had no Idea it was half so bad till I mixed among the body of the people. And tho' the produce of the Country Command more than six times it's former Value it is not Adequate to the Exorbitant prices you are Oblige to give for the Common Necessaries of life. [*In a half dozen damaged lines he discusses high prices of everything and blames speculators who add to the price and then distribute goods to peddlers, barbers, tinkers and shoemakers.*] all of whom are become Merchts [Merchants] in this Country, who again retail them out to a lower Class, and by the time an Article is consumed it will have half a dozen Masters, each of whom has his proft which falls at last on the backs of the poor Farmer, or planter, who are the only people that brings produce to Market. Our Assembly is indeavouring to put trade [on a] better footing but this has been so often Attempted with [out any good] effect, that I have little hopes from there delib[erations. They] have been two months Siting, and have as [yet done little?]. So soon as there business transpires, will come [about some?] thing that may be interesting.

We have a 20 [gun vessel?] aground at our Cape, she was in pursuit of the *Ratt*[*lesnake* a privateer?] which is also fast on a sandbank. All our state M [*obliterated*] are gone to attack and get of the Ship in which there is very little doubt of Success.

The Business of your Department I dairsay has fully imployed you. However I hope you have made it worth your while, and that you stand independent of thanks which is but a poor consideration for the many fatiguing hours you must have had, while others ware basking in the Sunshine of ease. I most heartily, and Sincearly Congratulate you on Mrs Greens recovery, and pray god to Continue you boath in health and prosperity. Make mine and Mrs Weedons Compliments Acceptable to her, and Believe me Very Affectionately Your Most Obdt Servt

G. WEEDON

ALS (MiU-C). Portions of the document are badly damaged. Where possible, reasonable conjectures have been substituted; in one case, where missing portions cannot be conjectured, the passage is abstracted.

1. James Monroe, the future president, was a twenty-one-year-old major on his way home after resigning as Lord Stirling's aide.

2. The battle of Rhode Island in August. (See above, vol. 2: 500–504.)

3. The reference is to the public acclaim denied Weedon and Greene for their roles at Brandywine and Germantown. It still rankled in both their minds, although Weedon would probably have agreed with the explanation NG made in a letter to Henry Marchant the previous summer, namely, that Weedon and his Virginians "being the general's [i.e., Washington's] countrymen, and I thought to be one of his favorites, prevented his ever mentioning a single circumstance of the affair." (See above, vol. 2: 471; for the battles of Brandywine and Germantown, see pp. 157n and 171n.)

4. Weedon, in a huff over being outranked by General Woodford, had "retired" temporarily a few months earlier and did not reenter the army until June 1780, after Woodford was captured at Charleston. (See above, vol. 2: 305–6, 362–64; for a more thorough discussion of the dispute, see Ward, *Weedon*, pp. 122–35.)

Colonel Clement Biddle to Moore Furman[1]

[Bound Brook, N.J., 1 December 1778. Has asked foragemasters to send forage as "Troops will be here in two or three Days."[2] He and NG wish to see Furman "on many Accounts." Will need fewer teams since Colonel Wadsworth says no provisions need go to North River until further orders. Biddle's brother [Owen] fears "Corn wont come up [to Trenton] in any Quantities til February or March." ALS (Nj) 2 pp.]

1. Furman was deputy quartermaster of New Jersey.

2. As noted below at NG to Furman, they were delayed.

To Moore Furman

Sir   Bound Brook [N.J.] December 2d 1778
    Your favor of yesterday I have receivd.[1]
    I wish to see you at this place as soon as possible. In the mean Time let all the Forage, Boards and Scantlins[2] be brought into this place as fast as may be.
    I am sorry to find our prospect of forage is so very indifferent; however we must do the best we can. A supply must be had by one means or other. If we are obligd to draw Forage at a greater distance we must use the more industry.
    I believe we shall Hut directly back of Bound Brook below the

Mountain. I am only waiting for His Excellencys approbation who is expected at this place tomorrow.[3]

Mr [Sidney] Berry is here and is doing every thing in his power to get things in readiness for huting the Army.

We propose to send away all our spare horses and if possible to engage the Country Teams to do the occasional duty in Camp. We wish those to consist principally of oxen Teams. They will live upon much less Forage; particularly the article of Grain.

We don't wish any more Flour or provisions of any kind to go on to the North River until we get a pretty good Magazine here. It is surprising to me how Pork came to be orderd Eastward [to New England] when so great a part of our Meat comes from that quarter.

I hope you will give the Convention Troops a quick and easy passage through your district. There is so active a quarter master with them I am in hopes they will give you but little trouble.[4]

You will let us hear from you by every opportunity and give me in a return, as soon as you can, of the quantity of Forage and Boards contracted for.

Please to make my most respectful compliments to Mrs Furman. I am with great respect your most obedient humble Sert

NATH GREENE

ALS (Nj).
    1. Letter not found.
    2. Scantling was lumber of generally small dimensions.
    3. Washington and the troops en route to Middlebrook were delayed by the British push up the Hudson. See Harrison's letters to NG of 5 and 6 December, below.
    4. On the Convention army, see above, NG to Davenport, 9 November.

From Henry Laurens,
President of The Continental Congress

[Philadelphia] 2nd December [1778]

Deliver'd Colonel Mitchell DQr Mr Genl an Act of Congress of the 30th Ulto for obtaining Forage for the Army.[1]

LB (PCC, item 13, vol. 2: 202, DNA).
    1. The act was in response to an appeal from General Sullivan in Rhode Island, who had informed Congress that towns in Connecticut and Massachusetts had plenty of forage—but at outrageous prices. (Hammond, *Sullivan*, 2: 408–9) Congress could only recommend to states in which army units were stationed that, when forage could not be obtained at "reasonable rates," the states, on application of the foragemasters, should take such measures as shall "be effectual, and most likely to procure a speedy supply." (*JCC*, 12: 1177) Few states took such measures.

To Nehemiah Hubbard

Sir   Bound Brook New Jersey Decem 4th 1778
Your favor of the 22d and 26 I have receivd.[1]

I am glad to hear you are in so great forwardness with your accounts and returns; they are much wanted on many accounts, but more especially to lay before the *Board of War*. I could wish to avoid multiplying Clerks, but if more is necessary to get the returns made agreeable to the Resolution of Congress you must engage them, for the returns must be had.

When ever a General Officer gives any order for a special purpose not in the regular channels of business, get it in writing; that will always appear, neither death, accident or design can defeat its operation. If General Gates gave you a verbal order to pay all the Accounts, incident to the Flour he Seizd let them be paid.

The pay of the Assistant deputy quarter master Generals is stated by Congress and cannot be deviated from. Those appointed to the Convention Troops can have no more pay than those appointed for other purposes. Their expences while upon this duty must be paid by the public.

Mr William Joyces terms were such as I thought would by no means answer and therefore gave myself no further trouble about him, as he said he should engage on board of the Brigg if he did not hear from me in a few days.[2]

You may [pay] subsistence money to all those you employ who are entitled to it either by contract or by any regulation of Congress.

Before I left Fredricksburg I sent you I think 30,000 dollars. It went to the care of Mr Stan[ton] at Danbury; doubtless you have been made acquainted therewith before this. I am not able to say how soon I shall be able to forward you a more liberal supply but hope it will not be many days first.

Major Bigalow made a mighty splutter about three or four bolts of Duck. I expected to have receivd 3 or 400 Bolts. However take what he has got.

I am very sorry to find you have let in an Idea that Col Hay had it in view to injure you by recalling the Smiths [i.e., blacksmiths][3] from Danbury. You may depend upon it, that a thought of the kind never enterd his heart. Perhaps he did not advert to the necessity of haveing a considerable number of Smiths at Danbury, it being a post where there was a great deal of transportation to be done, besides the necessary duty to be done for the Troops that were to be posted there. The order was given in consequence of a general Arrangement made for the division of all the Artificers to the several places where the army were to be cantond. Mistrust and jealosies are often productive of the worst of consequences and should be carefully guarded against, by those who from the nature of their business are necessarily connected. Col Hay has an exceeding good opinion of you and I am perswaded will do you every friendly office in his power. I have ever recommended to all my Deputies to cultivate the strictest harmony with one another. It contributes greatly to the ease and facility of all parties and gives dispach and success to Business.

I have given the necessary directions to have as many Smiths fixed at Danbury as the ocasional duty may require.

I am happy to find the Law of the State is now calculated to aid the quarter masters.[4] These are delicate affairs and must be improvd accordingly. I am with good wishes for your health and happiness your most Obedient humble Sert

NATH GREENE

ALS (Greene Papers: DLC).

1. Letter of 26 November not found.

2. NG had hoped to employ Joyce as a clerk. See above, Joyce to NG, 9 November.

3. Three brigades under General Putnam were stationed at Danbury for the winter. Udny Hay, the DQMG at Fishkill, had the supervision of an unusual number of artificers during the building of fortifications at West Point.

4. Connecticut had passed a law in October 1776 to compel "the furnishing necessary supplies and assistance to the Quarter Master General," but it had apparently never been properly circulated. The "Law" to which NG undoubtedly refers was a resolution passed by the Connecticut General Court in October 1778, directing that the act of 1776 "be forthwith printed." (Hoadly, *Records*, 2: 134)

See Map 1 for geographic references above.

To Colonel Charles Pettit

Dear Sir   Bound Brook [N.J.] December 4th 1778

I wrote you at Elizabeth Town that I was on my way to this place in order to fix upon a proper place for Huting the Army.

On my arrival here I find little or no preparation made for the accomodation of the Army; but I am told Materials are coming in from all quarters. I am in hopes in a few days a great plenty will be collected. Forage and Provisions are very scarce, great exertions will be necessary to get us a seasonable supply. We must depend on you principally for Grain.

I had Letters last night from Mr Hubbard and Bowen who both call very loud for money. General Sullivan demands the return of the Sum he lent to our department.[1] Col Hay is also very importunate for more Money notwithstanding the sum sent him the other day. I could wish to repay the Military Chest at any rate, for fear of a denial upon any future application. Col Wadsworth and General Sullivan I think are geting into a high quarrel, the former appears to be to blame; but this is no business of mine.[2]

Pray what is going on in Philadelphia? The intercourse between you and me seems to be as much cut off, as if you had become an Inhabitant of the Moon. I have not been favord with a line since you left Elizabeth Town.

I want to know when you will supply us with more Money and whether you have got a new Warrant, and if you have, for how much.[3] I also want to know the prospect we have for Forage from the Westward for I think our supplies will be very scanty here.

I intend to be in Philadelphia in about Eight or Ten days if possible. I had a Letter last Night from my brother who informs me Mrs Greene was to set out for Camp the 26th of last Month; if so She will be here in a few days.[4] I shall wait her arrival and then bring her on to Trenton, if her health will permit.

Please to write me upon the subject of our conversation when you left Fredricksburg. I think an explanation together with a recollection of the contract will put us upon an equal footing. My best respects to Col Cox and Mr Mitchel. I am with great regard your most Obedient humble Sert

NATH GREENE

ALS (Biblioteek der Universiteit van Amsterdam, Amsterdam, Netherlands).
   1. Letters not found. Sullivan had been partially repaid the money he had advanced in Rhode Island. See above, NG to Bowen, 29 October and Bowen to NG, 14 November.
   2. Sullivan had cause at first to be critical of the commissary department, if not of Wadsworth, who was then in the South. The quarrel grew out of the shortage of provisions in Rhode Island. By early November, Gen. Ezekiel Cornell reported that his brigade did not have "One Barrel of Flour or pound of Bread." (Hammond, *Sullivan*, 2: 420) Sullivan complained to Peter Colt, Wadsworth's deputy for the Eastern Department, but in the meantime he had impulsively hired agents to buy flour in Connecticut and New York in competition with the commissaries. When Colt criticized him for this unauthorized interference, Sullivan replied testily that he would stop when his troops were supplied. (Whittemore, *Sullivan*, p. 113) For some weeks Colt did little to supply them. As late as 29 November, for example, Colt's deputy in Rhode Island, Solomon Southwick, reported that he had no bread or flour nor did he know of any on the way. (Southwick to Sullivan, Washington Papers, DLC).
   On his return north, Wadsworth took up the cudgel for Colt. Unfortunately, Sullivan's combative nature led him to continue the fight long after Wadsworth had supplied the troops. Wadsworth reacted by having Sullivan's agent arrested; Sullivan countered by ordering a court of inquiry. The controversy finally ground to an end, and at the time Sullivan was given command of the Indian expedition, Wadsworth wrote NG, "I really do not wish him any evil." (See below, 23 April 1779.)
   Whittemore (*Sullivan*, pp. 111–15) covers the dispute but is somewhat unfair to his subject in glossing over Colt's failures.
   3. A warrant for $3,500,000 had been issued to John Cox for the department on 28 November, although the dollar was worth only 18¢. (*JCC*, 12: 1171)
   4. Letter not found. Catharine was in New Haven on 2 December and arrived at the home of their friends, the Abraham Lotts, near Morristown on the eleventh.

To Joseph Reed, President of the Pennsylvania Council

Dear Sir   Bound Brook [N.J.] December 4, 1778
I intended to have wrote you a full answer to your long Letter, but finding it impossible to get Time, I am obligd to just acknowledge the receipt of it, and to thank you for the information. You may rest assurd I shall not make an improper use of anything you may think proper to communicate to me.[1]
I am very sorry that our deputies interested themselves in the State politicks.
I expect to see you very soon in Philadelphia and therefore shall not enlarge upon any Subject.
I believe you have no reason to doubt my freindship for you, and I am sure I shall ever esteem myself happy in yours.
Col Pettit is every way to my liking. There is a most happy assemblage of good quallities in him, that are necessary to constitute the man of business and the confidential Freind. I am sir with great regard Your most Obedient humble Servt

NATH GREENE

ALS (NHi).
1. NG's brief comments are in response to Reed's letter of 5 November, above.

Memorial of the Noncommissiond Officers and Private Artificers Commanded by Lieut. John Bolton Posted at West Point

W[es]t Point [N.Y.] 4 Decr 1778
Humbly Sheweth that your memorialists Are very Happy under the Command of Sd Lt Bolton as your memorialists are intimately accquainted with him and Know him to be a Gentleman fully Acquaint and master of the Trade he professes, one who is a Soldiers Friend as well as to the Service of the United States of America. Your memorialists cant forget to mention to your Honour that Sd Lieut Bolton was a Magistrate in this State before these unhappy times commenc'd and gave due Satisfaction to the Public as well as Private in his Administration. A Gentleman we truly think deserves the Notice of his Superiors and inferiors. Your Memmorialists further observe that We are Orderd into Capt Sizers Company which is So very disagreable to us that for many reasons we are Sensable will make discord and be a determent to the Service who we all wish well too. Yr Memorialists Also are inform'd that Sd Lt Boltons Company must be Broak and put into Some Company or other. It is the Sincere wish and earnest disire of every Noncommisiond officer and Soldier

belonging to Sd Lt Bolton that we be put and annexed to Capt D. Pendletons Company Only But Shall not refuse going where your Honours in his wise Goverment Shall See proper to place us and your Petitioners as in duty Bound Shall ever pray[1]

STEPHEN CLAPP	PELEG BURDICK
STAN [?] PENNEL	PHINEHAS MAXSON
JOHN MILLS	ABIAL HATCH
SILAS KELLOGG	EDMOND ENTWISHEL [Entwistle]
ISIAH COOLIDGE	EBEN'R BELKNAP
JOSIAH WOOD	WILLIAM SHEEN
BEN'N FRISH	

DS (PPAmP).
1. John Bolton of Massachusetts and William Sizer and Daniel Pendleton of Connecticut were officers in the Artillery Artificers Regiment. Despite the men's protestations, they apparently agreed to join Sizer's company. See below, Udny Hay to NG, 18 February 1779.

From George Washington

Dr Sir   Elizabeth Town [N.J.] 4th Decr 1778.

I have to acknowledge the receipt of your last letters of the 30th Ulto and the 1st Inst. which met me on the way to this place.[1]

If Mr. Wallace can spare two rooms below Stairs, it will ⟨certainly⟩ make our quarters much more comfortable, as well as render them more convenient for public business. You will endeavour therefore[2] to concert measures with Mr Wallace for this purpose.[3]

I consider with you the line of communication to the Eas[t]ward much endangered, by leaving Paramus exposed, and shall order the Carolina brigade to that station and its vicinity.[4]

The New York paper of the 2⟨d⟩ speaks of the taking of Col. Ward and Captn Bradford, as an enterprise of ⟨much⟩ spirit conducted by tories, thro' a great many hazards. ⟨It has an ungenerous remark on the Colonel's former profession.⟩[5]

From a late application it is ⟨probable it will be⟩ necessary to detach a regiment to Trenton and another to Philada for the security of the public stores. As I think of breaking in upon Genl. Woodford brigade, you will in the plan for hutting have respect to this diminution.

I shall endeavour to reach the quarters you have allotted me ⟨,⟩ by that time Major [Caleb] Gibbs may have made his arrangements. I am ⟨D Sir Your most hble Sert.

GO: WASHINGTON.

P.S. Col. Moylan's horse will march to-day for their quarters at Lancaster.⟩[6]

Df (Washington Papers: DLC). Portions in angle brackets are taken from an unidentified typescript at MiU-C. It is apparent from an additional sentence and postscript that the typescript is of the recipient's copy.
1. Letter of 1 December not found.
2. The typescript reads: "You will be pleased. . . ."
3. The John Wallace house was at Raritan (now Somerville), about four miles west of Boundbrook. Washington remained there until June, except for six weeks he spent in Philadelphia in midwinter. NG had his quarters at the nearby Van Veghten House. See Map 5.
    Normally, the army did not compensate an owner for housing officers, because, as NG put the somewhat dubious argument, "the protection afforded by the Officers residing at a place" was equal to the trouble and inconvenience to the owner. Most householders were honored to have the commander in chief, but John Wallace was paid $1,000 by Washington for six months rent. (See NG to Sidney Berry, 23 June 1779, below.) On the Wallace house, see Ives, *Headquarters*, pp. 192–203.
4. Col. Thomas Clark's North Carolina Regiment.
5. On Ward's capture, see above, NG to Washington, 30 November. Rivington's *Gazette* on 2 December pointed out that Ward had been a schoolmaster in Boston.
6. Moylan's regiment, under Lieut. Col. Anthony Walton White, was delayed by the threat of a British push up the Hudson River. (See Harrison to NG, 5 December, below.) Washington issued new marching orders to the regiment on the sixth. (Fitzpatrick, *GW*, 13: 371)

To Colonel Ephraim Bowen

[Middlebrook, N.J., 5 December 1778. Sent Bowen $140,000, $20,000 of which was to have gone to Jacob Greene, but it is offset by amount Jacob owes for iron. ALS (MiU-C) 1 p.]

To Samuel Gray[1]

Sir   Middlebrook [N.J.] 5th Decemr 1778
    There has been frequent complaints made by the Artificers at Fishkill on account of the substitution of a Gill of Rice in lieu of half a pound of Flour. This is considered as a Greivance. There have been also complaints made that the Rum allow'd to the artificers has not been Issued agreeable to Contract.
    I have consulted his Excellency on these matters and he has referred the regulation to me.[2] You will therefore Issue in future to all Artificers, Waggoners, Colliers, and Boatmen and other Fatigue Parties on constant duty, one and a half [pounds] flour or Bread and one and a half pounds of Beef or other provisions of Equal substance and capable of affording the same support. You will also Issue daily a Gill of rum to all those intitled to draw an additional allowance to their Ration. If by any Incident any of the parties do not draw the Spirits the day that it becomes due, they may draw it afterwards. It is my Intention that Each man shall draw one Gill of Spirits for each day, and that no more be Issued to any party or set of men whatever under the direction of the Qr Mr General, his Deputy or assistant, unless he or they certify that the nature of their duty is such as to require an

additional allowance which certificate being produced to the commiss'y by the Commanding Officer of the party shall be a Sufficient warrant for him to Issue upon, and that there may be no impositions hereafter by persons drawing an additional allowance of their Rations who are not intitled to it. None shall be intitled to draw more than a common Ration except they can produce a Certificate or an appointment from the Qr Mr General, one of his deputies or their assistants that they have a right to draw more than a common ration.

NATHL GREENE

Cy (MHi).
1. Deputy commissary general of issues in the Eastern Department.
2. See above, NG to Washington, 24 November.

From Colonel Clement Biddle

MEMORANDUM RELATIVE TO FORAGE[1]

Rarriton [Raritan, N.J.] Decem 5 1778

The spare horses to be sent from Camp as soon as possible.

The Artillery Horses and their Waggon horses to be immediately sent away, as Country Teams who will find their own Forage can be had to haul Wood, Straw, Forage and [materials] for huting.

The Resolve of Congress directing that no Officer not entitled to Forage, should keep a horse within forty miles of Camp to be strictly complied with.

That no Officer keep more horses than are allowd by General Orders, which should be again pointed out and the necessity of saving Forage strongly urged, as there is not a sufficiency to be had in the Country to issue full Allowance for the necessary horses.

Racks and Troughs to be prepared to prevent waste of hay and Grain.

Orders for the same purposes as above to be sent to the seperate Departments and Detachments.

The Light horse to be enjoind to Oconomy in the use of Forage in Winter Quarters.

Are the Whole of the Marechaussé horse necessary in Camp? Those unfit for Duty should be sent away.[2]

Large hay Scales for Weighing loads of Hay to be erected and a hay yard inclosed as soon as the Artificers can be spared. Scales and Measures for issuing are Orderd.

The Above memorandum submitted to the Qu Mr Genl by his Most Obedt ser

CLEMENT BIDDLE

ALS (PCC, item 173, vol. 1: 289, DNA).
   1. The critical shortage of forage is evident in the peremptory tone of this memorandum, which Biddle undoubtedly prepared at NG's request.
   2. The maréchausée were mounted provosts, responsible for policing the camp.

From General John Cadwalader

Dear Sir,   Philad'a, 5th Decemr. 1778.
   I am much obliged for your concern for me *in a late affair*—It gives me great pleasure to hear my friends approve my conduct, as it would have added greatly to my uneasiness if it had been thought that my conduct proceeded from a turbulent Disposition.[1]
   Gen. Lee's tryal has been the subject of Conversation in all Companies for some time—Congress, I am told, have confirmed the sentence—three to one—I do not suppose he will ever serve again in our Army—I think it would have [been] better if he never had—[2]
   Mr. Dean's publication makes a great Noise—but this we are told is only a preface to what is to [follow]   ever will be ambitious and   every country. No doubt we have [our] share of them— when Facts are well ascertained and the writer signs his Name the publication have double force—I should be very sorry to see the day when a member or a number of the members of Congress dare not be attacked—I, too, have the highest respect for the Body, tho' I know some men of the most infamous characters among them—[3]One of the greatest grievances that occur to me, in the Army, is, the power Congress have of delaying the tryal, and final determination of the sentence of the C^t. Martial—By the management of a few, an officer may be kept out of command 'till he may loose every opportunity of distinguishing himself.[4]
   Gen. Arnold is become very unpopular [among the] men in power in Congress, and among those of this state in general—Every Gentleman, every man who has a liberal way of thinking highly approve his conduct—He has been civil to every gentleman who has taken the oath, intimate with none—The Ladies, as well those who have *taken an active part* (as our lowlived fellows will call it) as those who are good approved whigs, have been visited and treated with the greatest civilities—These are charges too absurd to deserve a serious answer—They may serve the purposes of Party or Faction, but can never injure the character of a man to whom his Country is so much indebted.[5] Mifflin is ruined tho' he has bullied Congress. He is now turned Legislator and is insignificant in a minority. A man of his [changeable principles] will not surprise me   him again at the head of   affairs; tho' I am convinced he can never again attempt the military.[6]

The Minister is a polite Gentleman and well calculated for the present barbarism of the Times.[7] His knowledge of mankind makes him overlook, tho' I cannot help thinking he must see some men and measures in true Colours. Where do you take Quarters for the Winter? I hope Mrs. Greene will be consulted—the amusements of Philadelphia I dare say would please her. I am just setting off on a visit to my family of little Fellows in Maryland—I shall be glad to hear from you when have leisure, and I now promise to be a more punctual Correspondent.

I am D[r] Sir, with great esteem

Your most ob[t]. humble Serv[t].

JOHN CADWALADER.

The Hon. Major Gen. Green,

Camp.

Col. Laurens.

Reprinted from *Lee Papers*, 3: 270–71. Italics and square brackets are the original editor's.

1. Cadwalader's duel with General Conway. See above, NG to Cadwalader, 10 November.

2. On Charles Lee's trial, see note, NG to McDougall, 8 November, above. Hours before Cadwalader wrote, Congress had ordered Lee's sentence "carried into execution." (*JCC*, 12: 1195)

3. The *Pennsylvania Packet* for 5 December printed a letter from Silas Deane that was to split Congress into two warring camps. It brought into the open a quarrel between Deane and Arthur Lee which had simmered since they first served together on a mission to France in 1776. In letters home, Lee had accused Deane of spending his time on private business, of misappropriating public funds, and of misrepresenting the role of the French government in the early years of the war. Whatever the basis for Lee's charges, he was an overly suspicious person whose testimony was always questionable. Benjamin Franklin sided with Deane, as did the French ambassador, Conrad Gérard.

Failing for months to get a hearing before Congress, Deane had taken to the columns of the *Packet* in desperation, condemning Congress as well as Lee. The letter made an enemy of President Henry Laurens, who resigned when a bare majority of Congress supported Deane; he was replaced by John Jay, an adherent of Deane. (*JCC*, 12: 1202–6) There ensued one of the bitterest newspaper wars of the period, finally bringing Thomas Paine into the fray. (See below, Paine to NG, 31 January 1779.)

As fond as NG was of both Laurens and Paine, he was squarely in the Deane camp, partly, no doubt, because of Wadsworth's friendship with Deane. A few months later, NG and Wadsworth became silent partners of Barnabas Deane, Silas's brother. In the end, Deane was the loser, spending his last years in bitter exile in England, virtually poverty stricken.

The Deane-Lee affair has divided historians almost as sharply as it did the Continental Congress. In 1926 Edmund Burnett called it a bone of contention that still served "to raise a growl." (*Letters*, 3: xxxii) The half-century since Burnett wrote has brought further "growls." Julian Boyd saw Deane as an intriguer and a self-serving businessman—if not a traitor. ("Silas Deane: Death by a Kindly Teacher of Treason?" *WMQ*, 3 ser., 16 [1959]: 165–87, 319–42, 515–50.) Coy Hilton James, who did not even acknowledge Boyd's contentions, accepted Deane's self-defense largely at face value. (*Silas Deane—Patriot or Traitor?* [Michigan State University Press, 1975]) The *DAB* had earlier been sympathetic to Deane, relying heavily on his defense in the *Deane Papers*, 3: 66–76, and on a vindication by Congress in 1842. A recent biography that treats Arthur

Lee objectively is Louis W. Potts, *Arthur Lee: A Virtuous Revolutionary* (Louisiana State University Press, 1981). For a thorough analysis of the effect that the Deane-Lee affair had on Congress, see Jack N. Rakove, *The Beginnings of National Politics* (Alfred A. Knopf, 1979), pp. 249–74.

4. He was undoubtedly thinking of Generals St. Clair and Schuyler, whose cases were held up for some months by a dilatory Congress. The original fault, as Cadwalader implies, was the Articles of War, which gave Congress the power to make a final determination when general officers were court-martialed.

5. The charges against Arnold are detailed by Joseph Reed, 5 November, above.

6. Mifflin was serving in the Pennsylvania Assembly as a representative from Philadelphia. (Rossman, *Mifflin*, p. 166)

7. The French ambassador, Conrad Gérard.

From Colonel Robert H. Harrison

Dr. Sir   Eliz. Town [N.J.] Dec. 5, 1778

His Excellency was informed last night by a letter from Colo Febiger to Lord Stirling that about 52 Vessels yesterday morning were proceeding up the North River with flat bottom boats and supposed to have troops and were as high up there as Closter Landing.[1] We cannot tell what their Object is, but the intelligence occasioned the General to send orders for halting all our Troops on the march, and himself and Lord Stirling to set out between four and five OClock this morning towards Acquackinunck [Aquakinunk] Bridge from whence they will proceed farther or return as circumstances may point out. The Enemy certainly must have some Object more than to divert us from Quarters, and I should suppose it One of three: to intercept our march, or to attempt a rescue of the Convention troops, or to attack the Highlands posts.[2] For the first and second, they must be too late and for the last I hope they are to weak. If Patterson and Learned's brigades are arrived at their ground, and they must be unless they have used the most cruel and wanton delay, the force in the Highlands must be sufficient to resist their whole Army, especially when we take into consideration the aid which may be derived from the troops at Danbury.[3] At any rate we are sure Nixons brigade was in the pass in the mountains; on the other side the Carolina [Regiment] at the Clove and several more [regiments] in the fort, which tho possibly they might not be equal to repel the Enemy if in full force would very probably be sufficient to maintain their Ground till succoured.

This movement of the Enemy as I observed before, hurried his Excellency away this morning when he desired me to acknowledge his receipt of your favor of yesterday[4] and said he could not determine which of the positions you mention best, without seeing them. Nor did he decide positively that I recollect as to his own quarters, but I believe Mr Wallace's is the place for such has been the run of conversation and *family expectation*.[5] You are very well acquainted with the General's ideas as to proper situation for the troops I should suppose, and I would fain hope the part you take will coincide with his sentiments. He designed to set out today towards the intended incampment, which would have obviated every difficulty but Sir Harry [Clinton] thought to interpose his manuvres. I dare say he will arrive as soon as or before the Troops, which may prevent some of the inconveniences you forebode.

I must request you to excuse this hurried scrawl, for in truth, [Alexander] Hamilton and Myself are immersed in thought and difficulties about our meeting Colos OHara and Hyde at Amboy on Monday not so much on account of the business, as because Amboy is destitute of meat, bread and all the &cs. that you can imagine but we are trying to put things in train.[6] I am Dr Sir yrs

ROB H H

DfS (Washington Papers: DLC).
    1. A few miles above Manhattan Island.
    2. Harrison's second conjecture was apparently correct. Kemble recorded in his journal of 5 December: "Sir Henry landed at Stony Point; the object of this Embarkation to cut off some of the Rebels conducting the Convention army to the Southward, as well as to facilitate the Escape of some." When they discovered the prisoners had crossed the river two days earlier, they returned to New York City. (Kemble, *Journal*, 2: 167–68) Washington by this time had apparently decided they were only on a foraging expedition. See Harrison's quote of James McHenry, another Washington aide, in Harrison to NG, 6 December, below.
    3. Gen. John Paterson's brigade had arrived at their new post at West Point; Gen. Ebenezer Learned's brigade (known as "late Learned's" since his resignation) were down river at Fishkill. John Nixon's brigade at Peekskill completed McDougall's division. The winter cantonments of the three brigades are listed in Fitzpatrick, *GW*, 13: 346; McDougall reported their arrival on 5 December, ibid., 13: 371. Gen. Israel Putnam had three brigades at Danbury.
    4. Letter not found.
    5. See note, Washington to NG, 4 December, above.
    6. In response to a letter from Sir Henry Clinton, Congress had authorized Washington on 19 November to name commissioners to discuss with a British delegation an exchange of American officers for officers in the Convention army. (*JCC*, 12: 1145–46) On 30 November, Washington had appointed two of his aides, Hamilton and Harrison, to meet with Col. Charles O'Hara and Col. West Hyde. (Fitzpatrick, *GW*, 13: 349, 358–59) Their efforts to find agreement on prisoner exchange were as fruitless as earlier ones. For further developments in prisoner exchange, see note at Council of War, 10 April 1779, below.

See Map 1 for geographic references above.

Major Ichabod Burnet to Colonel Clement Biddle

[Middlebrook, N.J., 6 December 1778. NG requests Burnet to inform Biddle that Washington will be at his quarters next evening. Wishes Biddle "could find us some Hay & Grain." (Excerpt from Charles Hamilton Catalog No. 140, 1981.)]

To Colonel Morgan Lewis

[Middlebrook, N.J., 6 December 1778. NG is not sufficiently informed concerning vessels and bateaux needed for proposed Canadian expedition.[1] He assumes Schuyler will be in charge of preparations. Lewis must judge the proper wages to be paid workers; should apply to Otis & Andrews for "Whatever you may want from Boston." ADfS (MiU-C) 3 pp.]

1. For the proposed collaboration with France on an invasion of Canada in 1779, see end of the note at NG to Washington, 28 October, above.

From Colonel Robert H. Harrison

Dear Sir   Eliz. Town [N.J.] 9 oClock pm Decm 6, [1778]

I wrote you yesterday from this place in answer to your Letter to His Excellency on the subject of quartering the Troops.[1] This minute Colo Hamilton received a Letter from Doctr [James] McHenry dated today at Paramus with the following paragraph "desire Colo Harrison to write to Genl Greene on the subject of his Letter respecting a change of ground for hutting. He may tell Genl Greene that the situation marked out in the first instance seems to His Excellency the most eligible, but that Genl Greene must be a more competent judge to which place the preference should be given."

With respect to the movements of the Enemy, the said McHenry writes thus: "We are informed by a Major of Militia that the Enemy's Vessels are near King's Ferry, and it is said that a body of about 2,000 men are as high up as Tarrytown. Their Object would appear forage and provision to be collected between Kingsbridge and the posts at the Highlands." Genl Wayne is ordered to Sufferans, Genl Muhlenberg to the same place. We shall move that way immediately."

Ham and I (this is against the rules of grammar, but it is consistent with those of modesty and the merits of the man, therefore I'll let it stand) shall set out tomorrow morning for Amboy by sun rise.[2] I have nothing more to add, except to tell you what I hope you already believe, that I am with very sincere respect and regard Yr friend and Obligd sert

R. H. HARRISON

ALS (Washington Papers: DLC).
1. NG's letter of 4 December concerning hutting has not been found.
2. For more on British activities and Harrison's assignment, see above, Harrison to NG, 5 December.

See Map 1 for geographic references above.

To Colonel Charles Pettit

Dear Sir   Middle Brook [N.J.] December 7th 1778

I am very happy to have it from under your hand that you are still among the liveing. I have not Time to give You an answer to many parts of your Letters of the 3d and 4th.[1] However there are two or three things which I shall just observe upon.

I have no objection to Major Eyres being disengaged from the public service upon the conditions you mention.[2]

I am sorry Col Mitchel gave people an opportunity to suspect that private property was transported at the public expence. These kind of circumstances where they lead to a suspicion altho clearly provd afterwards to be groundless, and that nothing was meant or intended to be done to the prejudice of the public interest; yet as the correction dont always keep pace with the report, It often injures the individual and all his connexions.[3]

Nothing can give me greater pleasure than General Reads [Reed's] appointment to the office of president, and what serves to heigthen the pleasure is, everybody is expressing their approbation.[4] I have a long Letter of his to answer which I shall embrace the first opportunity to perform and to congratulate him upon his appointment.

I thank you for your polite invitation to bring Mrs Greene to Trenton. She is on her way to Camp. I heard of her last Wednesday at New Haven. As soon as She arrives and the Camp is settled we will pay you a Visit. But you remember Col Cox insisted upon providing quarters for us and I should be sorry to hurt his feelings in so generous a business.

The Enemy have been up the North [i.e., Hudson] River. Before they made their appearance our Troops, baggage and Stores of every kind had got over. It is supposd their object was a large quantity of provisions that lay at Kings Ferry, which at their landing there, they had the mortification to find was all removd. They landed on both sides of the River, but I believe did little or no damage and are now returnd to the City again.[5]

The money arrivd safe agreeable to the Receipts given. It is a very seasonable and necessary supply; but much more will be wanted for the Eastern States.

The Expresses are waiting which prevents my adding anything more to this Letter.

You will please to make my compliments agreeable to Mrs Pettit and the young Ladies of your family and Col Cox and his family. I am with great respect and regard Your most Obedient humble Set

NATH GREENE

ALS (NHi).
1. Letters not found.
2. Pettit's conditions are unknown, but Washington did not consent to Maj. Benjamin Eyre's resigning as superintendent of the boat department. See below, NG to Pettit, 12 December.
3. For the charges against John Mitchell, see below, note, NG to Reed #1, 31 January 1779.
4. Joseph Reed had been elected president of the Pennsylvania Executive Council on 1 December. (See Reed to NG, 5 November, above.)
5. See above, letters of Robert Harrison of 5 and 6 December.

From Colonel James Abeel

[Morristown, N.J., 7 December 1778. Has not heard from NG recently. He has sent sugar, coffee, butter to NG, and will soon forward table linen. Requests a guard for stores at Morristown. LB (NjHi) 1 p.]

From General Charles Scott[1]

Dear Genl   Christiania Bridge [Del.] Decr 8th 1778
    I am unhappy to inform You that my indisposition has obliged me to halt at this Place for Several days, during which I could not but observe the wast of the Publick property In a most astonishing manner. I make no doubt that You are no Stranger to their Being a Large Magasine of Stors of almost every Kind Lodged at this place for our armey. There are of Course a Large Number of Waggons [wagoners] imployd who do not Earn the Salt to their bread, and no body Seams to give themselves any trouble or consern about them. I assure You my dear Sir it is truly alarming to See the Idolness in the Waggoners and the Willfull Wast of Forrage, all owing to the want of a proper person to Superintend this business.
    However unhappy I may be at the loss of time on the Road when on So Desirable a Journey I cannot but rejoice at the Misfortune when I Reflect that it has put it in my power to make this early Discovery of abuse which perhaps might not have happend untill Too late for Remedy.
    I do not know who to recommend to You to Take charge of this business, as I am not well acquainted with the people hear abouts, but would advise You to apply to Doctr McMakin and if he will under take it, You may Rest Satisfyed that every thing will be don agreable to Your wish. The Doctr and me has been saying Somthing about it. I think he may be prevailed on to undertake it. At any rate I would wish You to offer it to him, for this reason if no other Could be offerd. However that is not the case; that he has done as much as any person could Possably do in his way for the Country without any thoughts of a reward. He is on the Spot, a Man of property and a *Gentleman*. I

believe if You apply he will undertake it. He will Give Satisfaction I am Shure and Save ten thousand a Year to the Country.[2] I have In a great Measure Declind all thoughts of Resigning as I find it very Disagreable to my Frends. I have the Honour With all possable Respt Dr Genl your obt Serv

[signature mutilated]

AL[S] (NHi).
1. The author of the letter is identified by the handwriting and the docketing. Brig. Gen. Charles Scott (1739–1813) of Virginia had served ably in the battles of Trenton, Germantown, and Monmouth. He was captured at Charleston, S.C., in 1780, and upon his exchange was breveted a major general. From 1808 to 1812 he was governor of Kentucky. (DAB) Scott was en route to Virginia to settle some personal affairs and to improve his health, but he stayed on for some months to recruit men while his brigade remained at Middlebrook. (See his letters to Washington of 29 October and 6 November, Washington Papers, DLC)
2. NG's response to Scott's letter has not been found, but he did not employ "Doctr McMakin." Complaints continued about agents in Delaware and Maryland. See below, note at Hollingsworth to NG, 10 February 1779.

To Colonel Charles Pettit

Dear Sir   Middle Brook [N.J.] December 9, 1778

I freely forgive you for what is past, and to speak in the Scripture language, go and Sin no more. Your situation at Philadelphia and mine at Rhode Island were very similar. Family pleasures, the meeting of Friends, and a lazy habit had too much influence to leave one at liberty to be a very exact correspondent.[1]

The preparations here do not come up to my wishes or our wants, but I make no doubt everything has been done that could be expected. Mr Furman is very busy in passing Burgoynes Troops.[2]

I shall endeavor to make the Committee of Congress the best Estimate in my power. Colonel Biddle is at Sufferans. Upon the Enemys moving up the River His Excellency sent for him back again from this place. As soon as he returns we will attempt the business.

The Vote of the Committee appears to me was [in] part because they thought something must be done and they did not know what else to do.[3]

We are sending away all our spare Horses as fast as possible. I intend to get the Country Teams to do the ocasional duty in Camp. But after all the reduction we can make, our Numbers will be great; there are so many hangers on, of one kind or other. The grievance you complain on respecting the Supernumary Horses at Philadelphia and the neighbouring Posts, is a general Evil through all the Country, and it appears to me to be of such a nature as is hard if not impracticable to remedy it. I wish you would draw up a State of the matter and lay it before the board of War. However this may be a dangerous

Manoeuver for you to make. The Board having been all Summer indeavoring to digest your former queries, and not being able, will be outrageous at being perplexed with a new lot.

With respect to the Barrack Master General I think you had best temporise that business until I arrive in Philadelphia.[4]

There will be large Sums of Money wanted to the Eastward [i.e., New England] if certain preparations goes on to the Northerd.

I must close this Letter, there being not less than twenty People now in the Room wanting to do business. I intend to write you about the state of the Camp, our Winter quarters &c &c this Evening. I am with great regard your most Obedient humble Sert

NATH GREENE

ALS (NHi).
1. Pettit's letter to which NG refers has not been found.
2. The Convention army was passing through New Jersey en route to Virginia. See above, NG to Davenport, 9 November.
3. The request of the Supply Departments Committee has not been found, but it concerned the state of the forage, the reason NG wanted to see Biddle. See below, NG to Biddle, 10 December.
4. The "business" concerning Isaac Melcher, the barrackmaster general, is discussed in Melcher to NG, 25 January 1779, below.

To Colonel Clement Biddle

[Middlebrook, N.J., 10 December 1778. Encloses committee request on forage.[1] Biddle should see him on other forage matters as soon as weather permits. Meanwhile, Biddle should write deputies for returns. ALS (MiU-C) 1 p.]

1. Enclosure missing. The committee's letter is not in the PCC, but presumably it requested an up-to-date report on the forage situation as noted above, NG to Petit, 9 December.

To Colonel Ephraim Bowen

[Middlebrook, N.J., 12 December 1778. Wishes to know Olney's terms.[1] Will offer him $150 per month plus board and riding horse. Pettit pays $4 per day for excellent clerk. Encloses circular of 12 November.[2] Asks return of accounts by express rider who delivers this with some money and who is collecting accounts from deputies east of Hudson. Tents should be repaired; those not repairable are to be made into forage bags or hospital bedding. Tr (GWG Transcript: CSmH) 2 pp.]

1. On Olney's employment, see above, NG to Bowen, "before 21 November."
2. See circular to Bowen, 12 November, above.

Major Ichabod Burnet to Colonel Ephraim Bowen

[Middlebrook, N.J., 12 December 1778. NG wishes to pay for repairs to Mrs. Greene's carriage "as he does not wish to be indebted to the public for any kind of service in that way." Burnet asks about getting linen out of quartermaster stores. ALS (RHi) 1 p.]

To Nehemiah Hubbard

[Middlebrook, N.J., 12 December 1778. Sending $30,000 by express rider who will wait for returns requested in enclosed circular letter.[1] "They are wanted to lay before a Committee of Congress."[2] LS (MiU-C) 1 p.]

1. See above, NG to Hubbard, 12 November.
2. The Supply Departments Committee.

To Colonel Charles Pettit

Dr Sir   Camp Middle Brook [N.J.] December 12th 1778
I have wrote twelve Letters this Evening[1] and if I make this a short one you must not complain, for it is now past two oClock and I had been on horse back all day before I sat down to writing.

I acquainted His Excellency this Evening that I had given leave to Major Eyres to leave the public service upon conditions to engage again when ever called upon.[2] The General is not willing he should be granted this indulgence for he says he is certain he will be wanted more than he ever has been and that not long first. You will acquaint Major Eyres therefore that I cannot consent to his leaving the business.

Forage is prodigious scarce and we are under the necessity of keeping a large number of Horses until we get the Troops into Huts, after which I am in hopes to free ourselves in a great measure from the present burden. I think the business of huting will be over in the course of eight or Ten days, providing the Officers exert themselves; but the business is so disagreeable that I am afraid objects of pleasure will be more pursueed than that of geting the Troops under cover. Should that be the case our distress will be great as it will protract the Time for a number of days and we are unprepard with Forage for the present consumption.[3]

I have not seen or heard from Mr Furman but once since I came to this ground. The Convention Troops engrosses all his attention. It is rather unfortunate for us that they were going through the Jerseys the same Time we were.[4] We have promises from several quarters, but the supplies dont come forward as fast as our demand increases.

We are in a tolerable situation and not badly provided with everything necessary to our circumstances except Forage and Boards and I dont believe these are or will be to be had in as great plenty as our wants demand.

I wish to know what number of Tents will be had in Philadelphia by Spring.

When I was in Boston Messrs Otis & Andrew[s] informd me the Marine Committee had a large quantity of Duck by them, part of which they tho't might be had for the purpose of makeing Tents providing an order could be obtaind from the Board of War for the purpose. I wish you would consult them upon the subject as soon as possible for I am perswaded Duck will be a scarce article and there will be a large Number of Tents wanting, for the greater part of those now in use will be unfit for another Campaign.

Inclosd is a copy of Mr Beatys Letter.[5] I wish you would write to Mr Calhoun upon the subject and transmit him a Copy also, and desire his answer upon Mr Beatys proposition. I think they are both good men. I should be loth to offend either.

I had the pleasure to hear last Night of Mrs Greens being at Mr Lotts.[6]

When I began this Letter I did not intend to have wrote half as much as I have, but [one] thing after another kept crowding into my head and I put them down, by way of freeing myself from the trouble of thinking on them.

You will please to present my compliments to Col Cox. I am as I hope ever to be your sincere friend and well wisher

NATH GREENE

N.B. When Colo Cox was at Camp I had the promise of one or two Blls of Crackers and buiscuit. Mrs Greene will be in Camp in a few days and we have heard nothing of the Buiscuit.

ALS (NHi).
1. As seen above, only two have been found.
2. Maj. Benjamin Eyre was superintendent of the boat department. See above, NG to Pettit, 7 December.
3. It was some weeks before all hutting was complete.
4. The Convention army is described at NG to Davenport, 9 November, above.
5. See above, Beatty to NG, 27 November.
6. At Beverwyck, nine miles northeast of Morristown.

From Colonel Tench Tilghman

[Middlebrook, N.J., 15 December 1778. Washington is surprised that Pulaski's Legion has returned to Easton, Pa. He would order them

back to Minisink if they could be subsisted there since he thinks
"their coming down is only a pretence to get into more comfortable
quarters."[1] Wishes NG to inquire of Clement Biddle as to suitable
location. ALS (PHi) 1 p.]

1. Minisink, a frontier settlement fifty miles up the Delaware from Easton, was in
Sussex County, N.J., which was within the jurisdiction of Col. Robert L. Hooper at
Easton, Pa. Apparently the Minisink area could not sustain horses any better than
Easton. On 16 December, Washington ordered the legion to be subsisted wherever
Colonel Hooper should "point out." (Fitzpatrick, GW, 13: 402) In January the legion
was on its protracted journey to Georgia. See below, Pettit to NG, 10 and 11 February
1779.

See Map 3 for geographic references above.

From George Washington

Sir   Head Quarters Middlebrook [N.J.] 15 day of Decr 1778
    Without loss of time you will provide and deposit at Albany sail
cloath, rigging, pitch, Junk, Iron, and every other material for ship-
building.[1] I cannot at this instant give you either the kind or dimen-
sions of the vessels which are to be built as it is necessary for me to
advise with good naval judges on this occasion before I resolve, but
that you may have some data for your government, say, four square
rigged vessels of twenty guns each, or ten large stout row gallies.[2]
    You will have an exact account taken of all the batteaux which
now are or can be repaired, and got in order for hard service, by the
middle of April next, and transmit the same to Major Gen. Schuyler
at Albany. This account is meant to comprehend all the batteaux on
Hudson River, and such others as can be spared and transported from
the Delaware to the former. Information of this kind will enable Gen.
Schuyler to fix upon the number of new ones to be built, and your
deputy in that department[3] will receive orders from him accordingly.
    You are to form magasines of forage at Albany and other places
under the directions you will receive from Gen. Schuyler and you are
to provide at Albany a number of felling axes, 3,000, and a full and
complete assortment of intrenching tools; in doing those, regard is to
be had to such as can be spared from this and other posts, after the
hutting is completed. All new made tools should besides having the
public mark, be stamped with the initials of the makers name, that
impositions may more readily be detected and justice done the public,
as great complaints are made of the bad quality of our tools.
    It may also be necessary to provide bags for the transportation of
short forage [i.e., grain]. The number necessary will be best known
by a consultation with the officers at the head of that department and

the means of obtaining them. It will be proper also to know, whether a number of sleds (no matter how coarse and rough) could be had at a sudden call, and fat cattle sufficient obtained ⟨to draw them.⟩[4]

A number of ship and other carpenters should be provided at Albany for the various purposes there wanted. Their particular application will be directed by Majr General Schuyler.

Given at Head Quarters Middlebrook this 15 day of Decr 1778

GO: WASHINGTON

LS (CtN1C). Portion in angle brackets from ADfS, Washington Papers, DLC.

1. The OED defines *junk* in this sense as "Old cable or rope material, cut up into short lengths and used for making fenders, reef points, gaskets, oakum, etc."

2. Two days later Washington gave up plans temporarily for a possible invasion of Canada via Lake Champlain, although the use of boats was considered in a possible expedition against the Indians. See note at Washington to NG, 17 December, below. For the shift in plans from a Canadian invasion to an expedition against the Iroquois Indians, see note at NG to Washington, 5 January 1779, below.

3. Morgan Lewis.

4. Washington probably intended the phrase to read "and sufficient fat cattle obtained to draw them," but in writing the words *sufficient* and *obtained* above the line in the draft, he failed to put a caret beneath the first word, and his aide copied it as written above.

From George Washington

Dear Sir   Head Quarters Middle Brook [N.J.] 16th Decem'r 1778

As I expect shortly to be called upon by Congress to lay before them a general State of the Army with our Resources and prospects for the ensuing Campaign, I am collecting from the Gentlemen at the Heads of the several great departments their opinions of the present and future prospects of supplies in their respective lines.[1]

Your department (including Forage) being of the utmost consequence and the one in which I fear we shall be most distressed, I am to request you will draw me up such a state as will enable me to point out to Congress in a summary manner in what Articles you are most apprehensive of a deficiency, whether such deficiency is likely to arise from a real or artificial scarcity, and what will be the most probable means of remedying such evil. There are perhaps other matters, which do not strike me, which it would be proper and which you would wish to have represented to Congress. If there are I would wish you to include them, and I assure you that no exertions of mine shall be wanting to put them upon such a footing as will conduce to the good of the Service and to the ease and reputation of your office.[2] I am with great Regard Dear Sir Your most obt Servt

GO: WASHINGTON

LS (CSmH).

1. On 24 December, Congress appointed a committee of conference to meet with Washington, naming as members James Duane (chairman), Jesse Root, Meriwether Smith, Gouverneur Morris, and Henry Laurens. (*JCC*, 12: 1250) Beginning on 8 January, Washington directed a series of letters or memoranda to the committee or its chairman in which he described the numerous problems facing the various departments and his thoughts on the coming campaign. Comments on the quartermaster department were conspicuously missing, probably because NG presented them in person during his long stay in Philadelphia. (For the month of January the following communications from Washington to the committee are printed in Fitzpatrick, *GW*, 13: 485, 499; 14: 3, 26, 35, and 68.)

2. For NG's views on what was needed for his department, see below, NG to Pettit, 17 December.

To Colonel Charles Pettit

Dear Sir   Camp Middle Brook [N.J.] December 17th 1778

The Troops have not all yet arrivd upon the ground, but as fast as they arrive new difficulties arise. The affair of huting is naturally a disagreeable business, and the officers are difficult to please.[1] I am in hopes however they are all posted now and that we shall have no more moveing.

Upon takeing a survey of the Tents, I am really afraid but a very small part will be fit for the next Campaign. Col Abale [Abeel] says he has about two or three hundred Tents and Cloth to make five or Six [hundred] more. These are all the reserve Tents we have. I expect a part of those at Rhode Island, and a small propotion of those at Fish Kill and Danbury will answer again, but those we have with us are almost all ruind.[2] One Month of the latter part of a Campaign does the Tents more injury than all the rest. The Winds are generally high in the Fall, heavy storms repeatedly following one another wrecks and tears them to pieces prodigiously. To add to this injury the Soldiers build large fires at one end of the Tent, the heat and smoke of which soon rots the Cloth.

I was observeing some Tents that were exceeding good at Fredricksburg are now in a manner ruined. But these are evils that are unavoidable and therefore it signifies nothing to fret.

I observe by your Letter of the 12th that you are preparing a general plan for all the deputies to form their accounts upon.[3] I wish while your hand is in, you would make out proper blank returns for Stores, that there may be some uniformity in the returns hereafter, for it is almost an endless piece of work to reduce them to order in the manner they are now made.

You remark the demand for Money to the Westward is beyond conception. The demands from the Eastward are infinitely greater.[4] The much greater part of our Army is to the Eastward of the North

River in a more exhausted Country and where Money is of as little consequence as in any part of America. In a word money begins to be of so little value, that I am afraid to look forward. I think it will be much better and safer to send the Money to the Eastward than for them to send for it. Should the Deputies join their forces and send for the Money they may be detaind a great while upon expences and the knowledge of their errand may get abroad, by means of which they may be intercepted. Col Hay I find will want upwards of 150,000 dollars for the Fish Kill department to enable him to settle his accounts up to the first of December; this is exclusive of the Forage department. Mr Hubbard has large outstanding debts and a continual expence arising upon the Troops at Danbury, that his demand will be very considerable. He has made a demand upon Col Biddle for 150,000 dollars only for the forage department to pay for purchases already made. [Ephraim] Bowen is largely in debt but I sent him 140,000 dollars out of the last parcel you sent me. I am in hopes therefore his future demands will not be very considerable until towards Spring.

Col [Morgan] Lewis will have heavy demands upon us as great preparations are going on in that district for purposes already known to you. I sent Col Lewis an hundred thousand Dollars out of the two last parcels you sent me and still his calls are pressing.

I am in hopes [William] Smiths expenditure will not be very great this Winter and Col Chaces I think cannot be very large now the Convention Troops are removd but he has already contracted heavy debts on their account which will [have] to be discharged. I think we are near square with Mr Andrews and Mr [Jacob] Greene. Indeed I think the latter is indebted to us. I have sent a man to the Eastward to bring forward all their accounts.

After I wrote you respecting Moylans Regiment going to Baltimore the General alterd his mind and directed them to go to Lancaster [Map 3], but I find that complaints and difficulties stare us in the face from every side. I cannot believe Lancaster is so exhausted as it is represented. I fear Money is the great difficulty.[5]

I am very glad you dont interfere in the dispute with the Commisaries. Mr Blane is not one of the most prudent men in the World; he seems to have taken up an Idea that there are no honest men but what are in the Commisaries line, and that, that department is of more consequence than all the rest.[6] Col Wadsworth appears to be perfectly desireous of cultivateing the best understanding with the principals in our department. It is not always safe to judge from appearances, but he seems to be very sincere. However there is one thing I would just remark. I would not wish the Congress to think there was any great intimacy between us, for fear they should think we play into one anothers hands, and more especially as they have it in contemplation to change the principles upon which the business is done in both departments.[7]

I have enclosd you a Copy of a Letter from his Excellency to me. Tents and forage are the two great Articles for the opening Campaign. I must call upon Col Cox for one and Col Biddle for the other. You will please to communicate the Letter to the Col and desire him to transmit me the prospect to the Westward for a supply of Tents, Camp Kettles, Knapsacks, Waggons and Harness in a summary way as soon as possible.

Mrs Greene desires her compliments to you and Col Cox and to both your families. I am in hopes to get ready to set out for Philadelphia next Week. I am with great regard Your most Obd, humble Sert

NATH GREENE

ALS (NHi).

1. Private houses had to be found for the brigade and regimental officers, no easy task in crossroad settlements. See below, John Beatty to NG, 17 February 1779.

2. The troops at Middlebrook would have to live in tents for several more weeks.

3. Letter not found.

4. NG distributed money to deputies east of the Hudson River and Pettit to those to the west and south.

5. On Moylan's regiment, see above, NG to Pettit, 23 November.

6. Ephraim Blaine, a native of Carlisle, Pa., had been sheriff of Cumberland County before the war. In August 1777 he was appointed deputy commissary general of purchases, serving under Wadsworth after April 1778. In January 1780 he succeeded Wadsworth as commissary. (*JCC*, 8: 617; Heitman, *Register*) Blaine was the great grandfather of James G. Blaine, the celebrated senator from Maine who served twice as secretary of state. (*PMHB*, 2 [1878]: 471)

7. NG did not then anticipate that he and Wadsworth would become silent partners of Barnabas Deane. See Articles of Partnership, 4 April 1779, below.

See Map 1 for geographic references above.

From George Washington

Sir   Head Quarters Middlebrook [N.J.] 17th Decr 1778

I inclose you the copies of two letters for your consideration. The one my letter to Mr Wadsworth on the quantity of provision which he may be able by his utmost exertions to lay in at Albany, and on Connecticut River from No 4 (or Fort Charles) up to the lower Co'os inclusively, by the first day of February next; and whether he could keep a large army to the Northward regularly supplied?[1]

In his answer you will observe that a principal objection to our supplies being certain, is the precariousness of carriage.

Under the idea that the adequate proportion of flour may be

obtained for such an army as is supposed in my letter, you will determine whether it is in your power to give it a certain and uniform transportation.[2]

I shall expect your answer, and am Sir Your very hble servt

GO: WASHINGTON

PS. The above letter and the inclosures will serve to afford a more comprehensive view of the subject which I have already mentioned to you.

ALS (PPAmP).

1. As noted above at NG to Washington, 28 October, Wadsworth was optimistic in mid-November about supplying a large army at Albany and Co'os (on the upper Connecticut River). In the meantime, Washington was still blowing hot and cold on plans to invade Canada via those routes, depending on the latest intelligence or opinions as to British intentions. When he wrote Wadsworth on 16 December, he was again seriously considering the matter, probably at the behest of Congress.

He asked specifically if by February first Wadsworth could provide for ten thousand or more men at Albany and five thousand at Co'os, based on two different suppositions: the first, in case the British should evacuate the United States; the second, if the British should stay on but most of Washington's army would move north. (Fitzpatrick, GW, 13: 403–4) Wadsworth was still confident of providing beef in either case, but he had changed his mind about supplying flour and spirits, principally because of unforeseen shortages in Virginia. Only if the British pulled out could he promise sufficient flour, and even then in his judgment, it would be "impossible" for the quartermaster to furnish transportation. (Letter of 16 December, Washington Papers, DLC)

2. Before reporting to Washington, NG communicated with Wadsworth, as seen below. His letter to Washington has not been found, but he apparently agreed with Wadsworth on the impossibility of transporting sufficient flour.

Wadsworth's and Greene's opinions were enough to dampen Washington's enthusiasm. As he wrote Schuyler the next day, he was convinced "from the concurrent and definitive reports of the Quarter Master and Commissary General, that our resources are unequal to the preparations necessary for such an enterprise." (Fitzpatrick, GW, 13: 430) He agreed with Schuyler on the "importance of reducing Niagara at least if practicable" and thought it "prudent to be taking preparatory measures." He was "more induced to this," he wrote, "as the emancipation of Canada is an object, which Congress have much at heart." It was indeed.

Bit by bit the Canadian expedition was turning into an expedition against the Indians in upstate New York—with a possible strike at Niagara. See below, NG to Washington, 5 January 1779.

See Map 2 for geographic references above.

To Jeremiah Wadsworth

[Middlebrook, N.J., 17 December 1778. Refers to Washington's letter and enclosures above. In order to give Washington a "decisive answer," he must know what portion of the flour can be had near Albany and Co'os and from where the deficiency must be transported.[1] LS (CtHi) 2 pp.]

1. For Wadsworth's answer, see below.

From Jeremiah Wadsworth

[Middlebrook, N.J., 17 December 1778. In answer to NG's letter above, there would not be sufficient flour at Albany and Co'os by 1 February (Map 2); the deficiency must be made up from Pennsylvania, Delaware, and Maryland, with the possibility of some from New York in the spring. LB (CtHi) 1 p.]

To General Anthony Wayne

Dear Sir   Camp Middle Brook [N.J.] December 19, 1778
    I write by the request of the owners of the ground on which your Troops are going to hut.[1] They request that as much care and pains may be taken as possible to prevent the Rails from being burnt and the Wheet Fields from being fed. How far it will be possible to prevent these two evils you can best judge. The People will wait upon you upon the subject and more fully explain their wishes. This Letter serves only for an introduction as they say they are strangers to you. One thing is to be said in favor of the Inhabitants of this part of the Country, they are generally good Whigs,[2] and deserve all the indulgence that can be given them, besides which it will be for our Interest to keep them as good naturd as possible for our own ease and convenience.
    I wish you could engage Mr Vanest [Van Nest] to keep your Horses and receive pay for it. His forage shall be exempt in consequence of it. I am with great regard your Most Obedt humble Servt

NATH GREENE

ALS (PHi).
    1. They encamped south of the Raritan River and west of the Millstone (Map 5).
    2. Suspected Tories were treated less considerately. See below, Thomas Menzies to NG, 16 January 1779.

To Colonel James Abeel

[Middlebrook, N.J., 20 December 1778. Encloses invoice for stores to be sent to Albany as soon as possible. Captain Bruen[1] will come to Morristown to point out the tools "necessary for a set, each set must be put up in a seperate Box" for easy transport. Acknowledges Abeel's need for forage; supposes Morris County could provide it but "if not the Lord knows where we shall get the deficiency from."[2] LS (MiU-C) 1 p.]

1. Jeremiah Bruen of Baldwin's Artillery Artificer Regiment. He was promoted to major in November 1779. (Heitman, *Register*)
2. Abeel reported his progress on NG's order in letters of 21, 24, 27, and 30 December, below. In the letter of the twenty-first, he described the forage situation.

See Map 3 for geographic references above.

To John Hancock

Dear Sir   Camp Middle Brook [N.J.] December 20 1778
We have once more taken up our quarters in this ravaged State. Land transportation has become such a heavy affair and accompanyed with such an enormous expence, that we find it necessary to take a position favorable for receiving our provisions; a great part of which now comes from the Western States,[1] particularly Bread. The scarcity of Provisions and Forage is not a little alarming. Whether the scarcity is real or artificial in part I cannot pretend to say; but I believe the Peoples dislike to the currency is one great obstacle to our purchases.
The army is now a huting. I believe we are the first army that ever built themselves Winter quarters at the close of a campaign. The mode has an appearance of hardship and it is attended with many inconveniencies to the officers, but the Soldiers are very comfortable.[2] We can barrack the Troops in a short Time, and with little expence.
The Inhabitants are free from the distress that always attends quartering Troops upon them. The Morals of the people are preservd from the corruptions of the Soldiery, by keeping them in a collected State and under proper decipline which could not be preservd if they were to be contond [cantoned] in the Villiages.
The tryal[s] of General Lee, General Schuyler and St. Clair are all confirmd: the two last are honorably acquited, the former is condemn'd.[3]
Mr Dean and the Familys of the Lees have opend a paper War. I think from the Nature of the subject the disposition of the parties and quantity of matter it will be a long while before the dispute closes.[4]
His Excellency General Washington is going to Philadelphia in order to settle some points relative to a certain expedition in contemplation to the N———d [Northward]. He sets out tomorrow.[5]
By a Vessel just arrivd from St Estatia [Eustatius] we are informd the British Fleet has taken a large number of the Duch [Dutch] Vessels

coming to the West Indies. Their high Mightinesses have demanded them in peremtory terms and threaten upon a refusal some disagreeable consequences.[6]

There is nothing very interesting from N York. The Enemy appear to be waiting for instructions from Home. He has taken up a large number of Transports and appear to be in readiness to go or stay as his orders may direct.

The Estatia Vessel also brought an account that Count de Estaings Fleet was seen off the Island.

Please to make my most respecful compliments to Mrs Hancock. I am Sir with great regard Your most humbl Ser

NATH GREENE

ALS (PHC).
1. Pennsylvania, Delaware, Maryland, and Virginia.
2. A contrast with the preceding winter at Valley Forge.
3. See above, note at NG to McDougall, 8 November.
4. On the Deane-Lee dispute, see above, Cadwalader to NG, 5 December.
5. Washington left for Philadelphia on 22 December and arrived the same day. (Fitzpatrick, *GW*, 13: 452n)
6. St. Eustatius was a tiny Dutch-held island in the Lesser Antilles. It was a free port through which had flowed much of the European goods en route to the United States. In 1780 England captured the island, and although the French retook it, the island never recovered its position as an entrepôt. (Bemis, *Diplomacy*, pp. 160–61)

To Griffin Greene

Dear Sir   Camp Middle Brook [N.J.] December 21st 1778

I am favord with yours of the 5th.[1]

Mrs Greene is safe arrivd at Camp after a most disagreeable and distressing jorney. The Roads were never worse nor the Weather more disagreeable. Her health was somewhat impaird in coming, but George stood it out finely. He is a fine hardy fellow, full of play and meriment.[2]

We are this moment seting out for Trenton. I am going to Philadelphia, Mrs Greene continues at Trenton until my return.[3] The Weather is cold and the Roads very bad. I expect a very disagreeable jorney. Mrs Greene desires abundance of love to you and Cousin Sally and all the Family. I hope Duhy has got quite well before this will reach you.

I observe you have made a large purchase in dry goods with Messrs Clarke and Nightingale. Col. Cox who is here says dry goods are selling from £ 1500 to £ 2000 for every £ 100 Sterling.[4] Velvets are saleable if well chosen as to colours.

The best of Maderia Wine is very high at Philadelphia, upwards of 2000 Dollars a Pipe.[5] It is selling in the neighbourhood of Camp for 20 dollars a Gallon, but the quallity is but indifferent. West India Rum sells from four to five pounds a Gallon. New England Rum wont pay the transportation.

You will find it very difficult to get goods transported. Forage is scarce and Money so plenty that people dont regard it much. A little hard Money may be profitably laid out upon such an occasion. People will engage for such pay when they wont stir for any offer in paper money. In the quarter master department we can oblige them to go; but you will find it very difficult without giveing the most extravagant prices. What ever goods you send on, there should some good careful hand accompany them; otherwise your Liquors will be most intollerably adulterated.

It may not be amiss for you to lodge some good liquors at Albany in the course of the Winter; this is a secret hint.[6]

If Jacob has not got the writings done respecting the division of the brothers Estate I must beg you to get it done as soon as possible for I foresee a great deal of discontent and perhaps that may not be the worst of it.[7]

Being just upon the Wing I have not Time to write you half as full upon many matters as I want. I must refer [defer?] the matter until I get in to Philadelphia, where you may expect to hear from me next.

There is no change in European politics or in the State of the Enemy at New York. Go on and prosper. I am yours affectionately

N GREENE

ALS (OMC).
1. Letter not found.
2. Their son, George, who would be three years old in January.
3. NG stayed in Trenton for at least a week, arriving in Philadelphia before 31 December. In Trenton the Greenes were guests of the John Coxes at Bloomsbury. Catharine joined her husband in Philadelphia in mid-January.

NG did not return to camp until 9 February. During his absence the routine duties and correspondence of the department devolved upon Maj. Robert Forsyth, a deputy quartermaster. Sixteen letters to Forsyth from other deputies concerning departmental matters are in the Greene Papers, PPAmP.

4. These ratios put the value of the Continental dollar in specie at five to seven cents—only half the value assigned it in the table in Appendix I, where the ratio for December 1778 is shown as 6.84. It should be stressed, however, that the Continental dollar's long slide to virtual worthlessness could not be plotted on a country-wide, day-by-day basis; the value of the Continental dollar at any given time and place was what a buyer and a seller could agree on. By the end of April 1779, for example, when the dollar had generally dropped to half its December value, NG was reporting a ratio in Philadelphia no different from Colonel Cox's December figure. (See below, NG to Griffin Greene, 30 April 1779; NG's figures at that time are between seventeen and twenty to one.)

5. A pipe generally contained two hogsheads—or 125 gallons—and weighed over 1,000 pounds.

6. A reference to the probable expedition against the New York Indians and Niagara. See above, Washington to NG, 17 December and below, NG to Washington, 5 January 1779.

7. For background on the division of his father's estate, see above, vol. 2: 72–73, 104, and Indenture of 10 June 1779, below.

From Colonel James Abeel

[Morristown, N.J., 21 December 1778. Has received NG's of the twentieth. Stores and tools will "go forward" soon. Could get "a vast Quantity" of forage here if legislature would empower "proper Persons to take from Each Farmer only what they Could Spare. Horses are Dayly Dying for want of feed and unless some Method is fallen on to Procure forrage for the Teams Passing and Repassing to Kings Ferry the Publick will Suffer much in Horse Flesh."[1] LB (NjHi) 1 p.]

1. New Jersey did pass an impressment law but the reluctance of local officials to issue warrants against friends and neighbors often thwarted the law. See below, NG to Governor Livingston, 14 February 1779.

From Abraham Lott

Dear General   Beverwyck [N.J.] Decr 23d 1778
    Ever since I had the pleasure of seeing Mrs Greene here, I have been laid up with the Gout in my right foot;[1] the pain and confinement caused thereby has been tedious to me; but as it is going off am in hopes Soon to be out again. This trouble however has been light in proportion to the loss of my dear little Grandson (Colo [William S.] Livingston's son) who died the 15th Instant after a lingering and painful disorder of about Six Weeks: a loss the more Severely felt as it was the third son my daughter has lost this way. But knowing that all these dear pledges are only lent us, we have learned to Submit to the divine decrees of the great disposer of human events.
    Having an affair of great importance to communicate to and consult you upon, I intend to pay my respects to you,[2] as soon as my Pedestals will support me without the borrowed aid of Crutches and Canes; and as the Season approaches in which we generally have good Sleighing, make no doubt but shall be Accompanied by the females of the family, at least some of them.
    It seems by the latest Accounts from New York that the Enemy will not evacuate it this Winter. This has all along been my opinion, notwithstanding the repeated accounts we had from thence to the contrary. It appeared impossible to me that Transports could be provided to take off all their Troops, Horse, Stores of every kind, and the refugees, in the Short time they had allowed them after Sir Henry['s] return from Philadelphia. Besides I do not know whether the ministry of England would dare to give up New York and Newport without the Concurrence of Parliament. Add to this, if they mean to admit the American Independency, it will be better for them to Treat while in possession of those places than after they have Evacuated them. At any rate the Present meeting of Parliament will undoubtedly put An end to our doubts with respects to both these important points.[3]

The family are all in good health at this time and join in the most respectful Salutations to Mrs Greene, yourself and family, with Dear General Your Assureed friend and most obedt Servant

ABRM LOTT

ALS (PPAmP).
1. Catharine Greene had spent a week with the Lotts at Beverwyck before coming to camp. We are indebted to Mr. Alex Fowler of Boonton, N.J. for additional facts on Abraham Lott. (See above, vol. 2: 86n.) Mr. Fowler has an article on Lott in an upcoming volume to be published by the Morris County Historical Society. He believes that Lott was born in 1726, not 1714 as stated in the Lott genealogy. Beverwyck, he points out, was not owned by the Lotts, but by Lucas Von Beverhoudt, who lived in the main mansion while the Lotts lived in a lesser house on the estate. In 1783 the Lotts returned to New York City, where he was faced by enormous debts owed the state of New York. From 1786 to 1789 he was in debtors' prison, although, Mr. Fowler writes, "his comfortable downstairs room in the jail [from which he promoted the sale of land that had come down in his wife's family] was the scene of so much activity it seemed to be more of a business office." Whether he paid off all his debts is not recorded. He died in 1794.
2. The "affair" may have been a business deal. For example, see below, William S. Livingston to NG, 20 June 1779.
3. NG did not answer until 9 February 1779, but his letter has not been found. See below, Lott to NG, 14 February.

Colonel James Abeel to Major Edward W. Kiers[1]

[Morristown, N.J., 24 December 1778. Is sending entrenching tools that NG orders forwarded to Albany "Immediately by the first Sleds." Kiers should send grindstones that are ready to Morristown. LB (NjHi) 1 p.]

1. The addressee is listed only as "Major Kierse," but the assistant DQM with whom Abeel had been dealing at Kings Ferry was Maj. Edward W. Kiers.

From Colonel James Abeel

[Morristown, N.J., 24 December 1778. Is losing no time in forwarding items to Albany that NG ordered. Carpenter tools ought to be packed soon since sleds are preferable to wagons.[1] When men are hutted [at Middlebrook] he will repair tents. LB (NjHi) 1 p.]

1. The heavy snows of the past few days had smoothed out the rough roads for sledding but could not be counted on to last.

To Lord Stirling[1]

My Lord   Trenton [N.J.][2] Decemb 27, 1778
The situation in which I left the Army on account of Forage, the severe Weather that has happend since and the distresses that must have taken place among the Cattle [i.e., livestock] has given me many

uneasy feelings. Not because I have neglected anything in my power, but because the evil is in a great measure incureable under the present restrictions. Some months past a Resolution of Congress took place prohibiting under all circumstances the use of Wheat for forage. I foresaw the distresses that would follow and gave in a full representation to Congress, but they did not think it advisable to relax in the least from the determination they had taken.[3] Pennsylvania raises but little other grain besides Wheet. The transportation through New Jersey, together with the Troops quartered in it has consumd such quantities of Grain that it has been out of our power to lay up any Magizines and in many instances to furnish the supplies necessary for the dayly consumption. Our only hope has been from Virgina and Maryland but as the Farmers dont thrash out their Corn [i.e., grain] until very late in the fall no great supplies will be To be had from those places if the Winter is severe. There is now a great number of Boats froze up in the Delaware between this and Philadelphia loaded with Provisions and forage which we cannot at present get at. I am in hopes to be able to forward some forage from this place in a few days. I am also in hopes some considerable supplies will come in from Monmouth but if the deficiency should prove so great that the Cattle must perish or have recourse to some other modes to obtain supplies than has been hitherto been adopted, I hope your Lordship will furnish the Forage Master General with the necessary powers for the purpose. I know the measure is disagreeable but necessity must sanctify it.

I wish your Lordship to urge the officers to consent to send away as many of their Horses as possible to lessen the consumption of Forage in Camp. The Forage master will provide for them in the Country.

As your Lordship is a stranger in some degree to the State of the Forage department I thought it necessary just to give you the foregoing hints lest you should suppose the scarcity of Forage might be owing to the negligence of the Officers in the department. Full representations has been made to His Excellency from time to time, which I believe has been perfectly satisfactory.[4]

I have been detained at this place for several days past, the River being impassable. I am in hopes to cross on the ice tomorrow.

General Lee and Col Lawrens has had a duel in which the former was wounded in the back.[5] The cause of the duel I have not learnt, but it has been said General Lee affronted Mrs Washington at the Assembly before His Excellencys arrival in Town; but whether it is true or not I cannot tell.

Mrs Greene desires her compliments to Lady Sterling. I am my Lord your Lordships Most Obedient humble Sert

NATH GREENE

ALS (CSmH).
1. Washington had left Lord Stirling in command at Middlebrook while he was in Philadelphia.
2. NG had been in Trenton for several days with John Cox en route to Philadelphia.
3. The resolution, whose purpose was to preserve wheat for human consumption, was passed 26 October (*JCC*, 12: 1064). NG's "full representation to Congress" has not been found.
4. Stirling had already responded to a plea from Major Forsyth, NG's deputy at camp. See Stirling to NG, 28 December, below. When Stirling had insisted on Moylan's horse dragoons remaining in Elizabeth Town, he was probably not aware of the shortage of forage. See NG to Washington, 30 November, above.
5. The duel between Gen. Charles Lee and John Laurens occurred on 23 December, with Lee suffering a flesh wound. The incident is thoroughly recounted in Alden, *Lee*, pp. 262–64.

From Colonel James Abeel

[Morris Town, N.J.] 27 Decr 1778

Since I received your Order to forward the Stores to Albany,[1] I have been very Busy in procuring the Articles I had not by me which are Principally Sadlers and Smiths Tools, the first of which are very scarce. Five waggon Load are gone off already and more waiting for Sleads to carry them on as the Snow is so deep Waggons cannot go on. The principal part of the Carp't Tools I have already Sorted and Boxes prepared for packing up soon as [Jeremiah] Bruin Arrives whom I expect tomorrow. I am extremely sorry to tell you that the want of teams at this Place often Prevents my send'g the Stores forward as I would wish. I never receive an Order but the moment it comes to hand I set about fullfilling it.

I am intirely out of Money. The last small sum Mr Pettit sent me I had borrowed the greater part of and want to Pay off my Friends who were kind enough to lend it me. I should therefore be glad you would order on a sum to me as I am daily called upon by the different people I have Hors Shoes, Nail Rods &ca of, who all expect their Cash as they Deliver their Goods and would be discouraged should I disappoint them. Besides it will be impossible for me to settle my Accts untill I have Money to pay off People I have Contracted with. I some time ago spoke to the Genl [Washington] to Order all the Tents up to this Place soon as the Men are Hutted as I have made every preparation for receiving and repairing them so as they may be fit for Service in the Spring. I will have them Mended and sent to a Place of Safety to be washed and Dryed. Be fully assured that all the Attention in my power shall be paid to the Supplys of the Army and the Interest of the publick.

A number of Brigades who are in Quarters have their Tents scatterd about the Country and Perhaps in the Spring if the[y] are not all dryed will be unfitt for Service. Would it not be best to have them likewise Ordered on to me? I am Your most Obedt Hbl Servt

LB (NjHi).
   1. See above, NG to Abeel, 20 December.

From General Philip Schuyler

Sir   Albany [N.Y.] December 27th 1778

I have not had an opportunity by which to acknowledge the receipt of your favor of the 6th Instant which I received at Saratoga on the 18th Inst.[1]

Since my last to you I have been honored with a letter from his Excellency on the subject you allude to.[2] No exertions of mine shall be wanting to carry Into Execution his wishes.

I have by this conveyance transmitted Congress my resignation. Altho I shall return to private life I must Intreat you not to be thereby prevented from any application you may deem It necessary to make Either to promote the public Service or to do you In particular any. If Even I retired in disgust (which notwithstanding the various Ill treatment I have received is by no means the case) It would not Justify my witholding any Services I am capable of rendering my Country.[3] I am Sir with great regard and Esteem Your most obedient Humble Servant

PH: SCHUYLER

ALS (NHi).
   1. Letter not found.
   2. The subject was the possible invasion of Canada, which is discussed in a note at Washington to NG, 17 December, above.
   3. Schuyler had waited to resign until Congress approved the court-martial absolving him of responsibility for the loss of Ticonderoga in 1777—which Congress did on 4 December. (*JCC*, 12: 1186) Washington, uninformed of his resignation, asked him on 31 December to resume command of the Northern Department. In his response to Washington on 25 January, Schuyler turned down the command, although Congress did not accept his resignation until 19 April 1779. (*JCC*, 13: 473) In the interim, however, he made important contributions to the Indian expedition. Washington's letter is in Fitzpatrick, *GW*, 13: 469–70; Schuyler's to Washington is in the Washington Papers, DLC.

From Lewis Gronow and John Cloyd

[Chester County, Pa.] 28th day of December 1778

A Certificate for Alexander McCaraher Captn of an Artillery Company of Militia of Chester County, Pa. [to] Receive Fourteen Hundred and Eighty One Dollars and Seventy Eight Ninetieths for the Several Articles within mentioned, taken and Destroyed by part of the Continental Army, on their March from the [i.e., Chester] Valley to the Yellow Springs, on or about the 17th day of September, 1777. The said Articles being shortly after appraised by two respectable Inhabitants, of said Neighbourhood, The Loss of which hath been upon Oath declared. We therefore give the said Captn Alexander McCaraher this our Certificate to receive the sum abovesaid. As Witness our hands the 28th day of December 1778.

LEWIS GRONOW

JOHN CLOYD[1]

DS (PCC, item 42, vol. 5: 172, DNA) Enclosed with the certificate was McCaraher's list of missing articles.

1. As the army was leaving Valley Forge in June 1778, NG had authorized Justices Gronow and Cloyd to assess the damages sustained by "any of the Inhabitants in and about the present Encampment." (See above, vol. 2: 419.) McCaraher's losses, however, had occurred three months before the army encamped at Valley Forge and six months before NG became quartermaster. NG therefore forwarded the certificate to Thomas Mifflin, who told McCaraher he was not "impowered" to pay damages without an order from Congress. In September 1779, McCaraher petitioned Congress for relief, seeking to strengthen his claims by noting the similarity of his case with that of "Mr. Moore of Moore Hall," who had been reimbursed. (See above, note at William Moore to NG, 10 November.) Congress referred his petition to the Board of Treasury, and there it died as did many such memorials. (*JCC*, 15: 1104; the memorial is filed with the certificate, the list of missing articles, and a copy of NG's order of 1 June 1778 in PCC, item 42, vol. 5: 167, 170–74.) For a similar case that occurred before NG's appointment but which he did support, see below, NG to Jay, 20 February 1779.

From Lord Stirling

Dear Sir   Middle Brook [N.J.] Decembr 28th 1778

I have received yours of Yesterday's date. The distress for want of forrage is become so very great that Major Foresight [Forsyth] was obliged yesterday in Writeing to represent to me that unless a press Warrant was immediately granted to take forrage from the farmers of the Country it would be impossible to keep the necessary Cattle of the Army alive. In short that the Hutting of the Troops and all the other business of the Army must be at a Stand. Indeed I Clearly see that the very Existance of the Army depended on it; and however disagreeable the measure, necessity must Justify it. I therefore have given him a Warrant to Impress forrage, but yet as far as possible to observe that it be taken from the farmers in proportion to their Several Stocks on hand.[1] This Expedient may give us a temporary relief but unless it is Extended to the Counties which are remarkable for growing of Indian Corn, to wit Monmouth, Burlington and Glouster you may depend on it the distress will soon return in a greater degree than ever,[2] for it will then be incureable as the temporary Supply will be Exhausted and none to be had but at Such a distance that the Cattle [i.e., livestock] will Starve before it can be bro't in. I think you had better obtain a press Warrant from General Washington and immediately send proper persons into those Counties to get it bro't in by the Waggons of the Country, for you may be assured that the weather will give great obstruction to your Supplys from the Westward.[3]

The Cause of the Duel you mention I believe had its origin last Summer at Paramis. I have not been without aprehensions of it. But how happened it that the Wound is in the back? We have not a Word of News, every Avenue of Intelligence seems to be frozen up. It never was Colder in Lapland than we have had it for some days and yet I do not hear it has done any mischief to the men. Indeed by what I can learn the Army is more healthy than ever I knew it.

Lady Stirling Joins in her best Respects and good Wishes to yourself and Mrs Green with your Affectionate Humble Servt

STIRLING

Biddle is absent. I hope he is well imployed. I dont mean in a Christmas frolick.[4]

ALS (NjHi).
    1. In NG's letter to Stirling of 27 December, he had not actually requested a press warrant because he was unaware how much the forage supply had deteriorated in the week since he had left camp.
    2. The three counties, which bordered the coast south of Sandy Hook, were noted for growing Indian corn.
    3. Washington had issued a press warrant of one month's duration to get the army to Middlebrook. (See Washington to NG, 20 November, above.) As NG reported in his letter to Stirling of 31 December, he planned to ask Washington for another warrant.
    4. Biddle had gone to Monmouth County in search of Indian corn. As noted at NG to Livingston, 14 February 1779 below, the search was not an easy one.

See Map 3 for geographic references above.

From Colonel James Abeel

[Morristown, N.J., 30 December 1778. Because of items NG requested for Albany, he has no money for sixty sleds for camp.[1] Would be "Glad" if NG would give some money to the bearer and "hurry him back." LB (NjHi) 2 pp.]

    1. See above, NG to Abeel, 20 December.

To Lord Stirling

My Lord   Philadelphia Decem 31, 1778
    Your Lordships favor of the 28th I have receivd.
    I thank you kindly for the aid you gave to the Forage department. I felt exceeding uneasy at the scarcity of Forage, and had taken every measure in my power to procure a supply; but the consumption was so great and the Article so scarce, that my utmost endeavors were ineffectual. I believe Col Biddle was properly employed as he set out

through the Country to visit Monmouth [County] and to hasten on a supply of Forage as soon as possible.

I shall immediately communicate to His Excellency the contents of your Letter and endeavor to procure a more extensive Warrant.[1] I have but little hopes of geting any considerable quantity of Forage in any part of New Jersey except Monmouth, where I believe there is considerable quantities to be had.[2]

I am afraid there will be little or no forage to be had from the Western States until Spring. We have considerable quantitys purchaceed in Virginia and Maryland but it is too remote to derive any great benefit from it this winter.

The policy that the Congress have hitherto pursued in drawing all our supplies by land transportation, has been attended with truly bad consequences; it has mutiplyed our expences, and lessened our supplies. Land carriage is a most terrible expensive business, and is accompanyed with this difficulty that you cannot increase it beyound a certain extent however pressing the necessity. Besides which your supplies comes forward but slow; and generally attended with great waste, as they pass through many peoples hands.

This matter has been so fully represented to Congress that I am in hopes hereafter to be at liberty to make freer use of Water conveyance notwithstanding the public Stores are exposd to some risque and danger.[3]

There is nothing new in the City. Political feuds are very prevalent and luxury and extravagance beyound description. The City is crowded with people and all kind of diversions are going on which are no small embarrassments to public business.[4]

Mrs Greene is at Trenton where She will continue until my return to Camp.[5]

My compliments to Lady Sterling and the Gentlemen and Ladies of the family. I have the honor to be Your Lordships obedt Sert

N GREENE

ALS (Original in possession of David Coblentz, Raphine, Va., 1973).

1. No such letter has been found, but since NG saw Washington daily he may have asked him in person for a press warrant. If so, there is no evidence that Washington issued one.

2. On Monmouth County as a source of forage, see below, NG to Governor Livingston, 14 February 1779.

3. No letter to Congress on water transport has been found, but NG had discussed it in his letter above of 27 October to Washington, which Washington forwarded to Congress. For his early advocacy of water transport, see above, vol. 2: 319–20n.

4. Stirling responded to NG's observations on 4 January 1779, below.

5. She left the Cox's Trenton home the latter part of January to join NG in Philadelphia. (See below, NG to Griffin Greene, 25 January 1779.)

To General John Sullivan

[(   ) late 1778 [?]][1] Introduces Mr. Dusaw, the bearer, a French merchant of good character whom NG has known for years; he is interested in serving "our cause" in any way Sullivan can use him. ALS (NhHi) 1 p.]

1. Hammond, *Sullivan*, p. 477, places this at the end of 1778 without giving his reasons.

From Otis & Andrews

[Boston, 1 January 1779 [misdated 1778]. Asks NG to forward enclosed accounts to clothier general. LS (PPAmP) 1 p.]

To Colonel John Mitchell

[Philadelphia, 2 January 1779. NG attaches note to a long list of items needed to complete a row galley, asking Mitchell to procure enough of designated items for twelve boats, the material to be shipped to New Windsor, N.Y.[1] Cy (PCC, item 173, vol. 1: 315, DNA) 3 pp.]

1. Maj. Benjamin Eyre, superintendent of the boat department, was probably responsible for the three-page list of items needed for building a row galley with a keel of 50 feet and beam of 17 feet, to be equipped with two masts and forty 22-foot oars. NG checked off such items as hardware, canvas, rope, all of which could be procured in Philadelphia. The same items multiplied by twelve are listed in the Greene Papers, vol. 11: 77, PPAmP.

From Colonel Ephraim Bowen

[Providence, R.I., 2 January 1779. Has paid debts with $140,000 NG sent but needs more. Sold seventy horses per NG's direction, but they brought so little, General Sullivan had him stop the sale and put them on Prudence Island.[1] Good wagon horses sent to Connecticut to winter. ALS (PPAmP) 2 pp.]

1. Prudence Island was in Narragansett Bay. A British party from Newport later took the horses. See below, Bowen to NG, 8 February.

From Conrad Alexandre Gérard, Minister of France

Philadelphia January 2d 1778 [1779]

The Minister of France presents his compliments to Major General Green and prays him to give orders at Fish Kill to forward as soon as possible some linen cloth which is arrived there and is destined for the said Minister.

AL (PPAmP).

From George Olney

Sir   Providence [R.I.] 2nd Jany 1779
    Your offers for my services, as Auditor of Accounts in your department at Camp, are so near the terms I should have proposed, had you waited for them, that I do not think proper entirely to reject them, tho' I am unwilling to accept them without changing the form of the agreement.[1] While the currency continues at its present value, your terms may be consider'd as nearly adequate to the services; but it is in such a fluctuating and uncertain state, that, for my own security, I think it necessary to make the agreemt for hard money, or an equivalent in paper at the current rates of exchange. If therefore you will allow me eight pounds lawful money, in gold or silver per month, to live in your family free from expence, and to have equal privileges in every other respect, with the other officers in the department, I will set out for head Quarters as soon as Mrs Olney recovers (she being just put to bed) and I have provided convenient and suitable lodgings for her in my absence.[2]
    As this salary is really less than I have receiv'd previous to the War, for less important services; as I must necessarily be at a great distance separated from my family; and as the expences in travelling are so very high, I think you will be entirely justified in this agreement on the principle of justice to the public, as well as equity to an individual.
    I shall be glad to hear from you soon, and am with respect. Your Most Humble and Obedient Servant

                                                        GEO OLNEY

ALS (PPAmP).
    1. NG's terms are outlined in NG to Bowen, 12 December 1778, above. Bowen later said that it was not the salary that led him to accept but the possibility of advancement. (See Olney to NG, 30 August 1780, below.)
    2. He left Providence on 9 February. (Bowen to NG, 8 February, below)

From Colonel Jeremiah Wadsworth

Sir   Philadelphia January 2d 1779
    I am directed by the Committee of Congress, to import Ten Thousand Casks of Rice from South Carolina which is ready and I wish to have the Vessels provided for that purpose[1] directed to Abraham Levingston [Livingston] Esqr. at Charlestown South Carolina to be laden, and direct the Masters of such Vessels as you may think proper.[2] I believe Boston, Bielford [i.e., New Bedford, Mass.], Providence and Connecticut in New England [Map 2] will be the most proper places to deposite the Rice, a few Cargoes at Philadelphia.[3] I am, Sir, Your very humble Servant

                                                        JERE WADSWORTH

LB (CtHi).

1. The copyist, who was careless in transcribing Wadsworth's difficult hand into the letterbook, inserted a period and an "I" at this point, which would appear to distort Wadsworth's meaning as well as his syntax.

2. Abraham Livingston, a former clothing merchant in Charleston, was Continental agent in South Carolina.

3. New England was the principal destination of the rice. Despite the importation of grain from the Chesapeake region and New York, supplies of flour and meal in New England had dwindled by January to a critical level. (For conditions in Rhode Island, see note at Hubbard to NG, 6 February, below.) In a rare display of Continental unity, Congress took the initiative in bringing the rice from South Carolina, which had enjoyed a bumper crop. To the quartermaster general, however, fell the task of transporting the rice even though some was intended for civilian use. It was an enormous undertaking that would stretch out over the next six months.

The distance from Charleston to Boston by sea was almost a thousand miles. A hazardous voyage at best, in wartime a vessel had to run the gauntlet of British frigates and privateers—the latter, as NG wrote, being "as thick upon the coast as grass hoppers." (NG to Wadsworth, 19 March, below) The few ships already at Charleston needed to run the gauntlet only once, but most of the vessels and their crews had to be chartered in New England, thus exposing them to the hazards both going and returning. Many shipowners considered that Samuel Otis underestimated the danger when he reckoned the "real Risque" for the round trip at not more than 50 percent. (See Otis to NG, 11 February, below.) The vessels captured on their way to Charleston, moreover, endangered others, for as Charles Pettit pointed out, they "inform the enemy of the Scheme and induce them to cruize for those returning with a Cargo." (Pettit to Abraham Livingston, 30 April 1779, Greene Papers, PPAmP. On the capture of a vessel bound for Charleston, see below, Deposition of 10 March.)

Thus, it was weeks before a willing shipowner could be found and months until the last was engaged. (For a typical charter of a vessel, see 8 April, below.) The first ships to arrive in Charleston were further delayed by the South Carolina embargo. (See Livingston to NG, 27 February, below.) Although a number of vessels were captured, many miraculously got through, and great quantities of rice eventually reached New England. For the numerous letters on the subject, see index entries under "Rice" in this and the succeeding volume.

To Colonel Clement Biddle

Dear Sir   [Philadelphia] January 3, 1779

The Congress and the Board of Treasury have demanded the amount of the Debts due from the Quarter Masters Department up to the first of January. Please to have your letters ready to go Eastward as soon as possible upon the subject, and write to your brother to collect them from the Westward.[1] My letters are all ready to go off this morning. I am with much esteem yours

N GREENE

Tr (GWG Transcript: CSmH).

1. Clement Biddle's brother, Owen, formally became assistant commissary general of forage on 1 April. See his appointment on that date, below. The Hudson River was the dividing line between "Eastward" and "Westward."

From The Reverend John Murray

Dear Sir   Glouster [Gloucester, Mass.] Jany 3d 1779

From a heart replete with gratitude to the Divine being for bringing, and to you for kindly condscending to inform me you are brought to the close of another Campaign, accept of my warmest congratulations.[1]

Four Hostile seasons you have passed through unhurt! Blessed be the providing God under whose divine panoply you hav rode securely amongst inumerable dangers, and left death behind in so many frightfull forms. May the same goodness and mercy follow you to the close of your Militant state, till puting off the harness, you return with shouting to your lov'd retreat, to your peacfull dwelling, there to enjoy the dear bought fruits of all your toils.

It is but little I can know of the [dangers that?] turn up in the course of a Campaign. In this obscure Village so remote from the scene of action, we have no other Oracle to consult than the public paper; an Oracle that deserves as little credit as any that the ancient Pagans were deceived by. Yet I look forward with pleasure to the close of these tumultuous times, when from the pen of that great man you advert to [Washington], should the Father of spirits continue him long enough to finish the work he has begun, the world will have an opportunity of beholding in one view, in as elligant a form as it [is?] possible for [a] Historian to give it, all the great events that have marked this Era.

You Sir have been an eyewitness to the many surprising envents that has turned up since the commencment of this war, espcially through the course of this last Campaign. You have seen the British Troops surprised into a state of humiliation at Monmouth; and, when the Gallic Cock [Count d'Estaing] had called you to Rhode Island, then, spreading his wings, left you there to shift for yourselves, labouring under every disadvantage that can be conceived of, then, even then your enemies stood astonished at your undaunted heroism, and had a feeling proff [proof] that, in your lowest circumstances, without the aid of any foreign power, you were still a match for them.[2] I wish to see my haughty Country[3] brought to a proper sense of themselves, but I pray heaven no power but America may ever have the honour of applying caustic to cut off the proud flesh of that highly favourd nation. However I am so much of an Amerian that I participate with you in the pleasure it afforded in seeing our brave fellows chase the British bravos off the feild of battle.

I am happy to find from your pen that our affairs wear a better aspect than they did sometime back, both with respect to our friends and our enemies; and with you, look up with gratitude to him, who is mighty to save, and strong to deliver.

But what a chequered scene indeed! How gloomy the prospect when we turn to the dark side! And a dark side our affairs most certainly have. Our Money is the ghost of Money, whose voice sounds hollower every day. However, I have the pleasure to assure you, in a personal appearance it very rarely brings terror to me. You know it is an articl of commerce I deal but little in whether good or bad; yet it pains me to the soul to see its vallue sinking so fast, and the base measures that many of our professed Patriots pursue to obtain more of it, never considering that, like the Sybils Caves, it would increase in vallue as it decreased in quantity.

But dear Sir can [damaged] "our Officers begin at last to grow discontented." It is not [damaged] they have not been so from the begining? Neither am I surprised that a certain body of Men [i.e., Congress?] "begin to be jealous of the Army." I think I have somewhere heard it observed that, jealousy is bottomed in a consciousness of inability, but it is not always the case for, "the Army is jealous of them."

I have always thought our best Men were in the Army, without are dogs. I never was the thousand part so much afraid of foreign, as of domestic foes. In fact I don't know if it would not be good for us if we were well drub'd. We have got into a state of carnal security, as the Priests have told us, and we want to be rous'd out of it.

I tremble at "the appearance of *Faction* and the increase of corruption in our Politicks." "Private views" I have long since discovered to be, amongst us, "the bane of Public interest." In fine, the root of all evil has taken *deep* root downward and brings forth much fruit upward, and I am very much afriad, as England has done the work of America, we shall pay them in kind.

Yet, you are not discouraged! Surprising man! You are fit for a General. You have the heroism of [?] [damaged], the firmness of the Roman, and the faith of the Christian. Your faith seems superior to the faith of Abraham. When appearances were against him, he had the promise of Jehovah to support him, and therefore staggered not through unbelief. You have not the promise of Jehovah that we shall be *Independant*, and yet you are "fully persuaded we shall be a free and a happy people." Amen be it unto you; be it unto us according to your faith.

Yes Sir, I well know "you are making very large sacrifices," and your prospects are very gloomy. Honest Patriots must live by faith. They must be content to toil in this world, and reap their harvest in the next. I have always thought it would be your case and I know you are too well acquainted with Mankind ever to form any expectations from that quarter. No Sir.

> After a life of glorious toil endur'd,
> Britain repuls'd, and property secur'd:

Ambition humbl'd, no more cities storm'd,
Good Laws establishd, [*damaged*] reformed;
You'll close your labours with a sigh to find
The unwilling gratitude of base Mankind. Spect. Vol. 2 No. 101[4]

I pity your excellent Lady, her faithfull heart must feel many a painfull throb. When I was last at your mansion, I saw her cast a glance at your shadow[5] that hung in the parlour, and the rising sigh and falling drop, were outward and visible signs of inward and spiritual woe. In short you are both objects of envy and of pity.

Yet you are pleased to suppose that, *from the pulpit* I could convince you you have no reason to complain. If it would give you pleasure to hear me try, I heartily wish you had it. I will assure you it would make me very happy to have it in my power to contribute in any sort to the happiness of General Green. But *you have* reason to complain, *as a Patriot*, and as a *General*; but as a Man, and as a Christian that is an heir of a glorious Immortallity you have reason to rejoice and be exceeding glad.

You ask if the Priests are on [any better] terms with me than formerly.[6] I answer no, but their pride, and my humility will hardly admit of the reason you give; though I confess I have pride enough to be highly gratified by the generous partiallity you discover in the cause you hint at. Some time or other, when you have done with great matters, should that ever be the case, I shall be able to inform you how some of that crew have lately treated me, I have seen so much of the Preistly Order that [I can say] with the Old Patriarch, *My sons come not thou unto their secret, unto their Assembly, mine honour is not there united.* There is so much meaness of Soul and low cunning amongst them, that from my heart I dispise them as *Preists;* but they will soon drop the Preistly character, and then be no worse than other miserable sinners and with them, *saved in the day of the Lord, tho it be as by fire.*

My friends in this Town are highly gratified by your kind rememberance of them [particularly?] people where I lodge, and beg me to present their most respectfull compliments to you.[7] I have been much afflicted in the loss of several of my very worthy friends in this place since I have had the happiness of being connected with them, but this is my abiding consolation that I shall soon follow for

Tired of vain life I'd close the willing eye
Tis the great birthright of Mankind to die,
Blest be the barge that wafts us to the shore,
Where death divided friends shall part no more.

Please to make my compliments acceptable to your good Lady. I hope before the opening of the next Campaign to have the pleasure of see-

ing you. I have the honour to be, with great regard Your most obedient devoted servant[8]

JOHN MURRAY

P S I shall still indulge the pleasing hope of being honoured with a
line from you whenever you can find a seasonable opportunity.

ALS (MiU-C).
    1. NG's letter, from which Murray quotes here and there, has not been found.
    2. The campaign in Rhode Island is covered above, vol. 2: 476–513.
    3. Murray had left England in 1770.
    4. He paraphrased Pope's imitation of a portion of Horace's First Epistle as printed
in the *Spectator*. The original (as taken from Henry Smith's 1776 Edinburgh reprint) follows:

> *Edward* and *Henry* now the boast of fame,
> And virtuous *Alfred*, a more sacred name,
> After a life of gen'rous toils endur'd,
> The *Gaul* subdu'd, or property secur'd,
> Ambition humbled, mighty cities storm'd
> Or laws establish'd, and the world reform'd;
> Clos'd their long glories with a sigh to find
> Th' unwilling gratitude of base mankind.

    5. Probably a silhouette, a word that had just gained currency in France. It has not
been found.
    6. See above, vol. 2: 96n.
    7. He was staying at the home of a well-to-do shipmaster, Winthrop Sargent,
whose widowed daughter, Judith, later married Murray.
    8. On NG's friendship with Murray, the founder of Universalism in America, see
references in vols. 1 and 2, above.

From Colonel Walter Stewart

My Dear General   Fredericksburgh [Va.] Jany 4th 1778 [1779][1]
    I should think myself Inexcusable If I should neglect paying that
Attention to my friend and General, which I have Ever thought he
Merited, and has a right to Expect from me.
    Colonel Ball and myself have been much longer performing our
Journey to Virginia than I by any means expected when we left Camp;
But our friends in Philadelphia, and Baltimore, paid such Attention
to, and press'd us so Earnestly to be happy with them, that I cannot
help thinking we were a little Excusable in only travelling three
hundred Miles in five Weeks.[2]
    Since my Arrival in this Country I have been much pleas'd with
the great Hospitality and Hearty Welcome with which we were receiv'd by the Gentlemen whom we have yet Visited. They have really
done everything in their Powers to make our time pass Agreeably,
and the Company of our Mutual Friends Weedon and Spotswood has
Contributed not a little to our Happiness. With them I have pass'd

five or six days, talking over the Scenes which presented themselves to our Views while in the Army together.[3]

I am very Unhappy to find the Situation to which the People of this Country are drove for Want of Bread. Their Wheat is Entirely destroy'd by the Weavel, and the very Short Crops of Corn Occasions its Selling at 10 and Upwards per Barrel Consisting of five Bushels; the Common Price of Pork is from Thirteen to fifteen Pounds Virga Money per Hundred, and I am Inform'd difficult to be procur'd at those Prices. I was in great Hopes I should when I got here have the pleasure of finding our Money Valuable, but am sorry to say it is neither Scarce nor of more Value than it was at Philadelphia. What a happiness it would be to this Country if the Enemy should leave it for sometime. I am really Shock'd at the Idea of another Campaigne, unless Effectual measures are taken to lessen the Quantity of Cash in Circulation, and I dread the putting that in Execution will give our Credit such a stab as we shall severely feel. Providence Certainly heretofore has been kind to us, and on that kind Providence I fear we must depend in this Instance.

It makes me happy to find the Just sense the People throughout the Country in General have of General Lee. They are in this part of it Amazingly chagrin [to] find that a much severer sentance [has] not been pass'd on him. I am however Confidant it is Sufficient to rid the Army of his Company and am clearly of opinion his own Impetuous and Imprudent Conduct will soon rid America of a very bad member of Society.[4]

The Gentlemen here are much Exasperated against R H Lee. From what I can learn I Conclude his reign at an end, and firmly believe the *Junto* entirely routed.[5] That this may be the case is the sincere and fervent Wish of your Ever sincere friend

WALTER STEWART

P S I hope by this time you are happy in the Co of Mrs Green. If so make my best comps. to her, and all the Ladys of our Acquaintance about Camp. I hope our Lottery Tickets will be successful. It is really necessary. I shall do myself the pleasure of writing you from Williamsburgh where I propose being in a few days and hope to be able to shake you by the Hand the beginning of March

W S

ALS (PPAmP).
1. The docketing is 1779, corroborated by Stewart to NG, 29 January, below.
2. Stewart's objective in Virginia is not known. Since he traveled with Lt. Col. Burgess Ball of the First Virginia Regiment, his trip may have been social.
3. Gen. George Weedon was in temporary retirement in Fredericksburg; on Col. Alexander Spotswood, see his letter of 2 February, below.

Walter Stewart, 1756–1796, oil painting attributed to Robert Edge Pine
(Courtesy of The Henry Francis du Pont Winterthur Museum)

Joseph Reed, 1741–1785, oil painting by Charles Willson Peale
(Courtesy of Independence National Historical Park)

4. On Charles Lee's court-martial, see above, NG to McDougall, 8 November 1778. Stewart, who served under Lee at Monmouth, was one of the principal witnesses to testify against him.

5. Richard Henry Lee had been considered by Washington's associates as a prime mover in the "Conway Cabal." At this time he was involved in his brother Arthur's quarrel with Silas Deane. Ill health forced his resignation from Congress in April 1779, but he returned as a delegate in 1783 and soon thereafter was elected president.

From Lord Stirling

My dear Sir   Middle Brook [N.J.] January 4, 1779 10 oClock P.M.

I have had the Pleasure of receiving your Letter of the 31st Ultimo. The Forrage seems now to go on very well. I have heard no Complaints for three or four Days past and if the Roads continue tolerable I am in hopes all in that Department will do well for a time. But the Moment the Delaware is open again [i.e., thawed] you will I doubt not push on a grand Magazine to Trenton. Colonel Biddle I am perswaded is doing all in his Power to keep the thing alive; when I mist him he was doing his best in Monmouth, and I hope has in a great Degree succeeded. He is now going on a Plan which I am in hopes will prevent Clamour in this Vicinity, and takes off the Necessity of Impressment. This Measure must always be left for the last Necessity and kept for a dernier Resort. Your Sentiments with Regard to the Land Conveyance of Forage &c. are demonstrably just, and we had better run some Risques to avoid an enormous Expence which never secures us a proper Supply, and adopt a Plan that will give us a good Chance of a full Supply; this Accession to the usual Supplies will, if any thing can, secure us Sufficiencies. It ought to be adopted immediately that advantage may be taken of it while the Enemys Cruissers are oblidged by the Season to be off the Coast.[1] They cannot live there now, and doubt not you will make Hay while the Sun Shines, or in this very cold Season rather say while Boreas Blows. As far as my opinion goes I recommend the Measure strongly.

In Counterpart to all you tell us of the political Feuds, the Luxury and Extravagance prevalent in Philadelphia, we are here in the most perfect harmony, Simplicity and Eoconomy, and yet I wish you would enable us to be a little—what shall I call it—send us a little good Wine &c. and then I will tell you, and so doing I shall ever pray you and yours—Multos Annos &c &c &c

STIRLING

LS (NHi).

1. On NG's plan, see his letter of 31 December, above.

To Colonel Ephraim Bowen

Sir   Philadelphia January 5th 1779

The Commissary General has been directed by the Congress to make a large purchase of rice in South Carolina.[1] He has made application to me to procure him a sufficient number of Vessels to import the same into the Eastern States [i.e., New England]. You will charter therefore in the State of Rhode Island shiping enough to import 1,000 casks. It has been recommended by a Committee of Congress to give the importers a certain part of the Cargo for the charter of their Vessels; one quarter is proposed, and these are the conditions which are given to the merchants of this place for transporting flour to Boston, but it is thought advisable to give as high as one third, rather than not engage the Vessels in this way.[2] Whoever charters their Vessels upon these conditions, either for a quarter or third of the Cargo, run all risques both going and coming of their Vessel and such part of the Cargo as they are interested in for the freight.

If upon enquiry you find you cannot charter a sufficient number upon these conditions, you will charter to be paid in money upon the best conditions you can, and you will make your contracts either for the Owners to risque their Vessels or the public according as the different conditions of charter, rate of insurance now given, and chance of escape to be for the interest of the public.

The Vessels are to be fitted and sent off as soon as possible as the most favourable time for their going and coming safe, will be in February and March.[3] They are to go consigned to Mr Abraham Livingston, Continental Agent, Charles Town South Carolina, who is to load them back again: They may return to the same ports from whence they go, or to any other of the Eastern ports not further Eastward than Boston.

The most proper sized vessels for this business are from 80 to 120. Tons, but you may engage from 50. to 200. And if it should so happen that you cannot engage the Tonage requested you will advertise Mr Benjamin Andrews of Boston what you have engaged and what you are deficient.[4]

You will be very carefull not to let a single soul know the number of Vessels you want to charter, and take care to reduce all your contracts to writing[5] and let the business be set about immediately on the reciept of this Letter, and compleated as soon as possible.

You will write me from time to time of the progress you make in the business and the prospect you have of compleating it.[6] I am Sir Your most Obedient humble servant

NATHANAEL GREENE

N. B. You may contract for vessels at [New] Bedford and that part of the State of Massachusetts Bay. (Map 2)

LS (NcD).
1. See above, Wadsworth to NG, 2 January.
2. In proposing one quarter of the cargo, Congress was far from a realistic assessment of the risks involved. Even the one third that NG authorized proved to be too low.
3. The British blockade was least effective during the late winter storms.
4. On Andrews's accidental death four days later, see below, Otis to NG, 10 January.
5. For an example of a contract, see the agreement below of 8 April 1779.
6. NG wrote again on 27 January and Bowen responded on 8 February; see below.

To George Washington

Sir   Philadelphia January 5th 1779
The little leisure I have dont afford me a sufficient opportunity to go largely into the subject your Excellency requested my opinion upon. I have been oblig'd to write for two Nights past until after one oClock in the morning, and am now writing before Sunrise. Therefore I hope your Excellency wont think me inattentive to your wishes or regardless of the Subject.[1]

I think the fact is pretty clearly assertaind that there is a great scarcity of Provision and Forage. The Middle and Eastern States have been harassed very greatly for four Campaigns runing by means of which the Country has got much exhausted and the People sore with the hardships they have suffer'd, and the state of our currency added to the other two considerations renders a contracted plan and a breathing spell for the People absolutely necessary. No foreign Expedition should be undertaken while the Enemy remains formidable in these States.

There is three principal objects to be attended to in the plan of next Campaign. To take a position favorable for subsisting the army with ease and at the least Expence, To scourge the Indians at the proper season, and route [rout] the Enemy from N York should the state of the Garrison there render it practicable.

For the first, New Jersey is the most favorable position. Bread is the great article which is so difficult to transport. Meat can be generally drove to the Army. There must be a sufficient number of Troops at the North River to secure the communication with the Eastern States. There must also be a proper force kept somewhere in the Western parts of Conecticut to cover the Country with the aid of the Militia from the ravages of the Enemies parties. At and to the Eastward of the North River perhaps it may be necessary to keep near a third of the Army.

To scourge the Indians properly there should be considerable bodys of men march into their Country by different routes and at a season when their Corn is about half grown. The month of June will be the most proper Time. One division to move from Fort Pitt. One division by way of Wyoming and the other by the Mohawk River. The only object should be that of driving off the Indians and destroying their Grain and as soon as that is completed to return again. This must be done whether the Enemy continues in great or little force at N York.[2]

No offensive operations can take place against N York until green Forage can be had. Then if the state of the Garrison will admit of an Investiture, to commence the operations, which must be carried on either by the way of Long Island or attempt to effect a landing directly upon York Island [i.e., Manhattan]. The lat[t]er would be the most expeditious and effectual way of carry[ing] on the operations because it would bring the matter to a decision at once.

If we could get possession of Fort Washington and open a communication with Fort Lee it would greatly facilitate our measures. (Map 1) There must be a number of Battaues made for the purpose in the course of this Winter and Spring. If the operation goes on by the way of Long Island, The Battaues had best be made in Conecticut River. Continental Troops must be employed against the Indians or else the Work wont be half done, and should our collective strength here be unequal to the business of beseigeing New York, The militia can be easily called to our Aid. We cannot attempt the Garrison at N Y without double their force.[3]

If the Enemy should continue a Garrison at Rhode Island, The Country with what force there is there must protect themselves. Should we attempt N Y it will be necessary to make some appearances at Rhode Island as if that place was going to be beseiged at the same Time.

I am oblig'd to wait upon the Treasury board this morning which prevents my adding any thing further for the present. But I shall see your Excellency by and by [i.e., in a short time] and will converse further upon the subject. I am Your Excellencys obed Sert

N GREENE

ALS (Washington Papers: DLC).
1. Washington, who was in Philadelphia, had undoubtedly discussed the subject with NG in person. There is no evidence that at this time he solicited the opinions of other general officers on the coming campaign.
2. NG's suggestions in this paragraph for an expedition against the Iroquois Indians could almost serve as an outline of the Sullivan-Clinton expedition of 1779: its chief objective and suggested approach routes. Only his timing was off; the expedition, after innumerable delays, did not reach the Indian country until August.
The idea of an expedition against the Iroquois—and more especially the Senecas—did not originate with NG, of course. It had been urged upon Congress

many times by the frontier settlements in New York and Pennsylvania. In June 1778, Congress had ordered General Gates to mount an expedition into the Seneca country in central New York "in order to chastise that insolent and revengeful nation." (*JCC*, 11: 589) Gates, who responded by recommending to Congress that the United States "Steer clear of that hornet's nest, the Six Nations," managed to resist this order as well as subsequent pressures from Congress during the summer. (Nelson, *Gates*, pp. 199–201, discusses Gates's virtual disobedience of the orders from Congress while making plans for leading an invasion into Canada.)

It was the Wyoming Valley "massacre" in Pennsylvania in early July 1778 (where some three hundred whites were killed) that brought the issue sharply to the forefront. Local militia had been no match for Col. John Butler's Tory Rangers and some five hundred Indian allies. Congress spent many hours debating how to help the stricken area. On 27 July the Board of War wrote Washington, enclosing several resolves of Congress and asking for Washington's help. (The letter is in the Washington Papers, DLC.) Washington's main army at the time was at White Plains, N.Y., guarding against a possible British move out of New York City, while the remainder was preparing for an attack on Newport, R.I. Washington felt he had no troops to spare. He discussed the board's letter with Governor Clinton of New York and General Gates, both of whom agreed with him, as he told the Board of War in a letter of 3 August, that "a serious attempt to penetrate the Seneca settlements at this advanced season . . . was by no means adviseable." (Fitzpatrick, *GW*, 12: 262)

A somewhat less bloody attack, led by Col. Walter Butler (son of John Butler) and a band of Senecas, occurred on 11 November 1778 at Cherry Valley, N.Y. Washington learned of it in a letter from Gen. Edward Hand, which he received on 16 November and immediately sent to Congress. Although, he told Congress, "the only certain way of preventing Indian ravages is to carry the war vigorously into their own country," he regretted that this was "impracticable at this late season of the year." (Fitzpatrick, *GW*, 13: 264) He did ask Generals Edward Hand and James Clinton to meet in Albany to work out what protection they could for the frontier settlements during the coming months.

In December, Washington not only had to move his headquarters to Camp Middlebrook but was still much involved in preparing for a possible joint invasion of Canada with the French in the spring of 1779. (See note at NG to Washington, 28 October 1778, above.) On his arrival in Philadelphia on the first of January 1779 to consult with the Committee of Conference on the 1779 campaign, he learned that plans for collaborating with France in the spring had just been canceled by Congress. A week after receiving NG's letter of 5 January, Washington reported to the committee that, of three possible campaigns that might be considered for 1779, the army seemed driven to the necessity of "remaining intirely on the defensive, except such lesser operations against the Indians as are absolutely necessary to divert their ravages from us." (Fitzpatrick, *GW*, 14: 9–10) After discussing the advantages to the economy and currency of such limited objectives, he added, "I shall not enter particularly into the measures that may be taken against the Indians; but content myself with the general Idea thrown out, unless it should be the pleasure of the Committee that I should be more explicit." (Ibid., 14: 10)

The committee did not require him to be more explicit. It agreed with his limited objectives and left specific plans up to him. He confided to Gen. Lachlan McIntosh at Ft. Pitt of a general plan to carry the war into the Indian country in the spring and asked him to explore the country to the north of Ft. Pitt and to set about making limited preparations. (Washington to McIntosh, 31 January 1779, Fitzpatrick, *GW*, 14: 59) Eventually, an expedition was planned from Ft. Pitt under Col. Daniel Brodhead, who replaced General McIntosh as commander at Ft. Pitt in early March.

Washington had begun corresponding with General Schuyler in upstate New York in late January, asking his opinion of how best to approach the Indian country, whether or not in one body of men, how many troops were needed, etc. (Washington to Schuyler, 25 January 1779, Fitzpatrick, *GW*, 14: 45–46) By this time Washington agreed with NG that at least part of the expedition should approach by way of the Mohawk River in New York. Thus he could console himself, as well as Congress, that some of the preparations made for the spring invasion of Canada—especially the stores and boats laid up in Albany—would be used in the Indian expedition. Eventually, when it was decided to make a feint by way of Co'os on the upper Connecticut to deceive the British, some of the stores collected by Colonel Bedel's militia at Co'os would prove useful.

Thus was the transition made from the invasion of Canada to the Sullivan-Clinton expedition. From January until the early autumn of 1779, much of the quartermaster's time and correspondence would be spent on this expedition. On the expedition itself see below, Sullivan to NG, 12 May 1779.

3. Clinton later reported that as of 1 January 1779 he had 16,611 "effectives" in New York and adjacent posts, 13,830 of them fit for duty. He listed 5,071 fit for duty in Rhode Island. (Clinton, *American Rebellion*, p. 399n)

See Maps 2 and 3 for geographic references above.

From Colonel Israel Angell

[Warren, R.I., 5 January 1779. Has not heard from William Littlefield since he was granted leave at NG's request.[1] From excerpt in Charles Hamilton Catalog, no. 80, September 5, 1974.]

1. On Catharine Greene's brother William, see below, NG to Varnum, 9 February.

From the Board of War

[Philadelphia, 5 January 1779. Secretary Scull encloses list of articles ordered last April from France that should arrive before next campaign.[1] ALS (PPAmP) 1 p.]

1. The letter was probably handed to NG since he was at the War Office daily. The list has not been found.

From Colonel Udny Hay[1]

[Fishkill, N.Y., 5 January 1779. Has asked "the General" [McDougall] for court of inquiry on charges by forage department; needs hides for harness; debt owed artificers by former quartermaster general should be paid in clothes or money; needs money to pay General Gates's loan of $50,000;[2] Major Hale, who delivers this, will speak to NG on "subject of Cash with Eloquence, being truly sensible of the disadvantages arising from a want of it." ALS (PPAmP) 3 pp.]

1. For a biographical sketch of Udny Hay, see above, vol. 2:371–72n. We are indebted to Mr. Peter J. Price of Katonah, N.Y., for additional information on Hay. He was born in Scotland in 1739, attended Aberdeen University, and migrated to Quebec sometime in the 1760s, where he entered the timber business with his brother.

When NG resigned as quartermaster general, Hay also resigned. A friend and supporter of Gov. George Clinton of New York, he became state agent for New York, and there he remained throughout the war. In the 1780s he speculated in Vermont lands and became a resident of Vermont after 1790. During John Adams's administration, Hay was a leader of the Vermont antifederalists. In 1802 he was narrowly defeated in a race for Congress. He died in Burlington, Vt., in 1806.

2. See above, vol. 2: 418–19.

From Colonel Ephraim Bowen

Sr   Providence [R.I.] 6 Jan 1779

Inclosd are the Returns of Stores on hand and Men employ'd in the Department. As the Barracks are nearly Compleat at Tiverton &c I shall discharge all that can be Spared.[1]

General Sullivan absolutely Refuses to give any further Orders for the Payment of Damages, or losses, says it is not customary for the Commanding Officer of a Department to interfere in the least in the Q. M. Genl. Department, but that it is a Plan of yours to Saddle him. He directs me to acquaint you that he shall meddle no further in the Matter, and declares that General Washington Never gave Orders for the Payment for any thing lost. How true that Is, you are able to Determine.[2]

You'l Please to direct how I shall Proceed in this Matter, as I have Paid all but two or three in the way you formerly Pointed out.[3]

The Wages of the assistants in the Department are inadequate to the Services of many of them. If it could be Possible to give them Sixty Dollars per mo. I think it would be no more than Reasonable. I have Promisd those that are diserving as much as fifty, which I Beg you'l consent to.

As the Supply of Wood was uncertain in this town in Case the River Froze, or the Carting Bad, I applyd to the [R.I.] Council of War to direct a Sufficiency to be Brot in Weekly, which they Orderd to be done at Eighteen dollars per Cord. Just at the time a Bad Storm of Snow which Made the Roads impassable with Teams, Prevented the Supply for Several days, and as the inhabitants were destitute the Price Raised from 18 to 30, and even forty dollars. The Assembly Siting at this Time Pass'd an Act that the Army Should be Supplyd at the Current Going Price, and that wood, Teams, Horses, or any thing else Should not be taken from any Person without Paying him the Current Price.[4]

I askd Gen. Sullivan if I must give what was askd (which was the Currt Price) for wood &c. He declard I Should not, and that the Troops should take fuel wherever they could find it, with impunity till the Law was Repeald.

Nothing has been done Since. The Act will be Publishd in a few days when I will Send it you.

Benedict Arnold, 1741–1801, engraving by Benoit Louis Prevost
(*Courtesy of the National Portrait Gallery, Smithsonian Institution, Washington, D.C.*)

ADf (RHi).
1. Sullivan had stationed a Rhode Island battalion at Tiverton to protect the eastern shore of the Sakonnet River from enemy raids.
2. Bowen's dispute with Sullivan started in October 1778 and continued into February 1779. See above, Bowen to NG, 20 October; NG to Bowen, 27 October 1778; and below, Burnett to Bowen, 9 February 1779, and NG to Sullivan same day.
3. The reference is to NG's suggestion in his letter of 27 October 1778 that Bowen pay for the loss of impressed teams if Sullivan would not pay.
4. The Assembly action is discussed in Governor Greene to NG, 15 January, below.

Memorial of the Fishkill Carpenters and Wheelwrights[1]

Fish Kill [N.Y.] 6th January 1779

The Memorial of sundry Carpenters and Wheel Wrights, engaged in Public employment in Fish Kill Sheweth,

That your memorialists are for the greatest part, Refugees from the City of New York, who have been engaged in public service about two years, and some of us, since the beginning of the present War. That several of us have considerable large Families to support. That your Memorialist[s] cannot support themselves and Families on their present Pay, being only one dollar and an half per day, as every necessary of Life is risen to an enormous price. That your Memorialists are under the very disagreable necessity of leaving the service unless the Wages is raised, in some degree equal to the rise of the necessaries of Life.

Your Memorialists therefore humbly intreat your Honor, to take our Case under your serious consideration, and grant such relief in the premises as may be fit. And your Memorialists shall pray &c &c[2]

JOHN PARSELL	SQUIRE BAKER
THOMAS PARSELL	JOSIAH BALDWIN
ANDREW TEN EYCK	WILLM CRAWFERT
NEIL MC DONALD	JOHN LATIN
JOHN BELL	JOHN KINGSLAND
SAMUEL ROGERS	JAMES MC PHINNEY [?]
JAMES TUTTEN	WILLM PINE
WILLIAM L. PINFOLD	WILLM BURNS
JOHN CAMPBELL	JERRY TAYLOR[3]

DS (PCC, item 165, vol. 1: 83, DNA). Enclosed in Udny Hay's first letter of 9 January, below.
1. The memorial was addressed to the "Honble Major Genl Green."
2. The signers comprised less than a third of the carpenters and wheelwrights under Udny Hay at Fishkill. There were also bellows makers, plane makers, smiths, saddle and harness makers, sail and tent makers, and coopers—to the number of eighty. At Newburgh, Ft. Clinton, Kings Ferry, and Continental Village were another 350 under Hay, including—in addition to the categories above—masons, hostlers, straw cutters, batteaumen, and express riders. The fortification of West Point required many artificers. The complete roll is in Hay's report of 31 December 1778, PPAmP.

JANUARY 1779 [151]

The majority of artificers in the army were engaged in the construction of barracks, fortifications, and vessels, but they also made tools and equipment not available from private suppliers; those in the department of military stores made armaments. The organization of the artificers was a quasi-military one. Most were "privates" who took orders from superiors with titles such as foreman, captain, superintendent, lieutenant, or sergeant.

3. The artificers were given little relief by Congress and continued working at subsistence levels. As late as October 1780, the Board of War reported on the "absolute famine which now prevails" not only among the Artificers here but at all the posts at which they are employed." (*JCC*, 18: 969)

From William Smith

[Springfield, Mass., 8 January 1779. Is arranging at request of commissary for teams to haul not "less than 380" loads to Albany, including meat, salt, rum, and rice.[1] Impossible to engage wagoners at "26 2/3 dollars per Month on account of the Currency's being so depreciated." ALS (PPAmP) 2 pp.]

1. The supplies were being assembled for the Indian expedition. See note at NG to Washington, 5 January, above.

From Colonel Daniel Brodhead[1]

Dear General   Fort McIntosh[2] [Pa.] Jany 9th 1779
    I heartily wish It was in my Power to give you a shining Account of the Western Army, but as that is not the Case, beg you will excuse my Silence.
    General McIntosh is introducing a new regimental Plan, which being (as I apprehend) a partial one, may be injurious to the Service.
    I always understood that, Soldiers who were working as Artificers and Waggoners in your Department, were allowed something extraordinary for their Service. But General McIntosh insists on their Laboring early and late, and has forbid your Deputy in this Department, paying them a Shilling.[3] This I take to be Contrary to the customs of other Armies, everywhere, and has already caused some Desertion, and if practiced may be productive of much more. Besides I do not apprehend that Congress would Choose to have their Faithfull Soldiers so treated.
    I should therefore be exceedingly Oblidged to you for a line concerning the premises, for I have taken some pains to prevent murmurings amongst the Troops, but am at a loss what assurances to give them, and if it appears to you that it is right to deprive them of the additional pay, I will undertake for my own Men, that they shall not utter a whisper about it.[4] I have the Honor to be with the warmest Sentiments of Regard and Esteem your most Obedt Hble Servt

DANIEL BRODHEAD

ALS (OMC).
1. Commander of the Eighth Pennsylvania regiment.
2. The fort, some thirty miles northwest of Pittsburgh on the Ohio, had just been built. See Map 3.
3. McIntosh was unpopular with most of the officers in the vicinity of Ft. Pitt. At a court-martial of Archibald Steel (NG's deputy to whom Brodhead refers), McIntosh admitted he found great "opposition and indeed insult" to him among the members of the court. (Documents concerning the trial, dated 1 January 1779, are in the Washington Papers, DLC. The court unanimously found Steel innocent of McIntosh's charges. See Steel to NG, 20 February, below.)
   McIntosh met his match in Brodhead, who reported to Washington that McIntosh was "almost universally Hated by every man in this department both Civil and Military." (Brodhead to Washington, 16 January, Washington Papers: DLC) Washington tried to smooth matters over (15 February, ibid.), but complaints from others at Ft. Pitt continued to reach him as well as Congress. On 20 February, Congress relieved McIntosh of the command (ostensibly at his request) and asked Washington to replace him. Washington named Brodhead to the command. (*JCC*, 13: 213–14; Fitzpatrick, *GW*, 14: 194–95)
4. NG answered on 21 February, below.

From John Jacob Faesh[1]

Dear General   Mount Hope [N.J.] 9th Jany 1779
   By Colonl Abeels Team You'll receive Two Saddles of Venison, which I begg to accept of. I expect Some more; as Soon as they come in, I intend to do myself the pleasure of waiting on You and bring them along. Mrs Faesh joins with me in best Respect to the General and his good Lady. I remain with the greatest Regard Dear General Your most Obedt and humble Servt.

                                        JOHN JACOB FAESH

ALS (PPAmP).
1. NG had undoubtedly met Faesh through Lord Stirling, who had been associated with Faesh in the iron business. Faesh had come from Switzerland in 1770 and was the leading iron master of his day. As owner of the Mount Hope Furnace, which turned out cannon and shot as well as general ironwork for the army, he was one of the most prominent citizens of Morristown. He had originally spelled his name Faesch— the spelling used on earlier leases and deeds. Boyer, *Early Forges*, discusses him at length, pp. 23, 33, 44, 95, 120, 136–40.

From Colonel Udny Hay

Sir   Fish Kill [N.Y.] 9th Jan 1779
   Since Major Hale's departure from this I find the very extraordinary price of ten Dollars and a half per day offerd to Smiths and Carpenters is like to deprive me a second time of some of the most usefull men at this Post. Our Wheelwrights without something is done for them are determin'd to leave me, as are a considerable part of our Smiths, neither can I blame the men for accepting a good offer when in their power [?] but cannot help thinking they might with proper care have been engaged at a much lower rate. Mr Simmons has a sec-

ond time greatly depreciated our Money by the offer of so extravagant Wages, and [at the ?] same time raisd such a spirit of Discontent amongst those Artificers who remain that they do not the least part of their Duty with any degree of Cheer fullness.[1] In short, Sir, consider but the natural consequences which must arise from so sudden an addition of nearly five hundred per Cent to the Wages of those men who chuse to leave one Post to go to another, and you will readily conclude that my situation at present is extremely disagreeable. You may rest assured it is even suspected that I pockett *at least a part* of the Wages, which, as they say, I detain from the Artificers here and which by leaving this Post they can easily gett elsewhere. I am much affraid too it will greatly raise the price of our Best men who are to be engaged for next Campaign.

If Artificers must be had, and cannot be obtaind but at so extravagant a rate, had we not better gett them from the Regiments, and endeavour to fill up their places with a part of the Money which on this other plan of raising them the Continent must pay?[2] Enclosed I send you a memorial from some of the men in this Department addressed to you; to which lett me beg you will give an answer as soon as possible.[3]

I have in store a considerable quantity of Cordage; much more will probably be wanted to the northward. As we have a good rope walk erected within twelve Miles of this, and Mr Ivers is by contract oblidged to furnish us with about fifteen Tons more, should be glad to have your orders what sizes you think most necessary to make.

I have since my being here observed a very great loss arising to the public from a want of a proper public Tanner and Currier. I know a man who I believe is thoroughly capable of carrying on that business, and I fancy would either agree for so much pay per Month or take it by the job, whether this matter is carried on under the Direction of the Commissary of hides [or] under mine is to me totally indifferent but am thoroughly convinced if properly managed a great [dollar ?] benefit would arise therefrom. Be so good as give me your opinion on this subject.[4]

I must likewise mention to you the necessity I shall be under of paying higher Wages [to] the Country Teams than I have hither to done. Lett me beg you will forward the inclosed for Miss Van Wyck when convenient.

U H

The Commissaries pay at the rate of five and four pence per Mile for every five barrells of flour. We pay at the rate of five Dollars per Day, nor have we paid so much till very lately.

Having had occasion to write his Excellency the General upon some other business, I begd to know his determination about compleating the Works at West Point next summer.[5] Should that be determind on, a number of materials ought to be gott ready by me this spring. I am of opinion a very large number of Masons will be necessary. Be so good as lett me know your opinion on this subject.[6] We are or rather shall be in much want of saw Mill files, a Dozen of pair of scale [?] beams and the same number of steel yards[7] would likewise be necessary, if you think there will be much business this way next Campaign.

The saw Mill files I must beg you will order on as soon as possible from Philadelphia, and the other articles if you think they will be wanted.

I hope before the receipt of this, Major Hale will be on his voyage homeward bound and loaded with Money.[8] I am with due respect, Sir, Your most obed humble Sert

UDNY HAY

PS Since writing have a second address presented me which I enclose. If we raise the mens Wages, we depreciate the money. If we do not, the Post will suffer.

ALS (PPAmP).
1. Probably William Simmons. See Governor Clinton to General McDougall, 6 April 1779, regarding complaints about Simmons in Orange County—across the Hudson from Fishkill. (Clinton, *Papers*, 4: 693) In the next sentence Hay speaks of those men who were hired by Simmons at an increase of "nearly" 500 percent. If his men had been getting $1.50 per day (as they say in their memorial of 6 January, above) the *addition* would be 600 percent.
2. NG's answer to this query has not been found. As noted by Colonel Brodhead, 9 January, above and NG to Brodhead, 21 February, below, artificers were sometimes taken from regiments, but Hay undoubtedly needed many more than could be drawn from the regiments along the Hudson.
3. See memorial of 6 January, above. In his postscript Hay refers to a second memorial, but only one has been found.
4. He answered Hay about the tanyard on 10 February, below.
5. Hay's letter of 5 January is in the Washington Papers, DLC. Washington's answer has not been found, but he had consistently stressed the importance of West Point.
6. NG's response has not been found.
7. Steelyards were used for weighing.
8. NG did not receive this letter or the second one of this date below until well into February. In a note of 14 January from Middlebrook (below) Major Forsyth said Major Hale was delivering the letters to Philadelphia, but when Hale returned to Fishkill he discovered them, he wrote, in "my Portmanteau with my Cloaths." He called it a "most Shamefull piece of carelessness" for which he apologized. (D. Hale to Forsyth, 29 January 1779, Greene Papers, PPAmP)

Deputies and Agents in The Quartermaster Department

List of the Deputy Quarter Masters General and other Persons employed to make Purchases in the Quarter Master Generals Department, with the Terms on which they are severally employed; and the Sums of Money they respectively stand charged with January 9, 1779.

	Sums Charged in Dollars
Colo Clement Biddle, Commissary of Forage. He is to superintend the purchasing, collecting and issuing of Forage, with power to employ the necessary officers under him on such reasonable Terms as he can agree for. He is to receive for his own Trouble and private Expences three quarters of one percent on all his disbursements, and six Rations per day..............................	3,104,245

Pennsylvania

Robert Lettis Hooper Esqr, D.Q.M.G. for Northampton and part of Bucks in Pennsylvania and Sussex in New Jersey, 2 percent on his disbursements	897,353 30/90
John Davis Esqr, D.Q.M.G. for the West side of Susquehanna to the Allegany Mountains, 50 Dollars per Month and 1 1/2 per Cent	1,017,050
Archibald Steel Esqr D.Q.M.G. for Fort Pitt and the West side of the Allegany Mountain, 50 dollars per m[o], usual Rations and 1 1/2 per ct	740,000
Col: Jacob Morgan D.Q.M.G., the like pay &c........	483,000
George Ross Jun Esqr D.Q.M.Genl, part of Lancaster, 50 Dollars per Month, usual Rations and 1 1/2 per Cent	642,000
Cornelius Cox Esqr, D.Q.M.G, part of Lancaster, the like Terms, but he Accounts thro' Mr. Ross	
Robert Patton Esqr, D.Q.M.G., part of Lancaster, 50 Dollars per Month, usual Rations and 1 1/2 per Cent	341,000
Mr. Adam Zanzinger of Lancaster, an occasional purchaser of Ironmongery &c, 1 1/2 per Ct	13,360
John Mitchell Esqr D.Q.M.G., Philadelphia 50 Dolls per m[o], usual Rations and 1 1/2 per ct	1,468,868, 70/90
Cornelius Sheriff Esqr D.Q.M.G. to the division under the Command of Genl Smallwood, and for Chester Co'ty, 75 dollars per Mo, 6 Rations per day, and 1 1/2 per Ct on all Disbursements, except those for the Division to which he belonged ..	156,200
Hugh Runyan Esqr D.Q.M.G., part of Bucks Co'ty, 50 Dollars per Mo, 4 Rations and 1 1/2 per Cent ...	72,200

Col. William Cook D.Q.M.G., Northumberland, 50
Dollars per Mo, 4 Rations and 1 1/2 per Cent   63,000

Maryland

James Calhoun Esqr D.Q.M.G., Western shore, the
usual pay and Rations and 1 1/2 per Ct 274,210
Charles Beatty Esqr D.Q.M.G., Frederick County, 50
Dollars per Mo, 4 rations and 1 1/2 per Ct 73,000
Henry Hollingsworth D.Q.M.G., Head of Elk &c
[i.e., 50 dollars per mo, usual rations, and] 1 1/2
per Cent 315,688

Virginia

William Finnie Esqr. For the State, usual pay and
Rations and 1 1/2 per cent 170,000
Johnston Smith Esqr, Contractor for purchasing
Horses, Waggons &c in the back Counties. His
business ended last Summer, but the Accounts
not yet settled. Terms not exactly ascertained 274,000
Joseph Mitchell, ordered to erect Stables and provide
Forage for Horses out of Service in Berkly Co'ty
on Potommack. Terms not ascertained   7,720

Delaware

Francis Wade Esqr D.Q.M.G. for the State, 50 Doll's
per Mo, 4 rat's and 1 1/2 per Cent 228,837 30/90

New Jersey

Moore Furman Esqr D.Q.M.G. for the State except
Sussex County, 2 per Cent, including the pay of
his principal Assistant 1,102,257 11/90

New-York

Morgan Lewis Esqr, D.Q.M.G. Albany and Northern
District, 1 1/2 per Cent 359,000
Col. Udmy [Udny] Hay, D.Q.M.G. Fishkill &ca, usual
pay and Rations and 1/2 per Cent 591,419 45/90
It was expected that the Expenditures in Col
Hays district would have been proportionally
larger, and therefore his Commissions were fixed
at a lower rate, with a private Agreement however that they should amount to a certain Sum.

Connecticut

Nehemiah Hubbard D.Q.M.G. for the State, 1 1/2 per
Ct 483,600
Ozias Bingham, received for his district 10,000

Rhode Island
Ephraim Bowen D.Q.M.G. for the State 1 1/2 per ct . . . 471,000

Massachusetts
William Smith Esqr D.Q.M.G., Springfield and 30
miles round it East of the river, 75 Doll's per Mo,
6 Rations, and 1 1/2 per Ct 162,000
Thomas Chase Esqr D.Q.M.G. for the rest of the
State, 1 1/2 per Cent 512,000
Messrs Otis & Andrews Merch'ts in Boston, Agents
for purchasing divers Articles of Merchandize
per order. Their commissions not settled but they
ch'd [charged] 2 1/2 per Ct 197,000
Jacob Greene Esqr of Rhode Island, on the like Terms
with Otis and Andrews 120,000
Col: James Abeel Superintendant of Camp Equipage
&ca Qu'r Masters Stores, and the Manufacturing
Tents &c. Commissions not to exceed £ 1200 per
Annum   112,000
Major Benja. G Eyre, Superintendant of Ship Car-
penters and Boat Builders, 100 Dollars per Mo
and 2 1/2 per Cent on Disbursements 173,950
Mr James Davenport, D.Q.M.G. for the March of the
Convention Troops from Massachusetts to Vir-
ginia. Terms not ascertained 22,920
Joseph Webb Esqr, Connecticut, to purchase Tents
and Portmanteaus 4,000

With most of these it has been expressly stipulated and with all of
them understood that the persons under them are to be paid by
Salary and not to draw any Commissions.

The Deputies and Assistants for merely Military Purposes, Store
Keepers, Clerks &c are all on Monthly pay with the usual Allowance
for rations, and it has been given in Charge to every Deputy not to
keep any Clerk or Assistant on pay longer than the Service shall absolutely require.

Many of the Deputy Quarter Masters General are employed also
by Col. Biddle in the Forage Department and it is supposed they draw
the same Commissions on that Branch as they do on other Business in
the Departmt.[1]

D (PCC, item 59, vol. 2: 165, DNA).
1. The author of the document is not known.

From Colonel Udny Hay

[Fishkill, N.Y., 9 January 1779. Has learned that Washington has ordered clothing sent from Hartford to Fishkill. Hopes his letter of same
day [above] has convinced NG that artificers who have remained at
the post deserve encouragement by receiving some of the clothes and
that NG will intercede with Washington to this end.[1] ALS (PPAmP) 2
pp.]

1. As noted at Hay's letter above, this letter was not delivered to NG until February. Meanwhile McDougall had asked Washington for clothing for the artificers but
was told it was the province of the quartermaster. (McDougall's of 19 January is in the
Washington Papers, DLC; Washington's answer is in Fitzpatrick, GW, 14:85.) In a letter
to Hay of 10 February below, NG did approve their receiving clothing.

To Doctor John Morgan

Sir   Philadelphia January 10 1779
    I have receiv'd your several Letters requesting a certificate re-
specting your conduct as Director General and also of the state of the
General Hospitals in the Campaigns of 1775 and 76.[1]
    This address was not a little surprising and unexpected as you in
your publication in 77 seem to hold me up in the light of an accuser.[2]
However as you have thought proper to make the application I shall
not refuse a compliance.
    The Hospitals that were in the Neighbourhood of Boston, I was
very little acquainted with. I was remote from them and on an advanced Post within Cannon shot of the Enemy; which prevented my
visiting them very often. I think I never was at them more than once
or twice and therefore cannot pretend to judge of the care and attention that were paid to the sick or of the oeconemy established in them.
But as there were but few complaints against the Hospital department
while the army lay before Boston I immagine there was no want of
care or oeconemy.
    It is true there was some murmuring among the Soldiers about
going into the General Hospitals and there was some clamour among
the Regimental Surgeons respecting the Institution but they were not
considerable.
    When the Army movd to N York the scene changed. It had been
hastily drawn together, a great part of it was composd of the Militia of
the Country, who not being acquainted with that mode of living to
which they were there subjected to, and exposd to severe duty at the
same Time soon grew sickly. In this state of things complaints were
multiplied and the sick in many instances sufferd not a little.
    From the clamours that began to rage and from a desire to con-
tribute all that lay in my power to the comfort and accomodation of

the Sick I solicited you to establish an Hospital upon Long Island for the benefit of the Troops of which I had the command. This Hospital I visited almost every day and can speak with great certainty from my own observation that the Sick in it were well accomodated and provided for; and that your directions given to Doctor Warren (so far as I was a judge) appeared to be well calculated to promote good government and proper oeconemy.

You may remember I called upon you while I had the command on Long Island for the plan of the General Hospital. This I did as well to satisfy myself of your proper line of duty as to convince the commanding officers of Regim'ts that you had not such extensive powers as they seemd to conceive off.

It was from reading the Hospital establishment and finding you limited in your powers and seeing the distresses of the Regimental sick without the possibillity of a remedy, that I was inducd me to write to the General of the absolute necessity of some further provision being made for the Regimental Surgeons and the Hospitals under their care.

I do not recollect at this distance of Time that there were any complaints of the Sick suffering much in the General Hospitals. The complaints and sufferings of the sick were principally among the Regimental Hospitals, for want of medicine and other necessaries suitable to their situation and condition. And here I shall just observe that the sufferings of the sick must have been much greater than they were had it not been for the plan of furnishing the Regimental sick with Money to the amount of the value of their Rations, to enable those who had the care of them to provide such Articles as their several cases requird.

I remember great complaints were brought against you for withholding Medicine from the Regimental Surgeons. It was said you pleaded in justification of your self that you were not authorisd to do it as Director General, neither were your Stores equal to the demands made upon you and that if you had issued agreeable to the applications that had been made the General Hospital must have been without a proper assortment of Medicine.

However just your remarks, they were unsatisfactory to the army and gave rise to a great deal of censure and furnished a handle to insinuate that you were content so the sick did but die by rule.

It was about this Time, that I wrote to Congress from Fort Lee urging the necessity of enlargeing your powers, as well to give you an opportunity to silence the clamour against you as to do justice to the Sick.[3] I confess I felt the greatest anxiety upon the ocasion, not altogether on account of the sufferings of the present sick, but for fear of the disagreeable effects it might have upon the recruiting services.

On this account I could have wished you to have departed from the plan of the Hospital and to have rested the justification of your conduct on the necessity of the case and the call of Humanity that seemd to demand the measure.

From the little opportunity I had to observe your conduct I believe there was no want of assiduity or attention to your business. But with respect to the instructions given to the Surgeons of the Hospitals or the management or oeconomy observed in them, I am too little acquainted with the subject to give any opinion upon the matter.

With respect to the clamours of the Regimental Surgeons against you. I believe they originated rather in the Institution than from any personal ill treatment; as they made a confession to this import before a Board of General Officers that were directed by his Excellency to enquire into the matter, at N York.

I have not Time to go more largely into the Subject but I believe the state of the quarter Masters department in some part of the Campaign of 76 contributed not a little to the distress of yours. I have heard it frequently said you were very industrious in collecting Stores at Boston and I have heard General Knox repeatedly say you were diligent in saving them on the retreat from York Island; and that you exposd yourself not a little in the business.[4] I am Sir Your most humble Servt

N GREENE

ADfS (MiU-C). A printed version of the recipient's copy (*PMHB*, 43 [1919]: 77) is essentially the same but has been mistranscribed in places and changed somewhat in editing.

1. The only one found is dated 5 October 1778, which is abstracted above, vol. 2: 541. The subject of that letter was treated in vol. 1: 251n, 283–84n, and 312–13n. The letter was a long and somewhat self-serving defense of Morgan's tenure as director general and physician-in-chief of hospitals during 1775 and 1776. Morgan wrote in response to the appointment of a congressional committee on 18 September 1778 to inquire into his complaints, an inquiry that Morgan had sought since he was summarily dismissed in January 1777. As part of his defense, he asked NG for "a certificate of what you know of my Conduct, as Truth and Candour may authorize, for the manifestation of my Guilt or Innocence." He asked further for NG's general testimony of his "Humanity or Inhumanity to the Sick" and specifically whether he, Morgan, "appeared negligent or attentive to Duty; Upright or Dishonest."

2. In a so-called *Vindication* that Morgan published in 1777, he made a bitter, unfair attack on NG. As noted above (vol. 1: 284n) Morgan had been so hurt by his unexplained termination that he struck out at several people who had supported him. NG's decision to defend Morgan in this letter is a tribute to his objectivity as well as willingness to forgive.

3. This letter, of 10 October 1776, is printed above, vol. 1: 311–12.

4. The committee reported on 12 June 1779 that Morgan had conducted himself "ably and faithfully," and Congress the same day resolved that it was "satisfied with the conduct of Dr. John Morgan while acting as director general and physician in chief." (*JCC*, 14: 724)

From Lieutenant Baxter How[1]

[Pluckemin, N.J., 10 January 1779. "As the time is at Last Come"[2] for tents to be returned, asks where they should be taken. If to Trenton, he could bring back rum, "a Service to the Brigade." ALS (PPAmP) 1 p.]

1. How was brigade quartermaster in the artillery at Pluckemin. See Map 5.
2. The men were "at Last" in huts.

From Samuel A. Otis

Dear Sir   Boston Jany 10th ⟨1779⟩
With the strongest impressions of ⟨affection⟩ I take this first opp[ortunit]y to inform you my good friend ⟨and⟩ partner is no more. Returning to Town last Evening a friend took up one of his pistols which had been charged so long it was forgotten, and upon some observation relative to its ornament, Mr Andrews reached out his hand to take a nearer view, when unhappily it discharged. He was sitting in his usual agreeable manner, in Conversation with his amiable wife and unfortunate friend, when the fatal Shaft flew, pierced his head, and he expired without a groan or convulsion. The Community have lost a most valuable member by this sad accident, but his friends who knew his worth receive a dreadful Shock. Colo H, the unhappy Gentm in whose hand the ps [piece] discharged, loved him as his Soul, and I doubt not your manly breast will indulge a Sigh at this Catastrophe[1] [damaged] [there]fore proceed to observe that death haveing ⟨Dissolved the⟩ partnership which would otherwise have [damaged]able, the business devolves upon me and which ⟨I shall⟩ continue to execute in relation [?] to Morgan Lewis Esqr[2] and otherwise until further order, which shall be punctually executed by Your Most Humble Sert

SAM. A OTIS

ALS (PPAmP). Original torn in places; portions in angle brackets taken from a different version (possibly a draft by an assistant) written on the back of Otis's letter of 14 January, below.
1. NG had probably become acquainted with Andrews during a short stay in Boston in September 1778.
2. As deputy quartermaster at Albany, Lewis had made purchases from the partners.

From the Board of War

[War Office, Philadelphia, 11 January 1779. Board believes a deputy quartermaster should "reside at or near the Barracks built for the

Troops of the Convention [army] in Albemarle County Virginia." NG should direct him to provide barrackmaster with fuel.[1] Signed, Richard Peters. ALS (PPAmP) 1 p.]

1. NG's orders to William Finnie, the DQMG in Virginia, have not been found. For Finnie's problems with the Convention army, see his letter of 11 February, below.

From James Thompson[1]

Sir   Middlebrook [N.J.] 11 Jany 1779
Yours of the 7 Inst. I this Day receiv'd and Shall pay due attention to the Contents.[2]

I have us'd every means in my power for the preservation of the Cattle and have Sent of [off] as fast as I could collect, you will see by the inclosd return the number in Camp. The Pennsylvanians have the greatest number but them I expect to send out on Wednesday. I expect we shall be able to get Waggons in the Neighbourhood Sufficient to do the Brigad duty. For Extras I shall be poorley of [off] as those detaind for that purpose is mostly wore down. I fear we Shall want a much greater number of Waggons than I expected. Thers hardley one now fit for duty, and their being repaird with Stuff Just cut [i.e., green wood] will answer very Littel purpose, but even in that thers no prospect, the Season fast advancing and the Artificers otherwise imployed. Would recommend a much Larger number of new Waggons spoke for. And unless thers Harness Makers Oyl and Brushes sent from Philade[lphia] immediately, we must Loose all the Geers [i.e., harness]. They were turnd in when wet and muddy, then Frose and now beginning to thaw that Unless they are immediately washed and oyld they will wrot. I have Spoke to the DCG [Deputy Commissary General] of Hides for oyl but he cant tell when I can be supplyed. I have a great number of Waggoners now Idol whose times is near Expir'd and wont engage that I would employ in claening the Geers had I the materials for them to Work with.

I Shall miss no oppertunity of giving you advice of eny thinge material that may occur in my Dept while your Absent. From your most Obed Hum servt

JAMES THOMPSON

ALS (PPAmP).
1. Washington had appointed Thompson to succeed the incompetent Joseph Thornburgh as wagonmaster general on 22 December 1777—just as the army was making camp at Valley Forge. Thompson soon brought some order to the chaotic department, but by March he was so discouraged that he asked to be relieved of his command. (See his letter to Committee at Camp, 2 February 1778, PCC, item 192: p. 385, DNA; and Thompson to Clement Biddle, 2 March 1778, Washington Papers, DLC.) When NG took over as quartermaster general a few days later, he persuaded

Thompson to remain, which he did for as long as NG remained quartermaster. He received NG's heartfelt appreciation for having conducted one of the most trying jobs in the army "with ability and . . . the strictest honor and integrity." (NG to Thompson, 2 October 1780, below)

2. Letter not found.

From Samuel Barrett & Co.

[Boston, 12 January 1779. While lamenting the loss of "so capable, so honest, so generous and active and assiduous a Person as Mr. Andrews" they assume NG will want to replace him soon. Hope NG will "excuse so early an Application" for Andrews's place. Their references include General Heath and Commissary Wadsworth.[1] LS (PPAmP) 2 pp.]

1. On the death of Benjamin Andrews, see above, Otis to NG, 10 January. NG answered 9 February, below.

From John Erskine[1]

[Morristown, N.J., 12 January 1779.[2] On NG's orders he encloses express riders' accounts and a "Copy of Tavern Rates in Philad'a copied by a very Honest Fellow." Since their pay is $900 per month and expenses average $50 daily while traveling, their net is inadequate "to Recompence for the Service and Risk of their Horse, and wear of apparell."[3] ALS (PHi) 1 p.]

1. Erskine was in charge of the express riders.
2. The letter is mistakenly dated 1778.
3. On the express riders' compensation, see below, petition of 22 February.

From General James M. Varnum

Sir   Warwick [R.I.] 13th January 1779

Agreeable to your Directions Mr Mitchell has been removed, and Capt Tew put in his Place.[1] A most excellent Quarter Master! The Enemy on Rhode Island have been short of Provision. Two Days since a Fleet of thirty odd Sale came into this Port, mostly small Craft. Whether they bro't Provision or not, we have not learnt. The General Assembly have passed an Act empowering the Judges of the Superior Court and Magistrats to empress, after an Hearing, Articles for the Army, and making those who take, thro' any other Channel liable to an Action of Trespass.[2] General Sullivan is very angry and, I fear, there will be an open Quarrel between them. In consequence of this Act, every Article has raised one Hundred per Cent. I lament the Situation most of the Posts must be reduced to. They are without

Wood and Forage. Warren and Bristol I supplied In Time. The Brigade is disciplined and it is happy.

What will be the Event of the present Evils? Luxury, Chicanery and Dissipation of every kind prevail! The public Currency is of no Estimation, and the Troops, I fear, will soon resent the Injury. Wood Thirty odd Dollars pr Cord! Corn fourteen Dollars pr Bushell! Other Things in Proportion! Prices continually increasing, and the Army despised!

In November last I wrote the then President of Congress [Henry Laurens] for a Dismission from the Service. I have not obtained an Answer. This is cruel, as it leaves me at an Uncertainty how to dispose my Assignations! Should you be in Philadelphia when this reaches you, I shall esteem it an Act of Friendship if you'll mention it to the present Maximus [John Jay]; that I may know the Intentions of Congress.[3]

Mrs Varnum is well. My Brigade well provided and in perfect Health. Give my best Respects to Mrs Greene, and receive the sincerest Esteem of your most obdt humble Servt

J M VARNUM

ALS (PPAmP).
1. William Tew, a Rhode Islander, was in Col. Israel Angell's Continental regiment. (Heitman, *Register*)
2. See below, Governor Greene to NG, 15 January.
3. It is not known whether NG spoke to Jay, but in response to another letter from Varnum to Congress on 12 February, Congress accepted his resignation on 5 March 1779. (*JCC*, 13: 274) Two months later, Rhode Island named him major general in command of the state militia. (Bartlett, *Records*, 8: 544) In 1781 he was chosen as a delegate to Congress.

From Major Robert Forsyth

Dear Sir   Camp Middle Brook [N.J.] 14th Janry [17]79

The inclosed Letters from Colo Hay came to hand last Evening. They will be handed you by Major Hale who came in this Morning.[1]

Our Horses are all gone now except those with the Maryland Troops, who are exceedingly dilatory in the Huting Business. I have given Major Hale Mr Duers draft on Abraham P. Lott for 6,000 Dollars. It is of no use to me and Colo Hay is in much want. I hope you will do something respecting the Brigade Quarter Masters, they are much dissatisfied at present,[2] their Extra Pay is so small, and their being obliged to do duty for two other Departments for which they received no compensation. Please present my respectfull Complimts to your Lady. Your very Humble Sert

ROBT FORSYTH

ALS (PPAmP).
1. As seen in note, Hay to NG, #1 of 9 January, above, Hale inadvertently carried the letters back to Fishkill.
2. NG did not include brigade quartermasters in his recommendations below of 15 April to Jay. Undoubtedly he thought their pay should be considered along with line officers in the brigades.

From Samuel A. Otis

[Boston, 14 January 1779. Marine committee has cloth and anchors; should get them from the committee instead of buying. Preparing clothing and bags. Tents sent to Springfield. Everything is "intollerable dear, and what is more mortifying is upon the Rise." ALS (PPAmP) 2 pp.]

From Colonel William Palfrey

Dear General   Marlborough [Mass.] 14th Jany 1779
     Since my arrival in this part of the World, I have spent most of my time with my Family in the Country, where I can very seldom meet with an opportunity of forwarding a Letter to Camp, which I hope will in some measure apologize for my not writing to you sooner.
     A Report prevaild in Boston, some time ago, that you had been Kidnapped by the Tories and carried Prisoner to New York. This Report remaining uncontradicted for a while, gave great uneasiness to your Friends, but I have lately had the pleasure of hearing (by an officer from Camp) that you were safe and well, and still out of their Clutches.
     I have just returned from spending a Fortnight with our worthy Friend General [John] Hancock, who often mention'd you with great pleasure. He has been laid up with the Gout, but is so far recovered as to be able to attend the Assembly, which is now sitting. There seems to be a Coolness between him and General Gates, Neither they or their Ladies have visited each other. Genl G. seems not very well pleased with his Situation, and I beleive wishes most heartily to return to his Sabine Fields.[1] His [military] Family have been involved in Quarrells, almost ever since they have been in the place, which bid fair to proceed to such a Length that the Civil Authority thought proper to interpose. Mr Bob. Gates and Mr Carter have fought but it proved a bloodless encounter.[2]
     The Marquis has been on board the *Alliance* waiting above a Week in Nantasket Road for a Wind. I am informed they are to sail this Day.[3] The Winter has been uncommonly severe hitherto.
     All the Necessaries of Life are risen to such a Pitch as will probably, in a short time, totally stagnate the Circulation of Continental

Currency, unless Congress adopts some very spirited and decisive measures to support it. What a pity is it that some Locke or Colbert, could not start up and teach us the Art of Financing. An Art that we have been greatly deficient in, and ever shall be, so long as we want the foundation of a permanent, fixed medium to act upon: Had we proceeded with the Caution recommended in the good Book, of "first sitting down and counting the Cost," we should not perhaps have been involved in our present inextricable Labyrinth of Difficulties.

When I had the pleasure of conversing with you last, I told you of my intention to quit the Service; I do not see how it is possible for me to continue in it on the present footing, or indeed on any footing whatever. My Family is large, My Children all Young, Mrs Palfrey not of a very hearty Constitution and unable to support the fatigues, which a constant attention to provide for so many naturally requires—besides, I have not "a male in the House, not so much as a mouse" to assist her. Therefore I think, after four Years Service, in which I have spent great part of my Original Stock for the support of my Family, it is high time for me to turn my attention to some way of Business to prevent my being a Beggar, which must be the Case if I should continue in my present office another Year. Accordingly, as soon as I can place my Family in Boston, which will be in April next, I shall repair to Philadelphia, settle my Accounts, and resign my Commission.[4]

This Post will probably convey to you an account of the sudden Death of poor Mr Andrews, who last Saturday Evening was, by accident, Shot thro' the Head with a Pistol. This melancholy Event will probably oblige you to appoint some other Person to act as your Agent in Boston, and I beg leave to offer my Service to you for that purpose. As I have long been acquainted with Business in the Town I flatter myself I can serve you as well as any Person in it. I should therefore be much obliged to you to favor me with a Line on this Subject by the very first opportunity, and send a Duplicate for fear of Miscarriage.[5]

I had the pleasure of seeing a *plain* Brother of yours in Boston, who told me Mrs Green was with you, to whom I beg my best Compliments as also to General Knox and his Lady, to your worthy Assistants and all other my good Friends in Camp, particularly the General's Family, and beleive me most affectionately and truly Your Friend and humble Servant

WM PALFREY

For your amusement I send you a Price Curr[en]t of sundry Articles in Boston.[6]

ALS (PPAmP). An ADF at MH differs only in minor details.

1. Gates was not only unhappy to be at an inactive post, but in replacing the popular General Heath, he was not as warmly welcomed by Bostonians as he expected. (Nelson, *Gates*, p. 205)

2. Robert Gates was the general's son; his opponent was a friend of Gates's former aide, James Wilkinson, who had lost favor for his part in the "Conway Cabal." (Ibid.)

3. Lafayette did sail that day. Although the *Alliance* was buffeted by severe storms and threatened by mutiny, it made record time. (Gottschalk, *Lafayette*, p. 322; Idzerda, *Lafayette*, 2: 225–28)

4. Despite Palfrey's intentions of resigning as paymaster general, a post he had held since April 1776, he remained until 1780. He was appointed consul to France that year but was drowned when his ship was lost at sea. His grandson was the noted historian and editor, John Gorham Palfrey, incorrectly listed above, vol. 2: 109, as William Gorham Palfrey.

5. See NG's answer 11 February, below.

6. A short list that contains prices of such items as meat, butter, rum, sugar, and flour.

From Governor William Greene of Rhode Island

Dear Sir   Warwick [R.I.] 15th January 1779

With much Pleasure I received your favor by Coll Morgan a Gentleman who appears fully to answer my expectation after reading your favor.[1] I believe he is likely to accomplish his business without much difficulty.

I am very sorry to hear that after we have receiv'd so many blessings from the Supreme being of the universe, that luxury shou'd make its appearance instead of that Virtue which is really necessary to confirm and Support our Independance. For wherever luxury gits the better of Virtue it naturally tends to factions and every other evil Practice that will tend to sap the foundation of Our liberty. But such is our make that we cannot answer to Designs of Providence without his heavy Judgments; but it does really appear to me unaccountable that after the amazing Difficulties that Thousands who are now existing that have under gone every thing except the Agonies of Death, shou'd be so void of reflection as take to such Courses as tends to bring on the same Difficulties. The General Assembly who set the 28th of last month, among other things enacted that for the future, the Proper Officers, who are to see that the Army is properly provided with necessaries are to apply to persons who they think are likely to be possessed of them. And in case of his refusal to dispose of them at the going price, the Officer is then to report him to the Governor, Deputy Govr., Assistant or Justice of the Sup[erio]r Court, who are to Issue a Citation to the Sheriff, his Deputy or either of the Town serjeants to Cite such persons to appear before either of said Officers to assign his reasons why the articles apply'd for shou'd not be taken for the use of the Army, and if it shall appear that he had the articles to spare without great Ill conveniency, he is then to deliver them to the Officer who is to pay the going price therefore and the owner of the goods is to pay all reasonable Cost.

This act seems not to be Agreable to General Sullivan and what will be the Effects of it I am not as yet able to determine. The most difficulty seems to be, to find a Price that will go in such a way as to give general Satisfaction.[2] Query whether that can possablely be the case so long as Congress keeps the paper mill going? I really cant but wonder when I consider how amazingly the Currency has depreciated that Congress has not taken up the matter so as to recommend to the United States to Collect a sufficient sum by Tax to defray the expence of the Insuing Campaign, as it is my candit Opinion it is out of the Power of Congress to emit any sum that will add to the Value of what is already emitted. I am sencible there being such a demand for cash it makes it very difficult to stop the Mill of a Sudden, but had Congress about eght months past as I suppose that to be about the time they order[ed] the additional quantity that now Circulates order'd, or rather recommended a Tax about this time to have been paid in, it appears to me they might have put a Stop to any further emission for the present. I mention this to communicate my Sentiments to you who perhaps if of the same sentiment it may happen in your way to be Instrumental of something of the kind to take place.

Your youngest Child has been much Indispoz'd but is now bravely. The other I have not heard but that she is as well as common.[3]

I have been told that William Littlefields absence being so long has Occation'd some unesiness among the Officers of the Chore [Corps?] in which he belongs, and that he is left out in the pay Abstract. I thought it my duty to mention this that he might conduct as he thinks proper.[4] My Wife and Children desire their love to you, your Spous and Billy and please to except the same from your Sincere Friend and Kinsman.

W GREENE

ALS (PPAmP).
    1. Letter not found.
    2. The act was repealed at the session that began on 19 January. (Bartlett, *Records*, 8: 496)
    3. Cornelia was four months old; her sister Martha (Patty) was almost two
    4. On William Littlefield, nephew of the governor's wife and brother of Catharine Greene, see NG to Varnum, 9 February, below.

From Thomas Menzies

Sir   Fredericksburgh [N.Y.][1] Janry 16th 1779

While the troops lay at this place it was my lot to have Genl. Wayne's division, a Brigade Commanded by Colo'l Clark and Nixon's

Brigade Encamp'd on my farm, and the damage I have thereby sustain'd is Very great. Twenty four hundred and Eighty five Rods of my
fence was burnt which amounted to Upwards of thirty thousand
Rails, and all the Valuable timber on my farm distroy'd. I Enquir'd of
Colo'l Pettit before the troops March'd if he paid such damages. He
told me that he was not Authorized to pay for fencing or Rails, but for
what green timber the troops used he Would pay, and directed me to
get some reputable Inhabitants to View and acertain the Quantity and
Appraise the Same, which I accordingly have done. I have been since
told that I Ought to have got Vouchers from the Brigade Qr Msr but
this I was ignorant off, bisides it was imposible to Acertain the Quantity before the troops removed as They were dayly Cuting and hauling Wood. The Certificate of Appraisement has been presented to
Colo'l Hay but he says, tho' it is reasonable it Ought to be paid, that
he is Not Authorized to pay any such demand without an Order from
You Sir. I am therefore under the necessity of Applying to you (for
which freedom Sir I hope you will pardon me) and have sent the Appraisement by the bearer not doubting you will think it Just to pay it.[2]
I am with the Greatest Respect Sir Your Most Obedient Hum Servant

THOS MENZIES

ALS (PPAmP).
1. The army camped there from September to late November 1778.
2. NG's answer is lost, but in it he informed Menzies that he was not authorized to
pay damages. (Menzies to Governor Clinton, 9 August 1779, Clinton, *Papers*, 5: 186) It
is doubtful if Menzies was ever reimbursed. As a retired British officer living in Fredericksburg in 1775, he refused to renounce allegiance to England because he would
forfeit his pension, although he agreed not to aid the British. After first being confined,
he was allowed to return to Fredericksburg on parole, provided he stayed within six
miles of his house. (Ibid., 5: 185) Although six neighbors thought him entitled to damages and a local judge considered him a man of honor, other inhabitants, including
Hugh Hughes, former deputy quartermaster, questioned his loyalty. (Ibid., 5: 186, 255.
Menzies was exchanged in April 1781, ibid., 6: 781–84.) This suspicion of disloyalty
may have led Wayne and Pettit to choose his farm as a campsite, with the expectation
that Menzies might not have to be reimbursed for damages. When the army moved to
New Jersey from Fredericksburg, NG warned General Wayne to treat the owners of the
land where he planned to encamp with indulgence, since they were "generally good
Whigs." (NG to Wayne, 19 December 1778, above)

From James Thompson

[Middlebrook, N.J.,[1] 17 January 1779. Repeats from earlier letter his
need for harness oil. Country teams coming in. Has sent most Continental horses away. Maryland line still has some because they "Hut
sloly." ALS (PPAmP) 1 p.]

1. His location is conjectured.

To John Jay, President of the Continental Congress

Sir   Philadelphia 18th Jany 1779

It cannot be unknown to Congress that in the different Departments of the Army there are many Persons employed in the Character of Officers who have no other Commission than a kind of Warrant or Appointment from the Head of the Department in which they serve. They consequently have no Rank in the Army but are left on the Footing of private Soldiers as to Arrests and Modes of Trial. Amongst these there are many who from their Abilities and good Conduct are respectable Characters; their Feelings are therefore sensibly touched by being placed in a Situation which subjects them to Confinement in the common Guard House at the Will of even the lowest commissioned Officer in the Army for an offence of a trivial Nature, or perhaps for a supposed offence. The present Situation of Affairs affords so many Opportunities of acquiring Money in a private Capacity, and the publick Service requires the Employment of so great a Number of Men of Abilities for Business, that with all the Encouragement in our Power to give, it is found not a little difficult to fill the different Stations in the Staff Departments with Men of suitable Talents; it therefore seems requisite to remove from their View every Discouragement which can be laid aside without injuring the Publick in a greater Degree in some other Way. If Congress would be pleased, by a publick Resolution, to put these Warrant Officers on the same Footing with the Officers in the Line of the Army with respect to Arrests, Trials, and Punishment, it would probably have a good Effect on their Minds without working any Injury to the commission'd Officers or to the Publick. I have the Honour to be, with great Respect, Sir your most obedient and most humble Servant[1]

NATHL GREENE

LS (PCC, item 155, vol. 1: 79, DNA).
1. Congress referred NG's letter to the Board of War which declared on 5 February it was "entirely of his opinion." On the board's recommendation, Congress resolved on 16 March that warrant officers on the civil staff "be put on the same footing with commissioned officers, in respect to arrests, trials, and punishments." (JCC, 13: 321)

From Colonel James Abeel

[Morristown, N.J., 18 January 1779. Is sending six sleds. Will soon have sixty, some with "Boxes for Forrage," some for two horses, others for four. Tell Major Blodget[1] "the Ladys were pretty well this morning but have not quite got over their Fatigue." ALS (PPAmP) 1 p.]

1. NG's aide.

From Captain John Gooch

Dear Genl   Boston Jany 18. 1779

Our Speculators are laid all aback on account of the two Emissions being Shook with the Dead Palsey.[1] Their is many of them have large sums by them, some that have been Notorious Villians. I rejoice at their missfortunes. Others who again have fairly Bought and sold, I realy Pity. Most of our merch'ts have large sums by them so that the good and bad will indiscriminately suffer. For my part I'm in high Spirits on the affair. It must certainly have a Tendency to better our Currency of which we were in the greatest necessity, for in the space of three months it had depreciated at least 50 pr ct [%] and it is my real appinion had the Evil not been thus Timely remedied the Circulation would have ceased, as no person would have recived it, looking on it as no valuable Consideration for any thing they had to dispose of. This at once will give it a Value and the scarcisty prevent these monopolizing Villians Disstressing mankind. The prises of All the Necessaries of Life this Way is hardly Creditable were they to be mentioned. We have no news more than the News Papers will announce. Mrs Gooch as well as myself have been very much Indissposed the most of this Winter. She desires her Best Respects to you and Mrs Greene to whome be pleased to make my most Respectfull Compliments and belive me with the greatest Sincerity Your Most obedt and Most hble Servant

JOHN GOOCH

ALS (PHi).
1. The "Dead Palsey" refers to an action Congress had taken in early January (*JCC*, 13: 20–23) to reduce the amount of Continental currency by the "pretence," as Thomas Burke called it, that two emissions prior to 11 April 1778 had been "much counterfeited." (Burnett, *Letters*, 3: 542; Richard Henry Lee had called it, when first proposed, a "bold stroke in finance," sanctified by necessity. Ibid., 3: 495) Congress hoped that holders would take loan certificates in exchange for their Continental bills by June 1779. When, however, speculators were given the option of exchanging the old emissions for new bills, they not only avoided the disasters Gooch predicted for them but the measure also failed to reduce the amount of money in circulation. (Ferguson, *Power of Purse*, p. 45) Without the power to tax, Congress, in fact, had to fall back on printing more money, and far from reducing the amount in circulation, within five months another $35 million had been added. (Burnett, *Congress*, p. 406)

From Samuel A. Otis

[Boston, 18 January 1779. Is answering NG's letter to Andrews, Otis's deceased partner.[1] Ships for bringing rice from Charleston very scarce, although his search for vessels in various Massachusetts ports should soon bring results. Private adventurers give one half of cargo for transporting flour. If Otis must offer more than one third, he wants NG's "*positive* order." [Morgan] Lewis is pressing for his order, but Otis must have money first. ALS (PPAmP) 2 pp.]

1. Letter not found, but it was undoubtedly similar to his letter of 5 January to Bowen. See also Wadsworth to NG, 2 January, above. Andrews's death is described at Otis to NG, 10 January, above.

To Colonel Clement Biddle

Dear Sir,   [Philadelphia Jan. 20, 1779]
    I am favored with yours of the 9th, 11th, and 14th of this instant.[1] The great scarcity of the article of forage produces too general a cry to leave the least doubt of the reality of the thing. I am happy to hear from camp, that the distress among the cattle grows less and less. Major Forsyth and Mr. Thomson [Thompson] writes me that almost all the public teams are gone, and the country teams come in in greater plenty than was expected. There has been large sums of money gone eastward both for you and us. I hope nearly equal to the demands. A great sum will be sent to Major[2] Furman in a few days.
    I am sorry to hear the repeated complaints against Col. Bostwyck.[3] I think you had better give Col. Hay orders to provide forage for himself, if Mr. Bostwyck don't supply the post. Let him open a forage account for the purpose. I find the Governor and Council will do nothing more than recommend or enforce the old law; although this is far short of our wishes, yet it is much better to have them with us than against us.[4] I wish most heartily the forage and commissary line could unite their force and measures for getting the wheat manufactured; but I am afraid it is not to be done. The shorts [i.e., bran] would be a great relief to us.
    I have directed Col. Pettit to keep you in money at all events to pay for forage that is impressed agreeable to law.
    You inquire what you shall give your assistants in the forage department. Don't the resolution of Congress state their pay? I don't know what to say to the expenses. What do you suppose to be absolutely necessary for the purpose of subsistence?
    I shall procure an order from head-quarters for the division of Col. Sheldon's regiment. I agree with Mr. Hubbard they can be subsisted much easier and cheaper in a divided state than together.[5]
    The Governor and Council of this State complain that the State is overborne with cavalry and wagon horses. I have got an order for Pulaski's legion to go down into Kent and Sussex in the Delaware State. (Map 4) I don't think it advisable to order in horses out of Salem County, neither can Maj. Lee's corps be removed. There is nobody willing to receive the horses, and everybody desirous of getting rid of them.[6]

I drank tea with your good lady and sisters this evening. The spirit of dueling, intrigue, and cabal goes on here as much as ever.

Reprinted from Greene, *Greene*, 2: 165–66.
1. None found.
2. The copyist or printer undoubtedly misread NG's hand, since Moore Furman did not have a military rank.
3. Col. Andrew Bostwick was deputy commissary of forage under Biddle at Fishkill, N.Y.
4. On 10 February, Governor Clinton reluctantly gave Hay a press warrant for twenty-one days, with the admonition that it be executed by people who "have not rendered themselves obnoxious to the Inhabitants by past Controversies." (Clinton, *Papers*, 4: 558)
5. Col. Elisha Sheldon of Connecticut was commander of the Second Continental Dragoons. (Heitman, *Register*) Nehemiah Hubbard, DQM in Connecticut, was speaking of subsisting the dragoons' horses.
6. Biddle answered on 25 January, below.

To Nehemiah Hubbard

Sir   Philadelphia Jan. 20th 1779
I am favoured with yours of the 29th and 31st of December and the 9th of January.[1]

I note your observations on the pay of ADQM Generals. The resolution of Congress fixes them at 40 dollars, and there can be no deviation while that resolution remains in force or at least the passing of those accounts will depend upon the Auditors of Accounts. I wrote you early in the season on this subject and told you what pay could be given to ADQMrs[masters] Genl and that nothing further would be allowed by the public. However, this matter is an object of importance and requires more deliberation than I at present have time to bestow upon it.[2]

You must settle with Mr Bull upon the best terms you can. I agreed with Mr Davenport who went with the Convention Troops to Virginia for 75 dolls pr month and pay his expences. I should think this would be satisfactory to Mr Bull; but as there was no agreement made you must negotiate the business upon the best conditions you can.[3]

The Waggon hire with you is extravagant and the Farmers are intolerable in their demands, but it is out of our power to change either the Men or their demands. You must take unwearied pains to keep the prices of things down as much as possible; we can do no more.

I have forwarded you a large sum of money which I hope will be equal to all the demands upon you. Colo Pettit wrote you upon the occasion.

I have enclosed answers to all your queries except to those respecting the horses. I don't think myself authorised to give orders for the payment of horses lost in the Rhode Island expedition unless the owners can produce certificates that they were actually kill'd by the Enemy. The hire of horses you may undoubtedly pay provided the charge is reasonable.[4]

I think Mr Dickinson presented his account at Camp while the Army lay at Fredericksburg; the charges are extravagantly high and ought to be docked considerably; besides this objection to paying the account it should be paid by the Commissary of Military Stores. However if the man will agree to make the charges reasonable, pay it.

I apprehend a great scarcity of Forage the next Campaign, and therefore think it absolutely necessary to begin to provide a remedy. I wish you to enter into a written contract with a great number of Farmers (as many as will engage) to sow all the oats in the Spring they can, and that you will take all they raise and give the Market prices at the time of delivery, which you should fix at the most favourable part of the season for lowering the price. If you can engage the people generally in this business we shall have a plenty of Forage and upon our own terms.[5]

Do not fail forwarding the provision to Providence as fast as it may be wanted. There has been great complaints from that quarter already. I am impatiently waiting the arival of your accounts.

I hope Mrs Hubbard has recovered. Please to make my compliments to her [and to] Mr Wadsworth. I am Sir Your humble Servant

NATH'EL GREENE

LS (RHi).
1. Letters not found.
2. The salary of assistant deputy quartermasters (exclusive of commissions) had remained at $40 per month since Congress established the pay scale in May 1777. (*JCC*, 7: 359) For subsequent changes, see below, NG to Jay, 15 April.
3. See NG to Hubbard, 9 November 1778, above.
4. Reimbursements for losses in Rhode Island are discussed in NG to Sullivan, 9 February, and Sullivan to NG, 17 February, below. The quartermaster's responsibility in reimbursing losses is discussed above in NG's Orders, 1 June 1778 (vol. 2: 419–20).
5. See Hubbard to NG, 6 February, below.

From the Board of War

[War Office, Philadelphia, 20 January 1779. Since some people keep their horses in public stables without authorization, the board requests that NG "mark out some system" for determining those entitled to do so.[1] Signed by Peter Scull. ALS (PPAmP) 2 pp.]

1. If NG worked out a "system," it has not been found.

From Nathaniel Gorham

[Boston, 21 January 1779. Offers his "services" as an agent in place of the late Benjamin Andrews.[1] A member of the Massachusetts General Court he has just been appointed to the Massachusetts Board of War. Gives General Knox as reference.[2] ALS (PPAmP) 1 p.]

1. On Andrews's death, see above, Otis to NG, 10 January.
2. NG's answer has not been found, but he did not choose Gorham.

From Colonel Udny Hay

Sir   Fish Kill [N.Y.] 21 Jan 1779

I wrote you particularly by major Hale to which refers. I hope he is fully loaded with Cash, if our paper Currency deserves that name at present. Its depreciation here increases with a rapidity to me truly alarming nor can I think but we Gentry of the staff here had a tolerable share in that Disaster as many of us seem inclined to pay away the public money without paying much attention to the value we receive therefore.

Amongst other articles the price of teaming is raisd beyond all bounds; I have hitherto paid, to a two horse Waggon three Dollars per day if the horses and drivers were found [i.e., fed] by the public; if they found themselves, five Dollars or three shillings per mile, and notwithstanding the Commissarys have been giving near double that price. I have made a shift hitherto to gett a sufficient number of Carriages for the public service, but I find I cannot do that any more. The following is an extract from a Letter of one of the justices of the Peace to me on the subject: "I believe while sleding is good Teams might be had plenty [?] if you would give what the Commissarys give, but the price you give is not half that is common and usual price, and will not more than bear the necessary expences of man and teams, and it is truly hard for a man to find horses, slay man &c to work for nothing."

As a very [great?] number of Carriages are now wanted for getting in our [torn] and salt Provisions to the sundry places where it is [torn] wanted, I have agreed to give the current price in the Country paid by other public officers. The consequence will be that others will still bid higher.

I this day wait on Governour Clinton with a letter to lay before the Assembly, containing a plan for raising Carriages when wanted for public service, with more expedition and regularity than has hither to been done.[1] Amongst other requests therein is the following: That the State appoint three Gentlemen upon Oath to settle the price of Teaming every three months and that all public officers be regulated thereby.

I am truly perplexed about our Artificers. Ever since offers were made to men going to the northward of so high wages as is believed by the whole country is given there (6 1/2 Dollars per day) there has been nothing but a constant murmuring. Our Wheelwrights and Smiths are those men I am in most fear about.[2] They are engaged by the Month, and have given me warning that unless something is done for them at the end of this month they must look out for more Wages elsewhere. Though I am excessive loth to raise the price of either Wages or any thing else, yett I must confess that the Wages of Artificers have not kept pace with the rise of every commodity necessary for maintaining themselves and familys. They are at present paid at the rate of twelve shillings N. Y. Currency per day. Pray Lett me have your Commands on that head [as] soon as possible.

The Blanketts we had are extremely [?] small and the sheets (or rather a part of them) very bad. Respecting the Former, Colo Weiss has informd that you allow two for one, which we have communicated to the Artificers and I dare say they now are contented on that Score. The necessity I have been under of sending out those Gentlemen by whom the books should have been posted up has hither to prevented us from accomplishing that very necessary piece of business, which putts it out of our power to be so very regular as I could wish, hope however soon to find spare time for this business also.

I have lately had a return from a person sent on purpose to visit the Horses wintering in the upper part of the State. They are in general in a thriving way and I doubt not of having a number of Horses in good order for opening the Campaign with. I am with sincere respect Sir your most obed Sert

UDNY HAY

Inclosed you have a return of horses a wintering out.

ALS (PPAmP).
1. Hay's letter to Clinton of 20 January (a copy of which is in the Greene Papers, PPAmP) proposed that farmers with certain acreage be "Oblidg'd to keep Constantly either an Ox or Horse Team" that could be called out by a justice of the peace when needed by the army, the compensation to be determined by a group of three men. On 28 January, Clinton sent Hay's proposal to the legislature with his approval, but no action was taken. (Clinton, *Papers*, 4: 525) Clinton continued to provide Hay with limited press warrants. (Ibid., 559. Hay's clashes with justices over press warrants are illustrated by correspondence on pp. 566–68. See also his letter to NG of 10 February, below.)
2. See their memorial, above, 6 January.

To Colonel Clement Biddle

[Philadelphia, 22 January 1779. Sending money to camp. Believes he has supplied sufficient money to "Eastward States" so that they have no cause for complaint. Hopes to leave soon. "We spend money here not by hundreds but by thousands of pounds." ALS (PPIn) 2 pp.]

Major Ichabod Burnet to Colonel Ephraim Bowen

[Philadelphia, 22 January 1779. NG asks Burnet to acknowledge Bowen's letter of 2 January with accounts. Hopes blank forms for stores will be available next month. Sorry linen for NG and Burnet is delayed. Reports invasion of Georgia.[1] ALS (RHi) 2 pp.]

1. See below, NG to Sullivan, 26 January.

From John Jay, President of the Continental Congress

[Philadelphia, 22 January 1779. NG's letter of 18 January has been referred to Board of War.[1] Will report Congress's "Determination" at earliest opportunity. ALS (PPAmP) 1 p.]

1. See note at NG's letter.

From Lord Stirling

Dear Sir   Camp Middle Brook [N.J.] January 22d 1779
    I had the pleasure of receiveing yours of the 14th.[1] A Gentleman Just going past for Philadelphia gives me this oppertunity of Acknowledging it.
    Variety is the best sauce of life, as a proof of it I need only bring your own Evidence; when you say you are tired of Philadelphia and wish to Come to Camp. I thank God I am easily Satisfied, and should repine if I was ordered to be a month or two at that City provided Congress would pay my Expenses. I am much obliged to you for your promise of Attending to the busyness I took the liberty of troubling you with.[2] We have had reports of the Enemy's intending a Vissit to some parts of this State. Indeed it has been very Confidently asserted that they were landed both in Monmouth and Bergen Counties but there is no truth in either, that I can yet find. We have nothing else New. My best Compliments to Mrs Green and all friends and am very Sincerely yours &c.

STIRLING

Be so good as to desire Major Barnet [Burnet] to order the printers to send two sets of their News papers to me. I can not otherwise, get the New York papers.

ALS (PPAmP).
1. Letter not found.
2. It is not known what "busyness" NG was asked to attend to.

From Major Robert Forsyth

[Camp Middlebrook, N.J., 23 January 1779. Forwards Colonel Stewart's letter [of 4 January]. Adds: "No Cash. Not a Shilling." ALS (PHi) 1 p.]

From Colonel Henry Hollingsworth

[Head of Elk, Md., 23 January 1779. John Mitchell apparently requests him to pay more for "Waggonage" than "allowed by Orders." If there is a new regulation of 20 November "which Col Mitchell mentions I'll thank you to have it from under your Hand, as it will be requisite to have it from the first Authority."[1] LS (PPAmP) 1 p.]

1. Mitchell, DQMG in Philadelphia, was concerned with wagons in areas outside his own district. No regulation of 20 November has been found.

To Colonel John Davis

[Philadelphia, 24 January 1779. Wagon horses sent to Davis to be put "out to keep among the Inhabitants" for the winter. Davis should stress that farmers cannot be paid unless horses are in "good order" when returned. ALS (Davis Papers: DLC) 1 p.]

Colonel Clement Biddle to Moore Furman

[Raritan, N.J., 24 January 1779. In NG's absence he requests that Furman furnish, if possible, enough teams to transport two hundred barrels of flour weekly from Delaware River to New Windsor, N.Y. for the commissary department. (See Map 1.) Light dragoons cannot be sent from New Jersey. Has written "pressingly" to NG of Furman's immediate need for money. A friend is interested in "quality and price of your negro wench and Child."[1] ALS (Nj) 3 pp.]

1. Furman had advertised for sale "a stout Negro WOMAN, mostly used to country work, and her son about eight years old." (*N.J. Archives*, 3: 34) In January 1784 he freed his two slaves, "convinced of the iniquity and inhumanity of slavery." (Furman, *Letters*, p. x, which quotes the Hunterdon County records.)

From Captain Bartholomew von Heer[1]

Dear Generale   Milstone [N.J.] Jannuar 24the 1779
The present Situation which I am in respecting my Troop, in gitting them shoet [shoed] is impossible that the kand [they can] be
without a Blaksmidt, as your Department due not allowe a Priiss that
any Blaksmidt will work for me in this Naborhood and the Arteficers
are of a such a great a Distanz that it is impossible, that the Troop may
Rite of ten Mile Distanz for gitting their Horses shoet. I shall begg it as
a particulair favour that you would be so kind and consider, to grand
me one of the Blacksmidt Carts which will saeve a great deal Expenses
to the Public and liikeweise be a more convenience to gitting the
Horses in mor regulair Order as I expect James Career in one or two
Days to move with the halfe of my Troop to Molmouths [Monmouth]
County in which it is impossible when the Horses are not properly
shott [shod], that the[y] can due Duty, and as I expect that Duty will
be strang ther, I find great necessary that this would be the best convenience and the profitables Weg [way] to the public to being
supplied with one['s] Owne Blacksmit Cart, as I have the men who
kand [can?] act for that Buissness. I am in Expectation that it may not
be refased [refused] as it is to the benefit to the public and not to my
owne Interest. I am waiting with Respect for your Honours Answer.[2]
I which you will oblige your most humble and Obedient Servant

BARTHOLOMAW[3] VON HEER

ALS (PPAmP).
    1. He commanded the maréchausée (mounted provosts) from their establishment
in June 1778 until 1783. (See above, vol. 2: 427.) Despite von Heer's poor command of
English, Washington considered him an effective leader of a valuable corps. See, for example, Washington's letter of 1 June 1781, Fitzpatrick, GW, 22: 149–50.)
    2. NG's answer has not been found.
    3. Von Heer's contemporaries addressed him as "Bartholomew," which he ac-
cepted, as have historians since. He usually signed his name "Barthol'w."

To Griffin Greene

Dear Sir   Philadelphia January 25th 1779
    Your agreeable favor of the 5th of this instant came to hand about
Eight days since.[1]
    Nothing can give me greater pleasure than a line from my
friends. Family matters are nearest my heart, and accounts of them
the most pleaseing. It adds greatly to my happiness to hear your Son
is got well again and that Sally and the rest of the family are in good
health.
    I observe you have made a considerable purchase in Wines. I
think you will reap advantage from it. I told Col Cox and Fitzgerald

that if they intended to have any purchased they must not limit you in the price. However they did not think proper to put the business upon that broad bottom and therefore must be content with the disappointment.

I have inclosd you a price current of articles in this City. Dry Goods are most extravagantly dear and very scarce especially Silks.

The Currency is upon such a fluctuating footing that it is difficult to form any opinion about it. However I think the depreciation will be less from the measures taken to draw it out of circulation and from the firm assureances given the People that it will be redeemd hereafter at its full value. The great quantities that has been emited and the apprehensions of the Inhabitants that it was to die in their hands, has been the principal reason for its low ebb. The Congress are determined at all events to support its credit, as well from necessity as from a principle of justice. [2]

I think General Varnum is taken in, he expected the paper money would not be a Legal tender at the end of two years; and that you would be obligd to pay silver and gold. This appears very evident from the Nature of the contract.

However I dont think Houses are the best kind of Interest [i.e., investment] these Times and its a great doubt with me whether any of us will ever settle in Greenwich but dont let my private opineon interfere in the least with your plans or expectations.

I think you have done right in makeing as large purchases in wet and Dry goods as your stocks would admit. Altho I hope Money will not depreciate any more in the rapid manner it has, yet I have no expectation of its appreciateing in value for sometime to come; if it will hold its own it will be a great thing especially as the current expences of the War is so great and such floods of it constantly circulateing.

Mrs Greene is with me here and very happy. The Inhabitants are very polite, all the Ladies of the first class in the place have visited her. The respect that is paid her would not a little mortify her Enemies. I shall not name any, but you know who I mean. George is a fine fellow and universally admired.

The luxuries and extravagance of this City exceed any thing you ever saw. There has nothing been going on here but Entertainments, Assemblies and Balls. His Excellency General Washington has been here above a month and the Citizens have exerted them selves to make him as happy as possible. But I can truly say that I feel serious amidst festivity and gloomy among the most joyous. The extravagance of the Times is very unfriendly to a Republican Government and greatly enervates the National Strength. A mans expences here is almost at the rate of five pounds a minute. I am in hopes to get through our business and return to Camp in about Eight or Ten Days.

I am sorry I cannot oblige you with respect to Mr Rogers; but I have two Aids and the late Regulations of the Army obliges the Generals to take their Aids from the Line.

My love to Sally and all friends and Mrs Greene[3] also. Yours affect

NATH GREENE

ALS (OMC).
1. Letter not found.
2. On Congress's action, see note, Gooch to NG, 18 January, above. As seen there, NG was overly sanguine on the determination of Congress.
3. NG's stepmother.

From Colonel Clement Biddle

Dear General   Camp Middlebrook [N.J.] Jan: 25. 1779

I am favourd with yours of 20 and 22d inst with an Acceptable supply of Money from Colo Pettit who informs me he is prepared to furnish Mr Furman, which with the sums sent to the Eastward will leave all the posts in good Credit except Mr Hubbard, Colo Smith and Colo Lewis.[1] I beleive Providence will require a speedy supply and I have to replace 60 or 70,000 Dollars for which Genl Sullivan gave a Warrant.

We have rub'd on[2] tolerably well for Forage in Camp but my resources in Monmouth begin to fail and I fear will fall short before the river opens. There is a real scarcity of Forage in almost every state from the great land Carriage [i.e., transportation] both on public and private Account.

Mr. Flint has required Carriage for two hundred barrels of Flour weekly from the Delaware to the North River.[3] I have wrote to Mr Furman to order Carriages for the purpose but it will be extremely difficult to furnish the horses with Forage.

I shall send to Colo Hooper to provide at Coryells Ferry. [Map 3]

Our situation is distressing and Pennsylvania complains that we send too many horses there. This state think they are overburthened and I find in the Governors Proclamation a Clause which I fear will destroy the use of it. He cautions the magistrates not to take too much from the Inhabitants and I think they stood in no need of such advice.[4] Major Lees Corps[5] I believe fare pretty well where they are. The horses from Salem must have crossed before this time.

The Complaints against Colo Bostwick give me great pain. I fear he has not attended to my Orders to consult with and take Orders from Colo Hay.[6] Major Hale as he went through here on his return to Fish Kill told me he had accounts that Forage was coming in there in good quantities, therefore I shall wait to hear and if the Complaints continue will give the necessary orders to Colo Hay. In the mean time I shall write to him to purchase Forage if necessary.

I wish you would procure an order from Colo Wadsworth to his Deputies to purchase Wheat and deliver us the offall.[7] We have had little from them as yet and I wish to Obtain it on any Terms. Our demands are so much beyond what I can procure of other Forage.

The purchasers of Forage in districts are obliged to ride almost constantly and their Expences are great. If they keep an acct of reasonable Expence I think they should be allowd it, or we shall loose our best hands. There is no Pay fixed by Congress except for Forage masters who have Charge of magazines or with Brigades which is 40 Dollars a month. I have allowd them for Expences while moving from half a Dollar to a dollar a Day and twenty Dollars in lieu of Rations not drawn.

We wish for your Return and when you Arrive I must Request leave of Absence for a few Days as my presence in Philadelphia is absolutely necessary.

My Accounts from different Quarters are coming in by degrees and I shall arrange them as fast as I can.

The fleet that arrived at [New] York are said to be a second Cork fleet of 14 to 16 sail chiefly loaden with Forage—78,000 bushels of oats and one ship with 1500 barrels Flour. The first fleet which they depended on for Provisions is still missing. With Compliments to Mrs Greene I am Dr Sir, with respect Your mo: Obedt and very huml servt

CLEMENT BIDDLE

ALS (PPAmP).
1. Hubbard, Smith, and Lewis were deputies in Hartford, Springfield, and Albany, respectively.
2. Johnson, *Dictionary*, defines *rub* as "to get through difficulties."
3. Royal Flint was Jeremiah Wadsworth's deputy in the commissary department.
4. Biddle had written Governor Livingston of New Jersey on 14 January that although the forage department had sent two thousand horses to Pennsylvania and would receive forage from outside New Jersey when the rivers thawed, the desperate immediate need led him to ask if the governor would recommend to the magistrates that they execute the law for impressing forage. (*N.J. Rev. Correspondence*, pp. 139–40) Livingston responded the same day with a proclamation that asked the justices "vigorously to exert themselves" in executing the forage law, admonishing them at the same time "not to exact more grain or other forage in any district than the neighbourhood can safely spare." (Reprinted in *N.J. Archives*, 3: 33.) It was this clause that Biddle feared would destroy the effectiveness of the proclamation since the justices were in "no need of such advice." His fear appeared to be justified, at least in Monmouth County. See below, NG to Livingston, 14 February.
5. Henry Lee's dragoons.
6. See above, NG to Biddle, 20 January.
7. Offal in this case was the chaff, or husk, of wheat—a by-product of flour-making.

From Major William Blodget

Dear Sir

Rariton [N.J.] January 25th 1779.

Your Compliments by Major Forsyth's Letter was very acceptable, and I hope the return of mine will meet you with Mrs Greene in health.

I wrote you the 9th Inst, which I hope you have receiv'd.[1]

The Camp at present affords nothing worth relateing except, our own little amusements in the good fellowship way, which of late has [been] pretty frequent among us. We have made another attack on the General Hospital, and tho' many of the Departments signaliz'd themselves, yet, our's came of[f] with flying Coulors—we were really able to tell next day how we got home, which many of them coud not do.

I am very unhappy to acquaint you that our Friend Mr Benja Andrews of Boston, in examining a curious pistol, was by accident shot through the head, and died instantly. This comes in a Letter from his Partner Mr Otis.[2] I Truly lament his Death, not only as a man in whome the Public deriv'd great benifit from, but as a Friend and generous Companion: the Civilities I receiv'd from him merit my faithfull remembrance, and I feel doubly effected for Mrs Andrews whose Sencibility must greatly tend to make her wretched. As you are not unacquainted with them both, 'tis easy to conceive this peice of intelligence will not be acceptable.

We are favor'd with the Company of Mrs Livingston, Miss Gilly [Lott] and Miss Cornelia Lott, togather with Colonel [William Smith] Livingston, They are at Mr Coejemans and intend spending several days with us;[3] and in order to make Camp more agreeable to them, I am arranging matters so as to entertain them with a little dance tomorrow eve'ning, when we will do our possibles to make the departmant shine on the occasion.

I find by your favor to Majr Forsyth you are not only emerg'd [immerg'd] in business, but that the profits of the Quarter Masters Department are going fast; I can readily imagine it, from the prices of Articles—'tis well for me I am here, as I must necessarily make some small purchases if there, and as the Language of thousands is adopted—poor fifty Dollars not afford me a peep into the Assembly Room. I wish I cou'd see [Ichabod] Burnet for a moment under these circumstances? I think e'er this he must be grey, and shou'd he remain one Week longer, at his return I shall have an excellent substitute in him for a Portrait of Mathusalem [Methuselah].

Please to present my kindest regards to Mrs Greene, and believe me to be your Obedt Hble Serv

WM BLODGET

Colo Livingston with the Ladies beg the [their] Complimts may be presented to you and Mrs Greene. Be good enough to remember me to Genl Knox; his Lady is well and danc'd with us a few nights past at Mr Coejemans.

ALS (PHi).
1. Letter not found.
2. Otis to NG, 10 January, above.
3. Samuel Staats Coejemans (1722–81), an ardent patriot of Dutch descent, was proprietor of an imposing house and extensive holdings along the north branch of the Raritan River. (Hoffman, *New Jersey*, pp. 151–52) He was well known for his "open and generous" hospitality. (See his obituary, *N.J. Archives*, 4: 335 and sale of his estate in March 1782 on p. 374.)

From Major Robert Forsyth

Sir   Camp Middle Brook [N.J.] January 25th 1779

Yesterday I was honoured with your favour of the 22d Instant for which I beg leave to return my best Thanks.[1] You seem to write very feelingly of Family Duty. As you have had experience in that way, I take it for granted you must be right in saying the warm season is not so agreeable to preform in. However I must confess I ever thought the Spring months were best calculated for Enjoyment.

Inclosed you have a copy of Mr Flints request to the Deptment. Colo Biddle has wrote very fully on the subject to Mr M. Furman and thinks by way of Corryells will best answer the purpose.[2]

I perfectly agree with you, that the Artificers are a very Expensive set, and I am affraid they are by no means so industrious as I could wish them.

Mrs Livingston and the Miss Lotts are in Camp. Our *Beau Nash* [William Blodget] is making arrangements for giving them a Dance to Morrow Evening. I imagine we shall make out very well.

We are all out with our good Landlady. I believe she thinks we shall certainly go to the D——l, even poor Claiborne (of whom she had some hopes) she has given up for lost tho' I fancy she makes Blodgets and my Account Debit for aiding and assisting. I beg leave to refer you to Major Blodgets Ltrs for our internal movements lately. I have come off very well in all our Manouvres except the first Nights attack on the Flying Hospital. There I must confess I was caught. I have the Honour to be Yr Humble Servt

ROBT FORSYTH

ALS (PHi).
1. Letter not found.
2. See above, Biddle to Furman, 24 January and to NG, 25 January.

From Colonel Isaac Melcher[1]

Sir   Phil. 25 Jany 1779

I have taken the liberty to inclose orders reecd from the Board of War, as well as instructions given by me to those employd in my department which may be for the Government of those employ'd in your's in their applications for quarters, Stores or Barrack furniture and such other articles as is my duty to Supply.

I would beg leave to repeat to prevent future Misunderstandings what I concieve to be my principal duty. First, on the application of the Q.M.G. on the order of the commander in chief of any department, to provide and furnish such Barracks, store houses, and other buildings as may be deem'd necessary to accommodate the troops intended to be quartered. Secondly to supply them with such Barrack Utensils, as may be allowed them, with [fire?] Wood, Straw, soap and Candles as is customary in other armies, and it is my opinion no barrack master ought to be kept in pay where there are no Barracks except on some particular occasions, where troops are quartered in a town and in that case only so long as is necessary, and that the strictest *harmony* ought to exist between *your department* and mine particularly being often so necessarily connected, as well with every other which I assure you is the ardent wish of Sir your fr[ien]d and most obt hble Sert

ISAAC MELCHER

It is likewise apprehended my duty is principally confined to the troops in quarters as that of the QMG's is to those in the field.[2]

I M

Cy (PPAmP). The document is inscribed "True copy by his nephew Francis Shallus."

1. Isaac Melcher (sometimes spelled Melchior) was an early patriot whose father was a manufacturer of iron. (*Pa. Archives*, 5: 206) He accompanied General Montgomery to Canada in 1775 as brigade major, and in December 1776 he was appointed barrackmaster general of Pennsylvania with the rank of colonel. (PCC, item 42, 5: 1, DNA; *Pa. Col. Records*, 11: 51) The following year Congress made him barrackmaster general of the Continental army. (*JCC*, 9: 968)

2. Whether NG agreed with Melcher's demarcation of the boundaries between the two departments is not known. Charles Pettit reported a few weeks later that Melcher had forbidden Col. John Mitchell from purchasing wood or boards (letter of 15 February, below); and the dispute had not been settled when NG wrote the Board of War about it on 27 February, below. Within a few months most of Melcher's deputies were transferred to NG's department, but Mitchell did not win out by the transfer because Melcher continued in charge of the barracks at Philadelphia and Charlottesville. (*JCC*, 14: 645) In his report of 23 December 1779, Melcher listed as employees only those at Philadelphia and Pennsbury Manor, twenty-five miles north of Philadelphia, but none at Charlottesville. (PCC, item 78, vol. 16: 113, DNA) Congress later completely abolished the barrackmaster department and transferred all of its duties to the quartermaster. (Timothy Pickering to Alexander Hamilton, 20 April 1781, Washington Papers, DLC)

From William Smith

[Springfield, Mass., 25 January 1779. Entrenching tools NG ordered for Albany were missent to Springfield, N.J., but will be on the way by tomorrow along with stores and salt. ALS (PPAmP) 1 p.]

To Colonel Ephraim Bowen

[Philadelphia, 26 January 1779. Is "much in want" of Bowen's returns of stores, cattle, carriages, men he employs, and Sullivan's stores. Asks him to advance cash to Jacob Greene to complete orders if requested. Brigade quartermasters should make weekly returns to Bowen, who should make monthly returns to NG.[1] LS (MiU-C) 2 pp.]

1. In his letter to Sullivan this day, NG requested that Sullivan order the brigade quartermasters to comply.

To General John Sullivan

Dear Sir   Philadelphia January 26, 1779

I beg you to give the necessary Orders to the Brigade quarter masters and others under your command in the line of my department, for haveing Weekly returns made of all Stores in their possession or in the hands of the Corps to which they belong. These returns to be made both to yourself and Col Bowen.

His Excellency is at this place. We came here with an expectation of staying only a few days; but I am afraid we shall be detain two months.[1] The State of the Army and the business of the next Campaign are objects of our attention. The General as commander in chief, I as quarter master.

The Inhabitants of this City are in the high Road of luxury and extravagance. Such Entertainments you never saw as are given here. We poor fellows belonging to the Army could not pay the expense of one dinner under half a years pay. There is assemblies once a fortnight and private and public balls every Night. A man must get up by day light and go to bed at midnight to be able to go through the ceremonies of the City.

The Congress are going on as usual with slow deliberation. There is many factions in this State and abuse and dueling prevails.

The Enemy have made themselves masters of the Capital of Georgia and there is great apprehension for the safety of South Carolina.[2] My respects to the Gentlemen of your family. I am with great regard Your Most Obedt and humble Sert

N GREENE

ALS (Original in possession of Mary Lynn McCree, Chicago, Ill., 1975).

1. NG returned to camp on 9 February, a few days after Washington.

2. The attack on Georgia was a belated fulfillment of the British Cabinet's orders of March 1778 to strengthen Florida defenses and to take the offensive against St. Lucia and the southern colonies—orders that Sir Henry Clinton, then in Philadelphia, had wisely decided to ignore. (See above, vol. 2: 436n.) Five months later, Germain asked Clinton to carry out the orders as soon as his forces were sufficiently strong.

By late autumn Clinton decided the time was right. In a move that marked the renewal of Britain's southern strategy, Gen. James Grant sailed from New York on 3 November with troops for St. Lucia; three weeks later Lt. Col. Archibald Campbell followed with three thousand men bound for Georgia. On 23 December, Campbell's vessels dropped anchor at the mouth of the Savannah River. When word reached Gen. Robert Howe, the American commander at Sunbury, he set off with nine hundred men for Savannah, thirty miles to the north. "From start to finish," Kenneth Coleman has written, "the defense of Savannah was handled poorly." (Coleman, *Georgia*, p. 120) Squabbling between governor and militia commanders made a unified command impossible, while Howe proved an ineffective commander. After failing to oppose the British landings near Savannah, he deployed his men in what appeared to be a strong position between the river and a swamp south of the city, but the British managed to outflank his army by making their way through the swamp. Howe was completely routed, losing 83 killed, 11 wounded, and 453 captured. Campbell lost only 7 killed and 19 wounded. (Peckham, *Toll*, p. 56)

Gen. Augustine Prevost moved north from Florida to take the overall command from Colonel Campbell, and within a month the British controlled the thickly settled strips bordering the coast and the Savannah River up to Augusta. The restoration of royal government soon followed in the areas they controlled. Although the British drew back from Augusta and failed to subdue the Whig backcountry or to destroy a rival state government in that area, the new British strategy had nonetheless gotten off to a successful start. Except for the backcountry, which was torn by civil strife, Georgia was to remain in British hands until liberated in July 1782 by Gen. Anthony Wayne in the last major move of Nathanael Greene's southern campaign.

Despite the fears NG expressed above for the safety of South Carolina, Gen. William Moultrie turned back the British at Beaufort, S.C., in early February. In late April, General Prevost made his way to the outskirts of Charleston, but Gen. Benjamin Lincoln's forced march from Augusta caused the British to withdraw on 12 May to some of the coastal islands below Charleston. Not until May 1780 did they succeed in capturing Charleston.

The Georgia expedition is covered in Mackesy, *War*, pp. 230–34; Coleman, *Georgia*, pp. 116–26; Boatner, *Encyc.*, pp. 965–66, 980–82, 1033–34. A detailed account of Savannah's capture is Alexander A. Lawrence, "General Robert Howe and the British Capture of Savannah in 1778," *Georgia Historical Quarterly*, 36(1952): 303–27.

From William Smith

Sir   Springfield [Mass.] 26th Jany 1779

In conformity to your Orders giving Col Hay for building three Scows and a small Batteau at this Post which I recd at my first arrival here,[1] and your letter of June 12th, I immediately complyed theirwith, collected materials and set at Work the Artificers sent from Fish Kill by Col Hay for Said Purpose and completed them without Delay. I also engaged for one Year a Number of Boat men and built a small Barrack as conveniant Quarters could not be hired.

The Select Men of this Town were in Opposition to the Boats

being built of which I informed you by Letter dated the 21 June [1778].² They supposed it was unlawfull and would greatly injure the Person Licensed to keep the Ferry, and the whole was needless and waisting the Public Money. On informing them that it was your Orders that the Boats should be built, and that I should abide by them, they drew a Petition and Complaint to the Honourable Councel of this State representing many things that were not Facts, and desired that an inquiry might be made therein. In consequence of Which the latter part of November a Committee of three Members of the Councel arrived here. They requested I would give them a Copy of my Orders for Building the Boats, the expence for the same and services performed, which I complyed with. Similar Copys are herewith inclosed with the Petition and Report of the Committee, which report with respect to the wood is wrong. Ever since my appointment to this Post, I have Quartered at the House of Capt Pynchon, also my Assistant and servant.

It was not Possable for the County Ferryman to supply the Ferry for two hundred pounds per year, as he had not Boats sufficent, nor did I ever hear of any such proposal till it was mentioned to the Committee the latter part of November. If the Boats had not been built the Public service would have suffered. There is not private ones sufficent in the River to convey what is necessarily called for. When the Ferry men were not employed in the Boats they have been kept at other public service, and now the River is Frozen are in the Woods cutting Fuel.³

Excuse my troubling you with this long affair, but which I though[t] necessary you should be informed of, and wish your approbation of my Conduct if deserving.⁴ I am Sir your very Hble Servt

WILL SMITH

ALS (PPAmP).
    1. A copy of Hay's letter of 21 May 1778, which relayed NG's order, is in the Greene Papers, vol. 11: 89, PPAmP and is abstracted above, vol. 2: 397. To move men and supplies more quickly across the Connecticut River than could be done by the local ferry, the order called for building one scow capable of taking two teams of horses, two that could take one team, and a batteau that could carry four horses. "Genl Green," Hay emphasized, "has Ordered this matter to be put in Execution Immediately."
    2. See above, vol. 2: 443.
    3. Nathanael Greene, not William Smith, was the chief target of an eight-page memorial of 31 August 1778, which the selectmen of Springfield and West Springfield addressed to the Massachusetts Council. Smith, in fact, was not even mentioned by name.
    The memorial grew out of a clash between local interests and those of the Continental army that was typical of areas far removed from the unifying influence of enemy threats. After a long disquisition on the impropriety of wasting Continental funds, the memorial emphasized the extravagance of building the scows as well as the nearby "Elaboratory" (and even pleasure boats for the "amusement" of officers), all of which did "Double Mischief" by also raising local prices. But most of their ammunition was directed at the Continental ferry, which did great injury to "Mr. Gideon Leonard,"

whose ferry "from time Immemorial" had operated with "diligence and dispatch." If the army had had complaints, an easy remedy, they said, was available through the civil authority. Leonard, it continued, had not only lost the army's business but some of his regular passengers were taking the Continental ferry when on private business. The selectmen acknowledged that the Continental ferry was established on NG's orders, but they asked if this was not "an Instance of the Userpation of the Military over the Civil Government." It was their understanding, they said in closing, that in order to "prevent abuse," Congress had authorized the state executives (in Massachusetts, the council) to suspend subordinate officers; as selectmen they did not directly request such suspension but asked that a "public Enquirey be made into their Premises." (The congressional resolution of February 1778 to which the memorial refers is in *JCC*, 10: 139–40. The memorial, signed by William Pynchon, Jr., and nine other selectmen, is in the Greene Papers, vol. 11: 90, PPAmP.)

In November 1778 the Massachusetts Council sent a committee to Springfield to investigate. When the committee reported back to the council, they stated, surprisingly, that William Smith had established the ferry without a Continental order—this in the face of indisputable evidence that NG had ordered it. They may have ignored NG's role because of a hesitancy to tangle with the quartermaster general. They did not repeat the selectmen's charge that there had been a usurpation of authority by the military, concentrating instead on Smith's extravagance and the use he and others had made of public stores—especially firewood. In conclusion, the committee said the local ferrymen would be willing to do the army's transporting for two hundred pounds annually (considerably less than had been charged). (A "Coppy" is in the Greene Papers, vol. 11: 85, PPAmP.)

The only action the full council took on the report was to order President Jeremiah Powell of the Massachusetts Council to forward the papers to Congress on 16 January with a request for an investigation. Powell essentially let the papers speak for themselves, including the selectmen's charges of the "Userpation" by the military, only pointing out to Congress certain misdemeanors by Smith and others. Congress, in turn, sidestepped the issue by directing Washington to order a court martial. (*JCC*, 13: 163) The court found Smith innocent as concerned the Continental ferry because he acted on NG's orders, while it clearly upheld the quartermaster's inherent right to establish a ferry. Smith and others were also acquitted of any misdemeanors. (The findings are in Washington's orders of 14 May 1779, Fitzpatrick, *GW*, 15: 68–69.) Congress had made the quartermaster responsible for transportation; it did not detail how he should carry out his duties or set limitations on his means.

In the end, the town of Springfield, however, did not suffer. The "Elaboratory," or arsenal as it was also called, became the principal local industry, giving far more employment than was lost through other Continental establishments.

4. In his answer of 11 February, below, NG fully supported his deputy.

To Colonel Ephraim Bowen

Dr Sir   Philadelphia January 27, 1779

I wrote you the 5th of this instant to charter in the State of Rhode Island and in and about Bedford in the state of Massachusets Vessels enough to import 1000 Casks of Rice from South Carolinia. I wrote to Mr Benj Andrews to charter a suffcent number to import 4000 in the state of Massachusets Bay, his unfortunate death I am afraid will disconcert the business.

I hope you have not faild to complete what was requested of you; it is an object of the highest importance to the Interest and welfare of the United States. Pray dont neglect the affair. If you should be able to do more than is requested, please to let Mr. Otis, partner to Mr.

Andrews, know it, and if he should decline the business, let Messrs Miller and Tracy be acquainted with it, as they are requested to take the business up.[1]

The Express is just going and I have not time to take a Copy or correct what I have wrote. I am Sir Your humble Sert

NATH GREENE

ALS (Original in possession of David Coblentz, Raphine, Va., 1973).
1. On Andrews's death, see above, Otis to NG, 10 January; on rice shipments, see Wadsworth to NG, 2 January.

To Nehemiah Hubbard

[Philadelphia, 27 January 1779. If Hubbard has not chartered vessels to transport one thousand casks of rice from Charleston, as requested by NG, "pray dont *let there be a moments delay* as it is of the *highest importance* to the interest and welfare *of the United States.*"[1] ALS (MiU-C) 1 p.]

1. NG's letter of "about" 5 January not found. On rice shipments, see above, Wadsworth to NG, 2 January.

From Colonel Clement Biddle

Dear General   Rarriton [N.J.] Jan: 27, 1779

I had wrote to Colo Hay and Colo Bostwick when I received a very Acceptable Letter from the former in which he tells me they had got in Forage not only for a present supply but beforehand and he thought they should now do tollerably well. Also that the spare horses sent to recruit he found, on sending a person to visit them, were well kept and would be in good Order for spring.

We have rub'd on here tolerably well but begin to find it difficult to get in Forage. The latter Clause of Gov Livingstones Proclamation as I expected has in a great Measure defeated the intent of it, but it is of some Aid to us and Mr Marsh at Rahway has already got us 80 Tonns of fresh hay and some salt hay, great part of which is come on and coming when the roads are passible.[1]

Something must be done to repair the roads between here and Trenton, also from the Delaware to North River or they will be impassible. The men have been too much fatigued with hutting to turn out in any great Numbers for the roads.[2]

The Commissary Generals Application for Teams to convey two hundred barrels of flour weekly from the Delaware to Newborough or New Windsor I sent to Mr Furman and wrote to him and Colo Hooper to provide as much Forage as possible, but from the Accounts I have already repeatedly received from them I apprehend the greatest difficulty and almost impossibility of procuring any thing like a sufficiency. If the quantity to be sent is lessend or to be continued to the utmost I beg to be informd.[3]

Last Evening intelligence was received that the Enemy had brought a number of the Troops to Staaten Island and were making preparation to cross over to Jersey. Our Guards and Pickets were doubled, and the men kept their Arms in readiness. The Night was bad and no Account of their crossing.[4] They may *attempt* to disturb the post at Elizabeth Town, but I have no Idea of their Attacking us at this camp. If they should the troops will fight hard to defend their hutts. Would it be amiss to have the Brigade Artillery with us? The horses of the spare Teams and Regimental Teams Could be applied to hawl them without increasing our horses, for you know I am for keeping them to as few as possible.

The [artillery] park at Pluckumin have been very well supplied with Forage.

I hope to have the pleasure of seeing you soon in Camp. With Compliments to Mrs Greene, Cols Cox, Pettit and Wadsworth, I am with great respect Dr Genl Your most obedt huml servt

CLEMENT BIDDLE

The former situation of the Troops in Georgia and Carolina made it unnecessary to give any Orders[5] relative to Forage as there were few or no Teams employ'd.

It may now become an object for direction and I will write to the DQM Genl there if it is your pleasure and you will inform me his name. Yr ob

C B

ALS (PPAmP).
    1. On the governor's proclamation, see Biddle's letter above, of 25 January.
    2. It was often up to the quartermaster to maintain existing state roads. In March, for example, fatigue parties from Middlebrook were ordered by the quartermaster to repair various roads in New Jersey as far away as Trenton. (*Pa. Archives*, 2nd ser., 11: 423)
    3. Jeremiah Wadsworth had written Biddle from Philadelphia on 16 January that he had received an alarming report of imminent starvation in the posts along the lower Hudson River unless they received forty barrels of flour per day. (An extract of Wadsworth's letter in Biddle's hand is in the Greene Papers, vol. 4: 46, PPAmP.)
    4. Several such reports circulated during January and February, but no such raid occurred.
    5. Events in Georgia and South Carolina are discussed in note at NG to Sullivan, 26 January, above.

See Map 1 for geographic references above.

From Major Robert Forsyth

[Camp Middlebrook, N.J., 27 January 1779. Is sending "sundry Letters from the Eastward." Lord Stirling has received intelligence, which he has relayed to Washington, that the enemy intends "taking an Airing in Jersey," but Forsyth does not believe it will happen.[1] QM department ready to execute Stirling's orders. A group of young women and officers had "a most agreeable hop last Evening. . . . We kept it up till four in the morning." ALS (PPAmP) 2 pp.]

1. Stirling was in command at Middlebrook during Washington's absence in Philadelphia. On British incursions, see note above, Biddle to NG.

From Whitehead Humphreys[1]

[Philadelphia, 27 January 1779. As per his conversation with NG, he proposes to make Axes "Superior in Quality" to any made before and at current prices, which will "rise or fall in proportion to Coal, Iron, Steel, and Workmen's Wages."[2] ALS (PPAmP) 1 p.]

1. Humphreys was a steelmaker whose equipment had been commandeered during the British occupation of Philadelphia. (*PMHB*, 61 [1937]: 172)
2. He was among the first businessmen to insert the equivalent of a modern escalator clause in a contract.

From Colonel Francis Wade

[Wilmington, Dela., 27 January 1779. Has had no word on General Pulaski;[1] farmers who agreed to feed horses "have declared off"; corn at £3 per bushel puts him "to a stand how to Act"; NG's advice would be "Verry satisfactory"; roads are "scarce passable"; General Smallwood's ordering men back to regiments leaves Wade destitute of help; American troops guarding Convention troops are "Exceedingly troublesome," robbing the inhabitants, etc.[2] ALS (PPAmP) 2 pp.]

1. On Pulaski's Legion, see below, Pettit to NG, 10 February.
2. On Convention troops, see above, NG to Davenport, 9 November 1778.

From George Washington

Sir   Philad'a 27th January 1779
    You are hereby directed to provide with all convenient dispatch Twenty five hundred pack saddles of the cheapest and strongest kind, fit for the purpose of transporting Provisions, Stores and Baggage.[1] I am Sir yr most obt Servt

                                                              G W

Df (Washington Papers: DLC).
1. The pack saddles were for a proposed plan to "carry the War into the Indian Country next Spring," as Washington explained to Gen. Lachlan McIntosh at Fort Pitt, 31 January. (Fitzpatrick, *GW*, 14: 58–59) On the Indian expedition, see NG to Washington, 5 January, above.

From Joseph Reed, President of the Pennsylvania Council

[Philadelphia, 28 January 1779. If John Coryell "refuses reasonable Propositions" in settling the "Affairs of his Ferry" with the QM department, the council will give the department "all necessary Assistance."[1] ALS (PPAmP) 1 p.]

1. Coryells Ferry, fifteen miles above Trenton, had been used numerous times by Washington's army. See Map 3.

From William Moore Smith

[Philadelphia, 28 January 1779. Reiterates in a semiformal document William Moore's claims for damages as described in Moore's letter of 10 November 1778, above. He submits the document to "General Green's Consideration, whose Justice and Humanity will undoubtedly induce him to do every Thing in his Power for the Service of an ancient respectable Gentleman, whose Age and Infirmities, the General knows, must plead in his Behalf." Is sending this at NG's request "in Order to assist his Memory."[1] ADS (PPAmP) 2 pp.]

1. On the background and final settlement of Moore's claims, see note, Moore to NG, 10 November 1778, above. William Moore Smith, a twenty-year-old lawyer, was the grandson of William Moore and son of the noted educator, the Reverend William Smith, who had been imprisoned with Moore in 1758. (*PMHB*, 4 [1880]: 373–78)

From Colonel Walter Stewart

My Dear General   Williamsburgh [Va.] Jany 29th 1779
    I had the pleasure of Addressing you from Fredericksburgh which hope you receiv'd safe.[1] In it I mention'd my apprehensions for the Army on Account of Provisions. The farther we Travel South the greater we find the distresses of the People for Corn and Bread, and every Article much higher in price. I am Happy to find Congress have Ordered so large a Sum to be raised [?] in Taxation this year. That and Calling in the two emissions of   I am in hopes will at least give a check to this rapid depretiation which has unfortunately taken place all over the Continent.
    The Affair between Mr Deane and the Lees have Occasion'd much Conversation in this Country.[2] [We] found the People as low down as Fredericksburgh possess'd with very Just Ideas of those men

and their Colleagues in Congress, but Richard Henry [Lee] with a few Adherents have been very busy between that place and Williamsburgh. The People heard but one Story, and were from their Old Attachment to the Lee Family willing to believe it. However Col Ball and myself have been equally Industrious in placing things in a proper light, and I flatter myself the day is not far distant when the Junto will receive a Severe Shock by being depriv'd of one of the most Artful, designing and Wicked men the Country stands Curs'd with; I mean Richard Henry.[3] It is amazing to hear of his Artifice in this state in support a Popular Character, but the Peoples eyes are now Open'd and I doubt whether his Oratory and Weeping will again bring Tears and Lamentations (as Usual) for his sufferings from [the] Assembly; they have ever been Infatuated when he held forth to them, for whatever he said they were sure to believe.[4]

He has been very Industrious to make the Inhabitants of this Country Imagine that General Lee was the Salvation of our Army at Monmouth. No Circumstances has ever pleas'd me so much as my having been under his command that day. I have an Opportunity of Contradicting that Assertion with propriety; as I can safely declare it an Infamous falshood, they had likewise heard he had been in the Heat of the Action, and that he supported it for a length of time until the command was taken from him by his Excellency; this every officer who was in the field that day knows to be false, and that he never Intended to fight is equally clear to me by his asking Gen'l Wayne Why he had his men drawn up in front of the Enemys Artillery and Cavalry.[5] I am sorry to Trouble you so much on this Subject but it is one which nearly Concerns the Army and the Continent in General. It [shocks] me to find those men have even an advocate when those advocates know them oppos'd to the Interest of our Worthy General [Washington].

Williamsburgh I find the most Unsociable and least Polite place I have been in, in Virginia, but the Governor [Patrick Henry] is so [indecipherable] and pays so little Attention to the Officers of the Army that I dont Wonder People who are so naturally Inclin'd to, should follow his Example. We have been here two days, and only remain to dine with Old Ennis and a Mr Tazewell whom I came particularly recommended to. I find the old Continentals stick together whenever we meet, it makes me very happy to see it the case.

Poor Ball has not been so Successful as he could [have wish'd]. Old Mrs Taylor unfortunately heard he had Suffer'd a little [last] Campaign in [the] Wars of Venus; this and his having a son seems to distress her so much, that she has persuaded her Daughter to cast him off. I am happy to Inform you it has not entirely broken his Heart.

We set off tomorrow for James River, and shall push as Expeditiously as possible to Petersburg from thence to Fredericksburgh and hope to reach the Army early in April.

I beg my Respectful Compliments to Mrs Greene and his Excellency and all friends in Camp. You would be mightily pleas'd with the Generals Mother who is really a Sweet old Lady.[6] I am Just Inform'd a vessell is Arriv'd at York loaded with 200 Hhds Sugar, 200 Rum and a rich Cargoe of other Articles to [the] address of Mr Deane. I Am my Dr Genl yr Affect friend

W STEWART

ALS (MiU-C).
1. 4 January, above.
2. See John Cadwalader to NG, 5 December 1778, above.
3. On the "Junto" (or "Conway Cabal"), of which Lee was considered by Greene and Stewart to be a prime mover, see above, vol. 2: 277–78n.
4. Stewart wrote off Richard Henry Lee too soon. Although he was hurt politically by his part in the Lee-Deane affair and resigned from Congress in May 1779, he was later returned to Congress, even serving as its president. (*DAB*)
5. On Charles Lee's role at Monmouth, see above, vol. 2: 452–56n. Stewart's testimony at Lee's court-martial had helped to bring about Lee's dismissal. On his court-martial, see note at NG to McDougall, 8 November 1778, above.
6. They had visited Mary Washington when in Fredericksburg. If she entertained them, it could not have been lavishly, for two weeks earlier she had written her nephew, with possible exaggeration, that corn meal was too expensive, that she had not had a taste of flour, and had "never lived so poor" in her life. (Flexner, *GW*, p. 337)

To Major Robert Forsyth

Sir
Philadelphia January 30th 1779

Your favor with the inclosd Letters and returns from the Eastward came in last Night.[1]

I am happy to hear you are at Camp. I wish to be with you but am still upon the great Ocean of uncertainty.

To be sure the Spring is the season for Love; but if you stay in Camp until Spring you will have the hot season for a warm embrace, the agreeableness or disagreeableness of which I am a stranger, haveing always been absent from my Dulcinea in the Summer. However I dont wish to make your prospects more disagreeable than necessity obliges me.

Will the Enemy come out? Ten to one they dont all return again. I have not seen His Excellency this morning; but if there [is?] the least prospect of their Visiting you I am perswaded the General will fly to Camp and I shall come with him.

Please to let me have a Return of all the quarter masters Stores in Command, a return of the Stores at Elizabeth Town with the Troops there.

I want a Return of all the Artificers Brigades and Deputy quarter masters, Clerks &c.

The General has set Monday to return and notifyed the Congress, but I am afraid he wont hold his resolution.[2] Col. [Cornelius] Sheriff is now in Town. I intend to settle the matter with him respecting his relieving you. If he cant attend Claiborne must undertake. Please to innitiate him into the business for the purpose as I am determined you shall go soon at all hazzard.[3] Yours

N GREENE

If Col Hay has sent in any Returns lately of the Stores at Fish Kill please to forward them.

ALS (PCC, item 173, vol. 2: 65, DNA).
    1. Forsyth's letter of 27 January.
    2. Washington left the following Tuesday, 2 February; NG followed several days later.
    3. Richard Claiborne did replace Forsyth, who returned to Virginia and soon after became a deputy commissary under Wadsworth. See Forsyth to NG, 19 May, below.

To Colonel John Davis

[Philadelphia, 31 January 1779. To alleviate shortage of forage in next campaign he suggests that Davis contract with farmers to sow oats in the spring.[1] LS (Davis Papers: DLC) 1 p.]

    1. For another deputy's response and the farmers' lack of enthusiasm for the plan, see below, Hubbard to NG, 6 February.

From Joseph Reed, President of the Pennsylvania Council

Sir   Walnut Street [Philadelphia] Sunday 3 oClock [31 Jan. 1779]

    You will oblige me by informing me whether you have given any Directions or Orders to any Officer in your Department to settle the Account which was lately depending between your Department, or Gen. Arnold and certain Subjects of this State sent last Summer to Egg Harbour under the Direction of one Jesse Jordan since the Complaint on that Subject has been depending before Congress, or since Wednesday last, or if any Directions have been given by you on that Subject, Some Transactions having been mentioned to as having passed highly injurious to the Interests and Honour of the State as well as tending to dishonour the Department.[1] I am Sir Your most obed Hbble Serv

JOS: REED

ALS (PPAmP).
    1. See NG's answer below, written a few hours later.

To Joseph Reed, President of the Pennsylvania Council

Sir,   Col. Mitchel's [Philadelphia] 5 o'clock January 3d, [31st] 1779. Your favor of this day, dated at three o'Clock this afternoon, Is to me both surprising and unintelligible.[1] I have given no orders respecting the matter you mention. Col. Mitchel shewed me a Letter from General Arnold, and one that he wrote the general upon the subject, endeavoring to fix the principles upon which the party were to be paid for their services, at the same time observing he should obey the General's order, if he gave one. Col. Mitchel waits upon you to give you any further information you may want respecting the business. If there has been any thing done contrary to the honor or Interest of the state, it is a piece of inadvertence and all together without design. I have the honor to be, with respect, Your most obedient humble servt,

NATH. GREENE.

Reprinted from *Pa. Archives*, 7: 175.

1. To judge from Joseph Reed's curt letter above, one would not suspect that he and NG were friends, but Reed was undoubtedly writing in his official capacity at the direction of the radical executive council. (On Reed's switch to the radicals, see above, Reed to NG, 5 November 1778.) Reed's letter was "unintelligible" to NG only because of its purposefully vague allusions to "some transactions"; NG had known since early December that John Mitchell, his deputy in Philadelphia, was involved in Arnold's use of public wagons for private business. (See his letter to Pettit, 7 December, above.) During his stay in Philadelphia he must have learned much more about the incident since he stayed in Mitchell's house during his visit. Although he was ultimately responsible for either defending Mitchell's actions or removing him from office, NG, beset by other pressing demands and about to leave Philadelphia for camp, preferred to let the matter be handled by his assistant, Charles Pettit, who was, coincidentally, Joseph Reed's brother-in-law.

Mitchell's original involvement was an inadvertent one, arising from his inordinate desire to please those in high places. As a former merchant he knew his way around Philadelphia and as deputy quartermaster he was in a position to bestow favors on many people. Mitchell and his wife entertained the Washingtons and Greenes among others, and over the years he obtained sundry hard-to-get articles for Washington— from gilded calling cards to a carriage. Thus, when Benedict Arnold asked him for wagons and teams from the quartermaster department, John Mitchell was not the man to turn down a major general who was also commandant of Philadelphia. It was unfortunate for Mitchell that Arnold was so out of favor with the Pennsylvania radicals.

Arnold, the hero of Saratoga, had been named commandant of Philadelphia when the British withdrew from the city in June 1778 because a leg wound prevented him from taking a field command. From the moment he took up residence in the former headquarters of Sir William Howe, he began to alienate the Pennsylvania radicals. They eyed with suspicion his declaration of martial law (although mandated by Congress), and as the months passed they were infuriated by what appeared to them his arrogant manner, his questionable business dealings, and his lavish entertainments to which he invited relatives of suspected loyalists. (See above, Reed to NG, 5 November 1778; for a different view, see Cadwalader to NG, 5 December.) Arnold made no attempt to mollify his critics; in fact he openly defied them. More and more the opposition to him centered in the executive council, which was entirely controlled by the radicals. To make matters worse he won the undying enmity of its doctrinaire and spiteful secretary, Timothy Matlack, by refusing to reprimand an aide who had ordered Matlack's son, a militia sergeant, to run a demeaning errand. (Wallace, *Traitorous Hero*, 174–76)

It was amid the growing mistrust between Arnold and the council that, in October 1778, Arnold had asked Mitchell for wagons to transport the cargo of the *Charming Nancy*, in which Arnold had considerable financial interest, from Egg Harbor, N.J., to Philadelphia, a distance of some sixty miles. The request came on top of what the executive council had considered Mitchell's "excessive" call-up (under Pennsylvania law) of hundreds of wagons for hauling flour to the army. (*Pa. Col. Records*, 11: 588–89, 708) This did not deter Mitchell from complying with Arnold's request, and on 22 October he sent Jesse Jordan with a brigade of twelve wagons to Egg Harbor. (Ibid., 11: 680–81)

The council learned about the incident only when the wagon master of Chester County complained that Jordan and his men had not been paid. It began an immediate investigation. On 18 January, two weeks before Reed wrote to NG, the council ordered Mitchell to explain in writing Arnold's use of the wagons. (Ibid., 11: 672) Mitchell answered the next day. He declared that Arnold had agreed to reimburse the public service, and he justified his acquiescence with the assertion that he had "a greater number of Continental teams coming in than I expected" and that Jordan's absence posed no "inconvenience to the service." (*Pa. Archives*, 7: 160–61) Reed sent Mitchell's statement to Arnold with a request for an explanation. (*Pa. Col. Records*, 11: 674) Arnold's peremptory reply so offended the council that they immediately referred the matter to Congress, calling upon the delegates for "justice, and reparation of our authority, thus wounded by one of their officers." (Reed to Jay, 25 January 1779, *Proceedings of Arnold's Court Martial*: 12. For a full citation, see below, note at Pettit to NG, 26 and [27] February.)

Congress appointed a committee, chaired by William Paca of Maryland, to look into the allegations that Arnold had defied the council's civil authority and to "make report with all convenient speed." (*JCC*, 13: 115) On 3 February, when the committee had barely begun its investigations, the council made a formal complaint consisting of eight charges against Arnold, two of which concerned his use of the wagons. In the ensuing weeks, the Pennsylvania Council diligently gathered evidence for the committee, but Paca and his fellow members, not to be pressured, set about to make their own judicious inquiries. In the meantime, both Mitchell and Arnold continued to maintain that Arnold had been prevented from paying for the wagons by Jordan's failure to submit a bill. (*Pa. Archives*, 7: 213–20)

When NG wrote Reed on 4 February, he made no mention of the charges made the day before which implicated his deputy, nor did he respond to Reed's request of 1 February, below, for various written records. As he returned to camp on the fifth, disappointed by Congress's failure to cope with depreciation and troubled by the mounting criticism of his department, NG was relieved to leave matters in the capable hands of Charles Pettit. He was unable to foresee that, in the process of investigating Arnold's alleged offenses, the council also would uncover evidence about the wagon affair which would seriously implicate Mitchell, or that, for a few days, at mid-month, the council would turn its attention to his Philadelphia deputy and his assistant, Pettit, whose letters below, of 21, 25, and 26/27 February relate the extent of Mitchell's involvement with the council.

From Joseph Reed, President of the Pennsylvania Council

Dear Sir [Philadelphia] Sunday Evg [31 Jan. 1779]

The Council meeting this Evening, it will not be in my Power to spend it as I promised myself at Noon.

I received your Favour and shall communicate it to the Council. I did not suppose mine would be perfectly intelligible but if my Information was good Mr Mitchel would be able to explain it. At all Events in this Stage of the Business with General Arnold I think your Officers could not meddle with any Propriety to make that Gentle-

Clement Biddle, 1740–1814, oil painting by Albrecht Bernard Uhle after
Charles Willson Peale
(Courtesy of the Historical Society of Pennsylvania)

mans Situation better or worse, and I fear it will have disagreeable Consequences. If Mr Mitchel chuses to say any Thing on the Subject it will be best to be done in writing that it may not be capable of Misunderstanding or Misrepresentation.[1] I am Yours

J REED

I observed on the other Leaf the Council was to meet this Evening. It is upon the Business herein alluded to, so that if any Thing is to be offerd the sooner the better.

ALS (PPAmP).
1. On the Mitchell-Arnold affair, see note at NG to Reed, above.

To Joseph Reed, President of the Pennsylvania Council

Dear Sir   Philadelphia Sunday Evening January 31, 1779
I receivd your favor, of this Evening in answer to mine of this afternoon.
I was and still am so ignorant of the purport of your information and of any transactions haveing taken place in the quarter master department that has a tendency to prejudice the honor or Interest of this State, that your Letter appeard to me unintelligible. I wrote you in my first all that I knew about the matter and informd you that Col Mitchel would wait upon you to give any further information you might require.
There has two short Notes or Letters passed between Col Mitchel and General Arnold. If the Council are desirous of seeing them, the Col will attend.
I am perswaded there has no transaction taken place with a view of making General Arnolds case either worse or better. If there has anything happen'd that will have that effect it was without design.[1] I have the honor to be Your Excellencys most humble Sert

NATH GREENE

ALS (PPAmP).
1. See note at NG's first letter of the 31st, above.

From Colonel George Gibson[1]

[Camp Middlebrook, N.J.,[2] 31 January 1779. Details route by which the "Six nations may pass undiscover'd to the Cherokee, Chickashaw, Creek or Choctaw nations" in the South. ALS (PPAmP) 1 p.]

1. Gibson (1747–91) was familiar with the frontier, having spent several years as an Indian trader at Ft. Pitt and having led an expedition to New Orleans in 1776 to get

powder. His brother, Col. John Gibson, at this time was in command at Ft. Laurens in Ohio country. (*DAB*) On the proposed expeditions against the Indians, see above, NG to Washington, 5 January.
  2. Place not given, but his regiment, the First Virginia, was then in camp.

From Thomas Paine[1]

Dear Sir   [Philadelphia 31 January 1779][2]
  You doubtless think it strange I have not, as usual, called to see you. I have been out no where, and was resolved not to go out, till I had set every thing to rights. I know how it must end because I have it in my hands. The roguery will soon come out, and as I was determined to answer no questions upon the Subject, I thought it best to put it out of every body's power to ask me any, but finding you go tomorrow I must break thro' my resolve by calling upon you today.[3] I have acquainted his Excellency with the same reasons.
  Notwithstanding my absence, set me down as one of your most attached friends, and in return remember your Obt Hble Servt

                                                        THOS PAINE

P. S. If you should be away[?] when I call I wish you would leave word when you will be at home.

ALS (PPAmP).
  1. Paine had been a friend since serving as an aide to NG in 1776, during which time he wrote the first *Crisis*. (See above, vol. 1: 364, n3.)
  2. The place is determined by NG's presence in Philadelphia; the date is docketed on the verso and corroborated approximately by context.
  3. He refers to his involvement in the Silas Deane–Arthur Lee affair, which had split Congress into two warring camps and had brought about the resignation of President Henry Laurens. (See note, Cadwalader to NG, 5 December 1778, above.) In early December, Paine had taken up the case against Deane in the columns of the *Pennsylvania Packet*. Never noted for his discretion, Paine had quoted from secret documents that he had been privileged to see as secretary of Congress's Committee on Foreign Affairs. In so doing, he unwittingly embarrassed the French government, causing Ambassador Gérard to protest vehemently to Congress. The Lee faction saved Paine from outright dismissal but could not prevent his forced resignation on 8 January. For weeks he had, indeed, scarcely left his quarters. What transpired at his meeting with NG—or whether it ever took place—is not known. Although Paine and Greene remained friends, their relationship must have been strained during the following months, at a time when NG was arranging a partnership with Jeremiah Wadsworth and Silas Deane's brother Barnabas. (See below, NG to Wadsworth, 13 March #2.)

To John Jay, President of the Continental Congress

Sir   Philadelphia, 1st February 1779.
  In the different movements of the Army it frequently happens that the Inhabitants of the Country unavoidably suffer damages of various kinds for which Justice seems to demand that they should re-

ceive a Compensation from the publick.[1] There are two ways in which these damages usually happen one of which is the taking of such Articles on sudden Emergencies as the Army may stand in need of, which political Necessity will justify, and which reasonable Men will acquiesce in, the other is that kind of Trespass on private property which Armies in all Countries commit, partly from Necessity and partly from Accident and other Causes which even the best discipline does not wholly guard against. Such Articles as are taken for the use of the Army are usually paid for by the Quarter Master or Commissary; but the common Mode of ascertaining the Sums to be paid, by the Appraisement of Persons chosen in the Neighbourhood, is not unexceptionable, Experience having shewn that it admits of great diversity and Partiality in the Assessments; and though in many Instances the Parties receive more than may be justly due, they are frequently dissatisfied.

The incidental Damages which happen to Buildings, Gardens, Fields, &ca, whether necessary or not, are equally injurious to the Owner, and it may be no less politick than just, to establish some Mode for ascertaining Damages of this kind, and fixing how far Satisfaction ought to be made to the Sufferers. Great Mischiefs of this kind have already happened in many parts of the Country and the People call loudly for redress. They do not expect in all Cases a full compensation for their Damages, but they wish to see a Systematick Plan formed for the Distribution of Justice in such Cases by some known rule, that they may know what to rely on, and to whom they may apply for a common Measure of Redress. The want of such a regulation leaves Business in a state of Confusion and Difficulty. It creates discontent and an Unwillingness in the people to furnish Supplies for the Army. Some obtain pay at a higher rate than perhaps they are entitled to, while common Justice is withheld from others, the resolutions of Congress on this subject being not sufficiently explicit to direct the conduct of the Quarter Masters in one steady Line.

I would therefore beg leave to suggest to Congress the propriety of appointing certain Commissioners of proper Character and Abilities to hear and determine upon all Claims of this kind, subject to the Instructions of the Board of War, or such other Board as Congress shall be pleased to appoint, and to whom they shall report all their Proceedings; That the Commissioners be instructed to certify to the Quarter Master-General or to his Deputy such Assessments as are proper for him to pay, and in like manner to other Officers such as it may be proper for them to pay. There may be some Instances in which the Damages are so necessarily involved in the common Calamities of War that the Public cannot with propriety make any Compensation for them; and in others it may be doubtful by whom they ought to be paid: In every such case a Certificate may be given to the party injured, setting forth his Name, place of Abode, the amount of his Damages and how they arose, a Duplicate of which may be lodged in the War-Office as a record to be recurred [referred?] to when it shall be determined what farther Steps shall be taken respecting it. The Principles on which they are to be determined should, however, be previously settled as clearly and explicitly as may be, and the Commissioners instructed accordingly. In order to avoid Expence it may be well to appoint Officers of the Army to this Commission, as suitable Men may doubtless be found amongst them, who for some additional pay would execute the Trust with Fidelity. The Appointment of Officers might also be attended with a farther good Effect, especially if a set of Commissioners were to attend every separate Command or considerable Detachment of the Army, as they would be Witnesses of the Transactions and of course afford a constant Caution to the Officers in Command against permitting wanton Destruction, or the unnecessary Invasion of private property.

If Congress should think proper to adopt the Measure herein recommended, or any other that will be likely to effect the desired purpose, either myself or one of my Assistants will wait on such Committee or Board as they shall be pleased to appoint, to give such farther Information as shall be required.[2] I have the Honour to be, with the utmost Respect, Sir, your most obedient humble Servant

NATHEL GREENE

LS (PCC, item 155, vol. 1: 83, DNA).
1. A resolution to which Jay refers in his letter of this date, below, had undoubtedly triggered a discussion between NG and members of Congress on this perpetual problem. As noted at NG's Orders of 1 June 1778, above (vol. 2: 419–20n), he had paid for certain damages without authorization because Congress had failed to act. In the meantime, according to NG, Congress had forbidden such reimbursement. (NG to Sullivan, 9 February, below) No formal disapproval has been found, but NG may have been so instructed informally.
2. When Congress referred NG's letter to the Supply Departments Committee, that group dodged the issue by reporting the next day that "it would be improper to make allowance for wanton devastations which may be committeed, it being impossible to ascertain any precise mode in which justice will be done to Individuals or to the public." It added the observation, which was not likely to console those who had suffered from army depredations, that "in most cases remedy may be had against the Commanding Officer, whose duty it is to prevent such mischiefs." (JCC, 13: 133)
On 17 February, in another connection, the Committee on the Treasury, unable to cite a formal prohibition against the quartermaster paying damages, pointed out that such reimbursement was "not warranted by any Resolution of Congress and ought not to be made until some general rule may be established." (JCC, 13: 194) Congress, however, continued to avoid establishing such a rule, leaving the quartermaster to cope with complaints as best he could.

To Joseph Reed, President of the Pennsylvania Council

Sir   Philadelphia February 1, 1779

I have enquird of Col Mitchel respecting the threats thrown out against Jesse Jordan of confining him. He declares upon his honor that he never threatned Mr Jordan nor made use of any language that would admit of such an interpretation. When Mr Jordan first came to Town and demanded pay, he directed him to apply to General Arnold. The General refusing to give him his demand he returnd to Col Mitchel with a note from the General respecting his charge; and observd to Col Mitchel that if he could not have the whole of his demand he would have nothing and refusd to settle the affair. The Col told him he must settle it and that if he did not he would complain to the Governor and Council. Upon this he desird the Col to assist him in making out his account which he did. The Col also told the man that he must call and see the Governor and Council before he went out of Town to give them an account of the matter.[1]

As the Council may be inducd from Mr Jordans representation, and from Col Mitchel transactions in the matter to think he acted with a veiw of changeing the complexion of the business, I wish the Col may be called upon to appear before the Council to give them a narrative of his proceedings.

As I said last night so I say again I cannot immagin the Col has done any thing intentionally wrong.

The Clerks of the office and a Waggon Master was present when Mr Jordan was in the Office, neither of which heard any threats more than that he *Col Mitchel* would complain to the Council if he *Jesse Jordan* did not settle the business. I have the honor to be Your Excellencys most humble Servt

NATH GREENE

ALS (NHi).

1. Jordan, a wagoner in public service from Chester County, had been employed to transport private goods for General Arnold. See above, NG to Reed, 31 January, #1. He had come to Philadelphia on 29 January, some three months after the incident, to settle his account with Col. John Mitchell. At a Pennsylvania Council meeting of 30 January, Jordan testified that Mitchell, NG's deputy in Philadelphia, had threatened the wagoner that he would "make him a Prisoner" if he did not settle his account with General Arnold. (*Pa. Col. Records*, 11: 680–81)

From Joseph Reed, President of the Pennsylvania Council

Sir   Council Chamber Philada Feby 1. 1779.

I have just received your favour and can only say in answer, that Jordan has sworn to the particulars I mentioned, and as it seems to be the idea of Congress that we have no authority to call upon any persons against whom complaint is made in order to enquire into their conduct, 'till that point is setled we do not incline to see any more of their officers least we may subject ourselves to farther inconveniencies. Mr Mitchels representation will have its due weight if he thinks proper to make it in writing as I mentioned before.

In the meantime by the desire of Council I request you to Send us an office transcript of the entry of those waggons into the publick service and their discharge and also attested copies of the certificates given at the Ferries which it appears were made in the first case and given in the latter. The 21st October was the time which I mention to make the search more easy.[1] I am sir Your most obedient Servant

JOS: REED

LS (PPAmP).

1. NG did not comply with Reed's request for the various papers. See note above, NG to Reed, 31 January, #1.

From Udny Hay

[Fishkill, N.Y., 1 February 1779. Regrets he cannot get clothes for artificers engaged by the day. Promised wheelwrights, whose complaints were reasonable, their wages would be same as those in Philadelphia. Must give smiths and coopers same rate. Mr. Simmons (Col. Morgan Lewis's agent) has made contracts with artificers which Lewis will not honor. Is so convinced of the many evils that have come from Simmons's conduct "that I am determind to furnish the men who have been dupd by him with money to sue him, should I even be oblidged to pay it out of my own Pockett."[1] Wants to know daily wages of artificers to the "southward." Apologizes for late returns. Again asks for NG's opinion on establishing a tanyard.[2] ALS (PPAmP) 3 pp.]

1. On his earlier criticism of Simmons, see his letter of 9 January, above.
2. NG answered Hay on 10 February, below.

From John Jay, President of the Continental Congress

Sir

Philada 1st Feby 1779

The enclosed Copy of an Act of Congress of the 30th Ult: directs the Payment of sundry Accounts due to the Inhabitants of New York, for Provisions and Services supplied and performed immediately after the loss of Fort Montgomery. As these Sums have been due for more than a year, I am persuaded you will, without delay, provide for the Execution of this Act.[1] I am Sir, With great Respect your most obed't Servt

JOHN JAY

ALS (PPAmP).
1. Governor George Clinton had been in command of the troops that were "reduced to the Necessity" of taking flour, cattle, and forage from the inhabitants. After writing Congress "more than once" without results, he asked for help from Washington, who passed the letter on to Congress. (Clinton to Washington, 29 December 1778, Clinton, *Papers*, 4: 436, and Washington to Congress, 29 January 1779, Fitzpatrick, *GW*, 14: 52.) Jay wrote an identical letter to Wadsworth. (PCC, item 14, p. 39, DNA) The resolution is in *JCC*, 13: 124–25. NG answered 3 February, below.

Major Robert Forsyth
to Quartermaster of Maxwell's Brigade

[Middlebrook, N.J., 2 February 1779. NG requests that "you will immediately make out a return" of stores at Elizabeth Town and send it to him at Philadelphia.[1] ACy (PCC, item 173, vol. 4: 67, DNA) 1 p.]

1. Adjoining folios in item 173 have similar requests to Jacob Weiss at camp and the quartermasters of the North Carolina Brigade and an unidentified brigade.

From Colonel Timothy Pickering of the Board of War

[Philadelphia, 2 February 1779. Because of an uncertain supply of clothing from abroad, the board decided Mr. [Samuel A.] Otis should use his stock for the "military part of the army." Mr. Lewis should keep what had been sent him.[1] The fact that NG's agent is also the board's agent prevents the "mischief" of competition. ALS (PPAmP) 2 pp.]

1. Morgan Lewis's quartermaster employees (at Albany) were not considered part of the "military."

From Colonel Alexander Spotswood

[Fredericksburg, Va., 2 February 1779. Congress, which had not accepted his resignation in 1777, promised he should be the next brigadier from Virginia but has not communicated with him since. He will "demand" they comply. Asks NG to use his influence with friends in Congress.[1] ALS (MiU-C) 2 pp.]

1. Spotswood commanded the Second Virginia Regiment under NG at Brandywine. Washington, a relative by marriage, had tried to dissuade him from resigning but would not intercede to get him back. (Fitzpatrick, *GW*, 12: 306, 315–16) Despite Spotswood's efforts, Congress refused to name him brigadier or give him another regiment. As seen in his letter of 12 May, below, he reluctantly returned to farming.

To John Jay, President of the Continental Congress

[Philadelphia, 3 February 1779. Has directed Colonel Hay to reimburse citizens as per Jay's letter of 1 February. ALS (PCC, item 173, vol. 4: 69, DNA) 1 p.]

From Major Robert Forsyth

Sir   Camp Middle Brook [N.J.] 3d Feby 1779.
Your very agreeable Letter of the 31st was handed me this Moment.[1] Your faithful old John comes with his Bays in very good order. I am in Pain for Mrs Greene the Roads are so exceedingly bad.[2] I am respectfully Dr Sir Your humble servt

ROBT FORSYTH

ALS (PPAmP).
   1. Letter not found.
   2. The Greenes arrived back at camp on 8 February after a coach trip of several days. (NG to Gooch, 9 February, below)

From Samuel A. Otis

[Boston, 3 February 1779. To transport rice from Charleston, must pay half in freight or one third and insure it.[1] Asks NG's opinion. Needs money. Will forward nails, oakum, etc. to Col. [Morgan] Lewis tomorrow. ALS (PPAmP) 1 p.]

   1. See above, NG to Wadsworth, 2 January.

From Colonel Francis Wade

Sir   Wilmington [Del.] 3d Feby 1779
   I was handed your lettr of the 31st of last month[1] last Even'g and shall pay the necess'y attention to giveing the Encouragement and makeing the Contracts for Oats as you desire, but as to geting people to fulfill their Contracts at this day its not to be done and the mode that I hear has been and now is pursued, Vizt to Engage the prices now going for grain and the rise of the market at a Certain fixed time in my opinion must make Contracts Verry uncertain.[2]
   I have got the shallops in motion and have hopes Can give a helping hand towards a supply of forage, some are already gone up [the Delaware], and others on the way.[3] I seen some waggons going past here on their way to Dover yesterdy to be stationed there, by orders as the drivers informed of Colnl Blain [Ephraim Blaine].[4] I am at a loss to Conjecture the reasons for sending them, when I have ordered and now have there, at the Commissaries request as many

Teams as was thought necess'y for that service, and if more was wanted Can send them at a Call. I wish some matters before mentioned respect'g that gentns assertions Could be brought to an Explanat'n so as to have a line drawn and prevent his or any other person throwing out ungenerous reflections agt [against] the department. Theres a gent'n now in town Mr Whitehead Jones (who Mr Biddle knows) thats Employ'd by Coln'l Blain to purchase forage in this quarter, and was present at the time Coln'l Blain and I talked over those matters, and no doubt Can well remembr what I put up with from that gentn to prevent quarling. Until we come to a fair and Candid hearing, if on which, that it apears that I have in a single instance given that gent'n or his department the least Cause to Complain, I shall be ready and willing to make any submission that may be thought necess'y. I did Vindicate the honour of the department when he asserted in the presence of several gent'n that we had twice as many horses at Camp as was necess'y &c. However if you think it proper to pass the matter over unnoticed, I shall submit to your bett'r Judgem't[5] and am with respect and regards Sir Your most obed and most Hbble Servt

FRAN'S WADE

ALS (PPAmP).
1. Letter not found.
2. On contracting for oats in the field, see above, NG to Hubbard, 20 January.
3. A shallop was generally a two-masted vessel with lugsails for use in shallow waters. A smaller version was rowed.
4. Ephraim Blaine, the deputy commissary of purchases, did not normally provide transportation—the quartermaster's job.
5. NG's response has not been found.

From Joseph Reed, President of the Pennsylvania Council

[Walnut Street, Philadelphia, 4 February 1779. Asks that the council's proposal on Schuylkill Bridge made to NG's department some time ago be settled.[1] ALS (PPAmP) 1 p.]

1. NG, Pettit, and Cox had met with the council on this matter on 14 January. (*Pa. Col. Records*, 11: 666) See NG's letter below.

To Joseph Reed, President of the Pennsylvania Council

[Philadelphia, 4 February 1779. In answer to Reed's letter above, NG agrees to pay rent on bridge beginning the previous summer, less the cost of repairs.[1] ACyS (PCC, item 173, vol. 4: 71, DNA) 1 p.]

1. When the council did not accept NG's offer, Charles Pettit submitted a proposal to Reed on 20 February (Greene Papers, PPAmP) which became the basis for a settle-

ment a year later. The quartermaster department was to replace the damaged bridge in exchange for free tolls for the army and £ 700 annual rental from a "Tenant," who, in turn, would collect tolls from the public. (*Pa. Col. Records*, 12: 269)

From Colonel Henry Hollingsworth

Dear Sir   Head of Elk [Md.] 4th Febuy at night 1779

Your favr of the 2d I am Honnourd with,[1] observe the Contents, have dispach'd the packet to Mr Calhoon at Baltimore (who I embrace this oppertunity of wrighting you by). As to the price of waggoning, tis cartainly too high if it can be got done Lower, but tis not the case hear; whatever it may be in Philada, tis so different that I am now deficulted to procure waggons at 55/ to Continu[e] any time. As the present high price of grain has occation'd many of the owners of Teams to Leave the Sarvic and prepare for Farming, and many others will Leave it in a few days at any rate, which occation'd me to determine to make an ofer to them that those that would not enter for Six or twelve Months, should be immediately discharged, in hopes by this to get some of them to engage for that time so that we might have them to depend on, but if they can be had in plenty at 40/ tis better. I would recommend the engageing at Least fifty for this post, as I have more than that number of privat Teams now imploy'd (besides the two Bregades of Continantal Teams) and I am cartain the Hour I mention thier pay being redus'd to 40/ every Team will Leave the sarvic. I have therefore not mention'd it to any one, Least it should distress us before those come from Town.

I must also take the freedom to recommend that those Teams may be engaged for such a Length of time as you may think proper, as those which are discharged now, I fear will not willingly enter the sarvic in the Sumer Season, espetially while there is such incouragement for Farming. As to a Commission to my under Agents I am obliged to give such sallery, or wages, to each person commission'd by me as will incourage Gentlemen of Fortune, Carracteur, and Buisenis to undertake, and none others I dare entrust at the Distance some of them are from me. I have engaged to give to Capt John W. Veazey, who purchases in Ceacil [Cecil] and Kent Countys, nine pence per Bushell for all Corn, Oats, Rye, Flaxseed &c purchasd and sent me as Forage, and Mr Standly Byers who purchases in Dorset, Somerset, Worchester [Worcester], Wooster and Dorchester, the same.[2]

Colo Hemsley who I have Commissiond to purchase in Queen Anns, Talbert [Talbot], and Caroline Countyes, I have not fully agreed with as to his Sallery, or Commission. He refus'd the price the other Gentlemen acted for, and asked Ten pr Ct.[3] I told him I could not give any Such price, and mention'd that I did not know that I was Justifyable in allowing more than 40 Dollars pr Month which He smild at,

and assur'd me He had never done Buisenis for Mess's Willing and
Morris for Less, though He had done more Buisenis in one week for
them, than the whole ammount of the present purchase which would
confine Himselfe and two assistants for three to Six Months. He then
talked of finding and paying all Storage untill the Corn was Recd by
the Vessles, and to go to geting it into Stores immediately, which I
much incouraged as the Corn was then in the greatis dangure of
being purchasd by the Speculators, and we should be obliged to give
their price for it. We at Last agreed on no particular Sallery but that He
as a purchaser Should be paid an ample and sofficiant reward for his
Time and Expence, and as a Gentleman should not aske more, which
I agreed to give Him, not knowing a Gentleman in the District so capable of compleat'g the purchase. How far I may be sensurd, or
blamed for my conduct I cant say, can only say in this as in all my
other Conduct, that I have intended it for the best, and am not in the
Least afraid but it will turn out so, for at the distance I Live, and in
those [these] Corrupt times I dare not trust a man that could be Hired
at forty Dollars pr Month with fore of [or] five thousand pounds at a
time, nor if I did would the first Gentlemen of this State, who are
farmers, choose to Deal with, nor if they dealt, would some of them
be confin'd to Bargain by them. I lookd on it that Colo Hemsleys Carracteur, Influence, and Establishment, in those Countys, renderd his
Sarvise worth all the difference and much more.

As to the State of things at this post they are thus situated, all the
Forage that I have used through the winter and that sent on to Xteen
[Christiana] for Philada or Camp, has been collected in this County
only, nor have I re'd one Bushell from elsewhere, which has chiefly
been consum'd by the Teams in forwarding the Q Master, Comissary,
and Forage Stores (a few thousand Bushels Excepted sent to Xteen),
which must ever [?] be the case while such prodigeous quantityes of
provissions are to be forwarded this way, unless supplyd with Forage
from below, which I flatter myselfe will soon be the case as the Ice is
now all gone and the Bay clear, and I have wrote to every Forage Master to the southward of me, and to Each of the Gentlemen by me
commissiond, to forward as fast as possible Each a Load or two, so
that I am in hopes of a Speedy supply, which is much wanted hear.

I am now and have been for some time Forageing on Wheat nor
can I get any more Corn or oats untill it comes up the Bay, to Hasten
which every thing in my power has been done.[4] Three Vessles arived
hear this day with flower [flour]. An applycation made me by the
Commissary for fifty waggons more than I have (or have Forage for).
This Evnng a Bregade of waggons arrivd from Philada for Forage. I
having sent all I could possibly spare from hear to Xteen in time of
Frost [?][5] in order to send it to Philada or Camp, shall be obliged to

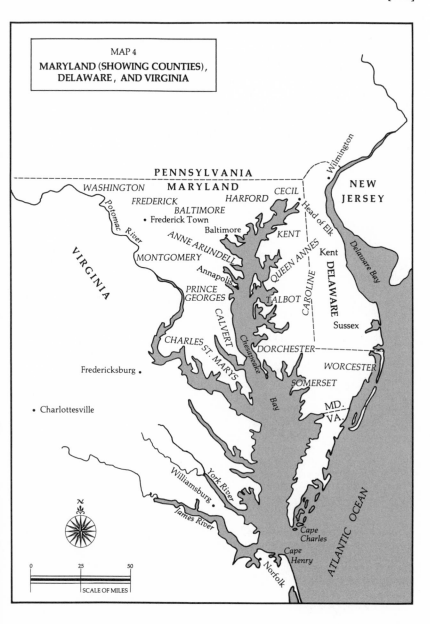

MAP 4

MARYLAND (SHOWING COUNTIES),
DELAWARE, AND VIRGINIA

send them down to Capt Veazey at Sasifrace [Sassafras, Md.], unless a Vessle arrives this night. No Quarter Masters Stores hear. My Accounts are made out, and now compareing with the Vouchers, flatter myselfe of coming up with them in Six or Eight days, or sooner if possible. No doubt I have tired you, Mus begg your Indulgence for the Length of this Letter, as I wish'd to be particelar and as tis by this only your Honnour can be Inform'd or your Most Humb Servt Directd

H HOLLINGSWORTH

PS Pray Ecuse erors as myselfe and the Clerks are too Busy to take a Coppy

ALS (PPAmP).
1. Letter not found.
2. In NG's answer of 14 February, below, he must have had Byers and Veazey in mind when he referred to Hollingsworth's appointing "the most capital Merchants" at such high commissions.
3. For a former justice of the peace and patriot militia colonel, William Hemsley demanded an outrageously high commission. Hollingsworth's counter proposal—to determine Hemsley's compensation *after* he bought the forage—was a most dubious business practice, however lofty the colonel's character. Surprisingly, NG did not comment on it in his letter of the fourteenth.
    The final settlement with Colonel Hemsley has not been found. While working for Hollingsworth, he was elected to the Maryland Senate and later represented the state in Congress. See sketch in *BDAC*.
4. "Forageing on Wheat" was strictly forbidden by a resolve of Congress of 26 October 1778, which was passed in order to reserve the scarce grain for human consumption. (*JCC*, 12: 1064) Whether Hollingsworth acted in ignorance or defiance of the resolution is not known.
5. That is, while the rivers were frozen.

See Map 4 for geographic references above.

From Colonel Thomas Chase[1]

[Boston, 5 February 1779. DQM Chase acknowledges NG's letter of 14 January and money. Has sent wine to NG and Major Lee. Among prices he cites are wood at $36 per cord and corn at $13 per bushel. ALS (PPAmP) 1 p.]

1. He was DQMG for eastern Massachusetts.

From Colonel Josiah Parker[1]

Dear General   Smithfield, Virginia February 5th 1779
    A length of time has elapsed since I had the pleasure of seeing you last, or indeed since hearing from you particularly. My friends Colo Stewart and Colo Ball being so good as to afford me a Visit in-

forms me that you are still General Greene and in the land of the living.[2] I shoud have thanked you long before this for the many civilities Which you granted me whilst in the Army but uncertain conveyances has hitherto prevented it, but be assured that a gratefull mind can never forget the happiness it experienced under your command. Being at to[o] great distance to expect to see you soon I can only request that if it ever lays in my power to construct any thing agreable for you or can by any means contribute to your happiness, that you will command me assuring you at the same time that it will give me real pleasure to serve you.

As Colo Stewart and Colo Ball has almost compleated the tour of Virginia I refer you to them for an account of the News of it. It woud be to[o] lengthy for an account of our laws and internal produce[?], and even the sentiments, complexion and disposition of the Ladies I refer you to them for.

I cannot expect to divert you from our Great National concerns but if a leisure moment shoud intervene It woud afford me real pleasure to hear from you.[3] I am very affectionately and with great respect Your Most Obedient serv

JOSIAH PARKER

ALS (MiU-C).
1. Parker had commanded the Fifth Virginia Regiment in Muhlenberg's Brigade, which fought under NG at Brandywine and Germantown. According to Heitman, *Register*, he resigned his commission 12 July 1778.
2. On Stewart's and Ball's Virginia trip, see above, Stewart to NG, 4 January.
3. An answer has not been found.

From Colonel Robert L. Hooper, Jr.

[Easton, Pa., 6 February 1779. Describes his transporting flour and clothing. Has some Continental teams, but in Sussex County[1] has hired "Country Teams" on the best terms he can get. Happy that NG approves his "Candid Account" of difficulties in providing forage for next campaign. Favors informing superiors of "disagreeable truths." Needs $100,000. For thirty or forty shillings can get a type of pack saddle with which he became familiar on western tours—"the Most Simple and best that ever was invented."[2] ALS (PPAmP) 3 pp.]

1. Hooper's territory included Sussex County, N.J., in addition to Northampton County and part of Bucks in Pennsylvania (See Map 3). Knowledgeable about the frontier, he played a major role in the spring and summer in supplying Sullivan's expedition. Among the most able and enterprising of NG's deputies, he was also commissary of forage and commissary of purchases. Not content with these duties, he still had under his care, by direction of the Board of War, a "very considerable Shoe Factory," which he had established and whose output he still distributed. (See his letters to Gen. Edward Hand, 15 January and 18 February 1779, Hand Papers, vol. 1, PHi. For a biographical sketch, see above, vol. 2: 331n.) Hooper's income must have been the envy of all those around him.

2. The pack saddles were for Sullivan's Indian expedition. See NG's correspondence with Hooper and John Cox during the following weeks.

From Nehemiah Hubbard

Sir   Hartford [Conn.] Feby 6th 1779
    I have to acknowledge your fav'rs of the 5th 20th and 27th of January.[1]

When yours of the 5th come to hand I was so unwell as to be confin'd to my Room and continued so for about a fortnight after. However Mr Jones took Unweried Pains to accomplish the business but to no Effect and had wrote Mr Benjn Andrews of Boston on the subject, but on hearing of the sad Accident that Put an end to his days, I desired him not to send it, as I would make another trial as soon as my Health would admit.

Immediately after I got about I employ'd Capt William Bull of this Town to go to every sea Port Town in this State to the Eastward of Fairfield and if Possible to Charter a sufficient Number of Vessels to Freight 1000 Casks Rice.[2] He writes me from New Haven that all the Vessels are fitting for the West Indies. Ten are now fitting at that Place, however hope he will meet with better success as he comes on to the Eastward. Will inform you of his success immediately on his Return. I could have got a sufficient Number of Vessels in this River [the Connecticut] without much Trouble but they are all froze in, and could not be got out in season.

I have Recd the Money forwarded per Colo Pettit, which amounts to 298,000 Dollars including 100,000 lent by Colo Jere Wadsworth for which he has my hearty thanks.

Your Plan to Remedy the scarcity of Forrage is an Excellent one, could the Farmers be Prevail'd on to enter into Contracts, but this I fear cannot be done;[3] were you acquainted with the Temper and disposition of our Farmers, you would be Convinc'd of the imposibilyty of obtaining a written contract from them. I have convers'd with several Farmers on this subject. They tell me they are willing to sell their Forrage for use of the Public, Provided they can get as much as from any other Person, and this they say can be done as well without as with a Contract. They say they are not Concern'd about a Market for their Forrage so long as the War lasts, and many other evasive answers. The Farmers are determind to Keep up the Price of every kind of Country Produce at all events lest the Merchants should get above them in the Price of Foreign Goods.

I have forwarded a Considerable Quantity of Provisions to Providence of late, hope you'll hear no more Complaints from that Quarter for want of Provisions.[4] Mrs Hubbard still continues very ill, tho' I hope she is something better. [I] am sir with due Respect Your obedt Servant[5]

NEHEMH HUBBARD

ALS (PPAmP).
1. Letter of 5 January not found.
2. For background on rice, see above, Wadsworth to NG, 2 January.
3. NG had suggested the plan in his letter to Hubbard on 20 January, above. Not surprisingly, farmers showed no inclination to commit themselves in advance during this inflationary period.
4. His reference is to Sullivan's quarrel with Wadsworth over provisions for the army in Rhode Island, which is recounted at NG to Pettit, 4 December 1778, above.

By January, provisions in Rhode Island—especially flour—had become so scarce that soldier and civilian alike suffered. The state, as Governor Greene informed Congress, "at the best of times . . . never raised bread-corn sufficient to support its own inhabitants," and with "nearly one-quarter of the best plow-land" in British hands, many people, he predicted, would starve—particularly "the poorer sort"—unless Connecticut and New York lifted their embargoes on grain. (See the governor's letters in Bartlett, Records, 8: 498–500) By the time Hubbard wrote on 6 February, supplies had reached the general population as well as the army.
5. According to the docketing, NG answered on 23 February, but the letter has not been found.

From Miller & Tracy

[Boston, 6 February 1779. They will endeavor to find vessels to transport rice if NG should wish.[1] LS (PPAmP) 1 p.]

1. No other correspondence with this firm has been found.

From Samuel A. Otis

Sir   Boston Feby 6th 1779
    Upon rect of yours of 5th Ulto to Mr A[ndrews], his Lady refering it to me, I found myself a little embarrassed, for as you addressed only to Mr A, I did not know whether it would be agreeable for me to take up the transports.[1] However I took upon myself to offer one third, and proceeded as observed in my last, and in the preceeding ones of 18th and 20th Jany, Since which your favr 27th of Jany pr express is come to hand, which being a warrant for my acting according to my best discretion, have this day procured a fine new Schooner of 120 tons,[2] and have a prospect of other vessels, and tho I can give you but little hope from my own address, my connexions at Portsmouth, Newbury, Salem, Marblehead, Plimouth, Nantucket &c are so good, in the commercial way, that if any applications will succeed mine must. To these places have applied for what Vessells I can get and upon the best terms possible.
    Have heard nothing from Mr Hobart, and as Colo Bowen informs

me he can do nothing I am at Liberty to make my application at Dartmouth [Mass.] or elsewhere, And as the Season is far advanced, and haveing conversed [with] Messrs Miller & Tracy, shall not wait your further orders, presumeing effectual measures will be taken to induce Mr Livingstone to attend to my applications, for demurrage will run exceeding high.[3] I hope also he will be authorized to supply such Vessells as I send with necessaries to fullfill their contracts for home passages, I mean in case of misfortune, Short provisions or other Emergency.

Colo Lewis's order was so repeatedly earnest to me, I supposed myself right in compleating a part of his order, but my Credit as well as Cash being [used?] up, can go no farther at present.[4]

The Class of people who let Vessells are not opulent, some cash therfore must be advanced these before it will be possible to get them to Sea; these considerations and the scarcity of duck (all in Town haveing already engaged) render an immediate Supply absolutely indispensible.

The bags, made of materials belonging to Board of War, in which I hope you will save me harmless, I have nearly done and shall go on in few days, and wish you would determine the heavy articles as anchors &c, before the frost breaks up or the travelling will be impracticable.

I cant get Russia duck (Most, I have imported and sold for 10 dollars) under two hundred, Ravens duck 50£ . I have a large quantity of each in my hands. What can the board of War do with it, but make it into Tents? I wish you could appropriate it.

The Two Silver Cups I send herewith, which Mr A bespoke [i.e., ordered], but were unfinished at his death.[5]

The bearer hereof haveing no money to carry him back, have advanced him 15£ which is placed to your Acct.

I have lost a kind father, a true friend, a most amiable wife, all within a few weeks, my heart sickens at the Scene, and I plunge into busyness to prevent reflection.[6] May you Sir experience none but agreeable vicisitudes is the wish of Your most obedient and Most Humble Sert

SAML A OTIS

PS As there is no hemp or rigging in Town a ton or Two in each vessel and a few barrells of Naval Stores on deck would take no rice room and help the Service I apprehend.

ALS (PPAmP).
    1. Letter not found. On Andrews's death, see above, Otis to NG, 10 January.
    2. Letter of 20 January not found. On South Carolina rice, see above, Wadsworth to NG, 2 January.

3. "Mr Hobart" was probably Nehemiah Hubbard, the DQM at Hartford; "Colo Bowen" was DQM at Providence. NG had asked both men to round up vessels for transporting rice. Miller and Tracy were Boston merchants. Abraham Livingston was the continental agent in Charleston who was shipping rice.

4. Morgan Lewis had assembled equipment for a Canadian expedition. See note, NG to Washington, 5 January, above.

5. Enclosed was a receipt for the cups signed by William Hunter to Joseph Edwards, the silversmith in Boston. The cups accompanied NG throughout the war.

6. Elizabeth (Gray) Otis had died 22 January, leaving five children, one of whom was Harrison Gray Otis, the future Federalist leader. (Butterfield and Friedlander, *Adams Family*, 3: 155n) The friend was his partner, Benjamin Andrews, mentioned in note 1 above.

See Map 2 for geographic references above.

Colonel James Abeel to Major Robert Forsyth

[Morristown, N.J., 7 February 1779. Has "12 Private Locks" for NG. Will forward candlesticks in a few days. Will be glad when NG is in camp for he is "moneyless and can do no Business without." ALS (PPAmP) 1 p.]

From Colonel Ephraim Bowen

[Providence, 8 February 1779. Finds no vessels in Rhode Island but could get two or three in Massachusetts to bring rice from Charleston at cost of half the cargo or one third if insured. At General Sullivan's suggestion he put horses to winter on Prudence Island, but Tories from Newport took "off what of them was in Tolerable case and kill'd all the rest but one or two."[1] ALS (PPAmP) 2 pp.]

1. NG comments on the loss below in his first letter of 23 February to Bowen.

To Samuel Barrett & Co.

Gentlemen   Camp Rariton [N.J.] Feby 9th 1779

Your favor of the 12th January has come to hand.

The death of Mr Andrews is much to be lamented, as the Public have lost a valuable Officer, and society a generous Friend.

Your kind offers to serve me, and the Public, merit both our thanks. My personal acquaintance with you was sufficient without any further referance, did it lay in my power to comply with your request: but the circumstances at present are such as puts it out of my power.

Mr Otis has served with Mr Andress [Andrews] in the business and (since the death of his partner) in his Letters to me has never signafyd an intention of declineing the Agency.

Shoud Mr Otis decline, I am under Promise to Colo Palfrey (shoud I make any sellection[?] in the appointment) so early as the last fall, as he proposes leaveing the Army and ent'ring into business.[1] Next to him Genl Knox applyd in behalf of his Brother; so that I find it out of my power to serve you in this instance, which if consistant woud give me pleasure. I am with Regard Gentm yrs &c.

Df (PCC, item 173, vol. 4: 79, DNA). That this unsigned draft was written at NG's direction is confirmed by the fact that it is an explicit answer to the Barrett letter of 12 January.
    1. This seems to be the best rendering of a portion of the draft that had been incompletely revised by cross-outs and interlineations. On Colonel Palfrey's application, see above, 14 January.

Major Ichabod Burnet to Colonel Ephraim Bowen

Dear Sir   Middlebrook [N.J.], Feb. 9th, 1779.
    General Greene desires me to write you and to inform you that no special damages done to the property of any inhabitant is paid for by the Quarter-Master General's department without an order from the commanding officer of the department, as the Quarter-Masters are entirely under the direction of the commanding officer within the department.[1] General Washington always gives orders for the payment of special damages done by the troops under his immediate command, and the Quarter-Master can have no sufficient voucher for the payment of such damages but the order of the officer commanding in the department where the damage is done. General Sullivan, I imagine, will have no objection to give such special orders if you assure him that His Excellency gives his orders for payment in like instances, which General Greene says is the case. General Greene also desires you will take the necessary measures to procure a sufficient supply of camp equipage for the troops now in Rhode Island for the ensuing campaign, viz., tents, knapsacks, canteens, camp kettles, &c.[2] You will immediately make this necessary provision without waiting for any further orders from the Quarter-Master General, as he thinks it is high time the measures were taken for supplying that part of the army. As our expresses go through you will have the earliest opportunity to forward the linen to me. I am yours, sincerely,
                                                        I. BURNET

Reprinted from RIHS, *Coll.*, 6: 225–26. When printed in 1867 the original ALS was in the Bowen Collection of R.I. Historical Society but was stolen about 1900. An ADfS, considerably shorter, is in PCC, item 173, vol. 4: 77, DNA.
    1. See NG to Sullivan, this date, below.
    2. The "ensuing campaign" was undoubtedly Sullivan's expectation of an imminent British attack on the western shore of Narragansett Bay. See Sullivan to Governor Greene, 16 January 1779, Hammond, *Sullivan*, 2: 493–94.

To Captain John Gooch

[Middlebrook, N.J., 9 February 1779. Thanks him for his "very pleasing" poetry, which shows his illness did not affect his "mental faculties." Is pleased there are no differences between Gooch and Colonel Chase.[1] Df (PCC, item 173, vol. 4: 91, DNA) 1 p.]

1. Thomas Chase was deputy quartermaster in Boston; Gooch, NG's old friend, was an agent under Chase. On the differences between the two men, see above, Gooch to NG, 24 and 25 October 1778.

To Nathaniel Gorham

[Camp Raritan, N.J., 9 February 1779. NG gives essentially same answer to Gorham's request of 21 January as he does to Samuel Barrett & Co., 9 February, above. Df (PCC, item 173, vol. 4: 81, DNA) 1 p.]

To Griffin Greene

Dear Sir   Camp at Middle Brook [N.J.] February 9th 1779

Your favor of the 16th of January I receivd while I was in Philadelphia and has lain by me unanswered ever since. The reason was I had wrote you the day before the receipt of it so fully upon every matter, that I was determind to wait a few days to see what changes took place in order to give you further information.

Your favor of the 2d of this Instant dated at Hartford was deliverd me this Evening.[1] I am very sorry to find you so much alarmd about your purchases; as I am afraid you will take some measures to get rid of your Stocks to your prejudice.

I have not the same apprehensions by any means that you have respecting the falling of the Stocks. If the Resolution of Congress will prevent Money depreciateing it will be a great thing. I do not expect it will rise in value much; if it will hold its present value I shall be happy.

If Stocks should fall in Boston I would sooner purchase than sell. Indeed if West India Goods fall greatly I would purchase all I could. West India Goods will rather rise than fall as the War now carrying on between the French and English will prevent cultivation and render our communication more difficult.

Good Wines are selling here at 20 Dollars a Gallon. It is still dearer in Philadelphia. But the Wines that I wrote you was selling at 30 Dollars was of the best quallity such as came in the *St James*.

You may depend upon it the falling of the Stocks in Boston is in a great measure effected by the Speculators in order to take advantage of the Markets. Commerce is not my Study but I am confident in the matter and wish most heartily you may not have taken any disadvantageous step before this reaches you.

I shall write you as soon as I can get an answer from Philadelphia where I shall write in the morning to learn the price of Wines of such quallity as you have for sale. Wines are an article of Merchandize that dont sell very high in large quantitys. It will be best therefore in my opinion to put it into some honest persons hand to sell for you. Part of it may sell with the Army; but there are but a few of the Officers that drink Wine—they are generally so poor they cant afford it.

Forage is so very scarce that I fear it would be impossible for you to get your Wines through the Jersys if you was to make the attempt to get them to Philadelphia before Grass is grown fit to subsist the Cattle.[2] Besides which it distresses my department in the Forage line which is already over charged with difficulties.

It is said the Kings speech has arrivd. He threatens us with new furies; but it is happy for us that his power is not equal to his will.[3]

There is late accounts from the West Indies which say Count de Estange has got a drubing in a Sea fight with Admiral Byron. The French Land forces met with a defeat in attempting to repossess themselves of St Lucia. The loss was considerable.[4]

The Enemy are in possession of Savannah the Capital of Georgia and the People not a little alarmd for the safety of Charles Town South Carolinia.[5]

It is beyound a doubt with me the Enemy intend to try the force of another Campaign. New York and Newport will be strongly Garrisoned and the Frontiers and the Southern States will be the scene of operation.

The Express did not arrive with your Letters within the Time you set, therefore I did not pay him any thing; but I believe he made all the haste he could. He was detaind at the North River.

⟨You should always make it a rule in commerce never to sell when Stocks are upon the fall. But buy when they fall and sell when they rise. If you intend to get any thing these Times you must not be frighted by every report but steadily pursue your purpose. Reports will rise and fall Stocks prodigiously, be careful therefore of their influence.

I have just returnd from Philadelphia, there is no material change taken place there. I think I may venture to assure you that you have nothing to fear if you buy ever so many Goods and all those you have already got will neat [net] you a profit before five months is at an end.

What I write you is in confidence, burn this Letter and improve the hint.

If this Letter should not overtake you before you get Home, Please make my compliments agreeable to Cousin Sally.

You will communicate everything necessary for Brother Kitts information as I have not Time to write him; besides which I am almost tird to death with writing and have a severe pain in my breast.

Give my kind love to him and desire him to remember me to his Wife.

Mrs Greene is writing brother Jacob and desires her love to you and Sally and to Kitt and Caty. I am yours affectionately

N GREENE

My hand shakes so prodigiously that I can hardly write at all.

Your Letter of the 16th was so very different from this last which you have sent with respect to Trade and commerce and of the rise and fall of Goods that I had not the least apprehensions that you would get alarm respecting the Stocks. I repeat it again dont be afraid to buy if the Stocks fall.⟩

LS (OMC). Material in angle brackets taken from undated fragments in Greene Collection, OMC.

1. Griffin's letters of 16 January and 2 February not found. NG's letter to which he refers is printed above, 25 January.

2. The term includes horses.

3. The king's speech to Parliament of 26 November 1778 had just been reprinted by American newspapers. Only those Americans who had expectations of a conciliatory gesture from the throne—possibly even British withdrawal from America—could have considered the speech as threatening "new furies." It was, in fact, almost innocuous. Focusing chiefly on the perfidy of France, George III did lump his former colonies with "all our enemies." But the threats were confined to his hope that against those enemies "the conduct and intrepidity of my officers and forces by sea and land" would be "the means of vindicating and maintaining the honour of my crown, and the interests of my people." (Murdoch, *Annual Register*, p. 732)

4. In December, Admiral Hotham had landed troops at St. Lucia, and they captured the French naval base a day before d'Estaing appeared. In attempting to retake the island a week later, d'Estaing suffered 1,600 dead and wounded compared with fewer than 200 British casualties. Admiral Byron was too late to prevent d'Estaing from slipping back to Martinique.

5. On the British offensive in Georgia and South Carolina, see above, NG to Sullivan, 26 January.

To Nehemiah Hubbard

[Middlebrook, N.J., 9 February 1779. Is "very impatient" to hear whether Hubbard has found vessels to freight rice from Charleston. If present pay is too low for good assistants in the department, what should it be?[1] LS (MiU-C) 1 p.]

1. Hubbard had written on 6 February (above) but his letter had not yet arrived; he repeated much of it when he answered this letter on 19 February, below.

Major Ichabod Burnet to Colonel Charles Pettit

[Middlebrook, N.J., 9 February 1779. General Greene is anxious for copies of returns. ACyS (PPAmP) 1 p.]

To Isaac Sears[1]

Sir   Camp Middle Brook [N.J.] 9th Feby 1779
    Your favour of the 10th December last, acknowledging the receipt of my letter of the 21st Novemr is now before me.[2]
    I with pleasure inform you, that the Pipe of Madeira safely came to Hand this day.
    Give me leave to thank you very kindly, for the trouble you have had in rendering me this obliging Piece of Service, and believe me Dr Sir Your Obdt Humble servt

FC (PCC, item 173, vol. 4: 89, DNA).
    1. Isaac Sears (1730–86) had known NG since 1776, when Sears, a New York radical, was administering loyalty oaths on Long Island. He was a successful ship captain and owner, who in 1777–83 operated privateers out of Boston. (*DAB*) In 1780 he became co-owner with NG's family of the *Flora*, a British vessel that cousin Griffin Greene raised from the waters off Newport.
    2. Letters not found.

To General John Sullivan

Dear Sir   Middle Brook [N.J.] February 9. 1779
    Col Bowen writes me that you refuse to give any more special orders for the payment for damages the Inhabitants sustains by the Troops under your command, and that you refuse upon this principle, that if it is right for the People to receive any consideration for waste commited upon their property, the quarter master has full powers to settle the matter.[1] You may rest assurd that is not the case. The Resolution of Congress respecting that matter wholly forbids the quarter masters paying any thing for damages. The property that is taken from the People and applyed to the public use I can order payment for, for the common and ordinary purposes of the Army; but waste I cannot meddle with, unless I have a special order; and His Excellency has granted a great number in the course of this Campaign.
    It would be a great hardship upon the quarter master to be obligd to pay money at his own risque for damages committed by Troops the Commander in chief of which refusd to give his order as a voucher to the account.
    My Instructions to Col Bowen upon that head are exactly the same as those given to every other deputy quarter master general and perfectly consistent with the line of conduct I observe myself with the

Army. I hope therefore you will acquit me of haveing any ungenerous intentions and continue your directions to Col Bowen as heretofore. I have the honor to be with the most perfect Esteem Your most obedient humble Sert

NATH GREENE

ACyS (PCC, item 173, vol. 4: 73, DNA).
   1. See above, this date, Burnet to Bowen.

To General James M. Varnum

Sir   Middle Brook [N.J.] February 9th 1789 [1779]
    Your favor of the 13th of January I received in Philadelphia.
    I am exceeding glad to hear that Capt [William] Tew is appointed Brigade quarter master, as I am fully persuaded he will make an exceeding good one.
    I am very sorry that there is a probabillity of a breach between General Sullivan and the State.[1] The local policy of almost all the States is directly opposed to the great National plan: and if they continue to persevere in it, God knows what the consequences will be. There is a terrible falling off in public virtue since the commencement of the present contest. The loss of Morals and the want of public spirit leaves us almost like a Rope of Sand. However I believe the State of Rhode Island acts upon as generous principles, and ever has done, as any one State of the Union.
    Luxury and dissipation is very prevalent. These are the common ofspring of sudden riches. When I was in Boston last Summer, I thought luxury very predominant there: but they were no more to compare with than now prevailing in Philadelphia, than an Infant Babe to a full grown Man. I dine'd at one table where there was an hundred and Sixty dishes: and at several others not far behind. The Growing avarice, and a declining currency, are poor materials to build our Independence upon.
    I beleive the Congress have it in contemplation to make some further provision for the Army but whether it is in their power, is a matter of doubt. I cannot agree with you that the Army is dispis'd: it is far from being the case in Philadelphia. The Officers were never more respected.
    The great Maximus will write you upon the subject of your resignation, and Mr. Ellery also.[2] Is your application serious, or is it only done to alarm the Congress, in order to make Them more attentive to the Complaints of the Army? The freedom of America must depend upon the Army and therefore, it is very impolitick to neglect it.
    There is a report prevailing in Philadel'a that Count de Estainge

has got a drubing by Admiral Byron's Fleet. The French forces also met with a defeat at St Laucia, which I suppose you have seen in the Papers.[3]

Our affairs are much against us to the Southward. The Capital of Georgia in the Enemys hands, and the People under great apprehensions for the safety of Charles Town, the Capital of South Carolina.[4] General Lincoln is drawing the Militia of the country together, in order to expel them: but I am not very sanguine upon the subject.

There is no European Intelligence of a late date: but I think from every movement here, and from the complexion of the last accounts we had from Europe, we shall have another Campaign. The Enemy will continue Garrisons at New York and Newport, in order to hold our Troops at Bay: and endeavour to ravage our Frontiers and make inroads upon the Southern States.

Make My and Mrs Greens compliments to Mrs Varnum. One thing I had like to have forgot, Col Angel wrote me a few days past, desiring to know what had become of Lt Littlefield: and inclos'd a Letter directed to him: ordering him without loss of time to join his Regiment.

If Mr Littlefield has transgressed, he stands responsible to you, who gave him the first leave of absence: and I hope, before this, has waited on you to account for his longer stay than his Furlough allowed him.[5] General Sullivan gave him a second Furlough to wait on Mrs Greene to Camp, which I dare say will be a sufficient apology with you for his absence.

Please to remember me to the Officers of your Brigade. I am with Sentiments of esteem and regard Your Most Obedient humble Sert

NATH GREENE

Tr (GWG Transcript: CSmH). NG's spelling and capitalization, which the copyist appears to have faithfully reproduced, were edited to fit the editorial standards of the 1850's—probably by G. W. Greene. Since the changes are readily identifiable, it has been possible to restore the transcript as the copyist left it.

1. See Varnum's letter of 13 January, above.

2. The "great Maximus" was apparently President John Jay; William Ellery was a R.I. delegate to Congress. Varnum wrote Jay on 12 February that, not having received an answer to a November request for his "Dismission," he would continue as a "Servant to the Public" only as long as it took to receive Congress's final order. Congress accepted his resignation on 5 March. (JCC, 13: 274; PCC, item 78, vol. 23: 161, DNA)

3. On the West Indies, see note at NG to Griffin Greene, this date, above.

4. See note, NG to Sullivan, 26 January, above.

5. William Littlefield, Catharine Greene's brother, had often overstayed a leave, but this time General Sullivan had apparently granted him an extension. See Varnum to NG, 26 February, below.

From Colonel Ephraim Bowen

[Providence, R.I., 9 February 1779. Is sending bill for NG's linen, which he has delivered to brother Jacob. "Am always happy to Recieve your Command whether in Public way or for your Private Acct."[1] ALS (MiU-C) 1 p.]

1. In December, Bowen had had Catharine Greene's carriage repaired at NG's expense. (Burnet to Bowen, 12 December 1778, above)

From Colonel Thomas Chase

[Boston, 9 February 1779. As per NG's instructions of 29 January [not found] he will apply to Navy Board for "Tent Cloath" for one thousand tents.[1] ALS (PPAmP) 1 p.]

1. The Marine Committee of Congress had approved NG's request if the Navy Board could spare "light sail Duck." (Samuel Adams to Navy Board, 1 February 1779, PPAmP)

From Colonel Henry Hollingsworth

[Head of Elk, Md., 9 February 1779. Needs an answer to his letter on hiring wagons.[1] Wagoners report they would "leave the sarvice" before accepting forty shillings. Has "Large supplys of Flower since the Frost Broke up but no Forage." The "Needfull" [i.e., money] is much wanted. ALS (PPAmP) 1 p.]

1. NG answered his letter of 4 February on 14 February, below.

To Colonel Ephraim Bowen

[Middlebrook, N.J., 10 February 1779. Asks about rice.[1] Suggests vessels might be found in Dartmouth and [New] Bedford, Mass. Reprinted from RIHS, Coll., 6: 226.]

1. NG had not received Bowen's letter of 8 February, above.

To Colonel Udny Hay

Sir   Middle Brook [N.J.] February 10, 1779
       Your favor of the 1st of this instant I recievd before I left Philadelphia but I had not an opportunity and Time to give it an answer, until my arrival here.
       If there is Clothing wanted for your artificers employed by the day it can be had providing a return is previously made for the pur-

pose. The Clothing must be charged at such rates as to free the public from any loss.

I have enquird of Col Wadsworth respecting the Commisary employing Teams. He says he cannot conceive what gives rise to the report unless the Commisarys have employed a few upon some pressing necessity. He desires you to state the facts to him respecting the matter in a Letter.

I am sorry to find the Artificers are geting discontented. You must endeavor to keep them as quiet as possible until we see what effects the late Resolution of Congress will have upon the currency;[1] and until we can have an opportunity to fix the price of the artificers generally.

If Mr Simmons was employed by Col Lewis to engage Artificers I could wish you not to enter into any disputes with him or give any support to the men for fear of creating some disputes between you and the Colonel.

I am not acquainted with the Wages given to the artificers employed by the Day, but will enquire.

Your plan for establishing a Tanyard is elligible providing a Company would undertake it upon their own account; but there is no possibillity of carrying on any business to advantage where you are obligd to hire all the people for the purpose. General [Lewis] Morris has a plan now before the Congress for establishing a Tan Yard in Sussex [N.J.]. Whether he will succeed I cannot pretend to say.[2] My respects to Mrs Hay. I am Sir Your humble Sert

NATH GREENE

ALS (PCC, item 173, vol. 4: 93, DNA).
  1. See note above, Gooch to NG, 18 January.
  2. The journals of Congress make no mention of General Morris's plan.

To Colonel Morgan Lewis

Dear Sir   Camp Middle Brook [N.J.] February 10, 1779
I wrote you the 26th of January from Philadelphia since which I have not heard from you.[1]

I am so much in the dark respecting the necessary preparations to be made at Albany that I hardly know how to give any instructions upon that head. The original plan is in a great degree discarded, an Expedition I expect will go on against the Indians; but the General has not yet determind by what Routes he will penetrate their Country which leaves me at a loss where to deposit Stores for the purpose.[2]

I wish you would make out an Account of your Stores, what you have already on hand, and contracted for, for the opening Campaign. What you expect from Boston from the Accounts you have had from there, and what you will want to compleat your assortment. The deficiency I will direct to be forward you from Philadelphia as we have a large assortment of almost every thing providing at that place.

The high Wages that was offerd for the Artificers for the Canada Expedition has playd fury among that class of people every where.[3] They began to leave off work and demand an increase of their Wages. In future where ever there is an Expedition going on, Each Post must endeavor to furnish a certain propotion and the conditions of pay be previously agreed upon. But our currancy is upon such an unstable footing that we are often obligd to take our measures from the circumstance of Time and place.

As the Treasury Board are very desirous of haveing some Estimate of the sums that will be necessary to close our accounts up to the second of March, I wish you would endeavor to make some calculation what further sums you will want to close your accounts to that Time.

You mentiond in one of your former Letters that your Assistants would leave you without an increase of pay. If you cannot detain them until the Congress has determind upon that point you must agree to give them some further allowance until you are further instructed upon this subject; keeping it as private as possible.

I mentiond to you in one of my former Letters the Necessity of haveing a number of Battaues notwithstanding the failure of the Canada expedition. Please to inform me what are your prospects. You will in your next also acquaint me whether the Iron is gone to Springfield. I am with the most perfect esteem Your Most Obedient humble Sert

NATH GREENE

ADfS (PCC, item 173, vol. 4: 97, DNA).
1. NG's letter not found.
2. Both Washington and Congress were again wavering in the decision to mount an expedition against the New York Indians and Niagara rather than directly north into Canada. (See note, NG to Washington, 5 January, above.) While still in Philadelphia, Washington gave NG verbal instructions to countermand any orders he had given to the quartermasters along the Hudson as a result of Washington's letter of 15 December, above. (On these verbal instructions, see below, 17 February and Washington's letter of 24 February.) As noted in the last paragraph of this letter to Lewis, NG refers to the "failure of the Canada expedition" that was discussed in his former letter—undoubtedly the letter of 26 January that has not been found.
3. See also the exchange between NG and Udny Hay, 1 and 10 February, above.

To General Israel Putnam[1]

Dear Sir   Middle Brook [N.J.] February 10, 1779

I receivd a Letter from you sometime past while I was at Philadelphia.[2] It has got mislaid which prevents my giving a proper answer to it. I recollect it was respecting the quarter masters department; that you had given an appointment to a Brigade quarter master to act as deputy quarter master general.[3] The Brigade quarter Master frequently does the duty of a Deputy quarter Master general without any special appointment. A General order for the purpose is sufficent.[4]

I should suppose Capt Starr will be able to procure all the necessary supplies in the quarter masters line for the Troops under your command and that the Deputy with the Troops will have only to attend to the Troops in Camp.[5] However if there is any thing that I can do to render the Troops more agreeable I shall chearfully do it.

I have just returnd from Philadelphia. There is the greatest degree of luxury prevailing in that place you ever saw. The Congress are over loaded with business, and ever will be, while they retain all their powers in their own hands. They should establish proper boards to free them from a great part of their present burthen, which prevents their bringing their business to some issue.

It is said the Kings speech is arrivd. He threatens us with new furies. The French in the West Indies are rather going by the Walls, and our matters wear rather an unfavorable complexion to the Southard.[6] I am with the most perfect esteem Your most obedt humble Sert

NATH GREENE

ACyS (PCC, item 173, vol. 4: 85, DNA).
1. This is the only letter from NG to Putnam that has been found.
2. Letter not found.
3. Putnam, whose division was at Redding, Conn. (Map 1), had asked Washington about appointing a division quartermaster. Washington, who was not certain this could be done under regulations, told Putnam that he "must therefore apply to General Greene." (Fitzpatrick, GW, 13: 455; Putnam's letter of 17 December is in the Washington Papers, DLC.)
4. In speaking of a brigade QMG's doing the duty of a "Deputy quarter Master general," NG was referring not to one of his state or district DQMGs but to a DQMG at the division level—Putnam's division, for example, comprising three brigades.
5. It is far from clear, but it would seem that it was Capt. *John* Starr who had taken on the duty of Division DQMG at Redding. (See NG to John Starr, 26 February, below.) Part of the lack of clarity is that the DQMG at the Danbury camp (part of Putnam's division) was *Ezra* Starr, and to add further to the confusion, the first names of the two men were not always used in the correspondence.
6. On the French Indies and Georgia (the "Southard"), see notes above at NG to Griffin Greene, 9 February and NG to Sullivan, 26 January.

From Colonel Udny Hay

[Fishkill, N.Y., 10 February 1779. Creditors' claims exhausted his cash. Needs $100,000 until March first. Asks suggestions on pay of "fatigue men," bateaumen, and artificers. His use of military force to get wagons caused justices to imprison a wagon master, to send a constable after an assistant, and to arrest Hay. Since the fort was almost out of flour, they may be more cautious. Has proposed a plan to the legislature for transporting stores. Believes NG can remedy the evil of commissaries paying double the amount Hay pays for teaming. Since no justices are nearby to attest to accounts, asks if Washington can appoint Major Hale to administer an oath. Forage masters will need money to pay people for keeping "Horses putt out to winter." Rope makers must know size of rope NG wants.[1] ALS (PPAmP) 3 pp.]

1. NG's letter of 16 February, below, is almost a point-by-point response.

From Colonel Henry Hollingsworth

Sir   Head of Elk [Md.] February 10th at Evening 1779
    Yours of the 2d is just now handed me, which I heartily thank you for.[1] The Complaints made to Congress I apprehend are occasioned by Purchasers not of my Appointing, but by Persons, who call themselves Public Purchasers and have come over or been appointed from a Neighbouring State, who I have more than once mentioned to Col. Biddle, one of which I detected in this County the other day, offering as the Farmers tell me three Pounds fifteen Shillings per Bus [bushel] for Corn.[2] But be this as it may I am certain every possible care has been taken by me to prevent such a Conduct. In the first place the cause of my appointing those Purchasers, was to prevent and suppress those I mentioned from the Deleware State, and other Speculaters, from Purchasing up the Corn, to the Prejudice of the Public, I being at such a distance as not to have a proper check on them.
    The Persons appointed are Gentlemen of the first Character and Fortune amongst us, two of them are employed by the Bus [bushel] rather than by the Month or a Commission on the Money, as by this they are encouraged to buy all they could, and yet have no Interest in raising the Price. The other, Mr William Hemsley, is to have an ample reward for his Service; nothing certain, untill we know what that is, this I rather chose than a Monthly Salary because there was greater encouragement for Industry. I also laid out the Districts into three distinct Districts, appointing to each (with his Orders) his District, with Orders not to Clash or interfere with each other and have ever given my Orders to them to deal at a certain Price, and not to give the rise, to any time, except in one instance, when Col. Hemsley was with me, in the time of the hard Frost. I requested he would at least endeavour to have one Load of Corn laid in some Store adjacant to the Navigable Water, on Wye River, and a Vessel prepared to take it in as soon as the

Weather opened, so that we might have a supply of Corn as early as possible after the Frost broke, for which Load only I desired he might give the Spring Markett, as he said the Markett was not fix'd and the Farmers would be unwilling to Sell on any other Terms, and this was to be done in case it could not be got without. Whether it was executed or no I cannot tell. All I know of it is that I have receivd none yet, and am in the greatest want.

This Morning sent off another sett of Letters Express to each of those Gentlemen to send me Forage immediately, all they have, Repeating my former Orders, not to deal but on fixed Prices, and that as low as possible, and to have a particular regard to each others District. Thus if the whole affair had been my own I could not have acted with more care and precaution than I have done.

However I shall make strict enquiry into this matter, and if any of my Agents have acted amiss they shall be accountable, and be dismissed. They are men of Fortune and Business. If they have erred 'tis with their Eyes open. They cant plead Ignorance.

I rec'd a printed Inlistment for Waggons of Colo [John] Mitchell and have tried this evening to get them to enter at forty shillings. They to a Man declare off and will not enter for less than 55/ or what the Legislature of Pennsylvania from time to time shall fix it at. Have prevailed on them to stay untill I hear from you, assuring them they shall not be detained after unless they choose it. I Submit it whether it would not be better, to engage them at what the Law allows, for six or twelve Months, as we shall want a number all the Season, and when the Season of Tillage come on, it will be difficult to get them. Will thank you for your full Instruction on this matter. If the Teams are to be dischargd let me know it by Giles, who I much want with Cash and am Sir your Most Humb Servt

H HOLLINGSWORTH

P.S. to the 10th. 11 of Febry 4 oClock A.M. Colo Mitchell wrights me regarding two Waggon Mastars Anderson and Caswell, who have contrery to orders left their Loading near or at Jinkins [Jenkins] Town. What the cause of their conduct may be I have no Idea, as the mattar is new to me, and those W M being gon to Xteen [Christiana] with their Bregades [of Wagons] I cant have an oppertunity of inquireing untill they return. As such conduct unless taken notice of will be Lyable to be practiced by others, and of course have a very bad tendency, Ile thank you for your orders therein. They have heartofore as far as I know behaved well.

The present prices of halling in the privet way hear makes it very dificult to know how to *act*. The present [price] is from £ 7/10 to 10 pounds per Day, and a very great deal of it to do, so that the waggoners rather look on it a virtue to stay in the Sarvic, and a priveledge to be dismiss'd, as by that they can be imploy'd for the present in a Sarvic much more advantagious, and be under no compultion to tary Longer than it sutes them, of course go to Farming in the Spring, and should we dismiss them I fear we should not get better. For though Mr John F McClenahan made the present information [i.e., charges] against Anderson and Caswell in which He did well, yet when imploy'd as a W Master He acted no better than some others.

On the whole I am so perplex'd that I know not how to *act*, to gather with want of Virtue in the Farmers, missbehavour in Shallopmen, Waggoners, and W M [Wagon Masters], no Law hear to call them to an account. For though we have Laws we cant Execute it in this County, not having a Court House or prison in it that any parson can have buisinis done at, tis so situated that ther is no geting at it, at this Season.[3] For though the Court sit (or rather ought to have sit) this week they have never been able to meet on account of bad weather, though the best I ever knew at this season. Pardon the Degretion. I mention it to convince you there is no doing buisinis in that way hear, that if there is any thing to be done with those W M, they may be call'd else where. I sent to Governor Johnson for the Late act of our assembly in order to take the earlyest oppertunity of stoping the prograce of the Speculators, who are the parsons that give the prices I mentioned for waggonage. On Examining the Act, I finde the clause which relates to transporting of goods is so inconsistant that it commands the very act it prohibits. As it was sent me in Manescrip I thought it an eror of the Clark [i.e., Clerk] but the Governor assures me the original is so. Of course no Stop can be put to those Leaches untill the Assembly sits again.

I have Sent a Coppy of the *act* to my Brother Levi Hollingsworth, where you may get it if tis wanted. I shall come up with my accounts as soon as I get a Supply of Forage, so that I can Leave the post without Inguring the Sarvice when I flatter my selfe of convincing you that the weak Nerves, and Small abillitys I have, has been Exerted in the Sarvic and am Sir your Most Humb Sart[4]

H HOLLINGSWORTH

ALS (PPAmP).

1. Not found.

2. One of the reports circulating in Congress implicated Hollingsworth, although not by name. It was in the form of a seven-page anonymous letter, dated 7 January 1779 and signed "A Friend to his Country." Somewhat less abusive than most anonymous diatribes against the supply services, the letter gained wide acceptance among delegates. After criticizing the commissaries in the Eastern Shore of Maryland and Delaware, the writer declared that "matters are not better managed in the Quarter Master General's department" and continued, "Money has been squander'd away in a most unreasonable manner for the Building of Stables, and the Purchase of Hay and Fire-

wood." The charges appear largely based on hearsay. The author, for example, had "understood" that agents on the Eastern Shore had manipulated the price of forage to increase their commissions and that one assistant deputy lived "in the expensive character of a Gentleman." (PCC, item 29, pp. 141–47, DNA)

In the spring of 1779, similar anonymous accusations were circulated widely by word of mouth or in newspapers. Maryland seems to have been the target for more than its share of complaints, some of them laid directly at the doorstep of Henry Hollingsworth. There is a natural temptation to suspect some underlying cause of so many accusations, but documentary evidence is lacking that would either prove or disprove specific charges circulated about him or his agents.

Before the war, Hollingsworth was a successful merchant at Head of Elk, the northernmost point of navigation of Chesapeake Bay. His family had long been prominent in the small settlement; Head of Elk, in fact, had once been called Hollingsworth. His brother Levi, a merchant in Philadelphia, had bought anchors from Nathanael Greene & Co. before the war. Henry also owned a grist mill and iron foundry, which during the early war years turned out bayonets and other military items. As a mill-owner and merchant, he fitted the pattern of other deputy quartermasters. Most successful deputies hired by NG's predecessor (many of whom NG retained) as well as the few NG added, had been merchants. What a distance he had traveled since 1775, when he had written to delegate Samuel Ward that "Merchants in general are a body of People whose God is Gain, and their whole plan of Policy is to bring Publick measures to square with their private interest." (See above, vol. 1: 140–41.)

It could be argued that the most important requirement for a deputy quartermaster (if not necessarily his agents) was a business background. A successful deputy needed experience in buying and selling, good judgment of men as well as goods, and the ability to handle money and to keep reliable records. He should also have drive and resourcefulness in acquiring scarce supplies. To be a successful deputy in acquiring scarce goods for a desperate army in times of tobogganing depreciation, it could be an advantage for a deputy to employ roughshod practices and be at times even a bit unscrupulous. The one quality often missing from merchant-deputies was the ability to oversee a number of absent and sometimes distant underlings.

The most common charge against deputies and their agents was that the commission system encouraged them to pay higher prices than necessary in order to increase their commissions. This argument had been quoted by Joseph Reed at the time of NG's appointment in March 1778 when his committee recommended the continuation of the system; Reed met the argument by pointing out that there were many far easier ways for a dishonest quartermaster to cheat than to raise the prices of the goods he purchased. (See above, vol. 2: 310–11n.) It seems quite likely, despite the lack of proof, that some of Hollingsworth's agents were not as scrupulous as they should have been and undoubtedly succumbed at times to the temptation to pay higher prices than needed in order to raise their commissions. Some may have found other ways to line their pockets. If the practice was as widespread as rumor had it, then Hollingsworth could be said to have been a lax administrator, a charge that could have been made against other of NG's deputies.

But what can be said of Hollingsworth's character? After getting to know him, NG would not have said that he had made a "God of Gain"—at least in the early war years. As a colonel in the Maryland militia, he had led a regiment to northern New Jersey in the spring of 1777 to help defend that state, and in November of 1777 he commanded the regiment in defense of Daniel Morgan's troops in the battle of Whitemarsh. In the winter of 1777 he returned home to find that the British had destroyed his mill and forge.

His patriotic sacrifices early in the war, of course, did not necessarily testify to his moral character. While no documentary evidence has turned up that questions his ethics or honesty during the time he served as deputy quartermaster, there were belated charges made in March of 1780 by the commissioners of accounts concerning an incident that occurred in February of 1778 before he was appointed quartermaster. At the end of January 1778, with the army at Valley Forge near starvation, Washington had appointed him as a commissary because of his experience as a grain dealer and former owner of a grist mill. Two weeks after the appointment, he had purchased flour "on his own," which he sold at a very substantial profit. His later defense was that he made the purchase before he had been notified of his appointment. He never explained why he did not sell the flour to the army at the price he paid for it when he received his appointment. More serious, however, was the discovery by the commissioners of accounts that the receipt supposedly given him for the purchase was a forgery, prepared later by one of his clerks. (The charges against Hollingsworth, dated 11 August 1780, are printed in *JCC*, 17: 728–30, under the date of 14 August. Hollingsworth's lengthy defense, which also contains some of the biographical data above, is in PCC, item 43, pp. 99–115, DNA, under the heading of a "Remonstrance, Memorial and Petition" to Congress. The document is undated, but the docketing indicates Congress received it on 25 March 1780.)

The case dragged on interminably. When the commissioners laid the charges before the Board of War, that group, unwilling to pass judgment, turned the case over to Congress. Unable to arrive at the truth of the allegations, Congress requested Gov. Thomas Sim Lee of Maryland to investigate and report back. (*JCC*, 17: 734) Hollingsworth was not brought to trial, but the governor laid the case before Judge Alexander Hanson of the General Court of Maryland. It was December of 1780 before Judge Hanson wrote his opinion. While not entirely exonerating Hollingsworth, the judge gave it as his opinion that there were "no grounds for instituting a criminal prosecution." It was almost two years before Congress expressed its satisfaction with Judge Hanson's report and dismissed the complaint. (*JCC*, 23: 746–47) During the months after March 1780, when Hollingsworth was under fire, NG and Pettit had stood by him, not knowing that he would eventually be exonerated.

To return to the spring of 1779, criticism of Maryland deputies continued until mid-April, at which time NG sent his aide, Major Ichabod Burnet, to investigate the matter first hand. On that investigation, see below, NG to Pettit, 15 April, and Hollingsworth to NG, 3 May.

3. Cecil County is in the northeastern corner of Maryland.

4. NG responded in letters of 14 and 16 February, but only the latter has been found.

From Abraham Livingston[1]

[Charleston, S.C., 10 February 1779. In answer to NG's request for rice, "the number of small [British] Cruisers in almost every Inlet on our Coast has rendered the transportation from the Country extreemly dangerous."[2] Will buy rice as soon as available and as soon as he has money. Since Congress still owes him, he has "resolved not to advance any private Monies." Colonel Wadsworth has not sent money for his portion. Encloses copy of charter for brigantine *Polly*, but owners require money. Must have money also to indemnify him "in Case of the Capture or loss of any Vessel" he charters. Rice now $2 bushel. ACyS (PPAmP) 3 pp.]

1. Livingston, a South Carolina lawyer, had been hired by Congress as a Continental agent in Charleston in April 1778. (*JCC*, 10: 311)

2. NG's letter of 5 January not found. On the plan for buying rice, see Wadsworth to NG, 2 January, above.

From Samuel A. Otis

[Boston, 10 February 1779. Acknowledges money. Has sent two vessels to Charleston for rice; has hopes for dozen or more soon.[1] To cover cost of freighting it is necessary to order 10,000 to 12,000 tons to net 6,000 in Boston. Concerned about cost of demurrage if ships not unloaded promptly. One-fourth of rice should be in small casks. Vessels could bring some naval stores. ALS[2] (PPAmP) 2 pp.]

1. Otis was far too optimistic about the number of vessels that would brave the British blockade.
2. Only the last third of the letter is in Otis's hand.

From Colonel Charles Pettit

[Philadelphia, 10 and 11 February 1779. Is "in midst of Bustle" routing Pulaski's Legion to Georgia by way of York, Pa., and through back country. Too far from Williamsburg for deputy Finnie to help. When money available must send someone to accompany the Legion.[1]

Pettit has thought deputies responsible for ferries, but if NG has agreed that Major Eyre should take charge, Pettit needs to know.[2] Encloses letter from Col. R. L. Hooper, who has paid extravagant amount for teams; more properly NG's or John Cox's business. At request of commissary, has asked Colonel Hollingsworth to erect stores at Head of Elk. Asks Mrs. Greene to be "Mistress of the Ceremonies for me on the like Occasion to Mrs. Washington."[3] ALS (PPAmP) 3 pp.]

1. The Legion had spent the early winter at Minisink, N.J., on the upper Delaware as a passive defense against Indians, but when upper New Jersey began to be stripped of forage for its hungry horses, Washington sent it to Delaware on 19 January. (Fitzpatrick, *GW*, 14: 24–25) There the Legion was stationed on 2 February when Congress ordered Pulaski and his men to join Lincoln in South Carolina following the fall of Savannah. (*JCC*, 13: 132; on Savannah, see above, NG to Sullivan, 26 January.) No one was happier than Washington at Pulaski's departure, but the burden of moving the Legion fell on the beleaguered quartermaster corps, which had just gotten the Convention army moved from Massachusetts to Virginia.
2. NG promised in his letter of 14 February, below, to look into it but no further communication has been found.
3. Martha Washington had accompanied her husband to Middlebrook the first week of February. (Freeman, *GW*, 5: 94)

To Colonel James Abeel

[Middlebrook, N.J., 11 February 1779. Asks about progress on spring preparations: how many tents repaired and how many new ones by April. "Much in want of" nuts and cider Abeel promised. ALS (NjR) 1 p.]

To General Alexander McDougall[1]

Dear Sir   Camp Middl Brook [N.J.] February 11 1779
I have not heard from you in the course of the Winter. I have just
returnd from Philadelphia where I spent a month in the most agreeable and disagreeable manner I ever did a month in my life. We had
the most splendid entertainments immaginable. Large Assemblies
and Evening Balls. It was hard service to go through the duties of the
day. I was obligd to rise early and go to bed late to complete them. In
the Morning a round of Visiting came on. Then you had to prepare for
dinner after which the Evening Balls would engage your Time until
one or two in the morning. Our Great Fabius Maximus [Washington]
was the glory and admiration of the City. Every exertion was made to
shew him respect and make his Time agreeable; but the exhibitions
was such a scene of luxury and profusion they gave him infinitely
more pain than pleasure. In a word you never saw such a degree of
dissipation prevailing anywhere as now prevails in Philadelphia.
    The Congress are over run with business and ever will be while
the[y] retain all their powers within their own body. They are allways
begining but never finishing business. They act from the spur of the
ocasion. I was in the City a whole month and upwards, and went
upon the special application of a Committee of Congress; and all the
business they did with me might have been done in a few hours,
notwithstanding I was pressing them to a decesion every day.
    It is said the Kings speech has arrivd who threatens us with new
furies; but it is happy for us that his power is not equal to his will.[2]
    The French appear to be going by the Walls in the West Indies
and our affairs to the Southard are not in a very promising situation.
General Lincoln is indeavoring to collect a force to repel the invaders;
but I am not very sanguine in my expectations, the Militia of the
Country being young in War.[3]
    Mr Morgan Lewis DQMG at Albany writes a Number of In-
trenching Tools that was orderd to that place was stopt at Fish Kill. I
must beg you to let them go on, and if more are wanted at your Post
they shall be sent.
    Mrs Greens and my Compliments to yourself and Mrs
McDougall and the Gentlemen of the family. I am with the most perfect esteem Your humble sert

N GREENE

ALS (NHi).
    1. McDougall was in command of the New York Highlands, including the new fort
under construction at West Point. His headquarters were at Peekskill on the east side of
the Hudson.
    2. See note at NG to Griffin Greene, 9 February, above.
    3. See note at NG to Sullivan, 26 January, above.

To Samuel A. Otis

[Middlebrook, N.J., 11 February 1779. Has Otis's letter of 18 January. Is "exceeding happy" he is carrying on business after Andrews's death. Otis can depend on NG's confirming his contracts. He should charter rice vessels on best terms possible, paying freight in money or rice as necessary.

NG's department needs cloth of all kinds, especially for tents and clothing. Understands a quantity is "lately arrivd at Boston."[1] If prices are dropping, asks Otis to buy $100,000 worth.[2] ADfS (PCC, item 173, vol. 4: 101, DNA) 3 pp.]

1. Most of the cloth and clothing that Otis handled was from France. Boston was the safest port for imports.
2. There was still hope that Congress's recall of earlier emissions of money would lower prices. See note at Gooch to NG, 18 January, above.

To Colonel William Palfrey

[Middlebrook, N.J., 11 February 1779. An answer to Palfrey's of 14 January. Andrews's death "a melancholy affair to his family as well as a great public loss." Has many applicants to replace him, but if new contractor is appointed, it shall be Palfrey as promised.[1]

Describes dissipation in Philadelphia. The Congress "retain all their powers within themselves instead of establishing proper boards;" thus they are "never finishing what they begin." King's speech is "a Milk and Water production," and Parliament is inquiring into the "State of the Nation" and "dismission of the present Ministry."[2] ALS (MH) 2 pp.]

1. Samuel Otis remained as "contractor" with a new partner; and as noted at Palfrey to NG, 14 January, above, Palfrey continued as paymaster general.
2. The report of the ministry's dismissal was an unfounded rumor. On the king's speech, see note at NG to Griffin Greene, 9 February, above.

To William Smith

Dear Sir   Middle Brook [N.J.] February 11, 1779
     Your favor of the 26th of January I have receivd with the inclosd proceedings of the Select men and Committee of Council.[1]
     The complaint and proceedings thereon is of a very extraordinary nature. There is no difficulty in finding out the cause of the complaint respecting the Boats and I suppose the purchase of the Wood Lot is the foundation of the other complaint. Such little dirty proceedings mark the temper of the People and the spirit of the Times.
     I can say with great truth that there is not a deputy of my ap-

pointing whose conduct I have higher opinion of, both for industry and Integrity; and you need not give your self the least trouble about the complaint, as it is founded in ill Nature and falsehood.

It will be necessary for you to act with great circumspection that no part of your suit may admit of misinterpretation. [Right] intentions and an honest conduct is not always sufficient security against the shafts of calumny and reproach.

What ever Stores are coming on from Boston let them be forwarded without delay. I am with the greatest regard Your Most Obed humble Sert

NATH GREENE

ACyS (PCC, item 173, vol. 4: 105, DNA).
1. See note at Smith's letter of 26 January, above, for background to the affair and the eventual outcome.

From Colonel James Abeel

[Morristown, N.J., 11 February 1779. His only cash is what he can "borrow of my Friends." Must pay for tools and horseshoes "dayly coming in." Sorry some axes sent to camp "are entirely without Steel." He can furnish cheaper and better iron articles than those from Pennsylvania. Since iron prices are rising, would it "not be best to purchase a Stock?"[1] Colonel Lewis can get bellows in Albany. ALS (PPAmP) 2 pp.]

1. NG's response has not been found, but that he approved the suggestion is confirmed in Abeel's letter of the thirteenth.

From Colonel Clement Biddle

[Philadelphia, Pa., 11 February 1779. Use of forage here "beyond all bounds and they must suffer unless the horses are Reduced." Colonel Pettit doing "all in his power." Pulaski's Legion is at York, Pa., waiting for money; Biddle will write DQM in Georgia about forage for them.[1] Can support our horses with difficulty "til the coming harvest." His stay in Philadelphia to be "short as possible." ALS (PPAmP) 2 pp.]

1. On Pulaski's Legion see above, Pettit to NG, 10 February.

From John Erskine

[Raritan, N.J., 11 February 1779. Mr. Weiss asks him to report that NG should order closing of the road that connects the two houses where stores are kept; he has too few sentries to guard against someone forcing the doors, as was done one night.[1] ALS (PPAmP) 1 p.]

1. Jacob Weiss was the deputy quartermaster at Camp Middlebrook.

From John Jacob Faesh

[Mount Hope, N.J., 11 February 1779. Sending "Two Saddles of Venison which Youll please to accept of." To wait upon him soon. ALS (PPAmP) 1 p.]

From Colonel William Finnie

[Williamsburg, Va., 11 February 1779. Received copy of Board of War's letter to NG of 11 January [above] enclosed in NG's to him of 15 January [not found], in which NG relayed Wadsworth's complaints about Finnie's handling of Convention troops.[1] It is his duty to defend himself and to point out defects of campsite near Charlottesville.

Soon after learning in late October where camp was to be, he sent five wagons of salt; then appointed "Mr. Moore," Colonel Aylett's assistant, to serve as quartermaster of the post.[2] As prisoners neared camp, Moore and Aylett requested forty or fifty wagons to haul provisions the seventy miles. He sent all he could find. He had no "regular Instructions" but reported his actions to Colonels Biddle and Mitchell. Sent money to Moore by an assistant, who reported the station was exposed to "numberless Inconveniences," including "as bad Roads as any in the Country" and a river, the north fork of the James, that swelled with "every little rain" to delay wagons.

In late January, Finnie went to Charlottesville, confirming that the seven-mile road from there to the camp was "horrid beyond Description" and that there would be insufficient water for camp in summer, which, coupled with the impossibility of supplying the camp, should induce Congress to discontinue it. He petitioned Congress to remove it to a "secure Place upon Navigation." The governor [Patrick Henry] and council also wrote.[3] "Nothing can be more groundless" than the charge that he had ignored Colonel Aylett's requests—the "only complaint that has ever been made against me."[4] He cannot reside at Charlottesville because he is needed "at, or near Williamsburg." The incessant cry for forage, "requires my utmost Exertions."

[Chesapeake] Bay and Capes [Henry and Charles] are infested by enemy cruisers and privateers. Two vessels, protected by armed vessel that he ordered, will sail up the bay to supply Camp Middlebrook.[5]

If NG thinks "reasons above . . . powerful enough to opperate in Favour of my opinion," Finnie, as NG recommended, will appoint Captain Rice to superintend the "Business" at Charlottesville. ALS (PPAmP) 7 pp.]

1. On Convention troops, see note at NG to Davenport, 9 November 1778, above.
2. Col. William Aylett was deputy commissary of purchases for Virginia.
3. Finnie's letter to Congress of 5 February was essentially the same as this letter to NG. (See PCC, item 78, vol. 9: 221, DNA.) The same day, Governor Patrick Henry wrote to the Virginia delegates, assuring them, according to Finnie, that from his knowledge of the Charlottesville area the prisoners could not be supported there. (Henry's letter was received in Congress the same day as Finnie's; JCC, 13: 190.) Finnie's and Henry's advice not only went unheeded, but their fears for the camp's survival were unjustified, for despite its shortcomings, it survived until October 1780, when British successes in the South induced Congress to move the remaining prisoners northward to Winchester, Va., and Frederick Town, Md. (Wall, "Convention Army," 202–3)
4. It was not the first complaint lodged against Finnie. (For example, see Washington to Lund Washington, 18 Dec. 1778, Fitzpatrick, GW, 13: 428.) NG, however, kept him on as a deputy during his tenure and after the war he even interceded with Congress to right some supposed wrongs done to Finnie. (NG to Richard Henry Lee, 2 January 1785, below)
5. On enemy privateers and cruisers in American waters, see NG to Wadsworth, 19 March #2, below. It is evident that Finnie was unable to make arrangements for armed vessels since Pettit wrote Congress ten days later that provisions could get through from Chesapeake Bay only if Congress provided protection. (See Pettit to NG, 21 February, below.)

See Map 4 for geographic references above.

From Abraham Livingston

[Charleston, S.C., 11 February 1779. He is "in treaty for the Chartering of two Ships and a Brigg that will carry together about 2000 Barrells Rice." Must insure vessels and pay high freight. He forgot to say yesterday "that few Seamen can be got to venture in Vessels that take even a full load of Rice."[1] ACyS (PPAmP) 2 pp.]

1. This letter, which was added to a duplicate he had made of his 10 February letter, was enclosed with a 27 February letter, below.

From Samuel A. Otis

[Boston, 11/15 February 1779. Has hired some vessels for 1/2 the cargo of rice at owner's risk; has insured others and offered them 3/10 or 1/3. Continent should insure vessels as "real Risque is not more than 50 pr Ct" while [insurance] offices charge 70 percent. Has completed most of Lewis's[1] order and has bought all the duck "I could lay my hands upon." Marine board delivered Major Chace[2] enough for 700 tents. Awaits NG's explanation if he has "order'd two persons to make provisions for the same parcell."³ In 15 February postscript he lists 17 vessels engaged to haul 4,990 barrels of rice. ALS (PPAmP) 3 pp.]

1. Morgan Lewis, DQM at Albany.
2. Thomas Chase, DQM at Boston.
3. Although NG apparently answered Otis's queries his letter has not been found.

From General John Sullivan

Dear Sir   Providence [R.I.] Feby 11th 1779
    I am honored with your favor of the 26th ultimo and have given the orders Requested.
    I wish his Excellency and your Endeavors for planning the next Campaign may be attended with Success, at the Same time Cannot help Expressing my fears that unless Some thing is done for the Army you will have no troops for the next Campaign. The Gaiety of the Philadelphians may perhaps be the Reason of the Slow movements of Congress. I beg you to give me Information from time to time of the Enemys Progress at the Southward. We have nothing new here Save that a party of the Enemy went Lately to Elizabeth Island for Plunder.¹ They first Landed at Buzzards Bay on the main [i.e., mainland], took 17 Cattle, drove them to the water Side, killd them on the Shore. The militia Came upon them and Beat them off without any part of their Booty. They then went to Elizah Island took two vessels Loaded with Flour and one Loaded with Tobacco. I had from Spies on the Island got Intelligence of their going off and immediately Drafted fifty Seamen from the Army well officered and put them on Board a twelve gun privateer which retook all the prizes with the men put on Board and would have taken the whole of the Enemy had not a Frigate come to their assistance.²
    I beg my Compliments to Mrs Green and the Gentlemen of your family and that you will believe me to be with the most Sincere affection and Esteem Dr Sir your most obedt Servant

                                                                    JNO SULLIVAN

ALS (PPAmP).
    1. Elizabeth Island is off the Massachusetts coast at the entrance to Buzzards Bay. See Map 2.
    2. The nearby British raid, and Sullivan's partially successful response to it, undoubtedly influenced the Rhode Island Assembly two weeks later to request that Sullivan "purchase and equip an armed vessel . . . for the defence of this state" and to do so in "conjunction" with Rhode Island. (Bartlett, *Records*, 8: 513)

From Colonel Morgan Lewis

Dr General   Albany [N.Y.] 12th February 1779

I was a few Days since Honored by the Rect of your favors of the 19th, 20th and 26th Ulto, all by the same Conveyance.[1]

The Instructions which General Schuyler has received from his Excellency "have rendered the large Preparations in this Department in a great measure unnecessary."[2] I could wish the first projected plan of Operations had been prosecuted, or sooner set aside. In the One Case, I flatter Myself our Department would have derived Reputation from the forward State of our Preparations: in the other, we should have saved a great Expence unnecessarily incurred. I had the Timbers hewed Out, a very Considerable part of the Iron Work for a Twenty Gun Ship prepared, and my Boat Builders in Such a Train, that they would have built One and Twenty Batteaux a Day, when I recd General Schuyler's Instructions to dismiss my Ship Wrights, Three Companies of my Boat Builders, and to reduce my whole System which I complied with Accordingly.[3]

You may rely on every Exertion in my Power to be prepared for the Expedition you Mention. And I do not doubt my Endeavors will be Attended with Success; Saving in the Articles of Forrage. Of Hay I have laid up Magazines to the amount of about Three Hundred Tons, A very Considerable part of which I shall be obliged to Transport upwards of Fifty Miles Land Carriage. I have therefore ordered it to be pressed into Bundles of about four or five Hundred weight. Grain we cannot procure in any large Quantities. Tho, could some mode be fallen on to Reduce the Quantity consumed by Officers Horses while in Winter Quarters, such as a Pecuniary compensation, we should be able to make a much more respectable Figure in that Article. The Officers of Colo Butlers Corps,[4] which Consists of between Two and Three Hundred Rank and File, Stationed at Scoharry, have consumed in the last Month, by the Forrage Masters Return, One Hundred and fifty one Bushels Grain: a much larger Quantity than they are entitled to. I have made Several Representations on the Subject to the Commanding Officer of the Department but the Evil still Exists and will continue as long as the Forrage Masters are Obliged to Issue on the orders of the Officers Commanding at a post.

The Season has been and still continues very unfavorable. We have had but little Snow, none of which has lain upon the Ground above Eight and forty Hours. Due attention shall be paid to your Recommendation of contracting with the Farmers for a Supply of Oats the next Summer.

I have as yet Received few of the Entrenching Tools you order'd from Springfield. They are Exceedingly ill made, and by no means adequate to the Purpose for which they were intended.

I wrote you some time since, that I had Engaged to give the Ship Wrights I have Employed, whatever wages Shipwrights might have been induced to come from Philada for. I am bound by my agreement to have them ascertained by the first of April.

I must therefore again Request you will furnish me with the Necessary information, that I may thereby be Enabled to Come to a final Settlement with them. What makes me particularly Solicitous on this Head is, that I was under the Necessity of advancing them more money than I Imagine their Pay will come to, and I am apprehensive I shall Experience great Difficulty in Obliging them to Refund, should a Ballance be found in my Favor.

Tis High time some Effectual Plan should be fallen on to Raise Batteau men for the Ensuing Campaigne. The Number we have hitherto been able to enlist do not amount to Ten Persons. Whether it be owing to a want of Confidence in the Promises of Public officers I know not, But 'tis Certain that the Suit of Cloathing offered them is not the least inducement. Were we to set that aside and give them Twelve Shillings or even Two Dollars a Day, I am Persuaded we should have them on very reasonable Terms, Considering the low State our Currency is reduced to, and it would be very little more Expensive to the Public.

A Common Laborer can get of a Farmer Three Dollars per Day and his Provisions, and were it not for the Hopes of being Exempt from Militia Drafts, the Public would not be able to procure them under that Sum. Your Immediate answer on this Subject will be highly Necessary.[5]

I hope you will not omit geting the wages of the A D Q M G raised, otherwise all those I would wish to retain in Service are Determined to Quit it.

The Conclusive Parragraph of your Letter of the 19th gives me uneasiness. I wish to know the Cause of your Embarrasments.[6]

The Principal Articles we Shall want from your Quarter will be Carpenters Tools, a Dozen Smiths Vices, some Scale Beams and Weights for the Commissaries.

Enclosed are Abstracts of my Disbursements and Returns for the last month. I am most Respectfully Dr Genl Your Obt Servt

MOR'N LEWIS

ALS (PPAmP).

1. Letters not found.

2. By mid-December Washington's ambivalence toward a Canadian expedition, either by way of Lake Champlain or Niagara, had given way to a firm questioning of its feasibility. (Washington to Schuyler, Fitzpatrick, *GW*, 13: 430) A month later, with the Indian expedition in the forefront of his thinking, he asked Schuyler to "put an immediate stop to all the preparations" for a Canadian expedition and to relay this to Colonel Lewis in Albany, assigning "him such Reasons for this sudden change as shall seem to you most prudent and plausible." (Ibid., 14: 19)

3. Lewis's efforts were not entirely wasted, for, as seen in NG's letters to him of 17 and 27 February below, some of the boats would be used in the Indian expedition.

4. Lieut. Col. William Butler of the Fourth Pennsylvania, whose regiment had been at Schoharie, N.Y., since October. See Map 3.

5. NG's answer was dependent on the information he requested in his letter of 21 February, below, to Benjamin Eyre. His letter to Lewis of 21 February, below, refers only to paying artificers more than Hay was paying at Fishkill.

6. The cause of NG's "Embarrasments" is not known.

From Colonel James Abeel

Sir   Morris Town [N.J.] 13th Feby 1779

Your favours of 11th and 12 Inst I have recieved.[1] I shall in a day or two send you Returns of all the Stores on hand. My Tent Makers are very Busy repairing the old and making the New Tents. You shall soon as possible have a particular return of them. I have by me a considerable Quantity of Choice Waggon Harness, Horse Shoes, a large parcell, far superior to any we had last Campaign which I am putting up in handy Boxes, strongly made to bear transporting. I have also a Number of Axes, and have some of the best workmen repairing [and?] New Steeling the old Axes. By the Return you will see the exact Number of every Article By me. The old Tents that cannot be made fit for Service I will make Waggon Covers and Forrage Bags of. Knap Sacks and Canteens I have a Considerable Number of and more dayly making.

A Number of Waggons are also sent to me by the Commanding Officer of the No Carolina Brigade. The horses belonging to them have been sent to Colo Sherrif in Chester County to recruit.[2] They still have in that Brigade Twenty two Teames the horses of which I am told are suffering much for want of Forrage. I shou'd think if the Publick horses were sent to recruit and they be allowed to hire private Teams when necessary it wou'd save the Publick some expence as the Teams are laying Idle one half of the time. I here inclose an Order for a hhd of Cyder which please to send for and let the Person that goes for it deliver the inclosed Letter. I shall send Mathews for some Nutts I have bought and send them to Mrs Green.

I shall be extremely glad to recieve some Cash as I have none but what I dayly borrow which are no small Sums.

Since Recieving your Letter I have purchased three Tons of Iron. Be assured I will loose no time in purchasing the Quantity you mention, but wish it had been more as it will rise amazingly. It has allready been sold for £ 400: per by Mr Faesh; this I have got is best refined and cost only £ 300.[3]

The Waggons I have recieved shall all be put in the best Order soon as possible. I am with respect Sir Your Most Hble Servt

JAS ABEEL

Mrs Abeel Joins me in Complyments to Mrs Green and the Genl.

Two days ago I sent to the Care of Genl Knox Two Saddles of Venison for you from Mr Faesh which I hope you have recieved.

ALS (PPAmP).
1. Letter of 12 February not found.
2. That is, to be restored to health.
3. For background, see Abeel's letter of 11 February, above.

From Colonel Udny Hay

[Fishkill, N.Y., 13 February 1779. Awaits NG's answer on artificers' wages. "The Wheelwrights we must not lose, nor can we possibly part with the Smiths." Has promised to settle wages by end of month.[1] ALS (PPAmP) 1 p.]

1. NG answered on 20 February, below.

From William Smith

[Springfield, Mass., 13 February 1779. Will need money for "transporting Provisions, Stores, and ammunition to Albany, clothing to Camp, lumber &c for the ordnance department."[1] ALS (PPAmP) 1 p.]

1. Normally called "Elaboratory" or arsenal.

To Colonel John Cox

Dear Sir   Middle Brook [N.J.] February 14th 1779

This moment receivd a Letter from Col Hooper. The inclosd is a copy of a paragraph taken from it, by which you will see that Pack Saddles may be had from 30/ to 40/ apiece.[1] To the best of my remembrance Col Mitchel contracted to give £ 15 apiece. The great difference in the price leads me to suspect some imposition among the tradesmen in Philadelphia or else the plan they are makeing the Saddles upon is more expensive than the nature of the service requires. I beg you to make immediate inquiry into the matter and give the necessary orders from the information you may receive for securing the public against any imposition or Subjecting her to any unnecessary expence in the plan of preparations.[2]

His Excellency is very anxious to see you. If Col Patterson dont arrive soon I could wish you to come to Camp for a few days that the General may have an opportunity to consult you and you can leave word for the Col to follow you.[3]

Make my and Mrs Greenes most respectful compliments to Mrs

Cox and the young Ladies of the family. I am with the most perfect respect Your Most Obedient humble Sert

NATH GREENE

ADfS (PCC, item 173, vol. 4: 107, DNA).
1. See Hooper to NG, 6 February, above.
2. Cox responded in his letter of the sixteenth, below.
3. On Col. William Patterson, see his letter of 14 February, below.

To Colonel Henry Hollingsworth

Sir   Camp Middle Brook [N.J.] the 14 Feby 1779
     Your favours of the 4th and 9th I reciv'd this day. I observe your remarks upon the Subject of Waggon hire. I cannot apprehend the danger you Suggest in proposing an alteration in the price. Interest is the Governing principle with the farmers as well as almost that of every other order of men. If you propose any terms to the farmers short of those advantageous which they can make in other Employ they will leave your service but if you will Impose new Conditions less benificial than they now have if they cannot better themselves elsewhere they will continue to Serve you; you have to Consider therefore the quan'ty of business you have to execute and the number of Teams that offer to engage in the Service from which you will Judge whether you have an advantage of the Farmers or they of you and upon this principle you must take your Measures. However I would recommend to you to make application to Colo Mitchell of Phila'a to see whether he could furnish you with a Sufficient number of Teams for any given time upon better terms than you can provide for yourself and if he cannot, engage a Sufficient number yourselfe for your Post as early as possible, as a certainty of having the business executed with dispatch and the Stores Conveyed on Seasonably, is of more consequence to the public than the little Saving in the Waggon hire.
     I also remark your observations, plan and Principles upon which you engage your under Agents as Contractors in the Forrage Line. I am too little acquainted with the geniuses of the people and so remote from the place where the business is executed that I cannot form a proper Judgement of the justness of your observations. However from the knowledge I have of men and business in General I cannot Conceive the most capital Merchants to be the properest persons for this Employ. Their Veiws an[d] expectations, are too high for the Consequence of the business and their Attention is too much engross'd about other matters to devote that time to this Service which is necessary to execute it faithfully. A good honest Farmer well known amongst the Inhabitants with a Tolerable knowledge of the forms of

business will be more likely to execute the trust with fidelity than a Merchant of high order besides which he will be content with Infinitely less Profit than the other Class of People. I should recommend therefore That such be employ'd at all places where there is not a very large Share of business to transact.

I am persuaded the Commissioners of accounts will with difficulty be brought to allow a larger Commission for the Several agents employ'd for the purchase of Forrage collectively more than one and a half per Cent and the sallary's Stated by the resolution of Congress. I presume you have acted for the best, but the reasons that influenc'd your Conduct may not Strike the Commissioners so forcibly as they did you. Good intentions is not always a sufficient Warrant to go upon where propriety and Occonimy must be obvious in every transaction to Justify our Proceedings under this consideration. I apprehend some difficulty in the Settlement of those affairs.

I am very happy to hear you are making very great Exertions to forward Provisions and Forrage, the latter of which Articles we feel an increasing distress daily. The resorces of this country are almost Exhausted. The people begin to grow Clammorous and refuse us any further Supplys. Our hopes and expectations therefore are entirely upon you—fail us you must not as ruin will attend us. It gives me pleasure to hear your accounts are in such forwardness. I wish them to be brought to a Settlement as soon as Possible as the business of this day is Conducted much upon the principle of the Circumstances of time and place which may not appear hereafter so fully as it does now. I am with good Wishes Your Most Obt Humble Servt

NATH GREENE

CyS (PCC, item 173, vol. 4: 115, DNA).

To Colonel Robert L. Hooper, Jr.

Sir   Camp Middle Brook [N.J.] the 14 Feby [17]79
   Your favour of the 6 Inst't came to me at this place with the Inclos'd extracts from Biddle and Wadsworth. I wish to be inform'd whether you could increase your contract for packsaddles from five to fifteen Hundred Shou'd it be necessary and whether you are Confident that those upon the Constructions which you recommend are the best Calculated for an Indian Expedition. This is an interesting Enquiry and I wish your answer to both points as soon as Possible.[1] I am happy to hear that you have your accounts in great forwardness as I am determined to press a settlement of all my accounts with the Commissioners of Congress at the close of the year. I hope the contract you have made with the farmers to Give them five Pounds pr

day was the result of necessity, being fully Convinc'd no other mode could be adopted more advantegious. I apprehend one evil from this Contract, that is the farmers in other Districts will lay hold of the president [precedent] to increase their Wages.[2] I am your most obt servt

N. GREEN

Cy (PCC, item 173, vol. 4: 113, DNA).
1. An "interesting Enquiry" was one in which the army had a vital interest.
2. Hooper responded to NG's letter on 18 February, below.

To Governor William Livingston of New Jersey

Sir   Middle Brook [N.J.] February 14, 1779

I have enclosd for your Excellencys information Copies of several Papers sent by Col Rhea to Col Biddle forage master General respecting the Wickedness and Villiany of some Magistrates in Monmouth County.[1] No 1 is an advertizement set up by Justice Abrams. No 2 is a copy of Justice Schenks Letter to Justice Foreman. No 3 is a paragraph of Col Rhea Letter to Col Biddle. No 4 Copy of the advertizement set up by the Officers in the Forage Line.

Your Excellency will observe the great difference in the prices offerd by the public purchasers and private engrossers. This advertizement of Mr Abrams can be set up with no other view than giving a price to all the produce in the Country, and it appears clearly to me to be a plan concerted with a design either to save the Grain in the Country or procure the Inhabitants an extravagant price for it.[2] That we are reduced to the necessity to impress Grain by the aid of the Magistrate is notorious. That the prices offerd by private purchasers will in a great measure govern the Magistrate in fixing the prices for grain taken for the use of the army is clear beyound a doubt. Therefore every such advertizement as Justice Abrams in the present state of things is a public injury and this measure is the more extraordinary as it proceeds from a Justice of the Peace who ought to give support to the public measures instead of embarassing them.

Your Excellency will observe in Justice Schenks Letter to Justice Foreman that the former repremands the latter for presuming to take Grain from Mr Benjamin Van Cleeff to whom he had given protection. This Van Cleeff has had the Rye in stack upwards of two years. He has frequently refusd to sell it, cloaking his real intentions with the very charitable purpose of reserving it for the use of the Poor. Justice Schenks protection appears to me to be directly opposd to the spirit and intention of the Legislator [Legislature] who directs the Magistrate to take from Time to Time from all the Inhabitants according to the wants of the Army, and in propotion to the Stocks the

People have on hand.[3] One Single Magistrate may give protection to all the People in a County and then what effect would the Law have or by what means would the Army be supply'd? I think it my duty to represent these abuses to your Excellency as early as possible that you may give a seasonable check to such public impositions.

The Resolution of Congress prohibiting the use of Wheat for forage, and the great failure of Grain in the Southern States last year, will render it absolutely necessary to draw from the Farmers here all they can possibly spare. I must intreat your Excellency therefore to give us all the aid the Law intended and such further assistance as the circumstances of the Army may render necessary.[4] I have the honor to be with the greatest respect Your Excellencys most obedient humble serv

NATH GREENE

ADfS (PCC, item 173, vol. 4: 109, DNA).

1. Among the papers that Biddle gave NG from Col. David Rhea, Biddle's deputy foragemaster, was a letter written 12 February describing his quarrel with the justices. (NG enclosed only a paragraph of this letter to Livingston, listing it as item "No 3.")

Colonel Rhea used no names in his letter, but the persons were identified in Justice Schenk's letter to Justice Forman which Rhea enclosed. (NG's item "No 2," excerpts of which are quoted in note 3 below.) On learning that Benjamin Van Cliff, a local farmer, had "a Quantity of Rye in the Sheaf," Rhea sent a "Mr. Knight" with a brigade of wagons to purchase it, but for fear Van Cliff would refuse to sell at quartermaster prices, he asked Justice Peter Forman to accompany Knight in order to impress the grain if necessary. This, Justice Forman did. Van Cliff accepted a receipt "without Oppisition," but as soon as the wagons were loaded, he applied to another magistrate, Justice Schenck, who would not "suffer" Knight to take any grain and forced him to unload. Rhea ended his letter to Biddle with the observation that "it is a Damnation Country to do Business with." (PCC, item 173, vol. 3: 37–38, DNA)

2. Although the nature of Justice Abrams's original "advertizement" is not clear from the copy NG received, it would appear, for example, that Abrams had listed the going price of rye and corn at $10 a bushel, compared with quartermaster prices of $4 and $6. (See PCC, item 173, vol. 3: 39, DNA.)

3. Justice Schenk had written Justice Forman an indignant letter for having later "made a Scoff" at the "precept" that Schenk had granted Van Cliff. Neither the chief justice of the state nor Governor Livingston, he assured Forman, would "superseed any Magistrates precepts without giving him a hearing." He thought Forman must have been aware that the legislature had made the magistrates "Guardians to the people," giving them authority to impress produce from "persons, disaffected and of sorded Dispositions who would withhold their produce," but it had not given authority to take from "those that would dispose of their produce for use of the Poor." Twenty-four families (all poor, according to Schenk) were dependent on the grain that Forman "undertook to seize." He reminded his fellow Christian that "he that regards not the cry's of the poor shall cry himself and shall not be heard." (Schenk's letter is in PCC, item 173, vol. 3: 41–42, DNA.)

NG's charge that Van Cliff was cloaking his real intentions under the guise of helping the poor is not documented, but as Governor Livingston was aware, it was not unusual for local magistrates to avoid issuing impressment warrants by such stratagems—especially in areas safe from the enemy. (The British had not returned to Monmouth in any numbers since the battle there in June 1778.)

4. Livingston responded on 17 February, below.

To Colonel Charles Pettit

Dear Sir   Middle Brook [N.J.] February 14, 1779

I exceedingly approve of your plan for accomodating Polaskies Legion on their march to Georgia.[1] If you know no more about the Rout than I do it will be difficult for you to make out one. I wish you may make a happy choice as it is a trust of considerable consequence. I am told one of the Corps was yesterday at Head quarters for the Route; his servant was with me not an hour since enquiring for his master, but I have not seen him. If he comes I shall direct him to you.

Money is exceedingly wanted here, and I am afraid of some disagreeable consequences will take place to the Eastward for not furnishing our Contractors with a proper supply of Money seasonably.

This moment receivd a Letter from Mr Sam Otis, Mr Benjamin Andrews partner. I send you a copy to convince you of the necessity of sending money to him immediately.[2] I think he will want upwards of 200,000 Dollars, Mr [Jacob] Greene about 50,000 or 60[000] at most.

These sums I wish you [to] forward as soon as possible as there is a prospect of making our purchases upon good terms if the fall of Stocks takes place which is now expected.

I wish you would apply to the Marine Committee and learn of them whether there has any orders gone to the Navy Board at Boston for furnishing our department with a quantity of Duck. If there has not desire them to forward one as soon as possible.[3]

I think it was a part of Major Eyres contract to settle all the accounts and measures necessary for the regulating the public Ferries; but I am not positive. I will look over the agreement and write you more fully upon the subject.[4]

I shall write to Col Hooper upon the extraordinary contract he has made.[5] I agree with you nothing but necessity can justify it. Forage is so scarce and our currency upon such a bad footing that measures must be taken according to the circumstances of Time and place. Under this consideration I cannot pretend to censure the Contract that Col Hooper has made; but it appears to be very extraordinary. Such precedents will produce more injury to the public service by effecting the prices else where than the consequence of the business considerd in an abstracted view.

I wish you would write to Mr Livingston[6] to Ship a small quantity of Hemp on board the Vessels that comes for Rice agreeable to Mr Otis recommendation.

Col Wadsworth says that Mr Livingston has drew on him for 20,000 dollars. He wishes to advance it on account of the draft given to our department for the purchase of rough Rice. When you are in cash please to pay to the deputies of that department the aforesaid sum.

Press the treasury very hard as our necessities begin to press us.

I have been writing to Governor Livingston today upon the rascallity of some of the Monmouth Justic[e]s, who are devising ways and means for avoiding the operation of the State Law for procuring Forage. I will send you a copy of the transactions in a few days that you may lay it before the Committee of Congress, and Treasury board to shew them the causes of the constant rise of goods.[7]

I observe Col Hooper says he can get Pack Saddles made for 30/ or 40/ a piece. If I recollect right, Col Mitchel told me the Tradesmen in Philadelphia asked him £ 15 each by the hundred. The great defference in the price requires some explanation. Please to enquire into it. I have enclosd you a copy of that part of Hoopers Letter, that you may be prepard for the purpose. I have wrote to Col Cox upon the subject.[8] If the difference is in the mode, and those of Col Hooper will answer equally well with those made in Philadelphia, that plan ought to be adopted immediately. If the Tradmen have imposd upon Col Mitchel (which I cannot suppose possible), the contract ought to be renderd void.

I am glad you have put in a written application for fixing the mode for settling our Accounts; I think the sooner the Vouchers are orderd in the better. I wrote for your opinion upon this matter. You will please to give it in your next.

I have faithfully conveyed your compliments to Mrs Greene, with the commission for her to convey your compliments to Mrs Washington, which I have no doubt will be punctually executed, you being a great favorite of hers. She desires her compliments in turn. Now you being my debter, I desire you to present my and Mrs Greenes most respectful compliments to Governor Read [Reed] and his family. I am with the Most perfect Esteem Your Most Obedient humble serv

N GREENE

PS Please to write Mr [Abraham] Livingston to furnish the Captains of Vessels charterd by Mr Otis with what necessaries may be wanted agreable to Mr Otis's request.

ADfS (PPAmP).
    1. See Pettit's letter of 10 February, above.
    2. Letter of 6 February, above.
    3. See note at Chase to NG, 9 February, above.
    4. NG's decision on the ferries has not been found.
    5. See his letter to Hooper, this day, above.
    6. Abraham Livingston in Charleston.
    7. His later letter to Pettit has not been found, but the "transactions" are described in a note to his letter to Governor Livingston, above.
    8. See letter to Cox, this day, above, and Cox's reply, 16 February #1, below.

From Jacob Greene & Company[1]

[Hartford, Conn., 14 February 1779. Requests that NG advance money to a Philadelphia merchant. LS (MiU-C) 1 p.]

1. The signature—Jacob Greene & Co—was not in brother Jacob's hand.

From Colonel William S. Livingston

[Beverwyck, N.J.,[1] 14 February 1779. Twice he used NG's quarters while NG was away from camp. Wadsworth's presence "absolutely necessary" when Livingston brings "Cag with Arrack" to camp.[2] ALS (PPAmP) 2 pp.]

1. The home of Abraham Lott, Livingston's father-in-law.
2. *Arrack* was a general term for liquor; a *cag* according to Johnson, *Dictionary*, held four or five gallons.

From Abraham Lott

Dear General   Beverwyck [N.J.] February 14th 1779

Your favor of the 9th reached me the 12th Current.[1] I had no right to expect an answer to mine of the 23d December from Philadelphia, while your time must have been so fully imployed between the Weighty affairs of State, and the Splendid entertainments and gay delights of the City. I was for a few days in that metropolis last November, and then thought it the most extravagant place upon the Globe. But from the different Accounts I have received Since, extravagancy, Luxery and Venality have since arisen to Such a pitch as almost to baffle all description. Is it not Surprising that the laudable Spirit of oeconomy and frugality, and let me add public Spirit, with which this Continent set out in the beginning of the Contest with Britain, should be so totally Sunk and lost, as not to leave the least traces behind? If melancloly and Stubborn facts did not carry full Conviction along with it, one could hardly believe that instead of the Patriot virtues of oeconomy and frugality so lately possessed by the Americans, a licentious Spirit has taken place by which every Vice is introduced, even into places far remote from Cities; and instead of public Spirit every Member of the Community seems to be Studiously imployed to enrich himself by Sapping[?] the Rights and Liberties of his Country and invalidating the Currency of the Continent.

These are Melancholy reflections, and unless a Sudden reformation takes place, forebode no good to the Cause in which we are so justly engaged. While we remained Virtuous, and endeavored as one man to work out the Salvation of our Country all things went well, and turned out more favorable than we had a right to Expect. But now the case is altered, dissentions have taken place. The Virtuous are grown few. Every Species of Venality has taken place: and God only knows where the evil will end.

For my part, I feel more alarmed at the present Situation of our Affairs than at the time you and the Small remains of our Army were pursued over the Delaware.[2] The time is now come which our Enemies have foretold, and in which by their publications in the New York Papers they Seem to Glory and Exult more than if they had Vanguished our army. I do not however, I will not dispond. I trust our Troops under the Conduct of his Excellency, and other valuable officers, will under the guidance and Protection of the Almighty live to free this Land; that so before long we may all peaceably return under our respective Vines and Fig trees; But am not so Sanguine as to think that will be the case this year.

I cannot believe Great Britain is brought low enough yet to own [i.e., acknowledge] our Indep[end]ancy, and if even Sound policy moved her to adopt such a Step, we cannot now close with it unless France Acquiesces in the matter. Here I will drop my present Subject; my Strength failing me: and shall therefore conclude with returning you and Mrs Greene the thanks of self and family for the friendly expressions of your regard. The Girls were greatly disappointed in not seeing Mrs Greene, and propose Soon to pay their respects to her. As soon as I can wear shoes and recover so much Strength as to Travel will also wait of [on] you. In the Interim am joined by Mrs Lott and family, with respectful compliments to Mrs Greene and Self, Dear General your assured humble Servt

ABRM LOTT

ALS (PPAmP).
 1. Letter not found.
 2. In mid-December 1776.

From Colonel William Patterson

Sir   Cumb[erlan]d County [Pa.] 14th Feby 1779

I received your favour pr Express this morning and intend to begin my Journey agreeable to your request to morrow. The confidence you are pleased to place in me shall not be abused.[1]

My Ill state of Body will not admit that I speed, therefore thought it best to send off the express with directions to make the best way he can for Philada. I am Your Obedient Huml Servt

W: PATTERSON

ALS (PPAmP).

1. Washington, busy preparing for the Indian expedition, had undoubtedly asked NG to write Colonel Patterson because NG's assistant, Col. John Cox, had recommended Patterson as knowing more about the "Indian Country between the Susquehannah and Niagara" than any man "that cou'd be met with." (Washington recalled Cox's words in a letter to Joseph Reed, 8 April. Fitzpatrick, *GW*, 14: 351) In late February, Patterson accompanied Cox to headquarters. Washington, following a meeting with them, wrote to Patterson on 1 March for detailed information on the area of the six Indian nations and "their dependent Tribes" and authorized him to hire "intelligent, active and honest Men" to gather intelligence. (Ibid., 14: 168–69)

Before Patterson responded, Washington received a letter from Joseph Reed reporting that two members of the Pennsylvania Executive Council, Col. Matthew Smith and Mr. John Hambright, had asserted from "personal knowledge" that Patterson was "unfriendly to the true Interests of America" and was suspected of having held "Intercourse with the Enemy." (Reed to Washington in an undated letter, tentatively dated in the Washington Papers, DLC, as "between March 29 and April 7" and filed at 7 April.) Washington, greatly disturbed, pointed out to Reed that if he had been "deceived in the Man, Colo. Cox is the author of the deception and is highly culpable." (Fitzpatrick, *GW*, 14: 352; in a letter to Washington of 9 April, below, NG revealed that he was no less disturbed.)

Whether Smith's and Hambright's motives were political or personal, the men appear to have accused Patterson falsely. His brother-in-law, for example, was the celebrated Pennsylvania patriot, Gen. James Potter, who later served on the executive council. John Cox, moreover, had not only recommended Patterson but continued to uphold him to Reed; and when Reed was challenged by Patterson to name his complainants, Reed admitted that no regular complaints had been lodged against him. (Patterson to Washington, 29 May 1779, Washington Papers, DLC) Colonel Smith's record was far from spotless. During the siege of Boston, for example, he and his company had disgraced themselves by their conduct during a mutinous uprising. (See above, vol. 1: 118n) Some time after the incident with Patterson, Smith was dismissed from the post of prothonotary of Northumberland County. (*Pa. Col. Records*, 13: 696) Finally, in Patterson's defense, Gen. Edward Hand, who had conducted an investigation for Washington, reported that the man bears "a good Character." (Hand to Washington, 26 April, Washington Papers, DLC)

At the same time, Hand gave Patterson poor marks as an Indian intelligence agent. Some weeks after Patterson's first report (which he sent to NG on 28 March, below), General Hand wrote Washington that Patterson knew "nothing of the country farther back than French Catherines Town [on the headwaters of Seneca Lake] . . . nor is he acquainted with the Six Nations Language." (See Map 3) He recommended that Washington stop Patterson from proceeding with the mission. (Hand to Washington, 26 April 1779, Washington Papers, DLC)

Although Washington incorporated a later report by Cox and Patterson into his summary of the area, by 11 June he had terminated Patterson's employment. (See NG to Patterson, 11 June 1779; two reports by Patterson and Cox are filed at the end of May in the Washington Papers, DLC.) Washington's final communication with Patterson was on 22 June 1779. (Fitzpatrick, *GW*, 15: 301)

From James Thompson[1]

[   ] [before 15 Feb.1779][2]

The Right honourable Major-General Green, Sir

The Cause of my Wrighting, to your honour, is through Necessity, which is Mother of invention. I have been in the Continental Service Ever Since this unhappy Contest began, I haveing Neither Lands nor Liveing to fight for, only a poore Distrest famaly of Small

Children, with my Wife. Nevertheless, my harts Desire was to Searve My Country, all that in me Lay, and I have Done it, Even untill now, but I finde by woful Expearrance, that I Cannot Serve any Longer unless my poore famaly is better provided for, then they have been, while I have been in the Service, and Espshaly Since I ingaged with Captn Wm Mills in the Artiffisial business. Twelve Months Last April I Left my famaly and have not had the happyness to See them untill I had a furlough, from the Captn 22d Novemr Last by order of Major General Putnam, for which I Desire to be thankful; to finde them a Live, in Such a time of Distress was grate Sattisfaction. But to finde them in want of allmost Every Necessary of Life it fild my hart and minde with trouble and Distress. I mean to acquaint you, Most Noble General, of the Differance thats made betwean my famaly, and the famalyes of the Sorldiers. There famalyes has fire wood at twenty Shillings, and mine at Thirty Dollars per load. They have Indian Corn at four Shillings per bushel, and I give ten Dollars, or Else not have it, and Every other artical in perpotion, and as I have Served as a Clerk, in Said Company, and am but Little wanted, therefore, unto you, Most Noble General, I humble Pertishion and harttily beg, for a Discharge, from the Service. I at this time only Stand as a Clerk to Said Company, appointed by Colo Baldwin, Last August, at the White Plaines, and if it Should be your honours will to Consider the Matter, and to grant my Request I Shall take it as the gratest favour, that your honour Can possablely besto on your Very humble, most obadient and unworth Servant[3]

JAMES THOMPSON

ALS (PPAmP).

1. Gen. John Glover forwarded this letter to NG with the covering letter printed immediately below. Glover's intercession remains a mystery, for he was stationed in Providence, while William Mills's company, to which Thompson belonged, was in Jeduthan Baldwin's Artillery Artificers regiment in the region of the Hudson River Valley. The most likely explanation is that Thompson's family lived in Rhode Island and that Glover was asked to investigate their plight. This James Thompson is not to be confused with Lieut. James Thompson, who signed a petition of artificers of 8 July 1779, below.

2. On Thompson's location, see note 1. The date is determined by Glover's covering letter below.

3. According to the docketing, NG answered on 7 March, but his letter has not been found. He undoubtedly acceded to Glover's recommendation. The plight of Thompson's family was only marginally worse than those of others in his company. In a petition of 8 February to Jeduthan Baldwin, Thompson's fellow artificers in Mills's company stated that unless those with families could make better provisions for them, their servitude would be "wors than Egyption Bondage." (Greene Papers, PPAmP, vol. 4: 86) As the Board of War pointed out in a report to Congress on 1 May 1779, artificers were more likely to have families "than the Men in Marching regiments" because the artificer corps, being stationary, either attracted men with families or induced "them to enter into Matrimonial engagements." (JCC, 14: 603)

For the widespread distress of the artificers and NG's efforts to correct it, see petition and note, end of February, below.

From General John Glover

Dear General

At head[quarters] [Providence, R.I.] Feby 15, 1778 [1779]
From Compassion (only) I am induced to mention the Distressd
Circumstancies of Thompsons Famely, which is Truly Great.[1] Could
he Consistent with the good of the service, be Dischargd I apprehend
he would be able to support them much better then its now in his
Power to do. I am Dear General Respectfully your most Obdt Sert

JOHN GLOVER

ALS (PPAmP).
    1. See letter immediately above.

To John Jay, President of the Continental Congress

Sir   Middle Brook [N.J.] February 15th 1779
I do myself the honor of transmiting to your Excellency the
proposition I made to Mr [Elbridge] Gerry in the Committee of conference for settleing the Sallary of myself, and my two assistants in
the quarter masters department for our future services. The conditions was the same I mentioned to your Excellency, that is 3000
pounds Sterling for each of us and our expences paid. Payments to be
made quarterly either in Sterling, Bills on France; or in hard money
here.[1]

I trust this proposition will appear so reasonable when the nature
of the services is considerd and the trust adverted to, that the public
will acquit me of takeing any unfair advantage of its necessity. I am
the more inducd to entertain this belief as I have confind my demands
to the sum your Excellency approvd of.

I also told Mr Gerry I was willing to go on upon the present Contract or accept of the above Sallary in lieu of it or quit the department
altogether. But as I would not wish to distress the Army or injure the
common cause by leaving the business suddenly I would agree to
serve a few months upon almost any Terms until the Congress could
have it in their power to make other appointments upon conditions
more to their likeing.

Col Wadsworth agrees to the same conditions I offer [to] serve
upon. I have the honor to be with great respect Your Excellys most
obed humbe Servt

N GREENE

ADfS (PCC, item 173, vol. 4: 119, DNA).
    1. While in Philadelphia, NG had proposed that he and his assistants, Pettit and
Cox, be paid by salary in the hope of quieting criticisms of the commission system by
which quartermasters were traditionally compensated. From the time of NG's ap-

pointment, the three men had shared a 1 percent commission on departmental expenditures. (See above, vol. 2: 308–13n.)

Much of the recent criticism arose because the depreciated dollar (then worth only ten cents) had pushed up departmental expenditures—and commissions—to astronomically high figures. Some ill-informed people blamed inflation on the high prices that quartermasters and commissaries were paying for goods and services; among such persons, NG received no credit for keeping the increase in expenditures lower than the rate of depreciation.

But the criticism to which he was more vulnerable was of the quartermasters' bountiful incomes as expressed in the equivalent of specie. During the first quarter of 1779, for example, the department was spending at an annual rate of 32,000,000 Continental dollars—or roughly 3,200,000 Spanish milled dollars, the 1 percent commission on which was the yearly equivalent of some 2,400 pounds sterling for each of the three. (JCC, 15: 1432) This was far above the income of a major general—an amount for which NG had once offered to work. Colonel Cox thought that their proposal to work for 3,000 pounds Sterling would "not only greatly redound to our Credit but likewise to our Comfort." (Cox to Pettit, 2 February 1779, PCC, item 173, vol. 3:9, DNA) It would, indeed, redound to their "Comfort" since it represented a 25 percent increase over their current income, but it is doubtful if such an increase would redound to their "Credit" with the public. Few men in America, in fact, had larger assured incomes.

The salary proposal was not considered seriously enough by Jay or the committee of conference to be brought before Congress, and it is doubtful if NG expected it. It is equally doubtful that he was serious in his offer to "quit the department altogether." Thus the commission system was allowed to stand. Most of the criticism in Congress was still aimed at the deputies and agents in the department, although Pettit did report on 8 April that a few members of Congress thought "Genl Greene was too grasping and was making an immense fortune." (See his letter below.) Pettit and Cox, of course, were equally reproachable but were less in the limelight. Outside of Congress, critics made less distinction between the lower echelons and the three top officials, and they grew more vociferous. In view of the money rolling in, however, the mounting criticism was not yet intolerable.

The Greenes enjoyed a higher standard of living than they had known, for which Catharine especially was grateful. But unfortunately for NG, whose chief financial concern was for the family's future security, a high current income was no assurance of future dividends. Although his commissions were the equivalent of 2,400 pounds sterling, they were actually paid in rapidly depreciating Continental dollars, which prudence dictated getting rid of as quickly as possible.

But where could one invest surplus money? There were no banks, no stocks, no bonds. Government loan certificates issued after March 1778 paid interest in paper money—a negligible return. (Ferguson, *Power of Purse*, p. 39) Three principal areas were open to the investor—ships, land, or business enterprises, for which NG had neither the time nor the business acumen. Thus, he turned to joint ventures with family, friends, and colleagues. During his tenure as quartermaster, his investments were varied and numerous. Examples of his ventures in the following months are seen below: in land, Burnet to NG, 10 March; in commercial enterprises, Wadsworth to NG, 13 March; in industry, to Jacob Greene, 20 and 27 March. In the following year he also took shares in several dozen vessels—mostly privateers—with a variety of people.

A principal ingredient of success in such ventures—good luck—was too often missing, and when he left for the South in October 1780, he reckoned his total worth at no more than £ 5,000 in "lawful hard Money" [i.e., specie], plus a farm in Rhode Island that was his share of his father's estate. In pointing out that much of the money "in trade may be all lost," he was more prophetic than he could have known. The summary of his holdings was included in a letter to Catharine, 21 October 1780, one of the few times he mentioned such matters to her. It was undoubtedly engendered by thoughts on his own mortality as he set off into an uncertain future.

To George Washington

Sir   Rarotan [N.J.] February 15, 1779

I have carefully looked over the plan for a Resolve of Congress.[1] There appears to me two defects in it. One is the Articls taken in the Commisarys and quarter masters line should pass through the principals of those departments instead of going to the Auditors as it must be suppoasd they are better judges of the necessity and proper application of the things taken than the Auditors can be. The other defect is there dont seem to be care enough taken in the instructions given to the officers that gives Certificates to guard against forgery. If there is a Resolution of Congress directing payment to be made for all Certificates signd by any officer there will be great danger from the strong temptation and the difficulty of detection of Peoples taking unfair advantages of the public. Indeed I think there is much more necessity to guard against this Evil than the misapplication or abuses of the officers. I beg leave to recommend the enclosd precautions as well to prevent impositions as to pave the way for a just and speedy payment.

The Resolve as far as it respects the Clothiers department appears to me to be upon as good a plan as can be adopted.

Certificates that are given for articles taken for the use of the Army by Commisiond officers to be signd with their Names at full length and the Rank they hold and if under a General officer to have the addition of the Regiment and State to which they belong. To be inserted in the body of the Certificate, the things taken, their suppoasd Value, the Time and place, for what purpose and the necessity of the measure.

The Certificate to be directed to the principal of the department and his deputies whose duty it is to provide the things so taken. The officer shall keep [exact?][2] copys of all the Certificates he gives and also transmit copeys to the nearest agent in the department giving him the necessary information respecting the business.

The deputies shall also transmit Copies of such Certificates as they pay off to their principals that inquiry may be made if necessary whether the giving the Certificates was necessary for the public service and whether the things taken has been properly applyed[3]

ADf (PCC, item 173, vol. 4: 123, DNA). Possibly incomplete. (See note 3.)

1. The proposed resolve had been drawn up by the Board of War to redress the grievances of citizens who had been unable to cash certificates that they had accepted in exchange for provisions, some dating as far back as the winter at Valley Forge— before NG became quartermaster. From their inception, certificates had proved troublesome, and sellers had regularly resisted accepting them. Shortly after taking office, NG had attempted to regularize them by the use of printed forms, but they remained difficult to cash and depreciated daily in value. (See above, vol. 2: 324–25.)

The Board of War first called the attention of Congress to the plight of those long-suffering citizens in a letter of 9 February 1779, following two days later with a tentative resolution to meet their complaints. (The letter is printed in *JCC*, 13: 275–77; the draft resolution, dated 11 February, is in the Washington Papers, DLC.) In its letter to Congress, the Board declared that even "the best whigs" were given certificates "which after a tedious circuity of application are still unsatisfied." The resolution proposed that the supply departments pay such claims, after first establishing their legitimacy, for which the department heads or deputies should be allowed "one half per cent. and no more" for their trouble.

On 11 February the Board sent a copy of their 9 February letter and a draft of the resolution to Washington for his "Perusal & Remarks," asking if he would either amend it or prepare a better plan before it was presented to Congress. (Richard Peters to Washington, 11 February 1779, Washington Papers, DLC) Washington turned both documents over to NG for his comment.

As seen in this letter, NG's chief comment on the draft resolution was to have the principals in the supply departments, rather than the auditors, approve the purchases. Most of his letter, however, consisted in suggestions for handling certificates in the future, which the board had not touched upon.

In drafting a reply to the board for Washington, Alexander Hamilton relied almost entirely on NG's letter to Washington, quoting or paraphrasing his words without mentioning the source. (Fitzpatrick, *GW*, 14: 130–32) On 5 March, Congress took up the resolutions, which involved the commissary general and clothier general also. After receiving assurances from the Board of War that the report was "exactly conformable" to Washington's sentiments, Congress approved the recommendations essentially as NG had suggested in this letter. (*JCC*, 13: 277–79) The resolutions insured a more businesslike handling of certificates, but sellers continued to accept them only as a last resort.

2. One or two words in NG's draft are obliterated. The word "exact" has been supplied from Washington's letter to the board, as the remainder of his sentence is almost identical to NG's.

3. NG's draft, ending abruptly at the bottom of a page, appears incomplete, but Washington's final recommendation on the subject to the Board of War ends at the same point. If NG added anything on a missing page, it apparently did not concern certificates.

From Colonel Ephraim Bowen

[Providence, R.I., 15 February 1779. Encloses the returns of stores, wagons, horses, and persons employed. As ordered, he has dismissed express rider to headquarters. "About fifty Sail of [British] Transports . . . observ'd coming down the Sound" [Long Island Sound] but cannot say if Troops aboard.[1] Ordered canvas for knapsacks for Glover's and Varnum's brigades. ALS (PPAmP) 2 pp.]

1. On 26 February, Capt. John Garzia in Warwick, R.I., reported to General Sullivan that there had arrived at Newport on 25 February "37 Sails, 5 of which was Ships the Others of Various Rigg." (Hammond, *Sullivan*, 2: 521) They may have had troops aboard, but they represented no threat of a British offensive in Rhode Island.

From Colonel Robert L. Hooper, Jr.

[Easton, Pa., 15 February 1779. Advanced money for Convention troops en route to Virginia; can provide kegs for Indian expedition; infantry of [Pulaski's] Legion en route to Georgia; sent oats for

Washington's horses; eight loads chopped rye ready, two being sent; teams contracted for at Sussex Court House; commissaries should send flour; the Hoopers hope for visit from Mrs. Greene. ALS (PPAmP) 2 pp.]

From Colonel Charles Pettit

Dear Sir   Philadelphia 15 Feby 1779
    Your Favour of the 12th was delivered to me yesterday.[1] You may imagine from the number of Demands upon me that I cannot sit very easy under the Delay of Cash—not a single Dollar has come to my Share from the Treasury since your Departure. I have at length obtained a warrant for 1,500,000, but it has been so long in coming that I could distribute it all in one Day if I had it, but it is yet untangible.[2] After this Day I believe I come next to be supplied, and the moment I can get it I shall send some to you, and to the Eastern Contractors. Mr Biddle hands me in a List of upwards of 500,000 which have for some Time been demanded from him.
    The Treasury Board have evaded my Application for a Form of Accounts; telling me Mr Trumbull the Comptroller of Accts[3] is expected shortly, when the different Chambers will be established, with whom I may consult on Business of that kind. The Truth is the Business is beyond the reach of the Members of the Board and as I doubt not they will appoint Gentlemen skilled in the Science to the different Chambers of Accounts I am glad to find it will be entirely referred to them. In the mean Time I will endeavour to frame a model for our Department and send it round. But I foresee considerable Difficulties in collecting and examining the Vouchers, and deciding upon the different Articles of the numerous Accounts we have to examine.
    Col. Mitchell has recd a Letter from Col. Melcher forbidding him (or warning him against) purchasing any Wood or Boards, all of which he says you agreed to be within his Department. I have advised him for the present to take no notice whatever of the Letter.[4] In the mean Time I should be obliged to you to state in writing the several Matters the Board of War promised to report to Congress that I may know exactly how far to go when any conversations arise on the Subject either with the Board or on any other Occasion, and it may be necessary to jog their Memory occasionally to get the Business done.
    Considering the Route I find it necessary for Genl Pulaskie to take, I think it expedient to send a Person to preceed him as a Qur Master and Forager the whole of the Way. But as this Person must act independantly of the Deputies, going through an entire new Country, he must have a sufficient Supply of Money with him, and cannot set out till that is obtained.[5]
    Some Intelligence has been received by Congress which is as-

serted to be kept a profound Secret. All we are told concerning it is that it is of high importance, and good; but for political Reasons must not be divulged; that some particulars must not be published at all. Various are the Conjectures out of Doors—among others, that Spain has announced our Independency and proposes a Treaty of Amity and Commerce with a Loan of 10 to 15 millions of Dollars and to join immediatly in the War unless G. Britain shall submit to proper Terms of Peace. Much more you may suppose is fancied, but something of this kind gains the greatest Credence. The Truth is, I believe that Congress as a Body are not yet possessed of the Matter. The Minister of France has communicated something to some Members; and is to have an Audience, I believe today, to make a formal tho' secret Communication of it.[6] I carry my Ideas on the Subject farther than Spain. I suspect there are Workings in the different Courts of Europe which are important to our Alliance and which perhaps ought not to be known out of the Cabinet, lest our Enemies should derive something from it. In the mean Time we are deriving some Good from it in its Effects on Commerce. Rum, which was rising rapidly, has fallen two or three Dollars per Gallon. Hard Money which had risen to 10, or 12 for one I am told has been sold at 7. and that a Gentleman offered for £ 6,000 to pay £ 1000 hard [i.e., specie] by the first of June, and these good Effects seem to be still increasing. In addition to this a Tax Bill is in forwardness which it is expected will raise 8 or 9,000,000 of Dollars in this State within the Year which must work in favour of the Currency of Money.

While I am writing, a Letter comes in from Mr Hubbard which I shall inclose to you.[7] Considering the State of Affairs at Carolina I doubt the propriety of sending Vessels thither for the present. I shall mention my Thoughts of the Matter to the Committee for their Consideration.[8]

I received yesterday a Return of Stores from Fishkill which I suppose came from your Quarters tho' I had no Letter with it. As all Matters relating to Stores falls into Col. Cox's Division of the Business I shall send him all I have recd and in future they had better be directed to him. In the mean Time I shall add this of Col Hays to the Genl account formed from such Returns as I have and send you a Copy herewith.

If anything more shd occur before I send this away I will begin a new Leaf. In the mean Time I will close this with compliments to Mrs Greene and assurances of being Dr Sir your most obed hum'l Servt

CHAS PETTIT

I do not know whether the whole of Col. Hay's Return is added or not. The Clerk had it in hand and I believe had not finished it. He being out when the Oppor'ty offers I send it as it is.

ALS (PPAmP).
1. Not found.
2. The warrant had been approved on 11 February. (*JCC*, 13: 176) Warrants were always issued to NG or to an assistant rather than to the department.
3. Jonathan Trumbull, Jr., the son of Gov. Jonathan Trumbull of Connecticut, had been appointed the first comptroller of the treasury in November 1778; he resigned in April 1779. (*JCC*, 12: 1096; 13: 490) Later in the year he was elected a commissioner of the Treasury Board. Active in Connecticut affairs, he served as governor from 1797 until his death in 1809. A recent biography is John W. Ifkovic, *Connecticut's Nationalist Revolutionary: Jonathan Trumbull, Junior* (American Revolution Bicentennial Commission of Connecticut, Hartford, 1977).
4. This was a jurisdictional dispute between NG's Philadelphia deputy and the barrackmaster general, Col. Isaac Melcher. See above, Melcher to NG, 25 January.
5. Pulaski's Legion was en route to Georgia. See above, Pettit to NG, 10 February.
6. For the past week Philadelphia had buzzed with rumors of an impending Spanish alliance. As early as 18 January the *New York Gazette* had reprinted a letter from London which speculated on the possibility of the war being extended to include Spain, but the recent rumors originated in Congress, a fertile ground for nourishing such rumors since it had tried for two years to involve Spain. Floridablanca, Spain's shrewd foreign minister, was reluctant to enter the war and was emphatically opposed to recognizing the independence of the United States—a condition that he wisely foresaw as boding no good for Spain's relations with her American colonies.
He did hope to win back Gibraltar and Minorca by threats to join France in the war. Several times in 1778 he held the threat over England by offering to mediate the conflict, but was rebuffed. It was his virtual ultimatum to George III in October 1778, relayed to President Jay by the French Minister Gérard on 8 February, that sparked the hopes of Congress. On the fifteenth, Gérard appeared before Congress, where he was less sanguine on the prospects of Spanish involvement than he had been in his letter to Jay. The only prospect he held out for Spanish financial aid was a "subsidy" for American troops to conquer Florida, which was then to be turned over to Spain. Thus, the prospect of concrete Spanish aid was far from rosy, but individual delegates, grasping at straws, chose to see vast possibilities ahead. As is evident in Pettit's letter, as well as in letters below of the sixteenth from NG to Hay and Cox to NG, their fanciful hopes soon became the basis of rumors. Briefly, the Continental dollar rose in value, then fell as it became obvious that Spain was no warm friend of America. Not until 21 June did she declare war on England, and then not as an ally of the United States. Spain, in fact, had no intention of recognizing American independence. Monetary aid was also slow in coming and disappointingly small. A recent estimate is that Spain's total contribution during the war was on the order of $600,000, compared with France's $8,000,000—both in specie. (Higginbotham, *War*, p. 235) The road ahead with Spain was to prove a rocky one. (Bemis, *Diplomacy*, chapter 8, is still useful on the relations with Spain.)
7. See above, 6 February.
8. Since the British capture of Savannah in late December and Augusta a month later, the safety of Charleston was much in doubt. In a letter of 19 February to William Whipple of the Marine committee, Pettit pointed out the hazards in getting ships to Charleston for rice and asked for the committee's advice. (Greene Papers, PPAmP, vol. 4: 79) Charleston was not captured until May 1780, and in the meantime a number of rice ships did get through the British blockade.

From Colonel Charles Stewart[1]

[Kaen's Quarters, N.J., 15 February 1779. Necessary to keep temporary magazine at landing on Raritan. Bridge there "wants repairing"; fears accident to wagons. He supposes NG would have noticed the condition if he had traveled "that way lately." ALS (PPAmP) 2 pp.]

1. A former colonel in the N.J. militia, Stewart had been commissary general of issues since 1777.

To Justice [   ] Dunn[1]

Sir   Camp at Middle Brook [N.J.] February 16th 1779

Col Thomson [James Thompson] the Waggon Master General informs me you detain a Continental Waggon under pretence of its being employed in conveying Contraband Goods; and that you propose to confiscate the same.

I shall state the facts and then leave you to act as you please.

Col Blain Deputy Commisary General made application to Col Thomson to send a Waggon to General Maxwells to fetch a Box of things from thence to the Army.

Col Blain being entitled to a public Waggon from the nature of his appointment, the Waggon Master General sent the Waggon without the least hesitation.

This is the first hint I have had of the affair. I neither knew that the Waggon was gone nor the service that it went upon; and if I had, I should have had no suspicions of any property being to be conveyed in it that was Contraband; Especially as it was to be brought from General Maxwells.

Officers frequently make application to have baggage conveyed from one place to another; the officers in the Waggon department cannot be supposd to know the Contents and therefore cannot refuse to perform the duty.

I am perswaded when you reflect a moment you will see the impropriety of your conduct and discharge the Team. However if after this information you presume to detain it I shall prosecute you in behalf of the States.[2] I am sir Your humble serv

N GREENE

ADfS (PCC, item 173, vol. 4: 125, DNA).
1. The draft was addressed to "Esqr Dunn. Justice of the peace near Quible Town." Quibbletown was between Middlebrook and Elizabeth Town, where General Maxwell's brigade was stationed. See Map 1.
2. It is not known whether Dunn released the wagon or whether NG had to "prosecute" him.

To Colonel Udny Hay

Sir

[Middlebrook, N.J.] Feby 16 [17]79

Your favour of the 10th to me and the 11th To Major Forsyth are recd.[1] I am sorry to find the numerous host of vouchers renders a large reinforcement of money necessary. These kind of claims lie like hidden mischief. They ruin a man before he is aware of being in danger. I wish some mode could be adopted by which the constant expences of the Department could be known, but I am afraid it is impracticable.

Agreable to your application made to Major Forsyth I have sent you Thirty thousand Dollars which I hope will enable you to pay off your arrearages agreable to your Advertisements. I shall also write to Philadelphia to have the remaining seventy Thousand forwarded as soon as the state of our finances will admit, but I am afraid the money will not come in seasonable as you wish, there being many pressing demands now ag't the Department, and the other great Departments of the Army by their Claims upon the Treasury, together with the late heavy Drafts from the Southard will render it difficult for us to supply all the wants of our several Agents.

You desire to know by what means I expect a supply of Fatigue men for your Post for the ensueing Campaign to which I can only say, you must provide yourself by the best ways and means you can. The present prospect of our Currency growing better, together with the agreable news now circulating that Spain has come into the Alliance, and offers us the loan of thirteen Millions of Dollars, opens a prospect of wages falling instead of Rising; therefore I should recommend to wait a fortnight or three weeks, and see what effect these circumstances will have upon our Money, on which the price of labour will depend.[2] However, I do not mean that you should neglect any measure necessary for the carrying on of your business, for the sake of the prospect of this saveing. You must judge from the circumstances, and take your measures accordingly.

I am sorry you have got into a dispute with the Justices, as they are like the Watchmen upon the Tour [tower] to give the cries to the people. This order of men are generally confident and conceited; obstinate and vindictive, and when they have such a Battalion of Constables to carry into execution their devices, its difficult for poor honesty to resist their force. If you have come off victorious in the present instance, by alarming their fears, I advise you to settle the difference, and bury the hachet.[3]

I should be glad of a Coppy of your proposed plan to the Legislature for furnishing our Department with Teams in future. If it is already pass'd into a Law, with any amendments, pleas to transmit me a Copy of that also.[4]

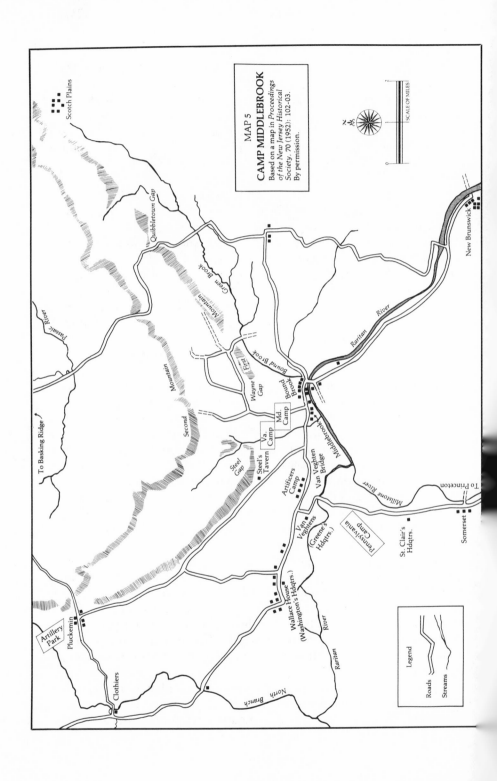

MAP 5
CAMP MIDDLEBROOK
Based on a map in *Proceedings
of the New Jersey Historical
Society,* 70 (1952): 102–03.
By permission.

SCALE OF MILES

Scotch Plains

Quibbletown Gap

Green Brook

First Mountain

Passaic River

To Basking Ridge

Second Mountain

Wayne's Gap

Bound Brook

Middlebrook

Steel's Gap

Steel's Tavern

Va. Camp

Md. Camp

Artificers Camp

Van Veghten Bridge

Van Veghten (Greene's Hdqrs.)

Pennsylvania Camp

Milstone River

To Princeton

Raritan River

New Brunswick

Somerset

St. Clair's Hdqrs.

Artillery Park

Pluckemin

Wallace House (Washington's Hdqrs.)

Raritan River

North Branch

Clothiers

Legend

Roads

Streams

I wish it was in my power to remedy the evil you mention, that is, The different prices of Waggon hire, and the ill consequences that result from it, but the Commissaries are not under my controul and therefore I cannot restrain them. One general price would certainly be more satisfactory to the Inhabitants, and far less expensive to the public. To effect this, every department that requires any transportation, should govern their prices by ours as ours is infinitely larger than all the rest; and our Agents so station'd, as to be better judges of the ability and disposition of the People than any others can pretend to be.

I cannot conceive that General Washington is authoris'd to give any powers to a Person to administor an Oath that is not Warranted by a Resolution of Congress. I should recommend that Major Hale apply to Governor Clinton, who I think can Clothe him with authority for the purpose.

You will please in your next to let me know the extent of your prospects in the article of Tents. I am Sir your Humble Servant

N GREENE

Cy (PPAmP).
1. Hay's letter to Robert Forsyth, the deputy who acted for NG while he was in Philadelphia, is in the Greene Papers, PPAmP.
2. On the rumors about Spain, see above, Pettit to NG, 15 February.
3. In Hay's quarrel with the justices of the peace (one of whom had him arrested), he had the sympathy and support of Governor Clinton—at least as far as the governor's authority extended. On 10 February, the same day that Hay had written to NG, the governor had issued a twenty-one-day impressment warrant to Hay and his agents, to be used principally for acquiring horses and wagons. He admonished Hay, however, to use agents "such as have not rendered themselves obnoxious to the Inhabitants by past Controversies." (Clinton, *Papers*, 4: 558) When one Justice "Umphrey" refused to comply with the warrant, Hay reported this to Clinton in hopes that he could push the legislature to pass an amendment to the impressment law that the governor had laid before them in late January. (Hay's letter to Clinton of the fourteenth and one to "Mr. Umphrey" of the eleventh are in ibid., 4: 566–68. The governor's message of 28 January is printed on p. 525.)
4. On Hay's plan for the New York legislature, see note at his letter to NG of 21 January, above.

To Colonel Henry Hollingsworth

Sir   Camp Middle Brook [N.J.] 16th Feby [17]79
Your favour of the 10 Inst I have receiv'd. I wrote you so fully on the 14th of this Inst upon the Several matters which you request answers to in these Letters that it is unnecessary to add on the Subject.[1] I recollect your having mentiond several times the Interferance of purchases from the neighbouring Districts. I have as repeatedly Injoyn'd a Discontinuance of such practices as I have receiv'd Complaints, but I am afraid the orders has not had full affect as the evil still

Continues. I have no doubt of your attention and industry. I only wish you to continue the same Degree that you have done heretofore.

You must deal with the Waggon Masters, Mr Anderson and Caswell, as will be just to them and have a tendency to Correct a future evil of the Kind. How far their former merit may serve to atone for their present offences I leave for you to Judge.

The Extravagant offers made for the Conveyance of private property opperates as a severe Tax upon the public. The ambiguity of State Laws and the popular Principle that pervades Public Counsel renders it very Difficult drawing any aid from the Cival Majestrate in Support of the Public business, this Policy is too prevalent every where for the good of the Common Cause. I am too Sensible from my own Experience of the want of Virtue in the farmers, the infidelity of Shallop men and Waggoners to have render'd your Cathalogue[2] necessary to work a Conviction of the truth of your Observation but these are the Materials with which we have to work and if our Success is not equal to our Wishes the Charge is not against us, but against the Temper and Disposition of the People. We can only use care and Industry and if that fails under the guidance of our best Judgement we stand Acquited from any negligence.[3] If you shall need any further advice upon any matters you will write to Mr Pettit at Philadelphia. I am Sir Your m't Obt H Servt

N GREENE

Df (PCC, item 173, vol. 4: 133, DNA).
1. See above.
2. Johnson, *Dictionary*, defines a *catalog* as "an enumeration of particulars."
3. These thoughts could stand as NG's consoling credo during the trying months that lay ahead.

Colonel Ephraim Bowen to Major Ichabod Burnet

[Providence, R.I., 16 February 1779. Made provisions for knapsacks; has tents and cooking utensils for troops here. Encloses return of stores by which NG can make an estimate. ALS (PPAmP) 1 p.]

From Colonel John Cox

[Bloomsbury, Trenton, N.J., 16 February 1779, 11:00 P.M. At NG's request is sending a horse that appears "recovered of his Lameness." Repeats rumors on Spain and their effect on prices.[1] Pennsylvania tax to raise "8 to 10 Million." Report of two Continental frigates bringing five or six enemy armed vessels to Chesapeake. News from Egg Harbor that "our Schooner Hunter" brought in a prize.[2] ALS (PPAmP) 2 pp.]

1. See note, Pettit to NG, 15 February, above.
2. If the news was true, the *Hunter* was one of the few privateers of many in which NG owned shares which ever took a prize.

From Colonel John Cox

Dear Sir   Bloomsbury [N.J.] Feby 16th 1779

I this morning Received your favor of the 14th Inst. and will immediately enquire into the reason of the very great difference in the price of the Pack Saddles and give such orders as will be most condusive to the public Interest. I imagine those mentioned by Col. Hooper must be the kind commonly made only by the Indian Traders, which are made with a Slight Pad and Cross Tree, to which the Load is slung. If so I question their answering the common purpose of the Army unless very great attention is paid to the making of them. Besides I am confident he must be greatly mistaken in the price as they formerly in the cheapest of Times cost from 20/ to 30/. However, I will immediately write to him on the subject and if they can be had even at three pounds [i.e., 60/] order five hundred of them made so soon as possible.[1]

I dispatched an Express to Col Patterson immediately after you left us [at Trenton] and am in hourly expectation of either seeing or hearing from him. The moment he Arrives I will (tho very unfit) accompany him to Camp and shoud he not come in a few Days and I continue to mend I will set out alone and leave the necessary directions for him to follow.[2] Mrs Cox and family join me in most respectful Compliments to Mrs Green and am very sorry we cannot do ourselves the pleasure of partaking with you at Pluckemin on Thursday next.[3] I am with sincere Esteem Dear Sir Your Obed Hbl Servt

JOHN COX

ALS (PPAmP).
1. John Cox had undoubtedly been influenced in his opinions by John Mitchell, whose price, as NG noted in his letters to Cox and Pettit of 14 February, above, was considerably higher than Hooper's. Neither Cox nor Mitchell were as knowledgeable as Hooper on frontier matters, and in the end NG decided that the Hooper packsaddle was cheaper and better for the Indian expedition. (See below, Hooper to NG, 18 and 25 February, and NG to Hooper, 20 February.) Gen. Edward Hand refused to accept those from Mitchell. See Claiborne to NG, first letter of 6 May, below.
2. See Patterson to NG, 14 February, above.
3. The Coxes missed a memorable evening, which broke the tedium of camp life for NG and his fellow officers at Middlebrook. On Thursday, 18 February, Gen. Henry Knox and his officers staged at their artillery headquarters at Pluckemin, five miles northwest of NG's headquarters (see Map 5), an "entertainment" to commemorate the first anniversary of the French Alliance. It had been postponed from the sixth because Washington was in Philadelphia, although once back in camp he was unsure of attending because he feared the British would use the occasion for an attack. When it did not materialize, he joyfully joined the celebrants. (Fitzpatrick, *GW*, 14: 122) Judging from a lengthy account in the Trenton paper, the affair was not one likely to be forgot-

ten in the lifetime of those present. In addition to the officers, this included, according to the newspaper, "Mrs. Washington—Mrs. Greene—Mrs. Knox; the gentlemen and ladies for a large circuit around the camp" and "a vast concourse of spectators from every part of the Jersies." Any disappointments with the alliance must have disappeared in the festivities.

The celebration was opened about 4:00 P.M. with "the discharge of THIRTEEN cannon." Then a select company assembled in the academy at the artillery park "to a very elegant dinner" with many toasts to America's "liberties, empire—and independence." In the evening "a very fine set of fire-works" was displayed at the point of a "Temple" constructed for the occasion. It was a remarkable structure, some one hundred feet long, consisting of thirteen arches, each highlighted by an illuminated painting with accompanying "mottos." The paintings, by some unheralded artist, depicted such scenes as the battle of Lexington; the British burning of American towns; the decaying empire of Britain, consisting of "fallen spires—ships deserting its shores—birds of prey hovering over its mouldering cities—and a gloomy setting sun." In the adjoining arch was a painting of America as a rising empire with a "splendid sun emerging from a bright horizon." Other arches depicted Louis XVI, Benjamin Franklin, Saratoga, generals fallen in battle and now "in Elisium," and finally "peace with all her train of blessings" with a background of "flourishing cities—ports crowded with ships—and other emblems of an extensive empire, and unrestrained commerce." When the fireworks were finished, the company concluded the celebration by "a very splendid ball." (N.J. Gazette, 3 March 1779) General Knox reported that some seventy ladies and "between three and four hundred Gentlemen" danced all night. (Quoted in Fitzpatrick, GW, 14: 122n)

From Colonel Lewis Morris, Jr.[1]

Dr Genl   Head Quarters Providence [R.I.] Feb 16th [17]79

You will pardon me for requesting the favor of you to direct and forward the enclosed Letter to my Brother [Jacob]. I should not trouble you Sir with the requisition, if I had not been informed that the Family have moved from Princeton to some other Part of the Jersies, and I am at a Loss to determine where.

I have nothing particular to communicate in our Department, except that a Report prevails upon the Bridge, there are a Number of Transports standing down the Sound. Perhaps these may have Troops on board to reinforce Genl Prescott. If so their Object probably is this Town. I wish it may be, from a certainty that their utmost Exertions cannot dispossess us of it; and unless we have some object to call the Soldiery into the Field, and divert them from their present State of Security and Idleness, I am apprehensive the Pleasures and Dissipation of this Place will be as fatal to the Soldiers of the American Army, as those of Capua were to the Soldiers of Hannibals.[2]

I would inform you that the State of Massachusetts has voted a thousand Dollars to each of their Field Officers, and two hundred Pounds to each Captain, and so on to the Subalterns in Proportion, as a Compensation for their Services;[3] and have likewise agreed to make up the Depreciation of the Money both to officers and Men.[4] I hope this noble Example will be adopted by the other States Not from a selfish Motive, but to pacify the common Soldiery who are principal

Sufferers in the present State of currency. Such a Step would lull their Clamours, lay them under a greater Obligation to their Country and add Vigor to our operations in the ensuing Campaign. My Respects to your Lady and Family and I have the Honor Sir, to subscribe myself your humb servt

LEWIS MORRIS JUNR

ALS (MiU-C).

1. Morris was the son of Lewis Morris of Morrisania, a general of the New York militia who had fled with his family to Princeton in 1776. Lewis, Jr., at this time was General Sullivan's aide, but in June 1779 he became NG's aide for the duration of the war. See letter from Gouverneur Morris, his uncle, to NG, 19 May, below, and *DAB*.

2. The British did not attack Providence. Sullivan's army, soon to be commanded by Gates, continued to form an essentially passive defense around the perimeter of Narragansett Bay, allowing the men the usual "Pleasures and Dissipation" that Morris decried.

3. In saying that Massachusetts had "voted" its officers various sums of money, Morris was in error. The officers of Glover's Massachusetts brigade at Providence had petitioned the legislature to grant their families the same aid that had been extended to the families of noncommissioned officers and private soldiers of Massachusetts in an act of 10 October 1777. That act required each town to provide "necessaries" to the families of men who had signed up for three years or the duration, not as a gift, but to be repaid by the men when their pay was "made good." A town that failed to act would have to pay the state up to five times the value of the goods denied.

In response to the officers' petitions of January 1779, the Massachusetts lower house on 4 February (concurred in by the executive council on 6 February) agreed to provide £ 300 to families of captains, chaplains, and surgeons; and £ 150 to families of subalterns. As with noncommissioned officers and soldiers, the amounts were not given but "advanced" and were to be "deducted from their Wages" later. (A printed copy of the act of 6 February 1779 is in PCC, item 74, p.101, DNA.) It includes some of the provisions of the act of 10 October 1777.

4. Morris was on sounder ground in referring to the promise of Massachusetts "to make up the Depreciation of the Money." In a somewhat abstrusely worded passage of the act cited above, the legislature reiterated a promise made in the act of 1777 "against Monopoly and Oppression" to make good to officers and soldiers (or heirs of those who had died) the Continental wages for which they had been engaged, "taking for a Measure of their Wages the Prices set to the Articles enumerated in the same Act."

A table of depreciation, listing each month between January 1777 and January 1780, was drawn up by a committee of the Massachusetts legislature on 11 January 1780. It was to be used to "settle & adjust the Ballance due each officer and Soldier" and was based on the average prices of beef, Indian corn, sheep's wool, and leather. By January 1779 the table listed the rate of depreciation at 9 to 1. How the state could possibly afford to make up for such depreciation, not to mention the 40 to 1 rate by January 1780, the committee did not say. (A manuscript copy of the committee's table with a preamble is in PCC, item 74, pp. 107–8, DNA.)

From Colonel Charles Stewart

[Kaen's Quarters, N.J., 16 February 1779. Sickness obliges him to leave camp. Needs express to Philadelphia. ALS (PPAmP) 1 p.]

From Asa Worthington[1]

[Raritan, N.J., 16 February 1779. Because of "an overplus of Cattle" in vicinity of camp asks if an artificer—"an Ingenious Young man"—can help for few weeks. ALS (PPAmP) 1 p.]

1. He was inspector of cattle in the commissary department from November 1778 to January 1780. (*JCC*, 16: 65) His letter below of the seventeenth asks for considerably more than for an artificer.

Circular Letter to Deputy Quartermaster Generals

[Camp Raritan, N.J., 17 February 1779. Encloses resolution of Marine Committee of Congress asking for charges against French fleet. Cy (PCC, item 173, vol. 4: 137, DNA) 1 p.]

Verbal Instructions of George Washington to Nathanael Greene[1]

Sir   Raraton [Raritan, N.J.] February 17, 1779

It has been determind by a Committee of Congress appointed to confer with me upon the practicabillity of carrying on a Canada expedition that it is not in our power to prosecute it with a prospect of success; and therefore the preparations are to be discontinueed. You will countermand all the orders you may have given in consequence of mine given to you at the Rarotan the 15th of December past. But nevertheless as the preparations have gone great lengths towards providing materials for the Battaeus and Gallies, You will still go on with them and complete a suffecent Number of Battauex for the original plan of the expedition and have all the Materials provided for the Gallies agreeable to the Invoice made out by Major Benjamin Eyre except such articles as I have marked against. Take this and deposit them at Albany by the middle or last of April.

This order is not meant that any measures should be taken for providing any Timber or Plak [Plank] for the Gallies or have any men held in pay to be in readiness to build them.

AD (PPAmP).
1. This puzzling document in NG's hand appears to be instructions to NG which Washington gave him verbally. It is especially puzzling because in a letter of 24 February, below, Washington wrote that he wished to "repeat the verbal instructions" given NG in Philadelphia, which countermanded the instructions given him on 15 December, above. It is possible that Washington repeated at camp the verbal instructions first given in Philadelphia, for as noted at NG to Morgan Lewis, 10 February, above, NG had received such orders while in Philadelphia.

Whatever the circumstances, the evidence is convincing that NG was the intended recipient of the instructions and that it was Washington who gave them. In the first instance, despite the document's being in NG's hand, he left it unsigned and wrote his own name as the addressee in the lower left corner of the last page. He was, moreover, the only recipient of Washington's letter of 15 December, above, about the "Canada expedition." The evidence is equally convincing that the instructions were Washington's. Two statements in the document could fit no one else: first, the Committee of Congress was appointed to confer about the Canadian expedition (among other matters) with the "Commander in Chief" and with no one else (*JCC*, 12: 1250); and secondly, the orders from Washington to NG of 15 December, above, are referred to as "mine."

To Colonel Morgan Lewis

Sir   Middle Brook [N.J.] Feby 17th 1779
    I Saw a letter yesterday from General Scuyler to His Excellency General Washington wherein he informs him that the materials are prepar'd for building a large number of Batteaux, in which Letter he also suggests the propriety of making a sufficient number for the purpose of the first expedition.[1] He offers two reasons for the measure, one is, that it will be attended with little additional expense. The other is, that boats will be in readiness for any other offensive operations that the change of circumstances may render necessary to persue hereafter. His Excellency appear'd fully satisfy'd that the business of the Batteaux building go on, providing circumstances are as General Schuyler has hinted. You will persue it therefore until you hear further from me, and in the mean time, give me a full account of the state of the Materials provided for the purpose. It is not meant that a new expense should be incur'd in providing materials, but only those Manufactur'd into Batteaux that are already collected.
    By Letters from Philadelphia, I am inform'd that a Spanish Vessel that has lately arriv'd there brings the agreable intelligence that Spain has acceeded to the Alliance, and offer'd the Loan of thirteen Millions of Dollars. This circumstance bids fair to put a different face upon our Currency. The Speculators in the City are in the greatest consternation for fear of a very great fall of the Stocks.[2] I am Sir Your most obedient Humble Servant

Cy (PCC, item 173, vol. 4: 135, DNA). The subject matter of the letter reveals the author as NG.
    1. The letter that Washington received on 16 February was written by Schuyler on the fourth. (Fitzpatrick, *GW*, 14: 121)
    2. As noted above at Pettit to NG, 15 February, the rumors about Spain were far rosier than the reality.

From Colonel John Beatty[1]

Dear General
    Commiss[ar]y Pris[on]ers Office [Raritan, N.J.] Feby 17th 1779
    Herewith you will receive a Letter for Colo Greene, as also his

Parole and Certificate of Exchange. The General will be kind enough to transmit them to him by the earliest Opportunity.

Business preventing my coming to Camp at the time Head Quarters was fixed at Middle Brook, the Gentn of the Army improved their early arrival at this Ground in procuring for quarters all the Houses in the Vicinity of Camp and Head Quarters. The duty of my Office requiring a constant and almost daily Attendance on the Commander in Chief, I cannot find within the Circuit of several Miles any House convenient except the one I now live in, which indeed might answer my purpose were it not for The Revd Dr Belmain of the Virginia Line, who had previously taken Possession of the only Spare Room in the House.[2] The nature of his Duty, I conceive might with equal regularity and punctuality be gone thro'h was he removed to a greater distance, and I have no Doubt, there are Houses as near to the Line to which he belongs, wherein he might be equally well accomodated. I am sorry to trouble you on such an occasion, but will thank you to point out the proper measures to be pursued for his removal, or I must be obliged to provide new Quarters.[3] I am with great Respect Dear General Your most Obd Hum'l Servt

JNO BEATTY

LS (PPAmP).
  1. Colonel Beatty (1749–1826) had succeeded Elias Boudinot as commissary of prisoners on 28 May 1778 after having been a prisoner himself for eighteen months. A graduate of Princeton who had studied medicine under Benjamin Rush, he was one of four brothers who served as officers during the war. He resigned under somewhat of a cloud in March 1780 but lived on to hold several public offices in New Jersey. (DAB)
  2. Alexander Balmain was chaplain in Muhlenberg's brigade. (PCC, item 173, vol. 1: 197, DNA)
  3. Providing housing for officers was one of the more annoying chores added to the quartermaster's principal duties. Since Beatty wrote thenceforth from Camp Middlebrook, NG presumably moved the Reverend Balmain to other quarters.

From Governor William Livingston of New Jersey

Sir   Morris Town [N.J.] 17 Febry 1779
  I have received your favour of the 14th instant with the inclosures, and am sorry to hear that any of our Magistrates should furnish any matter of complaint, either for delinquency in duty or excess of authority; in both which respects I have reason to believe that some of them have rendered themselves culpable. For while some are remiss in assisting the army according to the true spirit of the Law; others have been oppressive in granting warrants for cutting wood without summoning the owners to try his disaffection, or any proof of his refusal, and that by the acre, instead of the cord. Certain it is that for every breach of duty, they are amenable to the Law; but that I have

any particular authority to exercise over them, in consequence of their conduct, is far from being evident.[1] I shall however take occasion to lay the papers before the privy Council, and it would give me real pleasure to be instrumental in the execution of the Law for supplying the army according to its wants and in proportion to the stock people have in hand, and the necessities of their neighbours that have none at all. I am with great Esteem Sir your most humble Sr

WIL LIVINGSTON

ALS (PPAmP).
1. Livingston had issued a proclamation on 14 January requesting the justices to execute the forage laws. See above, note at Biddle to NG, 25 January.

From Colonel John Mitchell

Dear Sir   Philada 17 February 1779
I have the pleasure of your esteemd favors of the   and 15 Inst. The former gave me the pleasure of hearing you were safe arrived at Camp with Mrs Greene, and George, which as the Roads were bad both Mrs Mitchell and me were antious to know.[1] I beg leave to assure you we had particular pleasure in contributing in any degree to your pleasure and convenience while here, and that we are Happy in your being pleased with what was in our power to do. Believe me that my esteem and respect for Genl Green will at all times make every service in my power to render him or his Lady will give me real satisfactions and hope you will never think of the pleasure you gave us by your Company as any favor or Obligation.

I am sorry it is not in Mrs Mitchell's or my power to be at Camp at the Exebition, it is not possible for me to be absent from the Office at this time. I have sent Mrs Greens shoes by the bearer. Mrs Mitchell Joins me in most respectfull Complimts to you and your Lady, and am with real esteem and respect Dr Sir Your most Obed huml Sr

JNO MITCHELL

ALS (PPAmP).
1. Neither letter has been found. One or both undoubtedly supported Mitchell in his quarrel with the Pennsylvania Executive Council. (See above, NG to Reed #1, 31 January.) George was the Greenes' three-year-old son.

From General John Sullivan

[Providence, R.I., 17 February 1779. Was unaware of resolution of Congress that NG mentions in letter of ninth but "Shall in future pursue the Measure pointed out by the practice in the Army." ALS (PPAmP) 1 p.]

From Asa Worthington

Sir   Rariton [N.J.] Feby 17th 1779
By Colonel Wadsworth's diriction's I am to request you to order that the Slaughter House now began in Camp may be speedily Compleated. At present there is nothing done but the Frame.

Among the many reasons that Induce me to Urge the matter, is the following. The Cattle after being drove 150 and 200 miles from Camp, and being badly suplied with forage on the road, will certainly loose considerable flesh, and by the time they get here are falling away fast, and was they ever so well suplied with forage, it would be a dificult matter to prevent their further falling away. But this is so far from being the case, that it is with the greatest dificulty we can give them a slight Foddering once in two days, and give me leave to add, that in my humble opinion 1000 Dollars pr day will barely make good the Loss of flesh from the beef Cattle now in the neighborhood of Camp. This Circumstance will I hope convince You of the necessity of having it Emediatly attended to.

And that all the Cattle may be killed as soon as they arive at Camp, and the wast in Flesh, and Consumption of forage prevented, I wish a large Vatt May be made at the slaughter house to salt the meat in as it is Killed, as there cannot be a sufficient quantity of barrels Procured for that purpose. I will give directions concerning the Construction of the Vatt when the Artificers are ready to work on it. I am Sir Your obt servant[1]

ASA WORTHINGTON

ALS (PPAmP).
1. NG's answer has not been found, but presumably Worthington's request was carried out.

From Colonel John Cox

[Bloomsbury, Trenton, N.J., 18 February 1779. Is well enough to accompany Colonel Patterson to camp.[1] Compliments to Mrs. Greene from all, including "the Young Ladies." ALS (PPAmP) 1 p.]

1. On Patterson's trip, see above, his letter of 14 February.

From Colonel Udny Hay

[Fishkill, N.Y., 18 February 1779. In answer to NG's letter by Captain Pendleton, Hay has not heard "a single Complaint since the men were Joined [to] Capt Sizers Compy."[1] Pendleton, who talked to Captain Bolton, "is fully of my opinion." LS (PPAmP) 1 p.]

1. NG's letter has not been found, but it concerned the artificers' petition of 4 December 1778, above.

From Colonel Robert L. Hooper, Jr.

[Easton, Pa., 18 February 1779. Has NG's of the fourteenth. Expects "Legion Infantry" to reach Nazareth tomorrow.[1] Confident that packsaddles he's recommended are "of the best Construction for an Indian Expedition," a judgment founded on long experience and corroborated by General Hand. "They are more Simple, light, cool and easy to the Horse." Can complete 1,000 by April. Needs cloth and thread for pads.[2]

Admittedly, "Five Pounds per day for a Four Horse Team" is high; but he had to pay it because Pennsylvania law allows even more. ALS (PPAmP) 2 pp.]

1. Pulaski's Legion was en route to Georgia. Nazareth was ten miles west of Easton. See Map 3.
2. Hooper had first recommended these packsaddles in a letter to NG of 6 February, above. On NG's decision to order Hooper's instead of Mitchell's, see note at Cox to NG, 16 February #2, above.

From Colonel Udny Hay

[Fishkill, N.Y., 19 February 1779. Entreats NG for blankets to replace those borrowed from General McDougall, whose men "are now suffering for want of them." Blankets formerly received "so bad that they have been estimated at two for one."

Great difficulty to get teams. "Oldest man in the Country never remembers . . . a winter near so bad for the business of Transport."[1] However, they have not suffered, nor will they. ALS (PPAmP) 2 pp.]

1. Because of lack of snow for sleighing.

From Nehemiah Hubbard

Sir   Hartford [Conn.] Feby 19th 1779
I have Recd your favour of the 9th inst. wherein you say you have not recd a line from me since you wrote me from Philadelphia.

I Wrote you the 4th inst per[1] one of your Returning Express's giving some account of my ill success in Procuring Vessels to Freight Rice from South Carolina.[2]

I must now Repeat the old story. I then wrote you I had sent Capt William Bull of this Town along the sea Shore in quest of Vessels. He return'd after a Cruise from New Haven to Stonington without Procuring a single Vessel, or even geting the least encouragement. Soon after the [Connecticut] River being in a fair way to break up, I took a trip from this to Saybrook in hopes of Procure[ing] some Vessels in this River. Indeed I had encouragement from several Persons who were owners of Vessels then froze in, that in case the River should break up in season, they Should be very fond of the Voyage, and would fit them out upon the terms Propos'd, that is one third Part of the Cargo. However when I come to talk with them in earnest they had to make calculations on the Profit of the Voyage, and consult the other owners, as every Vessel in this Part of the Country has from Eight to Thirty two Owners which are all to be consulted And Agreed with, and after making one two or three Journeys, they will find out that they cannot fit out their Vessels under one half of the Rice. They are determind not to Charter their Vessels for Money at any Rate, and after all my Trouble and fatigue I am not certain of but one Vessel of 60 tons which will be Ready to sail Next week, tho' I am in some hopes of Procuring a Schooner of 100 Tons, the owners will give me an Answer on Monday next. However I find every thing Uncertain till I get it into my own hands. I never undertook a Piece of Business in my life that cost me so much Trouble and fatigue to so little Purpose, but it's not in my Power to Alter either the minds or disposition of the People.

I forwarded my Accounts and Return of stores by Gurdon Wadsworth the 17th of Jany and here inclose a Return of all Persons employ'd in the QM Genl department in this State, Teams &c.

I am very much at a loss what good Assistants in the QM Genl Department may be had for. I however think they ought to be Paid in some Proportion to the Business they Transact. Eighty Dollars for the lowest and One Hundred and twenty Dollars per Month with subsistance for the highest Class, I believe will be as low as they can be had for.

They are however willing to serve on the same footing as at other Posts. I am sir with the greatest Esteem your Obedt sert

NEHEM HUBBARD

NB I had forgot to mention I have wrote Messrs Miller & Tracy and inform'd them of my ill success in Procuring Vessels, and in case they did not succeed Mr Benj'n Andrews, to Present it to the Proper Person.[3]

NH

ALS (PPAmP).
    1. Hubbard wrote on 6 February, not the fourth. See above. For Connecticut port cities, see Map 2.

2. On bringing rice from Charleston, see above, Wadsworth to NG, 2 January.
3. On Andrews's death see Otis to NG, 10 January, above. The firm of Otis & Andrews was succeeded by Otis alone and later Otis & Henley.

To Colonel Udny Hay

Sir   Middle Brook [N.J.] February 20th 1779
    Your favor of the 13th by Major Stewart was this moment deliverd me.
    It is impossible to fix the Wages of the Artificers by the day. The money is so fluctuateing and more especially while the merchants give wages according to the necessity of their concerns. We have no Artificers by the day here and very few if any at Philadelphia, except Shipwrights therefore it will not answer for you to govern your wages by their's. Major Stewart informs me the People are desirous of going to the Northerd in expectation of geting higher pay. You may assure them that they shall have no employ to the Northerd for I will write to Col Lewis not to hire a man of them upon any account whatever and you will please to transmit him a list of their Names and occupations in order that he may be properly informd.[1]
    I am determind that where ever any Artificers leaves one post to get higher wages at another that they shall have no employ. In future I will follow this principle as far as possible. There may be some cases which will require a variation.
    You will in the present instance indeavor to fix the Wages upon some reasonable footing; if after which they refuse to Labour I will promise them they shall have no employ in the quarter masters departm't. I am Sir Your humble Sert

N GREENE

ADfS (PCC, item 173, vol. 4: 143, DNA).
    1. On the artificers' grievances under Hay, see note at their petition of 6 January, above. "To the Northerd" from Fishkill the men could go up the Hudson to Albany, where Morgan Lewis was deputy. See NG's letter to Lewis this day, below.

To Colonel Robert L. Hooper, Jr.

[Middlebrook, N.J., 20 February 1779. Has Hooper's of the eighteenth. Sorry 1,500 packsaddles not possible, but he will expect 1,000. Desires them "branded with the makers name." ADfS (PCC, item 173, vol. 4: 151, DNA) 1p.]

To John Jay, President of the Continental Congress

Sir   Middle Brook [N.J.] February 20th 1779
This will be handed your Excellency by Mr Robert Temple. He made application to me for the balance of an account due him for things taken on his Farm near Charles Town for the use of our Army when the Enemy lay in Boston in the year 1776.[1] This account is founded upon an estimation made by himself and approv'd by three Gentlemen appointed by Colo Thos Chase D Q M General at Boston, for the purpose of surveying his Farm. I have examin'd its contents, and find there is a very small part of it comes under the head of damages.

I am perfectly well acquainted with the whole History of that affair. His Orchards were cut down for Abatis. His nursery was cut up for Fascines and Pickets. His fences were burnt for fuel for the Soldiers, and his walls were pull'd down to get Stones to underpin the Barracks. His Houses and out Houses were made use of for Barracks, and sav'd the Continent a larger sum in the expence of building than the value charg'd.[2]

The Resolution of Congress touching losses under such circumstances admits of this interpretation; that every kind of property taken for the use of the Army by which it is benefited shall be paid for at a reasonable rate. This distinction will draw a just line between that kind of injury which is incidental and unavoidable in all Wars, and which can never admit of any restitution and that kind of compensation which is due to a person for property taken not by contract, but from the necessity of the case.

This acco't is founded, not upon a principle of damage, but upon the value of property received for the use of the Public. What distinction there can be made in the state of the acco't between the benefit the Public received, and the injury the Party sustain'd in the state of the charges, I cannot pretend to say, but I believe nothing very considerable.

This transaction took place long before I had any connection with the Quarter Masters Department, and therefore I cannot take any measures necessary to bring it to a settlement; but as it is an object of great importance to Mr Temple and as he is desirous of bringing the acco't to a settlement upon the general principles which the Quarter Master General settles with others under similar circumstances, I thought it but just to him, and necessary for the information of Congress to give them the foregoing state of facts respecting Mr Temple's loss and also to explain my Ideas respecting the Resolution of Congress upon the subject of damages, that they may rectify me, if I mistake their intentions.[3]

One thing more I will just observe, that the difficulty of procuring wood and Stones near to the place where the Army lay renders those articles more valuable as it sav'd a great expence of hauling. I have the honor to be With due respect Your Excellencies Most obedient Humble Servant

NATHL GREENE

LS (PCC, item 155, vol. 1: 91, DNA).
1. According to Temple's memorial of 26 February 1779, written in Philadelphia, the losses occurred in 1775. (PCC, item 41, vol. 10: 71, DNA)
2. Although Washington had issued strict orders in 1775 against soldiers burning fence posts or cutting fruit trees, Congress had distinguished, as does NG here, between depredations by soldiers on the one hand, and the seizure of property for their survival or for the use of the army on the other. A thin line often separated the two. When Mrs. Harriet Temple reported the damage in August 1776, Congress ordered the quartermaster (then Mifflin) to "make her a just compensation." (JCC, 5: 699, 713, where her name was spelled "Harriot.") And yet in May 1777, while expressing sympathy for other citizens of Charlestown who had suffered from "the calamities of war," Congress regretted "the inability of the United States to afford the solicited relief." (JCC, 7: 365–66)
3. Congress made a final settlement with Temple on 6 March 1779. On the recommendation of the committee that considered his memorial and NG's letter, it ordered the "late quartermaster" to pay Temple "14,006 2/3 dollars" in addition to an earlier sum paid him. (Specific damages are spelled out in the resolution, JCC, 13: 288–89.)

To Colonel Morgan Lewis

Dear Sir   Middle Brook [N.J.] February 20, 1779
The Artificers at Fish Kill that are employd by the day are very clamorous about their wages.[1] They insist upon haveing them raisd. They urge in support of their claim the Wages given by you to the Northerd;[2] and threaten to leave that Post in order to engage with you. I have directed Col Hay to transmit you a list of their Names, with their different occupations annexed that you may know them; and should they leave that Post and come to Albany you will please to refuse them any employ. I have authorisd Col Hay to assure them that they shall have none if they go there; and you will govern yourself accordingly.

The different Agents in the quarter masters department must endeavor to support each other in keeping down the Wages of the Artificers for they are riseing to an intollerable heighth. I am with great esteem and regard your most obedient humble Sert

NATH GREENE

ADfS (PCC, item 173, vol. 4: 139, DNA).
1. See memorial of artificers under Hay, 6 January, above.
2. See note, NG to Hay, 20 February, above.

From Colonel James Abeel

[Morristown, N.J., 20 February 1779, Sunday morning. Tells NG how to get five barrels of cider. ALS (PPAmP) 1 p.]

From Colonel Clement Biddle

Dear General   Philadelphia 20 Feb: 1779

I wrote you a few Lines in haste the 17th inst: since which I have forwarded Two shallops to Trenton with about 1800 bushels of Grain and I have been calling on every person who can give us any Aid to hasten it forward that we may subsist our horses til the ensuing harvest.

I am sorry to learn from Colo Finnie of Virginia that their bay [i.e., Chesapeake] is full of the Enemy Cruisers which prevent him from sending any Forage to the head of Elk and as I had great Dependance on him and must fall far short if that Conveyance is stopd. I have represented the Case to Colo Pettit to lay before the Committee of Congress and desire them to take some measures to clear the bay, which I think may be done by sending the Gallies and a Brig'n [brigantine] from Baltimore to join those of the State of Virginia.[1]

I have wrote to every person to send what Forage they can to Camp and in Case Mrs Biddle's situation should Keep me a few Days longer in Town I hope your horses will not suffer and I shall leave nothing in my power undone to help you from the Southward.

We have for some time been told by Members of Congress that they have some foreign Intelligence of great importance in our favour which was not proper *yet* to be divulged and they keep it to themselves.

Foreign Alliance and a Loan are the general Surmises, but it had a strange effect on the speculators—hard money fell from 11 to 8 for one—Rum fell 30/ per Gallon, but both have again risen to their highest rates and unless the good News transpires the prices will continue to rise, but I have some hopes that the publication of the good news may add to the value of our money which is in a most melancholy situation at present.[2]

I shall be much Obliged to you for any Intelligence you may have at Camp. We have various reports from thence but nothing certain.

Nothing new from Carolina. A paragraph in the Virginia paper says there has been an Action and 83 killed on both sides, but Congress I beleive have no Intelligence.

The parties in Town run very high but I am not inclined to attend so much to them as to give you any Account of them at present.

Charles Pettit, 1736–1806, oil painting by Charles Willson Peale
(Courtesy of the Worcester Art Museum)

Mrs Biddle joins me in Compliments to Mrs Greene. With great respect I am Dr General yr mo: Obed servt

CLEMENT BIDDLE

ALS (PPAmP).
1. See Pettit's letter of 21 February, below.
2. On the rumors about a Spanish alliance, see above, Pettit to NG, 15 February.

From Colonel Archibald Steel

Sir   Pittsburgh [Pa.] Febry 20th 1779

I receivd your's of the 20th of January last and Observe the Contents. It is beyond a doubt I have fallen under General McIntosh's Displeasure, but I flatter myself have Maintain'd a Good Character with my Contrymen in General. I am sorry I differ in this point with the Gentleman whome I have the honour to represent here. I mean with respect to our Oppinions of the Genl. It is true I have for Some time past Suffer'd in Character and Person proceeding from premidated, Groundless, and Low Artifice to screen himself from the Censors of his Contry. I shall ever Dispise a Person of his turn.

The Charges ran high as you Justly remark, but the Court has Acquitted me of the whole. Had my resentment not run so high I should have perhaps been by this time on a Good footing with the Genl.[1] I am Conscious it is my duty to Cultivate harmony with my Commanding Officer, but this is impossible for any Generous soul to do with Genl McIntosh when Acting under him.[2] I cannot suffer any Ungenerous Insults from any man and Let them pass with Impunity. I have my failings, at the same time I have my resentments.

I am preparing my Accounts as fast as possible and promise myself the honour of presenting them to you and flatter my Self they will Meet with Your Approbation, considering the Many Difficultys I Labourd under. I gave Genl McIntosh a Return of stores on hand. Colo Brodhead made an additional List of what Stores he thought would be Necessary for the Insuing Campaign. I have made sundry Applications to the Genl of this Nature, but have Never receivd his Answer. As early as Last November I Applied to the Genl for his directions on this head, Informing him that this early Application was to prevent any Disappointment. I yet remain in the dark. Let me assure you it is with the Greatest Difficulty I retain a single Person in my imploy from a pack horse man upwards. As for my own Part, the Breach is so great Between the Genl and me that I think it never will be heal'd. I Have the Honour to be your Most Obed and Most Hble ser

ARCHIBALD STEEL

FEBRUARY 1779 [283]

ALS (PPAmP).
1. In mid-December, Gen. Lachlan McIntosh, commander of the army at Ft. Pitt, had charged Steel with a variety of infractions, including neglect of duty, incapacity for his office, delaying the transporting of provisions, spending his time upon private concerns, embezzling and suffering others to embezzle, repeated disobedience and contempt of orders, and finally insulting the commanding officers. A court-martial, presided over by Col. George Morgan, commissary of issues for the area, acquitted Steel of all charges. The court was satisfied that the "general distresses of our country, Colonel Steel's want of money and other causes mentioned by different evidences" had been the causes of his failure to transport Colonel Morgan's flour over the mountain. (The charges and the quotations of the court are in Washington's general orders for 21 April, Fitzpatrick, GW, 14: 423. A forty-six-page report giving McIntosh's version of events leading up to the court-martial is in the Washington Papers, 1–21 January 1779, DLC.)
2. Steel does not appear to exaggerate. McIntosh reported to Congress that he "found so much opposition and indeed insult" to himself both in court and throughout the camp that he dismissed any inquiry the court intended. Congress received his request for retirement from Ft. Pitt the same day it received his report on Steel. (February 20, JCC, 13: 213) When Congress requested Washington to name a successor, he appointed Col. Daniel Brodhead. (Fitzpatrick, GW, 14: 194–95)

To Colonel Daniel Brodhead

Dear Sir   Middle Brook [N.J.] February 21, 1779
Your favor of the 9th dated at Fort M Intosh I have receivd.[1]

General McIntosh can best judge how far it is practicable to make Soldiers labour from day to day that are engagd to fight only and do their other tour of duty. We have given to all the Privates £ 4.10 per Month that have been employed as Artificers; but as the plan he proposes will be a public saveing I wish it could be adopted so far as it respects my department as quarter master General, for the expenditure is much greater than I could wish and yet I know of no way of contracting it.

I am told Mr Steel is under Arrest. If he is guilty of the charges brought against him he deserves to be hangd; but human Nature is acted upon by so many different causes that I am in hopes the grounds of the complaint may partly originate from resentment and not altogether from misconduct; however that must appear from the tryal. I had conceivd a very good opinion of Mr Steel and it was confirmd by General Hands warm recommendation. I wish I may not be deceivd as it would hurt my feelings exceedingly.[2]

I am told General McIntosh has got into some disputes with almost all his officers, pray what is the matter with you? Are you grown more factious or is his dicipline more severe? I always thought him an exceeding attentive officer and highly worthy respect.[3] I am with the most perfect esteem Your Most obed and hum Ser

N GREENE

ALS (PCC, item 173, vol. 4: 153, DNA).
1. Letter not found. Ft. McIntosh, which had been erected in November 1778, was located thirty miles northwest of Pittsburgh, where the Ohio River turned abruptly toward the southwest.
2. On Steel's arrest, see his letter of 20 February, above.
3. McIntosh's difficulties with the officers under him and his replacement by Brodhead are also discussed in Steel's letter, above.

To Major Benjamin Eyre

Sir   Camp Middle Brook [N.J.] February 21. 1779.
Col Morgan Lewis D Q M G at Albany has enterd into some contra[c]t with his Shipwrights respecting their wages which he wishes to be determind upon as soon as possible. You will please therefore to fix the wages upon the principles he has contracted and enclose me a certificate thereof that I may transmit it to him. I have enclosd you an extract of his Letter to shew the agreement.

I wish you to reduce the wages as low as possible and not violate truth and candor. The best mode for affecting it I must leave to your judgment.

I wish your answer as soon as may be and am with the most perfect esteem your most obedt humble Sert[1]

N GREENE

ADfS (PCC, item 173, vol. 4: 157, DNA).
1. Lewis had asked for an answer in his letter of 12 February, above. Neither Eyre's answer to NG nor NG's answer to Lewis has been found.

Memorandum from Colonel James Abeel[1]

[Morristown, N.J. 21 Feb. 1779]
Genl Green will please to write to Genl Knox about letting three Sail Makers he has in his Brigade come up to Morris Town to help repair the Old Tents. They will not be wanted more than a Month.[2]

He will also please to give Orders to Capt Bruen to send me the Six Carpenters that are at N[ew] Brunswick to help repair Twelve Waggons I have at Morris Town and prepare a Number of Tent Poles as we have by no means a Sufficiency for the Tents on hand.

If some of the Gent'n in Pensilvania were stopt from making Axes untill they paid more Attention to their Smiths it wou'd be of service to the department as many have no Steel at All and are entirely unfit for Service.[3]

The Genl will be kind enough to order me what Cash can be spared soon as possible as the Quantity of Iron ordered to be purchased and the Horse Shoes engag'd will require a Considerable Sum besides the Call of about 25 Artificers I have dayly employ'd. As the

Genl will be more at leasure in a few days I will do myself the Pleasure of either calling on him or writing very particular to him about
the department.

JAS ABEEL

ADS (PPAmP).
1. Since Abeel normally communicated with NG by personal letter, it is likely that
this third-person memorandum was directed to an aide.
2. Neither NG's request to Knox nor Knox's response has been found.
3. He had first complained of inferior axes in a letter of 11 February, above.

From Colonel Charles Pettit

Dear Sir   Philadelphia 21st February 1779
   I have at length got a little Money, and tho' I am surrounded with
Demands for it, and I know the publick Interest is suffering for want
of it, more particularly in the forage Department, in divers Places, I
have according to your Desire appropriated the first Fruits for Camp
and Boston, and shall send herewith to Mr Otis 200,000, to Mr [Jacob]
Greene 55,000 and to you for Camp 77,000 Dollars, out of which you
will be able to supply any small neighbouring Demands; particularly
Col. Abeel will want some, and I know not how otherwise to get it to
him, for believe me it requires no small Degree of Fortitude to resist
the pressing Demands this Way so far as to save this Sum for the
Eastward [i.e., New England]. By the Time I had got the Warrant
lodged with the Treasurer I found the immediate Demands upon me
exceeded in Amount the Sum it would produce, vizt 1 1/2 Millions. I
therefore wrote, rather in the pathetic Strain, to the Treasury Board,
stating the Wants of the Department and the Injury to the Publick
Interest occasioned by the Delays of Money, intreating they would
grant a farther War[ran]t and take Effectual Measures to enable the
Treasurer to supply the Money. I expect it will take him the Course of
this Week to furnish what is now due, in the mean Time I am promised another Warrant.
   Count Pulaskie is got in Town, waiting to settle his Accounts as
he alledges he is considerably in Advance for Congress. I have however sent off Mr. Faucet with Money and Instructions to provide for
the Legion. I was at much Pains in settling the Route and Plan, and at
length concluded on what I thought clear Conviction to send them by
way of Winchester and between the Mountains. A Copy of the Route
shall be inclosed.[1]
   I applied to the marine Committee sometime ago for an Answer
to your Letter of Application for Sail Duck. After sometime they sent
me a Copy of their Chairman's Letter to the Commissioners of the
Navy, which Copy I shall inclose herewith, and if I understand it right

it will be a sufficient Ground for you to draw an Order on them for the Duck in favr of whom you please.[2] I should suppose the order ought to be general as to the Quantity, leaving the Receipt of the Party to ascertain it, and you can limit him by Instructions.

I shall shortly take Occasion to write to Mr [Abraham] Livingston of Carolina on the Subjects you mention.

Respecting Pack saddles I find Opinions divided, but as I am not a proper Judge I have referred those I have conversed with on the Subject, to Col. Cox especially as it is in his Line. He has written to Col Mitchell about it, who asked my Advice whether he ought to countermand any of his Orders for them. I advised him not to do it unless he should receive Instructions so to do from you or Col. Cox.[3] Col. Cook of Northumberland tells me he can get such as are fit for carrying Bags completed for about £ 3. He says they need not Breechings nor Breast Plates for this Purpose, but that for Casks they do. He tells me those he proposes were used with Success the last War. I promised him to write to you or Col. Cox about it and to give him farther Instructions; in the mean Time, as we shall want a good many and in that Part of the Country, I desired him to set the Business on foot as far as 100 or 200.

I shall barely [i.e., merely] send Letters of Advice to Messrs Otis and [Jacob] Greene with the Money, and refer them to you for Instructions.

It occurred to me that the Manouvres of the Enemy to the southward might render it prudent to make some Alterations in our Plan of sending Vessels to Carolina. I therefore wrote to the Committee with whom the Plan was concerted, but have not yet recd an Answer. The rough Draught of my Letter is inclosed for your Information &c.[4] Having done this it will lie with them to countermand the Orders if necessary. I also inclose to you a rought Draught of a Letter to Congress respecting the Navigation of Chesapeak and Delaware [Bays].[5] I did not think it proper to mention the Affair of the Vessels to Congress; as the Plan was a kind of Secret not known to all the Members. Col. Finnie had written from Virginia to Col. Biddle that the Enemy's Cruizers had rendered the Navigation of the Bay unsafe, on which [he?] desired Col. Biddle to state the Matter in a Letter to me which I sent to Congress.

Mr President Reed [of Pennsylvania] informed me a Day or two ago that the Matter respecting the Bridges remained unsettled, that the Assembly were about to pass a Law on the Subject, and that the Council wished to know what footing to put it upon so far as respected the Quarter Master's Department.[6] After some Conversation on the several Points started, it was agreed that I should state Proposals in writing, which I did yesterday afternoon the Draught of which I send you herewith. (You will have rough Draughts enough, and Draughts rough enough.)

While these Proposals were copying I received a Letter from Mr Secretary Matlack, which discomposed that Calmness of Temper which my Friends sometimes flatter me that I possess. But before I introduce this Letter I must give you a short historical Preface. You know the Situation of Affairs respecting the Eggharbour Waggons when you left Town.[7] About a Week since I recd a Letter from Mr Secretary stating that Council had applied to you for an Attested Copy of the Entry of Jesse Jordan's Brigade of Waggons in the Quarter Master's Books and of the Certificates given at the Ferries he had crossed,[8] but had not recd an Answer or a satisfactory Answer or something of this kind. I have not the Letter now by me, but I think this is the Substance of it; however, it concluded with desiring I would furnish them with these Papers. I shewed this Letter to Col. Mitchell and desired him to enable me to give the proper Answer. He told me you had already given the President or the Council all the Answer that was necessary, that is, that he had no Entry of the Waggons save a Note in a Memorandum Book of the Day they arrived which was the 22d of October and that as to any Certificates at the Ferries he knew nothing about them. I thought the Affair of too small Consequence to interfere with much other Business which claimed my Attention and let it pass for two or three Days; but the first Opportunity I had with the President, I mentioned it to him as it is above stated. He said the Council were informed there was an Entry in a Book, which they wanted a Copy of. I told him that to shew my readiness to comply with the Desire of Council I would enquire more particularly into it and send them the best information I could get. I intended to look at the Book myself, but finding it inconvenient to go out, I sent the Letter to Col. Mitchell and begged him to furnish me with a minute answer to it and to send a Copy of such Entry as he had. He sent me a written Answer that he had no other Entry than as above ment'd that as he had given the W[agon] Mastr no Orders but to go to Genl Arnold, he knew not at what Ferry he had crossed nor whether he had given any Certificates or not; and that he should on all Occasions be ready to gratify the Council and hoped this would be satisfactory. This I inclosed to Mr Secretary [Matlack] in a short Letter of which I kept no Copy but it was of the Complaisant kind and free from Acid. But in Reply I received the obnoxious Letter I have mentioned of which I shall send you a Copy.[9]

I thought by taking the Air and going to Col. Mitchell's Office myself for the Paper required I might settle my Mind on the Subject. I therefore went and got the Entry extracted from the Book; but when I sat down to answer the Letter I found my Choler rather incresing than abating by Time. I believe it is a just Remark that a Temper slow to Anger requires proportionately longer Time to subside. I found myself full of Ire and knew not what Course to give my Pen. I wished to say something smooth as well as cutting but no Expressions would occur that hit my Fancy; however as an immediate Answer of some sort seemed necessary I mounted Pegasus with as taught a Rein as I could keep, and after the first Flounce he took off in the Course you will see. Finding him still ungovernable and apprehending he might run me among the Briars in the Way he was going, I wheeled him round into a Narrow Enclosure and dismounted. The inclosed first Draught will best explain to you the Expedients I have described. This Letter I sent last Evening. What it may lead to I do not know, but I am not yet cool enough to condemn it, tho' I can begin to laugh at the Figure it presents of my Mind at the Time.[10] As far as I am yet able to consider it, the Demand of the Council was rather of Favour than of Right, at least so far as not to admit of an authoritative Command; and I should have given at least plausible Ground of Suspicion had I acquiesced tamely in the Imputation of throwing "Delays and Difficulties in the Way of Enquiries into the Conduct of Publick Officers." But the repetition of these Words I found produced Ideas that would run me into greater Length than I intended, and that I might perhaps say something that I should on reflection wish I had not said, and therefore in that Stage I concluded to take a new Course and cut the Matter shorter. As this Matter is at present known only to the Parties, I would wish it to go no farther than to you and Col. Cox, and I have related it thus fully to you as Friends and Coadjutors as well because you are interested in my Official Conduct as to receive any Hints that may occur to either of you by which I may correct what is amiss. My Resolution to avoid intermedling in the political Disputes of this place, is unshaken, but they run so high that the most indifferent Actions can scarcely escape the Imputation of having such Views with one Party or the other.[11]

Within a few Minutes I have rec'd a Letter from Mr Calhoun informing me he has expended all the Money he has except about 15,000 Dollars of the condemned Emissions and asking a Supply of 150 or 200,000. I cannot send him any till the produce of the next Warr[an]t comes forth; Hooper, Davis, Morgan, Ross, Wade, Hollingsworth &c have all lived upon Expectation for some Time and the Forage Departmt here and in Virginia as hungry as a dry Cartwheel. Speaking of Virginia puts me in Mind of the Prisoners at Charlotteville. I am told they are wretchedly provided and so illy situated that they cannot be well supplied where they are. Col. Finnie has sent a Remonstrance to Congress on the Subject a Copy of which he inclosed to Col Mitchell which I have seen.

I shall, the first Time I can spare for it, frame a Model for the Accounts of the Deputies as I find little Room to hope for Assistance from the Board of Treasury or their Officers. I propose to send a Copy to each with directions for arranging and sending in their Vouchers up to the 28[?] of March; it will not be proper to call away their Vouchers till their accounts are framed and squared by them, and they arranged according to the Accounts.

You will think from the length of my Letter that I have no want of Leisure. Remember it is Sunday in which I have not so many Calls as on other Days, and having determined not to dine out I have the more Time for a Tete a Tete with you. But having a good deal to do before the Departure of this Express, I must leave you to amuse yourself with this Sheet till another Oppor[tunit]y. You see I have no Room left for compliments. The Ladies will excuse me.

CHAS PETTIT

ALS (PPAmP).
1. The Legion's transfer to Georgia is discussed in note at Pettit to NG, 10 February, above.
2. For the Marine committee's response, see Chase to NG, 9 February, above.
3. The decision on packsaddles is noted above, Cox to NG, 16 February, #2.
4. There is no evidence that the Supply Departments Committee countermanded its earlier decision (cited in Wadsworth's letter of 2 January, above). Pettit's copy of his letter of 19 February to Whipple is in the Greene Papers, PPAmP.
5. His letter of the nineteenth to Congress (ibid.) urged that "Measures may be taken to protect a Navigation so essential to the Welfare of the Army." Congress referred it to the Marine Committee, where it seems to have died. (*JCC*, 13: 213)
6. On the negotiations about the bridge in question and the eventual settlement, see above, Reed to NG and NG to Reed, 4 February. A copy of Pettit's letter of 19 February to Reed is in the Greene Papers, PPAmP.
7. See above, NG to Reed, 31 January, #1.
8. See above, Reed to NG, 1 February.
9. Matlack's imperious letter accused Pettit of obstructing the council's investigation into the Mitchell-Arnold affair. He wrote that "His Excellency the President [Joseph Reed] expected, from the Conversation which he had with you on this Subject, that you would have examined fully into this matter, and he now requests that you will do it and furnish the Copies demanded without delay." (Matlack to Pettit, 20 February 1779, Greene Papers, PPAmP)
10. Pettit angrily replied to Matlack that, had he not been acquainted with Matlack's signature, he would suppose the letter he received "not to be genuine." Pettit added that he could not "conceive that any Part of my Conduct has merited the Language it contains either from the Council or their Secretary." Further, he questioned the right of the Pennsylvania Council to summarily demand records at whim from the quartermaster's office. (Pettit to Matlack, 20 February 1779, Greene Papers, PPAmP)
11. For a discussion of political factions in Pennsylvania, see above, note at Reed to NG, 5 November 1778.

A Petition of Express Riders

[   ] Febr 22nd A.D: 1779

To the Honourable Major General Green;
We Your Humble Petitioners Sheweth; Whereas, we the Under Named Express Riders, Being Much Agrieved by the Extortion of the Publick at this Time, Do Humbly Desier of the Honbl Major General Green; to take this to Consideration to Raise Our Wages to Eight Dollars pr. Day. Otherwise, we Cannot perform the Several Duties Enjoined Upon Us, &c:

Subscribers E[xpress] R[ider]   *Subscribers*

ALEXR MC COLLISTER	JOHN LONG
JAMES DAVIS	ISAAC HUMPHREY
NICHLS CHRISTOPHER	METHUSELAH DAVIS
JOSEPH MARSH	MOSES AUSTEN
JOHN TUMERL	JOSEPH BURWELL
ISAAC LYON	NOAH FRENCH
WM DAY	ROBERT DUNN
MOSES LYON	ISAAC TITSWORTH

DS (PPAmP).

From Colonel Charles Pettit

[Philadelphia, 22 February 1779. Encloses powdering knife for NG. Asks NG to forward a letter to Jacob Greene. Arrival of Captain Cunningham from Martinique;[1] D'Estaing at Port Royal expects reinforcements. Cash sent to Samuel Otis, Jacob Greene, and NG. ALS (PPAmP) 1 p.]

1. The celebrated American, Capt. Gustavus Conyngham (or Cunningham, 1747–1819), had arrived in Philadelphia after a three-year absence during which he had successfully commanded several privateers off the coast of England. Conyngham's exploits were so daring that he became a legendary figure. A French print, published in 1779, depicted him "on the deck of his ship, standing in clouds of smoke, five pistols under his belt and a drawn sword in his right hand." The legend underneath the picture referred to Conyngham as the "terror of the English." (*PMHB*, 48: 358; *Pa. Packet*, 23 February 1779. A collection of documents relating to Conyngham's naval career has been published under the title *Letters and Papers Relating to the Cruises of Gustavus Conyngham: A Captain of the Continental Navy, 1777–79*, Robert Wilden Neeser, ed., New York, 1915.)

From Major Samuel Shaw

[Quarters of the Artillery, Pluckemin, N.J., 22 February 1779. Asks NG to decide about forage rations for a horse left by Colonel Harrison.[1] LS (PPAmP) 1 p.]

1. Col. Robert Hanson Harrison, one of Washington's aides, was in Virginia.

To Colonel Ephraim Bowen

[Middlebrook, N.J., 23 February 1779. Answers Bowen's letter of 8 February. NG is persuaded Bowen has done everything possible to charter vessels for transporting rice from Charleston, so the department cannot "be subject to censure for negligence." In taking horses from Prudence Island, Tories "have play'd you a fine trick,"[1] but wintering may have cost more than their value. Wages for Bowen's assistant are high, but "you had better give a high price for a good man than employ a bad one for nothing at all."[2] Must have monthly returns. Suggests taking General Sullivan's advice on new tents needed. LS (RHi) 2 pp.]

1. See above, Bowen to NG, 8 February.
2. George Benson was assistant deputy quartermaster stationed at Providence. See Bowen's "Return of Men Employ'd in the Quart'r Mast'r Gen's Department . . ." 15 February 1779 (PPAmP).

To Colonel Ephraim Bowen

[Middlebrook, N.J., 23 February 1779. Has Bowen's letter of 9 February. Thanks him for "attention to my private affairs." Expects George Olney "will give me great ease and assistance in my business." Is in "daily expectation" of news from Congress respecting the Spanish ship "lately arrived, which has fallen the Stocks so prodigously in Philadelphia."[1] Tr (GWG Transcript: CSmH) 1 p.]

1. On Spain's involvement in the war, see above, Pettit to NG, 15 February.

To Colonel Thomas Chase

Dear Sir   Middle Brook [N.J.] February 23, 1779
Your favor of the 5th and 9th I have receivd.
In your Letter of the 9th you acknowledge the receipt of one of mine of the 29th of Januy and say the Navy board has got Duck and that you will apply and get a sufficient quantity to make a thousand Tents. I have no copy of that Letter, but to the best of my recollection I requested you to enquire of the Navy Board whether Duck might be had and not positively directing it to be made into Tents.[1]
The Express was just seting out as I wrote which prevent my takeing a Copy.
In the fore part of the Winter I wrote to Mr Benjamin Andrews one of our contractors to get a 1000 Tents made;[2] and to get the Duck if

he could of the Navy Board to save laying out more Money than was necessary. His untimely death left the business all at an uncertainty[3] and I was by no means certain whether Mr Otis would pursue the affair and complete the orders, therefore I addressed myself to you that if the first order faild you might engage in it and execute it agreeable to the instructions before given Mr Andrews. Since I wrote you Mr Otis writes me he has undertaken to finish the business. I wish you to consult with him and get about a thousand or twelve hundred Tents made between you. I beleive a greater number will not be absolutely wanted and I don't wish to lay out a farthing more money than cannot be avoided; but if 2000 should be made they wont come amiss as it is but prudent to have some in reserve which we shall not upon the first calculation.

The providing of Tents comes under the head of Camp equipage and therefore is not properly in the line of the quarter masters duty appointed for a Post which has been the cause why the business was not addressed to you in the first place. There are few if any of our deputies that provides Tents. Col Abale [Abeel] is a Agent for Camp Equipage under the direction of Col Cox who is contractor for the whole department.

Let me hear from you by the first convenient opportunity. My best respects to Mrs Chace. I am Sir with respect your most obedient humble Servt

N GREENE

ADfS (PCC, item 173, vol. 4: 173, DNA).
    1. Letter of 29 January not found.
    2. Letter not found.
    3. On the accidental death of Andrews, see above, Samuel A. Otis to NG, 10 January.

From Colonel Alexander Hamilton

Dr Sir   Head Qrs. [Middlebrook, N.J.] Feby 23d [1779]
The General has given me some memorandums for instructions to you on the subject of the Northern preparations.[1] He is however undecided on one point. How far the preparation for vessels ought to be pushed. It was his wish when the resolution to discontinue the former plan was taken to stop the provision for the vessels as well as other matters; and he is only induced to depart from this idea in consideration that a part of the materials have been already provided. It seems necessary to understand more clearly from you how far this business has gone; what quantity of materials are provided and actually providing; for how many vessels and of what kind. You can't I

know determine this matter precisely; but from the orders you have given and the reports you have received you may do it so far as may be sufficient to answer the purpose.[2] The General's idea is to stop as short as possible without leaving what is in hand incomplete. Be pleased to favour me with an answer by the bearer;[3] and to make it as particular as you can. I am D Sir Yr Most Obed hum servant

ALEX HAMILTON

ALS (PPAmP).

1. On the shift in plans from a Canadian expedition to one against the New York Indians, see above, NG to Washington, 5 January. In his letter of 24 February, below, Washington was more deeply involved.

2. On the bateaus being constructed in Albany, see above, Lewis to NG, 12 February, and NG to Lewis, 17 February.

3. NG replied to Hamilton later in the day. (See below.)

To Colonel Alexander Hamilton

Dear Sir   At my quarters [Middlebrook, N.J.] February 23 1779

Your favor of this morning I have receivd.

Inclosd is an extract from Col Morgan Lewis Letters respecting the state of the preparations to the Northerd.[1] From what His Excellency said to me in Philadelphia respecting the Battauex, of the probabillity of their being wanted for another purpose; and the desire he had to take advantage of the Enemy to the Northerd if a change of circumstances should put it in his power; and from the little additional expence that will be incurd in completeing the Batteaux seeing the preparations have gone so far I have been inducd to suffer Mr Lewis to go on with the finishing the Boats without taking any steps which will increase the expenes [expenses].

There is bought for the Gallies part of the Riging and Sails. Some part of the Iron work is made and now makeing. There is some of the Articles bought under the head of Gunnery but what I am not well informd. However I beleive there is no provision made for the Gallies but that can be sold without much if any loss should the General think it advisable.

I will wait upon the General either this Evening or tomorrow morning and will satisfy him in any other points of which he may wish to be informd. I am Sir Your humble ser

N GREENE

ADfS (PCC, item 173, vol. 4: 161, DNA).

1. See above, Lewis to NG, 12 February 1779.

To Samuel A. Otis

[Middlebrook, N.J., 23 February 1779. NG acknowledges Otis's letter of 3 February and refers Otis to his letter of 11 February "upon the subject of the Vessels and the prospect of the Money." ADfS (PCC, item 173, vol. 4: 171, DNA) 1 p.]

To Colonel Jeremiah Wadsworth

[Middlebrook, N.J., 23 February 1779. NG encloses a copy of [Nehemiah] Hubbard's letter of 6 February concerning chartering vessels for rice. Has written Mr. [Samuel] Otis to "Charter at any rates, as the Rice must be had."[1] Asks Wadsworth to give further directions on the matter to Hubbard, Otis, and Bowen. LS (CtY) 1 p.]

1. Although NG says he wrote Otis on the "13th," he is referring to his letter to Otis of 11 February 1779, above.

From Colonel Udny Hay

Sir   Fish Kill [N.Y.] 23d Feb 1779
    I am favoured with yours of 17th inst.[1] The charges against the French fleet will I am affraid be very difficult to be made out, as we cannot ascertain the Provisions sent to them by Carriages we paid for, from the Provisions sent to our Army at the eastward, never having recd any regular information thereabouts. Shall write you more fully on that subject in a few days.
    I recd the thirty thousand Dollars which will help me in jogging on some time, but could wish the other seventy thousand may be forwarded as soon as possible that I may be enabled fully to settle my accompts.
    Your advice respecting the Artificers and fatigue men shall be punctually obeyd as far as circumstances will admitt.[2]
    The little dispute with some of the justices is tolerably well settled.[3] I stand so well with the Country in general, notwithstanding some of these Gentlemens insinuations that I was extremely arbitrary and made use of military force when altogether unnecessary, that I have had influence enough to gett many of them to subscribe a [i.e., in] writing begging that Military force may be made use of where people refuse or neglect turning out when the justices order. This I have shown to some of the justices, who I believe are now fully ashamd of their Conduct, and I have only one little affair against me on account of unwarrantable impresses at present and that I believe will be withdrawn as I have threatned to publish the whole to the world and hold him up to the Army as a disaffected Person, of which

he seems much affraid. I have as you advised buryed the Hatchett very deep, nor shall it be raisd again till the public service absolutely requires it. These are not the people I would wish to contend with, as victory would give no honour to the Conqueror.

Enclosed I send you my first letter to the Governour proposing a new mode of raising teams, a rough Sketch of the bill as it now lyes before the Senate, and the observations, in consequence of their desire I have made thereon.[4] I shall be extremely glad to hear your opinion on the whole, with such amendments as you may think necessary. You shall have an exact and particular account of my prospect of Tents in a few days.

Having an opportunity to send this as far as Haverstraw at present [Map 1], I have only to add that I am with Gratitude and respect, Sir, Your most obedt and very humble Ser

UDNY HAY

ALS (PPAmP).
    1. See NG to the Deputy Quartermasters, 17 February, above.
    2. On NG's advice to Hay, see letters of 10 and 16 February, above.
    3. For a discussion of Hay's dispute with the New York justices, see note at Hay to NG, 10 February, above.
    4. See note at Hay to NG, 21 January, above.

From James Thompson

Sir   Camp [Middlebrook, N.J.] Feby 24. 1779
    The season fast advancing and the Prospect of another Campaign makes it necessary for me to point out some difficulties that may arise in that part of your department under my care, both for the Public Interest and the better to enable you in your industurous efforts for the good supplying the Army &c with that so highly necessary (for the moving so large an Army and so valuable a Quantity of Stores) as Waggons, Teams and Waggoners; the two former there is little danger from, but the latter many difficulties and much danger, as have been fully experienced in the former Q M Gen's [Mifflin's] time, and are not altogether free of it at present. The greatest part of our Cont[inenta]l Teams with the line of the Army have been obliged to be supplied with Waggoners from the Line. The consequence was fatal to many good Teams. There was no way of obliging them to take care, or any mode of punishment for neglect. The only resource was to turn them off and get another Soldier, which was only adding to the distress. We have been Labouring to procure Waggoners from the different parts of the Country, many have been procured, but the time so soon expires, that there is very little service from them being engaged for one year only, and many of them totally ignorant when enlisted, and

when they just come to a knowledge of their duty the year is expired, and even were there any advantage to the public in engaging them for that time we are deprived of it. We have the trouble of Enlisting them and Cloathing them and the Line through a large Bounty added to the many reflections [i.e., criticisms] against a mans continuing in the Waggon Service, reinlist them for the war though they are but just Enlisted and have Nine or ten Months to serve.

I have here pointed out the inconveniencies attending the Waggon Department for want of Waggoners, and would beg leave to recommend that some steps may be fallen on to enable us to procure Waggoners, which I think can only be done by giving the same Bounty and engaging them for that particular Service for the war, whereby we may reap the benefit of learning them their duty and making them accountable for the Teams. Much may be said on account of the Bounty and Wages. As to the Bounty at this time it does not exceed the Expence attending the sending W Condrs [Wagon Conductors] to recruit them, wheras by the Advertising I flatter myself they would engage with the DQM Gen's at the different posts. The Wages appear high when compared with the Soldier's, but remember his duty comes by turns, and not laborious but the Waggoners duty has no end Day or Night.

I therefore submit the whole to your superior Judgment and doubt not but you'l take such steps as may be conducive to the public good and enable us to procure Waggoners.[1] From Your most Obedt servant

JAMES THOMPSON

LS (PPAmP).
1. After receiving this letter, NG immediately wrote to Washington about the urgent need to recruit competent wagoners. See below, same date.

To George Washington

Sir   Middlebrook [N.J.] Feby 24th 1779
I find from experience in the Quarter Master's Department the greatest difficulty in procureing Waggoners. These are a class of men that are difficult to be found, and are so essential to the movements of the Army that there is nothing to be done without them.

The encouragement that was given last Campaign appear'd to be very high, and the pains that was taken to enlist men for the Waggon service was very great, and yet a very small part of the necessary number could be found.

The discontent given to the Officers from employing Soldiers for Waggoners, and the inconveniences that Your Excellency has found from this practice in the loss of Discipline, together with the diminution of the strength of the Line in detaching for this service, renders it necessary that some other measures be fallen upon to provide Waggoners for the Army.

Were these the only evils, the injury would not be so great, but there is a much greater waste of Horseflesh from improper Persons being employed in this service, than there would be if proper Waggoners were provided, and those kept constantly to that business.

The duty is disagreable in itself. The Waggoners are greatly expos'd being Night and day without the common comforts and conveniences that Soldiers enjoy in a well regulated Camp. These hardships are multiplied by the abuse they are often subject to from the Officers of the Line, who from a mistaken opinion, think every body has a right to correct a Waggoner. From the nature of the service, the hardships they endure, and the abuse they are subject to, I find it very difficult to get any to engage.

The bounty that is now given—which is a Suit of Clothes—and the Wages, which is Ten pounds a Month, has but a feeble influence, when People are giving from twenty to Thirty Pounds per Month for service much easier and more agreable. I think therefore, there is not the least prospect of obtaining a sufficient number, upon the present conditions.

Upon the whole it appears to me that the duty is disagreable and the expence of procureing Waggoners for a short time so enormous, and the shifting Waggoners so destructive to Horseflesh as well as perplexing to the operations of a Campaign, that the public had much better submit to the expence of enlisting Waggoners for the War, and give them the same bounty which is now given to Soldiers, and allow them such Wages and Cloathing as others can be procurd for upon Annual Service, than persue the present mode. The bounty is considerable, but the expence of Annual Enlistments and supporting Waggon Conductors while out upon this service is equally so; besides which the Department is always in distress, and the business in a state of uncertainty.

The Season is fast approaching when Waggoners will be wanted and I have received the fullest testimonies from our Agents that not a Man can be engag'd upon the former encouragement, nor none of those detain'd who have been in service before. Therefore I must beg Your Excellency's advice on this matter as soon as possible as a delay may be destructive to the operations of the Campaign.

The only effectual remedy will be to endeavour to engage Waggoners for the War, and in the end I am perswaided it will be by far the less expensive, altho it may appear otherwise in the first instance. I am With the most perfect esteem Your Excellency's Most Obedient Humble Servant[1]

NATH'EL GREENE

Cy (PCC, item 173, vol. 4: 177, DNA).

1. During the winter of 1778–79, NG's deputies reported continual difficulties in hiring and keeping competent wagoners, especially because the duties were difficult and the wages insufficient. Sidney Berry, deputy quartermaster in Somerset, N.J., complained that "the Waggon Conductors and Waggon Drivers Belonging to the army is the worst men I ever saw." (Berry to Moore Furman, 7 December 1778, Nj). James Abeel, one of NG's deputies, had also complained about the "great abuse in the Waggon Mast'r Gen'ls Dept." (See vol. 2: 427–28.) In his letter of 22 October 1778, above, Abeel wrote that "the waggoners plunder whenever they have an opportunity." See also, Charles Scott to NG, 8 December 1778, above.

As early as March 1778, shortly after assuming his duties as quartermaster general, NG informed Henry Laurens, president of Congress, of the difficulty in obtaining conscientious wagoners. "Hundreds [of horses] are lost for Want of good Conduct in the Drivers. The Loss of one Horse amounts to almost a Drivers Wages for a whole year." (See above, vol. 2: 322.) In order to attract and keep good, reliable men, NG recommended an increase in the "encouragements" offered to wagoners—better salaries, additional bounties, and enlistments for at least a year, and possibly for the duration of the war. Greene's suggestions to Laurens apparently went unheeded, and officers were often forced to assign soldiers from the Continental line to wagon duty because of the dearth of regular wagoners. As seen in Pickering's letter of 26 February, below, this caused administrative problems, and the men chosen from the line for wagon service were often undesirables whom officers wished to remove from the ranks. Speaking of artillery men and wagoners recruited in this manner, Washington wrote that the officers "contrive, as is very natural, to divest themselves of the very worst Men under their command." (Fitzpatrick, GW, 14: 344)

When he received Wagonmaster Thompson's urgent letter of this date (above), NG renewed his efforts to establish the wagon corps on a uniform basis by writing to Washington, who forwarded NG's recommendations to a committee of congress (Fitzpatrick, GW, 14: 158). NG then sent Thompson to Philadelphia to intercede with the committee. (See below, NG to Duane, 9 March.) On 16 March, Congress passed a resolution authorizing the commander in chief to "take proper measures for causing to be enlisted such a number of waggoners as he shall judge necessary for the service, to continue therein to the end of the war." In addition, each wagoner would be granted, besides "pay, clothing, and subsistence," the same bounties granted to volunteers who enlisted in the Continental battalions for the duration of the war. (JCC, 13: 320–21) This resolution added to the "encouragements" that NG had been seeking for the wagoners, but it did not increase their £ 10 monthly wage. He felt that Congress should have left wagoners' salaries to the discretion of the quartermaster general, who could regulate them according to the fluctuation of the currency. (See below, NG to Washington, 24 March, and NG to Jay, 25 March.)

Washington sent NG's additional recommendation to Congress (Fitzpatrick, GW, 14: 289). President Jay referred the matter to the Board of War. (See below, Jay to NG, 4 April, and NG to Board of War, 7 April.) In a letter to Jay of 15 April (below), NG again stressed the need to attract honest and reliable men to the wagon corps by offering competitive wages. "For want of such men," he wrote, "I will venture to say the publick suffers, and will suffer five times as much as the difference in pay between what good and indifferent men may be employed at." Greene's letter must have had an effect: on 17 April, Congress passed a resolution that gave the quartermaster general a free hand, with the "concurrance of the Commander in Chief," to "regulate the pay, clothing and subsistence of the waggoners so enlisted, in such manner as shall be best adapted to circumstances, and most conducive to the good of the service." (JCC, 13: 467) NG had not received word of this resolution when he wrote GW from Middlebrook on 19 April 1779 (below), almost in desperation, about the urgent need for wagoners. Washington replied on the same day that Greene should make a representation to Congress on the matter in his forthcoming trip to Philadelphia (Washington to NG, 19 April, below). Greene then laid before the committee a request to enlist as many wagoners as possible for the ensuing campaign, and Congress complied in a resolution passed on 23 April 1779 empowering the quartermaster general "to employ so many waggoners as shall be necessary for the use of the army, upon the best terms on which they can be obtained, provided such terms are approved by the Commander in Chief." (*JCC*, 14: 503)

From Colonel John Beatty[1]

[Middlebrook, N.J., 24 February 1779. Requests a horse for the bearer, Lt. Col. William Dark of Virginia, a prisoner on parole who was returning to his captivity in New York. ALS (PPAmP) 1p.]

1. Beatty was the commissary general of prisoners. Sir Henry Clinton had ordered all American officers on parole to return to New York. (See Joshua Loring to Beatty, 20 October 1778, PCC, item 78, vol. 14: 247, DNA, and 31 October 1778, PCC, item 147, vol 2: 377, DNA.)

From Colonel Clement Biddle

[Philadelphia, 24 February 1779. "Mrs Biddle safely in bed with a Son"; Biddle will leave for camp soon. Will "set everything I can in Motion to feed our horses at Camp." Quantity of forage consumed here is "amazing." ALS (PPAmP) 1 p.]

From Colonel Udny Hay

[Fishkill, N.Y., 24 February 1779. Lt. [Eliphaz] Kingsley comes to camp to settle wheelwrights' accounts. Hay proposes a new system for paying wheelwrights "without putting any person to the trouble and expence of going to head Quarters for that purpose." Asks NG's opinion. ALS (PPAmP) 2 pp.]

From Colonel Nehemiah Hubbard

[Hartford, Conn., 24 February 1779. Jeremiah Wadsworth has issued orders to give the merchants one-half of the cargo, "the owners to Victual, Man, and Run all Risks, which will Undoubtedly induce the Merchants to fit out their Vessels." Two schooners and a sloop will be sailing shortly from Connecticut.[1] Will set out in quest of more vessels. Transportation of provisions is expensive because of the great distance involved—"from the North River quite to Providence." Needs $150,000 for quartermaster supplies; $100,000 for forage. Brushes, curry combs, and main combs are needed for Colonel Sheldon's dragoons, but "the Artificers Refuse to make them till they can be Assured of their Pay and Price." ALS (PPAmP) 2 pp.]

1. For procuring rice from South Carolina. See above, Wadsworth to NG, 2 January, NG to Hubbard, 9 February, and Hubbard to NG, 19 February. One of Hubbard's contracts for transporting rice from Charleston is printed below, 8 April.

From Colonel Jeremiah Wadsworth

Dear Sir   Hartford [Conn.] Feby 24th 1779
    I arr[i]ved here on Sunday and found my Family well. But I believe the Body Pollitick in this State are in a sad decay, that Idea of paying of the Bills at a great discount or not paying them at all has been too deeply impressed on the minds of the People to be easily eradicated. I am afraid we shall find much difficulty in procureing the supplies which New England can furnish. A delegate now in Congress has told his Sentiments publickly, When at Wethersfield on his way to Congress to be against paying of the Bills at their nominal Value.[1] Nothing cou'd save the Currency here but the farmers geting great Sums of it. They will perhaps think they have more than their share.
    I am not surprised at General Sullivans ordering a Court of enquiry next Monday to enquire into the conduct of the Com[missar]ys for supplying his command.[2] The Issueing Com[missar]y thus[?] Issues Rum by a General order to the officers and takes money for it at a moderate price; 1/6 per Day for Sauce [i.e., Vegetables] to each Soldier, an allowance in cash for Soap over and above the usual one &c &c. I think a court of enquiry necessary and as it is composed of officers of his Army who have been much indebted[?] Perhaps they may find what he wants by the enquiry. Oblidgeing me to quit my office to attend to these damd quarrels will be but a Small Evil compared with the ruine[?] that must happen if one command is so differently dealt by from another. I am persuaded a more important enquirey will soon be necessary. I will if possible avoid a quarrel but haveing already born too much I can not promise to hold out long, and if I begin I must wade thro.[3] Farwell, God bless You and keep you from the Evils I feel. I am Dear Sir Your Sincere freind and most obed Servt

JERE WADSWORTH

ALS (PPAmP).
    1. The delegate has not been identified.
    2. For an account of the Wadsworth-Sullivan quarrel, see note above at NG to Pettit, 4 December 1778.
    3. NG responded to Wadsworth on 6 March, below.

From George Washington

Sir   Head Quarters Middle Brook [N.J.] 24th Feby 1779
    I have given the Commissary General orders to lay in a Magazine of four Months provisions for twelve hundred Men at Fort Pitt; and another of the like quantity for one thousand Men at Sunbury, both to be formed by the first day of May next and exclusive of the quantities

necessary for the subsistence of the Troops in those quarters.[1] I have directed him if possible, to draw his supplies for Pittsburg from the Frontiers of Virginia, and those for Sunbury from the West side of Susquehannah. You will consult with him and afford him the necessary aid respecting the transportation.

You will endeavour to obtain as soon as possible, and in as secret a manner as the nature of the case will admit, a list of all the Vessels from the Falls of Susquehannah (above Harris's Ferry) to Wyoming, estimating the number of Men and quantity of provisions they are capable of carrying, and distinguishing public from private property, and those which may suit the upper, narrower and shallower parts from such as are adapted to the lower, wider and deeper parts.[2]

You will please to furnish me with a Return of all the Stores which shall be in your department on the first day of every Month, and the places where they are, to be made as soon after that day as the particular Return from your Deputies can be collected and drawn into a General one. You will cause the same to be done by the Commissary of Forage in his department.

I take occasion, in this place, to repeat the verbal instructions given you in Philad'a for countermanding the orders you may have issued in consequence of former instructions to you of the 15th December last,[3] except so far as relates to an Indian Expedition upon a smaller scale, preparations for which are to be prosecuted agreeable to the directions which shall be received for that purpose from Major Genl Schuyler. Though you are to proceed no further in providing Materials for the Vessels of force, the Articles which may be already procured are to be carefully deposited for future use in such manner as will best secure them from waste and loss.

Given at Head Quarters Middle Brook this 24th Feby 1779

GO: WASHINGTON

LS (PPAmP).
1. See Washington to Wadsworth, Fitzpatrick, GW, 14: 98n, 113–14. Sunbury was on the east bank of the Susquehanna River, some seventy-five miles south of the New York border. See Map 3.
2. The Indian expedition was finally under way. For background, see above, NG to Washington, 5 January.
3. See Washington's Verbal Instructions to NG of 17 February, above.

From Colonel Henry Hollingsworth

[Head of Elk, Md., 25 February 1779. Acknowledges NG's letters of 14 and 16 February. Thanks NG "for your cautions."[1] Is experiencing great difficulty in procuring forage. "A few Small Shallop loads of Corn from Virginia" and elsewhere have arrived and will be sent to camp. Expects shortage of wagons has prevented supplying "any quantity worth mentioning until now." Asks NG to inform Colonel Biddle as he has "not time at present to wright Him." In a postscript, Hollingsworth writes that he is enclosing "a few Verses by a young Lady a Friend, who asked me to deliver them."[2] ALS (PPAmP) 1 p.]

1. For NG's "cautions," see above, NG to Hollingsworth, 14 February 1779.
2. The sixteen stanza poem by "Plebia" that Hollingsworth enclosed is a plea for justice and mercy on the part of military leaders in waging war. A typical verse reads: "That Charity which thinks no ill / Is pacific and kind / Makes Heroes greater Heroes still / and shows a noble mind."

From Colonel Robert L. Hooper, Jr.

[Easton, Pa., 25 February 1779. Has been contracting for packsaddles. Can procure 1,500 saddles by mid-April or sooner. Will be with NG "tomorrow evening." ALS (PPAmP) 1 p.]

From General Henry Knox

[Pluckemin, N.J., 25 February 1779. Will send tent makers to Morristown. Washington wishes Knox, NG, and the adjutant general to meet respecting "Armorers [?], Conductors, &c." Mrs. Knox sends compliments to Mrs. Greene; it would not be "prudent" for her to travel "under her present circumstances."[1] ALS (PPAmP) 1 p.]

1. A daughter, Julia, was born in the spring.

From Colonel Charles Pettit

Dear Sir   Philadelphia 25 Feby 1779

In my Letter of Sunday last I entertained you with a narative of a Correspondence I had been drawn into with the Council of this State,[1] which, as it is carried on in my official Character, I think it best that you and Col. Cox (who I suppose is now with you) should know as minutely as possible, especially as something serious seems to be growing out of the Subject, tho' not in consequence of this correspondence. Monday afternoon I received an official Letter from the President [Joseph Reed], to which I wrote an Answer the same evening, copies of which I inclose to you as they will explain themselves from the information I have already given you.[2]

Tuesday passed over without any farther movement. Yesterday morning I received a verbal Message by one of their Clerks that the Council would be glad to see me at their Chamber. I attended immediatly, not knowing what Turn they meant to give the business and therefore was preparing my mind for an attack in case it should happen. However, they all rose to receive me and very complaisantly seated me near the President, who from the Chair introduced what he was charged with by assuring me of the good Opinion of the Council. Then followed a recapitulation of the Circumstances of their Application to you about the 1st of this month for the desired information. Some compliments on your candor and disposition to cultivate a good understanding with the civil authority, but that you had not answered that part of the request, which was supposed to be owing to the many Things you had to attend to at setting out for Camp, but they imagined you had either left it in charge with me or given orders to Col. Mitchell to do what they had required. In this expectation they had waited till the 16th when they made their first request to me.[3] That the Delay of the Information was the more injurious to their Business as the Committee of Congress had frequently called upon them for Evidence in support of their charges against Genl Arnold which had been thus withheld from them. That they thought it comported best with their Station to negotiate with the principal in the Departmt rather than a Deputy and therefore as you were not here they called on me, and as I had seemed not so clearly to approve or understand Letters coming from the Secretary the President had signed the Letter to me. This I took in the Light of a sort of an appology to take off the unfavourable feelings I had expressed. I made a short return of Professions and assurances, and held myself ready to hear what farther should be offered.

Some things not favourable to Mr Mitchell were said, and that it was with some difficulty they had avoided including him in the charge against Genl Arnold, that they could not help thinking he had endeavoured to conceal the circumstances of this affair and that his conduct was highly blameable, that they were now more than ever convinced of it from an alteration in the marginal note of the Entry of Jordan's Teams before he gave a certified copy of it, and the obliteration of an entry in the same Book which they supposed had been the entry of the return or discharge of those Teams, that the Secretary had inspected the Book and committed his remarks to writing. They then demanded of me to produce the Book to them. I told them I did not look upon it to be in my Custody but that I would advise Mr Mitchell to wait on them with it either by himself or one of his Clerks. They said they would have nothing to say to Mr Mitchell in the affair, that all the Books belonging to the Department were virtually in my Custody wheresoever they were (that is as standing in the place of the QMG) and they should look to me for it; that I might send it by whom I should please but they would receive it only as from me; that they were clear they had a right to this Demand and to expect a Compliance. I gave them some of the first reasons that occurred in Opposi-

Quarters at Middle—Brook 5\

A Return of Quarter-Master General's Stores in the *first Virginia* .... Brigade commanded by

Brigadier Gen'l Woodford . April 27th 1779 .—

Camp Equipage and Materials, viz.	2d	3d	5th	7th	11th	TOTAL	Tools, viz.	2d	3d	5th	7th	11th	TOTAL
Marquees,	•	•				—	Broad axes, .	2 .					. 2.
Horseman's tents,	•	•	3	/	• 2	6	Narrow axes, .	40	14	23	10	5	106.
Common tents,	•	•					Hatchets, .						
Bell tents,	•	•					Adzes, .						
Tent poles,	•	•			3	3	Crosscutsaws, .				/	/	2.
Tent lines,	•	•					Handsews, .	2	/	/		/	5.
Tent pins,	•	•					Saw-sets, .						
Camp kettles,	43	38	32	18	21	151.	Drawknives, .	2				/	3.
Knapsacks,	65	101	44	100	17	327.	Chissels, .				2		3.
Haversacks,	7					70—	Gouges, .	/		/		/	3.
Wooden bowls,	13	17	15	5	9	59—	Augers, .	2	/			/	4.
Pails,							Iron squares, .						
Canteens,	20	16	21	16	9	82.	Rules, .						
Bags,							Compasses, —						
Leather portmanteaus,	2 .	/ .	5	. 3	. 11.		Pincers, .						
Leather valieces,							Hammers, —			/			/
Canvas valieces,	/	2 .				3.	Gimblets, . —	2		/			3.
Saddlebags,							Files, . —			/		2	3.
Iron cups,							Guages, —						
Pots,							Chalk-lines, .						
Sheets of tin,				/		/	Shovels, .	18	2	6	2	6	16.
Brass kettles,							Spades, .	12	2	2	2	5	23.
Iron Mongery, &c. &c.							Picks, .	9	/	/		5	16.
Tomahawks,	/	3	/	4		9—	Fascine hatchets, .						
Scythes,							Fascine knives, .						
Wedges,	3		2	2	2	9.	Drilling tools, .						
Frows,	4		/		2	7—	Waggons and Horses, viz.						
Crowbars,							Covered waggons	/	•				/
Scythstones,							Open waggons, .						
Grindstones,		/	/		/	3.	Waggon horses c. p.						
Whetstones,							Ditto ditto p. p.						
Cutting-boxes,							Riding ditto c. p.						
Cutting-knives,							Ditto ditto p. p.	4	4	3	2	3	16—
Wheelbarrows,							*Troughs*		/				/
Handbarrows,							*Wm F. Master*						
Cranks		/	/	/	8		*Riding Houses*						/
Jacob of Commissary							*C. P*	/					
C. Fritter	/	— — — — —	*Stillards*	/					
W. Banter	4	— — — —	*C. Boyes* .	/					
Stillards	/	— — — —	*C. Kettle* .	/					
N. Bos	4	— — — —	*C. Joon* .	/					
C. ditto	4	— — — —	*C. Knife* .	/					
C. Boyer	/	— — — — —	*N. Ayes* .	/					

An example of a quartermaster return
(Courtesy of the American Philosophical Society)

tion to the right, but at the same time told them that tho' I could not agree with them in opinion on that point I did not think it necessary to put it in issue as I thought prudence so far dictated a compliance with the Request, that I would ask the Book from Mr Mitchell for the Purpose and advise him to deliver it, but that I should not interpose any official authority to obtain it.

I immediatly went to Mr Mitchell and asked him for the Book, at the same time telling him the footing I had put it upon and the purpose for which I asked it; he gave it to me without hesitation, desiring me to tell them it was a mere memorandum book in which his Clerks occasionally made such memorandums as they pleased and altered them at their Pleasure.[4] I waited on the Council with the Book and told them what Mr Mitchell had desired me and also the readiness with which he complied with the Request. Their Ire seemed raised against him. They read to me his pressing Letters for calling out a great Number of Waggons 11 to 1300 from the 25 Sepr to the 1st of Octr and then compared it with his Certificate published by Genl Arnold mentioning that these Waggons could be spared without Inconvenience and hinted at some other misdeameanors.[5] I endeavoured to hold up to view some softening circumstances, but as it appeared like throwing oil on a fire I desisted. Their Expressions plainly indicated a Prosecution. I told them that if they had any Matters of charge worthy of a prosecution he should be immediatly put on Trial by a Court of Enquiry or Court Martial as the Circumstances should require. I was immediatly told they should not trouble me nor the Q M Genl with that Business as they could proceed in another Way on the Resolution of Congress of last Year.[6] They desired me to leave the Book with them as they wanted to shew it to the Committee of Congress and would send it to me, but charged me not to return it to Mr Mitchell as he ought not be trusted with it again till this Matter should be settled lest more alterations should be made. After asking if they had any farther commands for me I made my Bow and retired. I thought it right to apprize Mr Mitchell of the ground he stood on without however painting it in the strongest Light or mentioning any irritating Circumstance.

This morning he received a Letter from the Council dated yesterday notifying him that they intended to proceed against him on the Resolution of Congress of the 9th of Feby 1778 unless he should forthwith shew Cause to the contrary. He called upon me to advise him how to proceed in it. I advised him to wait on the Council, and ask for a Copy of the accusation and Copies of the Evidence to support it and desire Time to answer it. Here the matter stands at present. I wish you were on the spot as I think you might afford some mediation that might be useful. From the essays I have made towards it I see no prospect of doing good by farther attempts at least while the fever is up. I therefore think it best let it alone lest I should do mischief. Mr Mitchells conduct in this business has not been so discreet as I wish; but I do not believe he has had any evil Intentions nor that the circumstances fairly admit the high colouring the Council are pleased to give them. Whether the Resolution of Congress (I shall inclose you a Copy) will warrant this mode of proceeding, Congress being here, and I also on the spot, is not altogether clear; but be that as it may, if they choose to declare him an improper Person for the Employment, either by directly displaceing him or otherwise, it may be improper to contend with them. On the other hand Mr Mitchell is a valuable and useful Officer and I should be unwilling to lose the Benefit of his Services or to let him suffer unjustly. The Affair is of a very delicate Nature and I must confess is not a little embarrassing.[7]

I have written thus fully that you may be the better able to advise me in it. I would write more but Major Story calls on me and seems in haste. I am (I say it to both of you) Dr Sir Yours sincerely

CHAS PETTIT

ALS (PPAmP).

1. For background on the Mitchell-Arnold affair, see above, NG to Reed, 31 January, #1, and Pettit to NG, 21 February.

2. In a formal letter to his brother-in-law, Reed attempted to assuage Pettit's anger by telling him that "the Council entertain too favourable an opinion of your prudence to suppose you would if properly informed countenance any unnecessary delay." Despite his conciliatory tone, Reed added that the council differed "totally" with Pettit concerning their power to examine quartermaster records. We "do not ask the certificates as a matter of favour, but of clear and undoubted right," Reed wrote. (Reed to Pettit, 22 February, Greene Papers, PPAmP) Apparently mollified by Reed's tone, Pettit assured the council that he was doing everything possible to assist them in their investigation. Although Mitchell's conduct had been "erroneous, and betrays at least a want of Caution," Pettit wrote, he was satisfied that Mitchell had not deliberately withheld information from the council. Pettit reaffirmed his "earnest Desire that every Abuse in the Department in which I have the Honour to be placed should be corrected, and that there is not any Person employed in it to whom I have any Attachment that would induce me to wish to screen his Mal Practices from Detection." (Pettit to Reed, 22 February 1779, Greene Papers, PPAmP)

3. It is not clear why NG took no action after receiving Reed's letter of 1 February, above, requesting copies of the quartermaster records. NG's response to this letter of Pettit's has not been found.

4. The information that the memorandum books in Mitchell's office had been altered was the most potentially damaging challenge to Mitchell's claim that he was innocent of any wrongdoing. On 24 February, Secretary Timothy Matlack told the council that he had stopped by Mitchell's office in order to inspect "the original entry in Mr. John Mitchell's memorandum book," which concerned Jordan's wagon trip to Egg Harbor. Matlack discovered that a note written in the margin by the entry had "been altered in a darker coloured Ink and a different hand writing." (Pa. Col. Records, 11: 706–7) When Pettit produced the book for the council's inspection, they discovered not only that "the alteration plainly appeared" but that the last entry was "totally obliterated, not by a common erasure, but by a black blot, done with evident design totally to conceal the entry there made, consisting probably of two lines." (Pa. Col. Records, 11: 707) In testimony before the council on the twenty-fifth, Mitchell admitted that the "blot in his Memorandum book of the 30th of October, 1778, was done by his order, to

conceal a Memorandum entered by his Clerk, of that date" concerning the return of the wagons from Egg Harbor. Mitchell further revealed that the obliteration had been made "after the charge against Gen'l Arnold for having used the Public Waggons . . . had come to his knowledge." (*Pa. Col. Records*, 11: 708) Thus, it appeared that Mitchell had attempted to expunge the evidence of Arnold's wagon use from the official records.

5. See above, note at NG to Reed, 31 January, #1.

6. The resolution authorized the "supreme executive powers of every State" to "give attention to the conduct and behaviour of all continental officers, civil or military, in the execution of their respective offices" and to investigate "any reprehensible conduct of any other officer" (i.e., those appointed by Congress) and to report the same to Congress or the commander in chief (*JCC*, 10: 139–40).

7. Although Mitchell's behavior gave credence to the Pennsylvania Council's accusations of a "cover up," he was eventually exonerated. See below, Pettit to NG, 26/27 February, #2.

To Colonel Clement Biddle

Dear Sir   Middle Brook [N.J.], February 26th 1779

Your favours of the 11th [and] 20th of this Instant, I have received.

I am glad you are forwarding the grain up to Trenton as fast as possible. Our supplies from this State, are growing less and less, and I expect by and by will totally stop coming in. The Inhabitants in Monmouth begin to get clamorous at the great quantities of Grain drawn from thence.[1]

What a shame it is that a few little Cruisers in Chessapeak Bay should cut off our communication. The Continental Frigates, and State Gallies, are all in a State of Inactivity. More enterprize and better oeconomy is absolutely necessary in the Navy Department of American affairs. I wish to God there was an Admiralty Board for the direction of these matters. While the business is done by Members of Congress, nothing but delays are to be expected; for they have not time to attend to the business.

Inclosed is an extract of General Washington's order for sending in Monthly Returns.[2] You will give the necessary orders for sending in the Returns. The Genl says He will admit of no excuse. It will be absolutely necessary therefore for your Agents to be punctual. Give them instructions to notify you constantly of their contracts, as well as of Forage on hand.

I wish you to make your stay as short as possible in Philadelphia after Mrs Biddle is in Bed, but don't wish you to return before, nor to leave her until she is in a good way.[3]

Make my and Mrs Greenes compliments to her; To General Wilkinson and his Lady; and Docr Hutchinson and his Spouse. I beg leave to congratulate the last Couple upon their happy union, and wish them unchangable felicity.[4] I am With sincere regard Yours.

NATHL GREENE

LS (PPAmP).

1. See above, NG to William Livingston, 14 February.

2. Washington specifically asked for forage returns in his letter to NG of 24 February, above.

3. Mrs. Biddle had just given birth to a son. See above, Biddle to NG, 24 February.

4. Dr. James Hutchinson (1752–93), surgeon general of Pennsylvania, had recently married Biddle's sister, Lydia. Gen. James Wilkinson was the husband of another Biddle sister, Ann. (*DAB*)

To Colonel Ephraim Bowen

[Middlebrook, N.J., 26 February 1779. Duplicate of circular to Deputy Quartermasters General, same date, below. RIHS, *Coll.*, 6 (1867): 227–28.]

To Colonel John Davis

[Middlebrook, N.J., 26 February 1779. Asks Davis to assist Col. Ephraim Blaine, deputy commissary general of purchases, in forming magazines at Sunbury and Pittsburgh according to Washington's orders.[1] "It will be absolutely necessary therefore to keep the business as secret as possible." LS (Davis Papers: DLC) 1 p.]

1. In his letter of 24 February, above, Washington asked NG to aid the commissary with the formation of the magazines in western Pennsylvania. See Map 3.

Circular Letter to Deputy Quartermasters General

Sir   Middle Brook [N.J.] February 26 1779

Inclosd is an extract of General Washingtons orders to me respecting makeing him Monthly returns;[1] he has demanded them, repeatedly, but as they have not been sent in regularly by the Deputies, It has been out of my power to comply with his Orders.

I am now to request you to send me immediately a return of all the quarter Masters Stores in your possession, and the Forage on hand, and contracted for.

You will make a seperate return of any Stores Manufactureing, by whose order, and how soon they will be complete.

I must have Monthly returns in future to be sent in at the begining of every month.

As his Excellency the commander in chief, The Congress, and the Board of War, all require Monthly returns from me, I must insist upon their being regularly furnished Monthly and cannot admit of any excuse.

Blank returns may be had of Mr Pettitt in Philadelphia. I am Sir Your humble Sert

NATH GREENE

ADfS (PCC, item 173, vol. 4: 189, DNA; a duplicate to George Ross and John Davis is in the same volume, p. 193. A duplicate to Moore Furman is in NjP, one to Ephraim Bowen in RIHS, *Coll.*, 6 (1867): 227–28).
1. See above, Washington to NG, 24 February 1779.

To Moore Furman

[Middlebrook, N.J., 26 February 1779. Duplicate of circular letter sent to deputy quartermasters general, same date. LS (NjP) 1 p.]

To Colonel Udny Hay

[Middlebrook, N.J., 26 February 1779. Inquires about repair of wagons "for the opening Campaign."[1] Asks Hay to send a return of "Public Waggons" in his district, informing NG how many are "fit" and how many need repair. Those beyond repair "had better be taken to pieces" and their parts used to repair others. ADfS (PCC, item 173, vol. 4: 185, DNA) 1 p.]

1. The Indian expedition.

To Captain John Starr[1]

[Middlebrook, N.J., 26 February 1779. Asks about repair of wagons. Needs an immediate return of all wagons "with the Division of the Army under the command of General Putnam." ACyS (PCC, item 173, vol. 4: 187, DNA. The index to the PCC mistakenly lists the recipient as George Starr.) 1 p.]

1. Starr appears to have been General Putnam's division quartermaster at Redding, Connecticut. See above, NG to Putnam, 10 February, and Map 1.

From Colonel Charles Pettit

Dear Sir   Philadelphia 26 [and 27] Feby 1779
    My last Letter left Mr Mitchell in the Council Chamber, or at least gone from me for that purpose.[1] He returned to me after 3 o'Clock having spent two or three Hours in Council, and appeared to me more cut down than I have seen him on any occasion before. By his Account of the Interview no high Words had passed between the Parties, but he seemed to have discerned a settled Resolution in them to push a Prosecution against him and to be his Judges, and heard Opinions of his conduct uttered that pierced him deeply and seriously—amongst others, that had it not been for this Enquiry the matter would probably have passed over silently and the Expence of the Waggons saved to Genl Arnold. The alteration in the marginal

note of the mem. Book and the obliteration of a subsequent Entry; are dwelt on as strong marks of a fraudulent Intention, and indeed they are unfortunate Circumstances which it would have been much better had never happened; for as they first stood as far as I can learn they amounted to little or indeed nothing of a criminal Nature.[2] You may remember that Mr Mitchell before you left Town gave the Council a written narrative of the sending these Waggons to Genl Arnold. Sometime afterwds the Genl called on him for a certificate accomodated to his Views and produced one ready written for him to sign, which he declined and after some time gave him the one you have probably seen in the News Paper, which was a mere copy of the one he had given the Council, with the addition of some Circumstances about the mode of paying the hire. Council have now called upon him for a narrative of the negotiation between him and the Genl about that Certificate, which he has given or means to give; but his desire to keep out of the scrape has made him give any Certificates with so much apparent Reluctance that he has offended both Parties by it; and his caution in wording them has heightened the offence by concealing or dropping some circumstances as they say; and in short every new step seems to increase poor Mitchell's Difficulty.[3] He has pressed it upon me to endeavour to soften the matter. I have, with truth, assured him of my disposition to do it if I could see a probability of attempting it with Success, but the temper of the times does not admit of such an interposition. I might involve myself in the consequences, but see no probability of its alleviating his Distress by it. This Morning I wrote a Letter to the President [Reed] on the subject, merely as a private and friendly one, expressing my sense of Mr Mitchell's conduct, that it had been indiscreet and deserved reprehension as such, but that from the whole Tenor of his conduct in office I thought it deserved a favourable construction and therefore as well as because there were no appearances of his being interested in it.[4] I could not suppose he had designed a fraud or to cover that of another. I also stated some difficulties we should labour under if they should suspend him. He answered my Letter in the same friendly style; but intimated a different opinion of Mr Mitchell's conduct, expressing his wishes however that my opinion might be justified. I see no hope from this Letter of any consolation for Mr Mitchell, unless some things I suggested in mine should lead to a train of thinking that may imperceptibly dampen the fire.

The President however is not the leading man in this matter. I have reason to believe he was the means of preventing Mr Mitchell from being joined in the accusation against the General. Mr Mitchell shewed me this morning a Draught of a Letter he was preparing to send to the President with the Narrative above mentioned. It was something in the peccavi style[5] but expressing more apprehensions from the colouring they might choose to give in a publication of these Matters than from a loss of his office. I suppose he has sent it but I have not seen him since. Here the Business stands at present. If any thing farther occurs before I have an opportunity of sending this to you I will add it. I shall blend no other matter with my Letters to you on this Subject. As I write to the moment without regard to what is to follow, it will be more likely to give you a true state of the transaction, and may serve hereafter to correct my own Ideas of it if they should wander or my memory play the knave with me. This minutely travelling over the ground again and recording the transactions serves as a memento to aid me with circumspection in my own conduct in the Business. 27 Feby This morning Mr Mitchell has been with me again, he expresses great Concern that the Council suspect him of want of candor and a desire to conceal the Truth and declares his willingness to make the most explicit declaration of the Facts in any manner the Council shall desire not inconsistent with the Character of a Gentleman. He has desired me to convey this Declaration to the Council which I have just done in a Letter to the President.[6]

[*not signed*]

AL (PPAmP).
1. For background on the Mitchell-Arnold affair, see above note at NG to Reed, 31 January, #1; Pettit to NG, 21 February; and Pettit to NG, 25 February.
2. See note at Pettit to NG, 25 February, above.
3. Mitchell's statement before the council on 26 February and Reed's response are in the *Pa. Archives*, 7: 207–8. The "certificate," i.e., Mitchell's version of the incident, appeared in the *Pennsylvania Packet* of 23 February. From the beginning of the investigation in January 1779 until its end with Arnold's court-martial in January, 1780, Mitchell gave several different accounts of his role in the wagon incident.
4. Pettit continued to believe firmly that Mitchell had no financial interest in the ship's cargo transported by public wagons from Egg Harbor.
5. I.e., admitting guilt.
6. On 1 March, Mitchell wrote a long letter to Reed on the wagon affair, giving his version of the events in detail. (*Pa. Archives*, 7: 213–20) The council then referred Mitchell's case to Congress. William Paca's congressional committee, named to look into the charges against Arnold (note at NG to Reed, 31 January, #1, above) examined John Hall, Mitchell's clerk, about the memorandum book alteration. Apparently satisfied by Hall's testimony, the committee reported on 20 March that "no Evidence appears to prove that the said Col. Mitchell, in ordering and directing the said John Hall, his clerk, to make the said alterations and obliterations, has acted criminally or fraudulently." (*JCC*, 13: 345) Thus, Mitchell was exonerated.
Soon after, in late March, Congress resolved that Arnold, who had been asking for a court-martial since early February to clear his reputation, be granted his request, ruling that several of the Pennsylvania Council charges, including the two concerning the wagons, should be heard by a court-martial. (*JCC*, 13: 184, 412–17) Both Mitchell and his clerk, John Hall, appeared as witnesses at the court-martial, which met in Raritan in December and January, 1779–80. The court found Arnold innocent of any wrongdoing in the charges levied against him by the Pennsylvania Council. It did, however, criticize his conduct in making an "improper" request for the public wagons. The court held that while Arnold had intended to reimburse the public for his private use of the wag-

ons, his request to Mitchell, because of the "delicacy attending the high station in which the general acted, and that requests from him might operate as commands," was "imprudent and improper, and that, therefore, it ought not to have been made." The court then sentenced Arnold, who had resigned his Philadelphia post the previous March, to receive a reprimand from the commander in chief. (The proceedings of Arnold's court-martial were first published in 1780, and reprinted under the shortened title of *Proceedings of Arnold's Court Martial*, New York, 1865. The verdict appears on p. 145; much of the printed testimony pertains to the wagon affair. See also, *JCC*, 16: 161–62, and Fitzpatrick, *GW*, 18: 222–25.)

Although this 26/27 February letter from Pettit is marked "Answered," what was undoubtedly an interesting reply from NG has not been found. Mitchell's behavior in the wagon affair, both in lending the wagons to Arnold and his subsequent actions in attempting to "cover up" the evidence, were clearly suspect. In fact, Mitchell was named in a similar case in March 1779. John Gardner, a wagoner with the Continental service, complained to the Pennsylvania Council that Mitchell had ordered him to Morristown, N.J., to deliver a load of rum, sugar, coffee, and brandy. After returning to Philadelphia, Gardner discovered an advertisement in a New Jersey paper for the goods, offered for sale by the merchant to whom Gardner had delivered them. (*Pa. Archives*, 7: 241–42)

But NG was reluctant to censure or criticize his deputy. NG himself escaped implication in the Mitchell-Arnold affair, although his assistant, Charles Pettit, had been criticized briefly. (See above, Pettit to NG, 21 February.) Members of the Pennsylvania Council seemed to hold NG in high esteem. Joseph Reed, writing on 24 March 1779, referred to him as "not only a brave, valuable, and amiable Character, but my particular friend." Reed further wrote that "there is none, the Commander in Chief excepted, to whom I would sooner wish to see any Mark of Respect and Attention shown." (*Pa. Archives*, 7: 263) NG was concerned about his deputy's reputation (NG to Wadsworth, 19 March, #1, below) but it is clear that his personal relationship with Mitchell precluded harsher forms of criticism or action. NG, for example, was staying at Mitchell's house during his January-February sojourn in Philadelphia when the wagon affair first came to light. Mitchell, moreover, was extremely effective in supplying NG and other Continental officers with difficult-to-obtain personal items. (See above, note at NG to Reed, 31 January, #1.) However, it is impossible to separate the attacks on Arnold and Mitchell by the Pennsylvania radicals from the political schisms that existed between radical and conservative at the time. In the months following Mitchell's exoneration by Congress, his unpopularity with the radicals increased. (See below, Pettit to NG, 20 March and 24 September 1779.) Ultimately, NG's failure to dismiss or censure his deputy in Philadelphia was as much a reflection of his desire to remain aloof from the political factions in Pennsylvania as it was testimony to his personal regard for Mitchell and respect for his usefulness as a deputy.

From Colonel Charles Pettit

Dear Sir   Philadelphia 26th [and 27] Feby 1779

Having been at the Assembly last Night I want to recover a Debt from Somnus[1] which he seems inclined to pay me, but the Evening or Sunday is all the time I can find free enough from Interruption to write Letters, and therefore tho' I have already given you this evening near two of my crowded Pages on a subject which has made frequent calls on me lately, I must stain another Page or two on the Subjects of your favour of the 23d and other matters of business.[2]

I have sent forward to Col. Cox all the Returns of a late Date that I had. I believe there were few or none from the southward among them, nor do I recollect to have seen any; perhaps Col. Cox may have some of them as I believe he wrote for them some time ago. I had not an Idea of declining any part of the Business that might happen to be out of my appropriated Line when occasion might require it, by making the Observation you mention. I only meant to hint to you where you might be more likely to obtain what you wanted as I had not the Power of giving it to you completely. While I am on this Subject it may not be improper to remark that I find it impossible to give that personal Attention to the Accounts that I would wish and intended. The procuring, receiving and distributing of Money, the receiving and answering of Letters and Applications from different quarters, and negotiating Business with the different Boards and Committees of Congress with the Etcetera which every Day brings forth, find me full employment pretty constantly even [though] now the round of dining and spending Evenings is pretty well over. While you were in Town, I felt but part of this as a good deal of it fell on you, and will always light on the highest step of the Stairs for the Time being at the Seat of Congress. I therefore perceive plainly that it will be a vain Expectation in me to think of wading through all the vouchers of the Deputies and Contractors as I had intended. This Business must nevertheless be done and some Person of sufficient Capacity must be employed in it, and it will alone be full Employment for any one Person. Indeed it ought to be almost his only employment for it is a Business that will not bear Interruption. I shall nevertheless give the Accounts all the Inspection I can and be at Hand to examine points of difficulty which must be reserved by the Person through whose Hands they pass. I have again been with the Treasury Board and their Officers to try to settle a Plan; they refer me to Mr Trumbull who has been for some time expected but is not yet arrived.

Before this you will have received all the Money I have been able to get; in this I include what is sent to Boston. Mr Biddle has immediate demands on him here for 600,000 Dollars. As the Forage Branch seemed to demand it most I gave him a Draught for that Sum, and tho' I have not interfered with him for a Week and he has hunted the Treasurer closely, I do not believe he has yet got half of it. I have pressing Demands from all Quarters and have not yet answered any one of them but those I have advised you of. I have mentioned this to the Treasury in strong Language both in writing and in daily Conversation with the Members, but get nothing but fair Words and promises which they give me as freely as I would wish. A paltry dispute with the signers about their Wages has occasioned some delay, but I have been told that is ended. I shall steadily pursue the measures most likely to obtain the necessary Sums; but they are fallen behind hand and at best it will take time to recover.

One of my Late Letters will have given you my present Idea respecting the collecting and sending in the Vouchers. I do not think it will be best to call them in so frequently as you mention as it will prevent their coming so well digested into order as might be wished. The Deputies however should draw them in from their Assistants as fast as they get their Accounts, and every Deputy should methodize all the Accounts of his District and arrange the Vouchers to send in at certain Periods which I think cannot be shorter than quarterly, to wit the 1st of March, June, September and December. As soon as I can possibly do it I mean to frame a model with Instructions on these Points which I will send to you for your correction and approbation. Johnston Smith is now in Town,[3] and his accounts are under Examination. Pray tell me what Reward and Allowances I may agree to as well on his own Expenditures as those over which he had a superintendancy.

I had given my Idea to Mr Biddle nearly in the manner you mention respecting the Carolina Business, but not quite so fully, I shall discourse him again on the Subject.

You will read General Arnold's Affair in some measure in my other Letter respecting Mr Mitchell. The Committee of Congress have not yet reported on the Charges of the Council; the latter think the Business unduly delayed and are much dissatisfied, as they seem to think they are not treated with the respect which has been usual in the like Cases.[4] From some hints I have heard I suspect they are making farther Enquiries into certain transactions about the purchase of Goods on the first coming to Town and it may be that the Clothier Genl and his Agents may be singed in the course of it.

Genl Pulaskie talks of setting out tomorrow.[5] Yesterday I recd a Note from Mr Peters[6] desiring I would give him an Estimate of the Expence of the QM Department for an Army of 6000 Men for one Year as well as I could do it on short Notice. I framed an Estimate in a few Lines and sent it to him amounting to about 1,500,000 Dollars besides transportation from the Places where Articles should be procured to the place of consumption. I supposed 200 purchased Teams, 200 spare and riding Horses, Tents equal to 1500 common ones. I believe the number of Horses was too low, the whole making but 1000. Please to form an Estimate for such an Army as minutely as you can and send me; it may be of farther Use.

Thus far I have written of this Letter on a Gallop without stopping. I must now pause a while to consider what is next to be said, and perhaps take a nap in the mean Time. But lest I should forget it, pray send me a Copy of what you have written to Mr [Abraham] Livingston of Carolina, as I may otherwise not properly accomodate what I say, to it.

27 Feby

This morning brot me a short account from Col. Cox of the

Enemy's being out. The next Account I expect will be of their going in and then an Embarkation.

I intended this Day to have gone to Trenton, but Mr Mitchells critical Situation, and the Number of People waiting for Money and other Business induces me to postpone it for some Days. The present Situation of Affairs make me afraid to be a Day absent, and yet I could wish my Duty permitted me to be out of hearing of it.[7]

My best Respects to Mrs Greene and Compliments to our Friends. I am Dr Sir sincerely yours

CHAS PETTIT

ALS (PPAmP).
1. The classic god of sleep.
2. For Pettit's long letter on the Mitchell-Arnold affair on this date see above, 26/27 February, #1. NG's letter of 23 February has not been found.
3. Johnston Smith was a contractor for horses and wagons in the backcountry of Virginia.
4. See above, Pettit to NG, 26/27 February, #1.
5. General Pulaski and his Legion had been ordered to Georgia. See note at Pettit to NG, 10 February, above.
6. Richard Peters, secretary to the Board of War.
7. Although this letter was marked "Answered," no response has been found.

From Colonel Timothy Pickering of the Board of War

Sir   War Office [Philadelphia] Feby 26 1779

A few days since we saw a certificate of discharge given by a waggon conductor to a soldier who had been employed in his brigade as a waggoner; and Colo Mitchell informed us measures were taking to reduce the number of waggons and consequently of the waggoners. Seeing many of these are soldiers, if they are merely discharged by the waggon conductors, they may never join their regiments, nor their officers know what is become of them, or take any steps to find them, imagining they are still waggoners; and thus numbers will be lost to the service. We therefore conceive it necessary that you issue orders to all your deputies under whom any soldiers are employed as waggoners, to suffer none to be discharged, unless at the same time they are delivered up to their regiment, or to some commissioned officer who will give his receipt for them and undertake to convey them to camp or to their regiment.[1] Lists also of such discharged soldiers should be transmitted to you, specifying their names, regiments, times of discharge, and to whom delivered up. These lists to be given to the Adjutant General who will cause inquiry to be made whether the persons therein named have joined their corps. This or a similar regulation we think might answer valuable purposes: if a better occurs to you, we wish it may be pursued. Should you deem any general order requisite in the case, you will be pleased to communicate it to the Commander in chief. It appears likewise to be extremely necessary that accurate lists should be kept of all soldiers employed as waggoners, shewing their names, regiments, where and under what waggon conductors they are employed; and the latter should be accountable for all in their brigades. Perhaps too it may be expedient that monthly returns should be made you of all waggoners, and the casualties happening to them, and that the commanding officer of each regt should be regularly informed of the situation of his men in your department, thro' the Adjt Genl to whom copies of the returns made you might be transmitted. But these matters we submit to your consideration; wishing only that some regular plan may be struck out and adopted for the advancement of the public service in this regard, so long as a disagreeable necessity compels us to thin our ranks of soldiers to make waggoners. We are, Sir, very respectfully, your most obedt servants. By order of the Board

TIM. PICKERING

ALS (PPAmP).
1. No evidence has been found that NG issued any orders to his deputies on this matter. He was, at the time, pressing for measures to ensure a permanent reliable corps of wagoners that would eliminate the necessity of drafting soldiers from the Continental line to serve in the wagon corps. (See above, note at NG to Washington, 24 February 1779.)

From Colonel Charles Stewart[1]

[Camp Paramus, N.J., 26 February 1779. Encloses returns of stores and tents ("Marquees, Horseman's tents, Common tents, Bell tents &c"), also a return of "Riding Horses which draw forrage." Will send a return of wagons. Is drawing stores from Morristown, which is more convenient than Middlebrook. ALS (PPAmP) 1 p.]

1. Stewart was brigade quartermaster of Thomas Clark's regiment. See Clark to NG, 27 February, below.

From General James M. Varnum

Sir   East Greenw'ch [R. I.] 26th Febry 1779
    Your agreeable Letter of the Ninth instant has been received. As it is not by me I cannot recollect all its Contents; But am very glad that Corruption has taken as deep a Root in Philadelphia as the other large Towns in the Union. This will lay the Foundation for that Chastisement from the Enemy which will reduce the People to a Degree of Indig[nation] the only Situation in which their Fears can be alarmed, and their hidden Sparks of Virtue, if any they have, rekindled to a

Blaise. To prepare the Way to this Event with more certainty, it seems to have been wisely adjusted that the Circumstances of the Army should be so distressing as to create Discontent; that this should Alarm the Citizens, and convince them that in Democrasies there should be no Servitude, and that the God of Nature never intended the Safety and Happiness of Millions should result from the Toils and Hardships, and unpaid for Labors of a generous Few. Let the Indolent and idle be subjected to as many Exertions as those who have served their Country four years in the Field, we need not fear the Rage of the Universe. For my own part, when I wrote Congress in November last, my inttentions of leaving the Army were sincere. From the most agreeable Attachments the Resolution was painful, but hard Necessity urged it by every cogent Motive. Not receiving an Answer from them, about a Fortnight since I sent a positive Resignation, and am now entering into Business with an extensive Prospect.[1]

The General Assembly are now setting and have ordered fifteen hundred Men raised for one Year from their respective Enlistments. They give the Men forty five Pounds bounty, and a compleat Suite of Cloaths, besides six Pounds Monthly in Addition to continental Wages.[2] I wish Colo [Christopher] Greene could be promoted to the Command of my Brigade. It is well disciplined, but I fear will suffer. Tho' out of Course here permit me to observe that I would sooner have lost my right Hand than left the Army could there have been any kind of Provision made suitable to my Rank and Expences.

Mr Littlefield's Absence has been attended with no disagreeable Circumstances saving that he should have notified his Colo or me of Genl Sullivan's Permission. The matter is over.[3]

The People at large are uneasy with their Delegates, and many have urged me to enter the Senatorial List; but as their Provision is adequate only to a bear Subsistence, I shall decline. The Governor will stand without Opposition. I shall come in for the Place of Attorney General, and, if so inclined, Major General of Militia; but as the latter is a Place of Trouble without Profit, I am not fully determined in my own Breast.[4] The State have ordered a Tax of sixty Thousand Pounds, to be paid by the sixteenth of April next towards raising their Troops.[5] Unless Congress will advance them a Sum of Money, their extreme Poverty cannot admit of their accomplishing this great Object towards the general Defence. Your Sollicitations in this behalf might be advantageous.[6] I should write Congress myself upon the Subject, but am apprehensive it would not be attended with any great Success, as they will esteem me scrupulous [i.e., doubtful] of the Omnipotence of their Power.

At a leisure Moment I shall address the Great General Washington upon the Reasons of my Conduct in retiring to private

Life.[7] Nothing can make me so unhappy as to be under his Displea
sure but I hope to convince him that I act with Propriety. To him be
pleased to make my sincerest Acknowledgments, with every Senti
ment of Duty and Affection. To the Gentlemen of the [family?] I feal a
sacred Attachment; be pleased to mention me with the most cordia
Friendship; As likewise to Mrs Greene; and be assured that I am, with
unfeigned Respect, your constant Friend and very humble Servant.

J M VARNUM

ALS (CSmH).
1. Congress accepted Varnum's resignation on 5 March. See above, note at Var
num to NG, 13 January.
2. The act was passed at the February 1779 legislative session. See *R.I. Acts*
1779–80, pp. 14–17.
3. On Capt. William Littlefield's extended absence, see above, NG to Varnum,
February.
4. At the May 1779 session, the R.I. General Assembly reelected Gov. William
Greene. William Channing was reelected attorney general and Varnum was chosen
major general of the R.I. militia. (Bartlett, *Records* 8: 529–30, 544).
5. Tax was to be paid "in any of the bills of public credit emitted by the Congress
excepting the emissions of May 20, 1777 and April 11, 1778." (Bartlett, *Records*, 8: 509)
6. No record has been found of NG interceding with Congress.
7. If Varnum did inform Washington about his reasons for retiring from the army
the letter has not been found.

To the Board of War

Gentlemen   Middle Brook [N.J.] February 27th 177[

When I was before the Board I represented to them the necessity
of haveing a speedy determination to my proposition to free the Warrant officers from confinement as a private soldier, Which the Board
were good enough to promise should be decided upon immediately.
Since my return to Camp there has been several complaints and the
murmurings and discontent upon this subject growing worse and
worse every Day. The injury the Public service will receive from a
delay induce me once more to press the Board to a decision.[1]

There is the affair also respecting the Barrack Master undecided.
Col Melcher has lately wrote to Col Mitchel upon a point which renders it necessary for the Board to draw the Line between the two departments to prevent any further disputes.[2]

I am happy to see by a Resolution of Congress the business of the
Portmantauex decided upon.[3] I am with great respect Your honors
Most Obedient humble Sert

N GREENE

ADfS (PCC, item 173, vol. 4: 25, DNA).
1. Congress acceded to NG's request in a resolution of 16 March. See above, note
at NG to Jay, 18 January.

2. Melcher, barrackmaster general, had written Mitchell, said Pettit, "forbidding him (or warning him against) purchasing any Wood or Boards," supplies that NG had apparently decided were under Melcher's purview. (Pettit to NG, 15 February, above) On 25 January (above), Melcher had written NG asking for a recognition of the barrackmaster general's jurisdiction.

3. The question of whether or not to provide portmanteaus for officers at public expense had been pending before Congress since NG wrote Henry Laurens on the matter in June 1778. (See above, vol. 2: 420–21.) On 20 February, Congress finally resolved that "the portmanteaus and valeses furnished to the officers of the army by the quarter master general, pursuant to the orders of the Commander in Chief, be charged to the United States, and the officers permitted to retain them for their own use." (*JCC*, 13: 214)

To Colonel Morgan Lewis

[Middlebrook, N.J., 27 February 1779. Washington has directed General Schuyler to have bateaux made "for the original plan of the Canada expedition." Lewis is to take Schuyler's orders, NG writes, "notwithstanding anything I have wrote upon the matter." ACyS (PCC, item 173, vol 2: 187, DNA) 1 p.]

From Colonel Thomas Clark[1]

[Paramus, N.J., 27 February 1779. Is "concerned" because NG has not received returns;[2] weekly returns will be made punctually in the future. Tents sent to Colonel Abeel at Morristown are now needed as his "Soldiers are at too great a distance from each other to be easily collected for the purpose of Manouvering." ALS (PPAmP) 1 p.]

1. Col. Thomas Clark was commander of the First North Carolina regiment.
2. See above, Stewart to NG, 26 February.

From Major Benjamin Eyre

[Philadelphia, 27 February 1779. "On Tuesday Next I shall lanch the Ship *Genl. Greene* the State has made application for to Purchaise the Ship for Cruisur & I am reyly of the opinion that they will in sist on haveing her if they do it will be a great disadvantage to the Owners as the Cargo is Procurd & the Voyge plan'd." He asks the General [NG] to remind Colonel Batey [Beatty], the Commissary of Prisoners, to "exchange Mr. Francis Grice, "Ship Write of this City." Excerpt from *The Collector*, #875 (1981)]

From Abraham Livingston

[Charleston, S.C., 27 February 1779. Has engaged three ships and a brigantine to transport rice.[1] Asks NG to forward $300,000 without

delay. The *Conclusion* and the *Polly* remain at Charleston "in consequence of the Number of privateers which have of late made their appearance on this coast."[2] Hopes to procure more ships but it is
difficult since private vessels are being detained in port.[3] ALS
(PPAmP) 3 pp.]

1. Livingston had been arranging for shipments of rice. See above, Wadsworth to
NG, 2 January.

2. As seen in Samuel Otis's first letter of 17 May (below), the *Polly* arrived with a
cargo of rice at Dartmouth, Mass., apparently after having been captured by an American privateer, the *Providence*.

3. The congressional embargo, originally imposed in June 1778, restricted the ex-
portation of certain grains and other provisions from the states. (See above, vol. 2:
545n.) The state of South Carolina, its trade impaired by the embargo, refused to allow
the vessels with rice for the army to leave Charleston harbor. (See below, NG to
Washington, 26 April.) In letters to NG of 19 March, 3 and 8 April (none found),
Livingston apparently elaborated on the difficulties posed by the detention of public
vessels in South Carolina. Charles Pettit, answering for NG, wrote Livingston on 30
April that he had laid "extracts" of the letters and Livingston's "protest" before a congressional committee in the hopes of obtaining permission for the ships to sail (Greene
Papers, PPAmP). The next day, Pettit again wrote Livingston that as result of a letter
just received from Gouverneur Morris and a conversation with the Supply Departments Committee (of which Morris was chairman), he found there was a secret "understanding" between the committee and the governor of South Carolina. "The detention of the Vessels," Pettit wrote, "is rather the effect of a plan concerted between them,
which we must suppose to be founded on good reasons than a design in the Governor
to obstruct our measures." (Greene Papers, PPAmP) Pettit urged Livingston to obey the
directives of Morris and the Committee and "to cultivate that harmony and good understanding with the Government which is necessary to give the desired efficacy to
your Labours in the Public Service." (Pettit to Livingston, 1 May 1779, Greene Papers,
PPAmP) Pettit enclosed copies of his letters to Livingston and from Morris in his letter
to NG of 12 May, below. The embargo was eventually lifted.

From Major Hardy Murfree[1]

[Paramus, N.J., 27 February 1779. Has no horse and cannot purchase
one near Paramus "that will do to ride." Asks NG to assist him in
buying a horse as "it is a real Necessity." ALS (PPAmP) 1 p.]

1. Murfree was a lieutenant colonel of the First North Carolina Regiment. (Heitman, *Register*) There is no record of NG's response.

From Colonel James Abeel

[Morristown, N.J., 28 February 1779. Requires cash to pay for iron.
Also, the "great Number of Horse Shoes dayly coming in Occasion
many Dunners" for whom additional money is needed. Major Burnet
has inquired about a maid for Mrs. Greene. Will do everything in his
power "to procure a good honest Girl for her."[1] ALS (PPAmP) 1 p.]

1. NG also wrote about the maid for Catharine. See below.

To Colonel James Abeel

[Middlebrook, N.J., 28 February 1779. Acknowledges Abeel's of same date. Has received $70,000, most of it already dispersed. Will send money to Abeel "As soon as it arrives." Would be "exceedingly oblig'd if Abeel would procure a maid for Catharine, preferably "to buy a good Negro Girl that has been in a Gentlemans family."[1] ALS (RHi) 1 p.]

1. Abeel did find a maid, but whether for hire or purchase is not known. See his letter of 15 March, below.

From Hugh Smith[1]

[Camp Middlebrook [?], N.J., 28 February 1779. Would be "Exceedingly obliged" if NG would order an express rider to carry mail to Philadelphia. The request is necessary because he "Cannot find a Man for Money." ALS (PPAmP) 1 p.]

1. Hugh Smith (also Smyth), the postmaster at army headquarters, did not indicate he was writing from Middlebrook. (Fitzpatrick, GW, 14: 345)

Petition from the Officers of Artificers Companies

To the Honorable the Quartermaster General of the Army of the thirteen United States of America.

The memorial and Petition of the Officers of the several Companies of Artificers in the Service of the United States, in behalf of themselves, humbly sheweth. That, We received Orders in the Year 1777, by virtue of Authority from the then Q. M. General of the American Army; to recruit Artificers to serve in the Continental Army; intituled to all the privileges and perquisites granted by Congress to the Battalions in Sd Army; therefore have been at great expence to Raise Artificers for the above purpose; men eaqual to their duty. That our encouragments were, all the Privileges and Perquisites granted by Congress to any Officers serving in the American Army.

Therefore expected when calld upon to march (or as soon as circumstances would admit) to be Commission'd and have Rank among ourselves Eaqual to the Line, and thereby Authorized to exercise Military discipline, and lead our Men into the field of Action in conjunction with the Line whenever circumstances required: (which some of us have been call'd to) the Men were therefore acquainted at the time of inlisting that they were to take Arms whenever needed, which they readily agreed to, and still show a resolution, and determination, to risk their lives in defence of their Country.

We also expected we had an undeniable right to all the State, and Continental Stores of Cloths &c, as much as any Officers in Sd Army; indeed we expected the Advantages of the State and Continental privileges and perquisites in all respects.

We have served about two years (and trust we have not forfeited our encouragements by misconduct) without Obtaining any of the Privileges which we expected: we are not vested with any Authority, but barely our recruiting Orders; and good order government and subordination, so efficatious and Necessary, and on which the safety and prosperity of an Army, or Nation, so much depends, is greatly embarrised; by reason of not having the authority of the Officers established.

The supposition appears to us absurd, (if any there be) that men should be inlisted into continental Service on the Establishment; and to Join the Army, intituled to all the Privileges and Perquisites, subject to all the Rules and Regulations thereof; Sworn to be true to the United States, and to serve them honestly and Faithfully, against all their Enemies or Opposers whatsoever, &c, and the Officers not authorized to lead and govern them; or to put the Laws in execution by which they are obliged to walk: indeed should the question be asked, what Officers are you, or what authority have you? We could not answer with propriety; that we were Officers, or had any Authority.

We are continually liable to Insults, and if insulted, no other way to get satisfaction than any Privates have; and if Captivated by the enemy shall undoubtedly be treated the same as privates; and if we claim any Rank, with the utmost contempt; not being able to show authority for our claim.

We have not recev'd the benefit of State Privileges to which we belong; or the advantage of the Continental Stores of Cloths &c altho' repeated applications have been made.

Application has been made by the Officers belonging to the State of Connecticut, to their Assembly, for the privileges granted by that state to all Commission'd, and S[t]aff Officers serving in the Army; but were intirely denied; with the answer, that the Artificers were not known, as they were not raised by the State, did not count for the State, and that their application must be made to Congress, by whom they were raised.

As we have served the greatest part of the present war, in different Capacities and departments, we entered the service of our Country Conscious of the Justness of the Cause; with a View and determination to serve according to the best of our Capacities (life and health permitting) 'till the Independency of America should be established; Nothing doubting our situation would be made honorable; (and consequently agreeable) and our Service as acceptable to the States we belong, and the public in general; as any service whatever. But to our great astonishment, we find ourselves disowned by the states to which we belong, for engaging in the Glorious Cause of our Country without their particular encouragement or direction: and neglected or forgot by the Honorable Congress: and as we receive no privileges or perquisites from the States, or the Continent; have nothing but our Wages for the support of ourselves or Families; which at first tho' liberal is now (by reason of the depreciation of the Currency,) become of very little Value; and our Families are starving, or becoming beggars, while we are supporting the most glorious cause ever America was engaged in; or that's recorded in the annals of History.

We now consider ourselves, in a very disagreeable, disadvantageous and dishonorable situation, not confirmed in any thing, and exposed to every thing.

As we willingly exchanged the sweets of domestic life, for the fatigues and hardships of war: we are still willing and desirous to Serve our Country 'till the Liberties and Independency thereof shall be established: in case we can be upon eaqual footing with our Brethren, engaged in the same common Cause.

Still flattering ourselves, the good will and Influence of your Honor is sufficient to have our reasonable expectations fulfilled, and have us established in a Situation more Advantageous to the public, honorable to your department, and agreeable to us.

Altho' 'tis with reluctance we trouble your Honor with our situation, we find ourselves necessitated thereunto.

Therefore earnestly desire your Honor, to take our circumstances. into consideration; and Use your influence, that our Authority may be established with Commissions according to our encouragements, and have the Advantage of the Continental Stores of Cloths &c. and the other privileges and perquisites granted by congress to the Officers serving in the Army, confirmed to us; and that the Honbl Congress would concert some method, whereby our Men may count for the States to which they belong, that they and we may receive State privileges, that we may not be necessitated, (to support ourselves and Families,) to quit that service, which if persevered in, will render America United, Free, Independent, and Sovereign States.[1] And we in duty bound shall ever PRAY. Feb. 1779 Signed

⟨Captains.	Belonging to:	Lieuts	Belonging to:
J BRUEN	New Jer'y	E. LITTELL	New Jersey
WILLI'M MILLS	Mass't State	NATH'L CLARK	Mass't State
JERIUS WILLCOX	Connecticut	JOHN BOLTON	Massachusetts
WM SIZER	Do	THOS PHELPS	Connecticut
STEPHEN OSBORN	Do	LINUS HOPSON	Do

RICHARD LAMB	Do	JAMES HORTON	Do
MOSES COOK	Do	ELIPHAZ KINGSLEY	Do
ISAAC PURDEY	New York State.	JAMES ABORN	Massachus[etts]
PHINEAS PARKER	Massachusetts	JOHN TEMPLE	Do)

DS (PCC, item 155, vol. 1: 100, DNA). For reasons of clarity, portion in angle brackets transcribed from Petition of Artificers to Congress, February 1779. (PCC, item 155, vol. 1: 103, DNA)

1. NG enclosed this petition and the one described in the source note above, in a letter to John Jay of 6 March, below. As seen there, he stressed the importance of satisfying the artificer officers' demands because they were "a Class of Men so necessary to the operations of an Army that they cannot be done without." When Congress had taken no action on the petitions after some months, NG, who had been "impatiently waiting," again pressed for a resolution on the matter. After his initial appeal to Congress in March, he received another petition from the officers. (Artificer Officers to NG, 8 July, below) He was forced to use "all the influence and adress" that he could muster to prevent them from leaving the army. (NG to Jay, 30 August 1779) Finally, on 12 November 1779, Congress resolved that the officers in the companies of artificers raised by the quartermaster general be granted commissions "which shall entitle them to rank only in their own corps, and enable them to hold regimental courts martial" (JCC, 15: 1262). Four days later, Congress voted to recommend to the states that the artificers, both officers and soldiers in the quartermaster corps, be allowed "all the benefits provided for officers and soldiers in the line of their quotas of the continental battalions, except half pay." (JCC, 15: 1276)

To George Washington

Sir   at my quarters [Middlebrook, N.J.] March the 1 1779

Inclosd is your Excellencys queries with the Answers; they are not so particular as I could wish, but are pretty explicit to the most capital points.[1]

Should be glad to know whether you will want to see Col Hooper again, or have any orders to give for preparations in his district.[2] If the Troops should March from Easton to Wyoming the Col should have some previous notice of it.

I was mentioning to your Excellency the other day the necessity of haveing a number of Keggs prepard. Col Hooper can provide them, if instructed seasonably.

I shall make out a list of Stores and preparations to be made at Estherton, which if your Excellency approves, shall be glad of your orders upon it.

Col Patterson will wait upon your Excellency again before he goes.[3] I am with the most perfect esteem your Excellencys Most Obedient humble Sert

NATH GREENE

ALS (Washington Papers: DLC).

1. Washington's queries have not been found, but their nature is clear from NG's memorandum that follows.

2. For Washington's reply, see below, this day.
3. Col. William Patterson, like Colonel Hooper, had been called in as a consultant on the Indian country. See above, Patterson to NG, 14 February.

See Map 3 for geographic references above.

Memorandum on General Sullivan's Expedition[1]

[Middlebrook, N.J. March 1st 1779]

Middle Town ⎫
Estherton ⎬ Are proper plaices for depositing
Hunters ⎭ Stores for an Indian Expedition.

From the above places the Stores can go up the Susquehannah by Sunbury, Wyoming, and to Tioga, the last of which places is very near the Indian Settlements and the Country leavel into the heart of them.

Memorandum. The Boats that go up the Susquehannah should have a good Guard to go on in front of the Battauex near to the River. There are many narrow passes up and down the River, ocasiond by the High Lands juting down close to the Banks of the River.

The distance from Estherton to Tioga is one hundred and Eighty Miles from thence to Lake Ontario is Ninety Miles, all a free and open Country.

Boats can go from Estherton to Tioga until the Middle of May that will carry from five to Eight Tons and from the Middle of May through the season that will carry Two Tuns. The Navigation grows better and better the farther you go up the River the Waters being deeper and less rapid.[2]

There is in the Neighbourhood of Estherton a large number of Saw Mills which can be employed to saw boards for constructing Battauex.

By calculation there will be wanting 140 Battauex of the two Ton Size.

Watermen will be difficult to be got, the duty will be hard and dangerous. Great encouragement must be given as so much will depend upon the transportation of the Stores.[3] I think there will be upwards of 500 wanted. Each of the two ton Battauex will require 4 men and the larger boats 6 men.[4]

The Artillery can go up from Estherton to Tioga by Water there will be no crossing it from Easton to Wyoming.

Posts to be established upon the River.

Sunbury 50 Miles from Estherton
Wyoming 60
Wyalusing 30
Tioga 40 180

AD (Washington Papers: DLC).

1. Since both Washington and Greene were unfamiliar with the Susquehanna Valley route into the Iroquois country in New York, they had asked Col. William Patterson (14 February, above) and Col. Robert L. Hooper, NG's deputy in Easton, Pa., to confer. (NG's letter to Hooper has not been found, but in a letter of 9 March to Gen. Edward Hand, Hooper said he had been "called" to headquarters to give information on a subject that Hand had often "hinted" to him. Hand Papers, vol. 1: 70, PHi) Hooper was eminently qualified to give information, having surveyed and mapped portions of that part of Pennsylvania before the war, and he was to play a prominent part in supplying Sullivan's expedition. NG told him later that the expedition "must have faild without your particular aid and assistance." (See above, vol. 2: 331n.)

NG prepared the memorandum for Washington from notes he took while meeting with Hooper before 1 March. His notes are in PCC, item 173, vol. 1: 17. A few substantive differences between the notes and memorandum are noted below.

2. The notes included Hooper's statement: "There may be had upon the River about 12 Boats which will answer with a little repairing. These will carry from 5 to 8 Tuns."

3. The notes read: "Great Wages must be given to encourage People to engage."

4. Hooper had added: "Some may be had from Hartleys Regt."

See Map 3 for geographic references above.

From George Washington

[Middlebrook, N.J., 1 March 1779. Is favored with NG's of "this morning." Wishes Colonel Hooper to send "any draughts of the River or Country," to assist in planning for the proposed expedition. Has not yet decided on the route of march from Easton. Kegs should be prepared at Easton and Albany. Would like to see list of stores etc. at Estherton.[1] LS (MiU-C) 1 p.]

1. See below, to and from Washington, 2 March. For locations, see Map 3.

To George Washington

Camp Middlebrook [N.J.] March 2d 1779
Articles to be provided and deposited at *Estherton*,[1] for the ensuing campaign.
150 Batteaux of about two tons burthen to be immediately built.
10 boats to carry from 8 to 10 tons.
2 Travelling Forges.
1500 good felling Axes ground and helved [i.e., with handles], and boxed up.

20 Broad axes	Ditto	Ditto
500 Spades ⎫		
500 Shovels ⎬	Helved	
100 Picks ⎭		
300 Tents		
2000 Knapsacks		

2000 Haversacks
3000 Canteens
1000 Camp Kettles
2000 Fascine Hatchets
200 Fascine Knives
2000 Nails consist'g of 10d. 12d. 20d and a few small.
6 Setts Carpenters Tools, supposed 10 men in a set.
2 Setts Smiths Tools
50 Grass Scythes with sneeds whet-stones etc.
20 Sets of shoeing tools
6000 Setts horse shoes, with nails pointed, the ends of the Shoes turned up fit to set.
500 Pack Saddles
2000 fathom ropes suitable for packing and slinging Kegs &c &c
1000 Horse Slips
1000 Horse bells with straps to buckle on
500 Horse hopples [i.e., hobbles] of strong leather.
50 setts Harness, *compleat* including chains &c
50 Cross cut saws, with files suitable
6 Saw mill saws
1000, ax Slings with straps to buckle
50 Rheam Paper
20 lb Sealing Wax
10 Wafers
3,000 Quils
10 Dos. Ink powder
200 Orderly books
50 Ink Stands
100 Flat bottom Iron Candlesticks
100 Portmanteaus

NB All the articles that will admit of being packed, to be boxed up with two hoops round Each box, and every box to weight to as near 100 lb as possible and all marked and numbered.

FC (Washington Papers: DLC).
1. Washington requested the list of stores for the proposed Indian expedition in his letter of 1 March, above. NG's list was enclosed in Washington's reply, below.

From George Washington

Sir   [Camp Middlebrook, N.J.] March 2d 1779
   The foregoing list being submitted to me by you for consideration, I shall observe that if the articles therein contained are intended as an extra provision for the ensuing campaign and wholly designed

for such troops as may proceed by the way of Wyoming, I think the quantity two great, and that the following deduction may be made as an expedition of this kind, should be as little encumbered as possible.

500 felling axes
200 Spades
200 Shovels
1000 Knapsacks ⎫   It is to be presumed the troops will be provided
1000 Haversacks ⎬   with these articles.
2000 canteens ⎭
600 Camp Kettles
200 Fascine Knives
500 Horse bells
200 Hopples

Perhaps the whole 500, as every woodman knows how to make them equally good of hickory withes.

If on the other hand these things are to be considered as part of the general provision for the use of the army next campaign and can be procured on tolerable good terms in the Towns bordering on the Susquhannah they may as well be purchased there, as elsewhere, especially as it may be a magazine from whence the Troops at Fort Pitt may be supplied; the wants of which should be immediately ascertained and supplied, and a proper enquiry made into the state of these articles at Albany that there may be no want of them in that place.

GO: WASHINGTON

FC (Washington Papers: DLC).

From Colonel James Abeel

[Morristown, N.J., 2 March 1779. Acknowledges NG's letter of 28 February. Needs £ 3,000 for iron, which is scarce and expensive; has prevailed on his "Dunners" to wait for payment. Needs carpenters and tent makers. Is trying to procure a maid for Mrs. Greene but it may "be Impossible to Get a good Wench as they are very Scarce." LB (NjHi) 1 p.]

From John Jay, President of the Continental Congress

[Philadelphia, 2 March 1779. Communicated to Congress NG's proposals "on the Subject of your Office."[1] Encloses copy of a congressional act concerning portmanteaus and valises for officers.[2] LB (PCC, item 14, p. 56, DNA) 1 p.]

1. See note above, at NG to Jay, 15 February.

2. NG was "happy to see" the resolution concerning portmanteaus and valises. See his letter to the Board of War, 27 February, above.

From James McHenry

Sir Head Quarters Middlebrook [N.J.] 2d March 1779
His Excellency desires that you will give it in order to your deputies at Philadelphia, or elswhere, to furnish Col. Wm Patterson with such articles in your department as he may judge necessary in the execution of the service he is going on, with which you have been made acquainted.[1] I am Sir Your most hble servt

JAMES MC HENRY

ACyS (Washington Papers: DLC).
1. Col. William Patterson was gathering information, on orders from Washington, for the proposed Indian expedition. See note at Patterson to NG, 14 February, above.

To Griffin Greene

Dear Sir Middle Brook [N.J.] March the 4th 1779
Your favors of the 9th 20th and 23d of February by Mr Baker came to hand last Night.[1]
I am not very apprehensive of any disagreeable consequences from your being contractor. I suppose some people will think the benefit is greater than it is; and that the appointment is a favor to you; but I am perswaded it is not. I shall be happy if the profits barely compensates you for the trouble you take.[2]
This is a murmuring age and every body that handles public money must expect to be subject to some degree of reproach; as I know my intentions to be good I regard the speech of People the less.
When I was in Philadelphia the Committee of Congress appointed to confer with the General and my self took ocasion to say that they thought the profits I derivd from the quarter masters department was too great.
I told them I was very willing to relinquish it. The profits of the office was not the object that first inducd me to engage and the profits would be no motive for my continueing providing they would release me. But if they expected I would do their druggery with out a reward they were mistaken for I would not; and there the business stands.[3]
I am as willing to quit as to serve; if I was free from this office I should have a seperate command and altho it is less profitable it is more honorable; and if it is of less consequence to me in the present hour it may be of more importance to my family hereafter.
I wrote you from Philadelphia the moment I got information of the plan of Congress for sinking the two large Emisions of May the 20

of 1777 and April the 11, 1778. I was in hopes the Letter would have reached you seasonably. But Peoples opinions were various respecting the effect it would have—some of the most Sensible men in Congress were apprehensive it would rise Stocks and depreciate the money faster than any measure that had been taken; and it really had that effect in some of the Southern States for a Time.[4]

What made me write you that I was apprehensive you were selling your Stocks to a great disadvantage was owing to a Letter I receivd by a special Express from Mr Green at Hartford. From the manner he wrote as well as the matter I expected he would sell at all events at the prices he could get.[5]

I wrote him my opinion upon the state of affairs and desird him to take his measures accordingly and if he does I think he will reap the advantage of it. I founded my opinion simply then upon the state of the currency. What effects the Politicks of Europe may have upon Stocks or upon our money I cant pretend to say—People have various opinions [one or more pages missing]

AL (OMC). Incomplete.
1. Letters not found.
2. NG did not feel he was compromising himself by employing relatives as agents for the quartermaster department. See above, vol. 2: 404n.
3. For a discussion of the criticism and NG's reaction to it, see above, note at NG to Jay, 15 February.
4. On the congressional plan for sinking the emissions, see above, note at Gooch to NG, 18 January.
5. Probably NG's brother Christopher, who had gone to Hartford to sell wine. See below, Wadsworth to NG, 4 April.

From Colonel James Abeel

[Morristown, N.J., 4 March 1779. Received NG's letter of 26 February, with Washington's orders for prompt returns. Will send an account of supplies on hand, and, in future, will send returns "by the last of Every month." Deputies have been lax about forwarding monthly returns; "sending a Person round to them cost[s] the Publick a good Deal of Money." Is collecting stores and tents; also trying to procure forage in Bergen County. LB (NjHi) 2 pp.]

From Colonel Ephraim Bowen

[Providence, R.I., 4 March 1779. Encloses accounts and returns of stores. Has "Consulted" General Sullivan about tents; they are being repaired and will be ready by mid-April or sooner.[1] Horses are in short supply. ALS (RHi) 2 pp.]

1. See NG to Bowen, 23 February #1, above.

George Weedon, 1734–1793, pencil sketch by John Trumbull
(Courtesy of Yale University Art Gallery, gift of Mrs. Winchster Bennett)

From Colonel William Smith Livingston

[Beverwyck, N.J., 4 March 1779. Requests that NG support the appointment of a friend to a consulship.¹ Excerpt from Stan V. Henkels *Catalog #1005 (1909)*]

1. The friend may have been Henry Brockholst Livingston. See below, "To All It May Concern," 30 April.

From Captain John Gooch

Dear General   Boston March 5 [and 9] 1779

I was Honored with the Receipt of Your's of the 10th Feby¹ and I'll assure you though at the Time I recived it I was under a Severe fitt of the Gravail [i.e., kidney stones] a thrill of Pride intreduceded itself and pervaded my whole Frame. How should it be otherwise when I recive such Incomiums from Genl Greene? I am at present much afflicted with the Gravail and in very great pain. My Cup of Bitterness seems to be Large, but as every one thinks his Cup the Bitterest, I'll bare it with all the Patience possible and Drink it off without Murmureing.

I suppose you'l be presented with a Petition for Reliefe from A Number of the Officers on the [Q.M.] Staff.² I wish it may be approbated for they are realy in a most Disstressed Situation especially those that have Families, as I'll assure you it will take a Years pay for one Suit of Cloths any ways decent. Provissions are excessive high. Beef, Mutton and Pork at 4/6 to 5/ per lb, Flour at 20£ per ct [hundred weight], Rye twenty Dollrs pr Bushl, Indian Corn at 15 Dollrs pr Bushl and every thing of the Necessaries of Life in Same proportion. It was an unhappy affair for them being alow'd subsistance money instead of Rations as their Rations at this time would be far preferable to all their pay. The Inhabbitants here are in the greatest Disstress for want of Bread; at Least one half of them are Daily forced to go without. Money will not purchase it.³

This Letter was begun the 5 of March, it is now the ninth. The dreadfull Intervall has been fill'd with Pain more Excrutiateing than language can paint. Even at this Instant I feal more than I would wish the worst personal Enimy I have to undergo, but could I transfer it to the Tories I'd soon Render them incapable of doing further misschiefe. I'm reduced to Perfect Skelleton confind to my Chamber and for the most part to my Bed. My Pittying Friends often make me smile in the midst of my Pains. Would you think it they treat me Just as you would treat a favorite Dog, with Poor fellow what he undergoes. I fear Colo Biddle will censure but Sickness like mine cant do business. I cant Copy this I send the News for you and the Colo. Mrs. Gooch Joins with me in Best Respects to you and Mrs Green.

Heaven preserve you and yours from what I feel. And belive me with the Greatest Esteem Your most obedt and most hble Servant

JNO GOOCH

P.S I'd like to have forgot to Informe you it is very uncertain wether I shall recover. The Doctr begins to shake his head but I flatter myself the worst is over.

ALS (MiU-C).
1. The draft of NG's letter was dated 9 February. See above.
2. See Petition of the Employees of the Quartermaster General's Department at Boston, below, 12 March.
3. It was the shortage of flour that induced Congress to order rice shipped from South Carolina. See above, Wadsworth to NG, 2 January.

To John Jay, President of the Continental Congress

Sir   Middle Brook [N.J.] March 6th 1779
I have frequent applications from the Artificers belonging to the Army representing their disappointments and distresses.

Inclosed is one of their Petitions to me and another to Congress, which contain the substance of their grievances.[1]

The first thing complain'd of is, They have not Commissions similar to those that belong to the line of the Army. These Companies were all rais'd before I came into the Quarter Master's Department, but the Officers have never had either Commissions or Warrants to establish their authority. They think themselves entitled to Military Commissions, and found their claim on some verbal promises made them at the time they engag'd by order of the former Quarter Master General. How far the granting of Commissions to any Officers but those belonging to the Line of the Army may be consistant with the views of Congress I cannot pretend to say; notwithstanding they who claim them may be engag'd during the War, and necessary to its operations. I have printed Warrants in the stile of Commissions, which I give to all such who I appoint to any Office in the Department. These I conceive to be sufficient for all the purposes of Government. However, If The Congress thinks proper to indulge the Petitioners with Commissions it will be agreable to me.

These are a Class of Men so necessary to the operations of an Army that they cannot be done without; and little service is to be expected from any order of Men who conceive themselves to be impos'd upon and whose pay is insufficient for their support.

The second subject of grievance is, The pay of the Officers has not been rais'd in proportion to the depreciation of the Money, which those of the Privates generally have. They wish therefore to have an increase of pay equal to the depreciation of the Money, or to be furnishd with articles necessary for the support of themselves and Families, at such moderate rates as they were sold [told?] when they engag'd in the service.

Was this the only subject of their grievances I would not trouble Congress with it; as I conceive myself sufficiently authoris'd to do them that justice upon this head, that they have a right to expect, or the good of the Service may render necessary.

The third thing they complain of is, That they are not consider'd as belonging to any State and consequently cannot derive any advantages from allowances and provisions made by them for their Officers. They have made frequent applications to the different States to which they belong to partake of those provisions which are made for Battalion Officers with the Army, and for their Families at home, and have been constantly refus'd, not being considered as any part of their Quota which they are bound to furnish. This provision in the declining state of the Money is become an object of great importance.

The fourth and last thing which they consider as a grievance is, That they have not the prospect of future advantage of a Landed provision, which is made by the different States for the Battalion Officers and Soldiers, and here permit me to observe that I conceive their services so important as to render them equally entitled to the same advantages with those in the Line. The only benefit which we expect from this Class of People is from their labour; and it may be well to consider how far we may expect them to be industrious and faithful when they see the conditions of their servitude are less beneficial than another Class of Men whose fatigue and hardships are infinitely less and who is little more expos'd to danger or misfortunes.

I shall be glad of the sense of Congress upon these several matters, that I may know how to accommodate my conduct to the several subjects of complaint. In the present situation the Party are restless and uneasy for want of being inform'd of what they have to hope and expect.[2] I have the honor to be, With the greatest respect Your Excellencies Most obedient Humble Servant

NATH'EL GREENE

LS (PCC, item 155, vol. 1: 95, DNA).
1. See above, petition to NG, at the end of February.
2. NG's letter was read in Congress on 12 March and referred to a three-man committee (*JCC*, 13: 306). As seen in note at the Artificers' Petition, end of February, it was months before Congress acceded to some of their demands.

To Colonel Jeremiah Wadsworth

Dear Sir   Middle Brook [N.J.] March 6 1779

Your favor of the 24th of Feb came to hand a day or two since.

I am very sorry to find you and General Sullivan are in a fair way of renewing your trouble again, quarrel I mean.

I find you are in the gall of bitterness. Pray dont get too Angry. It will give your Enemy an unfair advantage over you. I read part of your Letter to His Excellency. He was very wroth at the measures taken at Providence. But I believe dont care to make a formal attack upon the party.[1]

I wish you had such a cool man as Mr Flint with you.[2] I am afraid of your heat and fire. Remember a good politician never gets angry but veiws every thing with as much impartiallity as if he want [wasn't] concernd.

General Sullivans Aid Major Courtland [Van Cortlandt] is here. I have just taken ocasion to hint the dispute between you and General Sullivan. He says the General has an exceeding good opinion of you; but Mr Colt[3] he thinks neglected his duty. The whole charge is leaveled against him without an intent to injure you.

Mr Joseph Webb has been with me a day or two. He is a fast friend of yours. He is gone to Philadelphia.[4]

I have enclosd you a list of Vessels taken up by Mr Sam Otis for the purpose of transporting the Rice from South Carolinia. I am in hopes there will a sufficient Number go. Mr Pettit applyd to the Committee to get orders for stoping the Vessels going to Charles Town for Rice upon the presumption that the place would be taken or the Harbour so blocked up that there would be no geting out or in. I have heard nothing further of it therefore conclude they did not agree with Mr Pettit. Things are gone too far to retract.[5]

I wish to hear from the Eastward what the voice of the people is respecting the business of our two departments, whether they think our Agents conduct their Affairs with honor, honesty, and oeconemy or whether there is high charges of Vilany and prostitution of public trust.[6]

I dare say your observations upon the currency are true; and I have no doubt of the Member of Congress makeing the remark in Weathersfield. I think he belongs at W_____[7]

I am afraid there are Members of Congress playing their old Game endeavoring to raise a popular cry against people they dare not attack openly. I was told by Col Hambleton [Alexander Hamilton] a few Nights past that more noise had been made against our Departments at Head quarters within a Week past than had been in the course of the year. Col Malcolm was there.[8] The principals are not yet included. The System is said to corrupt the Agents. This makes m⟨ suspect it springs from the fountain. However it is nothing but suspi⟨ cion and therefore I shall rest it for the present. But the moment I ca⟨ reduce it to a certainty I will leave the department.

Mrs Greene is well and desires her respectful compliments to yo⟨ and Mrs Wadsworth. Yours sinserely

N GREEN⟨

ALS (CtHi).
1. For a description of the Sullivan-Wadsworth controversy, see above, note at N⟨ to Pettit, 4 December 1778.
2. Royal Flint was assistant commissary of purchases. See above, note at NG t⟨ Flint, 3 November 1778.
3. Peter Colt, deputy commissary general of purchases for the Eastern Depart⟨ ment.
4. Joseph Webb, stepson of Silas Deane, had been actively working to secure th⟨ exchange of his brother, Col. Samuel Blachley Webb. See above, vol. 1: 258n.
5. See above, Pettit to NG, 21 February.
6. Wadsworth apparently reassured NG, with some exaggeration, that there ha⟨ been no criticism of the quartermaster department by the citizens of Connecticut. Se⟨ below, NG to Wadsworth, 20 March.
7. The delegate, as noted at Wadsworth's letter of 24 February, above, has not bee⟨ identified.
8. Col. William Malcolm, of the New York regiment that was being reorganized⟨ (Fitzpatrick, GW, 7: 93n)

From Abraham Lott

[Beverwyck, N.J., 6 March 1779. Thanks NG for the "Attention paic my Children." Lott's daughter, Cornelia, who is staying with the Greenes, "must take care not to overdo it in froliking." Wishes tc speak with NG about "a Matter lately hinted to You" by Colone⟨ Livingston.[1] ALS (NjP) 1 p.]

1. This may have been the business venture described by Col. William Smit⟨ Livingston in his letter to NG of 20 June, below.

To Nehemiah Hubbard

[Middlebrook, N.J., 7 March 1779. Answers Hubbard's letters of 1⟨ and 24 February, above. "Business of Chartering the Vessels is likel⟨ to be compleated soon."[1] Hubbard should pay Colonel Sheldon's anc George Marsh's bills. Although the bills for combs and brushes fo⟨ Sheldon's dragoons are high, they must be paid as "the Public Stand⟨ responsible." LS (RHi) 1 p.]

1. For the transporting of rice from Charleston, see above, Wadsworth to NG, ⟨ January. An example of Hubbard's agreement with shipowners is printed below, ⟨ April.

From George Washington

[Middlebrook, N.J., 8 March 1779. Has received only seven of twelve tablecloths ordered from Colonel Mitchell. Would like NG to "cause enquiry to be made at your Stores" for the missing ones. Desires NG's assistance in procuring a "sett of Queens ware" that Mitchell has been unable to supply.[1] ALS (NjMoW) 3 pp.]

1. John Mitchell, deputy quartermaster general at Philadelphia, did many personal favors for Washington, Greene, and other generals. See above, note at NG to Reed, 31 January #1.

To James Duane[1]

Sir   Middle Brook [N.J.] March 9th 1779

Inclos'd is a Coppy of a Letter addressd to His Excellency General Washington upon the subject of enlisting Waggoners during the War. He informs me He has transmitted it to the Committee of conference and waits their orders to give me an answer upon the business. Since I wrote to His Excellency I have had further accounts from different Quarters of the difficulty of procureing Waggoners, and I have made further trial upon those who are in service here, but without any success. Indeed they would not engage even for the bounty that is given to the Soldiers. The small number that we have a prospect of engaging, and the great number that will be wanted, makes me exceeding anxious to have an answer to my Letter to The General as soon as possible.[2]

For this purpose I have sent the Waggon Master General to the City,[3] from whom the Committee may have any further information that is necessary to govern their opinion with respect to the State of the Department. I have the Honor to be With great respect Your most obedient Humble Servant

NATH'EL GREENE

LS (PCC, item 155, vol. 1: 107, DNA).
1. James Duane (1733–97) of New York was one of the more industrious members of Congress. As chairman of the Committee of Conference that was appointed to meet with Washington in early 1779 and as chairman of the Treasury Board, he understood better than most delegates the problems facing the army—and especially the quartermaster department. He had been a staunch defender of Washington throughout the war and he extended his support to those close to Washington, including NG. After Gates's defeat at Camden in 1780, he was a principal advocate of giving NG the southern command, and at the end of the war, he was instrumental in having a captured British cannon inscribed to NG. (See his letter to NG of 20 October 1783, below.) A scholarly biography is Edward P. Alexander, *A Revolutionary Conservative: James Duane of New York* (New York: Columbia University Press, 1938).
2. See above, NG to Washington, 24 February.
3. James Thompson.

Deposition on the Loss of the *Friendship*

Be it known and manifest unto all whom it may concern that on the 10th day of March 1779 before one Wm Nesbitt one of the Justices assigned to keep the peace in Charlestown district in the State aforesd [South Carolina] and also a Notary public by lawful authority duely admitted and sworn, dwelling in Charlestown in said State, personally appeared Robt Craige Master of the Snow called the *friendship*, Joseph Peck and Anthony Flin marriners both belonging to said Vessell who being severally and duely Sworn on the holy Evangls of Almighty God depose that they sailed from Boston in the said Vessell on the 17th Day of Jany last past, that on 11th Feby Lat 32.57 No, Longt 78 West they were taken by the Ship *Unicorn* mounting 20 guns who sett these deponents on Shore at North Santee and these deponents arrived in Charleston on the 9th Instant.[1]

ROB CRAIGE

JOS PECK

ANTHONY FLIN

Therefore I the said Notary at the special Instance and request of the said Robt Craig did and by these presents do most solemnly protest[2] against the ship *Unicorn* on acct of seizing and takeing the said snow for all Losses damages Costs Charges and Expences hitherto sustaind or that may hereafter be sustained by reason of the grievances [?].[3]

Thus done and protested in Charlestown the day and year before written

In Testimonium Veritatis

WM NISBITT

Copy   JP and NP

1779

Cy (PPAmP). The document was enclosed in Otis & Henley to NG, 10 May, below.

1. The location given for the capture was about one hundred miles east of Charleston, toward which the vessel was bound for a cargo of rice.

2. Johnson, *Dictionary*, defines "to protest" as "to give solemn declaration of opinion or resolution" or "to give evidence of."

3. As seen in Otis & Henley's letter of 10 May, below, the value of the vessel was appraised at £ 4500. On the risks involved in bringing rice from Charleston, see note at Wadsworth to NG, 2 January.

From Major Ichabod Burnet

Sir   Newark [N.J.] 10th March 1779.

Agreeable to your request my Father[1] has purchased the Farm formerly possessed by Mr Booth containing One hundred and sixty nine Acres for which he is to give three thousand eight hundred and fifty pounds; also a small piece of woodland ajoining, containing 16 Acres for Four hundred and five pounds. There is a second piece of land of 60 Acres very contiguous to the farm, and mostly woodland which he intends to purchase.[2]

It is generally thought the farm was sold cheap, As there were but few people at the Vendue. Major Linn was almost the only person who bid for it.

I wish to know what you would have done with the place, as it will soon suffer unless the fences are repaired. There have several people applied to live on the place if you mean to have it rented.

I will ride up and view the place before my return to Camp.

If you do not chuse to have the other land purchased, please to let me know by the Bearer. I am Sir with respe[c]tfull compliments to Mrs Greene Your most Obliged humble Servt

I. BURNET

ALS (CtHi).
1. Dr. William Burnet, Sr., father of NG's aide, was a prominent physician in Newark. During the war he was active in the patriot cause, both as chairman of the Essex County Committee of Safety and as a presiding judge in the Essex County courts. Dr. Burnet also held a number of military appointments in the hospital department, including chief physician and surgeon for the Eastern Department. (*PMHB*, 3 (1879): 308–14)
2. As noted above, NG to Jay, 15 February, NG was hard pressed to find investment opportunities for his accumulating commissions.

From General George Weedon

My Dear Sir   Fredericksburg [Va.] March 10th 1779
I have not been Honored with a line from you these Several Months tho frequent Opportunities have passed this place from the Army, by whom I have understood you and lady were in health. The happiness this Intelligence affords would have been hightened by a confirmation under you[r] Own hand. And why not spare a few Minutes to gratify an old Acquaintance?[1] You have seen the Kings Speach; you have seen the Debates of the House of Commons; you are no stranger to the French Opperations in the West Indies, And I know of no one more able to judge (from Appearencies) of the British designs in America, from all of which I beg to know your Sentiments as to future events. Spain, it is said, has Acknowledged our Independence and will no doubt take an Active part with France. Great Britain (I should suppose) is pretty well drained of men and money at least too much so to engage in a war at this day, with the United Force of France, Spain and America. These considerations Added to the very small Advantages gained over us since the Commencment of the War,

make much in our favr and Ought to promise us every blessing, but on the other hand, have we improved by dear bought experience? Is our Army more formidable than Usual or is our Union, on which everything depends more General? I fear not. What can this be owing to? A House divided against it self. Parties run higher now, and are more prevalent than ever, but hope in God, that Virtue for which the American Army was ever Admired, still remains in our Camp notwithstanding the wicked efforts of some designing men who to Aggranddize themselves, and Creatures, would stop at Nothing. Is our Illusterous Genl Well? I hope his Magnanimous mind spurns at, and despises the Calumny of such Mortals as beneath his Notice, yet every grain thrown into the Oposite Scale will have a greater or lesser effect and must come into the Addition that makes against us.[2] The prices of every Necessary of life I look upon to be the most alarming Circumstance that Attends us, nor can I see how the Army is to be supplyed if the present rates keep up. Corn sells now for Twenty pounds pr Bussl, Pork £ 10, Beef £ 7.10, Flouer, £ 12 pr cwt, rum £ 4, Whiskey £ 3.10, Brown Sugar 17/ pr pound, loaf 20/ pr pound and everything else in proportion. I hope however that the late resolution of Congress, with the Taxes for the present year, will sink so much of our Money now in Circulation, as to make the rest Valuable.[3] Our Coast swarms with privateers, scarcely one Vessell in ten gets in safe, insomuch that our trade is almost totally destroyed, but for fear I should tire your patience shall refer you for other particulars to Colo Walter Stewart who has made the tour of Virginia and can Satisfy you in any thing you would wish to know respecting it. He has been some days with me, and leaves us tomorrow for Camp. He will deliver you the 4th Vol. of Enticks History[4] which was brought thro' Mistake with my Baggage, and which I never discovered till a few Weeks ago. You will I hope excuse me for such Neglect, and impute it to the right cause in my not knowing it to be in my possession when I left Camp.

Please make my most Respectfull Compliments to your little Companion who I hear has taken the field again with you. I shall expect to hear that Similar Consequences will attend her Vissit to Middle Brook, that did that of her Vissit to Vally Forge.[5] Believe me my Dear General Your Very affectionate Friend and Hbl Servt

G WEEDON

ALS (MiU-C).
   1. Weedon was on leave of absence from the army. See above, vol. 2: 362–64.
   2. No doubt Weedon had been speaking with his visitor, Col. Walter Stewart, about the "Conway Cabal" and subsequent factionalism. Stewart disliked Richard Henry Lee especially for Lee's defense of Gen. Charles Lee's actions at the Battle of Monmouth, with its implied criticism of General Washington. See above, Stewart to NG, 29 January.
   3. See note at Gooch to NG, 18 January, above.

Jeremiah Wadsworth, 1743–1804, pastel portrait by James Sharples
(Courtesy of Independence National Historical Park)

4. Probably the Reverend John Entick's *The General History of the Late War: Containing its Rise, Progress and Event, in Europe, Asia, Africa and America . . .*, a five-volume history, first published in London in 1763. Entick also wrote two other multivolume works on the British empire, both first published in the 1770s.

5. Nathanael Ray Greene was born at the end of January 1780. Their third child, Cornelia, was born after Catharine's visit to Morristown and Valley Forge in the winter of 1777–78.

To Nehemiah Hubbard

[Middlebrook, N.J., 11 March 1779. Will adopt mode that Hubbard proposes in separating the accounts of the French fleet "from the ordinary duties of the Department."[1] Regrets Hubbard's "poor success" in chartering vessels for the importation of rice. The demands of the whaleboat owners are unreasonable. Either "pay them agreeable to the Apprizement, or Return the Boats without any allowance for the use of them."[2] Will settle Mr. Huntington's accounts. LS (Beinecke Library, CtY) 1 p.]

1. See NG's circular of 17 February, above.
2. Hubbard had related his problems with the whaleboat owner in one of two letters to NG that have not been found (1 and 6 March), but NG summarizes the dispute in his second letter to Wadsworth of 19 March, below.

To John Jay, President of the Continental Congress

[Middlebrook, N.J., 11 March 1779. Has received Jay's letter of 2 March enclosing the congressional resolution on portmanteaus for officers. Wishes a "Coppy of the appointment of a Deputy Quarter Master General for South Carolina, and the Southern District" in order to send forms for returns.[1] LS (PCC, item 155, vol. 1: 115, DNA) 1 p.]

1. Undoubtedly Gen. Thomas Mifflin's appointee.

Petition of the Employees of the Quartermaster General's Department at Boston

Boston March 12, 1779

To the Honble Major General Green Quarter Master General of the Army of the United States of America

The Petition of a Number of the Officers Serving in Said Department

Humbly Sheweth, That your Petitioners have been in the Service in the Diferent Stations, and for the Lenght of time affixed against each respective Signers name and have Endeavored to give satisfaction in their several Offices, and have the satisfaction to find their

Endeavours have been approbated, and their Conduct hitherto not Reprehensible, but under the present Distressing Situation of Affairs when every species of Cloathing and Provisions are so scarce, and at so exorbitant a Price, that we find our pay inadequate, even to purchase Necessary Cloathing, and by being allowed by Congress but one Ration Per Day our Families must in the Present Situation of Affairs Absolutely Suffer, for the Necessaries of Life. We therefore are Necessitated from the Distressing reasons Above Mentioned to Entreat your Honours Interpossion, That we may have reliefe and be Enabled to Draw Cloathing from the Continental Store, as has been Allowed to the Officers on the Staff in the other Departments at reasonable prices.[1] And as in Duty bound Shall ever Pray

		months
JNO BUTTERFIELD	DWMG [Deputy Wagon	35
	[Master General]	
JONATHAN PARKER	Cond[ucto]r	23
RUFUS BENT	Do	12
JAMES PERKINS	Do	11
ROBERT BAGNALL	Do	10
WM PRICHARD	Do	8
WM PATTEN	Do	8
JAMES S LOVELL	Clk	16
WILLIAM SWETT	Clk to DQMG	20
RICHARD HUNEWELL	of Masons	32
JOSIAH WHEELER	Masr Carpen'r	44

DS (PCC, item 173, vol. 1: 25, DNA).
1. The petitioners call themselves "officers," but as wagoners, clerks, carpenters, and masons, they did not hold commissions. In his letter of 5 March, above, John Gooch advised NG that this petition would be forthcoming because of the mens' "Distressed Situation especially those that have Families." NG may very well have taken steps to obtain clothing privileges for the petitioners, but his letter to John Jay of 15 April, below, in which he asked that "staff officers" in the department be allowed to draw clothing, does not appear to refer to these men.

To Colonel Jeremiah Wadsworth

[Middlebrook, N.J., 13 March 1779. Wadsworth's account of the currency situation and prices in Connecticut "makes my blood run cold. . . . We are upon the Wheel of Fortune and must take our chance of the round of things." Provisions are costly and scarce; Virginia appears drained and the Convention troops are "in distress." William Finnie claims Colonel Aylett "has accusd him wrongfully."[1] Encloses two letters from Abraham Livingston about rice and has directed Colonel Pettit to forward money to him. "By the by money comes hard and is worth little when we get it." Does not need an auditor as Mr.

Olney is "one of the completeest accomptants I ever saw," but Biddle may need one. Biddle has just returned from Philadelphia, where, he reports, "party and faction rage in the City to a greater degree than ever. Many of the most obnoxious go secretly armd." A committee of Congress is still considering "General Arnolds affair"; the Pennsylvania Council feel slighted in their treatment by Congress.[2] ALS (CtHi) 3 pp.]

1. For background on Aylett's criticism of Finnie, see above, Finnie to NG, 11 February.
2. Charges against Arnold, which originated with the Pennsylvania Executive Council, were referred to a congressional committee. See above, note at NG to Reed, 31 January #1. The executive council subsequently became embroiled in a dispute with Congress over its handling of the affair. See below, Pettit to NG, 29 March.

To Colonel Jeremiah Wadsworth

Dear Sir   Middle Brook [N.J.] March 13 1779

I receivd your Letter of the 5th with the inclosd propositions for forming a commercial connection with you and Mr Barnabas Dean.[1]

I have such an entire confidence in your integrity and knowledge, that I submit the whole business to your direction. What ever conditions you put it upon I will accede to. It would be most agreeable to me not to be known to be in Trade and I think if it is not necessary for you to be known it will be best. We can serve Mr Dean and ourselves better in this way than if the connexion is open and avowd.

You know what a suspicious body we have to deal with and how necessary it is to appear to be free from any connexion that may lead to a misapplication of public Moneys. For let us be ever so honest they wont believe it. They have taken up an Idea that Principle lays no restraint upon a man when his interest demands a violation.

These are degradeing Sentiments to human Nature and mortifying to sensible minds; but the facts are true nevertheless that they entertain such Sentiments of all their Agents.

When you write to me upon these subjects write private on the outside of your Letter and put it under a double cover and on the outer cover direct in common form.[2] Yours affectionately

N GREENE

ALS (PHi).
1. Letter not found. The "commercial connection" between Deane, Wadsworth, and NG was made official on 4 April 1779. See Articles of Partnership, below.
2. On NG's concern for secrecy, see note at NG to Wadsworth, 14 April, below.

From Nehemiah Hubbard

[Hartford, Ct., 13 March 1779. Received NG's of 7 March. Needs cash; the wagoners under Major Skidmore "are continually calling on me for their pay." Six months teamsters are also "uneasy about their wages." They must now work "two days and a half for the price of one bushel of Indn Corn, when they formerly had three bushels for one days work."[1] Cy (RG 93, WRMS: DNA) 1 p.]

1. Nothing illustrates more graphically the social cost of inflation—especially to wage earners. It appears in retrospect that Congress had no alternative in 1779 to the printing of paper money; as Benjamin Franklin pointed out, it was also the one form of taxation that Congress could levy—albeit an involuntary one on the part of the taxpayer. Franklin also thought it a fair tax because it fell more heavily on the well-to-do, through whose hands the greatest sums of money passed. Franklin would have been hard pressed, however, to have convinced wage earners and day laborers of its fairness. In truth, it fell hardest on them because wages invariably lagged behind depreciation—usually far behind—while the well-to-do, especially merchants, were astute enough immediately to exchange their depreciating dollars for something of more intrinsic value. Most producers of scarce goods and commodities—such as manufacturers, farmers, fishermen, lumbermen—could usually price their products even higher than mere depreciation of the dollar justified. The wage earner or day laborer could seldom pass along wage increases so easily. Furthermore, since he had few reserves, he was often forced into accepting the wages offered him. (On Franklin's opinion, see Higginbotham, *War*, p. 290.) On the lag in wages for artificers, see their petition of 6 January, above.

From George Washington

[Middlebrook, N.J., 14 March 1779. He is "obliged" to weaken the post at Paramus in order to strengthen those at the Highlands.[1] Stores and provisions en route between Middlebrook and Kings Ferry should not be unnecessarily delayed lest the enemy have an opportunity "for insult or surprise."[2] Df (Washington Papers: DLC) 1 p.]

1. In a letter of 4 March from Peekskill, General McDougall reminded Washington that the enlistments of 847 men in his division would expire on April first. He added ominously that "My Spies among the Tories inform me the Enemy intend paying me a visit when the Time of service of those men expire." (Washington Papers, DLC) Fearful lest the British strike before West Point fortifications were complete, Washington ordered replacements sent to McDougall from Putnam's division in Connecticut and from the North Carolina regiment at Paramus, N.J. (Washington to McDougall, Fitzpatrick, *GW*, 14: 249–50) The British attack did not materiaiize.
2. The same letter was sent to Jeremiah Wadsworth (Fitzpatrick, *GW*, 14: 236n).

From Colonel James Abeel

[Morristown, N.J., 15 March 1779. Sends return of stores on hand in the county. In future, returns will be sent the first of every month. Is posting his "Return Book." Returns are late due to absence of principal clerk. Tent makers "go on Briskly" repairing tents; canvas is needed to keep them employed. Has made a "fine Contrivance" for washing tents and a water-powered grindstone for grinding axes. LB (NjHi) 2 pp.]

To George Washington

Sir　　　　　　　　　　　　[Middlebrook, N.J., 17–20 March 1779][1]

I have carefully looked over General Schuylers plan for an Indian expedition, and tho I think many of his observations are just, yet I am perswaded it will be attended with more risque and expence and be less certain of success, than if the Expedition is carryed on by the way of the Susquehannah.[2]

There is six great objects to be taken into consideration in the plan of the expedition. The force that is necessary, the hazzard they will run—The time for execution—The expence incident to the plan; and the certainty of execution.[3]

I think a moments reflection will convince any body that the Route by the Oneyda Lakes[4] will require a greater force and be ex-posd to more hazzards than the Susquehannah Route; besides it appears to me to be entering the Enemys country at one corner; and from the best accounts I can get, very remote from the Seneca Indians which is the principal object of the expedition.[5]

The difficulty of geting up Stores and provisions up the Mohawk River from Albany to Fort Schuyler are very considerable. The difficulty and expence of crossing into Wood Creek is also considerable. The Navigation down the Creek into Lake Oneyda is slow and tedious; and upon the whole after you have past the Lake and the Onowdago [Onondaga] River you are as remote or more so from the great body of the Senecas than you would be at Tioga.[6] The great object of the expedition should be to give the Indians a severe chastising, anything short of that will not compensate for the trouble and expence in preparing for the expedition. I have no doubt the Indians will be glad to come to terms when they see we are about to enter their Country in good earnest; but unless their pride is broke down and they sufficently humbled Little benefit will result from any Negotiations that may take place. The British will soon spirit them up to commit the same depredations again as they did the last Campaign. Therefore I think the plan of the expedition should be founded upon the principle of chastissing and humbleing the pride of the Indians and not trust to the uncertain advantages of a negotiation.

I think it will be wrong for us to take any measures with the hopes of surprising the Enemy, when those measures interfere with the main design. Our force will be too large and the movements too slow to effect a surprise upon a people who keeps such a good look-out.

The greatest objection I have to the route by the way of the Oneyda Lake is the contiguity to the Ontario. We have great reason to expect the Enemy will attempt to support the Indians. Indeed we have it from pretty good authority that reinforcements came up the Saint Lawrence last fall for the purpose. Should any considerable force be at Fort Frontenac when our Army has past the Onondago River they may easyly take post upon that River and totally cut off the Water communication and consequently the supplys of Stores and provisions. This will inevitably halt the Army to dislodge them; as it would be dangerous to push forward while the supplys were so precarious and a retreat so insecure. To halt the Army will delay the expedition and to divide the force will be too hazzarding a defeat. Therefore I think the Route ineligible, for should we dislodge the Enemy from the Banks of the Onondago they can easily retire to their Shiping and as soon as our Army attempts to move on into Indian Country they will return and play the same game over again.

The Stockade Forts altho they will considerably diminish our force, will answer no other purpose than that of giving security to stores within the command of the Works. [7]

General Schuyler proposes the Troops to move in two directions part by Land and part by Water and to form a junction at the Cayuga. The Troops that are to move by land are first to determin whether the Enemy are in force upon the Onondago before those in the Battauex moves forward. Suppose the Enemy should be found in force and our strength divided what may be the consequence of the discovery. This division appears to be without an object. If the Enemy is found in force the experiment is dangerous. If they are not in force there is nothing gaind.

The route appears to me to be long and tedious and so divided between land and Water carriage that it will require double preparations to enable the Army to move with ease and security. There should be a sufficient number of Boats for crossing the Lakes, Rivers &c. There must also be a proper number of Pack Horses sufficent to carry provision enough for the whole force after they leave the Cayuga, for such a length of Time as will be necessary to execute the plan of the expedition. This is indispensably necessary in order to execute the main design, but it will be found prudent upon another consideration, which is, supposing the Army to be defeated and the retreat cut off by the way which it enterd the Country, unless it has provisions to move with it in any direction that necessity may oblige it to take, The Troops may run the risque of starveing. I therefore conceive the number of Pack Horses proposed by General Schyler to be totally inadequate to the support and security of the Army.

I cannot think the General has allowed sufficent Time for the movements of the Army upon such a difficult Rout where the natural and physical obstructions are so great.[8] I am perswaded from common accidents it will take a third more Time at least And I should not be surprisd if the expedition should terminate with a few little brushes with the Onondagoes and Tuscaroras should it be enterd upon by the Rout the General recommends.

General Schuyler observes that the Susquehannah is a very shoal [i.e., shallow], rapid and difficult Navigation. This dont appear to be a fact from the best intelligence I have been able to obtain.

The Navigation is said to be exceeding good from Sunbury up to Tioga and from the Time you leave Sunbury until you arrive at Tioga the Navigation grows better and better.[9]

The route by the Susquehannah appears to me to be every way preferable to that which is recommended by Schuyler. The Stores can be convey'd to the borders of the Indian Country at a much less expence. The approches to the Seneca Country much less difficult and complex, the distance much shorter and the retreat infinitely more secure, in case of a defeat.

There being a greater quantity of Flour consumd upon the North River and to the Eastward of that, than that country affords. If the Expedition goes on by the way of Fort Schuyler the flour will be [have] to be transport from Pennsylvania; which will be attended with no small expence. I only mention this as a remote circumstance not as a capital objection.

Upon the whole I think the expedition may be carryed on by the way of the Susquehannah with a less force than by the other route; because the Troops may act more compactly, and there will be no necessity for leaving so many Stockaded forts in the rear for preserving the communication.

The hazard and fatigue will be less. The time shorter and the execution more certain. And when you add to this the great saving in point of expence I think there is no room to doubt which is the properest route to be made choice of.

General Schuyler proposes to alarm the fears of the people of Canada; by cuting Timber upon Lake George which will lead to a belief of an intended expedition by the way of Lake Champlain. I am perswaded he is entirely mistaken in his expectations of alarming the Enemy by such preparations; for should they be ever so fully convinced of such a design they would laugh at the scheme as impracticable.

I think the plan your Excellency has already adopted is infinitely preferable; because the Enemy knows they are vulnerable that way; and will take the alarm accordingly.

I really expect some very considerable advantages from the Coho [i.e., Co'os] Manoeuver; but from the other I should expect none; for I am perswaded it would be what the Enemy would wish.[10]

The plan which General Schuyler proposes for surprising the Onondagas I think eligible; and worth attempting. A scheme of this sort may be executed with a degree of secrecy and dispach that will give well grounded hopes for success. Should it fail, I dont apprehend any very bad consequences from it.

I give it clearly as my opinion that every farthing expence that is incurd in geting Ship timber and plank upon the North River for the purpose of building upon Lake Ontario will be totally lost; as the expence and difficulty of transportation will be greater, than that of geting it all out of the rough, upon the borders of the Lake, where it is to be had in great plenty. I am with the most perfect esteem Your Excellencys Most Obedient humble Sert[11]

NATH GREENE

ALS (Washington Papers: DLC).

1. NG did not date his letter, but Schuyler's letter to Washington, the subject of NG's comments, was written over a period of several days between the first and seventh of March. (Washington Papers, DLC) Washington did not record the date he received it, but he did note that a letter of the eighth from Schuyler arrived on the sixteenth—the normal time required for a letter from Albany to Middlebrook. (Washington made the comment in a postscript to a letter to Clinton, 16 March, Fitzpatrick, *GW*, 14: 248.) Assuming, then, that Schuyler's letter of the seventh arrived on the fifteenth and that Washington first read it carefully before handing it to NG, the earliest possible date for NG's comments would appear to be the seventeenth and the latest would be the twentieth—the day before Washington answered Schuyler. (Ibid., 14: 268–73)

2. As noted above at NG's memorandum of 1 March on the Indian expedition, Washington's unfamiliarity with the Iroquois country of New York had induced him to invite Colonels Patterson and Hooper to Middlebrook in order to confer on a proposed route by way of Pennsylvania and the Susquehanna River. A similar unfamiliarity with the route from Albany had led him two weeks earlier to query General Schuyler on that approach. (Letter of 11 February 1779, Fitzpatrick, *GW*, 14: 94–98) Few men of Washington's acquaintance were more knowledgeable about upstate New York than Schuyler—especially about those areas adjacent to the Mohawk and Seneca River valleys. In his detailed sixteen-page answer, he supplied Washington with an avalanche of facts as well as advice.

NG, like Washington, lacked a first-hand familiarity with the region, but also, like Washington, he was adept at interpreting the available maps. He had learned, moreover, a great deal about the Indian country from his conference with Robert L. Hooper, who was more knowledgeable than Schuyler about south central New York.

3. NG inadvertently omitted the sixth "object," which in the next paragraph he called the "principal object of the expedition"—namely, the chastisement of the Seneca Indians. Schuyler said the same in his letter to Washington. The Senecas' territory surrounded Seneca Lake, one of the Finger Lakes, located 150 airline miles west of Schenectady and half again as far by any practicable surface route.

4. NG undoubtedly meant to use the singular since there was only one Oneida Lake.

5. Washington had asked for Schuyler's judgment about three "suggested" routes. Schuyler gave reasons for rejecting all three. Instead, he suggested that a large contingent—perhaps 1,200 men—travel up the Mohawk River by boat to Ft. Schuyler, then portage one mile to Wood Creek, which would lead them to Oneida Lake. From the west end of the lake they would march overland to Onondaga, "which is less than thirty Miles . . . by a good Foot path and thro' a level and tolerable open Country," and thence by water to Cayuga. There they would be joined by a smaller contingent and the supply boats, which would have taken the longer and slower water route all the way.

6. Tioga was just inside Pennsylvania where the Chemung River joined the Susquehanna. It was thirty airline miles from the south end of Seneca Lake.

7. Washington had asked Schuyler whether stockade forts to protect supply magazines would be worth the time required to build them. Schuyler had recommended that stockades be built only at a few locations.

8. Schuyler estimated that it would require forty days for the army to reach Cayuga from Schenectady, twenty days to destroy the Seneca villages and return to Cayuga, and an additional twenty days to return to Schenectady, for a total of at least eighty and possibly one hundred days.

9. Schuyler was right about navigation on the upper reaches of the east branch of the Susquehanna, but NG was also right about the stretch between Sunbury and Tioga, where the rapids were fewer than downstream.

10. On 6 March, Washington had ordered Col. Moses Hazen's Canadian regiment northward to Co'os, N.H., on the upper Connecticut River as a feint to mislead the British. (Fitzpatrick, GW, 14: 204–5)

11. It is apparent that Washington incorporated NG's comments in his letter to Schuyler of 21 March. Washington was tactful in acknowledging that Schuyler had "weighty" reasons for recommending his plan, but he was frank to spell out the "considerations which upon the whole, determine me to send the main body by way of the Susquehannah." (Fitzpatrick, GW, 14: 268) The tentative plan that he shared with Schuyler was very close to the final plan of the Sullivan-Clinton expedition: 3,000 men were to approach the Senecas from the Susquehanna and Chemung rivers; some 500 were to attack "by way of the Ohio and Allegeni River"—the route that Col. Daniel Brodhead was eventually to take; and another 1,000 of New York regiments were to approach via the Mohawk. (Ibid., 14: 271) Washington did not say so but he probably envisioned that the New York regiments would take the route that he had suggested to Schuyler in his letter of 11 February and that Gen. James Clinton eventually followed in his juncture with Sullivan—namely, the Mohawk to Canajoharie and then a twenty-mile portage to Lake Otsego, the source of the east branch of the Susquehanna at the present site of Cooperstown, New York. For more on the expedition, see below, Sullivan to NG, 12 May 1779.

See Maps 1 and 3 for geographic references above.

From John Jay, President of the Continental Congress

Sir   Philadelphia March 17th 1779

Herewith enclosed are three Acts of Congress, one of the 12th Inst ordering the Return of some and Payment for the Remainder of the Goods taken from the Inhabitants of Philadelphia. Another of the 13th Inst calling for an Account of the Sale and Distribution of those Goods,[1] and a third of the 16th for enlisting Waggoners to serve during the war.[2] I have the Honor to be Sir With great Respect your most Obedient and Hble Servant

J. JAY

LB (PCC, item 14, p. 67, DNA).

1. Prior to the British evacuation of Philadelphia in June 1778, Congress had resolved that Washington should act to prevent "the removal, transfer or sale" of any goods belonging to the residents of the city until it was determined which goods had belonged to the British. (JCC, 11: 571) Accordingly, after the evacuation, General Arnold, commandant of the city, issued a proclamation calling on inhabitants having "European, East or West India goods, iron, leather, shoes, wines and provisions of

every kind, beyond the necessary use of a private family," to give an accounting of such goods so that the quartermaster, commissary, and clothier general departments could contract for them. If anyone attempted to sell or conceal merchandise, Arnold warned, their goods would be "seised and confiscated for the public use." He also asked for an accounting of public stores or effects belonging to "subjects of the King of Great Britain, or their adherents." (*Pa. Archives*, 6: 606–7)

In late July, Congress appointed a committee to work with a state committee to insure that inhabitants were equitably reimbursed for goods the army seized or contracted for and to ascertain what was the property of the British. (*JCC*, 11: 714) In October 1778, Congress asked the Board of War to supervise the appropriation of goods and to keep careful accounts of "quantity and quality, and of whom seized, or with whom contracted for." (*JCC*, 12: 1055) Not until December did the committee report back to Congress, and only after several postponements and additional petitions from financially pressed merchants over a period of several months did Congress finally act. (See *JCC*, 12: 1202, 13: 213; and PCC, item 78, vol. 15: 423, DNA.) The resolutions that Jay enclosed in the above letter were designed to remedy the petitioners' grievances. The first ordered the clothier and quartermasters general to pay the petitioners "from whom goods were taken for the public use, the current price of the same when the goods were taken." The clothier and quartermasters general were to give "a full account of the sales and distribution of the goods." (*JCC*, 13: 308–9) On 25 March (below) NG replied to Jay that he had given orders to Colonel Cox to carry the two resolves into execution. NG trusted that Cox, who had apparently been in charge of the contracts for the department in Philadelphia, would be able to give Congress a "satisfactory account of his conduct." There appears to be no further record of Cox's or NG's action on this matter.

2. NG was not entirely satisfied with the 16 March resolution on wagoners. See above, note at NG to Washington, 24 February.

From Henry Moffett

[18 March 1779. Moffett, a wagon conductor, complains that Maj. James Grier confined him "Contrary to a genl order" for neglect of duty. Moffett had been tried and acquitted.[1] Asks NG to "Interceed" with Washington to have Grier arrested for breach of general order.[2] ALS (PCC, item 173, vol. 1: 1, DNA) 1 p.]

1. Moffett's trial was held on 12 March 1779. Major Grier, of the Tenth Pennsylvania Regiment, had Moffett confined, he said, because of the "Non Attendance of the Waggoners and Teams and they not doing their Duty." After hearing testimony from Moffett and others, the court found him not guilty of the charges. (PCC, item 173, vol. 1: 5–7, DNA)

2. NG's response has not been found.

Memorandum from Colonel George Morgan[1]

[Middlebrook, N.J.?, March 18, 1779][2]

The Service has suffer'd from Want of Attention to the Water Carriage on Potomack.[3]

Six Batteaux sufficient to carry 100, or 120 Kegs of 100 lbs[?] each, and twenty Cannoes capable of carrying 30 Kegs each, should be kept on that River, for the Transportation of Stores to Skipton.

One Store House and a Coopers Shop, should be built at the

Mouth of Connecocheague, One at   s Landing on the Virginia Side and One at Skipton. Coopers should be stationd at each of those Places.

A Road may be opend from Fort Cumberland to Fort Pitt which will shorten the Distance 22 or 25 Miles in 81 [miles]. The New Road may easily be made a much better One for Waggons than the old One can be even with the same Labour and it leads through two plentifull Settlements for Forage Vizt The South End of Brothers Valley and Turkey Foot Settlement. I have directed it to be opend for Pack Horses, and to be surveyd. More than One half is already done.

The Service has sufferd, by Pack-Horse-Men, Drovers &c, employ'd by the Staff, being drafted into the Militia and heavy Fines being levied on those who did not attend the Call of the County Lieutenants.

4 Kegs of 3dy Nails wanted, to be sent to David Mitchel of Skipton. Also six Tent Cloths of 10 yds by 7____, 2000 Bags.[4]

D (PPAmP).
1. George Morgan (1743–1810), the merchant-brother of Dr. John Morgan, had served for three years as Indian agent at Ft. Pitt with the rank of colonel and also as deputy commissary of purchases for the western district. He resigned both posts later in 1779 to devote the remaining thirty years of his life to promoting scientific agriculture, first at his farm in Princeton and later near Washington, Pa. (*DAB*)
2. That Morgan was probably at camp when he wrote is indicated in NG's first letter to Wadsworth of 19 March, below. The date is determined by the docketing.
3. NG had asked Morgan's advice on improving transportation to Ft. Pitt in preparation for Brodhead's expedition against the Iroquois. (See note at Sullivan to NG, 12 May, below.) At NG's request, Morgan wrote Capt. Charles Clinton the following week, ordering him to expedite the building of the road from Cumberland to Ft. Pitt. (See Morgan to NG, 2 May, below.) For the location of place names listed in the memorandum and the suggested route to Ft. Pitt, see Map 3.
4. On the back of the memorandum NG's aide added the following: "Colo Morgan thinks that Colo Steels districts should take in Berkly, Shanodore [Shenandoah], Frederick, Hamshere [Hampshire] County's in Virginia; Washington's County westerd of the Allegany Mountains, and Maryland." Of the four counties in Virginia, all but Frederick bordered western Maryland across the Potomac.

To Colonel Jeremiah Wadsworth

Dear Sir   Middle Brook [N.J.] March 19, 1779
You may remember I told you I intended to send the President of Congress a copy of the propositions I had made to the Treasury Board as conditions of my future services. Inclosd is a copy of the Letter I wrote Mr Jay upon the subject. I did not know but he might forget the conversation he and I had; and instead of lodgeing my Letter among his private papers, lay it before Congress; therefore I put in a paragraph intimateing that I expected to be acquited of taking any unfair advantage of the publics necessity; as I had confind my demands to

the terms he approvd. This I did to stop the mouth of clamour for I think they will not dare to attack us after what has past.[1]

I wrote you in my last that Mr Flint and I was just seting out for Trenton. I went on purpose to see Mr Pettit and to learn the state of politicks in Philadelphia. Since we left that City, faction has run higher than ever. However it is subsiding a little. Col Mitchel has got into a hobble respecting the Waggons he furnished General Arnold. The whole affair is published and much to the Colonels disadvantage. The circumstances of his conduct in the enquiry appear much worse than the original transaction. Governor Read [Reed] is now in Camp; but I have had no opportunity to converse with him upon the subject yet.[2]

The Assembly of Pennsylvania have recommended it to Congress to give their officers half pay during life; and informing them at the same time if they do not, that they will.[3]

Col Morgan your deputy for the district of Fort Pitt was here to day. He refuses to act upon the usual commission. He says the business is so labourious and risky that he will not engage in it without a larger commision. He has represented the matter to Congress; and they have it now under consideration.[4]

The business of that district is so much behind hand, that I am afraid it will be difficult for us to get it forward so as to keep pace with the opening season. However I will try.[5]

I like Col Morgan exceedingly; and intend giving him a kind of general superintendance in my department as well as yours. That if the present Agents dont give him the necessary assistance in forwarding the provisions; to empower him to take such further measures as he may think the good of the service may require.

I have Letters from Mr Abraham Livingston. He says he has no money of yours in his hands; and refuses to advance as the public treated him very ungenteelly in protesting a bill he lately drew upon the Treasury for 10,000 Dollars. However he says he has charterd four or five Vessels part of which are ready to sail.[6] But I am afraid we shall have but little benefit from them as the Privateers are as thick upon the coast as grass hoppers. Livingston has drew upon me for 200,000 Dollars. I expected to have got the business done for about thirty thousand dollars.

Mr Otis of Boston informs me he has charterd the full complement of Vessels for the importation of 6000 Casks into that State. The conditions of charter and risque almost frighten me. One Schooner from the Eastward was taken on her outward bound passage. Our coast is alive with Privateers of late.[7] The Continental frigates are cruiseing for plunder instead of protecting our trade. Our Marine affairs are conducted by the maxims of good policy and sound judgment. Trade and commerce will flourish while under the auspices of such able managers.[8]

Col Sam Webb and his brother Joseph has been here for several days past. We had a little dance at my quarters a few Evenings past. His Excellency and Mrs Greene danced upwards of three hours without once siting down. Upon the whole we had a pretty little frisk. Mr Flint was at it. He is a very sensible fine fellow—few men possess greater abillitys than he does. We had a very agreeable time at Trenton, where Mr Flint had the pleasure of gazing upon the agreeable Miss Gracia Cox. Such looks and such squeezes as he gave her hand, plainly indicated his wishes.[9]

Miss Cornelia Lott and Miss Betsy Livingston is with Mrs Greene. This moment they have sent for me to drink tea. I must go. Give my compliments to Mrs Wadsworth and tell her I intend to call and see her the next time I come through Hartford. Yours affect

N GREENE

ALS (CtHi).

1. See above, NG to Jay, 15 February.

2. See above, note at NG to Reed, 31 January #1.

3. The Pennsylvania Assembly resolution on half pay was one of several resolutions designed to placate the state's Continental army officers who were complaining about their low pay and the depreciation of Continental currency. (Reed, *Reed* 2: 60–65) In May 1778 Congress had passed a resolution stating its *intent* to give officers half pay annually for seven years after the end of the war (*JCC*, 11: 502). In its resolution of 13 March 1779, the Pennsylvania Assembly voted to change the seven-year provision to run for a lifetime (*Pa. Archives*, 7: 244–45). Both NG and Washington favored a permanent pension for officers which would provide an incentive for them to continue in the service, but Congress failed to establish such a system. (See above, vol. 2: 259–61.)

4. Col. George Morgan is identified at his memorandum of 18 March, above. There is no record of congressional action on his insistence for higher commissions.

5. Archibald Steel was NG's deputy at Ft. Pitt. For the troubles that put the business in his district "behind hand," see Steel's letter of 20 February, above. Morgan was not given the "superintendance" of Steel's district as NG wrote in the next paragraph—perhaps because Morgan would not continue at the same commission.

6. Livingston was arranging for large shipments of rice as noted above, NG to Wadsworth, 2 January.

7. The British privateers were principally from New York and Halifax.

8. NG's sarcastic comment on the "good policy and sound judgment" of those responsible for marine policy reflected his frustration at the lack of American vessels to convoy the rice shipments through the enemy-infested waters.

9. Col. Samuel Blachley Webb was on parole. (See above, NG to Wadsworth, 6 March.) NG's quarters were at the Van Veghten house. Because of his limp, he seems rarely, if ever, to have danced. Royal Flint was assistant commissary of purchases under Wadsworth. Gracia Cox was one of six daughters of Col. John Cox.

To Colonel Jeremiah Wadsworth

Dear Sir   Middle Brook [N.J.] March 19, 1779

I forgot to mention in the long Letter, which I have just wrote you a circumstance respecting some Boats that was engagd last Summer in Conecticut River for the public service.

The Boats were apprais'd at the Time we took them. The owners this Winter demand a return of the Boats and pay for them at so much a day ever since we first took them; notwithstanding the Boats has not been in use one tenth part of the Time. The demand appeard to me to be so unreasonable that I gave Mr Hubbard orders to pay them the first appraisement and keep the Boats or else return them and allow nothing for their use. It is very possible their demands and my conditions are both out of the way. I wish you would enquire into the affair and direct Mr Hubbard to do what is right in the affair.[1]

Some person in the Trenton paper has given the system of the Commisary and quarter masters departments a little basteing. Chargeing the depreciation of the money to those causes. But at the same time speaks respectfully of the principals in those departments.

The piece is well wrote; but the writer is mistaken in the facts from which he makes his deductions.[2] I am with esteem and regard your most obed humble Sert

NATH GREENE

ALS (CtHi).

1. See above, 11 March, for NG's orders to Hubbard.

2. In a letter to the *New Jersey Gazette* (10 March 1779), "Caius" attributed the sudden depreciation of Continental money to the "arangements of some of the army departments." He objected to the "Quarter-Masters, Commissaries General &c" receiving commissions rather than fixed salaries because their profits would increase as the depreciation of money continued. "Caius" tempered his criticism by noting that he did "not mean to be personal, or to reflect on the Gentlemen at the head of these departments." Nevertheless, he urged substitution of "very *ample* salaries" for the present commission system. A week later, in the 17 March edition of the *Gazette*, "A True Patriot" was not so moderate in his remarks. "Here government sits as indiffrent spectators," the "True Patriot" wrote, "while Quarter-Masters and Commissaries, the unjust trader, the farmer and the mechanick, are contending for the prey; and they who get the greatest booty, are daily wallowing in dissipation, venality and luxury, at a time wherein thousands are groaning under the weight of intolerable distress." He appealed to the "community at large" for "evidence" of the truth of such misconduct, asking, "Is Congress only ignorant of these abuses, which the whole publick beholds with grief and concern?" Several months earlier, in response to similar allegations, Congress had asked the states to investigate alleged offenses in the quartermaster department, and although such investigations came to naught, criticism like that of "A True Patriot" continued to be published from time to time. (See above, notes at Marchant to NG, 5 November, NG to Bowen, 12 November 1778, and NG to Jay, 15 January 1779.)

To Jacob Greene

Dear Sir   Camp Middle Brook [N.J.] March 20 1779

I believe I shall interest my self in a 1/12 or 1/18 of Batsto Furnace. She goes into blast this Spring. My only motive is to accomodate your Iron Works. Her situation is very comodious for transporting Piggs to the Fulling Mill. A vessel that will carry 50 tuns can go up within half a mile of the Furnace; and the same you know can run up to the deep Hole at Wood Point [R.I.].

This Furnace is said to work to the most advantage of any one upon the Continent. Her stock of Wood and oar [i.e., iron ore] is inexhaustable. There is many thousand acres of Woodland that belongs to the Furnace, besides which there is a prodigious wood country for many miles round. I wish to have your opinion upon the subject. The mettle is said to be very good, but not equal to Livingstons or Sallisburys.[1]

I wrote Griffin a hasty Letter informing him, that there was an offer for his Wine of 14 Dollars a Gallon; and that he was at liberty to take or refuse it. I wish him to answer Col Biddl[e] upon the subject as soon as possible.[2] Wines are very high now in Philadelphia and upon the rise as is almost every thing else. If I was in your place I would not keep any large sums of money lying by me.

I have sent forward your Razors; whether they will ever reach you is very uncertain as they have been so unfortunate. I intended to have sent them by your Express; but by mistake they were neglected. George put them up by mistake and I never found they were with me until about three Weeks since. If they get back to you safe by mistake I shall be happy.

Mrs Greene is well and happy and desires her kind love to you and Mrs Greene.

My love to all friends. Yours affect

N GREENE

ALS (OMC).
1. NG did purchase a share in the Batsto Furnace, as did his assistants, Pettit and Cox. In a letter to Pettit on 10 May, below, NG had decided on two twelfths as his share, but in the end, Joseph Ball kept nine twelfths and sold Greene, Pettit, and Cox one twelfth each. (Pierce, *Iron in the Pines*, p. 128) Although one of his motives may have been to "accomodate" Jacob's iron works, it was not the only one. There is no evidence, in fact, that Jacob ever received iron from Batsto. NG's principal motive, it would appear (as noted at NG to John Jay of 15 February, above), was as an investment for his accumulating commissions.

The investment was undoubtedly urged on Greene and Pettit by John Cox, who had been sole owner of Batsto furnace from 1773 until he sold it to Joseph Ball in 1778, shortly after accepting the post as NG's assistant. (See above, NG to Cox, 25 November 1778.) Batsto, which had operated since 1766, was one of several iron works in the Pine Barrens of southern New Jersey, where bog iron, firewood, and waterpower were plentiful. It was located along the Batsto River, a branch of the Mullica River, which emptied into Little Egg Harbor thirty miles to the east. Under Cox's proprietorship the furnace had turned out a great variety of cast iron, including, after 1775, such items for the army as camp kettles, stoves, cannon balls, and shot. Although the furnace continued to operate throughout the war, from later evidence it appears that NG's investment was never very profitable.

For full accounts of the furnace see Pierce, *Iron in the Pines*, pp. 117–55, and Boyer, *Early Forges*, pp. 174–90.
2. See above, 4 March.

To Colonel Jeremiah Wadsworth

Dear Sir   Camp Middle Brook [N.J.] March 20th 1779

Your favor of the 15 of this instant, this moment came to hand.[1]

There being an Express ready to set off for Hartford I have only time to acknowledge the receipt.

I like the Letter you wrote to the General.[2] The language is manly and firm; and at the same [time] shews a proper disposition for peace and good fellowship.

What you say respecting the Department over which I preside I am very happy to hear. If the great public approves our conduct the Gentry at Philadelphia dare not do otherwise. However I wish I was well out of the troublesome business. I have told the General [Washington] sometime since that if there was any dissatisfaction either with him or the Congress, I should be happy to leave the business.

I dont think there will be any want of Vessels to transport the Rice from South Carolinia. My best regards to Mrs Wadsworth. Yours affy

NATH GREENE

ALS (MiU-C).

1. Letter not found.

2. Wadsworth's letter was to General Sullivan. On their dispute, see above, note at NG to Pettit, 4 December 1778.

From Colonel Charles Pettit

Dear Sir   Philada 20 March 1779

In my Absence Mr Faucet, whom I had appointed to attend as Qr Master to Genl Pulaskie's Legion, returned a second Time, having, by the General's order deposited the Money given him (execpt near 1000 Dollars he had expended) with Col. [David] Grier ADQMG at York Town [Pa.]. The Count [Pulaski] demanded 18 Waggons. The Board of War had limited him to 12. This order being shewn him the Count became enraged. Faucet returned frighted and would not consent to renew the Charge. I have therefore, on the Recommendation of the Board of War, appointed Capt Paschkee[1] to the Office and have just drawn up his Instructions and the Letters to Count Pulaskie and Col. Grier. I have been obliged to agree to allow him 80 Dollars per mo. besides his travelling Expences, for the Service of Qur Master and Forage Master which he calls double Duty. I had intended 60, but as he stickled for 90, Col. Cox stepped in as umpire and fixed it at 80. I wish this Corps were safely under the Care of Genl Lincoln. The Board of War as well as we I believe are heartily sick of them.[2]

Before this you will have had an Opport'y of seeing Govr Reed and perhaps have had an Opport'y of conversing with him. Such a

Conversation may not be unuseful both to you and him. To you, as it will give you Information of the Views, Designs, Suspicions, Apprehensions &c of the Government here; and to him as you will thereby have an Opportunity of giving him some Hints which they may profit by. He is a Man of Wisdom and a good deal of Knowledge of Mankind and of the Affairs of Government; but he is not entirely exempted from the Passions and Prejudices which designate the Frailty of Man. He means to do right, and I believe aims at it in all his publick Conduct, and of course has not a favourable Opinion of any thing that opposes him.

People in such a Situation are apt to think the Actions and Opinions of others should run in the same Channel with their own, and that wherever they deviate they must of course fall into Error. Impatient of Contradiction and fretted by Opposition, they are apt to think Measures necessary for the vindication of their own Honour which in a cooler Moment, as in others in a like Situation, they would think more prudently avoided. They are apt to consider their [view?] as the grand object of pursuit to which all others [must?] give Way; and of course they sometimes expect Compliance from their Friends without duly considering the Embarrassments they would occasion, or that one of the greatest Arts in Government is *the not governing too much*. These are general Reflections on the Subject; but they are not unapplicable to most of the Government [I have?] been acquainted with, especially in the Hands of [those?] not long accustomed to the Trade. My Situation [here?] is not a little embarrassing—On the one hand more perhaps may be expected from me by some, on account of my Connections, than might be proper for me to comply with; and on the other, this Apprehension may possibly make me too cautious of rendering what, in other Circumstances, I should find no difficulty in. In general I have little to do with the affairs of this Government; but I have mentioned to you some Characters in our Employ which they (the Persons in Power) wish out of it, and I find a growing Opinion that we do not wish to see their Faults disclosed nor to pursue the Means of Enquiry into [damaged] with respect to myself, I feel as an unjust imputation [damaged] in general as applied to these particular Characters, to which I am sure I have no undue Attachment.[3]

I am informed Pains are taking in the Country to get Signers to the *Republican Society*, and I am not without Apprehensions that some of our People may be unwarily drawn into it. I have therefore been consulting Col. Cox on the Propriety of writing a circular Letter to the Deputies in this State to guard them against [acting?] in any Measures of the kind. He approves it; but [says?] it would come best from you; or at least that if I were to do it I should say it was by your Desire. As Col Cox will be with you the Affair can be discussed between you; but if it is deemed proper, no Time should be lost or it may be too late for this Occasion.[4]

As I write to you on these Subjects as freely as I think, and often give you the unpremeditated thoughts of the moment in which I am writing, it may be prudent that my Letters of this kind should meet no Eye but yours or such as you may think proper on good Reasons to expose them to, that is, that they should not be left open to those who may occasionally see our ordinary Letters of Business. These free Communications between you and your Assistants are necessary to that clear understanding of each others minds even in matters of small moment which is requisite in the course of our official Business, in order to preserve an uniformity of Conduct; and on that account I wish to lay my mind fully and fairly before you that you may correct my Opinions by yours, and yours by mine as you find either ought[?] to prevail over the other.

Col. Cox has sent you one of the printed Copies of the publication of the Council respecting Genl Arnold in which Mr Mitchell [stands in a?] light not the most favourable. He thinks he is placed in a [worse] light than he deserves and seems to have a mind to mend it by some Publication of his own. The colouring, as it now stands in the Council's observations upon the Facts relative to the Book, may be rather high; but I am apprehensive he would not gain much by a publication. On the present footing the Composition will read with a view principally to other Objects and he will by most Readers be little thought on. When the Piece has had its Round in a small Circle, it will die away and be forgotten. If he goes to publishing he immediatly draws the attention of the multitude to his particular part of the Transaction and raises up a spirit of Enquiry concerning Facts which at best are not favourable to his Reputation. It will gain him no new Friends and may fix against him many who now stand indifferent or think nothing about it. The Council I am persuaded would be gratified if he should resign his office. That, however, is a Step that I cannot hint to him, as well because it is worth his keeping, as because, if he stood as fair with the People and their Representatives as he does with me, I know of no Person who would execute the Office better if so well. But I am not without my Apprehensions that they will make Business troublesome both to him and us as long as he continues in it. On this account, merely, if he were to propose resigning I would not dissuade him. On the whole I know not what advice to give him unless it be to be quiet and more guarded in future; and yet it seems but a natural Consequence of his Feelings that he should be anxious to struggle to get out of a Situation in which he must be uneasy.[5] Col. Cox will be with you to consult on these and other matters and on that account I say the less upon Business.

Mr Biddle has this Day shewn me a Resolution of Congress of the 5th Instant which seems to call upon us to pay off the old accounts of the Department. This is the first I have seen or heard of it; but as he tells me he has sent some Copies to Camp you have probably seen it. It may perhaps be proper to give some Instructions to the Deputies about it; and amongst other Things they must be instructed to keep the Accounts separate, as there is but 1/2 per Cent allowed to them and us [to do] the Business.[6] I am, with Respectfull Compliments to Mrs Greene Dr Sir your most obedt Servt

CHAS PETTIT

ALS (NjR) Portions damaged.
    1. Frederick Paschke, a lieutenant in the Polish army, came to the United States in 1776. He served in the Continental army as captain and quartermaster in Pulaski's Legion, remaining in the South as DQM under deKalb, Gates, and later, NG (JCC, 17: 431; PCC, item 41, vol. 8: 201–2, DNA).
    2. See note at Pettit to NG, 10 and 11 February, above.
    3. Pettit is probably referring to Mifflin appointees.
    4. The Republican Society, a loose-knit group of "Republicans," represented the conservative faction in Pennsylvania politics. (See above, note at Reed to NG, 5 November 1778.) In the Pennsylvania Gazette of 24 March, the Republican Society published an appeal "To the Citizens of Pennsylvania" signed by eighty-one men, setting forth their several objections to the state constitution. Among the signers were such Continental army staff officers as Clothier General James Mease, Deputy Commissary of Purchases Ephraim Blaine, and Superintendent of the Boat Department Benjamin Eyre. This overt intrusion of Continental staff officers into state politics, coupled with allegations that deputy quartermasters were involved in electoral politics (Reed to NG, above, 5 November 1778) prompted NG to issue a circular letter to his Pennsylvania deputies on 26 March (below) warning them against entanglement in the factional politics of the state.
    5. As noted above at Pettit to NG, 25 February, Mitchell, NG's deputy in Philadelphia, had apparently altered an entry in his memorandum book after the Pennsylvania Council had begun an investigation of his conduct in supplying public wagons for General Arnold's private use.
    6. The congressional resolution established a system of certificates, reimbursements, and commissions for articles contracted for by the quartermaster department. (JCC, 13: 277–79)

To Moore Furman

[Camp Middlebrook, N.J., 22 March 1779. Requests returns of stores, equipment, and persons hired by month in his district, one copy for Washington and one for Congress. Excerpt from Thomas F. Madigan Catalog (November 1928, Item 96)]

From Colonel John Davis

[Carlisle, Pa., 22 March 1779. Has sent returns of stores and "Abstracts" of cash expended; will continue to send them on a regular basis. Forage "is Got to A most Enormous price and Exceedingly

Scarce." Horses that NG ordered sent are "so Reduced and so Verry Poor" that many will be unfit for service until the end of May. Cy (Davis Papers: DLC) 1 p.]

To George Washington

[Middlebrook, N.J., 24 March 1779. In a letter almost identical to the one he would send to John Jay the following day, NG itemized his objections to the congressional resolution of 16 March concerning wagoners and asked for Washington's "instructions upon the business as early as possible."[1] LS (Washington Papers: DLC) 4 pp.]

1. NG had written Washington one month before about the absolute necessity of taking measures to recruit capable wagoners. See above, letter and note of 24 February, to Washington.

From General Alexander McDougall

My Dear Sir   Head Quarters Peeks Kill [N.Y.] March 24th 1779
    Your Favor of the 11th Ultimo reach'd me in due Time. But I have been so nailed to the Chair and Table I have not had Time to acknowlege it as I could wish, nor even now to do it.
    The Grand Army left me almost on bare Creation. I had to make Brick without straw. Every thing was Confusion. The Department had been so long without an Overseer, and every man his own master, that all was a perfect Chaos, If any thing can be called so.[1] Your Department was in the best state. I feared when Colonel Hughes left it, none would be found to fill his place. I think I was mistaken.[2] The Detention of Intrenching Tools was a Mistake. Nothing of the Kind was done. A Number of pick axes were much wanted at Kings Ferry; it was ordered to detain there as many as we could replace at Fish Kill, agreeable to Colonel Hay's Return of them. The rest, if detained must have been owing to want of Carriages, and not to any Order of mine. However, five Hundred Picks are wanted at the Post.
    What Don Quixot Scheme is it, that is in agitation to the North? Who are the projectors?[3] It gives me great pleasure to hear that Fabius Maximus[4] had so much Respect paid him in Philadelphia, but I am sorry to hear of the dissipated Manners of that Capital. It "augars" ill to America. Can the Country expect Spartan Virtue in her Army, while the people are wallowing in all the luxury of Rome in her declining state? If they do they are Novices in the Science of human Nature. Recluses and Enthusiasts may vainly flatter themselves with democratical Constitutions on paper, But the present Manners and forms of Government will not long exist together. They must and will lose their Energy. The Consequence is obvious.

From what I experiencd in the little Congress of New York, wherever a Supreme Council such as Congress aim to do every thing, very little will be done. They should lay out such parts of the Business, as do not require solemn Deliberation; and let the persons or different Boards answer for their Conduct with their Heads. The works at West Point are greatly retarded for want of Carpenters. I beg you will send on what can be spared. The Bomb proofs require so much Labor in framing that we make but slow progress, as there are many other pressing Calls for men in that Line. I have never been so hard pressed, in any period of my Life, from Revellie to Tattoo. I have lived a truly spartan Life since I sat down here. But this is not painfull to me. Matters now are near being in Train. I fear with you our Affairs in Georgia will be unprosperous, till the People recover from their Panick. What is the last authentic News from thence?[5] What is Congress, or the Army, doing with General Arnold?[6] Our Alliance with France is a natural one because it has for it's Basis mutual Interest; and neither of the Parties can have any important Temptation to recede from it. But I own to you, my Expectations from that quarter, are not so great or sanguine as that of many others. America must under God rely on herself. If all the Foreign powers of Europe were to accede to our Independency, they will not pay our Debts, or restore our Currency, the want of which will keep us in a languid State.

I cannot now add, but Mrs MacDougall's Compliments and mine to your Lady. I am your affectionate Friend and humble servant

ALEX: M'DOUGALL

LS (PPAmP).
1. McDougall was in command of the New York Highlands. See note at NG to McDougall, 11 February, above.
2. Col. Hugh Hughes had refused reappointment as deputy quartermaster after NG assumed command of the department in March 1778. See above, vol. 2: 329n.
3. The "Don Quixot Scheme" to which McDougall refers was the Canadian expedition, which had not been entirely abandoned by Washington and Congress. See above, NG to Morgan Lewis, 10 February.
4. George Washington.
5. See note at NG to Sullivan, 26 January, above.
6. See note at NG to Reed, 31 January #1, above.

To John Jay, President of the Continental Congress

Sir   Middle Brook [N.J.] March 25, 1779
Your Excellency's favour of the 17th of this Instant, with the three inclosed Acts of Congress, I have had the honor of receiving.

I have given the necessary orders to Colo Cox for carrying into execution the two Resolves of Congress respecting the goods taken from the Inhabitants of Philadelphia for the use of the Quarter Masters Department, after the Enemy left it last Spring. He transacted the whole of that business, and I trust will be able to give Congress a satisfactory account of his conduct.[1]

I am sorry to find the other Resolution of Congress respecting the Waggoners is put upon a footing which I fear will defeat its intention. The wages of the Waggoners is fixed at £ 10 per Month. I am persuaded that not a single man can be enlisted for this pay, if the bounty and perquisites were three times as large as they are. In my Letter of the 24th Feby to His Excellency General Washington, I recommended the giving the same Wages to those who enlisted dureing the War, as others might be hired for upon Annual service, with equal perquisites except the bounty. I am confident these are the only conditions upon which they can be induc'd to enlist.

In the fluctuating state of our money, the people will not engage for any length of time, unless the conditions of their pay is left to be govern'd by the state of the currency. To attempt therefore to enlist Waggoners upon the present state of the Resolution will only incur a fruitless expence and produce nothing but distress and disappointment to the Department. But if it was practicable to carry it into execution upon the present conditions, it still would be exceptionable, provided the money should ever appreciate to its original value or any thing near it while the War lasts. Their pay as it is now stated would be much higher than others might be hired upon. This would lay us under the necessity of dismissing them before the period of time for which they enlisted, or of continuing them upon pay much above the value of their services, or for what others might be procur'd to do the same duty.

Could we but enlist near a sufficient number of Waggoners to serve during the War, we could almost regulate the pay as we pleas'd, but while we are oblig'd to engage people upon the spur of occasion, they will ever take advantage of the public's necessity.

I wish I could flatter the Congress with the least hopes of success upon the present standing of the Resolve, but I have the fullest evidence that no terms short of those which I recommended to the General will answer the purpose.[2]

There is another part of the Resolve which appears impracticable to be carried into execution, but in a way which would be more expensive than useful. The Employment of Waggoners is so various, and generally so detach'd, that to have them Mustered and paid in the way directed, there must be as many Deputies as there are Divisions of the Army with which they may serve.

The mode which we have hitherto pursued is to have all the Waggoners Names Register'd in the Waggon Master General's Office, and the time and conditions upon which they were enlisted. The

Abstracts for payment are made out by the Waggon Conductors and presented at the Waggon Master General's Office for inspection. He upon finding them right gives an order upon the Abstract on the Quarter Master for payment. In the Quarter Master's Office the Abstracts undergo another examination by the Auditor of Accounts, who compares them with the former Abstracts and passes them for payment, upon being found just and proper. This I think to be the most eligible mode in the order of business, equally safe to the public Interest, and best accommodated to the payment of the Waggoners.

In the seperate Divisions of the Army, the same mode is pursued, and Returns made from the Depy Wagn Mast Genls Office to the Waggon Master Genl's.

It frequently happens in the course of the Winter that the Conductors and Waggoners are sent out into the Country for the purpose of recruiting their Cattle, and continue from the Army some Months, which would prevent their being Muster'd and paid in the way propos'd. While they are out on this service, the Conductors make weekly Returns to the Waggon Master General of the state of their Waggoners which serves as a check to their Pay Abstracts that may follow.

I am now endeavouring to form Blank-weekly Returns for the Waggon Department, which I hope will put this business upon the most regular and perfect footing of any that can be adopted.

Returns may be made from the Waggon Master Genls Office to the War Office, either Weekly or Monthly, as the nature of the service may admit.

It has been almost impossible to obtain Returns from the diff'rent branches of the Quarter Master's Department for want of the necessary Forms to direct the Agents in the business. This I am endeavouring to compleat and flatter myself, the Agents in future will be able to make regular returns once a month.

It was so late in the Season last Year, before I enter'd upon the business of the Quarter Master's Department, and finding it naked, distress'd, and in a state of confusion, The wants of the Army numerous and pressing, The business multiform and complex, Myself and the two Gentlemen my Assistants in a great degree strangers to the oeconomy of it, that I have never had either leisure or opportunity to digest it into such form and order as I could wish: and as I conceive, necessary for the just information of Congress, and for my own convenience, ease, and security. I have the honor to be Your Excellency's Most obedient And very humble Servant

NATHL GREENE

LS (PCC, item 155, vol. 1: 119, DNA).
	1. See above, note at Jay to NG, 17 March.

2. NG eventually succeeded in convincing Congress of the need for better pay and benefits to attract enough able men to the wagon corps. See above, note at NG to Washington, 24 February.

To Colonel Jeremiah Wadsworth

Dear Sir   Camp Middle Brook [N.J.] March 25th 1779
I receivd your agreeable Letter of the 19th.[1]

General Sullivan I find has turnd Lawyer again. I wonder what fee he had. Methinks he has gave a fine opening for some satirical pen. Suppose the Enemy had surprisd his post while he was playing the Cicero in Conecticut.[2]

I am sorry he interests himself so deeply in that affair, and still more so that he gives his tongue a latitude of reflection.

I intend to write him upon the general state of the Staff; of the difficulty of transacting the public business under the present embarassments; of the necessity of the Lines giving all the support in their power to the Staff, and the consequences that will follow from a want of it.

How is it possible for us to support the burden of our Departments if the General Officers adds to our difficulties. Such should extend their veiws farther than their own Posts. The question is not whether I can be supported here or there; but whether the system can be upheld.

Few men are as considerate as they ought to be. Private envy, and public slander mixes too freely with all public transactions. In the State of New York I find there has been some very illiberal attacks made upon the General Staff of your Department and mine. It is answerd I believe by Col Hay with great spirit and good sense.[3] General charges are always illiberal and ungenerous—The Child of Ignorance and ill Nature. The Public good is commonly the ostensible object while the secret veiws of party cabal and private interest are the leading motives. The public is often dupd in this way by designing men. I think it may be fairly provd that this policy is well calculated to serve the Tory interest and to distress the common cause. What can be more injurious to the public interest than the loss of confidence in the public officers? What more ungenerous than to punnish the innocent with the guilty? What more savage than murdering ninety nine good men for the sake of punnishing one Vilian? Are not all these principles and measures calculated to serve the Tory interest? and are they not the genuine offspring of a Tory disposition?

He that knows of any abuse of public trust and dont expose the persons is both a knave and a coward. The opportunity of knowing fixes the obligation for discovery. For how can viliany be detected unless it is known? How can the public expect to be faithfully servd when the virtues of the good and the vices of the bad are all coupled indiscriminately together?

General charges throws down all distinction of charactors. It destroys half the motives to virtue as well as gives many to those of Vice. The question is not whether the Departments are free from error; but whether the faults are as few as is to be expected from the natural disposition of mankind and the state of the business.

In such extensive, multiform, and complex transactions as ours, can it be thought extraordinary where so many are necessary to keep the wheels in motion, that a few should prove rascals.

There is a great overhawling in Philadelphia respecting the Goods taken last Spring. It is thought the Clothier General will appear rather in dark colours upon the enquiry.[4]

Mrs Greene is well and hearty. We are going to have a little hop at Pluckemin on the 30th of this month. Miss Cornelia Lot wants a partner. What a pity it is you are not here.

Please to present my and Mrs Greenes compliments to Mrs Wadsworth.

I have not seen Mr Flint for several Days. Yours sincerely

N GREENE

ALS (CtHi).
1. Letter not found.
2. On Wadsworth's dispute with Sullivan, see above, Pettit to NG, 4 December 1778.
3. Hay had answered critics in two letters, signed QUARTERMASTER, which were printed in the *New-York Journal*, 8 February and 15 March. See note at NG to Wadsworth, 14 May, below.
4. The reference is to goods taken by the army in the summer, not the spring, of 1778. See note at Jay to NG, 17 March, above. James Mease, the clothier general, was not the target of the inquiry.

Circular to Deputy Quartermasters General in Pennsylvania[1]

Sir   Middle Brook [N.J.] March 26 [17]79

The party, faction and cabal that has so long prevail'd in the State of Pensylvania against the present constitution has no doubt fix'd its partisans for and against it. I know not a more dangerous situation than that of falling into the Current of Party. People thus circumstanc'd are very apt to forsake the directing principles of equal justice which are so necessary to guide them thro the various duties of real life, and follow the particular views of party without regarding whom or what it effects upon the fair, just and generous principles of common right. He, who is under the influence of this temper, is an unfit Agent for public trust; he is not only incapable of an impartial line of conduct from his own feelings; but must naturally expect that every clog and embarrassment however detrimental to the public that will either serve to sink his reputation, or work his ruin, will be thrown in his way by the opposite party.

I have carefully attended to the politicks of that State, and think I may venture to speak with certainty, that the constitution has been gradually gaining ground from first to last. The firm footing which it now appears to have got in the minds of the people, induces me to think it but a folly to oppose its progress. But supposing the fate of the constitution was not yet decided and the minds of the people balancing for and against it, yet I think every public officer, from reasons of policy as well as a regard to the public interest should stand aloof, unconnected with either. It is both unlawful, as it respects the state, and unjust, as it concerns the public, to exercise any Official influence to effect any revolutions, or changes in government; which is nothing less than endeavouring to give an improper bias to the free sentiments of the people. This I conceive to be unlawful as it respects the state, unjust as it concerns the government, by mingling private politicks with public transactions, and improving powers for one purpose that were Delegated for another.

In the present conjuncture of affairs, when Money has but a feeble influence, when the supplies for the Army are scarce and difficult to be got, when public emergencies are too great for the powers of Office, and the influence of government necessary for its aid, both public and private policy point out the necessity of standing upon a friendly footing with those in power, and I think it but a piece of justice due to the interest of the Public (let your private sentiments be what they may) to observe such a line of conduct, while in Office, as may be best calculated to influence government to give you the necessary support. What hopes can a person have of discharging the duties of his Office with reputation to himself and to the satisfaction of the public, when he has not only to combat the difficulties that are incidental to the business, but to stem the stream of public resentment?

I am persuaded that it will be both for your interest and ease, as well as for the public advantage, to follow the line of conduct which I have pointed out. But for fear that the influence of party, or motives of private resentment, should propel you to a contrary conduct, I take the liberty of enjoying [enjoining] it upon you as well from a regard for your own reputation, as that of the public wellfare. I think my own character so much at stake as a private Gentleman and public Officer, and so intimately connected with every Agent employed under me, that both private policy and the public good render'd the foregoing precautions necessary, which I hope you will conform to, as well from duty as inclination.² I am, with esteem and regard Your most Obedient humble Serv

N GREENE

DfS (PCC, item 173, vol. 2: 53, DNA).
 1. The circular was sent to John Mitchell, John Davis, Cornelius Sheriff, Archibald Steel, Robert Patton, Jacob Morgan, Robert L. Hooper, Jr., and George Ross, Jr. In his letter of 20 March, above, Pettit had suggested that NG send such a circular. See the note at that letter. For an overview of Pennsylvania politics during this period, see above, Reed to NG, 5 November 1778.
 2. NG's unwillingness to have his deputies or himself become involved in the intricacies and machinations of Pennsylvania politics derived in part from the fact that he and Pettit had friends in both the radical and conservative camps and in part because such involvement was bound to weaken the quartermaster department at a time when he was desperately trying to round up supplies for the impending Indian expedition. But beyond such considerations was the fact that NG was opposed in principle to anything that threatened the usurpation of civil government by the military.

To Moore Furman

[Camp Middlebrook, N.J., 27 March 1779. Regrets impending loss of the "Country Teams" and directs that up to twenty-five Continental teams be provided to "supply their places." Notes that there is a great need to transport flour before country teams leave or the army will be "pinched by and by." ALS (Nj) 3 pp.]

To Griffin Greene

Dear Sir   Camp Middle Brook [N.J.] March 27 1779
    In yours of the 13th you inform me that you have got the writings nearly completed for the Division of the brothers interest.¹ If the original Deeds had been filled up in my Name sent forward by the Expresses, I could have signd them and sent them back again in the course of a fortnight at farthest. But as you have got the writings drawn in another way, I will give you any powers necessary to execute them upon that plan.²
    We have nothing new to inform you; but are in hourly expectation of some interesting intelligence from Europe and the West Indies.
    Money is rather upon the decline yet. The South Sea bubble which the Congress held up as having receivd great and glorious news has greatly injurd its credit.³ People were in expectation of some interesting events which was to put the Money upon a good footing; but when they found they were deceivd they thought the Money was upon a worse footing than it really was.
    Little artifice never produces any solid advantages to the party.
    Mrs Greene is well and desires her kind love to you and Sally.
    The Express is just going. I have not Time to add. Yours aff

N GREENE

ALS (OMC).
1. Letter not found.
2. On the division of his father's estate and NG's granting to Griffin Greene the power of attorney, see above, vol. 2: 73, 332–33, and below, NG to Griffin Greene, 30 April, and Indenture of 10 June, below.
3. He undoubtedly refers to the rumors of a Spanish alliance. See above, Pettit to NG, 15 February.

To Jacob Greene

Dear Sir   Camp Middle Brook [N.J.] March 27, 1779
I wrote you a few Days since respecting a bargain that I was about to make for Batsto Furnace.[1] I am not certain yet whether I shall be interested as I have had no certain intelligence upon the subject. I wish to have your opinion upon the measure and at the same time dont let any body know any thing about it but your self and Cousin Griffin. It will only serve to raise the spight and envy of those who dont wish me well. Keep it a secret from all the brothers; and particularly from old Aunt Cate.[2] It is not only necessary to be honest; but it is necessary to give no grounds for suspicion. Altho I have carefully avoided drawing out of the public funds more money than I am justly entitled to from the commissions arising upon the business, yet if it was to be known that I was making any purchases, it would be thought there was a misapplication of public Moneys.

You mentioned an intention of purchaseing out Uncle Johns part of the Iron Works; perhaps this other purchase may cooperate with your veiws. Iron is now selling for between seven and Eight hundred pounds a tun.[3]

Mrs Greene is well and George. I have not time to add. Yours

N GREENE

My love to Mother, Sister Peggy, Nancy Littlefield and all friends.

ALS (MWA).
1. See his letter to Jacob of 20 March, above.
2. Catharine Ray Greene, the aunt of NG's wife.
3. In depreciated dollars.

From Colonel Jeremiah Wadsworth

Dear Sir   Hartford [Conn.] March 27th 1779
Your several favours came to hand last Evening. Your letter to the President was well judged and I believe has puzled the *Jesuites*.[1] The Origin of all the Clamors was from *them*. Mr Livingston I fear has an Idea of keeping Money in his hands in Case of Loss of Vessels he Charters, at Sea, he hints such a thing in a late Letter to me.[2] If he has omitted to make the Purchases of Rice and kept Money in hand on

that acct: he has done Wrong and his being ill used by Congress is not a sufficient cause for so doing.

Your description of the happiness you enjoy at Cam[p] is pleasing. Your opinion of Mr Flint is pleasing to me. I know it is well founded. He has great Merrit and I hope to see him Com Gen.[3] I am glad to hear Miss C---'s [Gracia Cox] fine Eyes had such an effect on him. He will be better Company after he has been two or three times in Love.

I find Money does not come as I expected. I am hard pushed for Cash and if it grows worse and looses Credit as fast for a month to come, as it has the last month, I dont think it will be worth the transportation. I intend to come to Camp as soon as I can put my affairs in such a train that I can leave them. My business in Virginia is going wrong, and at Phila'a it dont go at all. What in the Name of God wou'd Hazens Regiment be sent this way for without the least previous notice; they will be in two days at Simsbury, not a Pound of flour or Bread Provided.[4] If I had the power of Creating Bread it might do to be Com Gen [Commissary General] but as it is I must Starve somebody.

Mrs Wadsworth joins me in sincere regards to Your self and Mrs Green. I shall finish the Affair with B[arnabas] D[eane] in all Next Week and send You a Copy.[5] I am Dear Sir Yours Sincerely

JERE WADSWORTH

ALS (CtHWa at CtHi).
1. See above, NG to Jay, 25 March. Chester M. Destler in his "Wadsworth," p. 99, believes that one of the leading "Jesuites" was Roger Sherman, a delegate from Connecticut.
2. See above, Abraham Livingston to NG, 10 February.
3. Wadsworth favored Flint as his successor if Congress had accepted Wadsworth's resignation.
4. On 6 March 1779, Washington had ordered Moses Hazen's "Canadian" regiment from Middlebrook to Co'os near Simsbury, as a feint in preparation for the proposed Indian expedition. (See Map 2 and NG to Washington, 17–20 March, above.)
5. See below, Articles of Partnership between Wadsworth, NG, and Barnabas Deane, 4 April.

From Nehemiah Hubbard

Sir   Hartford [Conn.] March 28th 1779
I have recd 1980 Dollars from Colo Pettit per the hand of Rich'd Skinner, but it was not Sufficient to pay my debts. The expenses of transportation is amazing. I have flour to transport from the North River to Providence. In this extreme bad season am obliged to pay 15/s per ton per mile and cannot get it transported under. I am also obliged to keep a large number of Six Months Teams for Genl Putnam's Division [at Danbury] and to transport flour to Providence

which is a very Considerable expense. According to my calculation I shall want 300,000 Dollars for the ensuing two months for use of the Quarter Masters Department and 200,000 Dollars in the Forage Department, of which I have informed Colo Biddle. I cannot possibly transport provisions without money to pay the teamsters immediately after they have done the work. I cannot impress teams in the greatest distress without depositing the money with the Justice. Must request you to send me a supply as soon as possible as the people are very unwilling to trust the public [i.e., the government], on account of daily rise of every article of Country produce or labor.

The bearer Richard Skinner informs me he has an appointment from you as express rider but I have never been able to procure a sight of it tho I've often desired it of him. He took out of the money he brought me £ 79 L[legal?] money for expenses for which have taken his receipt to account with you. I did not settle his bill of Expenses as I was unacquainted with the terms he agreed to serve. If he has engaged in the service any Considerable time should think he had better be kept in Camp as he is rather indolent and apt to keep out of the way.[1]

The assistants and clerks are very anxious to know if their wages are to be raised. Pray let me know what is to be done. I fear they will all leave me soon. Are the wages to be stated by Congress or the head of the department? If by Congress I fear it will be too late.[2] Cannot I promise them something will soon be done for thier relief? Am Sir your obedt Servt

NEHEMIAH HUBBARD

Cy (RG 93, WRMS: DNA).
1. Skinner's position as an express rider is discussed below, in NG's answer to Hubbard of 6 April.
2. NG did authorize a raise in pay for the assistants and clerks. See below, NG to Hubbard, 6 April.

From Colonel William Patterson

Dear sir   Sunbury [Pa.] March 28th 1779

I take liberty thro' you to inform His Excellency that I could not procure any suitable person that would undertake the Journey with *Hicks*;[1] however I've put matters on such a footing as not to doubt his bringing such information as will please. I convey'd him quite clear of the Frontiers above Fort Wallace, with the assistance of Capn [Lewis] Bush in Particular and the other Gentlemen Officers in General of Coll [Thomas] Hartleys Regt who received and treated me with great Politeness.

In duty to my Country request you will mention the feeble state of this County To Genl Washington, having little to depend on for their defence, save the Regt above mention'd, the officers are verry allert but the number of men I apprehend are too few, and from a hint dropped Yesterday Afternoon, I have reason to Apprehend that the Enemy intend soon to attempt a surprise at one of the Advance posts in this Quarter. In Consequence thereof, I made application to Capt Bush for a Soldier to ride my Horse express with this letter to Coll Cox in Estherton, to be forwarded from thence under his direction; If a small Blow should be struck on this frontier, the whole inhabitants will evacuate the County in twenty four hours, which will be extremely injurious to the publick, as there are many usefull men Among them for Boating and Driving pack Horses.

I find there are many more Boats (both large and middle Size) than I expected on this River.[2]

I forwarded Genl Washingtons Letter to Jammy Potter by express.[3] Must not neglect to mention that there are publick Stores of Provision and forrage in Penns Valey in this County without any force to Gaurd [Guard] them.

The people in general of the County wish for an Expedition to be carri'd on against the Indians &ec. And I have reason to believe that there may be Vonlunteers raised if their Service is required. When I have renderd all the secret Services in my Power, I have some thoughts of excepting your kind offer on the Staff Departmt should the Expedition you mentiond be carry'd on. I shall be verry unhappy if any thing containd in the above Letter should give his Excellencey or Genl Green any offence, as the Liberty taken is thro love for my Country. Your Obedt Humbl sert

W: PATTERSON

ALS (Washington Papers: DLC).
    1. As noted at Patterson's letter of 14 February, above, Patterson was not the expert on the Indian country that John Cox had led Washington to believe. In Gershom Hicks, however, Patterson seems to have been fortunate in carrying out Washington's instructions of 1 March to "employ intelligent, active and honest Men, qualified for the service by a knowledge of the Country and manners of its inhabitants." (Fitzpatrick, *GW*, 14: 168–69) Hicks had been captured by the Delaware Indians as a boy and later by the Shawnee. With a facility in both languages, he was a logical choice to undertake an intelligence mission through the Indian country. Hicks sometimes wore Indian dress to conceal his identity. (Dupuy and Hammerman, *People*, p. 341; Fitzpatrick, *GW*, 14: 170n)
    2. The Susquehanna River.
    3. Gen. James Potter (1729–89) was Patterson's brother-in-law. See note at Patterson's letter of 14 February, above.

To Colonel Jeremiah Wadsworth

Dear Sir   Camp Middle Brook [N.J.] March 29th 1779
    Last Night some of the produce of Conecticut River arrivd at my
quarters.[1] I have sent them round among the principal characters;
and I expect more than a hundred people will eat and drink your
health to Day. I take this early opportunity of returning you the hearty
thanks of all the interested. I expect 30 People to Dine with me tomorrow; and I am to spend the Evening at Pluckemin in the palace; where
there is to be a fine Ball. Thus you see we live by Eating, Drinking and
Danceing.
    Mrs Greene longs for your return to Camp. I hope you dont let
Mrs Wadsworth know what a prodigeous gallant you are.
    Biddle now passes current among the Ladies; but if you was here
he would deprec[i]ate like continental money. I dont immagin either
he or Cockran [Dr. John Cochran] wishes to see you among the
Ladys.
    I hope youl continue to send us the good creatures, not like
Pharoahs lean Cattle, But large, fat and plump ones such as they eat
up. In haste yours

N GREENE

Here comes Mrs Greene [shouting?] my compliments to the Col
and his Lady. You will receive and deliver them accordingly.

ALS (CtHi).
    1. The "produce" was salmon. See below, NG to Nehemiah Hubbard, 3 April, and
Wadsworth to NG, 8 April.

From Colonel Charles Pettit

Dear Sir   Philada 29 [and 30] March 1779
    Yesterday I recd a Line from Mrs Cox, mentioning that the Col-
onel was suddenly taken ill as he was setting out for Camp so that I
fear he will be laid up for some time.[1] Some days ago Mr Risberg
communicated to me a Complaint that Waggons could not be had at
Trenton to pass on the Flour to Camp so fast as it was wanted.[2] I immediatly wrote to Major Gordon by Express and this morning have
received his answer.[3] He says Mr Steel has complained very unjustly;
that the Waggons have been lately employed in carrying up Salt Provisions more than was necessary and that if there has been any want
of Flour at Camp it must be entirely the fault of the Commissary, as he
has sent it forward as fast as it was desired. I mention this lest you
should hear any Complaint of the like kind. These Complaints when
ill founded are injurious to the publick and unjust to our department.

Mr Steel has been told that he does not stand in the fairest light, and I suppose he does not like to wallow in the mud alone.

What shall I do for money? Of all the long list of Demands, amounting now to four millions and upwards, I have not been able to comply with any except 71,000 to Trenton and a little to Major Eyre, for some time past: not a Quire[4] for the Western Country, Carolina, Boston or any where else. Col Biddle has sent me a string of Wants amounting upwards of 600,000 eastward of Delaware besides Mr Furman. I have doleful Letters from Hollingsworth, Hooper and Davis, and strong intimations of want from divers others. The Treasury I find as closely besieged as ever, and every department falling in arrears and claiming its share of attention. The past week I have recd but 71,000 and a Draught to Eyre for 66,000 and that spared as a work of supererogation. This Week I may get a proportion of the product of the press, but that proportion will hardly exceed 5 or 600,000 and that is not equal to the growing of the demands besides arrearage. The forage department alone, which cannot bear neglect, will want the run of this supply for some time to come to keep it in necessary plight. What then is to become of other Wants? I have given the alarm to the treasury board and they to Congress in the manner mentioned in my last. Mr Duane told me I had spoiled his rest by it. I could not offer him any consolation nor make any appoley for it, but such as must increase his anxiety if he felt what he expressed. I therefore made no attempt to lessen his alarm. In short I feel so much alarmed myself that I think it behoves us to make such timely representations to them as will throw the blame of any deficiency that may happen in our department on the right shoulders.

Seeing little prospect of getting Gold lower than 11 for one I have purchased six pieces to repay the six I borrowed for you at that rate which has added to your debit 480 dollars.[5]

The discontent between certain parts of the Congress and the Council of this State is grown to a disagreeable height. In Genl Arnolds affair which has been for some time in the hands of a committee, the Council confined their Evidence to the affair of the Waggons.[6] The committee I believe have taken a good deal of pains in the inquiry, but the Council disliked their mode of proceeding and some altercation happened by letters in the course of it. The committee I hear have reported an acquittal. The Council charge them with unfairness in examining witnesses ex parté and seem much dissatisfied. A conference has been proposed to Congress by the House of Assembly to clear up some misunderstandings; the latter proposes that the Council should join in the Conference. To this some objections are made in Congress and it took up one day's debate in Congress whether they would confer with the Assembly if the Council joined in it. How it was determined I do not know, but I am told the Assembly will not confer on this matter separately. I believe it is the intention of the Council to pursue their other Charges against the Genl but I know not how or when. In the mean time he has purchased Capt McPherson's country seat for about £ 18,000 or £ 18,500, subject to a mortgage of £ 1600, but whether the latter is payable in sterling, hard money, or currency I know not; if the latter, it is a good purchase.[7]

The opposition to [Pennsylvania] Government seems to have become feeble, but the Council seem to think Congress give it weight. The NY members especially are said to cabal with the republican society, and that all the measures of Congress have a cast against this government. There may be some foundation for the suspicion, but I believe the superstructure is much too large for it. Jealousy, however, begets Jealousy, and the fruits of this suspicion will be the production of more and more ground for it. Congress will disregard and counteract the State, and the State will do the like to Congress, much I fear to the publick disadvantage. The greater officers of this State begin to talk of holding their councils at a greater distance from Congress; that is, that one or the other must move their quarters; and I should not be surprized to find that either Congress move to some other place, or the government move its seat to Lancaster. Even the president of Congress is not free from being suspected of taking part against this Government. I am much grieved at these appearances, and know more of them than I have wished to know, as I cannot safely attempt any good offices of mediation and therefore endeavour to pass them by silently. These disputes are ill timed. The common enemy are not yet sufficiently quelled and will profit by our contentions. The Factions of this State will probably add one Campaign to the difficulties of our grand struggle.

If I get any good news from the Treasury before I close this Letter you shall have it, but my present expectations are very small and, till I can get some Money I can think of little else. Letters upon Letters assail me, and even the express-riders are become importunate for their employers. I am Dr Sir Your Friend and hum Servt

CHAS PETTIT

30 March   When I wrote the foregoing I felt a cold growing on me. It was so bad last night as to let me sleep but little and that in a broken manner. I am unfit for business today and have attempted but little. Your favr of the 27 came to hand this morning with the circular Letters which shall go by the first opportunities as directed. I am taking some of Cochran's Pills today in hopes they will help me.

ALS (NHi).
1. On Cox's illness, see below, Pettit to NG, 13 April.
2. Gustavus Risberg was an assistant deputy quartermaster.
3. Peter Gordon, formerly a captain in the New Jersey militia, was now serving in the quartermaster department. (Heitman, *Register*)
4. Twenty-four sheets of uncut currency.
5. The Continental dollar, that is, had dropped to one eleventh its specie equivalent.
6. See above, note at NG to Reed, 31 January #1.
7. As a prelude to his marriage to Peggy Shippen in April, Arnold on 22 March purchased Mount Pleasant, John MacPherson's estate of ninety-six acres. (Wallace, *Traitorous Hero*, p. 174)

From Colonel Alexander Hamilton

Dr Sir,   Middlebrook N.J. March 31, 1779
    The General requests you will send some discreet person to Brunswick to ascertain the No of Boats in the [Raritan] River. A countryman that is judicious & trusty would give less suspicion than an officer. It should if possible be a person acquainted with the place. His inquiries will be the more easily accepted. The more hurry & dispatch the better. D S [Dear Sir] Yr obt Serv

A H
Aide de Camp

Tr (John C. Hamilton Transcripts: NNC).

Terms of Owen Biddle's Appointment as Assistant Commissary General for Forage[1]

Middle Brook [N.J.] 1st April 1779

Terms proposed for Owen Biddle Esqr A.C.G. Forage at Philadelphia for conducting the Business of the Department there.

1st   That he be allowed One Quarter per Cent by the States on all monies drawn by him, and expended in the district South West of the Deleware.

2d   That the same allowance be paid him by the Comy Genl of Forage to make up his Commissions. One half per Cent.

3d   The usual commissions to be paid him for purchases in his district of the City and County of Philadelphia.

4th   Necessary Assistants and Clerks to be allowed him.

5th   Office Rent to be paid by the States.

NB   The whole Accounts of the Department to be transmitted to

Philadelphia for settlement at the Office there by him or a deputy in the Office.

The Forage business being in great distress for want of a suitable Person to conduct it at Philadelphia, and not being able to procure a proper one for the purpose short of the above conditions, I am under the necessity of engaging Mr. Biddle, fearing the want of his Services should bring distress upon the Army, and confusion creep into the Department.

NATH GREENE

I Confirm the within on my part.

CLEMENT BIDDLE

DS (PHi).
1. Owen Biddle (1737–99) was an older brother of Clement Biddle, who noted his approval of the terms at the end of the document. Owen remained in the forage department until near the end of the war. For a biographical sketch, see *PMHB*, 16 (1892): 299–329.

George Washington to a Board of General Officers

[Middlebrook, N.J., 1 April 1779. Transmits three items concerning a dispute over rank among three Pennsylvania majors.[1] LS (Washington Papers: DLC) 2 pp.]

1. The dispute involved Majors Francis Mentges, John Murray, and Francis Nichols. The issue was resolved with the appointment of Nichols as a lieutenant colonel. (Fitzpatrick, *GW*, 14: 154, 323n, 347)

To Nehemiah Hubbard

[Middlebrook, N.J., 3 April 1779. Through General Putnam he has learned that Hubbard has three hundred good tents. If true, wishes they be sent to Redding (Connecticut). Thanks Hubbard for salmon and requests that he "continue to forward us a Weekly supply." ADfS (MiU-C) 2 pp.]

Articles of Partnership between Nathanael Greene, Jeremiah Wadsworth, and Barnabas Deane[1]

Articles of Agreement and Copartnership Entered into and made Between Nathanael Green of the State of Rhode Island and Jeremiah Wadsworth and Barnabas Deane Both of the State of Connecticut this Fourth Day of April 1779.

[   ] 4 April 1779

Article 1st That Nathanael Green and Jeremiah Wadsworth Shall Each of them put into Stock the Sum of Ten Thousand Pounds and that Barnabas Deane shall put into Stock the Sum of Four Thousand pounds and that he Shall pay Interest unto the Other Partners for the Sums they advance Over their Proportion of the Whole Stock in Partnership Untill he Shall furnish his Equal Proportion of Stock which Shall be Within the term of Nine months from the Commencement of their Partnership.[2]

2d That Each of the Above mentioned Partners Shall Furnish the Above Mentioned Sums within the Term of Three months from this time, at which time their Partnership Shall Commence.

3d That there Shall be Regular Accounts kept of all the Buisness Done in Partnership for which purpose a Proper Sett of Books Shall be Opened on the Day the Partnership Shall Commence, in Which their Accounts Shall be Regularly Entered, Which Books Shall be always Open to the Inspection of Either of the Partners.

4th That at the Expiration of Every Six months from the Commencement of this Partnership, or Oftner if Required Each Partner Shall be Furnished with the State of their accounts and of all Goods and Money on hand.

5th That no Money Shall be taken out of Stock by Either of the Partners without the Consent of the Other Two Partners.

6th That Bar's Deane Shall have the Direction and Management of the Buisness for which Service he Shall be Allowed A Reasonable Reward (Exclusive of the Hire of a Clerk and Other Charges Necessarily Ariseing on Trade). He Shall Steadily and Faithfully attend on Said Buisness and Shall keep a Regular Correspondence with the Other Partners, Advising them of his Proceedings; he Shall also attend to and Follow Such Directions and Advice as he may Recieve from them.[3]

7th That this Partnership Shall be Carried on in Such place or Places as Shall be Agreed on here After.

8th That the Firm of this Partnership Shall be Barnabas Deane and Company.

9th That this Partnership Shall Continue for the Term of Four Years from the Day of its Commencement.

10th That at the Expiration of this Partnership their Whole Accounts Shall be Closed and Equal Division made of all Mony, Debts, Goods on hand &c &c.

In Confirmation of the above and foregoing Articles of Agreement and Copartnership, We have hereunto Interchangeably Set our hands and Seals to Three Instruments of this Tenor and Date. The Day and Year First Mentioned[4]

BAR'S DEANE

JERE WADSWORTH

NATHL GREENE

DS (CtHi). NG affixed his seal, with his initials, beside his name as did the other two men.

1. Barnabas Deane was a younger brother of Silas Deane, under whom he had served as a merchant's apprentice and sometime master of vessels engaged in the West Indian trade. When Silas left Connecticut for the first Continental Congress he entrusted his business in Wethersfield and Hartford to Barnabas. In April 1775, as a lieutenant in the Wethersfield Volunteers, Barnabas marched to Boston, and following the capture of Ticonderoga, Governor Trumbull appointed him as a commissioner to supply the garrison. After NG died, Deane and Wadsworth continued their partnership until Deane's death in 1794. (For a biographical sketch, see J. Hammond Trumbull, "A Business Firm in the Revolution: Barnabas Deane & Co.," *Magazine of American History* 12 (1884): 17–28.)

2. For a discussion of NG's various investments during his quartermaster tenure, see above, NG to Jay, 15 February. Although not specified, the amounts of money, according to Wadsworth's biographer, were in Continental dollars. (Destler, "Wadsworth," p. 113) The dollar was sliding downward rapidly in value, but no adjustment seems to have been allowed for completing the contributions three months later.

3. The partnership was apparently expected to focus on trade and privateering, although Deane later invested in such diverse enterprises as distilleries and gristmills. As revealed in the future correspondence of Greene and Wadsworth, Barnabas Deane & Co. was never a very profitable business.

4. In a receipt attached to the document, Deane acknowledged Wadsworth's payment of £ 10,000 for himself and two payments totalling £ 5,000 that Wadsworth advanced for NG. On the amounts each partner eventually contributed and on NG's concern for keeping the partnership secret, see his letter to Wadsworth of 14 April, below.

From Colonel Ephraim Bowen

[Providence, R.I., 4 April 1779. Encloses returns and accounts for March. The forage master "has at last lost his Credit by reason of not Paying his Bills as he engagd."[1] Needs a considerable number of horses but since he has advanced money to the forage master cannot purchase them. ACyS (RHi) 2 pp.]

1. The forage master was Bowen, himself.

From John Jay, President of the Continental Congress

[Philadelphia, 4 April 1779. Has referred NG's letter about wagoners of 25 March to the Board of War.[1] LB (PCC, item 14, p. 79, DNA) 1 p.]

1. See above, NG to Washington, 24 February.

From Colonel Jeremiah Wadsworth

Dear Sir　　　　　　　　　　　　　Hartford [Conn.] April 4th 1779

Your favour of the 25 Ultamo came to hand yesterday,[1] the day before which, General Sullivan passed through this Town; on his way to Head Quarters. Cols [William Stephen] Smith and Morris [Lewis Morris, Jr.], his Aids, were with me, and told me the Action against session was droped. The General did not do me the honor to call on me or send for me, and I am not acquainted with his design respecting a Court Martial,[2] but wish he may insist on one as it will give me an opportunity to shew the World what is going on among the Servants of the United States, but I am so seriously afraid we shall Starve for want of Bread and that our currency will soon become worth nothing that I have less inclination to push on an enquirey and Court martial than I shoud have, had I liesure.

Your remarks are very just and were the General Officers to act on such principles as you inculcate our Department wou'd be more reputeable and the publick better Served; but as matters are now conducted we are in a fair way to be ruined, and the publick can not be well served. I have in Vain endeavoured to engage Persons of abillity and integrity to fill the places of some People in my Department, who are tired out with the constant and unremitting attacks that are made on it. I have determined to Resign.[3] Those Attacks have been principally in this Quarter from a Set of People of the lowest order and who were interested in haveing all order destroyed. The better Sort of People here are not so illiberal. The Answer to the Real farmer signed "Quarter Master" I have read and supposed Col Hay to be the author.[4] I think it well wrote and believe it will Silence that junto who are set on by that dam'd jesuit.[5] If we can get thro this Camp[aig]n I shall certainly quit, if it were only to have time to drag to light a Set of Rascals who are pouring out detraction and calumny from behind the Curtain and have neither Virtue or Courage eno. to shew their Heads. If I can see such a Magazine of flour provided as will insure a supply this Campa[ig]n I shall imediately quit the Service, and recommend R[oyal] F[lint] and flatter my selfe I shall be able to support him in that Quarter. I have some reasons for leaveing the Service which will not do to Put on Paper but as soon as I see You they shall be communicated. The Papers with B[arnabas] D[eane] were compleated Yesterday and shall be forwarded soon for your Signing &c.[6]

Mrs Greens health and the many agreeable little Parties You have must contribute greatly to alleviate Your cares. I hope Miss Lott was not long without a Partner. I shoud have been very happy to have been her Partner at Pluckemin. I shoud partake of some very agree-

John Jay, 1745–1829, oil painting by Gilbert Stuart and John Trumbull
(Courtesy of National Portrait Gallery, Smithsonian Institution, Washington, D.C.)

able diversions here if I was not haunted with numberless Applications, and perplexed with calls for supplies that nothing short of a creative power can Furnish. Is their any thing in the Mighty secret which Congress were big with some time since?[7] Will all this Labour of the Mountain bring forth only a Mouse? If it shou'd they will have less Credit than at present. Christopher Green [NG's brother] was with us last Week, is returned to E Greenwich was very well, his W____s [Wines] here are unsold. The overhauling in Phila'a is not unexpected to me. Let it go on. I know who dont fear it. Our General Assembly meet here on Wednesday next. I shall write them a letter which I hope will wake them up. If it dont may they Sleep the Sleep of Death. The Subject suited to a Satyrical pen which You mention has been handled in a Ballad and wou'd have appeared next Week if somebody had not gone Westward.[8] Besides what You mention, learning to dance, the last winter was introducd, and some other little Anecdotes. The Title of the Ballad was *"Jack* will never make a Gentleman, or a G____l." Farewell God bless You and a Small number more who deserve it. Their are not many Im sure. Mrs. Wadsworth and my respectfull Compliments wait on You and Mrs Green. I am with great sincerity Yours

WADSWORTH

ALS (CtHWa at CtHi).
  1. This letter is a virtual point-by-point response to NG's letter of 25 March noted by Wadsworth.
  2. On Wadsworth's dispute with Sullivan, see above, Pettit to NG, 4 December 1778.
  3. Wadsworth resigned on 4 June but Congress did not accept his resignation until January 1780.
  4. See above, NG to Wadsworth, 25 March.
  5. Identified at Wadsworth to NG, 27 March above, as Roger Sherman.
  6. See above, Articles of Partnership between NG, Wadsworth, and Barnabas Deane, 4 April.
  7. Wadsworth is referring to the rumored alliance with Spain that did not materialize.
  8. He refers to Gen. John Sullivan.

From George Washington

[Middlebrook, N.J., 5 April 1779. Wishes NG to provide powder horns and "the necessary compliment of shot pouches" for use in the western expedition.[1] Df (Washington Papers: DLC) 1 p.]

  1. See below, NG to John Cox, 6 April.

To Colonel John Cox

[Middlebrook, N.J., 6 April 1779. Relays Washington's request for four thousand powder horns and shot bags for the western expedition. He is not to "beaughtify or polish them further than is necessary." Notes that a supply of [cattle] horns may be obtained at Valley Forge. ADfS (MiU-C) 2 pp.]

To Nehemiah Hubbard

Sir   Camp Middle Brook [N.J.] April 6th 1779
You[r] favor of the 28th March has been receiv'd.

The Forage Department is a branch of the Quarter Masters Department; Colonel Biddle has his appointment from me, with full powers to appoint such, and so many in that business as the nature of the service may require. The reason why I mention this circumstance, is, your having frequently spoke of the Forage Department as if it was a seperate branch of business from the other, which I am apprehensive may lead you to take some measures with regard to the conducting the two branches seperate, so as to incur an unnecessary expence. It is intended that the Forage accounts shall be kept seperate, but not in a way that is to multiply expence.

I shall forward a Copy of your Letter to Colo Pettit, with orders to lay it before the Treasury Board for obtaining the necessary sums.

Mr [Richard] Skinner was appointed an Express rider for the Commissary's Department, at the special request of Colonel Wadsworth. I wish you would consult the Colo upon the subject. If Mr Skinner is not wanted as an Express rider for that Department, order him to Camp.[1]

I am not in want of the Horses you mention. Skinner rode one of them here, and is obliged to ride him back again, having no other, and therefore it is impossible for him to leave the Horse, if he was wanted.

The Pay of the Clerks and assistants must be raised, and you may assure them employed under you, that their pay shall be rais'd from the first of March.[2] I am Sir Your Hble Servt

NATH GREENE

ADfS (Bibliotheek der Universiteit van Amsterdam).
    1. See above, Hubbard to NG, 28 March for Hubbard's queries concerning Skinner.
    2. See above, Hubbard to NG, 28 March.

Major Ichabod Burnet to Moore Furman

[Middlebrook, N.J., 6 April 1779. Since NG wishes ten or twelve riding horses sent to Middlebrook, he doubts not that Furman "will make the necessary exertions" to provide them as soon as possible. ALS (Nj) 1 p.]

To Colonel Jeremiah Wadsworth

[Middlebrook, N.J., 6 April 1779. Hopes to see Wadsworth back in camp soon "that we may consult together upon matters respecting the transactions going on in our Departments."[1] ALS (CtHi) 1 p.]

1. Wadsworth had conducted the commissary business from Hartford since February.

To the Board of War

Sir   Middle Brook [N.J.] April 7th 1779

I received a Letter from His Excellency John Jay dated the 4th of April informing me that my Letter to him of the 25th of March, containing remarks on the defects in a late act of Congress on the subject of enlisting Waggoners for the war is refer'd to your Board.

I have to request your decision upon it as soon as possible; otherwise it will be of little use this Campaign: For people of that profession will engage themselves for the season to the Farmers, and it will be next to impossible to engage a sufficient number for the opening Campaign.

I can but lament that business of this nature which depends upon time and season should be delay'd until the natural advantages are lost.[1]

I am now making out a general return of the state of the stores in the Quarter Master's Department, which tho' not so compleat and exact as I could wish, will nevertheless, I hope, serve to give the Board the necessary information with respect to the state of my Department. I have the honor to be with great respect Your most obedient Humble Servant

NATH'L GREENE

DfS (MiU-C).
1. For NG's past efforts on behalf of the wagoners and his eventual success, see above, NG to Washington, 24 February and below, NG to Washington and Washington to NG, 19 April.

Benjamin Brown to Samuel S. Coejemans[1]

[Middlebrook, N.J., 7 April 1779. By NG's order wishes material left by James Abeel forwarded for the making of marquees.[2] ALS (PCC, item 173, vol. 1: 331, DNA) 1 p.]

1. Benjamin Brown was quartermaster of Jackson's Continental regiment. (Heitman, *Register*) Samuel Staats Coejemans, as noted at Blodget to NG, 25 January, above, was the owner of a large manor house near Camp Middlebrook, but he is an unlikely person to receive such an order. The recipient was more likely a relative.
2. Coejemans attached a note at the bottom relating that additional items were found.

To Colonel John Cox

Sir   Camp Middle Brook [N.J.] April 7th 1779
    I find by examining the issues of Portmantaeus and comparing them with the Number of officers that have a right to draw, by the late Resolution of Congress; that there will be wanting upwards of a 1000; which I wish you to give orders to be made as soon as may be.[1]
    Let them be made about three feet long; and one foot diameter; and completed with a chain so as to lock up.
    Many that were made last Campaign were very vile things; and scarce worth the transportation to Camp. I am to request that you give the most particular charges respecting the Manufactary of these, as the Officers will be more difficult now than formerly, from their haveing a right to claim, and it being our duty to supply them.
    I wish you to let me know how soon you think they can be got made. I am with esteem and regard Your Most Obedt humble Sert

NATH GREENE

ADfS (MiU-C).
1. For background on officers' portmanteaus, see above, NG to Board of War, 27 February.

Major William Blodget to Colonel John Davis

[Middlebrook, N.J., 7 April 1779. Acknowledges Davis's letter of 22 March[1] and directs that future returns be sent to NG instead of Charles Pettit. ALS (Davis Papers: DLC) 1 p.]

1. Blodget mistakenly wrote "March 23d."

George Olney to Colonel Udny Hay

[Middlebrook, N.J., 7 April 1779. NG requests that Hay prepare for Indian expedition "with all possible diligence." For every 126 common tents, he should make 9 horseman's tents and 1 marquee. Capt. Thomas Pendleton's artificers are ordered to "assist in the Works at West Point." Df (MiU-C) 1 p.]

Memorandum for General Greene from Jacob Weiss[1]

[Camp Middlebrook, N.J., 7 April 1779. NG to have orders issued that stores are to be drawn and distributed by brigade quartermasters, to whom regimental quartermasters are to apply for stores. Only articles "of a private Nature" will be available in camp while brigade and regimental quartermasters are available. NG to order the deputy quartermasters to furnish with "dispatch" their returns of stores issued since 2 March 1778, the returns to include portmanteaus. Lists the identifying letters that are stamped on canteens "found to be serviceable." Cy (PCC, item 173, vol. 1: 33, DNA) 2 pp.]

1. NG had undoubtedly asked Weiss, his deputy at Camp Middlebrook, to prepare the memorandum.

Agreement of Nehemiah Hubbard with Amos Hosford and Solomon Dunham

Hartford April 8th 1779

This Agreement made and concluded this 8h day of April 1779 between Neh'h Hubbard DQMG in behalf of the United States on the one part, and the Owners of the Schooner *Presdent* on the other part Witnesseth[1]

That the said Owners have agreed to send said Schooner well found [i.e., supplied] fitted and Navigated to Charles Town South Carolina at their own Cost and charge, where she is to be Laden with a full Cargo of Rice by Abraham Levingstone Esqr Contl Agent or persons by him appointed on account of the United States (The said Schooner to be at the Risque of the United States from the time of her Departure from Connecticutt River till her return into Port where she shall be Unladen) according to the Appraisment of three Indifferent Persons under Oath at Two Thousands Eight Hundred Pounds Lawfull Money which the said Hubbard engages on the Part of the United States shall be paid in case of loss either in whole or part, within Thirty days after sufficient Proof thereof, and when the said Schooner shall be so Laden she is to proceed to the Port of Nw [New] London or any other Port or Ports in the possession of the United States not to the Eastward of Boston, and their deliver two thirds of said Cargo of Rice both in Quantity and Quality to said Hubbard or some other Public Officer as shall be proper. The other third to be retain'd in full

Pay for all charges and freight. The said Hubbard further agrees that said Vessell shall not be detained any unreasonable time to Receive her freight from said Levingstone or other persons by him appointed to Load said Vessel. If she should be detained by said Levingstone or other persons by him appointed after her Arrivall in Charles Town South Carolina, then the said Hubbard to pay reasonable damages.

To this Agreement each party bind them selves, in the Penal Sum of Ten Thousand Pounds L[awful] Money which to be forfeit by the party failing to fulfill to the Other party. Witness whereof we have set our Hands and seals.

Witnesses

AMOS HOSFORD

WM CALDWELL   SOLOMON DUNHAM

NEHH HUBBARD

Hartford April 8th 1779

Cy (PCC, item 173, vol. 1: 319, DNA).
1. The schooner *President* was one of several vessels that Hubbard chartered. (See his letter of 24 February, above.) The agreement is typical of the many drawn up to charter rice vessels.

To Colonel James Abeel

[Middlebrook, N.J., 8 April 1779. Asks that tents be forwarded to Col. Morgan Lewis in Albany, including "400 good Soldiers Tents." ADfS (MiU-C) 1 p.]

From Colonel Charles Pettit

Dear Sir   Philada 8 April 1779
With some industry I have received about 11 of the 15 that was promised me on Monday.[1] The promise was made on the expectations given by the printers and signers, who have not kept their word; and they talk about good Friday, and Easter by way of excuse. I have now got another War[ran]t for 5 m[2] and shall hunt the Treasurer pretty close till I get it. I am not yet in a Condition to send to Carolina, but hope to do it in a few Days.

I am told a representation is to be made to the Jersey Assembly about the Waggons employed at Bloomsbury. Major Trent has been talking freely and publickly of the matter in this town and you know how forwardly such things are circulated.[3] I have mentioned this to our friend who I doubt not will rear at it, but it would be unjust to conceal from him things of this sort till they accumulate to a greater head. I am apt to think there is some foundation for your apprehensions respecting the grumblings set on foot by some members of C_____ [Congress]. A Gentn told me yesterday morning he had heard some murmurings of discontent against Quarter Masters in a kind of general way, that they made too much money, that the system of paying Commissions was a bad one, that Genl Greene was too grasping and was making an immense fortune. He did not tell me from whence he got it, but as he lodges in the same house with Mr Frost,[4] delegate from N Hampshire and I believe some other delegates, I supposed it to come from thence. These complaints however were in generals, and I could not learn that any particular fact was alluded to. We already know who is at the bottom of this; an artful, insinuating Man[5] in his situation has much mischief in his power, and I think it is odds that the clamor will rise to a considerable heighth before he has done and very probably will work a publick mischief as well as a private inconvenience to us. In what manner it can best be counteracted is a Question worth considering; to attempt following these people in all the Ramifications of their abuse would be endless and idle; and whether the other extreme.

Col. Ball of Virginia left a memo with me last fall to enquire for a Marquee he left at Bethlehem.[6] I wrote to Col. Hooper about it, who in answer told me he found it had been sent to Camp. In that Case it must have gone to the Use of the Publick, and Col. Ball ought to have some restitution. When I can find Col. Hooper's Letter I will send it to you; meantime I promised Col. Ball I would mention it to you.

[unsigned]

AL (MiU-C). Pettit failed to sign or address the letter. The writing and content establish beyond doubt that it was Pettit's. The content also establishes NG as the addressee. That NG received the letter is evident by the fact that it was with other Pettit letters in NG's possession at the time of his death.

1. Sheets of currency.

2. Pettit had received a warrant from the treasury for $5 million on 5 April. (*JCC*, 13: 420) As many letters in this period reveal, it was a constant struggle to keep the quartermaster department supplied with sufficient currency to conduct business. In 1779, the department received nineteen warrants totaling over $56 million. (*JCC*, 15: 1432) On the value of the warrants in specie, see above, NG to Jay, 15 February.

3. The reference is to Col. John Cox, NG's other assistant, who had apparently been accused of using public wagons around his estate of Bloomsbury. There is no evidence the charge was made to the New Jersey legislature or that it was true.

4. The "Gentn" has not been identified, but his fellow roomer must have been George Frost (1720–96), who served as a delegate from 1777 until April 1779.

5. He has been identified as Roger Sherman of Connecticut in Destler, "Wadsworth," p. 99.

6. Burgess Ball of the First Virginia Regiment.

From Colonel Jeremiah Wadsworth

Dear Sir   Hartford [Conn.] April 8th 1779
    Your agreeable favour came to hand last Evening dated the 29th
March. I am pleased to hear the Salmon arrived and it is a great addition to my happiness that my friends in Camp enjoy themselves so
well. I read your letter to Mrs Wadsworth. She says she is pretty well
acquainted with me and I lately gave her a Specimen of my Gallantry
at a little hop where I danced with at least Six pretty Girls and got
home at three oClock in the Morning &c &c. I am glad to hear Biddle
is current among the Ladies, indeed Cockran's being so pleases me
and I am certain I shall not have it in my Power to depreciate them,
and I am sure my inclination will not lead me to injure them in so important a matter as their being current with the fair and I know they
are both much greater Gallants than Your Hum'l Sert. Before this
reaches You a fresh Supply of Salmon will arrive sent on by Hubbard,
but at present the Water is too high to catch any fish. When it falls you
shall have more.
    Herewith are the Articles of Copart[nershi]p which if You ap-
prove You will sign them and return two to B[arnabas] D[eane] and
J[eremiah] W[adsworth].[1] Mrs Wadsworth joins me in respectfull
Compliments to Mrs Green and the General. Our assembly have appointed a Commitee to report on a law to be passd to secure stores &c
&c. They are much alarmed at the representations and I hope will be
Vigorous. I fear nothing short of Millitary Law will do our turn here
but I never saw the Assembly more Spirited or more Unanimous.[2] I
am just going to Wait on the Committee which forces me to conclude.
I am Dear sir Your most obedient Hum Servant

JERE WADSWORTH

P.S. The sooner we put the Money in the better. I shall put in mine
soon.[3] Please send back the papers as soon as possible.

ALS (CtHWa at CtHi).
    1. See above, Articles of Partnership, 4 April.
    2. The act as passed required "ascertaining the Quantity of Grain, Flour and Meal"
and to provide an immediate supply of bread for the army and the "necessitous Inhabitants of the State" as well as for securing "Other necessary Articles for the Army."
(Hoadly, *Records*, 2: 224–26)
    3. See note at Articles of Partnership, 4 April, above.

George Washington to a Board of General Officers

[Middlebrook, N.J., 8 April 1779. Presents to the general officers all
pertinent papers and resolutions pertaining to the arrangement of
officers in the Maryland line.[1] Df (Washington Papers: DLC) 3 pp.]

1. In his orders of this date, Washington requested the general officers to meet to discuss this issue. (Fitzpatrick, *GW*, 14: 346) A report of the board's findings is not in the Washington Papers, DLC, but Washington included it in a letter to General Smallwood of Maryland on 15 April, noting that he wished Smallwood to "communicate the arrangement and report to the line with my approbation of both." (Fitzpatrick, *GW*, 14: 393)

To George Washington

Sir   [Middlebrook, N.J.] April 9, 1779
Inclosd is a Letter receivd last Evening from Mr Patterson.[1]

The contents are not the most agreeable, and how it comes directed through me to your Excellency I cannot imagine.

He mentions there being a greater number of Boats upon the Susquehannah than he gave an account of when at Camp. Will it not be best to lessen the number orderd to be built; if the proper sizd ones can be had already fit for service?

I dont intend to trust anything in the quarter masters line to Mr Patterson; as I can easily evade his offer, and dont wish to trust more to any man of a doubtful charactor than cannot be avoided.

General Potter married Mr Pattersons Sister. From him more may be learnt respecting him than from any other person.

Is it your Excellencys intention to send great quantities of provision up to Wyoming before that Post is reinforced? Will there not be great danger of its being destroyed? I wish to know your Excellencys pleasure in the matter, as I design to send an Express to Estertown this Evening or tomorrow Morning, and will give directions accordingly.[2] I am with due respect Your Excellencys most Obedient humble Sert

NATH GREENE

ALS (Washington Papers: DLC).
1. See above, 28 March. Patterson's mission is described at Patterson to NG, 14 February, above.
2. The Wyoming Valley of the Susquehanna had been the scene of the July 1778 massacre of that name. The day after NG wrote, Washington ordered Gen. Edward Hand to proceed from Lancaster to Wyoming in order to take command. For securing the supplies to be gathered there, he directed Hand to "immediately set about throwg. up some new Works, or strengthening the old." The works, he added, could also protect a garrison. (Fitzpatrick, *GW*, 14: 354–55)

See Map 3 for geographic references above.

From Colonel James Abeel

[Morristown, N.J., 9 April 1779. Acknowledges NG's of 8 April. Tents to be sent to Morgan Lewis; will send NG a return of tents fit for service and those that may be repaired. Is preparing a sample of "Slings and Horns" with their cost for NG's approval.[1] LB (NjHi) 2 pp.]

1. See above, Washington to NG, 5 April, and NG to John Cox, 6 April.

Council of General Officers

[Middlebrook, N.J., 10 April 1779. Present: "The Commander in Chief"; Major Generals Sullivan, Greene, Stirling, St. Clair, de Kalb; Brigadier Generals Smallwood, Knox, and Woodford. Washington reports on the latest proceedings of the commissioners on prisoner exchange.[1] Notes that a memorial had been sent to Congress from captive officers who wish that their freedom be obtained[2] and that Congress has responded by giving Washington the power to arrange a cartel for the general exchange of prisoners and asking him to attempt "an equivalent of inferior for superior officers and the equivalent of privates for officers."[3] Washington, as a consequence, arranged for a meeting with the representatives of Sir Henry Clinton to be held on 12 April at Amboy, N.J.[4]

Washington thus requests from the council advice on an appropriate number of enemy privates "consistent with justice" that should be exchanged for the American officers held. The council responds: "What number of Private Men the Commissioners on our part may be authorised to give to procure the exchange and release of our Officers, We think they may give a Thousand but not a greater number."[5] DS (Washington Papers: DLC) 3 pp.]

1. For background on prisoner exchange, see above, vol. 2: 306n.
2. Congress had received a memorial from Gen. William Thompson and other officers who were then prisoners on Long Island, as well as a letter from the President of the Massachusetts Council concerning men from that state who were being held. (*JCC*, 13: 279–80)
3. The resolution was of 5 March. (*JCC*, 13: 280)
4. Washington selected Col. William Davies and Lt. Col. Robert H. Harrison as American commissioners. (Fitzpatrick, *GW*, 14: 361)
5. Despite the fact that several ratios of exchange were agreed to, a final schedule was not devised until March of 1780. The further step—exchange of prisoners by composition—did not commence until the end of 1781. (Bowman, *Captive Americans*, p. 112)

To Colonel James Abeel

[Middlebrook, N.J., 10 April 1779. Acknowledges Abeel's of 9 April and wishes him to write the quartermaster at Kings Ferry to forward tents to Albany. ALS (RHi) 1 p.]

Major Richard Claiborne to Moore Furman

[Middlebrook, N.J., 11 April 1779. Informs him that twelve horses have arrived[1] and that NG wishes six more sent, three "to be likely riding horses."[2] ALS (Nj) 1 p.]

1. See above, Burnet to Furman, 6 April.
2. Furman added on 15 April that he had sent six "Spirited and Active" horses, "not the Largest but well formd for strength and Duration."

From General Samuel Holden Parsons[1]

Dear Sir   Redding [Conn.] 11th Apl [17]79

I have to acknowledge the receipt of your favor of the 29th Ul'o which came to Hand this Day; please to accept my Thanks for the attention you have paid to the Subject of mine to you.[2]

I have not a Wish that his Excellency Should nor the most distant Suspicion that he has intentionally given any undue Preferance to any Troops under his Command but am Persuaded his Designs are upright and disinterested and I fully and heartily acquit him from all Blame; I wish I could, with equal Sincerity, say I beleivd the same Candor pervades the Conduct of all other Officers of considerable Rank which has uniformly been manifested in his Excellency's Administration.

But altho' I acquit him, I am as unfortunate as if my misfortunes arose from a Conduct in his Excellency which had worse motives for its Basis. I have I suppose from misrepresentations, lost the Confidence of the General and am not beleivd when I assert Facts, and in Consequence my Officers and Soldiers suffer exceedingly and Should I continue in Service under these Circumstances the Injuries they suffer from this opinion would in part be justly imputed to me. Some of the Facts which gave Rise to this Idea or at least confirmd me in a Beleif of that which I had been often told but did not credit are that [*several words missing*] I applied to his Excellency for Clothing for my Brigade, and as none had then arrivd in Camp he gave me an order on Majr Bigelow for Coats, Wescoats and Breeches sufficient for those who were wholly destitute; this I beleive he tho't a Favor. I certainly esteemd it so, but before I could arrive at Hartford there was not Cloth left Sufficient to answer the Order. When the imported Clothing arrivd in Camp the Connect't. Troops were excluded a Share on the Ground of this Order: the Blankets and Small Clothing which arrivd in Camp when I was there we had a full Share of but of none which arrivd afterwards, and the Reasons assigned were that we were to be supplied by Majr Bigelow. Yet I could not procure an Order upon him for a Single Shirt or Blanket and on Representations made of the State of my Brigade every Article was orderd to be forwarded to Head Quarters and he forbid to deliver any. All this I submitted to and beleivd in the great Variety of public affairs constantly before his Excellency he had forgot the particular State of my Brigade.

The Connec't Troops complaind they were naked. They had neither Shirts Blankets or Breeches. The Weather was exceedingly cold Stormy and severe; they had neither Clothing nor Hutts in the 2nd Brigade. The Discontents proceeded to much [several words missing] than in mine. They mutinied and mine were quiet. I left no Measures untried to calm their Minds and releive their wants.[3] I wrote to his Excellency. He gave me no Answer but in a Letter to Genl Putnam has Expressions respecting those Matters which affect me exceedingly.[4] He taxes me with a want of Decency in my Applications and intimates it is fully in my Power to prevent the Disturbances which arise from want of Clothing if I was inclind to, at least this is the Idea conveyd. I have not the Letter and cannot recite the Words. This I indur'd with as much Patience as I could, and tho' I knew him mistaken I was certain he intended equal Justice to his Troops. But soon after there came an Order to cloth the 2nd Regt and as I am informd a similar one for the whole of the 2nd Brigade to be us'd at the Discretion of Genl Huntington, Altho' that Brigade and every Regt in it had receivd a Similar Order on Bigelow to mine and at the same Time and had succeeded much better in getting it answerd. This confirmd me in a Beleif that his Excellency by misrepresentations had been led to beleive there was no Credit due to the Facts I had so often Stated to him respecting my Troops; and that I was rather disposd to make Difficulties than to heal them for I do not now beleive he ever designd to do Us Injustice and yet we have very greatly Sufferd beyond any other Troops under his Command. These are some of the Facts which induce me to the Opinion that 'tis dishonorable to myself and injurious to my Officers and Soldiers for me to continue in my present Command. I will never for these Reasons forsake the Cause of my Country, and it will require many more Instances of Conduct of a kind in which I may be an exceeding great Sufferer to make me entertain any Sentiments dishonorable to the uprightness and Purity of his Excellency's Government; another Man against whom the Tongue of Slander will not prevail may obtain that Justice which under present Circumstances I cannot ask for, and which I know I should have had if that Credit was given to my Representations which I am certain They deservd.

I am sorry to say I know there are Parties in the Army and Factions in Congress but I am of no Party nor am I an adherent to any Faction nor do I intend to Sacrifice my own Sentiments or Conduct to the private Designs and ambitious Views of any Person; I have a good

Opinion of some Gentlemen who are in the different Interests, but in their Party Concerns I have not any, the least Connection. I beleive these Measures have been exceedingly detrimental to the Interest of the Country and will disgrace our History and many Gentlemen of more Honesty than their Accusers will be disgracd by the Malevolence of their Enemies.

The Case of Genl Putnam I think to be a very conspicuous Instance of Ingratitude and Malevolence: I beleive We don't differ in our Sentiments of the man and however Wise he might have been to have chosen to retire to private Life at his Age it must greatly affect a feeling Mind to reflect upon the Measures taken to remove from office a faithful Servant who has grown old in honest Endeavors to do Good to his Country. And the Means us'd to induce him to relinquish his Office are such as render it impossible to retire with Honor and who can wish Disgrace to attend him in his last Days? I confess I think when the public have no longer Occasion for the Exertions of their Servants it requires no great Skill to dismiss them in a manner which will not wound the Feelings of a Good Man.[5]

I wish you every Happiness you can injoy in your elevated Station, and should be happy to hear from you as soon as the public Concerns will give Time. Envy and Detraction attend the honest and good but I beleive you have as small a Share as most good men have. I am Dr Sir with Esteem and Respect yr Friend and h'l Servt[6]

SAM'L H. PARSONS

ALS (CtY).
　　1. Parsons's brigade, composed of Connecticut regiments, was part of Putnam's division, which had its headquarters at Danbury, ten miles from Redding (also Reading). Since Parsons and Greene had not been especially close, his reason for sharing his intimate feelings with NG was undoubtedly because he thought NG might help restore Washington's faith in him.
　　2. Letter not found.
　　3. A "mutiny" had occurred in Jedediah Huntington's brigade which was quickly put down and the ringleaders jailed. Putnam wrote Washington on 5 January 1779 detailing the circumstances of the "mutiny" and recommending pardons for the jailed leaders. Washington responded on 18 January, explaining that he understood Putnam's feelings and left it to his discretion as to the "culpability of those in confinement." At the same time, Washington cautioned Putnam on the need for harsh punishment for mutineers in the future, with "the severest and most summary example" being made of the leaders so that the men would learn that "Mutiny will not only be ineffectual in procuring a Remedy, but involve consequences infinitely worse than the evil complain'd of." (Putnam's and Washington's letters are in the Washington Papers, DLC; Washington's is printed in Fitzpatrick, GW, 14: 20–21.)
　　4. Washington seldom responded to a letter more testily than he had to Parsons's letter of 23 December, and his response to Putnam rather than to Parsons was in itself a severe rebuke. Washington considered Parsons's letter, he told Putnam, "as containing some insinuations of the most delicate nature." Parsons had recounted at tiresome length the failure of Connecticut troops to share in the supply of foreign uniforms when their supplies from Maj. John Bigelow, the assistant clothier at Hartford, proved inadequate. Washington said he had approved the Connecticut troops' application to

Bigelow only after "repeated importunities" in which General Parsons "was principly zealous." (Fitzpatrick, GW, 13: 491–92) Aside from what Washington considered inaccuracies and false accusations in Parsons's letter, its general tone was not one to endear the author to the commander in chief. The letter, in fact, was essentially a criticism of Washington, thinly disguised in deferential language and contrived excuses. "I am sure," Parsons wrote, "the great multiplicity of Business in which your Excellency is ingagd must have occasioned our misfortune in this matter." In another place he was sure that nothing could have induced Washington to contribute to the shortage except his "not recollecting the State of these Troops." He complained, moreover, about Washington's failure to be more explicit in orders to Putnam concerning provisions that were going to the enemy in New York—orders that he, Parsons, might have to carry out—although he assured Washington that no one desired more than he "to comply strictly with the true Spirit of every Order your Excellency gives." (Parsons's letter of 23 December is in the Washington Papers, DLC. Washington's to Putnam of 8 January is in Fitzpatrick, GW, 13: 491–95.)

Washington's impatience with Parsons, if not his actual dislike, is revealed in another letter to Putnam of 10 February, in which he speaks of Parsons's absence with leave as a "matter of some surprize." He added that the intervals that Parsons had "already enjoyed and lately too, one would have thought sufficient," and he ended with this admonition, "We should not suffer ourselves to be led from the line of our service by a mere desire to see our friends, or to arrange affairs not really of the last importance." (Fitzpatrick, GW, 14: 90–91)

5. Parsons is referring to the manner in which the senior major general in the Army had been treated. Unquestionably, Putnam did not enjoy a close relationship with Washington. As noted above in vol. 1: 354n, Putnam was bypassed in the defense of Mt. Washington in 1776 while still technically in command, and his advice was virtually ignored thenceforth on questions of strategy and command. His assignments from the autumn of 1776 to December 1779 (when he suffered a paralytic stroke that effectually ended his military career) were for the most part routine or of less than major importance. In 1780 Parsons succeeded Putnam in command of the Connecticut troops.

6. For NG's response to this letter, see immediately below.

To General Samuel H. Parsons

[Middlebrook, N.J. After 11 April 1779][1]

[One or more pages missing] . . . to acquire honnor and glory at other peoples expence and risque. I call'd upon him for some ill naturd things he had said about me, but he denyed the whole.[2]

I would not wish you to take any hasty resolution in your affair. I am perswaded you are mistaken. The General is not apt to take hasty or unjust resolutions. I have thought sometimes he is not always attentive to the claims of his friends but the public weal is an higher object than private friendship; and therefore I suppose he thinks himself justifiable in dispensing with the claim. I am perswaded if there is any man in the Army that has a right to complain upon that score I have as just pretentions as any one.[3] I wish it was possible to collect and hold up to public view every Mans merit both in the Councel and the field. I am confident many charactors would appear very different from their present standing.

I cannot think the General would wish to fall out with you from reasons of policy as well as justice. It is a fact well known to the General that your influence is equal or superior to almost any mans in the State of Conecticut. Popularity you know is agreeable to human nature and flattering to every mans ambition; and I have no reason to think the General so much of a stoick as to be insensible to its charm; and consequently neglectful of the means of leading to it.

I have a most laborious and disagreeable office—subject to every species of reproach without the least share of applause. I undertook it at the special solicitation of the General and a Committee of Congress; and I have and expect to pay dear for my condesension.

I am in hopes to see the General to morrow when I will indeavor to sift upon him the subject [of] your complaint. You may expect to hear farther from me in a few days.⁴ I am with sinsere regard yr most Obedt humble Sert

NATH GREENE

ALS (OCIWHi). Incomplete.
1. The date is determined by Parsons's letter immediately above, to which this is an answer.
2. The man has not been identified.
3. See the complaints NG made directly to Washington on 21 July 1778, above, vol. 2: 461–63, and to Marchant about his treatment by Washington, ibid., p. 471.
4. It is not known whether NG interceded with Washington. If there was further correspondence on the subject, it has not been found.

From Colonel Charles Pettit

Dear Sir   Trenton [N.J.] 11th April 1779
Hearing that Col. Cox was ill again, and being desirous to be here at the sale of a certain Estate, I set out from Phil'a Friday Afternoon. On the way I met Major Burnet's Letter containing an extract from Mr Hubbard's,¹ which shall have due attention; but I cannot promise the money immediatly, having not yet recd the Sum promised me for last Monday; I shall however follow up the Treasury as briskly as I can and distribute what I get, but I cannot give to anyone his full demand without robbing others.

The Land went above my Idea of it's value. It is purchased by Mr Runyan and will amount to about £ 17,000.² I cannot find that any other Person is interested in it, and people are beginning to wonder how he can accomplish such a purchase. You can judge where Enquiries of this kind will land. The publick Money and the profits of Quarter Masters will be scanned and much talked of; and however fairly he may be entitled to make the purchase, or from whatever sourse he may derive the money to pay for it, the Clamour will rise against the Department. If I had been interested in the purchase according to the plan I had formed, I should not have appeared in it; tho' my pretensions to it are perhaps at least equal to Mr Runyan's.

Col. Cox keeps in an unfit state for Business, indeed he can scarcely sit up, and I fear it will be some time before he will be able to bear any weight of business; mean time a number of Things fret and Seize him and give undue Biases to his mind. I shall call on him presently in my way to Philad'a which I mean to reach this Evening.

I have also recd Major Blodget's Letter written in behalf of Mrs Greene, which shall be punctually regarded. Mrs Pettit and Betsy join me in best Compliments to Mrs Greene. I am Dr Sir Your most obedt Servt

CHAS PETTIT

ALS (NjP).
1. Letter not found.
2. Hugh Runyan was an assistant deputy quartermaster for part of Bucks County, Pa. He resided in Trenton and completed the purchase described on 4 May 1779. The purchase price was £ 12,767/10s or $35,000 in Continental dollars (about $2,500 in specie). He soon sold 188 acres of the tract. (PCC, item 59, vol. 2: 165, DNA; *N.J. Archives*, 3: 7–8n)

To General James M. Varnum

Sir   Camp Middle Brook [N.J.] April 12th 1779

Yesterday General Sullivan arrivd in Camp. I am happy to find him pleasd with the people of the State in general; but more particularly so with the Governor.[1] He speaks of him in the highest terms of respect and regard. Few officers have left a command with greater eclat than the General has that of Rhode Island; if we are to judge from the numerous addresses from the different classes of people.

General Gates is to succeed him. His temper is not so well adapted to the genius of the people, as that of General Sullivans; but perhaps a little management may remedy that evil.

I shall be happy to hear from you at all times upon the politicks of the State, in which I cannot help feeling myself deeply interest[ed] altho absent. In return you shall have the news from Camp and such other intelligence as may be either interesting or amuseing.[2]

I am told Capt Collins is to be oppos'd in his election for a Delegate.[3] I have taken some pains to enquire respecting his general conduct in Congress; and find the Delagates speak very hansomely of him particularly with regard to his integrity and uprightness. His education and abillities are not the most shining. But I have often remarked that ingenious heads sometimes perplex more than promote public business. When such Charactors are govern'd by proper Motives and the head and the heart go hand in hand they render important services to the public; but where they act a contrary part they have it in their power to perplex and embarass exceedingly.

We have no news from Europe by which we can interpret the Enemies intentions the next or coming Campaign. The last accounts from the Southward were favorable. The Enemies force on the decline; and ours increaseing rapidly.[4]

Count de Estainge has receivd a large reinforcement of Ships and land forces. Tis to be hoped that he will give [Admiral John] Byron a severe drubing; but I must confess I am not very sanguine.

We expect the Minister of France in Camp every hour. I expect nothing but Parade and Ceremony will reign during his stay. He is one of the politeest men you ever saw.[5]

Please to make my respectful complements to Mrs Varnum. Mrs Greene is abed and not very well. I am with great regard Your Most Obedient humble Sert

NATH GREENE

ADfS (MiU-C).
1. William Greene.
2. Varnum, who had resigned from the Continental army, was soon to head the Rhode Island militia. See above, Varnum to NG, 13 January.
3. John Collins (1717–95) was a delegate to Congress from 1778 until May 1781 and again in 1782–83. He served as governor of Rhode Island from 1786 to 1790. (*DAB*)
4. As noted above at NG to Sullivan, 26 January, the accounts were overly optimistic.
5. On Gérard's visit, see below, NG to Washington, 27 April.

George Olney to General Anthony Wayne

Sir   Camp Middle Brook 13th Apl 1779

Application has been made to the Q.M.G. for pay for a red-roan Mare, branded C.A., which a Countryman purchas'd at public Sale, order'd by Genl Greene; of which he had a certificate: This Mare, as appears by the deposition of three Men, you took out of a Pasture (near where the owner lay mortally wounded by his Waggon) on your March from Brunswick to the North River last Summer; but whether for public or private use does not appear.

I am directed by Genl Greene to request a line from you, as soon as possible, certifying your having taken such a Mare at that time, and the purpose for which she was taken, that he may have a proper voucher for the payment of the Money demanded for her, by the late owner's Widow, he having died soon after he met with the above mentioned accident. I am Sir Your Most Huml Servt.[1]

GEO OLNEY AUDR

ALS (PHi).
1. The outcome of this matter is not known.

From Griffin Greene

Dear Sir   Coventry [R.I.] April 13, 1779

I received your agreable Letter of 27 of March. You conclude it would been better for me to have had the writeings finished all but your signing and sent them to you to have compleated them. I should have don so had not you sent me a powar [of attorney] to have finished them myself which was deficient in not being sealed &c. I was also afraid if the Brothers was doubtful about my authority it might make some cavil; as far as we had gone.[1] I will relinquish my Powar as quick as the business is compleat. We have got the refusal of Patience Island for Several Weeks for Four Thousand Seven Hundred Dollars in Silver or Gould. This is one of the best spots of Earth I know of; take it all together it will keep 25 Cows, 6 Oxen, 4 Horses, 100 Sheep and 16 or 18 Hoggs besides young Stock and you may rais Grain enough for a large Family. We have been trying to get the Money but cannot as yet find it to be had. I hear it may be had for betwixt, at Bottom, 10 and 11 for one. Please to let us know if you think the purchase worth making and if you due how the exchange is with you or at Philadelphia.[2]

When I requested you to give us a quantity of Iron work to do for your Department last Spring you gave me for answer that Iron was much cheaper at the Westward and we could not afford our Tools as low as they might be made their. But now the cas is altered and Iron is not near as high hear as it is at Philadelphia and we can furnish the Continent as well and as cheap I make no doubt as any part of the Thirteen States. If you should be in want for any article and will let us know how low a price you can get it maed for we will under take to furnish you with dispatch if the price is not much lower than I expect they can be made and give a good profit. We shall have a Large stock of meterals for Iron making this year. Cant you get us the Building of some Large Vessel for Publick or private use or some thing that will give us a double manufactury?[3] Dont you want ten or twelve Dozen of Scythes for the Army? We have them that is good. We have laid out all our Money and have but little Bussiness at present. If you should see any plan you think worth pursuing shall be much obliged if you will communicate it to us.[4] Sally and my Best respects to Mrs Greene. I am Sir your Humble Sevant

GRIFFIN GREENE

ALS (MiU-C).

1. NG had given Griffin the power of attorney for settling the estate of NG's father. (See above, vol. 2: 332–33.) The final indenture, signed by the heirs, with Griffin signing for NG, can be found below, 10 June 1779.

2. A price in Continental money of approximately $47,000 to $51,000.

3. Griffin Greene was an enterprising and ingenious man, who later contrived a

diving bell and high-speed pump to raise a sunken British ship. See below, NG to Griffin Greene, 27 July 1780.
4. NG responded in a point-by-point fashion to this letter on 30 April, below.

From Colonel Charles Pettit

Dear Sir   Philadelphia 13 April 1779
    When I left Trenton on Sunday our friend Cox proposed, as soon as he should find himself able, to set out for Camp as well in pursuit of Health as to converse with you on buisness. His Constitution seems to have received a shock of a serious nature, that calls upon him to pay more regard to his health than to any other earthly consideration; and I think it not improbable that he will determine to meddle very little with business at least for some time to come and perhaps to withdraw from publick business all together. He me[ntioned?] something of this kind to me; and tho' it would be inconvenient both to you and to me, that he should now withdraw from us, I cannot, as his friend advise against it unless his health becomes better established than at present seems likely while he continues in the busy world. He does not need the emoluments of Office; his fortune is ample enough, and he begins to think so. He wishes for ease and society with his family and those domestic enjoyments, the hopes of which only can excite to that Industry, toil and bustle by which wealth is usually acquired. The great difficulty, with a Man who is lucky enough to get into the high road of gain, is to know when to withdraw from it with the best prospect of happiness; and constant experience shews that most men continue in pursuit of the means till it is too late to enjoy what they have acquired. An happy combination of circumstances seems to give Mr Cox as fair a prospect of a pleasing remainder of life, if he has but health to enjoy it, as the world can afford. His health is now precarious; business perplexes him, and he is apprehensive would destroy his capacity for enjoyment. If he now retires he may still recover vigor enough to enjoy Life; who therefore can doubt of the choice he ought to make? On the other hand, if his health would bear him out in it, I should think from his regard to us, his feelings as a patriot, and perhaps to his own reputation, he ought to continue at the oar till the vessel arrives in port or till we are all relieved together. But if, even in this point of view, the chances are against his being useful by continuing, that is, that his health will not bear him out in it, why should he risk the making so great a sacrifice? My wishes are very sincerely for him to continue to act with us, but considering all circumstances I cannot press him to it. Had I less personal Friendship for him and regard for his family than I have, if he were to reason in the train I have men-

tioned, candor would oblige me to give way to it, and these considerations give the arguments additional weight with me. After all, however, the opening season, change of air and proper exercise, may restore him to vigor of body and mind sufficient to go through with the business, and I heartily wish it may. But lest it should not, it may be prudent in us to consider what we are to do in case he should be under a necessity of dropping business. In such Case it will be incumbent on us to form new Plans, and make new arrangements, and these will require consideration and conference. I have thought much of the matter within a few Days, but cannot satisfy my self about it. These hints will of course turn your mind to the subject. Col Cox will probably be with you in a few Days and you will be able to read the state of his mind. I would wish however that not a hint of this business go beyond the triumvirate (unless he should think proper to mention it to the General) till we have some opportunity of comparing our thoughts.[1]

I have heretofore mentioned to you that I had obtained a War[ran]t for five millions.[2] I have at length finished the old one and begun upon this as far as 210,000 besides a draught in favr of Mr Biddle for one million which he begins to receive today but there are so many demands on the Treasury that neither he nor I can get our wants supplied. One million is ordered for the Paym'r at Camp and another for the southward, which will keep us back. I mean to send some by the Escort to the southward, to Mr. [Abraham] Livingston.

I do not recollect that I have mentioned to you an Expression of our friend Mr Duane when he returned me the several Letters I had laid before the Treasury board to shew them the wants of the Department, amongst which was yours to me which was written for that purpose.[3] He said your Letter had rather given some offence, by insinuating that other Departments had a preference in the distribution of money, or that ours had not due attention paid to it. I do not remember his exact words but this was the Sentiment. It was in a little tete a tete in a corner of the Room. I made him no other reply than something to this effect. That the wants of the department in which the publick Interest and our Reputations were so deeply concerned, called upon us to express our feelings and apprehensions to the board, but that I was confident it was not your Intention to give them offence, or to give them any unnecessary pain. I have not since heard a hint on the subject. Since that we have had some conversation on the subject of financing, and as he is at the head of the Treasury business I gave him some of my thoughts on that business. He seems to me to hold Opinions that are rather speculative than practicable, but seemed inclined to give way to some experiments tho' rather reluctantly, which to me appear absolutely necessary. He told me the schemes I ment[ione]d were under the consideration of Congress, and he believed something of the kind would speedily be adopted.

Genl. Lee who has been on the set out for Virginia for some Days is still in Town; I believe he has been detained by a hint in the Saturday's Paper of a Publication against him which has this morning appeared, and seems to gall him not a little. I saw him this morning at Breakfast. He affected to laugh it off, but his chagrin was visible; and he talked of a Cudgelling for the Author who, it seems was formerly an acquaintance of his.[4]

You have probably heard that Genl Arnold was married on Thursday Evening. Mr Clarkson is gone to the southward.[5] The Bickerings between Congress and this State are not yet settled and I fear some disagreeable Consequences will yet ensue from them. The partizans on both sides are getting so warped that they see almost everything relating to each other thro' a false medium by which means they take disgust often unjustly and thence give occasion of offence which would otherwise be avoided.[6]

I have just recd a Letter from Col. Cox by which I find he is getting better. I am Dear Sir, sincerely yours

CHAS PETTIT

ALS (NHi).

1. John Cox soon recovered from his illness and continued to serve as assistant quartermaster general until NG resigned.

2. The warrant was voted by Congress on 5 April. (*JCC*, 13: 420)

3. Letter not found.

4. The author was Hugh Brackenridge, editor of the *United States Magazine*, who questioned in a letter directed to Lee, "what sense of honour a man can have who has been seven or eight months in this city [Philadelphia] damning General Washington, Governor Livingston, Henry Drayton, and the Congress, and threatening to resign . . . and yet after all continuing to retain your commission." In reference to Lee's fondness for dogs, Brackenridge wrote, "Nor am I the only person in America or elsewhere who have taken you for a wild animal." (*Pennsylvania Packet*, 13 April 1779)

In a letter to John Jay, Lee reacted less to the virulent personal attacks than to Brackenridge's insinuation that he had counseled Gen. William Moultrie to abandon Ft. Sullivan during the battle of Charleston in 1776. At Lee's request, Congress reprinted in the *Packet* of 15 April the vote of thanks it had extended to him on 28 June 1776. (*Lee Papers*, 3: 333; *JCC*, 13: 442)

Lee subsequently issued a challenge to Brackenridge which was refused. Nevertheless, when he observed Brackenridge one day on a Philadelphia street, Lee, horsewhip in hand, gave chase to his tormentor. In an opera buffa scene, Brackenridge ran into a tavern and secured the door against Lee, who remained outside, uttering oaths, challenges, and curses. (Alden, *Lee*, pp. 273–74)

5. Matthew Clarkson (1758–1825), as a former aide of General Arnold, was at odds with the Pennsylvania Executive Council. He was on his way to the South as an aide to General Lincoln. (*DAB*; Brunhouse, *Pennsylvania*, pp. 62, 68)

6. For background on Pennsylvania politics, see above, Joseph Reed to NG, 5 November 1778, and Pettit to NG, 29 March 1779.

To Colonel Jeremiah Wadsworth

Dear Sir   Camp [Middlebrook, N.J.] April 14th, 1779

Your Letter oi the 4th I have receivd; and that of the 8th also with the enclosd papers; which I have sign'd and returnd.

You may remember I wrote you sometime since, that I was desirous that this Copartnership between Mr Dean, you, and my self, should be kept a secret.[1] I must beg leave to impress this matter upon you again; and to request you to enjoin it upon Mr Dean. The nearest friend I have in the World shall not know it from me; and it is my wish that no Mortal should be acquainted with the persons forming the Company except us three. I would not wish Mr Dean even to let his brother [Silas] know it. Not that I apprehend any injury from him; but he may inadvertantly let it out into the broad World; and then I am perswaded it would work us a public injury.

While we continue in the offices which we hold I think it is prudent to appear as little in trade as possible. For however just and upright our conduct may be, the World will have suspicions to our disadvantage.

By keeping the affair a secret I am confident we shall have it more in our power to serve the commercial connection than by publishing it.[2]

I have wrote to my brother Jacob Greene to pay you £ 5000 without informing him for what purpose or on what account. If you could advance the other 5000 until you come to Camp it would be very agreeable to me. If not I must take some other way of sending it.[3]

General Sullivan arrivd in Camp a few days since; but has not said a word to your prejudice that I can learn. I believe he is willing to play, childrens play with you: if you will let him alone, he will you.[4] He dind with me yesterday; and paid great compliments to the Staff at Providence without discriminateing. He is to have the command of the Indian expedition. I wish he may succeed better than heretofore. For altho he has never met with any signal disgrace, he has not been remarkably fortunate in success.

I am glad your Song did not come out upon the whole; as it would have created a perpetual War. However I expected something of the kind, which made me write you that I thought he had given a fair opening.

We expect the Minister of France here tomorrow or next Day. When there is to be great doings. The Cannon is to fire, and the Troops to parade and all the General officers are to ride out to meet him; to welcome him to Camp.[5]

I am afraid we shall make but a skurvy appearance; as our force is but small and those very rag[g]ed.

Mrs Greene is gone to Trenton to a Tea frolick given by Betsy Pettit. Mr [Abraham] Lott, Cornelia [Lott], Major Blodget and Burnet are all gone. There is to be a number of Ladys from Philadelphia; and some members of Congress.

Col Cox is very ill. I was to see him about Eight or ten days since. He has got a relapse of the same disorder he had in Philadelphia. I am really doubtful of his recovery. It is very unfortunate to me, at this critical season. I must take a ministerial comfort; all things work together for good.[6]

Col [Richard Kidder] Meade has just returnd from Virgina, and says your Letter writing fellow has made rascally work in the Department in Virgina.[7] A prodigious quantity of meat is upon the spoil, and every thing in disorder and confusion. He gives great praises to my agents there.

I had a Letter from Major Forsyth a few days past.[8] He stands ready to engage with you if you think proper to give him an appointment. But I am afraid you'l find old agents are like chronick diseases, difficult to shake off. Major Forsyth I am sure would answer your purpose extremely well providing you was fairly rid of *Aylet*. But I am afraid it will be some time before you can get rid of him.

Mr [Royal] Flint din'd with me to day; and is brave and hearty. We wish for another feast of Salmon. When may we expect it? Should they arrive while the Minister is here, they will be doubly welcome. I sent one of the last that came to Mr Jay President of Congress. Mrs Greene sent another to Governor Reads family.

I am glad to hear your Assembly are entering into spirited measures in aid of the commisarys and quarter masters Department.[9]

Unless the States will give more aid than they have done to these Departments for some time past, I think the Wheels will stop.

This State grows more and more litigious. The Pettifoging Lawyers, like frogs in the spring, begin to peep in great plenty. Besides this pest of creatures, not less pernicious to the peace and welfare of a State than the Locusts was to the growth of the Herbage in Egypt, There is a great multitude of Justices of the Peace who parade with the constables at their heels and are as formidable in numbers as a Roman Legion. This class of men to show their learning and improve their genius swarm about us like Birds of prey seeking whom they may devour.

You may remember I made an armer bearer of one upon my first coming to this ground and I intend to keep them runing upon every ocasion. If they want business they shall have it.

General Arnold is marryed. He has lately bought a House and farm near the City of Philadelphia. It belongd to McPherson. It is said he can have 10,000 pounds for his bargain.[10] If so his trade is better than all the commisary and quarter masters profits put together.

Mrs Biddle has got back to Camp again with a fine Son. You have been informd before that Doctor [James] Hutchison is marryed to Miss Lydia Biddle. She is coming to Camp soon. Mrs Shippen is already here and the Doctors [Shippen's] daughter. I hope you will bring Mrs Wadsworth which will form an agreeable set.

I believe your patience will be exhausted before you get through this long and disagreeable Letter. Please to present my compliments to Mrs Wadsworth and Ill bid you good Night. Yours sinserely

N GREENE

ALS (CtHi).
1. See above, Articles of Partnership, 4 April.
2. NG's concern for secrecy seems to have sprung from his reluctance to have anyone—even his brothers—know the amount of commissions that he and his two assistants were collecting. The constant criticism of the department (if not of its principals) was enough to account for this concern, although it is quite possible that he also experienced some sense of guilt in the face of the hard times that his brothers and long-time friends were enduring. From the time the letter was first published (in the *Magazine of American History* in 1884 and again in 1898 in the *Pennsylvania Magazine of History and Biography*), it has caused some students of the period to suspect more sinister motives on NG's part. The later cipher that he and Wadsworth adopted for their "business" letters deepened that suspicion.
3. According to Wadsworth's biographer, NG's total investment in Barnabas Deane & Co. was £ 8,333, Wadsworth's was £ 17,333 and Deane's, £ 14,707—all figures in Continental dollars. (Destler, "Wadsworth," p. 113)
4. For Wadsworth's problems with Sullivan, see above, Pettit to NG, 4 December 1778.
5. On Gérard's visit, see below, NG to Washington, 27 April.
6. On Cox's illness, see above, Pettit to NG, 13 April.
7. The reference is to William Aylett. See above, Finnie to NG, 11 February.
8. Letter not found. Forsyth did succeed Aylett as commissary in Virginia.
9. See above, Wadsworth to NG, 8 April.
10. On Arnold's purchase, see above, Pettit to NG, 29 March.

Colonel Clement Biddle to Moore Furman

[Raritan, N.J., 15 April 1779. Has consulted with NG concerning purchase and securing of hay for the year. "The route from Trenton and Coryells Ferry to Kings Ferry and New Windsor will probably be much frequented and the hay that lays near them on each side may be drawn to the posts establish'd on these routes." Hay in the eastern part of New Jersey to be left at farms, while that "exposed to the enemy" is to be used by the troops and teams located there. Magazines, no larger than thirty or forty tons, to be established "Ten to Twenty miles from the Coast."

Encloses blanks for returns that he has sought from deputies. NG hopes to increase wages of assistants, including those in forage department.[1] Directs that pastures be established for horses; requests accounts. ALS (Nj) 3 pp.]

1. See below, NG to Jay, 15 April.

To John Jay, President of the Continental Congress

Sir   Camp Middle Brook [N.J.] April 15th 1779
I have delayed writing to Congress for sometime upon a subject, in which the business of the Quarter Master General's Department is deeply interested, in expectation that there would be an alteration of the system, but hearing nothing upon this head, and knowing the Department to be in a critical situation, from which very disagreeable consequences may result by a further delay, I think it incumbent upon me to lay the matter before them, and to request their speedy determination thereon.

In May 14th 1777 The Congress passed a Resolution regulating the Quarter Master's Department.[1] Among other things, the wages of different officers were stated. At the time this resolve took place, the reward offered for such services might have been adequate thereto; but from the depreciation in the Currency since, and the decline of publick spirit, it will be absolutely necessary to give a further encouragement, or else the Department will be without the necessary Officers to carry on the business.

I have received Letters repeatedly from the Deputies in the Department, urging the necessity of raising the pay of the Staff employed under them on wages, without which, they would be under the necessity of adopting some other mode to employ them upon, or leave the business unexecuted.

Since I have had the direction of the business, I have made it my study to employ as few people upon Commissions as possible. But unless the Assistants (which have hitherto been upon pay) can have some further consideration it will be impossible to continue them in the service, or to Engage others fit and proper for the trust.

A Person fit for an Assistant Deputy Quarter Master General, should have a proper knowledge of the forms of business, be a man of activity and good judgment; of a fair character and of good repute. All these qualifications are actually requisite to execute the trust with that degree of method and reputation necessary to secure the publick from impositions. Is it to be expected that persons of this character, and with such qualifications will either engage or continue in a service attended with so much labour, fatigue, care and attention, for the pay stated in the Resolution?

The Waggon Masters and Forage Masters are also generally about to leave the Departmement, unless they can have an addition to their pay. The business of Waggon Masters is very laborious. People that are fit for this Employment are good honest farmers well acquainted with the Waggon service, Men of principle and honesty, and such as will take proper [care] of the Cattle and stores committed to their trust. It is absolutely necessary that they should be honest men, as valuable stores are committed to their charge. Is it probable that this class of people can be called forth into the publick service in so disagreeable an employment (so different from that ease and repose which they enjoy at home) for the little encouragement that is given? And for want of such men I will venture to say the publick suffers, and will suffer five times as much as the difference in pay between what good and indifferent men may be employed at.[2]

The pay of a Deputy Quarter Master General act[ing] with the army is 75 Dollars per Month. This is a trust of the highest importance, and I was in hopes when I first entered the Department to have had liberty to fill the places with Feild Officers but His Excellency has utterly refused not withstanding many would have been glad of the appointments and several did actually solicit them.

I cannot for the present pay get men of suitable abilities to fill these Offices. It is to be remembered that those employed now in the Quarter Master's Department, not belonging to the line have no benefit of Rank, future provision or advantage of supplies from the State stores, and therefore the present pay must be something handsome to induce people (possessing proper abilities) to engage in the business.

It is a mistaken policy in my humble opinion to fix the wages of People (necessary to fill these Offices) so low that none but the most worthless and indifferent of men can be had. That this will be the case is very obvious, if the present establishment continues.

I would recommend that all Deputy Quarter Masters General that do business upon Commissions, be allowed no pay or Rations. This will be a small consideration to each individual, but collectively, will amount to a considerable sum. But all such as do business on wages, wether with the army or stationed at a post, be allowed 200 Dollars per Month and the usual Rations.

And in order to get good men, and save the necessity of multiplying the appointments of a great number of Deputy Quarter Masters General I would recommend that the pay of Assistants be 140 Dollars per Month and the usual Rations.

That the pay of a Deputy Waggon Master Genl be 100 Dollars per Month and the usual Rations.

That the pay of a Waggon Master be 80 Dollars a Month, and the usual Rations.

The Commissary General of Forage always attends the main Army, with which, and with each seperate army a Deputy Commissary General of Forage to be allowed with the same wages and Rations as a Deputy Quarter Master General.

The Assistant Commisaries of Forage either attending the army to collect Forage on a march, or those employed in purchasing under the principle purchasers in Districts, to have the same allowance as the Assistant Deputy Quarter Masters General, those Offices requiring persons of equal qualifications with the Deputies, and Assistant Deputy Quarter Masters General. The Forage Masters who attend the Receipt and issues of Forage at Posts or Magazines, and one with each Brigade of the army, to be allowed the same as Waggon Masters.

And I would further recommend, that all those staff Officers who serve with the army, be allowed to draw a suit of Cloths out of the Continental Stores upon the same conditions as other Officers, provided they engage for a year or longer.[3]

The pay of Waggon Master and Assistants heretofore have been upon a footing. It is surprising to me how that could have happened, when the qualifications of the persons necessary to fill these offices are so different. I have the honor to be your Excellency's most obedient Humble Servant

NATHL GREENE

Cy (NHi). This document appears to have been made from the copy that Jay received. A less complete draft of 12 April—the last paragraph in NG's hand—is at MiU-C.

1. *JCC*, 7: 355–59.

2. For the background on NG's efforts to keep competent men in the wagon corps, see above, NG to Washington, 24 February.

3. As a result of this letter and NG's appearance before the Supply Departments Committee on 23 April, Congress, on 11 May, approved a resolution that in many places is virtually identical in wording to NG's letter. The delegates not only included all of his recommendations, but in one area they added inducements that NG had not included: this was the matter of subsistence, ranging from $40 per month for deputy quartermasters and forage masters down to $10 for wagon masters and brigade forage masters. (*JCC*, 14: 503, 574)

As to the issue of clothing for staff officers, it is unclear whether the resolution was carried out, since as late as October 1779 NG was being queried as to its application. (See below, Gooch to NG, end of June and 18 October 1779.)

To Colonel Morgan Lewis

[Middlebrook, N.J., 15 April 1779. Has ordered over four hundred tents sent to Lewis as well as oakum to caulk three hundred boats. "General Sullivan is arrivd to take command of the Indian expedition which I expect will go on by the way of the Susquehannah, but this is under the rose. However I expect a detachment will move by the way of Fort Schuyler into the Indian Settlements."[1] French minister Gérard is expected.[2] ADfS (MiU-C) 3 pp.]

1. The Ft. Schuyler route was Lewis's responsibility. (See Map 3.) On the Indian expedition, see below, Sullivan to NG, 12 May.

2. See below, NG to Washington, 27 April.

To Colonel Charles Pettit

Dear Sir   Camp [Middlebrook, N.J.] April 15th 1779

Your favor of the 12th came to hand yesterday.[1]

We are entirely out of cash and wish a supply as soon as possible. The greater part of the last sum that came to Camp I sent to Col Hay as he appeard to be in distress.

I have wrote to Congress upon the necessity of raiseing the pay of the Staff. I wish you would urge them to a decision thereon as soon as possible. For I apprehend the most disagreeable consequences from a delay.[2]

Capt [Mathias] Sadlers company of Artificers time of service is out. I wish you to reengage them upon the best terms you can.

I want them to attend the Indian expedition; but this circumstance you need not explain. We have but a few Artificers to what there use to be. Three Companys were dismissed last Fall at the North River; and none engagd since, that I begin to fear we shall be in distress upon this head.[3]

I have enclosd you Mr Hubbards Letter, as it shows the necessity of the most pressing applications to the Treasury Board as well as a speedy decision upon the pay of the Staff.

I am very sorry that Col Cox continues so ill. It is a very unfortunate circumstance at this season when so much is under his direction.

Is it not time to direct all our deputy[s] to send their Vouchers in order to a settlement of our accounts?

I must beg you to hasten the preparations under the care of Col Mitchell and others in the State of Pennsylvania. The first of May we shall want all the Camp equipage to be on its way to Camp.

Major Burnet is on his way to the Head of Elk. I have heard so many complaints from that quarter that I am determind to know the foundation thereof.[4] I am confident the Department never was in so good reputation every where else, as at present, Notwithstanding the little dirty scriblers abuse.[5]

Mrs Greene is at Trenton. I am yours sincerely

N GREENE

ADfS (MiU-C).
1. Letter not found.
2. See above, NG to Jay, 15 April.
3. The difficulties of retaining an adequate number of artificers in the Hudson River area are described in various letters, above, of Udny Hay and Morgan Lewis in the winter of 1778–79.
4. See Henry Hollingsworth to NG, 3 May, below.
5. He has not been identified.

From Colonel James Abeel

Major Genl Green   Morris Town [N.J.] 15th April 1779
   Your favor of 10th Inst I receivd this morning. The 400 Ten's and
Horsmans Tents went off on Sunday last. The Marquees and remainder of the Horsmans Tents go off this day. The want of waggons
have prevented my sending them sooner. There is some great defect
in this departmt or the Q M'r has his hands too full of other Business
to provide them as he never took the pains to go himself and procure
them let the Service require it ever so much. He makes his Sole dependence on his Waggon M'r and the Justices when if he was to go
himself he might at any time procure them by good words and going
in person. It is needless for me to acquaint Mr Furman as I cautioned
him before he was appointed but he still thought proper to appoint a
Man who a few days before was turned out the Commy's Department
for misconduct.[1] A Company of Artificers sent by Capt Brewen
[Jeremiah Bruen] to go to the Northward has been detained three
days for the want of a Waggon to carry on their Tools and Should still
be detained longer was I not to provide for them. For my part I think a
Man ought to be appointed who would pay his whole Attention to
the Interest of the Publick and whose private Business ought to give
way to other of more Consequence. He Acts as Clerk to the Court,
paymaster to the Militia &c which gives him employment enough,
besides being the Head man of one of your Psalm Singing Societys
and which should Business Require his Attention ever so much he
would not neglect. The General may be assured I have no private
views in writing thus as the Man treats me with all the Civility he can,
but I do it solely for the good of the Department which suffers by his
inactivity.
   By desire of Major Claybourn [Claiborne] I have sent you 10 yds
Russia Drilling which cost last Summer 20/ per yd. I will endeavour to
procure Mrs Green some Loaf and Brown Sugar, none to be had in
Town. I have been tampering several Days with Duychencks about 1
doz Cups and Saucers. He will not let me have them unless I pay him
two Barrels Flour for 6 Cups and 6 Saucers which is too dear. I have
wrote to New Ark to get them and the Sugar. I am with Regard
                                                          J ABEEL

LB (NjHi).
   1. Abeel's complaints were directed at Joseph Lewis, the assistant deputy quartermaster at Morristown. In a letter to NG of 17 April, below, Abeel referred to Lewis as
"a Sly designing Fellow." Such an opinion was not held by Lewis's superior, Moore
Furman, one of NG's most respected deputies. Although Furman noted in a letter of 9
June, below, that the "Post at Morris Town has been attended with more difficulty to
manage . . . then [than] all the rest," he described Lewis as "both capable and very attentive to Business," having "as much influence in that county as any man in it."
   As a result of Furman's evaluation of Lewis as well as the informed opinion of

others, NG wrote to Abeel on 12 June, below, that he had found the complaints against Lewis groundless and hoped that "the little bickering" between you "may not embarass the public service in future and rob the public of both your services."

The bickering continued, however, despite NG's attempts at peacemaking. After charges and countercharges by both men, NG decided to hold a court of inquiry concerning the issues. (See below, NG to Abeel, and NG to Lewis, 3 September.) In a letter to Lord Stirling of 14 September, below, NG expressed the hope that a court would "be able to reduce the matter to a certainty." He believed the complaints originated "more from personal enmity than from any substantial evils" that actually existed.

The outcome of the inquiry has not been ascertained, but in letters of 21 and 28 October, below, Abeel once again renewed his attack on Lewis, to which no response from NG has been found. Since both men remained in the service of the department well into 1780 and continued to reside in Morristown, some accommodation must eventually have been reached.

From Captain John Gooch

[Boston, Mass. [?] 15 April 1779. "Beyond the Expectation of everyone I'm once more crawling up to Life." Sends his and his wife's regards. "I am Dr Genl liveing or dying sick or well most affectionately" your servant.[1] ALS (MiU-C) 1 p.]

1. On Gooch's illness, see above, Gooch to NG, 5 [and 9] March.

From Jacob Greene

[Coventry, R.I., 15 April 1779. Contemplates building a "20 gun ship." General Gates is at Providence.[1] British forces at Newport "said to be 6000." Excerpt from Stan V. Henkels, *Catalog*, No. 1005, (1909)]

1. Gates had assumed the command vacated by General Sullivan.

To James Duane

Sir   Camp Middle Brook [N.J.] April 16th 1779
    I have had frequent conversations with you upon the Quarter Masters Department. You being at the head of the Treasury Board, President of the Committee for confering with the General, and perfectly acquainted with all the secrets of Congress, as well as their opinions and sentiments respecting men and measures; I wish to explain myself further upon my own situation than I have hitherto done. I shall be very candid, and expect you to be so.
    It has been hinted to me, that some members of Congress think I am too griping in my demands, and am making a fortune too rapidly. As this is an insinuation of a personal nature, and implies a charge of taking an ungenerous advantage of the public necessity, I feel myself not a little hurt at it.

There is not a man in the army that has been a greater slave to public business from the infancy of this war than I have, and I flatter myself no one more useful in the humble station in which I have serv'd. I have been in every action that has taken place with the Grand Army since the commencement of the War, except those upon Long Island and at the White Plains; and altho I have never deriv'd any great Military merit, yet no one has been more expos'd, or more intent upon doing his duty. I think therefore I may claim some merit, as I make very great sacrifices in leaving the honors of the Line at a season when I had the fairest prospect of reaping personal advantages by my future services.

I have never spent a single moment in attending to my own private affairs since I enter'd the army;[1] nor have I been at my own home above an hour, and that, on the march from Boston to New York except when I went upon the Rhode Island expedition last Summer and then I was at home but about a fortnight. I trust therefore it will not be thought I am unreasonably attentive to my own private interest; especially when it is known I left large stocks in trade which I have been oblig'd to leave to the direction of others with a transfer of the greater part of the profits to negociate the business.

The emoluments arising from the Quarter Masters department, I freely confess is flattering to my fortune, but not less humiliating to my military pride. I have as fair pretentions to an honorable command as those who hold them; and while I am drudging in an Office from which I shall receive no honor, and very few thanks I am looseing an opportunity of doing justice to my military character. And what adds to my mortification is, that my present humiliating employment is improv'd to pave the way for others glory. There is a great difference betwixt being rais'd to an office and descending to one. Had I been an inferior officer, I might have thought myself honor'd by the appointment; but as I was high in rank in the army, I have ever consider'd it as derogatory to serve in it. It was with the greatest difficulty that I could prevail on myself to engage in the business. Nothing but the wretched state that the Department was in, and the consequent ruin that must follow, added to the solicitations of the General and Committee of Congress, could have procur'd my consent. It was not with a view to profit; for the General and the Committee of Congress will remember that I offer'd to serve a year, unconnected with the accounts in the military Line, without any additional pay to that which I had as a Major General. But as this plan did not comport with their views I told them that I would serve upon the same conditions which Colonels Cox and Pettit could be engag'd upon, and I have no more now than they have; notwithstanding my situation subjects me to a double share of care and fatigue, and holds me responsible for every failure. My emoluments are far less than the Commissary General's while the duties of my office are infinitely more perplexing and troublesome.

I think I may venture to take some merit in reducing Mr Cox's terms when he first enter'd the Department. For the Committee of Congress would have been under the necessity of giving him a higher commission which he insisted upon; and which he relinquish'd only from my intreaties being added to the Committee's reasons. And however high you may consider the late proposition which I made to Congress as a reward for future services, it was far short of what the other Gentlemen concern'd in it thought themselves entitled to. And I believe they would not have been brought to engage upon such terms as were offer'd had I not told them that was what the President of Congress and the Gentlemen of the General's family had advis'd to.

I did not solicit the appointment in the first instance, neither am I solicitous to hold it. I wish but to know the inclinations of Congress to gratify their wishes. I undertook the business with a flattering expectation of meeting their approbation, but I can have no hopes of succeeding, if they consider my rewards higher than my merit. I will appeal to facts for my fidelity. The distress of the army and the confusion of the Department at the time I enter'd the business, are notorious. I wish but to have the state of the Department at the two periods, now, and the last Spring, fairly contrasted for my own justification. I wish the General also to be call'd upon, and every other Officer in whatever department, to know whether they have not had every assistance that they had a right to demand from the Office, or that the state of the Country would admit. And also whether the business has not been conducted with as much oeconomy and order as could be expected in the confused state in which I found it, and from the complexity of its nature.[2]

I found the line of the army and the staff almost at open War. The difference subsisting between them I have been happy enough to heal, and to restore a mutual good understanding. In a word, I have had a very laborious task.

The business of the Department has been very expensive. The decline of the Currency, the avarice of the people, and the plan of the war, has render'd it unavoidably so. I have study'd oeconomy as much as in my power; and am persuaded there has been but little wanton waste of public property. I cannot add more industry or attention to the business than I have done. If my past conduct is not satisfactory, it is my wish to quit a business wherein I cannot please.

I have been in expectation of a new system ever since I left Philadelphia. I gave you all the assurances in my power of seconding your measures in any plan you should think proper to adopt. I have given you the conditions upon which I would act under it; which, by the by, are far from being thought unreasonable. On the Contrary, the terms are consider'd moderate and equitable. How it got abroad into the world I know not; but it seems it has and thus are the people's sentiments respecting it. It is to be remembred that the Quarter Master General in all armies is always liberally rewarded, as he receives no honor and laurels from all his toils.[3]

From the nature of the duty, and the importance of the trust, the time and qualifications necessary to execute the office in all its branches, it cannot be thought that my proposition was a Child of avarice, or a Creature of extortion. So perfectly satisfied am I with respect to the rectitude of my own actions, that I have not the least objection to the whole world's being made acquainted with every circumstance and transaction. I have always wrote and spoke my mind freely to Congress, and the Committees acting under them; wherein I have thought it necessary for their information for the public good. In doing this, I trust I have always preserv'd that decency and respect which is due to so honourable a body. But if plain truth and matters of fact give offence, It is the matter and not the man that is faulty.

I find difficulties enough that are incident to, and inseperable from the office. If these are multiplied by prejudices and discontent, the task will be render'd intolerable.

Previous to my engaging in the business, the Committee of Congress and the General promis'd me all the aid that Congress or the different States could render, in aid of the business committed to my care. From some states I have had it, while in others, I have met with almost every embarrassment. I only mention this circumstance to shew what a broad bottom I took this business up upon, and to observe at the same time, if the basis is to be contracted, I shall not hold myself responsible for consequences.

Thus Sir, I have given you my sentiments upon my present standing, and wish for yours with equal freedom that I may act a part consistant with my own honor and the public wishes.[4] I have the honor to be With great respect Your most obedient Humble servant.

NATHL GREENE

LS (PCC, item 155; vol. 1: 127, DNA).

1. An obvious exaggeration, but measured against his military duties, the time he had spent on private affairs was slight. For a discussion of his business ventures during the war, see above, NG to Jay, 15 February.

2. For the background on NG's acceptance of the post of quartermaster general, see above, vol. 2: 308–11n.

3. NG had offered to serve for a yearly salary of £ 3000 rather than receive a commission. See above, NG to Jay, 15 February.

4. An answer to this letter has not been found, but Duane, who was friendly with NG (as noted above at NG to Duane, 9 March), was undoubtedly one of those who urged Congress to express its confidence in Greene and Wadsworth. (See below, NG to Jay, 27 April and note.)

To Colonel Ephraim Bowen

[Middlebrook, N.J., 17 April 1779. Acknowledges Bowen's of 4 April. Is trying to obtain money for Bowen but "The Treasury is amazingly hunted." General Glover's brigade has been put in readiness to march;[1] Bowen is to provide "Teams, Tents, &c &c." LS (MiU-C) 1 p.]

1. See below, Governor William Greene to NG, 27 April.

To Colonel Charles Stewart[1]

[Middlebrook, N.J., 17 April 1779. Washington desires intelligence concerning the "Great Swamp."[2] NG invites Stewart for dinner as "I am a Widower and all alone." ALS (MH) 1 p.]

1. The letter was addressed simply to "Col Stewart," but Commissary Charles Stewart is identified by his knowledge of the Pennsylvania frontier. (For example, see Washington's opinion of his expertise in a letter to Sullivan of 8 May, Fitzpatrick, *GW*, 15: 19–20.)
2. The "Great Swamp" lay between the Delaware and Susquehanna rivers. Washington was planning the road that was later built for the Sullivan expedition through what was called "twenty miles of horrid rough gloomey country." (Whittemore, *Sullivan*, p. 124) See Map 3.

From Colonel James Abeel

[Morristown, N.J., 17 April 1779. Has sent off four wagons of iron for Udny Hay. Blames the "Q Mr at this place" for lack of wagons, lack of forage, which has caused horses to perish, and the loss of public stores. "In short he is a Sly designing Fellow. I am tired of finding fault with him."[1] Sends resolves of Congress.[2] Returns are being prepared by a printer. LB (NjHi) 2 pp.]

1. The reference is to Joseph Lewis, as noted in Abeel's letter of 15 April, above.
2. See below, Jay to NG, 18 April.

From George Washington

[Middlebrook, N.J., 17 April 1779. Requests that a horse be furnished Maj. [Caleb] Gibbs since his was lost in the evacuation of New York in 1776. ADfS (Washington Papers: DLC) 1 p.]

From John Jay, President of the Continental Congress

Sir   Philadelphia 18th April 1779
    Your favor of the 15th Inst was delivered to me last Evening, and shall be communicated to Congress in the Morning. A Speedy decision, on the measures recommended in it, is important. The determination of Congress on the Subject shall be immediately transmitted.
    Herewith enclosed is a copy of an Act of Congress of the 17th Inst, providing for the Enlistment of waggoners, and repealing a late Act on the Subject.[1] I have the Honor to be With Respect and Esteem your most obedient Servt

LB (PCC, item 14, p. 90, DNA).
    1. See *JCC*, 13: 467. The act that was repealed had been passed on 16 March. (*JCC*, 13: 320–21) For more on this issue see above, NG to Washington, 24 February.

To Colonel Thomas Chase[1]

[Raritan, N.J., 19 April 1779. Hopes that tents from Boston for troops in Fishkill will soon be forwarded. Expects army to "take the Field earlier than common." For the New York troops "a disappointment . . . will be attended with very disagreeable consequences." He cannot explain, but reasons are "waity and substantial." FC (MiU-C) 1 p.]

    1. This note was also sent to Otis & Henley in Boston and William Smith in Springfield.

To Colonel Christopher Meng[1]

Sir   Camp [Middlebrook, N.J.] April 19, 1779
    You are to proceed to Fish Kill Danbury and Reading [Redding, Conn.] and there examin the camp equipage of all kinds particularly of Tents. Get a return of each Regiment under the command of General McDougal and General Putnam and see whether there is Tents and other kind of Camp Equipage sufficient at the above places for the Troops under the command of the aforesaid officers. If there is any deficiency bring an account of what it is.
    You will leave a copy with each Brigade quarter Master of the propotion of Tents to be allowed to a Brigade.
    You will make your stay as short as possible so as to execute this order. I am sir Your humble Ser

N GREENE

ADfS (NBLiHi).
    1. John Christopher Meng (1750–1833) was an assistant deputy quartermaster who helped James Abeel with camp equipage. He had been a lieutenant colonel in the

Pennsylvania militia, although NG generally addressed him as "Mr." (Heitman, *Register*)

To Colonel Udny Hay

[Middlebrook, N.J., 19 April 1779. Mr. Meng has been sent to examine tents.[1] "The most indifferent of the Tents should be left for the Troops which Garrison Westpoint as they will be the least exposd." Anticipates earlier operations than usual. ADfS (MiU-C) 1 p.]

1. See above, NG to Christopher Meng, 19 April.

To Captain Ezra Starr[1]

[Middlebrook, N.J., 19 April 1779. Has sent Mr. Meng to examine tents and camp equipage.[2] Expects earlier spring operations than usual. ADfS (MiU-C) 1 p.]

1. Assistant deputy quartermaster at Danbury, Conn.
2. See above, NG to Meng, 19 April.

To George Washington

Sir   Camp [Middlebrook, N.J.] April 19th 1779

I wrote Your Excellency the 24th of February upon the necessity of enlisting a Corps of Waggoners for the War. There is almost two Months elapsed, and nothing decided upon the question. The season is now almost past for engaging this Class of people; the operations of the Campaign near at hand; and the army without Waggoners. What is to be done in this case is the question. I must beg your Excellency's advice in the matter; as not a moments time is to be lost in determining decisively upon the affair.[1]

With the utmost exertions and with the most liberal encouragement, I am persuaded it will not be in our power to procure one half the necessary number that will be indispensably necessary.

Inclos'd is an estimate of the number that will be wanted to act with the army, besides all those employed in conveying Provisions, Forage and Stores upon the different communications. But these being generally private property Teams, find their own drivers.

From the different accounts I have had from the Deputy Quarter Masters respecting the wages given for private employ, and from the opinion of the Forage Master, and Waggon Masters General, I don't think there is the least probability of engaging Waggoners short of between thirty and forty pounds a month. Wages are rising daily, and the difficulty of engaging men for this business hourly increasing.

The undecided condition that this business has lain in before Congress and the Board of War, will not only greatly increase the expence; but multiply the difficulties, as well as disappoint us of getting a proper complement of Waggoners for the various purposes of the army.

There is nothing now left, but to try to engage as many Waggoners as we can, and upon the best terms we can. I shall set about the business with all immaginable diligence the moment I receive Your Excellency's Instructions.

I have pointed out the number and expence and Your Excellency will judge of the expediency. I am With due respect Your Excellency's Most Obedient Humble Servant

NATHL GREENE

Estimate of public Teams which will require Waggoners to drive them including the Artillery Drivers, necessary to attend with the army.

		Brigades
1st	North Carolina	1
	Virginia	3
	Maryland	2
	Pensylvania	2
	Do Detach'd	1
	Jersey	1
	New York	1
	Connecticut	2
	Rhode Island	1
	Massachusets	4
	Newhampshire	1
		19
Each Brigade 4 Regiments 4 Teams		16
	Brigadier General	1
	Intrenching Tools	1
	Spare Ammunition	1
	Commissaries Teams	4
	Forage Teams	4
	Traveling Forges	2
		29
29 Teams each to 19 Brigades		551
2d	Artillery	
	38 Pieces with Brigades	38
	38 Ammunition Teams for Do	38
	Park 30 Field pieces	30
	Ammunition Teams for Do	30
	Spare Ammunition	50

	Baggage Teams	8
	Commissaries Do	6
	Forage Teams	20
	Traveling Forges	6
	Artificers of Artillery	4
		230
	Calvalry and Marachausse	
	Pulasky's Legion	12
	Colo Moyland	6
	Colo Baylor	6
	Colo Bland	6
	Colo Sheldon	6
	Major Lee	5
	Colo Armands	4
	Marichausse	3
		48 [2]
4	Generals and staff of the Army	
	Commander in Chief	12
	Major Generals 10 each	20
	Quarter Master General	3
	Adjutant General	1
	Comy Genl of purchases	1
	Comy Genl of Issues	1
	Comy Genl of Forage	1
	Pay Master General	2
	Auditors of the army accounts	1
	Muster Master General	1
	Waggon Master General	1
	Judge Advocate General	1
	Comms Genl of Prisoners	1
	Provost Guard	1
		47
5	Quarter Master Generals Stores	40
6	Commissaries teams attending the army	50
7	Do Forage Teams	60
8	Hospital	20
		170
9	Engineers and Corps of Sappers	10
10	Artificers of the line for tools	15
	and Baggage	25

Total 1071 [1119]

NATH GREENE
QMG

LS (Washington Papers: DLC).
    1. In addition to NG's of 24 February, above, see also his letter of 24 March to Washington and Washington's reply immediately below.
    2. NG failed to include the 48 teams in his grand total of 1071, which would thus have been 1119.

From George Washington

Sir   Head Quarters Middle Brook [N.J.] April 19th 1779
    I have received your letter of this day containing a representation on the subject of Waggoners. It will be impossible, in the reduced state of the army, that the number required can be furnished by drafts from the line. No alternative therefore remains but to engage them otherwise in the best manner and on the best terms you can; and as the time presses, on account of the early movement of the army which is intended, not a moment is to be lost in setting about it. As you are going to Philadelphia,[1] when you arrive there, you can report to Congress or the Board of War, the measures you are taking and the necessity that dictated them and receive their further directions.[2] I am Sir your most Obedt ser

Df (Washington Papers: DLC).
    1. NG left for Philadelphia on 21 April and returned on the twenty-seventh.
    2. For a discussion of this matter, see NG to Washington, 24 February, above.

To Colonel Udny Hay[1]

[Middlebrook, N.J., 20 April 1779. Encloses Washington's letter of 19 April. Wagoners to be enlisted for McDougall's troops for "Nine Months only." Hay should engage them "without fail as the General is determind not to allow them to be had from the Line of the Army." Desires copies of the enlistment agreements. "The people that you employ should not know how many is wanted or that the order is as positive as it is." ADfS (MiU-C) 2 pp.]

    1. A copy of this was sent to Ezra Starr in Connecticut.

To Jacob Greene

[Middlebrook, N.J., before 21 April 1779.[1] Asks about the family. As regards Jacob's sons, it is his opinion that the "Natural disposition of Children should be carefully consulted; and the reigns [reins] and the spurs occasionally made use of as circumstances renders necessary." It is "absolutely necessary" that cousin Griffin answer Colonel Biddle "for decencys sake. Pray give him a hint upon the subject." Hopes the Westerly farm may not be "impoverished as it is hard bringing land too again that has been once injurd."[2] No news on British plans; reports developments in South Carolina and West Indies. "We expect the Minister of France at Camp every day." A fortnight's ceremony is planned.[3] ALS (MWA) 2 pp. Incomplete.]

1. The date is determined by the fact that when NG left camp on 21 April for a week's trip he was still expecting the French minister "every day." When he returned, he learned the minister had arrived in his absence.
2. The Westerly farm, which had been acquired by NG's brothers with assets from their father's estate, became NG's share of the estate. (See Indenture of 10 June, below.) It had been purchased from Gov. Samuel Ward's heirs, one of whom was the wife of NG's brother Christopher.
3. On Gérard's eventual visit to Middlebrook, see below, NG to Washington, 27 April.

To George Washington

Sir   Trenton [N.J.] April 21st 1779

I have this moment receivd a Letter from Col Mitchel, informing me of the Minister of France haveing postpond his visit to Camp. On my arrival at Philadelphia I shall wait upon the Minister, and will indeavor to learn the precise time he sets out and give your Excellency the earliest information.[1]

By several Letters I have receivd on the Road I find the preparations for the Indian expedition will be defeated, unless we can get a better supply of cash. Horses is not to be had without the money in hand; and we cannot get a supply to execute the orders given. It is impossible for us to make Bricks without straw. Neither will it be in our power to put the Army in motion at the Time your Excellency has fixt unless we are better supported with the needful. However nothing shall be wanting on my part. The business and preparations are in great forwardness and nothing will be wanting depending upon us; but Horses and not these if cash can be had equal to our wants; but without it nothing is to be done.

I intend to lay the matter before a committee of Congress and advertize them of the consequences. On the one hand your Excellency is pressing to have your Orders executed faithfully and punctually, and on the other the means necessary for the purpose, are delayd and withheld. I conceive my situation to be very disagreeable. I am held responsible without the power to perform.[2] I am with great respect and regard Your Excellency Most Obedient humble Sert

NATH GREENE

ALS (Washington Papers: DLC).
1. On Gérard's visit, see below, NG to Washington, 27 April.
2. NG met with the Supply Departments Committee on 22 April and reportedly informed them that the department was "considerably in debt, and that the orders he has

received from the Commander in Chief cannot possibly be complied with . . . unless he can receive very considerable supplies of money." (*JCC*, 14: 503) Congress responded with an appropriation of $5 million for the department, which Pettit received about 20 May. Further demands of the Indian expedition forced NG to request two additional appropriations of $5 million each, which Congress approved on 4 and 22 June. (*JCC*, 14: 570, 686, 757; see also Pettit to NG, 11, 12, 19, and 21 May, and NG to Wadsworth, 14 May, below.)

To Colonel John Davis

Sir   Philadelphia 22d April 1779

You have already received Instructions to procure for the publick Service in the western Country from 700 to One thousand Pack Horses; as many of these as can be got on hire you will procure in that way, the Residue must be purchased. You will engage for this purpose some proper Person to act as superintendant, who will have the Direction and oversight of their Conduct; you will also appoint proper Persons to act as Horse Masters over the companies or droves assigned them, with proper drivers for the smaller sub-divisions.[1] The Wages to be given for these several Employments, cannot now be exactly ascertained; it must therefore be left in a great measure to your Discretion which is much relied on as well from your standing in the publick service, as your knowledge in that particular kind of Business. You will be careful to employ Men of suitable Abilities and Capacity for the Stations you place them in, and agree with them on such Terms as, on the whole, you shall find will be most for the Interest of the United States.

A number of Teamsters, or Waggon Drivers are wanted for the Teams of the Army. You will please to enlist as many suitable Persons for this purpose as you can procure so that they be at Camp in the course of the next Month. It will be best to enlist them for nine Months or the end of the Campaign at the Option of the Quarter Master General. The Wages to be given them cannot yet be ascertained; but it will not be less than forty Dollars per Month and a Suit of Cloaths by way of Bounty.[2] However, the enlisted Waggoners will be put all on a Footing and you may assure those you engage that they shall receive the Wages which shall be established; if you can engage one, two or even three hundred proper Men for this Business they will be wanted. I am, Sir, your humble Servant

NATH GREENE

Cy (WaU).

1. These were pack horses.

2. The forty-dollar figure and the suit of clothes were set out in the resolution of Congress of 17 April. (*JCC*, 13: 467–68)

To George Washington

Sir   Philadelphia April 22, 1779

I waited upon the Minister of France this morning, and find he sets out for Camp on Tuesday next.[1] He has recoverd a tolerable share of health and seems in perfect good humour. It is said he has been detaind by Congress for some days past; but on what account is a matter of speculation.

There is a report secretly whisperd about town that there has some overtures of Peace been made by Great Britain through Don Juan [de Miralles] to the Minister of France and by him to the Congress, but not in an official line, and it is said the conditions are such as are totally inadmissable. The fishery to be wholly given up to Great Britain. From the best information I can get I think there is some foundation for the Report, and that in consequence of it, there is a strange and unaccountable tardiness laid hold of the Minds of the Members of Congress. Every preparation and public exertion seems to be discouragd and embarassed.[2]

I suped with Governor Read [Reed] last Night, and he threw out several hints of the kind, which I find confirmd by others today.

I have laid my business before Congress, and requested a special Committee may be appointed to hear me, or that I may be heard before Congress. I expect an answer every moment, and have sat down to write in the meantime.[3]

I am fully convinced that it will be totally out of my power to procure the necessary Horses for the Indian expedition or to put the Army in motion by the time your Excellency has fixt without a very large supply of cash, which we have but a poor prospect of geting. The Boats and Stores I believe will be in readiness seasonably.[4]

I am more and more convinced there is measures taken to render the business of the quarter masters Department odious in the Eyes of the people, and if I have not some satisfaction from the Committee of Congress respecting the matter, I shall beg leave to quit the Department. I think I shall leave it upon as good a footing as is possible to put it under the present difficulties.[5]

I am informd General Lincolns Leg is likely to render him incapable of holding his command to the Southward. Should that be the case, and I leave the Department I am now in; I should be happy to obtain it.[6] I am with great respect Your Excellencys Most Obedient humble Sert

NATH GREENE

ALS (Washington Papers: DLC).

1. On Minister Gérard's visit, see below, NG to Washington, 27 April.

2. As noted earlier, Spain's repeated offers to mediate between England and the United States had been refused by George III, but the outcome was still in doubt in

America. (See note at Pettit to NG, 15 February, above, on the efforts to bring Spain into the war.) In response to the French minister's insistence upon knowing the minimum terms upon which the United States would accept a peace treaty, Congress had begun a five-month debate in March. The New England delegation did not succeed in making the Newfoundland fisheries one of the minimum terms.

3. NG did indeed write to Congress on this date as noted in *JCC*, 14: 503, but the letter has not been found.

4. He did succeed in getting money, as noted above at his letter to Washington of the twenty-first.

5. For similar expressions of NG's dissatisfaction, see below, NG to Washington, 24 April, and NG to Jay, 27 April.

6. General Lincoln had suffered a severe leg wound during the battle of Saratoga which left him permanently lame. There may have been reports circulating around Philadelphia that the injury was once again troubling Lincoln, but he remained in command of the Southern Army until his surrender to the British in May 1780 at Charleston, S.C.

From George Washington

Sir   Head Quarters Middlebrook [N.J.] 22d April 1779[1]

I received yesterday evening your letter of the 21st.

At this time I could have wished there had been no obstructions in the way of completing our Indian preparations. I would imagine however, that your personal representation to a committee of Congress, on the subject of your letter, will procure an immediate and necessary supply of money; which you think is the only thing wanted on the present occasion.

But Should this application fail and in order to prevent further delay, I enclose you a letter to Congress, with a blank date, pressing the supply.[2] But I would not have this communicated unless your own application should not operate agreeable to the intention. I am &c

Df (Washington Papers: DLC).

1. If Washington's date of 22 April was correct, then NG's letter of the twenty-first arrived in Middlebrook the same day it left Philadelphia—not impossible, but unlikely—while Washington's letter required two days to reach NG on the twenty-fourth. It seems more likely that Washington wrote on the twenty-third; in which case each letter would have reached its recipient the following day.

2. As seen below in NG's letter of Saturday, the twenty-fourth, he decided before Congress reconvened on Monday, the twenty-sixth, to make use of Washington's letter. Whether he or someone in Congress dated Washington's undated letter is not known, but it was recorded in the journal as being dated the twenty-third, along with another letter from Washington of that date. (*JCC*, 14: 511)

In his letter to Congress, Washington echoed NG's opinion that unless NG "receive an immediate and ample supply of money the preparations for the Indian expedition in particular and for other operations with which we must open the campaign, will not be completed in the time appointed in my orders to him, and required by the exigency of our affairs." He amplified the need for horses, which if not supplied by mid-May "at furthest, our whole plan will be defeated." He ended with the expectation that "Congress will not hesitate to grant the necessary supply." (Fitzpatrick, *GW*, 14: 438)

From Silas Deane

[Philadelphia, 23 April 1779. Sends papers by Col. [Samuel] Webb that are part of Deane's defense against the charges levelled at him. Hopes they "may be communicated to the Gentlemen of the Army."[1] Comments on possible action by Congress on the currency. Sends his compliments to Mrs. Greene as well as a fan from France to replace her broken one. Wishes her "an Agreeable Journey, when marching Orders oblige her to leave you." ALS (RHi) 2 pp.]

1. For background on Deane's dispute with Arthur Lee and the resulting factionalism in Congress, see above, John Cadwalader to NG, 5 December 1778.

From Colonel Jeremiah Wadsworth

[Hartford, Conn., 23 April 1779. Acknowledges NG's of 14 April, which contained papers relating to their partnership.[1] Hopes Sullivan will be successful. "I really do not wish him any Evil."[2] Notes currency is of little worth and "hardly deserves the name." Will return to camp and Philadelphia as soon as possible. ALS (CtHWa at CtHi) 1 p.]

1. See above, Articles of Partnership, 4 April.
2. On a dispute between Sullivan and Wadsworth, see above, NG to Pettit, 4 December 1778.

To George Washington

Sir   Philadelphia April 24th 1779

Your Excellencys favor of the 22d was deliverd me this afternoon.[1]

I am happy to find you have wrote so fully to Congress upon the disagreeable consequences that may follow from starveing the quarter Masters Department at this critical season. I wish it may have the desird effect and rouse their attention; but I must confess I am afraid the stupor is so great that nothing can alarm their fears or promote a spirit of industry. I had but very little prospect from my own application of obtaining the necessary supplies of Cash. What additional influence your Excellencys Letter will give to my reasons and representation, time only can manifest.[2]

The treasury appears to be hard prest on every side, and the demands at this Time are infinitely greater than is in their power to satisfy with the greatest exertions upon the present plan of striking Money. The truth of the affair is there has been a great degree of Negligence and want of timely attention to prepare seasonably for the present demands. When I was in Town in the Winter I reported to the

Treasury Board what I thought would be absolutely necessary for the quarter Masters department to the 2d of March, Not one half of which have we been able to get altho everything has been urged to induce them to satisfy our wants.

On my arrival here I laid your Excellencys Letter respecting Waggoners before a Committee of Congress.[3] They immediately confirmd it by a Resolution; notwithstanding they had been hammering upon the business for almost two Months off and on; and finally had put it (before the receipt of your Letter) upon a very restrictive plan.

The business of financeing is in a poor way. There is no plan formd or scheme digested for mending our Money. There is a thousand projects on foot; but none appear to be taken up on a practical footing.

There is complaints and murmurings in Congress against the people of this State and the people of the State complain against the proceedings of Congress. It is said days and Weeks together are spent upon the most triffleing disputes in the World; and those generally of a personal Nature. What will be the issue of this policy I know not.[4]

I have wrote Circular Letters to all the Deputies in my Department on the East side of the Susquehannah; to enlist as many Waggoners as they possibly can by the middle of next Month; and to have all the public Teams forwarded so as to be in Camp by that Time.[5] I expect our Waggon Horses will fall short, as our Agents have but a scanty supply of money. However I will do the best I can.

I wish to know whether I must increase the Number of Pack Horses. Orders has been given for 1000, but General Sullivan thinks near 500 more will be wanted. It dont appear so to me; but I am not a good judge of the business.[6]

The Board of War are out of Lead; and I fear the Ammunition will not be ready timely. This is only conjectural.

I wrote Your Excellency before that the Minister of France sets out for Camp on Tuesday next. Don Juan [de Miralles] will accompany him.[7]

There is a French ship just arrivd from the West Indies; but I cant learn that she brings anything new.

I intended to have set out for Camp tomorrow; but I believe I shall not be ready until Monday in the forenoon.[8]

I have desird Congress to give me leave to resign as I apprehended a loss of Reputation if I continued in the business. They are not disposd to grant my request at all. But unless they change the system or publish their approbation upon the present, I shall not remain long in the business. I will not sacrifice my Reputation for any consideration whatever. I am willing to serve the public but I think I have a right to choose that way of performing the service which will be most honorable to my self. I should be willing to serve in the Department I am in, for a proper consideration, if I could serve without loss of Reputation; but not without.[9]

I believe it has been a received opinion that I was so very fond of the emoluments of the quarter Masters office, that nothing but absolute necessity would induce me to quit it. I will not deny but that the profits is flattering to my fortune but not less humiliating to my Military pride; and he who has entertaind such Sentiments is a stranger to my feelings.

While I had a prospect of pleasing your Excellency, the Army, and the Congress the service was agreeable, but if a combination of circumstances changes those prospects, Nothing shall induce me to continue in the business, even if the profits is made five times as large as they are.

There is a great difference between being raisd to an Office and decending to one; which is my case. There is also a great difference betwext serving where you have a fair prospect of honor, and laurels, and where you have no prospect of either, let you discharge your duty ever so well. No body ever heard of a quarter Master in History as such or in relateing any brilliant Action.

I engag'd in this business as well out of compasion to your Excellency as from a regard to the public. I thought your task too great to be commander in chief and quarter master at the same time. Money was not my motive. For you may remember I offerd to serve a year unconnected with the Accounts without any additional pay to that which I had as a Major General. However this proposition was rejected as inadmissable. Then I told the Committee I would serve upon the same terms that Mr Cox and Mr Pettit could be engagd upon; and I have nothing more now, altho I have a double share of duty, and held responsible for all failures.[10]

Before I came into the Department your Excellency was obligd often to stand quarter master. However capable the principal [Thomas Mifflin] was of doing his duty, he was hardly ever with you. The Line and the Staff were at War with each other. The Country had been plunderd in a way that would now breed a kind of civil War between the Staff and the Inhabitants. The manner of my engageing in this business and your Excellencys declaration to the Committee of Congress that you could stand quarter master no longer are circumstances which I wish may not be forgotten as I may have ocasion at some future day to appeal to your Excellency for my own justification.

One thing I can say with truth and sincerity that I have conducted the business with as much prudence and oeconomy as if my private fortune had been answerable for the disbursements. And I believe your Excellency will do me the justice to say the Department has coopperated with your measures as far as circumstances were to be governd by me; and this you had reason to apprehend would not have been the case had I not taken the direction of the business. And here in justice to my Colleagues I shall mention that I think them entitled to your Excellencys personal esteem from the warmth of their wishes and a desire to promote your ease and convenience.

I am more acquainted with Mr Pettit's Mode of doing business than I am with Mr Coxes; but I think the public under great obligations to the former for his method, and oeconomy. I am with the most perfect esteem Your Excellencys Most Obedient humble Sert

NATH GREENE

ALS (Washington Papers: DLC).
1. As noted at Washington's letter, it may have been written on 23 April.
2. On the substance of Washington's letter to Congress, see note at his letter of the twenty-second.
3. The reference is to Washington's letter of 19 April, above.
4. On the strained relations between Congress and the Pennsylvania government, see above, Pettit to NG, 20 March.
5. See NG's letters to Udny Hay and Ezra Starr of 20 April and to John Davis of 22 April, above.
6. Washington's letter of 4 May, below, asked that NG fill all of Sullivan's requisitions "so far as is consistent with the general directions you receive from me."
7. On Gérard's trip to camp, see note at NG to Washington, 27 April, below.
8. He did not leave until Tuesday, the twenty-seventh.
9. NG may not have known that his friend Gouverneur Morris, the committee chairman, had summarized NG's testimony for the members of Congress the day before. General Greene, Morris said, "informed your Committee that the jealousies and suspicions which have prevailed with respect to the mode of paying for the services rendered in his Department [i.e., the commission system]; the very considerable tho' unavoidable expenditures, and the obloquy to which he finds himself exposed thereby, lay him under a necessity of resigning his office . . . unless it can be held consistent with his reputation: wherefore he prays that Congress will take his Department into their early consideration." (JCC, 14: 503) The committee and the Board of War agreed thereupon to confer with NG and report back on Saturday, the twenty-fourth. They did not report on the twenty-fourth but on 11 May, as noted above at NG to Jay, 15 April. Congress substantially approved NG's recommendations on pay scales for deputies and assistants. In the meantime, for the record, NG wrote a detailed and explicit letter on the subject to John Jay. (See below, 27 April.) Congress, however, did not vote to abolish the commission system, and short of that drastic step, there was little that it could do to stay the tide of criticism of the supply departments, although by a resolution in June it did reaffirm its approval of Greene and Wadsworth. (JCC, 14: 695)
10. For background on NG's acceptance of the quartermaster general post, see above, vol. 2: 308–11n.

From George Washington

Dear Sir　　　　　　　　　　Middlebrook [N.J.] Aprl 24, [177]9
　　Your letter of the 22d came to my hands about 9 o'clock this day. I thank you for the information contained. After the minister has actually set out, I should be glad to be informed of it by exp[r]ess and (if

the knowledge can be obtained readily) to be informed of his stages, and the hour he may be expected in Camp.[1]

I am sorry for the difficulties you have to encounter in the department of Quarter Master, especially as I have been in some degree instrumental in bringing you into it. Under these circumstances I can[n]ot undertake to give advice, or even to hazard an opinion on the measures best for you to adopt. Your own judgment must direct. If it points to a resignation of your present office, and your inclination leads you to the southward, my wishes shall accompany it; and if the appointment of a successor to General Lincoln is left to me, I shall not hesitate in prefering you to this command, but I have little expectation of being consulted on the occasion.[2] With truth and sincerity I am Dr Sir Yrs &c

GO: WASHINGTON

ALS (Concord [Mass.] Free Public Library).
    1. On Gérard's final plans, see below, NG to Washington, 27 April.
    2. As noted above at NG to Washington, 22 April, Lincoln's leg injury did not prevent him from continuing in his command. Washington, however, was indeed prophetic in saying that he would not be consulted on an eventual successor to Lincoln, as Congress appointed General Gates in June 1780 to head the Southern Army without soliciting Washington's advice.

To George Washington

Sir   Philadelphia April 26th 1779
    Your Excellencys favor of the 24th I had the honor of receiving last Evening.

I din'd yesterday with the Minister of France and find him still determind to set out for Camp tomorrow. He sets out at seven in the morning and intends lodging at Trenton. On Wednesday he will be in Camp if no accident attends him; but at what hour cannot be ascertaind as the place he dines at is not yet determind on.[1]

I intend to wait upon him sometime this morning and learn more particularly his stages. Don Juan [de Miralles] accompanys him.

I thank your Excellency for your generous and obligeing offer. Most certain my inclinations lead me to a resignation. My reputation I value more than any advantages of gain; and I consider it in great danger.

I wrote your Excellency lengthy upon this subject yesterday and therefore shall say but little upon it to day. I intend to write to Congress to day upon the subject of my apprehensions and determination; and if they dont give me those kind of assurances which is necessary to guard my reputation from Malice and detraction I shall insist upon leaveing the business.[2]

The politicks of Congress are really alarming and the state of the financeing asstonishing, where they will end time only can unfold.

Mr Holker made many enquiries yesterday respecting the temper and disposition of our army.[3] He seemd desirous to know whether peace upon a plan of Independence agreeable to the state of the alliance would be satisfactory. The fishery to be confind to the limits of the states. This would well nigh ruin the Eastern States. Upon the whole I think there has been some overtures made upon the subject of peace. It is said Russia on the part of England and Spain on the part of France are to stand Mediators. This is merely conjectural. Mr Jay says the Congress have no official propositions of peace; but I believe it is beyound a doubt there has been debates upon the subject for several days past Particularly with regard to the fishery.[4]

I spent last Evening with Governor Read [Reed]. I took ocasion to hint that General Sullivan was to command the Western Expedition. He took the alarm at once, and insisted he had no hopes of success if he was to direct the operations. So deep are the prejudices of human Nature. I had several hours conversation with him: and I believe satisfied him as far as is possible that the appointment was the result of the maturest deliberation. We were in private.

If I leave the quarter master Department I should be glad of the South Carolina appointment. However I shall wish to consult your Excellency upon the offer.[5]

We have an agreeable piece of intelligence from the Eastward; which is that Col Cambell and thirty or forty officers and Six or Eight Sail of transports bound for Europe were taken lately by a couple of our Frigates, and carried into Boston.[6]

I had Letters last night from South Carolina which indicates a great disgust between the State and the Congress. They think themselves neglected. There is a large number of public Vessels now on pay in the Harbour loaded with Rice which want to sail but the State is so much sourd that they wont grant exclusive priviledges to the Continental Vessels from the embargo.[7] The Express is waiting. I can only add that I am with esteem and affection your Excell obt Sert

NATH GREENE

ALS (Washington Papers: DLC).
    1. On his trip to camp, see NG's letter of 27 April to Washington.
    2. See below, NG to John Jay, 27 April.
    3. Jean Holker (1745–1822) was a French merchant who had accompanied Minister Gérard to America as the French consul general. In association with such financiers as Robert Morris, Holker used his position to acquire considerable wealth, largely through speculation. He resigned and returned to France in 1781 after his government prohibited further commercial enterprise by its representatives. (Marquis de Chastellux, *Travels in North America in the Years 1780, 1781, and 1782*, trans. Howard C. Rice [Chapel Hill: University of North Carolina Press, 1963], 1: 330–31n)
    4. See note at NG to Washington, 22 April, above.

5. On the possibility of NG's taking over General Lincoln's command, see above, NG to Washington, 22 April, and Washington to NG, 24 April.

6. On 17 April the American privateers *Warren, Ranger,* and *The Queen of France* captured seven of nine British transports that were bound for Georgia from New York, laden with provisions and dry goods. When the vessels were brought to Boston, a lengthy struggle ensued between the captains of the privateers and the Navy Board over the distribution of the prize shares, the total of which was reported to be £ 80,000. (William James Morgan, *Captains to the Northward: The New England Captains in the Continental Navy* (Barre, Mass.: Barre Gazette, 1959), pp. 157–62; *Boston Independent Chronicle and Universal Advertiser,* 22 April 1779)

7. See above, Abraham Livingston to NG, 27 February.

From Governor William Greene of Rhode Island

Sir   Providence [R.I.] 26th April 1779
The order received by General Gates from his Excellency General Washington for General Glovers Brigade to hold themselves in readiness to march on the shortest notice, greatly distresses the Inhabitants of this State. You are well acquainted with the weak and misarable state we are in, which renders it unnecessary for me to be particular, But I must entreat you in the most earnest manner to use your utmost influence with his Excellency, to reconsider the order, unless there should be an equal number sent here to supply their places, previous to these marching out of the State.[1] I am, Your Sincere Friend and Hble Servt

WM GREENE

Cy (Washington Papers: DLC).
1. Washington had issued the order on 17 April. (Fitzpatrick, *GW,* 14: 398) Similar instructions were sent to General Putnam's troops stationed at Danbury, Conn. The cause of the readiness alert was the fear that the British would attempt a move up the Hudson River against the American installations at Fishkill and West Point. NG wrote Washington on 6 May, below, but by that time the threat had diminished, and Washington rescinded his orders soon after. (Fitzpatrick, *GW,* 14: 397; 15: 74–75) See Map 1 for these geographic references.

To John Jay, President of the Continental Congress

Sir   Philadelphia 27th April 1779
When I had the honor to meet a Committee of Congress on Fryday last, I took occasion to mention to them my apprehensions that some Reports which were spread abroad concerning the Quarter Masters Department, would have a tendency injurious to the Public Service, by souring the minds of the People, and rendering it difficult to obtain the necessary Supplies for the Army; but as this part of our conferance was not committed to writing and may not have been considered in so serious a point of light as I intended, I take the liberty of communicating it more fully to your Excellency by Letter.[1]

The Gentlemen appointed by Congress to Assist me,[2] as well as myself, begin to be alarmed at the murmurings and complaints which have of late been spread abroad, to the prejudice of the System, and management of our Department. It is scarcely possible to govern a Department so extensive, and which requires the employment of so many Persons in different places, without giving opportunities to dishonest men in the detail of the Business, to take undue advantages; but from the care we have taken in the choice of our Agents, and the attention which has been paid to the Oeconomy of the business, we have reason to believe there have been as few of these abuses as could reasonably have been expected. We therefore believe that these growing clamours are founded on general Suspicions rather than on Facts, and propagated from improper Motives. And tho' we are conscious of having faithfully discharged our duty to the best of our Abilities, we are nevertheless apprehensive that injurious Imputations, however unjust, may reach our Reputation and that unless these evil Reports are speedily corrected, Jealousies and Discontents may grow among the People to the Injury of the Publick Service. I cannot but consider the Department as in a critical Situation; and should the prejudices of the People throw new difficulties in the way of the Business, it cannot fail of producing some disagreeable consequences. We therefore request the favor of Congress to signify their Sense of our Conduct.

If the present System on which our Agents are employed, is thought to be prejudicial to the Public Interest, and that a new one ought to be adopted, we have already declared our willingness to give aid to such a measure.

Our highest Ambition has been to give satisfaction to the Army, and to merit the approbation of Congress. These ends we have assiduously endeavoured to obtain; but if our past services have no Claim to this Honour, we have no hopes of succeeding in future, and would wish to give place to abler hands. We pretend not to be regardless of the pecuniary reward we derive from the Publick, but a fair reputation and the esteem of our fellow Citizens we value at a much higher Rate; no pecuniary consideration would therefore induce us to continue longer in the present employment, than is consistent with their preservation. We did not solicit our appointment, neither have we a wish to hold it, if our merit is less than our Reward.[3] I have the honor to be with great respect Your Excellency Most obedient humble Sert

NATH GREENE

DfS (MiU-C).
    1. As noted above at NG to Washington, 24 April, Gouverneur Morris had made a very brief summary of NG's testimony before the committee.
    2. Charles Pettit and John Cox.

3. Wadsworth made the same request. As a consequence, Congress on 7 June passed a resolution expressing full confidence in Wadsworth and Greene and even praising many of the "inferior officers" in their departments. (See below, Jay to NG, 8 June.)

To George Washington

Sir   Trenton [N.J.] April 27th 7 oClock in the Evening [1779]

His Excellency the Ambassador [Gérard] is now at this place. He sets off for Camp at 7 oClock in the morning and intends dining with your Excellency.

I have this moment arrivd here. I left Philadelphia between two and three this afternoon. Before I left Town an Express arrivd from Georgia that brought dispaches from General Lincoln. He says there has been two little skirmishes lately in both which we gaind some advantage over the Enemy.[1]

General How [Robert Howe] is arrivd in Philadelphia with his family and intends seting off for Camp in a few days.

Col Cox sends off immediately a light Waggon with a Sturgen and some Shad for Headquarters. It will travel all night and arrive seasonably to have the fish for dinner.

It is most probable the Ambassador will arrive about 4 oClock in the afternoon. He breakfasts at Princetown. Don Juan [de Miralles] is in company with him. They all lodge to Night with Colo Cox. Lord Sterling and Governor Livingston is here.[2] I am with great respect your Excellencys most obedient humble Sert

NATH GREENE

Col [Tench] Tilghman arrivd in Phil'd last night.

ALS (Washington Papers: DLC).
1. Lincoln was in the vicinity of Augusta, unaware that British General Prevost was marching northward along the coast in an attempt on Charleston. But as seen above in the note on British southern strategy (NG to Sullivan, 26 January), Lincoln turned Prevost back at the edge of Charleston on 12 May.
2. In keeping with the gala reception that Congress had given Minister Gérard on his arrival in July 1778, a corps of Philadelphia Light Dragoons had accompanied the minister's party to Trenton. Sources vary as to the date of their arrival at camp, but all agree that once the party had settled in, they were treated to a gala military display. As described by Dr. James Thacher, who was present, a stage was erected for the spectators, which included, in addition to the foreign dignitaries, "Mrs. Washington, Mrs. Greene, Mrs. Knox, and a number of other ladies, who had arrived in their carriages." At a signal of thirteen cannon, Dr. Thacher continued, "the great and splendid cavalcade approached in martial pomp and style," at the head of which rode Lighthorse Harry Lee and his dragoons, followed by Washington and his generals (including NG) on horseback. As the generals reached the viewing area, they dismounted and joined the ladies and honored guests. All then watched as the army "performed the field manoeuvres and evolutions, with firing of cannon and musketry." As a finale, the troops marched past the reviewing stand in formal salute. (See Thacher, *Journal*, p. 162, and *N.J. Archives*, 3: 291.)

From Nehemiah Hubbard

Sir   Hartford [Conn.] April 27th 1779

I have recd a letter from Colo John Cox of the 19th Inst requesting me to purchase one hundred and twenty five horses and thirty oxen to complete the Teams at this post. And I have this day recd a letter from Capt Starr enclosing a copy of yours to him,[1] with a copy of his Excellency's orders respecting waggoners &c. The prospect of Enlisting waggoners in this State at present is but trifling. You may however depend on our joint endeavors to Enlist the number wanted.

Cash will be necessary to purchase the horses and to pay the first months wages of the waggoners if I should enlist any which will be a very great embarrassment, as I am entirely destitute, though I have borrowed nearly thirty thousand dollars. The rapid depreciation of our currency makes it impossible to do business without money. I have daily horses offered me for sale but cannot purchase for want of cash, and the rise of horses is nearly as rapid as that of grain.

No news of Mr Jones since he left headquarters. Hope he will soon come on with the money. The scarcity of flour in this part of the Country induces me to ask if I cannot be supplied from the Issuing Commissary Store from time to time as may have occasion for. I have never drawn any thing from the Commissary store since my appointment, and should not ask it now if flour Could be purchased. However if it is not Customary, and the other Deputies do not receive any benefit from that quarter I will still try to do without it.

I am called on to know in what manner we are to settle with the inhabitants of Reading for the damage done by the troops under Command of Major General Putnam, in encamping on their farms, cutting their wood &c. Your directions will be esteemed a particular favor by your Obedt humble Servt[2]

N HUBBARD

LB (RG 93, WRMS: DNA).
1. See above, note at NG to Udny Hay, 20 April.
2. In NG's answer of 2 May, below, he ignored Hubbard's plea for money and his request to be supplied from the commissary store, but NG did answer his inquiry concerning the handling of damages by Putnam's troops.

To Jacob Greene

[Middlebrook, N.J. 28–30] April, 1779.[1]

You mention the envious dispositions of Mr —— and Mr ——.[2] I expected nothing better from the first of these gentlemen; the last, I thought had more principle than to be wholly under the influence of a spirit of detraction; but it is as impossible for a person to be appointed to a place of either honour or profit, and not be subject to the attacks of the malevolent and envious, as it is for the sun to shine and vegetation not to spring.

I feel the attacks of such people daily, but as I am conscious of having faithfully discharged my duty, I regard them the less. There have been great pains taken of late to draw a cloud over my department, from the amazing disbursements that have taken place. But as that has been owing to the depreciation of money, and not to want of economy, I regard it the less. However, it is a popular subject, and the people in general seem to be better pleased at finding their servants rascals, than at finding them honest and faithful to their trust. I have just returned from Philadelphia, where I have been to make a representation of the growing clamours. I have told the congress I will not serve them at the risk of my reputation, and if they think my reward greater than my merit, I wish to quit the business; or if my past services are not satisfactory, it is my desire to leave the department, as I have no hopes to conduct the business more to their satisfaction. This representation I have made in writing, to which they have given no answer.[3] But they give me all the assurances in their individual capacity that I can wish or desire, "that they have the most perfect confidence in my justice and integrity, as well as ability and attention." However, these assurances did not satisfy me, as I knew they might vanish like smoke, at a future day, and would not serve as vouchers to the public for my justification.

Excerpt reprinted from Johnson, *Greene*, 1: 130–31.
1. Johnson referred to the letter only as having been written in April 1779; the dates are determined by the fact that NG did not return from Philadelphia until 28 April.
2. The two men have not been identified.
3. See above, NG to Jay, 27 April.

To Colonel Udny Hay

Sir   Camp [Middlebrook, N.J.] April 29, 1779
Your favor of the 8th of April has been receivd.[1]

I have not said anything to the General as yet respecting the Clothing, he grants every thing of that sort with so much reluctance that I am loth to say any thing to him upon the subject.

You may venture to give our Artificers forty five dollars a month and with that they must be content.

I have just returnd from Philadelphia where I have been to get something done for the Staff. I recommended to allow Assistants 140 Dollars a month, Waggon Masters 80 and forage Masters the same. I think the whole will pass in Congress.[2]

We shall furnish you and Mr Bostwick with a new supply of cash as soon as possible; but I assure you it is very difficult to get sums equal to our wants. The Treasury grows tardy and is pressed on every side for money. I hope the people wont pretend to withhold the public Horses if the cash is not ready to deliver them at the time necessity shall oblige us to call for the Cattle.

I cannot say I admire your plan for purchasing Horses. To advertize that you are in want will give Cattle an immediate rise. If you were to employ private contractors I should think it would answer a much better purpose. The people need but be informd of the public wants to take advantage of their necessity. It will answer no valueable purpose to conceal the persons Names with whom you contract after the public are made acquainted that Horses are wanted. If Horses were plenty and people anxious for the business your plan would be elligible; but in the present State of things, I believe it will be productive of more evil than good.

I have not wrote to General M Dougall yet respecting a court of enquiry. If there has been any regular complaint a court of enquiry is necessary; otherwise I think not. To clear yourself of what you are not accusd, appears singular. I would not wish you to issue the advertisement you mention promising a reward to all persons who will appear and accuse you or any of your Agents. It will have too much the air of a bravado. Innocence is ever at ease and wants nothing of the bluster of a coward to support itself.[3]

I must beg your utmost exertions to have everything in readiness as soon as possible to put the Troops in motion. You must write to Mr [William] Smith to hasten forward the Stores from Springfield [Mass.].

Let your Tent Makeers make as many Horsemans Tents as possible as we shall fall greatly short in that article and in the articles of Markees. I am Sir Your humble Sert

NATH GREENE

ADfS (RPB).
1. Letter not found.
2. See above, NG to Jay, 15 April.
3. For more on this issue, see below, Hay to NG, 11 May.

To Colonel Robert L. Hooper, Jr.

[Middlebrook, N.J., 29 April 1779. Promises aid in obtaining a fair trial for Hooper.[1] When NG met with Congress, he stressed the need for cash. Has directed Pettit to give preference to Hooper's needs, which "are large and will require to be first executed." The need for packhorses and wagoners is detailed along with the need for Hooper to name a superintendent of packhorses.[2] ADfS (MiU-C) 3 pp.]

1. It is evident that Hooper had related the particulars of his trial in two letters to NG of 20 April, but they have not been found. The trial apparently grew out of charges made to a committee of Congress in 1778 by some of Hooper's political enemies who accused him of making improper use of public wagons. In a report of 23 January 1779, the committee recommended to Congress that a formal court of inquiry hear the evidence. Congress acquiesced by requesting Washington to order a court-martial. (*JCC*, 13: 106–7) There is no evidence, however, that a court-martial was ever held. For Hooper's earlier difficulties with the Pennsylvania radicals, see above, vol. 2: 424–25, 429–30.

2. On the need for wagoners, see also NG to Udny Hay and Ezra Starr, 20 April, above. For Hooper's response to these requests, see below, Hooper to NG, 5 May.

To All It May Concern

[Middlebrook, N.J., 30 April 1779. Certifies that Henry B[rockholst] Livingston served with NG in the campaigns of 1777 and 1778. He showed himself "as a good and gallant Officer" at the battles of Monmouth and Rhode Island. "As an Officer of merit, spirit and activity I desire to recommend him to the Notice of all Strangers."[1] ADfS (PCC, item 173, vol. 1: 321, DNA) 1 p.]

1. The recommendation was requested by Livingston when he was entering the foreign service. See below, William Blodget to Livingston, 1 May 1779; Heitman, *Register*.

To Griffin Greene

Dear Sir   Camp at Middle Brook [N.J.] April 30th 1779

I receivd your obliging Letter of the 13th.[1]

I did not propose to have the writings of partition sent to me to be sign'd because I had any objection to giving you the necessary powers but because I thought it the most expeditious and effectual mode and would save reconveyances. I have signd the power inclosd me by brother Jacob and with you to exercises it in all cases whatsoever until I revoke it.

I cannot think your plan of purchaseing the Island of Patience will be consistent with your views of business.[2] It is a good farm; but it will rent but for a trifle and it will make a prodigious draft from your Stocks. If you intend to quit trade altogether and have an inclination after the War to live upon the Island your self, I think your scheme eligible. But in no other light. You are much mistaken in your calculation respecting the rate exchange between Continental and hard Money. It is now in Philadelphia from 17 to 20 for one, and was upon the rise a few days since.

It is hardly possible for me to conceive how Iron can have got below what it sells for to the Westward where is the great manufactory for this article. We want large quantitys of Iron at Springfield [Mass.] upon Conecticut River where there is a Labotory [laboratory]. Mr [William] Smith is my agent there. You may write to him, and let him know your terms, and the quallity of your Iron and the quantity you can furnish at certain periods. I will also write him to apply to you if he can be furnished upon as good terms as to the Westward.

I dont think your plan of Ship building will answer your expectations in the present declining state of the currency. The depreciation will exceed all your profits. As soon as the Vessel is begun the accounts commences and all the depreciation that happens from the time the Ship is began until completed is so much deduction from your profits; and as the progress of this business is slow your profits will be small. However I submited it to your consideration and better judgment.

You say you have laid out all your Money and have little or nothing to do. The greatest profits that have been made in this State of late has been in Land purchases. A great number of Tory Estates have been sold which lay in large tracts of Land. I knew a man the other day that made 20,000 pounds only in the purchase of one farm. Did you and Jacob purchase Uncle Johns part of the Forge and Iron Works. I think you had better; if you ever intend to drive any great strok of business. For that will always hang over you like a rod in sook [?]. And you know he will be always ready to take advantage of your Necessity.

I shall be much oblige to you for a true state of the settlement of partition and stocks between me and my brothers as soon as it is completed.[3]

If you should come across any good Shirting Linnen which can be had upon good terms please to purchase Cloth enough for half a dozen Shirts.

The Minister of France is now in Camp and all things are in the *beau mon* [monde]. Parade upon Parade and Bow upon Bow. He is one of the politeest men of the age and appears to be very honest and candid. I admire him very much.[4] The Alliance with France is a most happy affair. It alleviates a thousand of our distresses and serves to check the great projects of Britain.

Jacob writes me that Patty is upon the decline since the warm weather commenced. I wish you would urge the necessity of having her frequently dipt; and pray them to give her as little food as she can possibly subsist with. It is impossible for her to recover her perfect shapes while she is cramed continually with food. The cold bath is a most sovereign remedy to a relaxed habit.[5]

Mrs Greene desires her kind love to you and Cousin Sally.[6] You will please to present my best respects to Sally. I am with Affectionate regards Your most obedient humble Sert

NATH GREENE

I will write you in my next respecting the Scythes.

ALS (OMC).
1. This letter is a virtual point-by-point response to Griffin's letter of 13 April, above.
2. Patience Island was a mile-square area off the entrance to Greenwich Bay, a part of Narragansett Bay long familiar to NG.
3. On the division of the estate of NG's father, see Indenture of 10 June, below.
4. On the visit of Minister Gérard, see above, NG to Washington, 27 April.
5. Martha Washington (Patty) Greene was suspected of having rickets. See above, vol. 2: 337.
6. Sarah Greene, Griffin's wife.

To Colonel Robert L. Hooper, Jr.

Sir
Camp [Middlebrook, N.J.] April 30th 1779[1]

I want you to employ a good trusty person to find the nearest and best rout for the conveyance of intelligence from Wyoming to Fort Schyler. Regard must be had to the safety of the dispaches as well as the distance and goodness of the Roads. A communication of intelligence will be necessary from those two Posts and the sooner the Rout is marked out the better.

It will be necessary in order to convey intelligence with the greatest dispach to have stages within about thirty miles of each other; at each of which a good faithful rider must be posted. The fidelity of these people must be unquestionable as matters of the highest importance will pass through their hands. The safe and faithful conveyance of which will greatly depend the safety of the Troops and success of the Indian expedition.

Your People brought into Camp ten Horses having lost two upon the Road.

Please to make my and Mrs Greens best respect to Mrs Hooper. I am Sir your humble Sert

NATH GREENE

ADfS (MiU-C).
1. NG may have misdated this draft. In Hooper's letter of 5 May, below, he refers to NG's request for information on the route from Wyoming to Ft. Schuyler as being dated 29 April and as having answered it on the thirtieth. The communication route would link Sullivan's and Clinton's armies.

To Nehemiah Hubbard

[Middlebrook, N.J., 30 April 1779. Has just returned from Philadelphia, where he asked for a more ample supply of cash for the department, but the Treasury Board is greatly pressed and "depreciation increases the demand hourly." Believes Congress will make a "generous and handsome" raise in pay for the staff.[1] Wishes tents, portmanteaus, and horses furnished Putnam's troops for their possible move.[2] LS (NjHi) 2 pp.]

1. See above, NG to Jay, 15 April.
2. See above, Gov. William Greene to NG, 26 April.

To Colonel Jacob Morgan, Jr.

[Middlebrook, N.J., 30 April 1779. Is aware that Morgan has not "entered into warm party disputes," but circular on 26 March had to be sent to all deputies in Pennsylvania.[1] Important that needed wagoners and wagon masters be provided. "It is an object of great importance with the Army and very interesting to my ease and convenience." Teams are desired in Camp by the second week in May. Wishes twelve grindstones "with Cranks" to be sent to Estherton. ADfS (MiU-C) 2 pp.]

1. Morgan's letter of 6 April, in which he apparently complained, has not been found.

To Colonel Jeremiah Wadsworth

Dear Sir   Camp [Middlebrook, N.J.] April 30th 1779

I have receivd your two last letters with the inclosd Alphabet of figures to correspond with.[1] The plan is very agreeable which is proposd. But in addition to it will it not be best to take upon us a fictious [fictitious] name? This will draw another shade of obscurity over the business and render it impossible to find out the connection. The busy World will be prying into the connection and nature of the business; and more especially as a letter of Mr Deanes has lately been intercepted in which it is pretended great things are discoverd and dangerous combinations formd. Whether there has been any Letter intercepted and if there has whether it contains anything of the kind that is represented, I am by no means certain. It is said he is forming one of the greatest Commercial Houses in the World; and has a plan for Land jobing of equal extent.[2] I know not what it all means; but believe it is the effects of Malice and detraction; which I can assure you was never more prevalent.

I have just returnd from Philadelphia where I have been to settle several matters with Congress respecting my department. The fixing the pay of Waggoners and Staff officers. But my principal business was to lay before the Treasury the impossibillity of executing the Generals orders without a more punctual and liberal supply of cash. Former promises have been renewd; but the truth of the affair is, the plan for strikeing money is really incompetent to the demand, with the greatest degree of industry; and there is no great share of that. The great Departments of the Army press the Treasury on every side. The South Carolinia expedition has created great draffts upon the Board; and embarasses their affairs.[3] The Lord knows what will be the consequence.

I find that certain members of Congress are endeavoring to spread among the people that the avarice and extravagance of the Staff are the principal causes of all the depreciation of the money; and I saw a report of the Treasury Board to the Congress to this amount altho not in the same terms.[4]

Inclosd is a Letter I wrote the Congress upon the subject. There was great professions and assurances of the most perfect confidence of Congress in the abillity, fidelity, care, attention, and integrity of the principals of each Department; but as these were only personal assureances by individual members and not as a body I thought it most prudent to write them the enclosd copy of a Letter. I have receivd no answer to it yet. What it will produce is difficult to conjecture.[5]

There is great disputes in Congress; and there has been warm work between them and the State of Pennsylvania respecting the Courts of Admiralty.

I shall be happy to see you here as soon as you can render it convenient. I think it will be necessary both for your interest and Reputation. The General enquires after you with great earnestness.[6] Things dont go on well in the preparations for the Indian Expedition upon the Susquehannah.

Mrs Greenes and my best respects to Mrs Wadsworth. I am with sincere regard your most obedient humble Sert

N GREENE

ALS (CtHi).
    1. The letters to which NG refers have not been found. The "Alphabet of figures" was a cipher that was designed to keep outsiders from determining the partners' investments. Two sets of ciphers are in the Barnabas Deane Papers, CtHi. On NG's concern for secrecy see his letter of 14 April to Wadsworth, above.
    2. Nothing is known about the intercepted letter, but NG was speaking of Silas Deane, who had been under fire for months. (See above, note at John Cadwalader to NG, 5 December 1778.) The very day that NG wrote Wadsworth, Deane was again complaining to Congress, because, as he said, "when returning to the character of a private citizen in the mercantile line, I can not sit down easy under imputations injurious to my character." (Wharton, *Correspondence*, 3: 150)

3. NG is referring to the expedition of General Lincoln. See above, NG to John Sullivan, 26 January.

4. On 31 March the Treasury Committee had written a long report on financing the war, which it did not submit to Congress until 22 April. The committee declared that "a general opinion prevails that one cause of the alarming expences in these Departments [commissary and quartermaster], arises from allowing commissions to the numerous persons employed in purchasing for the Army; and that a very general dissatisfaction has taken place on that account, among the citizens of these United States." (*JCC*, 13: 492) The report did not point to the principals in the departments.

5. See above, NG to John Jay, 27 April.

6. Wadsworth was reported by Washington to be in Middlebrook on 26 May. (Fitzpatrick, *GW*, 15: 156) He then set off for Philadelphia for talks with Congress. Following these discussions he journeyed to camp at Smith's Clove, N.Y., to which the army had just moved from Middlebrook. (Destler, "Wadsworth," p. 114)

From Colonel Robert L. Hooper, Jr.

Sir   Easton [Pa.] May 5th [30 April][1] 1779

The nearest Rout from Wyoming to Fort Schuyler is on the Indian Path to Lachawanick, then to Aninguage or Cookhouse, thence thro' Springfield to the Mohawk River at Stone Rauby [Stone Arabia], but this rout, tho' the nearest and best, is thro' the woods and very unsafe and at this time very impracticable. The next rout is on the Road, marked on my map, to Lachawanick, Schoholy, then to Delaware but from Lachawanick to Delaware the Country is uninhabited and as the Extent is great I think the rout will be unsafe and improper. The next and in my Opinion the only Rout that can be marked out for safety is to Colonel Stroud's, thence to Minisink and keeping on the Essopas [Esopus] Road leading to Kingston to a certain distance where, no doubt, there is a Road that leads to the settlement on Schohary Creek, thence to Fort Hunter on the Mohock River and by the common Rout to Fort Schuyler formerly Fort Stanwix. This rout, tho' 25 miles further than to go by Schoholy, brings the dispatches in one day into the inhabited parts of the country and thro' the whole rout there can be no danger of their falling into the Hands of the Enemy. When you are pleased to inform me on which Rout you have determined I will immediately Station Trusty and Proper men to ride as far as Schohary.

I once mentioned to you, that at this Place and at Bethlehem there is forty two Prisoners of War, Officers and Privates, some Brittish and Brunswickers. I have no reason to say that the Gentlemen will forfeit their Parole but they must become acquainted with our Movements and opperations, this place and Bethlehem being in the Rout of our Army, therefore I think they ought to be removed to some place out of the rout of our Army. You was pleased to approve of my Sentiments, but I cannot move them without an Order.[2]

Mrs Hooper is on a Visit to her Friends in Trenton. You'll please to present my Compliments to Mrs Greene and assure her that I'll take great Pains to procure two Genteel Horses for her. I am sir Your most humble st

ROBT LETTIS HOOPER

ALS (PPAmP).
1. Hooper should have dated his letter 30 April. As he wrote in his letter of 5 May below, this is a copy of a 30 April letter, which he feared NG had not received.
2. NG's order has not been found, but presumably the men were moved.

See Map 3 for those place names that can be accurately located.

Major William Blodget to Colonel Henry B[rockholst] Livingston

Dear Sir   Camp Middle Brook [N.J.] May 1st 1779
General Greene directs me to enclose you the Certificate you requested.[1]

We have just come from reviewing part of the Troops, which made an elegant appearance and the French Ambassador, and Don Juan [de Miralles] (who were present) shew'd great marks of their approbation. The Ambassador has been several days in Camp, and all possible attention has been paid to him and the Don. After the Review, the Baron Stuben gave an invitation to the Ladies, Genl Officers etc to partake dinner with him, w'ch was serv'd up in a most superb manner, and highly pleasing. The French Minister sets off for Philadelphia in the morning.[2]

Should you go into foreign Service except my good wishes; may you reap Laurels equal to your desires, and return safe to your Friends with immortal honors. I am with Regard Dear Sir Your very Hble Servt

WM BLODGET

ALS (MiU-C).
1. See above, To All It May Concern, 30 April.
2. For more on the visit of the French minister, see above, NG to Washington, 27 April.

From Robert Traill[1]

[Easton, Pa., 1 May 1779. Sends maps that Colonel Hooper forgot to enclose with his letter of 30 April. ALS (PPAmP) 1 p.]

1. Traill was Hooper's assistant for Northumberland County.

To Nehemiah Hubbard

[Camp Middlebrook, N.J., 2 May 1779. Acknowledges Hubbard's letter of 27 April. Asks that he provide General Putnam with horses. Since Washington will not permit use of soldiers as wagoners, Hubbard must enlist those needed. Suggests appointing "a number of good honest Farmers" as wagon masters to help enlist wagoners for a brigade of twelve or fourteen teams. NG will allow wagoners "Twenty Pounds a Month, Pennsylvania money, and a suit of Cloths." As for damages done farmers, Congress allows for "no damage at all," but Hubbard can reimburse them for goods taken for use of the army as long as "the public is not imposed upon."[1] LS (MiU-C) 2 pp.]

1. On reimbursing citizens for damages done by the army, see above, NG to Jay, 1 February.

From Colonel Thomas Chase

[Boston, 2 May 1779. Tents sent to Springfield; procurement never so difficult; men ask "5 Dollars a mile for Carting"; at Chase's request the Massachusetts General Court has directed a number of towns to send him teams, but few have complied; is sending lead to Board of War. ALS (PPAmP) 1 p.]

From Colonel George Morgan

Sir   Princeton [N.J.] May 2d 1779

Although the annexd Extrat of a Letter does not communicate the full Intelligence I could wish, I do myself the pleasure to transmit it to you, that you may see I have not been inattentive to the small matter you were pleased to commit to my charge.[1] I have not yet received advice from the Gentleman I directed to open the Road from Turkey Foot to Fort Pitt; but I doubt not its being speedily done, as he is a Man of Activity, and every way qualified for the Service to complete which I sent him three thousand dollars. I therefore take the liberty to request that you will transmit an Order to me for this Sum and the Amount of Captain Clintons demand, the whole being six thousand five hundred dollars, for which I will acct. Or, if you please, your D Qr Mr Genl for the Department may settle and pay the Acct for I would not wish to interfere with him in any Advantage of Commission. It will be a sufficient recompence to me if I have in this Instance, promoted the public, and render'd you an agreeable Service.

In spite of the delays of the Treasury, I have been able to make as ample Provision in the Commissarys Department, as could have been expected; and Colonel Steel tells me he has 600 Horses engaged in transporting Flour from Skipton, to which place it is now carried by Water to the great Saving of Time and Expence.

The principal Delaware Chiefs, with a Number of their Attendants are on their Way to Philadelphia. I have directed them to proceed immediately to Head Quarters, that his Excellency may be inform'd of their Dispositions and Intentions, and give such Orders in consequence, as he may think proper.

I think to detain them here two or three days, to repose themselves and that I may commit to writing every thing they have to communicate, as thereby his Excellency will have the less Trouble. I wish they could be pd some Compliment on their approach to Head Quarters.[2] I am with great Respect Sir Your very obedient hum Servt

GEO: MORGAN

P. S. I inclose Capt Clintons Survey of the Road which please to return to me.[3]

ALS (PPAmP).
    1. The copy of the letter he enclosed was from Capt. Charles Clinton, written on 20 April from Ft. Cumberland, Md. It concerned only part of the "small matter" NG had committed to Morgan's charge, which is explained in Morgan's memorandum of 18 March, above. Captain Clinton reported that he had opened the road from Turkey Foot to Ft. Cumberland except for four or five miles. The road was apparently designed for packhorses, because, he wrote, the men he employed were of the opinion that there were so few stumps it might easily be made into a wagon road. (The letter is in the Greene Papers, PPAmP.)
    2. Morgan accompanied the Indians to Middlebrook, where Washington addressed them on 12 May. His speech, which Morgan undoubtedly helped to write, is in Fitzpatrick, GW, 15: 53–56. The army was paraded to impress the Indians with the prowess of America's fighting men. (Thacher, Journal, p. 163, describes the visit with a note of condescension.)
    3. Clinton's survey has not been found, nor has NG's answer to Morgan. On the construction of the road to Ft. Pitt, see note at Sullivan to NG, 12 May, below.

See Map 3 for geographic references above.

From James Thompson

[Middlebrook, N.J., 2 May 1779. Price of span of horses he examined for NG is "double their Value." Will look for another. ALS (PPAmP) 1 p.]

Colonel Clement Biddle to Moore Furman

[Raritan, N.J., 3 May 1779. NG wishes to confer with Biddle and Furman in Trenton about applying to the New Jersey Assembly for aid. ALS (Nj) 1 p.]

From Colonel Henry Hollingsworth

Dear General   Philadelphia May 3d 1779
    Your favor of the 14th of April by Major Burnet I received at Elk
on the 29th[1] and sho'd have answered it from thence had I not been
certain of an Interview with the Major in this City, to answer which I
do declare every charge against me in that Letter untrue, and must
have been reported to your Excellency by slanderous Tongues, or
dissapointed Persons, who wish to rise by pulling at my Skirts; and as
they have had the advantage of the first charge, were I differently cir-
cumstanced it might make me uneasy; but when I consider that it is
by Maj Genl Green whose impartiality and candor and Justice is so
well established in every Part of America and that the inquiry is made
by the Judicious Majr Burnet, I am happy in receiving the Charges, as
I doubt not but it will in the End be a means of coming at and exhibi-
ting the aggressors to Public view, a thing I have long wished and
endeavoured for, as will now fully appear by the Copys of Letters inclosed which have been sent to yourself and the different Gentlemen
to whom directed, the Originals of which Major Burnet has done me
the Kindness to peruse, and can certify they are the same in Substance.[2]
    My first Charge is Loss of the Peoples confidence which as your
Excellency very justly observes, must be occasioned by misconduct. I
doubt not but that I have my Enemies, but I really do not know them
be they who they may,[3] I am certain they may act from one of the
above Principles, and am clear there is no man in the United States
who has done as much Business as I have for the Public, in as many
different Departments, with a fairer Character with the unprejudiced,
and those that see and know most about my Conduct. Majr Burnet
was so good as to signify that he suspected that I was disrespected by
Govr [Thomas] Johnson. So far is it from being so (which I doubt not
the Majr is satisfied off) that every matter and thing relative to Buying, Storing, removing, and every other measure that is to be done
with the State property in the County where I live, is intrusted to me,
although I have often entreated that it might not be the case, as I had
too much to do for the States in General, and I have ever been so
happy as to live on the most friendly terms with that Gentleman, for
when Govr Johnson of his own Knowlege says that I have done
amiss, I shall be as unhappy as if General Green had said it. As to the
charges against me coming through Members in Congress as I have
ever entertained the highest Opinion of that respectable Body, I am
sorry for it, but Members in Congress may and have been imposed
upon, it is more than probable that the Person who means to injure
my Character tho unknown to me, dispairing of any report he co'd
make himself has inveigled himself into the notice of Certain Mem-

bers of his acquaintance the better thereby to succeed in his Malevolence.

The Charge of Putting my Relations into Office as my Assistants will I flatter myself, assist me to confute the rest, as I never have had any assistants of any relations, at any rate, since my appointment to the D Q M Gs Place or the Forage Department, until the first of April last when I appointed my Brothers son a Youth about Fourteen Years Old to keep Tally at the town landing. This I did from experiencing that no other Person co'd do the Business as well, he living on the spot, and can attend to unload the Vessels continualy without Loss of time, not having any occasion to absent himself on Account of Diet. He has attended regularly to unloading and Keeping Tally since he was Eight Years Old, and as the Public by me occupy my Brothers Wharfs and Stores often to his very great prejudice, though I believe he never was heard to complain, I thought it my duty to appoint his Son, to give a sanction to my occupying his Warehouses &c. It was from the above reasons not because he was my Brothers Son that [I] employed him. I have ever been so very cautious on this Head since My Appointment that I have not employed one of my Brothers in either of the Departments, and though much distressed for an assistant this Spring, (as one of my old ones had left me) one of my younger Brothers being drove in by the Indians, from Muncy, and entirely out of Business, and so continuing, yet never co'd think of appointing him, though I know him to be very capable, and worthy of any appointment that I co'd possibly give him.

As to Appointing Colo Donaldson Yates as a DFMG I sho'd not have the least objection was not my character attacked. Let me have the privilege of first clearing myself from those malicious aspersions and I shall always be happy who may be appointed so that they are honest and capable Men. Such I think Donaldson Yates Esq. to be.

Colo Biddle has not wrote me on the Subject but he has my approbation after I have had the Liberty above requested. As I never Solicited an Office so neither do I mean to Solicit a Continuance any longer than is agreeable to my Principal in Office.

I heartily thank your Excellency for your Impartial inquiry, and am with Compliments to Colo Biddle Dear[4] Sir Your very Obedient and most Humble Servant

H HOLLINGSWORTH

P.S. A proper distinguishment not being made between Quarter Master and Commissary business has I am very sensible been the occasion of many, if not the whole of the Complaints. I made Maj. Burnet sensible of the same to whom I beg leave to refer you to, for further and more particular information.

ALS (PPAmP).

1. NG had sent his aide, Ichabod Burnet, to investigate conditions in Maryland because, as he wrote Pettit on 15 April (above), he had heard so many complaints he was
determined to "know the foundation thereof." NG's letter that accompanied Burnet
has not been found, but Hollingsworth's answer indicates that NG held back none of
the complaints that had reached his ears or eyes. On earlier complaints of Hollingsworth's district, see his letter of 10 February, above, and note.

2. The copies of the letters have not been found.

3. In defending himself against a different set of charges in March 1780, he named
Tobias Rudulph, the commissary general at Head of Elk, as "the only enemy I have,"
although in the same letter he added that "Mr. Yates" (Col. Donaldson Yates mentioned later in this letter to NG) had tried for two years to supplant him as quartermaster, citing a letter from NG to verify the assertion. He named the men in a letter to the
Board of War in March 1780. (PCC, item 43, pp. 99–115, DNA)

4. What answer NG made to this lengthy apologia is not known. In the end, Hollingsworth's letter must have been less persuasive than Burnet's findings in the matter
of convincing NG to keep Hollingsworth on as a deputy. No written report by Burnet
has been found, but it is clear from Pettit's letter of 5 May, below, that, during the return
trip to Camp Middlebrook, Burnet convinced Pettit that most of the criticism of Hollingsworth was ill-founded. It is doubtful, however, that Burnet could have learned
enough in the time he spent in Maryland to have exonerated all of the agents in the district. Since Hollingsworth was his host, moreover, it would be surprising if Burnet was
not somewhat prejudiced in his host's favor. As noted at Hollingsworth's letter of 10
February, above, he was an effective deputy in a district that was a prime source of fod-
der. It is doubtful if Hollingsworth and his agents were any worse or any better than
most of the deputies and agents in the department. In any case, he remained in office
throughout NG's tenure.

From Nehemiah Hubbard

[Hartford, Conn., 3 May 1779. Until he receives money he is unable to
purchase 110 horses and 38 oxen for General Putnam or to transport
any provisions, including flour for Rhode Island. Must also have
money to contract for forage.[1] ALS (PPAmP) 2 pp.]

1. Shortly after Hubbard wrote NG, he received almost $400,000, but by 13 May,
when he next wrote, it was all spent.

From Lieutenant John Cotton[1]

[Croton River, N.Y., 4 May 1779. Desiring to be "perfectly Acquainted" with duties of brigade quartermaster, he is applying directly to "the Fountain Head, where the Streame is Pure." Also asks
why Colonel Hay should not allow an increase in the half dollar a day
that Cotton receives for furnishing the brigade with a horse.[2] ALS
(PPAmP) 1 p.]

1. Cotton was quartermaster of Nixon's brigade.

2. NG's answer has not been found.

From General John Sullivan

Dear Sir   Millstone [N.J.] 4th May 1779

The Letters which accompany this to the Board of War and Colo Proctor are of great importance and ought to be forwarded as Soon as possible. I wish you to give orders that Such Letters as Come from me Directed on publick Service may be immediately forwarded. The Reason of my mentioning this is because a Letter of mine Directed to General Knox upon Business of importance was not Received by him untill Three Days after Sent to your office. I am very Respectfully Sir your most obedt Servt

JNO SULLIVAN

ALS (PPAmP).

From George Washington

Sir   Middle Brook [N.J.] May 4th 1779

Having already fully explained to you the plan of the Western expedition against the Indians of the Six Nations, and the preparations necessary in your department, I am now to inform you that Major General Sullivan is appointed to the command of this expedition, and to desire that you will comply with his immediate requisitions for every thing which falls within the province of your department so far as is consistent with the general directions you receive from me relative to the operations of the Army at large.

I must request you will immediately inform me, with as much precision and certainty as possible; when you will have ready the number of the Waggons and all other matters in your department requisite to enable me to make a general movement of the army, and take the field, agreeable to former directions. You are so well acquainted with the urgent motives to a speedy movement, that I am persuaded, I need not press you to make every exertion in your power for that purpose.

Given at Head Quarters Middle Brook May 4th 1779[1]

G WASHINGTON

LS (PPAmP).

1. Since there was nothing new in this document (Sullivan had been commander of the expedition for a month), Washington obviously wrote it for the record. In the draft, Hamilton had first written in a complimentary close, then scratched it and added the formal ending, docketing it as "Instructions." (The draft is in the Washington Papers, DLC.)

Washington issued formal instructions to Sullivan on the same day, ordering him to move out from his camp at Millstone, N.J., to Easton, Pa., where he was to lay out a road toward the Susquehanna. (See Map 3.) Before decamping, he was to "make every necessary arrangement" with NG and Wadsworth relative to his supplies. (Fitzpatrick, GW, 14: 492)

To General John Sullivan[1]

Camp [Middlebrook, N.J.] May 5th 1779
Colonel Van Schoike has given the Onondagoe Tribe of Indians a very pretty drubbing: he surprised them in their castle, killed twelve of their Warriors, took thirty prisoners (two of which are Sachems) burnt their town, destroyed a great Quantity of provisions, arms, and Amunition.

After which he returned to Fort Schuyler without any loss . . . [2]

Tr (Peter Force Transcripts, Series 7E, Edward Hand Papers, DLC). Extract.
1. The addressee is determined by Sullivan's answer of 10 May, below.
2. Col. Goose Van Schaick of the First New York Regiment at Ft. Schuyler led five hundred troops in an attack on the Onondaga settlement on 21 April. They destroyed the town, which consisted of fifty houses, killed seventeen warriors, and took thirty-two prisoners. (Peckham, *Toll,* p. 59)

From Colonel Robert L. Hooper, Jr.

Sir   Easton [Pa.] May 5th 1779
I wrote you the 30th Ulto in Answer to yours of the 29th Ulto and sent the Maps which I hope you have receivd. Inclosed is a copy of my Letter which, as you have not acknowledged the receipt of it, I have inclosed for your Perusal.[1]

I returned Yesterday from Bucks [county], where I hope to raise about 48 Teamsters, having engaged four Substantial men as conductors and they are now trying to Enlist Teamsters, but they refuse to serve under One hundred Dollars per Month nor will the Teamsters enlist for less than Sixty Dollars per Month. I have Nevertheless engaged these Men and some others to procure Men and have Promised them Your Answer in three days. On these Terms and the Cloaths You Offered as a Bounty with giveing One Months Pay Advance, I think I can raise near One Hundred Men by the twentieth of this Month, Provided I am furnished with Money equal to the Demands Your Orders will Occasion.[2] I receiv'd from Colonel Pettit on Saturday last One hundred and Seventeen Thousand two hundred and fifty Pounds, the whole of which Sum I have Paid for Horses, Forage &ca and as double that Sum will immediately be Wanted, I request You'll be pleased to direct that it shall be paid to me as soon as Possible, for I cannot spirit the People with whom I am connected to act without Money. On Tuesday next I shall send to Camp one Brigade of Teams compleatly filled and I think in the Course of a Week one More which Succession I shall try to continue till I am forbid.

I have about five Hundred Horses Purchased and the Pack Saddles almost compleated. I told You in a former Letter that they were compleated, thinking that I had Linnin sufficient *for the Padds,* but I find myself Mistaken. I want near One Thousand Yards. I sent an Express to Mr Abeel but he can't help me to any. I have People out in every Quarter in Search of Tow Linnin, but the getting of it is uncertain. Therefore if You'll please to give me an Order to receive it where it is to be had, I will send for it, otherwise this unavoidable Accident will Occasion a delay in compleating the Saddles.

I shall be able to Provide a Proper Person to direct the Pack Horse Men, but I beg to be informed how these Men are to be classed. It is sufficient to have Two Men to Ten Horses, Consequently 100 Horses will require Twenty Men over whom One Conductor may be Sufficient. You'll be pleased to inform me how many Pack Horse Men will be wanted and how many Men and Horses each Conductor is to have in his Care.

Forage is very Scarce. It is not to be had in my District in sufficient Quantities to subsist the Pack Horses &ca Thro' to Wyoming, and from Pocano Point to Wyoming the Country is a Barren Desert. I can Scarcely find Sufficient to Answer the calls at this Post. I therefore request You'll be pleased to mention this to Colonel Biddle, that timely Provision may be made. I am head over Heels in debt for the Forage Department.

In Answer to Your Letter of the 3rd Instant, I promise You my close Attention to General Sullivan and his Orders and that every Measure shall be Pursued in my Power to push on the expedition.[3]

The Horses shall be my *Particular care* but I fear I cant get them so soon as Mrs Greene will Expect them nor can I Positively say more than that I will use my best Endeavours and I think I shall Succeed.

My Letter, of which the inclosed is a Copy, was sent by Mr James Gore one of your Express Riders to whom I paid three Guineas for Major Burnet.

Your Friendly and polite Attention to me and the unfeigned regard I have for Your Candour and Strict regard to the Rules of Justice will ever command the Attention of Sir Your much Oblig'd and most humble St[4]

ROBT LETTIS HOOPER JUN

ALS (PPAmP).
1. The letter he enclosed is printed above, 30 April.
2. NG's answer has not been found, but he apparently approved Hooper's terms.
3. Letter not found.
4. The reference is to NG's consideration while Hooper's court-martial was pending. (See note at NG's letter of 29 April, above.)
Hooper played a key role in supplying Sullivan's expedition against the Iroquois. At least fifteen of the letters he wrote to NG during May have survived (all at PPAmP); none of the many NG wrote him during the month has been found.

From Colonel Morgan Lewis

[Albany, N.Y., 5 May 1779. Has NG's of 15 April. With arrival of tents, he is now prepared for [Indian] expedition, due to leave Albany on Monday.[1] Without cash he must soon make "an Elopement." ALS (PPAmP) 1 p.]

1. In mid-April Washington had ordered Gen. James Clinton's army to rendezvous at Canajoharie, N.Y., on 10 May (Fitzpatrick, *GW*, 14: 397). But as noted below at Sullivan to NG, 12 May, events kept General Clinton in Albany until 15 June.

From Colonel Charles Pettit

Dear Sir   Philada 5 May 1779

The Day after you left me, a million of Dollars were suddenly popped upon me, which, that day and the next, I dispersed as follows:

To Mr Biddle ----------------------	122 [000]
Mr Hollingsworth -------------	114
Mr Ross -----------------------	228
Mr Patton ----------------------	114
Mr Wade ----------------------	66
Mr Hooper --------------------	312

[$]956,000   the rest in smaller Payments not worth putting down in this Acct. Mr Ross's Messenger is again returned as hungry as ever. Mr Furman is also calling loudly for Money and a Man from Col. Davis is waiting in Town for 3 or 400,000. Mr Biddle and Mr Mitchell are also quite out and the sound of Calls at a greater Distance assault my Ears and threaten to be clamorous. How soon I shall be able to allay these clamours does not appear. By tomorrow I hope to dispatch about 200,000 to So. Carolina. I laid Extracts of Mr Livingston's Letters before the Committee; and on Friday obtained a Conference with Mr Morris as Chairman. I find there is a secret understanding between them and the Govr of Carolina about the detention of the Vessels.[1] In my next I mean to send you Copies of my Letters to Mr Livingston and of one from Mr Morris to me which will give you more full information of the State of that business. You may remember Mr Livingston complains that he has not copies of the charter Parties [?] and in one Case no Letter with the Vessels from the Eastward [i.e., New England]. It may be well to write to the Agents that way on this Subject, and also to stop the sending any more vessels. You will please to write to them, or inform me of the orders you have heretofore given them, as I do not know, except Mr Otis, who have sent vessels from the Eastward, nor what Instructions you gave them.

I went up to Trenton on Saturday afternoon. On Sunday Major Burnet came up, having arrived here after I set out on Saturday. Yesterday we returned together and found Col. Hollingsworth in Town with whom I have had some conversation; but neither his engagements nor mine have admitted of so much leisure for it as I wished. I am apprehensive much of what has been said against the conduct of business in that district is ill founded and arises from improper motives.[2] You will form some Judgment of the matter from Major Burnet's Report, and there are some farther circumstances which I hope soon to have explained which may give farther Light. The Major's acct of Things in that Country will bear rather harder on a neighbouring district and will afford ground for farther Enquiry and Consideration. It appears to me necessary to erect some Stores and perhaps a wharf at the Head of Elk, in this case I believe it will be best to take a long lease (say 20 years) of a suitable Lot, and whenever we have done with the Improvements we can sell them for the Remainder of the Leases; from what I can learn at present, a Lot of Mr Hollingsworth's will be the most proper; but Mr Risberg is to go down next week to view the place, and I have a good opinion of his Judgment and Candor. I have been spoken to on this subject by some members of Congress in a manner that makes the expediency of erecting some Stores there more apparent than it was before. Mr Chase,[3] however, took occasion to press it on me, in the presence of Mr Morris and the Maryland Delegates, to open another Communication from Back Creek, a branch of Elk, to Hamburg in the bite [i.e., bight] of New Castle; but the more I have enquired into the matter the more I am disinclined to it; and by his earnestness in pressing it I am apprehensive his motives were not merely the publick Good; especially as I find the Facts do not exactly correspond with his stating of them. It appears to me best, from present appearances, not to be hasty in taking the forage Department out of Mr Hollingsworth's Hands. You will learn my reasons for this from Major Burnet. But I have not given any Directions in the matter, as I am not acquainted with the Reasons on which you and Col. Biddle came to a determination. Mr Owen Biddle came to ask my Advice about it. I gave him my opinion, but declined either directing or advising in it for the Reason I have mentioned, which I also mentioned to him. He agreed in opinion with me, and I believe will delay the matter till he hears farther from his Brother.

I am told Mr Ross is giving monstrous prices for Teams, particularly one Team that Mr Mitchell refused giving more than £ 1500 for and turned it away. It is said Mr Ross has since purchased at £ 1800. This matter must be farther enquired into. Mr Ross does not stand fair with the better people of this State independantly of his Connections with the opposers of the Constitution, and I fear the Department will the more easily be wounded through the tenderness of his Sides. More however is said against him on the score of incapacity and other Circumstances of unfitness for the office than for direct malpractice, but in either case the Department at large and especially the Head of it suffers.[4]

Col. Cox set out on Monday morning to visit his Brother at Holly, who was thought to be near his exit—he talked of setting out for Camp this week, where you will probably have an opportunity of conversing more with him than I had, from his sudden departure for Holly.[5]

Mr Davenport's accounts are now under Examination. They are rather confused and ill vouched owing to the incapacity for Accounts of some of his Assistants whose vouchers are not so regular as they should be.[6]

I have give Major Burnet, his money running short, one hundred Dollars which I have charged to the office in Camp. Please to let it be entered as so much Money sent by me to Camp. I am Dr Sir Your most hum Servt

CHAS PETTIT

P. S. I have paid Col. Hay's Draughts in favor of Mr Faesh and Col. Ogden.

ALS (PPAmP).
1. On the detention of the vessels in Charleston, see note at Livingston to NG, 27 February, above.
2. For background, see above, Hollingsworth to NG and note, 3 May.
3. Probably Samuel Chase who had been a delegate from Maryland until 1778, when he failed to be reelected because of questionable business dealings. (See above, vol. 2: 242n.)
4. George Ross, Jr., was deputy quartermaster general for the southern part of Lancaster County. Despite Pettit's criticism of him, Ross stayed on in office.
5. Colonel Cox's brother, William, died the day after Pettit wrote. See below, John Cox to NG, 8 May.
6. James Davenport had accompanied the Convention troops on their removal from Massachusetts to Virginia. See NG's letter to him, 9 November 1778, above.

From Colonel Charles Pettit

Dear Sir   Philada 5 May 1779
I lately mentioned to you that I had engaged as many Shares in the Batsto Works as made up three sixth parts of the whole. Colonel Cox chooses to content himself with one half of a sixth. After you and I have drawn each a sixth part there remains therefore half a sixth unappropriated. It is now at my risk and I am content to keep it unless you choose to divide it with me. You will please to signify your Determination on this Subject and I would wish you to form it from

Considerations respecting yourself only, for be it either way it will be pleasing to me. If you adopt this offer we shall have 2 1/2 twelfths each, otherwise you will have two twelfths and I shall have three.[1]

You sometime ago mentioned to me a purchase of Land to the eastward, that is in East Jersey, and offered me half of it. I think I told you that if you meant it as a speculation I would take the Concern; but that if you meant it as an Estate as I took your offer to be a mere effusion of Friendship, I would decline it, as I would not interfere in your plans of realizing your money. I believe some other matter claimed our Attention and left the Matter unsettled. Pray how is it? Am I interested or not? I would have you determine this entirely by your own Feelings and I shall be satisfied it is right, be it one way or the other; but it ought to be determined and I do not recollect that I drew any conclusion from what passed.

On Saturday it was reported the *Hunter* Privateer in which we hold 1/16th, had taken a Jamaica Ship; but it seems she came off with a Flea in her Ear after an Engagement with a Ship from Liverpool. She is returned into Port and the Captain thinks the Vessel not fit for the purpose. The owners have therefore concluded to sell her; and this morn'g they consulted me about buying a new Brig[antine] for Capt Douglas which will mount 16 Guns. To effect this will cost near £ 80,000 of which the sale of the *Hunter* and her late prize will produce between 50 and £ 60,000. I have a good opinion of the Captain of the proposed Brig: and of the scheme save that they ask about £ 20,000 more for the Brig than she cost; but at the present depreciation I do not know whether she could be built for less. She was launched about 3 weeks since and will be soon ready. I gave Mr Clark, the acting owner, my opinion against giving so great an Advance, but told him that as our share was small I would not stand in the way if the rest of them thought proper to pursue it.[2]

I believe I told you I had relinquished the 1/4th I had taken in a new Brig with Mr B. McClenahan. She carried too little Cargo in proportion to the value of the Vessel to make any Profit unless she should take a prize and her Force was too slender to expect that, unless by great accident.

I have taken 1/4th of the two burnt Frigates which were bought for about £ 12,000. One will serve to repair the other and Major Eyre tells me they are a good pennyworth. I am Dr Sir Your Friend and huml Servt[3]

CHAS PETTIT

ALS (MiU-C).
    1. For background, see note at NG to Jacob Greene, 20 March, above.
    2. The privateer *Hunter* was owned by the Philadelphia firm of (James) Vanuxem & (Lardner) Clark, although NG's aide, John Cox, had signed a $10,000 bond with Capt. John Douglass on 1 January 1779 in applying for letters of marque and reprisal. The

schooner mounted twelve carriage guns and carried a crew of sixty. (PCC, item 41, vol. 7: 37–38, DNA) The firm apparently did not sell the *Hunter*, since they applied for another letter of marque and reprisal on 2 July 1779. (PCC, item 196, vol. 8: 24, DNA)
    3. NG answered on 10 May below.

To Moore Furman

Sir   Camp [Middlebrook, N.J.] May 6th 1779
    I have just return'd from a Visit to your House. I expected to have had the pleasure to see you at Home. I had many matters which I wished an opportunity to consult you upon; but as I am not like to have that pleasure seasonably, I must have recourse to my pen.[1]
    The General has given me orders to have the army ready to march by the 15th of this month; I wish you therefore, to hasten the purchasing of Horses as much as possible.[2] I believe we have Waggons and Harness in great plenty, and therefore dont wish you to purchase any of either.
    The Army will move towards the North River, which will render it necessary to convey the provisions upon that Route, before the Troops begin their March. Provisions must be lodged at Morristown and Pompton.
    I wish you to engage all the Transportation upon the different communications to be done by Country Teams, as we shall want all the Continental Teams with the Army. I think it will be best to open different communications for the benefit of Forage, and to form stages at about thirty Miles distance from each other. This will render the business more convenient and agreeable to the Farmers. In forming the Transportation upon this Plan, you can fix the time to perform the stages in, and oblige the Carters to do their Duty faithfully.
    If we could get the transportation done by the Ton or Hundred weight, I am persuaded it would be a great saving to the Public.
    Mr Caldwell has sent me his resignation.[3] It will be necessary for you to appoint a person to supply his place, If you think the Agents already active there, incapable of doing the Duty. There is great Complaints against Mr Lewis of Morristown. He appears to be incapable of doing the Duty of such an important Post, and one that will soon become still more so.[4]
    It will be necessary to get forward the Provisions and Stores, as fast as possible from Trenton, as the General [Washington] dont wish any great Magazine to be formed there, after we move towards Morris.
    I wish you to let me know as soon as may be, the number of Horses you can furnish, that I may know how to take my measures. I hope you will exert yourself to provide us as many Waggoners as possible, as the General will not allow us to draft any from the Line. I

wish you to get good Country Farmers for Waggon Masters and such as will do their Duty faithfully.

You will naturally see the necessity of keeping the movement of the Army a secret, as too early a discovery may be attended with disagreeable consequences. Please to inform me whether any further aid can be had from [New Jersey] Government, by any Law which they can enact, to aid the Department either in Procuring Waggons or Forage.[5] I am Sir yr very Hble Serv

N GREENE

LS (Nj).
1. Furman lived in Pittstown, twenty-odd miles west of Middlebrook. What took NG to the area is not known.
2. It was the end of May before Washington gave orders to move the army toward the Hudson. See his letter below of 31 May.
3. The Rev. James Caldwell was assistant deputy quartermaster at Springfield, N.J. He continued to serve as assistant forage master. See below, NG to Caldwell, 3 November 1779.
4. The source of NG's opinion of Joseph Lewis was James Abeel. As noted at Abeel's letter of 15 April, above, Furman helped to change NG's mind.
5. Furman answered on 7 May, below.

Colonel James Abeel to General William Maxwell

[Morristown, N.J., 6 May 1779. Is ordered by NG not to issue horsemen's tents without his orders. Maxwell's brigade should soon have an ample supply of tents. Abeel has ready for Maxwell a marquee that "Spreads 21 feet in Length, 13 Wide with a Bed Room." ALS (PPAmP) 1 p.]

To George Washington

Sir   Camp [Middlebrook, N.J.] May 6, 1779

I have just receivd a Letter from Governor Greene upon the recall of Glovers brigade from the State of Rhode Island.

I shall make no comments upon it. The weak and distressed condition of the State your Excellency is as well acquainted with as I am. You are also equally as well acquainted with the Enemies force being greatly superior to that of ours. All this was known at the time the order was given.

I should be very glad if the common interest would admit of their continuance there; but if it will not what can be said? However as an application is made to me to urge their continuance, I think it my duty to lay the Letter before your Excellency for your consideration. I am your Excellencys obedient Sert[1]

NATH GREENE

ALS (Washington Papers: DLC).
   1. The reasons for Washington's first ordering the removal of Glover's brigade, then rescinding his order, are noted at Gov. William Greene's letter of 26 April, above.

From Colonel Ephraim Bowen

[Providence, R.I., 6 May 1779. Encloses his accounts; unless a "*Speedy Supply*" of money arrives he cannot buy a "Single Tun of Hay"; inventory of tents includes a number he has had to condemn as "Old Canvas"; R.I. state officials and members of Congress are reelected.[1] ALS (PPAmP) 3 pp.]

   1. Gov. William Greene and Lt. Gov. Jabez Bowen were first elected in May 1778. The R.I. delegates to Congress were Stephen Hopkins, William Ellery, Henry Marchant, and John Collins. (Bartlett, *Records*, 8: 529–30)

From Major Richard Claiborne[1]

Sir   Eastertown [Estherton, Pa.] May 6, 1779
   I arrivd at this place yesterday, and am sorry to inform you that matters are not in such order and forwardness as I expected to find them. I enclose you a return of what stores have been received from Colonel Mitchel, likewise of those sent to Wyoming. Colonel Cox is not at home but his Assistant Mr Berryhill informs me that no accot of the stores to be deposited at this place has been sent them, neither do they know from whom the stores are to come. However, those that have been received are from Colonel Mitchel, and by a comparison of the two Returns, you will find what are on hand. The pack-saddles are so rediculously made and of such an improper model, that General Hand will not receive them.[2] The axes are not much better than Tom-hawks and either break or bend, so that they are of no service in a little time after they have been in use. In short, the greater part of the stores are so slightly done; and many of the materials so indifferent, that they will not answer half service.
   On my way I call'd on Colonel [Jacob] Morgan at Reading, and found his stores in good order and of a very good quality. He has a large number of exceeding good falling axes, well ground, helv'd [i.e., handled] and boxd up. Colo Patton also at Lebanon has his stores in very good order and well made.[3] So that unless Colonel Mitchel is to supply this place altogether, I would advise that what stores can be furnish'd by Colonel Morgan and Colonel Patton already made, be had in preference, as they are by far the best which I have seen. These posts are the nearest to Easterton, and the stores ready whenever they may be call'd for, which will save a great expence in the carriage as the farthest is but little more than a days journey.

As the pack-saddles procur'd by Colo Hooper are of the best construction and as some are wanted immediately, I think they had better be forwarded, as General Hand will not have any of those until they are made after the same manner as Col. Hoopers.

I have seen Major Eyres and he informs me that thirty one two-ton batteaus will be ready to lanch next Satturday.[4] Sixteen are already in the River, and when loaded with two-ton weight draw but six or eight inch water. Not a Batteauman has yet been engag'd, but I have every encouragement that we shall have enough in a few days. Mr Hughling and Mr Alexander are Gentlemen of property; well acquainted with the River, and of great influence. These I have sent for, and shall engage them if possible, to take charge of a certain number of Boats, and to proceed immediately to engaging Boatmen. I propose to have them engag'd for a certain term of Months, and to allow them such a price, as may be concluded on when Colo Cox arrives. To employ men by the day I conceive to be very improper as it would then be at their discretion to continue or quit, and by this means the execution of the business would be in a state of uncertainty, and the men unsubjected to rule or order.

The stores that have been sent from this were exported in 8-, 10-, and 15-ton batteaus, and deposited at Sunberry [Sunbury], where they are to remain for General Hand's further orders, as he conceives it to be dangerous sending them to Wyoming yet. These kind of Batteaus, I am inform'd by Mr Berryhill, may be procur'd in a short time, as they chiefly belong to Mr Hughling and Alexander, and are the most proper for carrying the stores to Wyoming, as the water is sufficient to support them, and it takes no more men to man them than the small Boats now building. The two-ton batteaus may go on building, as none of the kind are to be hired, the Inhabitants having only large boats and Canoes.

As I am unacquainted from whom the stores are to come, and your orders to me specify nothing upon this head, I must remain inactive in the matter; but shall confine myself to have every thing in a proper channel, and then return to Camp. I have the honor to be With the greatest respect Your Most obedient Humble servant

RICHARD CLAIBORNE

ALS (PPAmP).
    1. NG had appointed Major Claiborne as a special DQM in September 1778 without a specified area of responsibility. As a troubleshooter for NG he did much to assist the Sullivan expedition. Estherton, on the lower Susquehanna River, was an important entrepôt for supplies from southern Pennsylvania.
    2. For background on packsaddles, see above, John Cox to NG, 16 February.
    3. This account of Patton's fitness does not agree with Pettit's assessment of Robert Patton, who was deputy quartermaster general for the northern part of Lancaster County. See Pettit to NG, 7 May, below.
    4. Benjamin G. Eyre was Superintendent of Boats under NG.

See Map 3 for geographic references above.

From Major Richard Claiborne

Sir   6 oClock PM 6th May 1779 [Estherton, Pa.]
    Since my letter to you of this morning I have consulted Colonel Cox upon the method and terms of engaging Batteau-men, and find that it will be impossible to procure them without very great wages.[1] I have seen a letter from Colo John Cox of the 1st of May to his Brother upon this subject, wherein he mentions that it is expected at Head Quarters, every thing in the Quarter Masters Department at this place, will be in readiness by the 15th of this Instant and directs that Batteau-men be had upon the lowest terms possible. How matters have been conducted and what is the reason that every thing is so backward, I cannot conceive but I see very little foundation for such expectation. The Boats are not yet one fourth compleat, and even if they were, I hear of no stores to load them, nor can I understand from whom they are to come. I hope that no more will be sent from Philadelphia, when better can be had from one fourth the distance.
    We shall proceed tomorrow to appoint some Boat-conductors and send them out to engage Batteau-men. Colo Cox has mentioned several to me who are men of property and by whom alone, men can be engag'd. This being the case, it will be impossible to prevail on them to quit that ease and repose which they enjoy at home to undertake a business so laborious and dangerous, under twelve, and perhaps not less than 15 Dollars a day. These men have signified to Colonel Cox their inclination to engage in this business, and that they could perhaps get men at four dollars, but was doubtful whether under five dollars a day.
    General Hand has directed that the stores be sent and deposited at Sunbury, which will be done accordingly by the large boats as fast as they arrive at this place. There are nine large boats now in service which will be sufficient to convey the stores from this place. In the mean time I hope a sufficient number of Batteau-men will be engag'd to take the stores from Sunbury with the two-ton batteaux to any place they may be order'd to.
    Colo Cox is now writing to Colonel John Cox upon the same subject. I have the honor to be sir Your Most obedient Humble servant
                                             RICHARD CLAIBORNE

PS The Batteau-men to engage for four months, unless sooner discharg'd.

An example of a Boat Department return
(Courtesy of the American Philosophical Society)

ALS (PPAmP).

1. As noted above in the quartermaster list of 9 January, Cornelius Cox was a deputy quartermaster reporting to George Ross, Jr., at Lancaster. The brother of John Cox, NG's assistant, he had served in the Northumberland militia in 1776 and 1777 before assisting Ross. His duties before and after the Sullivan expedition centered on providing boat transportation on the Susquehanna. John Cox was a surety for Cornelius in his job as paymaster in the militia. See John Cox to the Committee of Safety, 12 November 1776, Gratz Collection, PHi. Cornelius's responsibility for the boats on the Susquehanna is seen in Ross to NG, 14 January 1780, below, and Cornelius Cox to John Mitchell, 15 March 1780, PCC, item 78, vol. 5: 449, DNA.

From General William Maxwell

[Elizabethtown, N.J., 6 May 1779. His brigade has been ordered by Washington to prepare to march.[1] Begs NG to issue orders for tents, portmanteaus, and especially teams to transport essential food and materials. ALS (PPAmP) 2 pp.]

1. See below, Washington to NG, 6 May.

From Colonel John Mitchell

[Philadelphia, 6 May 1779. Will do all in his power to see that NG's orders for "Tents, Markees and Horsemens Tents" are filled satisfactorily and on time. Some marquees have been issued to general officers in addition to portmanteaus. "Nearly all the Stores we were to send to the westward are gone, and the Military Stores go this week."[1] Has taken "all the pains Possible" to procure wagoners. ALS (PPAmP) 2 pp.]

1. These were for the Sullivan expedition.

From George Washington

Sir   Head Qrs. Middlebrook [N.J.] 6 May 1779.
    The first Jersey Rgt is under marching orders, and it is prob'le will move on this route the day after to-morrow.[1] Gen: Maxwell writes me "we have not got our portmanteaus nor waggons. Our tents are not taken out of the Store at Morristown for want of waggons."[2] This respects the whole.

    I have thought it best to give you this notice, that there may be no delay on the above account, as the whole brigade is under marching orders. I am sir your most hble servt

                                             GO: WASHINGTON

LS (PPAmP).

1. On 4 May, Washington had ordered Maxwell's brigade to join General Sullivan. (Fitzpatrick, GW, 14: 494)

2. See Maxwell's requests to NG, above, 6 May. The excerpt is from Maxwell's letter of 5 May, Washington Papers, DLC. On 14 May, below, NG was assured by his deputy James Abeel that Maxwell's brigade had been supplied with "every thing sufficient in the Return."

From Moore Furman

Sir   Trenton [N.J.] 7th May 1779

I am very sorry I had not the pleasure of seeing you at my House. Col. Biddles Letter came too late for me to get home that Night and Concluded you would not stay all the next day, and therefore concluded my return then would be too late.[1]

The want of money prevents my being able to execute orders as it would be in my power to do with good Supplies. I have received none since about 5th Last month and then but a Small Sum, hardly a Dollar in the hands of the Department in this State and all Calling in the most pressing manner. I sent an Express down to Philada as soon as I Came here, who is not returned. Hope he will bring some. I could send about Sixty Wagons immediatly but cannot get Drivers, the People not liking to go to the Army, and receiving higher Wages at home. I can send about Forty Teams next week, and if money comes today, about Fifty Horses; will make up as many more Teams as I can get Drivers for. I shall not Contract for any more Wagons or Harness after this untill further orders.

I Suppose the Commissary General [Wadsworth] will send Orders respecting the forwarding the Flour &ca when any here. At present belive there is not a Barrel of Flour or Pork at this Post.

There is about Two hundred Teams, Private Property, now in the Service at this Post and will take in all I can get more. It will be easy to fix Convenient routs for the Teams to the North River, but how to get a Supply of Forage I know not. I will get all I can carried by the barrel or Ton [?][2] but Forage is so nearly gone between here and the North River that fear little will be done by Chance Teams.

Mr Caldwell writes me he has resigned and I shall not be able to keep many more unless their Salarys are Raised. Col. Cox advises me to do it.[3] I wish for your Approbation. Hope to be at Morris Town soon, also Springfield. Belive Majr [Daniel] Marsh will do very well in that County if he will undertake, if not will get another.

The Assembly of this State appears to be very willing to give every aid to the Army in their power, but dont find they think any further Laws necessary for Collecting Forage; those already in Force being Sufficient to Collect what there is in the State at the Current prices, and they dont think it reasonable to limit the prices in this State while others are Left free.[4] Indeed its of very Little Consequence wether it be fixed or not for the little now in the State, but wish to see some Limitation to the Supplies necessary for the Army before the next Crop comes in, for if something is not done that will fix some bounds to the prices, fear it will take more Continental money to purchase than can possibly be made. I am Sir Yr most Obt Humble Servt

M FURMAN

ALS (PPAmP).
    1. See above, Clement Biddle to Furman, 3 May.
    2. He may have meant "tun" which Johnson, *Dictionary*, defines as two hogsheads.
    3. See above, NG to Furman, 6 May.
    4. NG had asked if New Jersey might help. See above, NG to Furman, 6 May, and Biddle to Furman, 3 May.

From Colonel Christopher Greene

Dear Sir   East Greenwich [R.I.] 7th May 1779
    As we never have had the Arrangement of the Officers in my Regiment Established by the War Office, I have Taken the freedom to Inclose a Copy there of to his Excellency with the exception of Lt Rogers who has resign'd. As the Officers who stand fair for promotions are uneasy at not having that Justice done them, must take the liberty to ask my friend's Assistance in hastening the Arrangement back Should it meet with his Excellencies Approbation.[1]
    I have also mentioned Captain Arnolds Misfortune and Expressed a wish that he might be permited to fall into Business, and not be in the Regiment, but to have every Advantage as if he belonged to it. Whether it will be Consistant or not I am not very Capable of Determining. Should you think it is, I wish your Assistance.[2]
    The same Prox as last year is elected for this Except Doc'r Babcock in the room of Mr Tanner.[3]
    Genl Gates gives Very good Satisfaction in this department which makes us still happy in a Commander.
    I have expressed a wish to be call'd from this State. Tho' I wish it, it is not from any dislike I have had or can expect to have from those superior to me in command, but bearly [barely, i.e., merely] from Troops rendering better Service to the public abroad than at home. However if it is thought must for the good of the Service that my small Services be done here, I most Cheerfully Submit.[4] Mrs Greene's and families best respects to your Self and Lady. I am Dear Sir with the most perfect Friendship your Very Huml servt

C GREENE

If Genl. Sullivan be in Camp please to present my Most Respectful Compliments to him.

ALS (PPAmP).
1. NG was a third cousin as well as a friend. Colonel Greene's letter to Washington of this date is in the Washington Papers, DLC.
2. Thomas Arnold, one of NG's oldest friends, had lost a leg in the battle of Monmouth in June 1778. In his reply of 30 July 1779, Washington wrote that the only provision for keeping disabled officers on full pay was that they enter the invalid corps, to which Arnold was transferred in November 1779 and where he remained until 1783. (Fitzpatrick, GW, 16: 20)
3. The "Prox" was the slate of candidates. See above, Bowen to NG, 6 May.
4. NG undoubtedly interceded for the Rhode Island regiment that had once served under him, but it was not until January of 1781 that the regiment left Rhode Island. (Rochambeau to Washington, 10 January 1781, Washington Papers, DLC) For Christopher Greene it was a fateful move, for he was brutally killed by a party of De Lancey's Tories at Croton, N.Y., four months later.

From Colonel Jacob Morgan

[Reading, Pa., 7 May 1779. Has received NG's of 30 April. Forage is scarce and he is attempting to purchase it at "Twenty Dollars per Bushell." Wants "nothing but drivers to send off Forty Teams."[1] ALS (PPAmP) 1 p.]

1. Shortly after Morgan dispatched the above letter, he had the opportunity to send a duplicate by express, adding only a postscript on his supply of axes, harness, and kettles. That letter is also at PPAmP.

From Colonel Robert Patton

[Lebanon, Pa., 7 May 1779. Has met with Richard Claiborne. Since some stores have suffered damage, suggests they be sent up the Susquehanna River quickly. Will forward all of his stores—a "Considerable Quantity." Upon receiving instructions from John Mitchell and John Cox, fifty teams will be sent to Philadelphia. ALS (PPAmP) 1 p.]

From Colonel Charles Pettit

Philadelphia 7th May 1779

Do you expect me, my dear Sir, to make bricks without straw? Or do you desire to get rid of me by a publick Execution for making money? I have laboured faithfully to obtain the necessary supplies of Cash, but I cannot obtain it so fast as is necessary. I have, it is true, distributed a good deal lately, but it has not been till the occasions were so pressing that it seemed as if another Day's delay would have been fatal; and I have been kept so far behind hand that these occasions are continually surrounding me. Tomorrow I hope to get off some money for Carolina, and as soon afterwards as I can, I will send you some, but you must not expect much unless you have a pleasure in being disappointed. In the way I have mentioned, however, the Warrant is exhausted, that is, it is all drawn for tho' not all yet paid. I have applied to the Board for five millions more which I have told them should be paid in the course of this month. I have yet recd no answer.[1] Congress are now sitting on another Egg for restoring the credit of the Money and seem to promise themselves great matters from its produce;[2] but they do not yet understand one another as to its contents. They seem to agree in one point; the stopping of the press at a given sum; but I fear they will delay the measure till the sum is emitted and then they will have nothing in hand to work upon till the measure takes effect. The intermediate time will drive them to expedients which will probably ruin the Plan and leave us in a worse situation than before, and perhaps risk the running aground all standing and away go the masts by the Board. Some of the Gentn I have conversed with seem to have Ideas that I think adequate to the purpose; but others particularly my worthy house mate, are disposed to stop so far short that I fear it will be ineffectual.

Mr Steel was in Town since you left me and will be here again in a few days. You know I never had a high opinion of him, but I never knew enough of him to have a bad one. I would pay so much regard to Genl Macintosh's representations of him as to enquire more minutely into the points he fixes on, and so far as he relates facts I should give them credit, but I should make great allowances for his *Opinion* on account of the Terms he and his quarter master were on during their campaign.[3] If it should be found expedient to displace Mr Steel, I believe it would be well to give the whole district to Davis as a purchaser; but I should think it expedient to appoint an active, clever fellow as Quarter Master to attend the Army who should receive the Supplies from the purchasers and apply them; for it rarely happens that the same person is thoroughly fit for both purposes.

I have heard very little said of the workings of your Letter in Congress; but I believe it will have some good effect and I see no danger of ill from it. I believe I have already told you it was referred to the Committee, and there it will probably go to sleep unless we revive it.[4]

I dined with His Excy the Minister of France[5] at Col. Cox's on his return from Camp, and derived great Pleasure from his appearing to be much pleased with what he had seen.

In consequence of a Letter from Mr Erskine I have purchased a reflecting Telescope which I shall forward by the first Opportunity.[6]

I have this day wrote to Col. Cox, respecting some dissatisfactions arising from the Conduct of our officers in some places, particularly Lancaster and Delaware. Of the latter Major Burnet will give you some account and also respecting Mr Calhoun's complaint of some Orders sent to Beatty.[7] These things seem to me to require a strict scrutiny and reformation; and I am apprehensive the reputation of the department has already suffered by the conduct of some of these Gentlemen. After a few reformations to the westward I flatter myself we shall stand on good ground notwithstanding all the calumnious reports of—what shall I call these cavillers? But some reformations are necessary.

I have also wrote to Col. Cox about the Col. [Robert] Patton you and he recommended to the General. He will shew you the Letter. I fear that man will disgrace the recommendation if he does not do worse. I have received information about him in divers ways. Genl Smallwood's Chaplain, Mr [Joseph] Montgomery, lives in that Quarter, and I imagine he can give you some account of his goings on. You will see Mr Montgomery at Camp.[8] I am Dr Sir Your affect'y huml Servant

CHAS PETTIT

ALS (PPAmP).
1. For a discussion of the acute money shortage in the quartermaster department, see above, NG to Washington, 21 April.
2. It is not certain what "Egg" Congress was sitting on. Pettit may have been referring to the step that Congress took a few days later to meet three days each week in an attempt to solve its financial problems. Or he may have been speaking of plans to limit the amount of currency in circulation and to tax the states heavily. The summer passed before they took any concrete steps toward either goal. It was not until 3 September that a resolution was adopted that limited the amount of currency in circulation to $200 million, a limit that was reached in a few weeks. Thus, the resolution did little to stem the tide of depreciation. For the time being they were no more successful in agreeing on taxing the states. (See Burnet, *Letters*, 4: xii–xvii; *JCC*, 15: 1019; Ferguson, *Power of Purse*, p. 46.)
3. On the dispute between Steel and McIntosh, see above, Steel to NG, 20 February. Despite NG's impatience with Steel for not getting his returns in on time, Steel remained in his post throughout NG's term as quartermaster general.
4. See above, NG to Jay, 27 April.
5. Conrad Alexandre Gérard. His visit to camp is described above at NG to Washington, 27 April.
6. Robert Erskine (1735–80) was the distinguished map maker and engineer, who had been geographer and surveyor general of the Continental army since July 1777. For more on this multitalented patriot, see Albert H. Heusser, *George Washington's Map Maker: A Biography of Robert Erskine*, 1928; reprint edition edited with an introduction by Hubert G. Schmidt (New Brunswick, N.J.: Rutgers University Press, 1966).
7. On Ichabod Burnet's trip to Chesapeake Bay, see above, Hollingsworth to NG, 3 May. The dispute between deputies Charles Beatty and James Calhoun is discussed at Beatty to NG, 27 November 1778, above.
8. Robert Patton later left the quartermaster department at an undetermined date.

From Colonel Jeremiah Wadsworth

Dear Sir   Hartford [Conn.] May 7th 1779
    I have recd Your favour of the 30th Ulto and agree with You that
we had best give the Name &c but more of this when I see You which
will be soon. The General [Washington] cant be more anxious for my
being in Camp than I am to be thier. I am not detained here by Private
business. The moment I can leave my Department in such a situation
that it will not go intirely to wreck I will set out for Camp.[1] Nothing
shall detain me long as I am satisfied their are persons more busy to
injure the Department than to serve the Country, who have unfortunately too much power and I know it is more than time I was near
them.
    I Like Your Letter to Congress.[2] What I shall say or do when I go
their is uncertain but if I was to go their without seeing You I feel what
it would be, but Your coolness and good advice has tamed me often
and I now see the advantage of haveing followed it, and will ask it
again when I see You. Mrs Wadsworth presents her Compliments to
Mrs Green and the General. If she had not a young brat at her breast I
dont know but she woud accompany me to Camp for here we have
no rest day or Night. Eternal noise confusion and dirt are the Portion
of this Neighbourhood. Here are all in a group DQMG, Purch[asin]g
and Issue[in]g Com[missar]y, Oxen, Horses, Carts, Waggons and the
Devil. I had rather be in Bedlam. Your supply of Cash to Hubbard was
seasonable; he had borrowed my last Shilling and every other bodys.
He was just giveing up the point and resolved to die, indeed we must
have all died; the transportation was allmost at an end. I shall bring
my next Letter myselfe. I am Dear Sir Your very hum S[ervan]t.

                                                    JERE WADSWORTH

ALS (PPAmP).
    1. On Wadsworth's eventual return to Middlebrook, see above, note at NG to
Wadsworth, 30 April.
    2. See above, NG to Jay, 27 April.

From Colonel John Cox

Dear Sir   Mount Holly [N.J.] May 8th 1779
    I this moment Recieved your favor of the 6th Inst.[1] in answer to
which I am to inform you that every possible step in my power hath
been taken to expedite the necessary preparations as well for the intended Indian expedition, as for the Army at large, and I flatter myself that most of the Articles Ordered to be deposited at *Estherton* are
now their and those for Fort Pitt on their way up. But it is impossible
for me to say with any degree of precision when a sufficient number

of Waggons, Horses &c requisite to enable His Excellency to make a general movement of the Army can be in readiness. I am induced to believe that the greatest part of the Stores in the Quarter Masters Department necessary for this ensuing Campaign are prepared, and it being now several Days since I ordered them forwarded to Camp I doubt not their being their in Time. I have a sufficient number of Waggons with the necessary Harness ready and a considerable number of Horses purchased, but have not been able till within a few Days past to procure ample Drivers without which the Teams cannot be sent to Camp. I am in hopes the late Resolution raising their pay will enable the Deputies to procure them.[2]

I cou'd have had a sufficient number of Horses bought long since if the Treasury cou'd have furnished Cash, and the Country, Forage, but being obliged to wait for the former, till within a few Days past, and for the growing of the grass to supply the place of the latter, the business has been unavoidably retarded till within these ten Days past. However, you may rest assured that every possible exertion is now making in the different States to raise and Equip the number required and from Letters I have lately Recieved from the different Deputies I have great reason to believe their will be a very handsome supply at Camp by the middle of this month at farthest, by which I have ordered. I expect all the Stores and every Team that can possibly be furnished with a Driver will be at Head Quarters. Col. [George] Ross writes me that Horses begin to come in fast and that he expects to have five hundred in a short Time. Col [Robert] Patton has 40 Teams compleatly equiped which I have ordered to Camp *immediately*. I expect Col. Morgan will send by the middle of the month at least as many, as he waits only for Carters. Col. [John] Mitchell is raising Teams daily and will send them on so fast as they can be Equiped. In a word every Deputy to whom orders have been given for the purpose writes me that they are making every possible exertion, but for the want of Cash are not able to do half as much as they cou'd were they amply supplyed.

I have ordered the Portmanteaus sent forward to Camp without loss of Time, and the Powder Horns and shot bags to Easton as you directed.

If we can engage Carters I hope we shall be able to raise a sufficient number of Teams without the aid of Government. I have been so much indisposed latterly that I have not had it in my power to sound the Legislature touching our Department, but shall at my return.[3] I have wrote both to Easton and Susquehanah repeatedly within these few Days past urging their utmost exertions and doubt not every things being done that can possibly be effected to expedite the Business committed to their management.

I shall write you more fully in a few Days. My Brother William who has for many years past been severely affected with the gout was violently seized with it in his Stomach a few Days ago, and the night before last took a final leave of all his Friends and paid that Debt which we must all ere long discharge. He is to be buried this afternoon. My best Regards wait on Mrs Greene and am with sincere Esteem Dr Sir Your most Obed Hble Servt

JOHN COX

ALS (PPAmP).
1. Letter not found, but it appears from Cox's response that NG had made some pointed inquiries about the delays in preparations.
2. See above, NG to Washington, 24 February 1779.
3. On Cox's illness, see above, Pettit to NG, 11 and 13 April.

From Moore Furman

[Trenton, N.J., 8 May 1779. Encloses a letter [not found] via the express. Seventy wagons to be loaded tomorrow and sent to camp. ALS (PPAmP) 1 p.]

To Moore Furman

[Camp Middlebrook, N.J., 9 May 1779. Found Furman's letter of 8 May on return from church.[1] Asks him to order "ten or twelve tolerable good riding Horses." Likelihood of having to transport large quantity of salted provisions and stores to camp during next fortnight will make "an extraordinary demand for Teams." ALS (Abeel Collection: DLC) 2 pp.]

1. A rare mention of his having attended church.

From Colonel John Mitchell

[Philadelphia, 9 May 1779. As requested in NG's of the seventh [not found], he will send as much linen as possible to Colonel Hooper, who failed to mention earlier he needed it. Asks where to send stores for galleys. Will send as many of other articles ordered as are "possible to be procured." ALS (PPAmP) 1 p.]

From General Israel Putnam

Dear Sir   Reading [Conn.] May 9th 1779
    I have not had opportunity or leisure to acknowledge the receipt of your obliging Letter of the 3rd Ultimo before this time, as it came to

hand whilst I was on a journey to the Eastward from whence I have just returnd. I need scarcely tell you, that your attention to the Troops under my Command and myself, is particularly agreeable to me.[1]

As we seem to be preparing to take the Field, and two Brigades have already movd from this ground, frequent applications have been made by the owners of the Land in the Vicinity of the Encampments for Orders to procure payment for the Wood, Timber and other Articles furnish'd for the use of the Division. I have deferr'd giving any, or taking the matter up partially, as I think it highly necessary for some general rule to be adopted, by which justice may be done to individuals, and the public not injured. For I find a strange disposition prevailing universally, to get as much from the Continent, as they can possibly obtain.

These accounts I suppose come within your Department, and are to be paid by some of your Deputies or Assistants, but I wish to know how, or in what manner this ought to be done, for I never can endure to see such enormous prices paid by the Continent, as I know some of the Inhabitants are disposed to receive. I wish you under these circumstances to suggest such methods as you think will be most conducive to the public good.[2] I am with great regard your most obed Servt

ISRAEL PUTNAM

LS (PPAmP).
1. Letter of 3 April not found. See above, Parsons to NG, 11 April, and NG to Parsons, "after 11 April," for problems that Putnam's troops had experienced with the supply services.
2. NG's answer to Putnam has not been found. Whether the landowners to whom Putnam refers furnished supplies willingly, or whether the troops took them without authorization, he does not say. If the troops *did* act without authorization, a determination had to be made as to whether they did so for survival or as an act of vandalism. On this thorny issue, see above, vol. 2: 419–20; William Moore to NG, 10 November 1778; NG to Jay, 1 February; and Jay to NG, 17 March.

From William Smith

[Springfield, Mass., 9 May 1779. Acknowledges NG's of 19 and 29 April [neither found]. Encloses requirements for transportation. Sent 495 tents to Colonel Hay at Fishkill; also 86 to Albany before receiving NG's corrected orders. Will send at once to Fishkill 470 more tents and twenty-one hogsheads of shoes and hose.[1] ALS (PPAmP) 2 pp.]

1. It would appear that Smith had received most if not all the above supplies from Otis & Henley in Boston.

To Moore Furman

[Camp Middlebrook, N.J.] May 10, 1779

The want of money has become one of our principal evils. The general he gives extensive orders and expects the most punctual execution, but the Treasury Board leaves me no power or means to fulfill them. My case is most like that of the Israelites, I am ordered to make brick without straw. The Treasury Board when I was in Philadelphia promised me five millions of dollars that week I left it, they have not fulfilled one fifth part of their promise, and in this situation business goes on.[1] I am glad you have stopped your purchasing of wagons as I am persuaded we have a plenty. You will continue your purchases of horses until you are further instructed. . . . When I was in Philadelphia I represented to Congress the necessity of increasing the pay of the staff.[2]

Excerpt from Robert F. Batchelder *Catalog* #18 (1977).
1. Congress did vote $5 million the next day (*JCC*, 14: 570) For background on the quartermaster department's acute money shortage during this period, see above, NG to Washington, 21 April.
2. For congressional action, see note above, NG to Jay, 15 April.

To Moore Furman

[Middlebrook, N.J., 10 May 1779. "Eighteen good draft horses" wanted the next day for the Artillery Park.[1] LS (Nj) 1 p.]

1. Furman complied with NG's request. See below, Furman to NG, 10 May.

To Colonel Charles Pettit

Dear Sir   Camp [Middlebrook, N.J.] May the 10, 1779

Your favor of the 5th by Major Burnet I have had the pleasure to receive.

I am content with one sixth of Batsto Furnace providing it is agreeable to you. If not I will hold another 1/12. You will therefore decide upon the affair agreeable to the suggestions of your own inclinations.[1]

I think the conversation we had in your Chamber upon the purchase I had made in East Jerseys must have slipt your Memory; upon informing you that I had bot it with a view for a settlement at some future day. It being contiguous to New York you declind having any thing to do with it. I first wrote you upon the subject, and afterwards on my arrival in Philadelphia you enquird respecting my plan and views in the purchase and observd if it was with an intent to speculate, you would take an interest in it, if not you should decline it. I told you it was my original intention to prepare it as a retreat from business; but that I would either make it an object of speculation or otherwise as should be most agreeable to you. I am perfectly willing to put it upon the same footing now.[2]

I observe you have interested us in the burnt Frigates. One thing I shall just remark to you—that is the *Board of War* when I was in Philadelphia hinted to me that there had been some insinuations thrown out by Major Eyres people that he misapplyd the public stuff by picking out the best of it for his own private use. I would wish the Major to transact the business in such a way as to leave no door open to traduce his reputation. However, the Board of War acquited the Major by rejecting the information against him with the utmost indignation. Mr Peters said he believed Major Eyres to be as honest a man as the World afforded.[3] Such kind of concerns where the same person has the direction of public and private property; and where it cannot be demonstrated to have been honestly conducted I would wish to avoid any connection with; as it will raise imputations to our prejudice that we from the Nature of the business cannot remove. I submit these hints to your consideration.

The express is going and I have not time to add only that I am yours

N GREENE

ALS (CtY).
1. For background on the Batsto furnace, see note at NG to Jacob Greene, 20 March, above.
2. For a discussion of NG's various business investments, see note at NG to Jay, 15 February, above.
3. Richard Peters was secretary of the Board of War. No action was taken against Benjamin Eyre.

From Doctor Thomas Bond

Dear Sir   [Middlebrook, N.J.?] May 10, 1779

Your Boy has gone thro' the Small Pox, the few he had are dried away and he is now as fit for Service as ever.[1] He is a fine Boy and has behaved in my family so as to merit the Esteem of it. It gives me pleasure to have had this Opportunity of testifying to you and Mrs Green the Obligations I was Under for your repeated Civilities. Be pleased [to] present my most Respectful Compts [Compliments] to her and inform her that next Week I will Visit her and bring Along Miss Bond. Give some Orders about the Boy, he may join you as soon as you please. Your Obd hum Ser

THOS BOND

ALS (PPAmP).
1. NG's son, George Washington Greene, did not actually have smallpox. He had gone through an unpleasant period of inoculation.

From Colonel John Cox

Dear Sir   Bloomsbury [N.J.] May 10th 1779

In Consequence of your favor of the 6th Inst I gave immediate Orders to every Deputy in the Department who had been furnished with directions for procuring either Horses, Waggons or Stores of any kind, to forward them to Camp with all possible expedition and doubt not they will pour in upon you in a few Days from every quarter.[1] Col Mitchell writes me that a number of Teams and spare Horses will leave Philadelphia for Camp this Day and tomorrow and that a considerable quantity of Stores will at the same time be forwarded to Trenton by water. I have ordered Waggons to be ready to receive them the moment they Arrive. The Markees and Horsemans Tents are going on with all possible dispatch. Col [Jacob] Morgan writes me that he has sixty Waggons ready and Teams for them nearly compleated, but that it is not in his power to procure Drivers for them *all*. However, part of them will go on to Camp loaded with Stores this week and the rest as fast as Drivers can possibly be enlisted. He informs me he has a considerable number of very extraordinary Axes, of which I have ordered 300 sent to Estherton to be forwarded up the Susquehanah. Col Hooper wrote me sometime ago that he had 1500 pack Saddles then ready which being a greater number than will be wanted at that Post, I have ordered three hundred of them immediately sent on to Susquehanah, that General Hand may be supplyed with both kind and take his choice.[2]

They write me from Susquehanah that they find great difficulty in procuring Watermen and that they cannot be got under four or five Dollars per Day. As the Waters are now high and will admit of Boats of 8 or ten tons burthen going I have advised their sending all the Stores up in them in preference to the Batteaus, as they will not require more than half the number of Hands, at the same time sending up the small Boats as fast as they can be maned, as they will be wanted to go up the small branches of the River. Col Davis writes me that by the middle of May he expects to have five or six hundred pack Horses Equiped and ready to start from Carlisle, that he finds very great difficulty in procuring the number of Waggons necessary and that it will not be in his power to engage one Driver on the Terms proposed as the Farmers are giving six Dollars per Day for common labourers, that he has forwarded fifty or sixty waggon loads of Provisions and Stores to the Westward within a few weeks past and that he is using every possible exertion to forward the remainder.

I have wrote to Major Claybourne as also to Ross and Patton[3] requesting they wou'd meet and examin the Stores in that quarter and select out such as may be wanted for the present expedition that have not been forwarded from Philadelphia and that the remainder be im-

mediately sent on to Camp. I am with best wishes Dear Sir Your obed
Servt

JOHN COX

P S Col Pettit writes me that he is in the greatest distress immaginable
for Cash and that the demands on him multiply hourly.

ALS (PPAmP).
1. NG's letter of 6 May has not been found. Four days later, in another letter that
has not been found, he asked Cox to have supplies sent instead to the Susquehanna region for Sullivan's expedition. As seen in Cox's first letter of 11 May, below, he was unable to reach all deputies in time to change the order.
2. General Hand had complained about the quality of packsaddles furnished by
John Mitchell. (See Claiborne to NG, 6 May #1, above.)
3. Richard Claiborne, George Ross, Jr., and Robert Patton.

From Colonel John Davis

Dear Sir   Carlisle [Pa.] 10th May 1779
Your favour of the 2d Inst. is now before me.[1] Your directions respect'g the Tents shall be strictly complyed with. As to Flax Linen I
cant buy any at the price you ment[ione]d. Tow Linen is from 22/6 to
25/-. I am altering your pack Saddles and will get them to Answer
every purpose with a Very triffling Expence. I am almost frightened to
death about the Scarcity of forage and the difficulty of procuring
Waggons. The demands on me for Teams to transport Provis[ion]s to
the Westward and to remove the Flour from Fred[eric]k County in
Maryland, and from this place to Harris Ferry, (to load the Boats) is so
great that I am apprehensive I shant be able to procure a suff[icien]t
Number of Teams to remove the remd'r of the Stores that are here to
Fort Pitt, till the Spring Crops are in the ground. All the Rye in this
part is Much Injured with the frost, and the farmers are engaged putting in all the Corn and Oats they possibly can. Your Teams arrived
here Yesterday. I shall load them back and let them return as soon as
possible. I sent off this Morning One Brigade of Waggons and a
Brigade of pack Horses with provis[ion]s for the Militia at Hannas
Town. I Expect to get Colo Bayard Stores Sent off by Thursday.[2] I
think I have now about Six hund'd pack Horses in the Diff't parts of
my district, hired and purchased. My Dear Sir let me hear from You as
frequently as possible, and Advise me on every Matter relating to Our
departm't, as I wish to discharge my duty as punctually as possible. I
am Sir with the greatest Esteem Your's Sincerely

JOHN DAVIS

Cy (PPAmP).
1. Letter not found, but it obviously contained NG's orders for supplying the Indian expedition.

2. Stephen Bayard was lieutenant colonel of Daniel Brodhead's regiment at Ft. Pitt. He was just starting work on the construction of Ft. Armstrong, located northeast of Ft. Pitt on the Allegheny River. See *PMHB*, 15 (1891): 252, and *JCC*, 14:601.

From Moore Furman

[Pittstown, N.J., 10/11 May 1779. An answer to NG's of the ninth. Will forward twenty horses, half for riding. More than one hundred barrels of salt beef sent to Pittstown instead of to camp. Will send it on when teams available. Expects to see NG Wednesday. [Postscript of 11 May]: In response to NG's request of the tenth has sent eighteen draft horses. ALS (PPAmP) 2 pp.]

From Colonel Robert L. Hooper, Jr.

Sir   Easton [Pa.] May 10th 1779
    I received your Letter of the 5th Instant last evening.[1] I am just returned from the Centre of Northampton County where I called a Meeting of the most leading Men. Many of the Conductors allready employed were present, and I am clear in my opinion that the Conductors, the Teamsters and Pack horse men cant be had under the Terms I have mentioned.[2] I studey Frugality, but such and so great is the depreciation of our Currency that there is no fixing prices for tomorrow. The Business must be done or our Independance will not be secure.
    I have been luckey in geting 500 yds. of Tow-linnin; but to avoid every inconvenience that may happen from sudden orders, I have ordered the twelve Teams I intended for Camp tomorrow to proceed to Philadelphia and to bring to this Post one thousand Pack-saddles and eight hundred yards of Linnin suitable for Padds.
    General Sullivan has wrote you about the Pack Horses.[3] When I receive your Answer I will, if ordered, send on all the Horses to Camp. Believe me, worthy Sir, that I am as busey as I can be in the Affairs of your Department and (you know I have seldom failed in my promises) you may rest assured that every thing will—*shall* be done here to General Sullivans satisfaction.
    Please to present my com[plimen]ts to Mrs Green. I think I have a good prospect of procuring her a pair of Horses and that I have *actually* secured for her 30 lbs Butter.
    I thank you for the News.[4] It is great. Genl Sullivans Orders only leave me time to say that I am very respectfully and sincerely Sr Yr most hble ser

                                                    R L HOOPER JUN

ALS (PPAmP).
    1. Letter not found.
    2. His terms are outlined in his letter to NG of 5 May, above.
    3. See below, same date.
    4. This may have been news of Van Schaick's raid on the Onondagas. See NG to Sullivan, 5 May, above.

From Captain Baxter Howe[1]

[Artillery Park, Pluckemin, N.J., 10 May 1779. Needs more horses to carry out General Knox's orders that the artillery be prepared "to move Tomorrow." ALS (PPAmP) 1 p.]

    1. Captain Howe of Massachusetts was in the Second Continental Artillery. (Heitman, *Register*)

From Colonel John M. Mitchell

Sir   Philadelphia May 10th 1779
    I have sent by Mr Black, Forty Portmantaus, five dozen Calf Skins and   Sheep Skins, the Portmantaus for General Maxwell Brigade and the Other Articles for the Harness makers at Camp. Have Sent Some Linen to Colo Hooper this day, and will Send off the Kegs, Shot pouches, and powder horns with Seventeen Portmantaus for Colo [Oliver] Spencers Regiment at Easton. On Tuesday Fifty good Horses will leave North Wales for Camp, On Wednesday Fifty more, and on Saturday Fifty more, and from Pottsgrove Fifty will go to Camp this Week. Have orderd in all the Brigades of Continental Teams I have; if I can get Carters will be able to Send you Sixty good able well found Teams to leave this on or before Sunday next. The Men who are gone out to Inlist are not Yet returnd, and price given by Farmers, and other private persons is more than even the Twenty pounds per Month, including the value of the Clothing. All the Stores are packing up to go to Camp. No time Shall be lost in Sending them on. They will be Shippd this Evening for Trenton. Where is Captn Sadler's Company of Artificers to go and when must they leave this?[1] I am with esteem and respect Sir Your most Humble Servt
                                    J M MITCHELL

ALS (PPAmP).
    1. Mathias Sadler was captain in Jeduthan Baldwin's artillery artificer regiment. (Heitman, *Register*)

From Otis & Henley

Sir   Boston May 10th 1779
    Inclosed is Copy of Protest of the Capt of the Snow *Friendship* taken up as a Transport for Rice and insured by your order behalf of the Continent.[1] This with other Losses which may be hourly expected, render a remittance immediately necessary.
    Inclosed is Invo of 2 hhds [hogsheads] Woolens which we designed for Colo Lewis and am respectfully your most Humble Serts

OTIS & HENLEY[2]

The *Friendship* apprized by indifferent [i.e., disinterested] men £ 4500.

LS (PPAmP).
    1. The "Protest" is printed at 10 March, above.
    2. A biographical sketch of David Henley is printed below at NG's letter to him of 12 May.

From General John Sullivan

Dear Sir   Head Quarters Easton [Pa.][1] May 10th 1779
    Mr Hoopers being out of town yesterday prevented my answering your Letter untill this morning. I find Mr Hooper will not have a Sufficiencey of Pack Saddles but has Sent off to Philadelphia for a Sufficiencey. Everything Else Seems to be in as good order as can be expected. He has about Six hundred Horses which I find by your Instructions to him are to be Sent on to Camp. I wish to know by a Line whether these Horses are Intended for me and if So whether there is a necessity for Sending them on to Camp. I thank you for the Information Respecting Colo van Schaike and Congratulate you on the happy event.[2] I am Dear Sir very Respectfully yr most obedt Servant

JNO SULLIVAN

ALS (PPAmP).
    1. Sullivan, having been ordered from his camp at Millstone, N.J., on 4 May, arrived at Easton on the Delaware on 7 May. (Whittemore, *Sullivan*, 121)
    2. See NG to Sullivan, 5 May, above.

(Table from Anne Bezanson, *Prices and Inflation during the American Revolution*, p. 65. With permission of The University of Pennsylvania Press.)

SPECIE EQUIVALENTS

THE RELATION OF CONTINENTAL MONEY TO SPECIE
December 1775–April 1781

Year & Month	Ratios — Webster Merchants	Ratios — Specie	Ratios — Commodity	Median corrected by three-months moving average — Webster Merchants	Median — Specie	Median — Commodity
1775						
Dec.		1.04				
1776						
Jan.						
Feb.						
Mar.				110.4		
Apr.				120.6		
May				135.5		
June				136.1		
July		1.08		133.4		
Aug.				136.0		
Sept.		1.14	1.75	126.0		
Oct.		1.25	1.75	126.0		
Nov.		1.25				
Dec.		1.50	1.50	151.8		
1777						
Jan.	1.25		1.44	171.4	154.0	142.4
Feb.	1.5	1.50	1.85	157.2	150.5	139.5
Mar.	2.0	2.00	2.06	139.7	127.8	124.1
Apr.	2.0	2.50	2.26	137.1	134.0	137.7
May	2.5		2.16	128.4	107.2	144.5
June	2.5	3.72	1.80	125.8	112.7	159.2
July	3.0	3.06	2.36	123.0	97.0	136.5
Aug.	3.0		3.50	138.0	123.6	148.4
Sept.	3.0	3.00	2.50	154.7	139.4	151.2
Oct.	3.0	3.00	3.22	148.3	151.3	155.0
Nov.	3.0		2.90	174.2	186.0	175.8
Dec.	4.0		3.78	158.1	204.3	178.5
1778						
Jan.	4.0		3.08	138.4	213.2	191.4
Feb.	5.0	2.71	2.54	141.6	212.0	196.3
Mar.	5.0		4.50	144.4	243.6	198.4
Apr.	6.0	2.28	4.60	142.8	221.2	153.8
May	5.0	3.53	5.74	153.3	234.5	152.7
June	4.0	4.00	4.72	178.3	201.1	158.5
July	4.0		4.16	182.9	195.0	171.0
Aug.	5.0	4.17	5.00	174.3	185.4	172.4
Sept.	5.0		5.00	171.6	195.5	167.3
Oct.	5.0	4.00	5.40	152.7	165.8	145.9
Nov.	6.0	5.72	6.34	155.2	159.4	145.0
Dec.	5.0	6.84	6.47	157.4	153.3	151.5

Year & Month	Ratios — Webster Merchants	Ratios — Specie	Ratios — Commodity	Median corrected by three-months moving average — Webster Merchants	Median — Specie	Median — Commodity
1779						
Jan.	8.0	8.00	7.99	141.0	136.7	138.5
Feb.	10.0	9.91	9.95	138.9	143.0	134.5
Mar.	10.5	9.77	11.50	130.9	150.4	127.2
Apr.	16.1	12.17	16.21	106.5	137.5	117.8
May	23.0	16.46	17.12	108.9	139.0	120.5
June	20.0	17.67	20.07	111.8	128.9	111.2
July	19.0	19.62	25.12	112.9	112.9	94.8
Aug.	20.0	21.72	25.10	117.2	116.1	95.8
Sept.	24.0	22.24	26.82	144.7	144.8	132.8
Oct.	30.0	30.00	28.68	154.4	161.9	158.0
Nov.	38.5	36.00	34.88	176.8	179.7	178.1
Dec.	41.5	42.22	45.60	193.9	200.9	191.9
1780						
Jan.	42.5	40.00	43.30	169.9	178.6	166.7
Feb.	50.0	45.25	47.73	174.1	183.9	181.7
Mar.	62.5	61.50	57.51	167.0	171.5	176.5
Apr.	60.0	61.21	57.98	170.4	170.5	176.0
May	60.0	59.67	61.20	178.9	181.8	180.6
June	60.0	56.30	59.10	167.1	171.9	163.6
July	62.5	61.38	66.08	161.5	165.7	157.0
Aug.	70.0	70.00	72.87	154.9	157.8	151.6
Sept.	75.0	72.33	73.08	149.4	156.5	149.1
Oct.	77.5	70.00	76.98	145.6	154.0	148.5
Nov.	90.0	86.87	87.68	141.2	147.3	146.1
Dec.	100.0	99.54	93.74	137.9	138.0	142.8
1781						
Jan.	100.0	103.33	98.54	122.7	124.5	128.5
Feb.	110.0	102.50	103.72	132.0	134.7	137.0
Mar.	127.5	125.00	123.02	113.7	123.1	125.7
Apr.	167.5	146.67	139.74		118.3	

Items Furnished by Quartermaster Department

This list was gleaned from letters of NG and from reports of his assistants and deputies during 1778–80. It is not exhaustive.

SOLDIERS' ACCOUTREMENTS

Bayonet Belts
Blankets
Canteens
  Tin
  Wooden
Canteen Straps
Cartridge Boxes (cartouches)
Cartridge Paper
Clothing:
  Body Coats
  Breeches
    Leather
    Worsted
  Caps
  Great Coats
  Hats
  Hose
  Hunting Frocks
  Hunting Shirts
  Jackets
  Mitts
  Overalls
  Petticoats
  Regimental Coats
  Shirts
    Cotton
    Linen
  Shoes
  Stocks
  Stockings
  Trousers
  Vests
  Waistcoats
Compasses

Haversacks
Holsters
Ice Skates
Iron Cups
Knapsacks
Knives
Lances
Leather Soles
Mess Bowls
Muskets
Portmanteaus (leather)
Powder Horns
Rifles
Shot Pouches
Snow Shoes
Spontoons
Spoons
Valises
    Canvas
    Leather

CAMP EQUIPAGE
Bags
Barrels
Buckets
Bowls (wooden)
Candles
Door Locks
Dutch Ovens
Firewood
Hand Irons
Iron Boxes
Iron Dogs (fireplace?)
Iron Pots

Iron Spoons
Kegs
Kettles
  Brass
  Iron
Kettle Covers
Lamps
Lanthorns (lanterns)
Mop Tubs
Pails (wooden)
Rope
Salt
Snow Shovels
Speaking Trumpets
Stew Pans
Stools
Stove Pipe
Stoves (iron)
Surveying Chains
Table Knives
Tar Brushes
Tar Pots
Tarpaulin
Tent Buttons
Tent Cord
Tent Hooks and Eyes
Tent Lines
Tent Pins
Tent Poles
Tents
  Bell
  Common
  Horsemen's
  Marquee
  Walled
Tin Funnels
Tin Measures (various sizes)
Trenchers
Tubs (washing)
Water Buckets
Wooden Bowls
Wooden Plates

FORAGE
Barley
Bran
Buckwheat
Corn
Flaxseed
Hay
Meal
Rye
Straw
Wheat

GUNNERS' STORES
Gun Carriage and Gun
Howitzers
Junk for Wads
Ladles
Linstocks
Match Rope
Pins for Gunshot
Powder Buckets
Prickers
Pump Nails
Rammers
Sheep Skins
Sheetlead for Aprons
Shot
  Double-Headed
  Grape
  Langrage
  Round
Sponges
Stools for Gunshot
Swivels
Tomkins
Worms

STATIONERY SUPPLIES
Account Books
Dictionary
Glue
Ink Powder
Ink Stands
Lamp Black

Letter Books
Orderly Books
Paper
  Common
  Folio
  Letter
  Post
  Wrapping
Pen Knives
Quills
Sand (for blotting)
Sealing Wax
Wafers
Writing Desks

TOOLS AND HARDWARE
Adzes
  Carpenters
  Coopers
  Foot
Anvils
Augurs (various sizes)
Awl Hafts
Axes
  Broad
  Coopers
  Filling
  Narrow
  Post
Barrows
  Hand
  Wheel
Bellows
Bill Hooks
Bit Stocks
Bits
Bolts
  Eye
  Round
Boxes
  Cutting
  Carpenters
Buttresses
Cables

Caulking Tools
Chalk
Chalk Lines
Chisels
  Cold
  Wood (various sizes)
Compasses
Coopers Tools
  Bits
  Bung Augers
  Compasses
  Frows
  Jointer Irons
Copper Hoops
Cordage, Coils of
Corking Irons
Crowbars
Drilling Tools
Files
  Crosscut
  Flat
  Half Round
  Hand Saw
  Pitt Saw
  Rasp
  Rat Tail
  Square
  Tennon Saw
  Whipsaw
Gauges
Gimlets
  Small
  Spike
Gouges
  Carving
  Framing
Grindstone Cranks
Grindstones
Hammers
  Masons
  Riveting
  Shoemakers
  Sledge
  Stone

Handbarrows
Hasps
Hatchets
  Fascine
  Nailing
  Shingling
Hinges
  Chest
  Closet
  Dovetail
Intrenching Tools
Iron Squares
Iron Stands
Iron Wedges
Jacks (mason's)
Knippers
Knives
  Cutting
  Draw
  Fascine
  Paring
  Scalping (for skinning)
  Shoemakers
Locks
  Chest
  Hand Cuff
  Hooks or Hook Locks
  Padlocks
  Small Closet
  Stock
  Thumb Latches
Marking Irons
Mattocks
Maul Rings
Mauls
Nail Rods
Nails (various sizes)
  Common
  Ribbon
  Shingle
  Spikes
Paint Brushes
Pickaxes
Picks

Pincers (Pinchers)
Planes
  Grooving
  Jack
  Long
  Smoothing
Plugs
Pump Hooks
Pumps
Punches (shoemaker's)
Rakes
Rasps
  Flat
  Round
Rivets
  Long
  Small
Rules
  Sliding
  Two-Foot
Saw Files
Saw Sets
  Cross-Cut
  Hand
  Tent
Saws
  Compass
  Cross Cut
  Framing
  Half-Round
  Hand
  Mill
  Panel
  Pit
  Tennant
  Tent
  Whip
Scales
  Brass
  Steelyards
  Tin
Scale Beams
Scale Weights
Scrapers

Screw Drivers
Screw Plates
Screws
Scythes (brush scythes)
Scythe Stones
Shears
  Fullers
Shoemakers Needs
  Leather Soles
  Pegs
  Punches
  Sides Seal Leather
  Tacks
  Thread
  Upper Leather Sides
Shovels
Sledges
Smith's Tools
  Anvil
  Awl Hafts
  Awls
  Bellows
  Hammers
  Tongs
  Vices
Spades
Spikes
  Plain
  Barrel
Squares
  Iron
  Wood
Staples
Steels (for cutting boxes)
Tackle Blocks
Tentmaker's Equipment
  Bodkins
  Geese
  Hooks and Eyes
  Leather Palms
  Needles
  Scissors
  Thimbles
  Thread

Wax
Tomahawks
Tongs (smith's)
Trowels (mason's)
Turk Knives
Vices
Wedges
Wheelbarrows
Whetstones
Wood Squares

TRANSPORTATION ITEMS
(LAND)
Bands, horse
  Back
  Belly
  Breast
  Breech
Bell Collars
Bells (for packhorses)
Branding Irons
Bridle Parts
  Bits
  Buckles
  Wheels
Bridles
  Blind
  Snaffle
Calf Skins
Cart Bodies
Cart Boxes
Carts
Cart Saddles
Cart Wheels
Chains
  Artillery
  Breast
  Cart
  Draft
  Halter
  Horse
  Lock
  Oxen
  Stretch

Tongue
Chain Traces
Coilers
Collar Buckles
Collars
Cruppers
Curry Combs
Doubletrees
Dung Forks
Feed Bags
Feed Boxes
Forage Bags
Girth Webbing
Girths
Hair Combs
Halters
  Blind
  Rope
Hames
Hame Straps
Hame Strings
Harness ("horse furniture")
  Buckles
Harness Leather
Hay Forks
Hay Rakes
Hobbles
Hogskins
Holsters
Horsehides
Horses
  Express
  Pack
  Riding
  Wagon
Horsemen's Caps
Horse Shoes and Nails
Iron Traces
Leather Lines
Linch Pins
Nose Bags
Ox Carts
Oxen
Ox Shoes

Ox Slings
Ox Yokes
Pack Saddle Trees
Pillions
Reins
Rope
  Tarred
  White
Rope Traces
Saddle Bags
Saddle Cloths
Saddle Pads
Saddles
  Cart
  Pack
  Riding
Saddlers Tools and Gear
  Awls
  Bodkins
  Hammers
  Palms
  Saddle Buckles
  Saddlers Strainers
  Saddle Straps
  Saddle Trees
  Stirrup Irons
  Stirrup Leather
  Stirrups
  Thimbles
  Thong Skins
  Thread
Shoe Brushes
Shoeing Tools
Singletrees
Sledges and Sleighs
  Log Sleighs
  Sleds
Snaffle Bolts
Stable Racks
Stable Mangers
Surcingles
Swivel Straps
Tar Pots
Wagon Bodies

Wagon Clouts
Wagon Covers
Wagon Harness
Wagons
  Close-Bodied
  Covered
  Four-Horse
  Open
  Two-Horse
Wagon Screws
Wagon Whips
Water Buckets
Wheel Rims
Wheel Spokes
Wheels
  Cart
  Wagon
Whiffletrees

TRANSPORTATION ITEMS
(WATER)
Anchors
Blocks
Boat Furniture, Boxes of
Canvas
Chain Plates and Bolts
Chains
Clamps for Gun Carriages
Clamps for Swivels
Deck Nails
Gimbals
Grappling (hooks ?)
Hoops for Masthead
Lynch Pins and Hoops
Main Yard
Marline
Masts
Oakum, Barrels of
Oarlocks
Oars
Pitch Kettles
Pitch Ladles
Pump Gallows
Pump Hooks

Pumps
Ring and Eye Bolts
Rope
  Tarred
  White
Rudder Fro
Sail Needles
Sails
Shole Pins
Spunyarn
Straps for Yards
Suits of Colours
Tar
Thrums for Mops
Vessels
  Barges
  Bateaux
  Durham Boats
  Gun Boats
  Pettiaugers
  Row Galleys
  Schooners
  Scows
  Skiffs
  Sloops
  Snows
  Wagon Boats
  Whale Boats
  Xebeques
Winches
Wythes for Yards

UNFINISHED PRODUCTS
Bees Wax
Brimstone, Barrels of
Calf Skins
Canvas
Charcoal
Cloth
  Brown Linen
  Drilling
  Hemp Cloth
  Linen Cloth
  Oznabrigs

Rovena Duck
Russia Sheeting
Sail Duck
Tow Cloth
Glass, Boxes of
Glue
Hides
Iron Bars
Lime, Bushels of
Linseed Oil
Lumber
  Oak
  Pine
Neats Leather

Oil, Barrels of
Paint, Kegs of
Rosin
Sheepskins
Sheet Iron
Shingles
  Cedar
  Pine
Steel
Tar, Barrels of
Tin, Sheets of
Twine
White Lead
Wire

INDEX

n; and R.I., 215n, 317, 318n; and tanyard, 226 and n; and Abraham Livingston, 233 and n, 370; and Pulaski's
Legion, 234n; and Charlottesville camp,
238, 239n; Va. delegates to, 239n; and
Finnie, 239n, 288; and Pettit, 239n, 286,
289n, 313; and certificates, 257–58 and
n; and rumored alliance with Spain,
260, 261n, 280, 281n, 291 and n, 368,
369n, 382 and n; and Gérard, 261n,
433n; and administering of oaths, 265;
and protection of ships in Chesapeake
and Delaware Bays, 280, 286, 289n; and
fighting in S.C., 280; and Pulaski, 285;
and wagoners, 298n, 350, 351n, 361 and
n, 363–65 and n, 384, 416 and n, 418,
420, 426; and Philadelphia, 305, 350–51
and n; and John Mitchell, 311–12n;
embargo imposed by, 320n; and George
Morgan, 353, 354n; and half pay for
officers, 354n; and McDougall, 362; and
Cox, 362; and the Pa. Assembly, 374–75,
402, 426, 428n, 441; and Pa. politics, 375;
and petition from prisoners on Long
Island, 391n; and factionalism, 393–94,
425n; and Collins, 397; and possible
peace overtures, 423 and n, 424n, 430;
and command of Southern Army, 429n;
and charges against Hollingsworth,
446–47; and Head of Elk improvements,
453; R.I. delegates to, 458 and n. See also
Board of War; Committee at Camp;
Committee of Conference; Foreign
Affairs Committee; Jay, John; Laurens,
Henry; Marine Committee; Navy Board;
Supply Departments Committee; Treasury Board
Continental Village, N.Y., 150n
Contracts: for forage, 174, 215 and n, 307,
308; for oats, 207, 208n, 241; Wade on,
207; for boats, 216, 299n; for packsaddles, 246, 250, 302; for teams, 246–
47, 249, 259; for shipwrights, 284; Cox
makes in Philadelphia, 351n
Convention army, 19, 22n; flour for, 24;
movement of to Virginia, 26n, 47, 50,
51–52 and n, 58, 69, 88 and n, 95, 173,
234n, 258, 454n; James Davenport and,
51–52 and n, 157, 173, 454 and n; bread
for, 71 and n; and crossing Hudson
River, 81; and Finnie, 83n, 238–39 and
n, 288; DQM's and, 96; possible rescue
of, 105, 106n; prisoner exchange and,
106n; passing through N.J., 110, 111n,
112; barracks for, 161–62; guards for,
192; and Charlottesville camp, 238–39
and n, 288; in distress, 343
Conway, Thomas: duel with John

Cadwalader, 56, 57n, 103, 104n
"Conway Cabal": Mifflin and, 15; Reed
on, 44, 45, 46n; and Richard Henry Lee,
139, 142n, 195n; Wilkinson and, 167n;
Walter Stewart and, 194, 195n; Weedon
on, 340 and n
Conyngham, Gustavus, 290; biog. note,
290n
Cook, Moses, 324
Cook, William: QM district of, 156; pay of,
156; and rations, 156; commissions paid
to, 156; money and, 156; and pack-
saddles, 286
Cookhouse, Pa., 442
Coolidge, Isiah, 100
Cooperstown, N.Y., 350n
Co'os, N.H.: and proposed Canadian
Expedition, 28n, 29n, 118, 119n, 348,
350n; flour at, 120; and the Indian
Expedition, 147n, 348, 350n; militia at,
147n; Hazen's regiment to, 370 and n
Cordage. See Rope
Cork, Ireland, 182
Corn: to Trenton, 94; from Va., 126, 301;
from Md., 126; and N.J., 129, 130n; price
of, 139, 164, 192, 209, 212, 229, 248n,
254, 269n, 332, 340, 345; and the
Indians, 145; scarcity of, 193, 215n; and
speculators, 210; from around Chesa-
peake Bay, 210; purchase of, 229; trans-
portation of, 230; planting of, 475
Cornell, Ezekiel: troops of short of provi-
sions, 98n
Corn meal, 195n
Coryell, John, 193
Coryells Ferry, N.J./Pa.: carriages at, 181;
flour transport and, 184; QM department and, 193n; and Pa. Council, 193
and n; and the army, 193n; and route to
Kings Ferry and New Windsor, N.Y., 405
Cotton, John: letter from, 448; and Udny
Hay, 448; horse of, 448; QM of Nixon's
brigade, 448n
Council of General Officers: and rank of
Pa. officers, 377 and n; and the Md. line,
389–90 and n; on prisoner exchange, 391
and n
Council of War: absence of, xi; on British
strategy, 3–6 and n
Courts-martial: of Charles Lee, 35n, 47n,
49–50n, 55, 56 and n, 103, 104n, 121,
142n, 195n; of Schuyler, 49, 50n, 121,
128n; of St. Clair, 49, 50n, 121; and Congress, 103, 105n; of Archibald Steel,
152n, 282, 283n; of William Smith, 189n;
of Benedict Arnold, 305, 311–12n; and
John Mitchell, 305, 306–7n; and artificer
officers, 324n; Wadsworth and, 380; and

Lebanon, Pa., 51, 458
Lee, Arthur: and dispute with Silas
  Deane, 104n, 121, 142n, 201n, 425 and
  n
Lee, Charles: and GW, 35, 402n; court-
  martial of, 35n, 47n, 49–50n, 55, 56 and
  n, 103, 104n, 121, 142n, 195n; Reed on,
  43; John Cadwalader on, 103; duel with
  John Laurens, 126, 127n, 130; and
  Martha Washington, 126; and Virginia,
  139, 402; Walter Stewart and, 139, 142n,
  194, 195n; and Battle of Monmouth, 194,
  195, 340n; Richard Henry Lee defends,
  340n; and Philadelphia, 402 and n; and
  Pettit, 402; unfavorable letter about in
  Pennsylvania Packet, 402 and n; and
  Drayton, 402n; and Congress, 402n;
  threatens to resign, 402n; his fondness
  for dogs attacked, 402n; and John Jay,
  402n; Brackenridge attacks conduct at
  battle of Charleston, 402n; challenges
  Brackenridge, 402n
Lee, Henry ("Light-Horse Harry"), 13;
  light horse under, 172, 181, 182n, 433n;
  wine to 212; teams for, 419
Lee, Richard Henry: and "Conway
  Cabal," 139, 142n; and Congress, 142n,
  171n, 195n; ill, 142n; and quarrel with
  Silas Deane, 193–94; Walter Stewart
  and, 194, 195n, 340n; defends Charles
  Lee, 340n
Lee, Thomas Sim, 233n
Leonard, Gideon, 188–89n
Lesser Antilles, 122n
Letters of marque and reprisal, 455–56n
Lewis, Joseph: Abeel's complaints
  against, 410–11 and n, 456, 457n; wagon-
  masters and, 410; and Furman, 410 and
  n; as paymaster to the militia, 410; and
  the commissary department, 410; DQM
  at Morristown, 410n; NG and, 456, 457n
Lewis, Morgan: letters to, 33, 107, 226, 271,
  279, 319, 408; letters from, 50, 53, 241,
  452; returns and, 81; and bateaux, 114,
  115n, 293, 319; money and, 117, 156,
  181, 452; QM district of, 156; commissions paid to, 156; DQM at Albany,
  161n, 182n, 239, 240n, 242n, 387; and
  Otis & Andrews, 161 and n, 172; and
  artificers, 205, 226, 277 and n, 279;
  clothing and, 206; employees of, 206n;
  nails and oakum to, 207; and the Indian
  Expedition, 216, 217n, 452; and Hubbard, 216; and entrenching tools, 235;
  and bellows, 237; and Canadian Expedition, 241, 242–43n; and contracts for
  oats, 241; and shipwrights, 284; tents
  and, 387, 390, 408, 452; and Ft.

Schuyler, 408n; woolens to, 478
Lexington, battle of, 268n
Light horse (American), 13; and Conn., 4,
  172, 173n; and Pa., 4; as escort for CG,
  67; GW fears conduct of, 81, 82n; to
  Baltimore, 81, 82n; and Stirling, 82n,
  127n; to Lancaster, Pa., 82n, 100, 101n,
  117; Colonel White commands, 89n,
  101n; and Elizabeth Town, 90, 91–92n;
  pursue Loyalists, 91, 92n; and forage,
  102; under Henry Lee, 172, 181, 182n,
  433n; and N.J., 178; combs and brushes
  for, 299, 336; under Sheldon, 336; teams
  for, 419; and Gérard reception, 433n. See
  also Connecticut light horse; Philadelphia light horse
Light horse (British), 194
Lincoln, Benjamin: and proposed expedition against Florida, 64n; and S.C.
  defense, 187n, 235, 433 and n, 442n;
  and S.C. militia, 224; and Pulaski's
  Legion, 234n, 357; leg wound of, 423,
  424n, 429n; and command of the
  Southern Army, 423, 424n, 429 and n;
  surrender of at Charleston, 424n; GW
  and successor to, 429 and n; near
  Augusta, Ga., 433n. See also Southern
  Army
Linen: table linens, 34; bed linen, 35, 60,
  66, 69 and n, 176; for NG, 66, 109, 112,
  177, 225; from Fishkill, 132; for Burnet,
  218; for shirts, 438; for packsaddle pads,
  450–51, 476; Hooper and, 470, 477; flax
  linen, 475; tow linen, 475, 476
Linn, Janus, 339
Liquor: estimate of needed, 5; rum, 83
  and n, 101, 122–23, 151, 161, 167n, 195,
  260, 280, 300, 312n, 340; Wayne's troops
  allowed, 88; for Canadian Expedition,
  119n; adulterating of, 123; and Albany,
  123; and Wadsworth, 251; at Middlebrook, 251 and n; brandy, 312n;
  whiskey, 340
Littell, Eleazer, 323
Little Egg Harbor, N.J., 356n
Littlefield, Nancy (CG's sister), 369
Littlefield, William: overstays leave, 147,
  168 and n, 224 and n, 317, 318n; brother
  of CG, 168n, 224n; NG on, 224; and
  Varnum, 224; furloughs for, 224 and n;
  accompanies CG to Middlebrook, 224;
  and Sullivan, 317
Liverpool, England, 455
Livestock: "recruitment" of, 3–4, 6n, 364;
  support of, 5; lost in R.I., 22; forage
  and, 70, 220, 221n, 274; subsistence of,
  78; to draw sleds, 115; distress among,
  125, 129; preservation of, 162; and Middle-

417, 421, 423, 425, 429, 433, 457; *letters from,* 31, 75, 100, 114, 115, 118, 192, 300, 326, 327, 337, 345, 377, 382, 389, 415, 420, 424, 428, 449, 462; headquarters of, xi, xiii; NG and, xi, xii, 15, 49, 92, 94n, 135, 270–71 and n, 293, 298n, 301 and n, 324 and n, 337, 357, 395, 396 and n, 412, 413, 414, 427, 429, 431 and n, 456; and Canadian Expedition, xii–xiii, 27–31 and n, 114–15 and n, 118–19 and n, 128n, 241, 242n, 292–93 and n, 319, 362n; and possible attack on New York City, xii, 76 and n; unsure of British intentions, xii; reluctant to release troops, xii; joined by Martha, xiii; and the Indian Expedition, xiii, 145–46n, 193n, 226, 227n, 242n, 253n, 301, 308 and n, 326–28 and n, 346–50 and n, 382, 383, 390 and n, 415n, 421–23 and n, 424 and n, 449 and n; receives faulty intelligence, 5–6n; desires expresses, 6; and inventory of grain, 7–8 and n; queried over abuses in commissary department, 8n; and QM department, 9 and n, 228n, 407, 427; sends troops to Boston, 11–12 and n; and hutting of troops, 14n; and "Conway Cabal," 15, 45, 142n; horses needed for, 21; lists troops fit for duty, 22n; and winter quarters for troops, 32, 74, 107; and bateaux, 33 and n, 319; criticism of, 35, 43–44, 340n, 394–95n; and Charles Lee, 35, 194, 402n; requests tools, 50; wishes QM for Convention army, 50; approves invalid soldiers' use as wagoners, 62 and n; to N.J., 65; asks after CG, 67; and impressment of forage, 68, 69n, 70, 78 and n, 81, 129, 130n, 131 and n; and relations between commissioned and warrant officers, 72–73 and n; Gouverneur Morris letter to, 74, 75n; joins Martha, 75n; and Philadelphia, 75n, 101n, 121, 122n, 126, 127n, 145n, 146n, 180, 186, 192n, 227n, 235, 267n, 270n, 293, 301 and n, 361; reports on strength of army, 76–77n; wishes army to remain at Fredericksburg, 81; and the light horse, 81, 82 and n, 83n, 90, 91 and n, 92n, 101n, 117; Custis stepson of, 83n; and complaints at Fishkill, 83 and n; and Congress, 91, 196, 283n, 298n, 307n, 329, 424 and n, 425, 426, 428n; and Bound Brook, 95 and n; stays at Wallace home, 100, 101n, 105–6; and artificer complaints, 101; orders troops to halt, 105; to Aquakinunk, 105; winter quarters for, 105–6; and Middlebrook, 106, 110, 146n, 187n, 195, 196n, 234n, 267n, 270n; and

prisoner exchange, 106n, 391 and n; and proposed Eyre resignation, 109n, 112; and Clement Biddle, 110; and Pulaski's Legion, 113–14 and n, 234n; and Committee of Conference, 115, 116n, 146n; and draft of letter, 115n; and forage department, 126; leaves Stirling in command at Middlebrook, 127n; and tents to Morristown, 127; and Schuyler, 128n, 271, 349n, 350n; and Northern Army, 128n; and plans for campaign of 1779, 144–45 and n, 146n, 186, 240; and Board of War, 146n; and Cherry Valley attack, 146n; prefers defensive strategy for army, 146n; and compensation for damages to civilian property, 148, 218, 222, 279n; Brodhead reports to, 152n; and command at Ft. Pitt, 152n, 283n; and West Point, 153–54 and n; and clothing for artificers, 158 and n; and the sick on Long Island, 159; and Von Heer, 179n; and charges against William Smith, 189n; intelligence from Stirling, 192; and battle of Monmouth, 194; and the Lee family, 194; and John Mitchell, 197n, 337 and n; calling cards for, 197n, carriage for, 197n; and Thomas Paine, 201; and payment for N.Y. goods taken, 206n; related to Spotswood, 206n; and division QM's, 228n; and Hollingsworth, 233n; and Cox, 244, 401; Lott and, 252; Reed and, 253n, 312n; and Patterson, 253n, 324, 329 and n, 372 and n, 390; and General Hand, 253n, 390n; and certificates, 257, 258n; oats for horses of, 258–59; and administration of oaths, 265; fears British attack, 267n; and John Beatty, 272; Harrison aide of, 291n; and wagoners, 296–99 and n, 337, 361 and n, 363, 417–18, 420, 426, 434, 444, 456; and Wadsworth, 300, 301n, 335, 441, 442n, 468; and armorers, 302; and returns, 307, 308 and n, 330, 360; and magazines in western Pa., 308 and n; to reprimand Benedict Arnold, 312n; and discharged soldiers, 316 and n; and Varnum, 317–18 and n; and portmanteaus and valises, 319n; and Hooper, 324, 437n; and Sullivan, 335, 449n; tablecloths for, 337; dishes for, 337; Weedon and, 340 and n; and McDougall, 345n; and Iroquois country, 349n; and charges against a wagon conductor, 351; dances with CG, 354; and pensions for officers, 354n; and Potter, 372; and intelligence from Raritan River, 376; and general officers on arrangement of Maryland line, 389, 390n; and provisions to

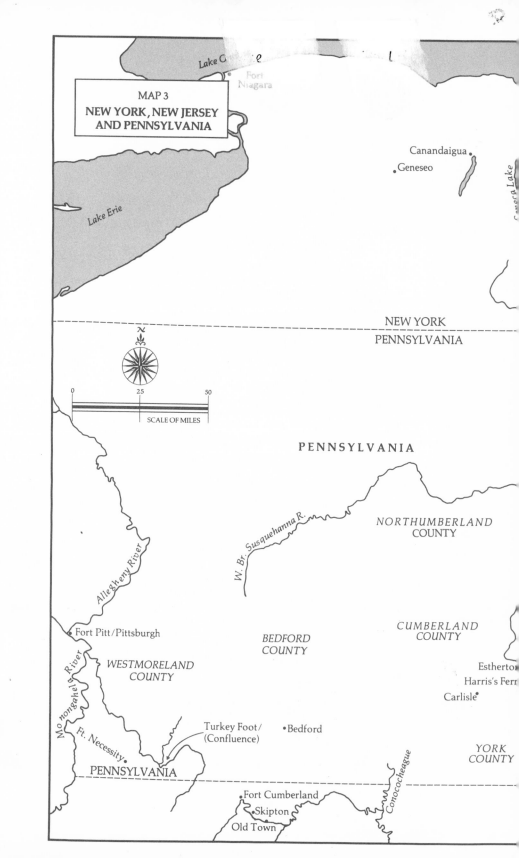

MAP 3

NEW YORK, NEW JERSEY AND PENNSYLVANIA

Lake C___e

Fort
Niagara

Canandaigua •

• Geneseo

Cayuga Lake

Lake Erie

NEW YORK
PENNSYLVANIA

N

0   25   50

SCALE OF MILES

PENNSYLVANIA

W. Br. Susquehanna R.

*NORTHUMBERLAND
COUNTY*

Allegheny River

Fort Pitt/Pittsburgh

*CUMBERLAND
COUNTY*

*BEDFORD
COUNTY*

*WESTMORELAND
COUNTY*

Estherto__

Harris's Ferr___

Carlisle •

Monongahela River

Ft. Necessity •

Turkey Foot/
(Confluence)

• Bedford

Conococheague

*YORK
COUNTY*

PENNSYLVANIA

• Fort Cumberland

• Skipton

Old Town